PAUL S. ANDERSON

PROFESSOR OF EDUCATION
SAN DIEGO STATE COLLEGE

LANGUAGE
SKILLS IN
ELEMENTARY
EDUCATION

LANGUAGE

SKILLS IN

ELEMENTARY

EDUCATION

THE MACMILLAN COMPANY, NEW YORK
COLLIER-MACMILLAN LIMITED, LONDON

Fifth Printing, 1966

Library of Congress catalog card number: 63-8188

THE MACMILLAN COMPANY, NEW YORK
COLLIER-MACMILLAN CANADA, LTD., TORONTO, ONTARIO

Printed in the United States of America

Photograph on title page, courtesy Burbank Public
Schools, Calif.

ACKNOWLEDGMENTS

*Grateful acknowledgment is made to the
following for permission to use excerpts from
the copyrighted works cited.*

APPLETON-CENTURY-CROFTS, INC., *Teaching
English Grammar,* by Robert C. Pooley, copyright © 1957 by Appleton-Century-Crofts,
Inc., reprinted by permissioin of the publisher, Appleton-Century-Crofts.

ASSOCIATION FOR CHILDHOOD EDUCATION IN-
TERNATIONAL, "Helping Children to Create,"
by Lois Lenski, from *Childhood Education,*
Nov. 1949, Vol. 26, No. 3, reprinted by
permission of the Association for Childhood
Education International, 3615 Wisconsin
Ave., N. W., Washington 16, D. C.

BENNETT, JOAN RODNEY, "Locomotive," by
Rodney Bennett, copyright 1941 by Rodney
Bennett, reprinted by permission of the au-
thor's estate.

BRUCE PUBLISHING COMPANY, "350 Most
Useful Spelling Words," from *A Basic Spelling Vocabulary,* by James A. Fitzgerald, copyright 1951 by Bruce Publishing Company,
reprinted by permission of the publisher.

BURGESS PUBLISHING COMPANY, *Resource
Materials for Teachers of Spelling,* by Paul
S. Anderson, copyright 1959 by Paul S.
Anderson, reprinted by permission of the
publisher.

CALIFORNIA STATE DEPARTMENT OF EDUCA-
TION, *California Journal of Elementary Education* (Feb. and Nov. 1961), and other state
publications.

THE CHRISTIAN SCIENCE PUBLISHING SOCI-
ETY, "Clouds," by Helen Wing, from *The
Christian Science Monitor,* reprinted by per-
mission of the publisher.

DENVER PUBLIC SCHOOLS, *Curriculum Bulletin No. 93495, 1955.*

DOUBLEDAY & COMPANY, INC., *Wag Tail Bess,*
by Marjorie Flack, copyright 1933 by Marjorie Flack Larsson, reprinted by permission
of Doubleday & Company, Inc.; "Mice," from
Fifty-One Nursery Rhymes, by Rose Fyleman, copyright 1932 by Doubleday & Company, Inc., reprinted by permission of
Doubleday & Company, Inc. and The Society
of Authors, London.

E. P. DUTTON & CO., INC., "Presents," from
Around and About, by Marchette Chute,
copyright 1932, renewal 1960, by Marchette
Chute, published 1957 by E. P. Dutton &
Co., Inc. and reprinted with permission;
"Listen to the Wind," and "Aeroplane," from
Another Here and Now Story Book, edited by
Lucy Sprague Mitchell, copyright 1937 by
E. P. Dutton & Co., Inc. and reprinted by
permission of the publisher.

EXPRESSION COMPANY, PUBLISHERS, "Red
Squirrel," by Grace Rowe, from *Choral
Speaking Arrangements for the Lower Grades,*
by Louise Abney and Grace Rowe, by per-
mission of Expression Company, Magnolia,
Massachusetts. Copyright 1953.

FAIRBANKS, ALASKA, PUBLIC SCHOOLS, children's poetry published by Don Mortenson's
class, 1960.

FISHER, AILEEN, "Coffeepot Face," copyright
by Aileen Fisher and reprinted by permission
of the author.

GINN AND COMPANY, "Check List for Reading
Readiness," from *Manual for Teaching the
Reading-Readiness Program,* rev. ed., by
David Russell, *et al.,* copyright 1961 by Ginn
and Company, reprinted by permission of the
publisher.

Grade Teacher magazine, "Soft Is the Hush
of Falling Snow," by Emily Carey Alleman,
reprinted by permission of the author and
publisher.

GRAND RAPIDS, MICH., PUBLIC SCHOOLS, *Study
Guide for the Language Arts.*

HARCOURT, BRACE & WORLD, INC., "Counting," from *Windy Morning,* copyright 1953
by Harry Behn; "Trees," from *The Little
Hill,* copyright 1949 by Harry Behn; *Patterns*

in English, by Paul Roberts, copyright 1956
by Harcourt, Brace & World, Inc. All re-
printed by permission of Harcourt, Brace &
World, Inc. "Little Sounds," © 1958 by
Beatrice Schenk de Regniers from *Something
Special,* reprinted by permission of Harcourt,
Brace & World, Inc., and Wm. Collins Sons
& Co. Ltd., London.

THE HORN BOOK, INC., "One Day When We
Went Walking," by Valine Hobbs, copyright
1945 by The Horn Book, Inc., reprinted by
permission of the publisher.

HOUGHTON MIFFLIN COMPANY for "A Prayer
for Little Things," by Eleanor Farjeon, copyright 1943 by Houghton Mifflin Company;
Improving Your Language, by Paul McKee,
copyright 1957 by Houghton Mifflin Company; *Come Along* Teacher's Manual, by
Paul McKee, copyright 1957 by Houghton
Mifflin Company; *Bright Peaks,* teacher's
edition, by Paul McKee, copyright 1958 by
Houghton Mifflin Company, reprinted by
permission of the publisher.

THE INSTRUCTOR, "Phonics Clinic," by Selma
Herr, copyright 1957 by Selma Herr; "You
Can Teach Handwriting With Only Six
Rules," by Max Rosenhaus, copyright 1957
by *The Instructor;* "Three Cheers for Peter,"
by Alice Hartich, copyright 1961 by *The
Instructor,* reprinted by permission.

LAIDLAW BROTHERS, PUBLISHERS, "Song of
the Pop-Corn," by Louise Abney, from *On
the Way to Storyland,* copyright 1961 by
Laidlaw Brothers; "The American Flag," by
Louise Abney, from *From Every Land, Book
6,* copyright 1961 by·Laidlaw Brothers, reprinted by permission of the publisher.

LE CRON, HELEN COWLES, *Little Charlie
Chipmunk,* reprinted by permission of the
author.

J. B. LIPPINCOTT COMPANY, "A Letter Is a
Gypsy Elf" and "Indian Children," from *For
Days and Days,* by Annette Wynne, copyright 1919, 1947 by Annette Wynne, published by J. B. Lippincott Company.

LOS ANGELES CITY SCHOOL DISTRICTS, poems
from *Speech in the Elementary School* (Publication No. 479, 1949).

THE MACMILLAN COMPANY, "The Cat," from
Menagerie, by Mary Britton Miller, copyright 1929 by The Macmillan Company,
reprinted by permission of the author and
publisher.

MC CULLOUGH, CONSTANCE M., *Handbook for Teaching the Language Arts,* copyright 1958 by Constance McCullough, reprinted by permission of the author and Paragon Publications.

MC GRAW-HILL BOOK COMPANY, INC., *Are You Listening?* by Ralph G. Nichols and Leonard A. Stevens, copyright © 1957 by the McGraw-Hill Book Company, Inc., reprinted by permission of McGraw-Hill Book Company, Inc., and Willis Kingsley Wing.

NEW YORK CITY BOARD OF EDUCATION, "Teaching Spelling" (Curriculum Bulletin, Series No. 6, 1953–54), reprinted by permission of the Board of Education of the City of New York.

RECREATION magazine (February 1950), "My Mother Read to Me," by E. H. Frierwood, reprinted by permission of *Recreation* Magazine.

RICHARDS, ROSALIND, "Antonio," by Laura E. Richards, from *Child Life Magazine,* copyright 1935 by Rand McNally and Company, reprinted by permission.

RIVERSIDE, CALIF., CITY SCHOOLS, "Second Grade Spelling Word List," copyright 1959 by Riverside City Schools.

SAN BERNARDINO, CALIF., COUNTY SCHOOLS, *Language Arts Guide.*

SAN DIEGO CITY SCHOOLS, "Independent Reading Activities in the Primary Grades," by Marie Lovell; "Creative Criticism," by Lillian Layton; "Oral and Written Language," with special acknowledgment to Elizabeth Stocker; *Language Arts Curriculum Guide for Grades 1–6.*

SAN DIEGO STATE COLLEGE, Campus Laboratory School for children's writings from the *Junior Aztec,* reprinted by permission of the Campus Laboratory School.

SCIENCE RESEARCH ASSOCIATES, INC., for "Listening Skill Builder No. 1," reprinted by permission from the *Instructor's Handbook, SRA Reading Laboratory, IVa,* by Don H. Parker. Copyright 1959, Science Research Associates, Inc.

SIDGWICK & JACKSON, LTD., "Choosing Shoes," from *The Very Thing,* by ffrida Wolfe, reprinted by permission of the author's representatives and the publishers, Sidgwick & Jackson, Ltd.

TASH, MERRY LEE, "To the Boy That Sits in Front of Me"; "Hobbies"; "Poems"; "Dear Mom"; reprinted by permission of the author and Clover C. Tash and Lloyd C. Tash.

TUCKER, SUSAN, "A Question to God," reprinted by permission of Gordon H. Tucker.

UNIVERSITY OF MINNESOTA, "Finger Plays for Young Children," Leaflet No. 11, reprinted by permission of the Institute of Child Development and Welfare.

YALE UNIVERSITY PRESS, "Bundles," from *Songs for Parents,* by John Farrar, copyright 1921 by Yale University Press, reprinted by permission of the publisher.

Dedication

This book is dedicated to the four teachers who influenced my interest in the language arts. Elizabeth Russell taught me to be specific in my work. Paul McKee urged me to help children demand meaning from the words they used. Robert Pooley revealed to me the beauty of the English language as it is expressed in literature. Virgil Herrick caused me to question so much that seemed to be fact.

To the Student

Teaching in the elementary schools involves hundreds of tasks. No one has ever made an effort to list all of them. Teachers have acquired skill in much the same way that a good parent learns to care for a family or a physician learns to treat his patients. Part of teaching proficiency comes from the memory of the way we were taught, part comes by learning from the experience of others, and part is based upon our own willingness to work at tasks that we feel must be accomplished. A methods course in the language arts is designed to prepare you to teach by having you relate your own childhood efforts to speak, read, and write to those of young learners, to inform you about what others have learned who have worked in this area, and to present ways of working with problems you will face. Some of these problems will have rather specific solutions, while others are predicaments that are never completely resolved. Just as the medical profession has been baffled by the common cold, the teaching profession continues to face unsolved problems. But with better teacher training and greater awareness of child psychology, more and more children are learning to read well, write with ease, speak expressively, and think efficiently.

The problems of teaching the language skills provide the basic organization of this book. Chapter 1 describes the place of the language arts in the school curriculum, outlines the interrelationship of language and culture, and gives a brief summary of the children who will learn in our classrooms. These problems are concerned with the reason for doing things rather than the procedures used in instruction. The following chapters emphasize the many ways teachers accomplish their goals. In these you will be able to detect my own personal philosophy. You will also find suggestions that appear to contradict this point of view. My purpose has been to present many ways to guide the learning of children. Do not hesitate to be critical of ideas and procedures presented in these chapters. Be slow to make judgments, but if some of these ideas and methods are found wanting, cast them aside and seek others.

Throughout the text specific devices, exercises, and activities are suggested. The front line of the educational battle against ignorance is in the classroom where the teacher and learner are face to face. What happens in these classroom experiences must be something read, something written, something learned. Theory is practical in that it helps a teacher determine which of many devices and techniques to use. The great unknown to anyone outside your classroom is a knowledge of the individual child with whom you work. It is your ability to know this child and combine this knowledge with the information of a methods course that will determine your success as a teacher.

Preface

As the space age unfolds, we are dramatically aware that the children we teach may one day reach other planets. It is equally important to recognize that our children must solve many problems that will determine how we will live on earth. Basic to these responsibilities is the ability to communicate. Through the skills of language, children must be able to clarify their thoughts, establish goals, plan together, and share ideas with others.

My work has caused me to visit schools in Colorado, Wisconsin, Texas, Tennessee, and California. In these schools, I found teachers who were aware of the responsibilities that are the heritage of our children. From these teachers I learned much that is presented here. It was not until my work involved the training of student teachers that the need to bring this information together became apparent. This book is not intended to cover all of the subject matter required for teaching the language arts. It is planned to help beginning teachers obtain successful classroom results as they start their teaching careers. With experience, more aspects of the language arts will assume importance and, I hope, encourage teachers to become scholars in the true sense— dedicating some of their time and energy to the research needed in this field.

Questions have been asked at the conclusion of some of the discussions to encourage evaluation or application of the ideas presented. These may be used for class discussion but are primarily to encourage the student to react to the material or summarize his own ideas.

Although a vast number of books, articles, theses, studies, and reports in the language arts have been consulted in the preparation of these chapters, no attempt has been made to include references to all of them. The implication and application of such knowledge has been stressed throughout the book. A beginning teacher not only needs to know *how* to do her work in this field, but also to understand *why* certain procedures are followed. It is hoped that practice will lead to questioning, questioning to further study, and further study to improvement of instruction in the language arts.

Individual students whose work at San Diego State College has been of great help in the writing of this book include Don Chamberlin, Mary Geesey, Margaret Gott, Leonard Kidd, Lillian Layton, Martha Miller, Theran Phalen, Lylith Ramsey, Myretta Snyder, and Huber Walsh.

The author's colleagues, Margaret Brydegaard, Patrick Groff, Charles Daniels, Robert Nardelli, and Mildred Epler have made suggestions that considerably improved the book's usefulness to teachers. The librarians Frances Schalles, Lillian Spitzer, and Doris Adams have given continuous help locating references and curriculum guides.

Deserving special mention are the author's wife, Verna Dieckman Anderson, and his typist Mrs. Francis Offner, who gave unstintedly of their valuable service during the compilation and editing of this material.

PAUL S. ANDERSON
San Diego State College

Contents

LANGUAGE
SKILLS IN
ELEMENTARY
EDUCATION

Chapter 1

The Language Skills and the Children We Teach

WHAT ARE THE SKILLS OF LANGUAGE?

Let us start by thinking together about the miracle of language. A word can cause us to sink into the deepest despair or lift us to inspired behavior. Words we share with our family, community, and country become a bond that unites us.

When a way to write words was discovered, man was no longer dependent upon the memory of listeners; meanings became more uniform and understanding more certain. Written words were a link with all generations to come, and as time passed became man's link with the past. Civilizations have disappeared, leaving only ruins and relics from which we attempt to interpret earlier ways of life; others, though buried under desert sands, seem almost contemporary because of written records, which tell us about their religion, education, business, and even the intimate gossip of their times.

Today, more language power has been given man through such developments as television, radio, and the telephone. It is possible for one speaker to have over a hundred million listeners. Distance and time are no longer barriers to the use of language. We take for granted such things as intercontinental telephone service and amateur radio operators who talk with others at sea or in other lands. Telstar has added to this power by two-way, intercontinental, live television transmissions between Europe and the United States.

One of the rewards of teaching is the satisfaction that results from helping a child grow in his ability to communicate ideas in speech and writing. Just as a parent proudly reports the first word the child speaks, so a teacher shares the child's development of a new vocabulary, his first written story, and his achievement when a degree of reading skill has been mastered. And just as a parent worries about the child's future, so are teachers concerned when a child is not competent in his use of language. A student who fails to achieve competence in language faces life with an unfair handicap for which the school must accept responsibility.

In many of our schools the daily program is divided among different subjects;

1

of these reading, spelling, handwriting, and composition are in the language arts area. If separate periods are provided for literature, speech, and phonics, they are also part of the language arts program.

Although we divide the school day into subject periods, the skills of language are used throughout the day. The receiving skills are listening and reading, while the sharing skills are speech and handwriting. Each one of these skills is related to the others, both as to the mental processes involved and the function of each in communication. Speech has no purpose unless associated with listening; the mental processes you employ to understand and evaluate the ideas on this printed page are almost identical to those you would use in listening to a teacher present these ideas orally.

The skills of speech, writing, reading, and listening are usually grouped together as "the tools of communication." The word *communication* has an interesting meaning. When one individual has had an interchange of thoughts or ideas with another, we say that communication has taken place. To be *in communion* means to share a mutual understanding or feeling; normally, this communion is an exchange of ideas on a common basis of understanding, since both words stem from the Latin *communis* or "common." If we separate the ideas shared from the writing, speaking, reading, and listening skills, the ideas become the *content* of communication. For this reason one sometimes hears the statement that the language arts have no content and must always use social studies, science, or other information in order to have ideas to share.

One result of this idea has been a tendency on the part of some to neglect instruction in the skills themselves and to concentrate on factual information; a few teachers have felt that if the child has enough to talk or write about, the skills needed will develop without planned instruction.

Others believe that the mastery of skills in the elementary school will give the child the ability and security needed to grow in knowledge. The entire lifetime of an individual who reads with ease and expresses himself clearly and comfortably is a learning experience. To attempt the mastery of many volumes of social ideas or scientific facts during the elementary school years places an artificial pressure on both teachers and students which may result in failure to provide adequate competence in language skills.

As a teacher or a future teacher you are personally concerned with communication because it is a necessity of teaching. What you are trying to do in the classroom is to communicate to children, to aid them in their efforts to communicate with you and with others. There are times when you will completely misunderstand your college teachers, just as your students will fail to understand you. Sometimes the words cause this misunderstanding. A group of kindergarten children were quite puzzled about what the teacher meant when she asked them to "tiptoe." More often, the same words will be used with different meanings, the one speaking the word thinking of one meaning and the person hearing the word associating it with another. The fact that many of our common words such as "run" have many different meanings accounts for partial or faulty communication.[1] Another factor is experience. Words such as *river, wagon, car, lake,* recall different images to each of us. Only when an experience is completely shared does total communication take place. Fortunately, complete and exact communication is not always necessary for adequate understanding.

Teaching is not just telling. Communication involves more than words. The derivation of most words for teaching imply "showing," "showing how," "showing what," or "showing why." The word is derived from the Anglo-Saxon *taecean* and is akin to the German *zeigen* "to show." In Latin *doceo* means "I show, point out, inform, tell," as does the Greek *didasko* and *deik-nymi*—originally "I show or point out," but ultimately, "I teach."

The term *art* is used to describe some-

---

[1] The 500 most commonly used words in English have over 14,000 dictionary definitions. See William V. Haney, *Communication: Patterns and Incidents* (Homewood, Ill.: Irwin, 1960), p. 48.

thing that is personal, creative, and original. In contrast, the word *skill* may indicate something mechanical, exact, impersonal. When we spell a word we do not offer a creative original version of the word but merely give an exact mechanical rendition of the accepted form. Yet when we write a poem we seek to express something personal and original. Some teachers stress the skills of language instruction with emphasis upon correct usage drills, grammatical classification of words and frequent testing. Others would place their emphasis upon the personal expression of ideas by students, feeling that in doing so they are helping them develop the art of language. A modern language program is concerned with both.

1. How was the school you attended organized with regard to the subjects included in the language arts?

2. In class, try an experiment to note the difference between the sender and receiver as far as complete communication is concerned.

> The teacher says, "When I was a little girl (or boy) . . ." How old was the child you pictured in your mind?
> The teacher says, "The dog barked." What kind of dog did you picture? Age? Color?
> The child says, "My grandmother lives in the country." What picture do you see? Is the place a farm, ranch, or suburban area? How old is the grandmother you picture?

3. Use the word *strike* with as many different meanings as you can devise. Look in the dictionary to see how many are listed. How might words of this nature interfere with communication?

4. One problem of communication is the stereotyped association people have with certain words. What is your image of a teacher, scientist, Dutch boy?

WHAT ARE THE OBJECTIVES OF INSTRUCTION IN THE LANGUAGE PROGRAM?

In education we attempt to give direction to our work by deciding what our objectives are. Teachers have stated these objectives in many ways. One statement that has been traditional and widely understood by parents is that the purpose of the elementary school is to teach the three R's: reading, 'riting, and 'rithmetic. These subjects in the minds of many are fundamental or of first importance. The fact that elementary schools were called grammar schools is another evidence of this thinking.

Contrary to some opinions, the schools of today still consider the skills of the three R's as fundamental for life success. Teachers have discovered so much about child psychology that they are able to approach the task from the learner's point of view. The more we know about a child the better we can decide when he will need and use certain skills, when these skills will be most meaningful, and how his interests and attitudes are influenced. When these decisions have been made, a subject

can be organized *psychologically,* or in the way it is learned. If we look at the skills apart from the learner and attempt to define what should come first, second, and third, we say that it is organized *logically.* You will find that in practice we use both logical and psychological organization of materials to gain the results we seek.

One group of teachers [2] has stated their objective in the following manner:

Students need experiences which will help each one to:

1. Develop language powers to the extent permitted by his own ability. This will be dependent upon emotional security as well as intellectual capacity.

2. Understand himself as an individual and as a member of the group.

3. Develop his ability to employ listening, speaking, reading, and writing in the solution of problems confronting him as an individual and as a member of the group.

---

[2] Oakland Public Schools, *Language Arts Course of Study* (Oakland, Calif., 1954).

4. Improve his ability to secure personal satisfaction through competent use of language in getting and sharing ideas.

5. Develop sufficient skill in language usage to make his meaning clear to those with whom he wishes to communicate.

Another group makes this type of statement: [3]

We believe . . .
Language is a universal tool of communication.

Effective communication—oral or written —is based on straight thinking and sincere feeling.

The student's power in the language arts will develop through meaningful experiences, both group and individual, rather than through unrelated drill assignments.

Language mechanics—grammar, punctuation, and spelling—are important skills for effective oral and written expression. These skills must be acquired through purposeful drill and significant use.

Language can contribute to the growth of the individual personality and to the unification of all peoples.

Language skills instruction is a day-long activity, supported by a period set aside for it.

The content of the language program is as broad as the student's interest and need, and draws from all areas of individual and group activity.

You will find other statements made by educators in your area that will help you set up guidelines for your class; some list the needs of each age level or grade, others list the specific skills each grade should master. Some suggest that the textbooks selected provide the objectives needed, others indicate the behaviors expected of children at each grade level. In time you will determine your own objectives in terms of your philosophy as a teacher.

Carefully determined objectives are needed today more than ever; the day is past when teachers can get results merely by following the path or the road they trav-

eled as students. In this age of the super-highway and space exploration, the wrong turn can be costly in both time and energy unless one knows where he is going from the beginning and how to get there.

1. What do you believe at this time about the following statements?:

a. The schools are doing a better job teaching the fundamentals than in the past.

b. Language and spelling errors can best be corrected through drill.

c. All children in the class should have the same spelling book.

d. The fact that there are children in the fifth grade who have a reading level of third grade and below indicates that the schools have failed to teach reading properly.

2. Would you approve of instruction in social courtesy as a language arts objective?

3. How may writing about fears contribute to the emotional maturity of a child?

To be a teacher of the language program you must feel with a deep conviction that the way a child uses his language is important to him both as a student learning to communicate his needs and feelings to others and as an adult requiring mature language skills to meet the problems of a complex society. You will need to have mastered such skills as handwriting, spelling, reading, and oral expression. Along with these basic skills you will need a sensitivity to the beauty expressed through words in poetry and prose, an understanding that words are only the tools of communication with others, and an awareness that thoughts and ideas are the ends or goals for which such skills are perfected. Above all, you must possess a desire to grow in language power as you teach and work with children and as you establish yourself as an individual growing toward teaching competence.

The following partial inventory of teaching knowledge will help you direct your efforts as you become a teacher of the language skills. As the course proceeds you may wish to check your progress.

[3] Tulare County Schools, *Tulare County Cooperative Language Guide* (Visalia, Calif., 1949).

Burbank Public Schools, Calif.

Self-Evaluation Form for Language Teachers

Rate your present skill or knowledge for each of the following aspects of teaching the language arts.

	Satisfactory	Improving	Needs Attention
1. I understand the historical background of the language I teach.			
2. I know how children master language before starting to school.			

Rate your present skill or knowledge for each of the following aspects of teaching the language arts.	Satisfactory	Improving	Needs Attention

3. I know how language instruction fits into the school day.

4. I can explain how reading, writing, listening, and speaking are related.

5. I know what the National Council of Teachers of English is and can name the current publications of that group.

6. I know the educational leaders in the field of language arts instruction.

7. I can give a parent a reference that will help guide the recreational reading of her children.

8. I can intelligently purchase books for a classroom library.

9. I know of books that should be read to children.

10. I can hold children's attention as I tell a story.

11. I know how to share a picture book with little children.

12. I can teach a finger play to a child and explain its importance to his parents.

13. I know how to encourage children to read good literature.

14. I can suggest a variety of book-report techniques to children.

15. I know where to get information concerning a book fair.

16. I know the sources of poetry that are appropriate to the children in my class.

17. I can read poetry well.

18. I know how to direct children in simple verse choir experiences.

19. I can recognize different types of speech defects.

20. I know how to distinguish the speech defects that I can help and those that need a speech specialist.

21. My own voice is free from irritation to those who listen to it.

22. I know how to listen to children.

23. I can discuss with a supervisor the im-

Rate your present skill or knowledge for each of the following aspects of teaching the language arts.	Satisfactory	Improving	Needs Attention

portance of teaching listening in my classroom and give examples of classroom emphasis on listening.

24. I can write print script.

25. I can write neatly and legibly on the chalkboard.

26. I can write a note to a parent and not be embarrassed by my handwriting.

27. I know the reasons why I teach handwriting the way I do.

28. I know how to help a left-handed child write well.

29. I know why our spelling book is organized the way it is.

30. I know how to individualize spelling instruction.

31. I know how to make the spelling period interesting to children.

32. I am able to help children to write creatively.

33. I know the relationship between oral and written composition and use it in my teaching.

34. I understand how standards of performance are established and how to use them to foster improvement in composition.

35. I can plan and produce an assembly program.

36. I know what type of work in composition to expect of children in the separate grades.

37. I understand the fundamentals of basic grammar.

38. I understand the conflict between teaching grammar and functional usage in the grades.

39. I understand the significance of readiness in all learning experience.

40. I know how the textbooks in spelling, penmanship, language, and reading are usually organized and used.

41. I can teach a beginner to read the ma-

Rate your present skill or knowledge for each of the following aspects of teaching the language arts.	Satisfactory	Improving	Needs Attention

terial in the books designed for the first grade.

42. I understand the strength and weaknesses of phonics as applied to spelling and reading.

43. I know of material designed to be used with children who are below grade level in reading.

44. I know these magazines and read them to keep informed concerning the language arts: *Elementary English, N.E.A. Journal, The Reading Teacher, Elementary School Journal, The Instructor,* and *The Grade Teacher.*

45. I can identify these authors of children's books: Doris Gates, Florence Means, Laura I. Wilder, Marjorie Flack, Virginia Lee Burton, Dr. Seuss, Beatrix Potter, Lois Lenski, Astrid Lindgren, Holling C. Holling, and others who have received special awards.

46. I can plan a lesson for one period of reading, a three-day sequence in composition, and for three groups in a single skill for a week.

47. I can make purposeful worksheets in handwriting and reading or know sources of such material.

48. I can give a talk at the P.T.A. explaining the significance of the skills of language arts for children in the space age.

49. I recognize the issues that exist in the language program and seek solutions that will work in my classroom.

50. I am aware of the importance of research in education and seek to keep informed.

WHAT ARE THE CULTURAL INFLUENCES UPON INSTRUCTION IN LANGUAGE?

Abilities in speaking, listening, thinking, reading, and writing are not developed apart from the group life in which each individual learner finds his securities, his values, and his language patterns.

A culture is usually considered to be

the sum total of all the material achievements, customs, beliefs, and values of any group of people; it includes the people themselves and their institutions as well as their ways of communicating and interacting with each other. A culture cannot be viewed merely as an aggregate of parts but must be seen as a human society in which various aspects of the whole are interrelated in a functioning way. Art, literature, and values emerge from the group's social experiences. Thus a culture is a dynamic and changing pattern, always being created by its members and in turn always conditioning the behavior of those who create it.

The American culture pattern furnishes the wider cultural context in which all American schools function. Democratic values and methods, together with a common basic language, make it possible for the United States to be a national or political cultural unit.

Culturally determined goals in language teaching make language a social tool for such purposes as understanding oneself and other people, relating oneself to the world through literature, finding personal satisfaction through expressive and creative use of language to solve personal and group problems, developing discriminative power to detect the purposes behind the written or spoken symbols, and evaluating the reliability of the spoken and printed messages. These goals have grown out of the modern setting of cultural activities. The conditions of living in today's world make it important to listen to and evaluate a radio or TV broadcast, to read and interpret a newspaper intelligently, and to speak, write, read, and listen with concern for integrity, logic, and honesty of expression.

The establishing of newer goals in a position of primary importance demands a new cultural integration of values and events. This integration is a slow process. It is not easy for people to see that the familiar, fundamental three R's may become still more fundamental with a recognition of the purpose for which reading, writing, speaking, and other language tools are used.

The culture holds the values which determine the opportunities for learning in the schools. Such questions as who will go to school, for how long, what kind of building, and who should teach are answered in different ways by different cultures. Laura Ingalls Wilder in *These Happy Golden Years* describes a culture which felt that a few weeks of school in midwinter was adequate.

The culture determines what the interests and experiences of school children shall be. What a child reads, speaks, and writes about is influenced by the family and community in which he lives. Children are most interested in the learning activities they can experience in their learning environments.

The culture determines the meanings that children attach to words and statements. A child raised on the prairies of eastern Colorado has no experience to relate to the word "woods." Eventually through pictures and descriptions he has a meaning but it will never be as complete as that of a child who has watched a forest change through the seasons, known the fun of seeking wild fruit and nuts, or participated in the gathering of maple sap. The Navajo child whose dwelling has always been a hogan does not use, hear, or read the symbol "house" with the same meaning as the child who has lived in a brick bungalow.

The culture determines when learning experiences shall be introduced and the sequence in which skills shall be developed. As knowledge from the fields of child development and social anthropology has accumulated, leaders in education are finding that the cultural patterns of age and grade expectations in a middle-class society do not always agree with what is known about children's intimate growth patterns; the culture often expects learning to occur before the child is ready for it. However, the expectations provide a strong stimulus for learning, and when the timing of the expectation is not out of adjustment with the individual's growth pattern this cultural influence is in favor of educational achievement.

The culture tells what kind of speech is expected of both boys and girls. The little boy is respected for speaking like a male, but scolded, teased, or otherwise punished for speaking like a female. The father serves as a model of the sex culture which the boy is encouraged to learn.

A child speaks the way his family and neighborhood speak because this is the group with which he has made first identifications. To identify with a person or group means to form a strong emotional attachment. A child's first identifications are the result of his human need for love and membership in the group. When a child identifies with someone, he unconsciously imitates that person's speech patterns. He is prone to retain these early speech habits, for they give him an identification badge; they are the symbols by which he proves his belongingness to a group. The extent to which a child speaks correctly or according to the school standards indicates the patterns that are in the security-giving group life surrounding him.

It is significant to note that the social group, even more than the family, provides the pattern for speech imitations after early childhood—more specifically, the peer group to which an individual belongs during later childhood and adolescence. The school must then accept the child as he is and help him to have pleasurable, satisfying experiences with the school group, so that he will want to change his language badge for the one used in school.

When teachers begin to understand the middle-class expectations for rapid training they will more clearly see why early reading and writing have become symbols of status. A child who learns to read early proves his and his parents' worthiness by this important cultural achievement. Fear of losing face with their group causes some parents to pressure children into reading before they show readiness for it. Teachers, too, are sometimes sensitive to their status position and exert similar pressures on children for early reading performance.

The cultural expectation for learning to read during the first year of school experience was established at a time when children were beginning the first reader at the age of seven, eight, or even nine years. It has persisted in the culture pattern, although the age for beginning first grade has been lowered. It was once culturally acceptable to leave school without having mastered reading.

Language instruction is dependent not only upon a child's inner maturational pattern but also upon his experience background and his opportunities for learning. A teacher must respect every child's commonplace experiences. She should dignify some of the everyday incidents of life and thereby help the child feel comfortable about his own home life and group experiences. An example of how this may happen is related by a teacher of a small school. Ten-year-old Jerry, who seemed active and interested outside of the schoolroom but who had never volunteered to share any of his interests in writing, said that he "didn't want to write anything." Jerry had never been to a circus, his only experience with airplanes consisted of watching them fly overhead. He did not have a horse or a pet. The teacher's concern for Jerry's lack of interest in sharing experiences led her to a discovery. Hitherto she had asked children to write about the unusual, or the exciting, or the very, very new experiences which only certain children had. She now changed her approach and encouraged them to write about such everyday occurrences as skinning a knee, getting wet in the rain, or running a race; Jerry then made some attempts to write about these "commonplace" experiences. Later, he wrote rather well about "Hurting My Thumb."

Similarly, a child who comes from a home where a foreign language is spoken or where language opportunities are limited may not be as ready for reading as is the child from a more favorable environment. The school must both supplement and complement the cultural nurturing of language growth.

1. Modern suburban neighborhoods tend to group people of similar income and aspirations. How would this influence the language instruction in the school?

2. A boy in the fourth grade of a suburban school is having trouble in reading. The parents had planned to send the boy to live with his cousins on a farm for the summer. However, the school now plans to have

a special remedial summer school. What would you advise the parents to do?

3. Children in your school use a great deal of profanity. This reflects the language heard at home. What action would you suggest to your fellow teachers?

WHAT CULTURAL INFLUENCES ARE REFLECTED IN THE ENGLISH LANGUAGE?

A major factor in our culture that concerns us is the English language itself. An understanding of the development of English will help to explain the spelling of certain words, the structure of our sentences, the growth of vocabulary, and the changes in usage.

A number of the early outside influences on the language of Britain came from Rome. Julius Caesar, as early as 54 B.C., reconnoitered on British soil and established friendly contacts with various chieftains. The Roman conquest was not completed until a century later and was marked by periods of savage resistance. The completeness of the cultural impact on the Britains is not known; the many Roman ruins throughout Britain would indicate a thoroughgoing Romanization of the country. For a period of almost four hundred years the Romans were in complete control of Britain.

Later the influence of Latin was extended by the activities of the Church. By the sixth century Christianity had spread throughout all of England. Christian converts were among the Anglo-Saxons who conquered England after the Romans left; the Welsh and British inhabitants were for the most part Christians before this time.

There are over 450 words of Latin origin found in Old English; these include: *cheese* (cāseus), *mint* (monēta), *seal* (sigillum), *street* (strata), *kitchen* (coquīna), *cup, plum, inch, wine, abbot, candle, chapter, minister, noon, nun, offer, priest, inscribe* (scribere), *cap, silk* (sericus), *sack, pear, cook, box, school, master, circle, spend, paper, term, title.*

The influence of Latin has continued through the years. Sometimes the borrowed words have come through French, Spanish, or Italian, but many retain their original form or drop an ending. One recognizes the Latin derivation of words like *censor, census, genius, inferior, quiet, reject, legal, history, individual, necessary, picture, nervous, lunatic, interrupt.* The Latin prefixes *pre-, pro-, sub-, super-, anti-,* or endings *-al, -ous, -ty, -ble, -ate, -ism, -tion, -ize, -ic,* are often used with words from other sources.

Of the 20,000 words in full use today about 12,000 are of Latin, Greek, or French origin.

The original speakers of the tongue from which English was born were Germanic dwellers on the eastern or European coast of the North Sea from Denmark to Holland. These Anglo-Saxons and Jutes had undoubtedly raided the British shores even before the Roman departure in A.D. 410.

When the last legions were summoned back to defend their Italian homeland, the Britons started fighting among themselves. The Jutes were called in by the British King Vostigen to assist him, after which they settled in Kent. The Saxons did not arrive until 477 and the Angles in 547. Many of these came as mercenaries lured by the promise of land, which was divided as war booty.

By the beginning of the seventh century this Germanic language which we call Anglo-Saxon emerged from the confusion and turmoil of the British conquest to take its place among the modern tongues of Europe. Among the factors thought to have influenced this development were the wide acceptance of a single religion and the unity of the seven kingdoms to resist the Danish invasions.

The sounds of the language resembled those of modern German rather than those of modern English. The little *c* always had the hard "k" sound. The letters *j, g, v,* were not used; *f* suggested our "v" sound; *h* was more like the "ach" of German. One additional letter, þ, called *thorn,* was used for one of the "th" sounds; we still use it in such signs as "Ye Olde Shoppe." We have lost the "u" sound, and *i* has replaced *y* in many words. Nouns had four cases: nominative, genitive, dative, and accusative. Adjectives were declined to agree with the word modified. Our little word *the* could assume any one of twelve different forms to show gender, number, and case. There were only present and past tenses.

Only a small percentage of our vocabulary today is Anglo-Saxon. If one were to take two thousand Anglo-Saxon words at random, one would find only a little more than five hundred still in use; however, these would include many of our most common words, such as: *man, wife, child, horn, harp, coat, hat, glove, hall, yard, room, bread, fish, milk, house, home, hand, thumb, head, nose, ear, eye, arm, leg, eat, work,* and *play.*

The Anglo-Saxon ability to form compounds led to expressions in which the original elements are almost lost. *Good-by* or *good-bye* is a corruption of "God be with you."

Some words from the Anglo-Saxon have picturesque word origins. *Spider* means "spinner" and *beetle* "biter." *Strawberries* once were berries strung on a straw. The poll in *poll tax* is the old word for *head.*

In spite of the Latin influence in the Church, such Anglo-Saxon words as *god, gospel, lord, Holy Ghost, sin,* and *doomsday* survived. In isolated dialects some Anglo-Saxon forms have resisted change; *larned* is used for "taught," *mooned* for "lunatic," *hundreder* for "centurion," *foresayer* for "prophet," and *gainraising* for "resurrection."

In the year 787 piratical rovers from Scandinavia first visited England, and for more than a hundred years continued to make landings primarily for the sake of pillage. In 840, thirty-five shiploads of Danes landed in Dorset; in 851, three hundred and fifty ships came up the Thames

and apparently for the first time wintered in England. Eventually they became so numerous that, for the sake of order, Alfred the Great made a settlement whereby half of England had its own Danish king; at one time all of England was ruled by these Danish kings. (When you say "They are ill," you are speaking old Norse, from which has descended modern Danish.) At least 1,400 localities in England have Scandinavian names.

Such words as *steak, knife, dirt, birth, fellow, guess, loan, sister, slaughter, trust, wart, window, odd, tight, skin, happy, ugly, wrong, scare,* and *though* are among our language heritage from the Danes. The *-son* of our family names replaced the *-ing* of the Saxon. (Washington actually means "Wasa's children's farm.")

Such doublets as *no—nay, rear—raise, fro—from, shatter—scatter, shirt—skirt, ditch—dike,* and *whole—hole* are a part of the divided language loyalties of the Islanders. The first is Saxon, the second Norse.

The future tense (which had hitherto been expressed by the present, "I go tomorrow"), the pronouns *they, their, them,* and the omission of the relative pronoun *that* in such expression as "the man I saw" were Scandinavian introductions in our language.

The Scandinavian invasion was not limited to the British Isles. Just as the Danes were settling in England, other Norsemen were invading the coast of France. As the British secured peace by granting an area to the invaders, so those in France were granted the region centering about Rouen. These Normans accepted both the religion and the customs of the Franks. Indeed, this acceptance was so rapid that the grandson of their Viking leader Rolf (or Rollo) could not learn his ancestral language at home but was sent away to learn Norse. Thus it was that when these Normans invaded England they not only brought with them the French language but vestiges of Scandinavian as well; indeed, other languages than these were spoken by the forces under William, Duke of Normandy. There were mercenaries from Spain, Italy, and Germany.

The struggle between the hardy race which had been developed in England under the wise policies of Alfred the Great and this Norman force was a long and bitter one. The Anglo-Saxon nobility finally was reduced to the level of their own peasants. Their language was scorned and ignored as being fit only for inferiors. With their defeat, the land was divided among the conquerors.

At the dawn of the thirteenth century there were three languages in England: French was the literary and courtly tongue, Latin the language of the Church and legal documents, and Anglo-Saxon that of the market place.

Conquerors cling to their own ways as long as they plan eventually to return to their homeland. While the Normans were occupying England their forces were defeated in France, and most of them gave up all thought of returning to that land. This changed their attitude toward the Anglo-Saxons and the language they spoke. In 1349 English was reinstated in the schools and in 1362 Parliament was reopened in English. During this time, hundreds of words came into the language. Some were words that one class might acquire from another, such as: *baron, noble, dame, servant, messenger, story, rime, lay.* French law terms remain in use: *fee simple, attorney general, body politic, malice aforethought.* In our kitchens, we use *sauce, boil, fry, roast, toast, pastry, soup, jelly, gravy, biscuit, venison, supper, salad, saucer, fruit, cream.* The French words *beef, veal,* and *pork* remain along with the Saxon *ox, calf,* and *swine.* Our present word *island* represents a blend of Saxon *iegland* and the French word *isle.* Among our synonyms, we have French and Saxon words in *acknowledge, confess; assemble, meet; pray, beseech; perceive, know; power,* and *might.* The words associated with the arts are French, or Late Latin through

French: *amusement, dancing, leisure, painting, sculpture, beauty, color, poetry, prose, study, grammar, title, volume, paper, pen, copy, medicine, grief, joy, marriage, flower.*

Many of the terms of the modern square dance are French. When one "sashays to the corner" the word is an adaptation of *chasser* which means *to chase;* and *do si do* is *dos-à-dos,* or *back-to-back.* Many military terms are French: *army, navy, host, enemy, arms, battle, siege, sortie, defense, soldier, guard, spy, lieutenant, anchor, rank, vanquished, conquer.*

But the most important thing that happened during these years was a tremendous simplification of the language. No longer were nouns and adjectives declined. One form of each word emerged as the one most frequently used. One authority says with a note of regret that if the language had remained neglected by scholars for another hundred years it might have emerged with a great purity of expression and meaning determined on basic usefulness to a people blessed with considerable common sense.

In review then, the English language contains words, patterns of speech, and spelling that were influenced by historical developments. Starting with the ancient Celtic, we next found the Latin influence of the Roman invaders. The basic language structure is Teutonic as introduced to the British Isles by the Angles, Saxons, and Jutes. This in time was influenced by the Danes. With the Norman invasion, we have noted both the French and continuing Scandinavian influences. Because of the Church, the Latin influence continued through the years. While trade with other lands has influenced our vocabulary, these are the major historical sources of the English language we use today.

1. Open any page of a large dictionary and note the indicated origin of the words.

2. Explain this statement: While half the words in common usage are of Latin or Greek origin, half of the words on any one page will be Anglo-Saxon in origin.

WHAT RECENT CHANGES HAVE TAKEN PLACE IN THE ENGLISH LANGUAGE?

With the development of printing, a number of important changes came into the language. The English printer, William Caxton (1422?–1491) made the works of Chaucer (1343–1400) available to the general public beginning in 1477; he is famous for printing the first book in English in 1475 (*The Reccuyell of the Historyes of Troye*).

Something happens when words are reproduced in print; they achieve an importance and dignity they did not possess in manuscript form. The very act of duplication or making copies seems to grant authority to the printed word. The spelling of a word or the sentence structure that appears in such an important literary effort places the stamp of social and cultural approval upon the form; at any rate, we can trace many of our instructional problems in language to these first printed books.

One of the problems was that of spelling. The word *guest* appears as *gest, geste, ghest, gheste; peasant* as *pesant* or *pezant; publicly* as *publickly, publikely, publiquely; yield* as *yeild, yielde,* and *yilde.*

Often it was a printer's effort to make words seem more consistent or even more scholarly that determined the form used. The silent *b* in *debt* and *doubt* originated on the premise that the original Latin forms had *b.* An early form was *det* or *dette.* The *gh* in *delight* and *tight* is a result of analogy with *light* and *night.* A number of words such as *won* in which the *o* represents the sound of *u* were an effort toward spelling reform. When such words are spelled with *u* the handwriting tends to become a confusing series of upstrokes.

It has been estimated that 10,000 words were added to the language during the Renaissance, and they became widespread through the press. Shakespeare added such words or expressions as *accommodating, apostrophe, dislocate, frugal,* *heartsick, needle-like, long-haired, green-eyed, hot-blooded.* Words such as *capacity, celebrate, fertile, native, confidence,* and *relinquish* were called "barbarisms," and were understood by few readers.

No description of this time would be complete without reference to the King James Bible of 1611. It is estimated that less than 6,000 different words are used in this translation and that fully 94 per cent of these were part of the common speech of the day. The translators were apparently concerned with reaching the masses in a language that would be understood by all. Hence it was up to them to use the best-known words.

Some words are repeated with great frequency (*and* is used 46,277 times). While there is monotony in some parts, the text is usually very clear in spite of the profound ideas expressed. While Shakespeare shows us the range of thought that can be expressed with many (15,000–17,000) words, the Bible demonstrates almost the same range with only a few (6,000).

Today a highly literate adult is not likely to have a recognition vocabulary of much more than 150,000 words. Of this number a few will be used over and over again. One-fourth of all our spoken words consists of a repetition of the words *and, be, have, it, of, the, to, will, you, I, a, on, that,* and *is.*

Since the invention of printing, new words have been added to English in many ways. Some are borrowed from other languages, others have been created for new products, and still others seem to be accidents or the results of misunderstanding foreign speech. If a person who spoke Anglo-Saxon were to listen to us today, he would have a very difficult task understanding all that is said.

From the Italian we find these words: *design, piazza, portico, stanza, violin, volcano, alto, piano, torso, 'cello, vogue, sere-*

nade, trombone, broccoli, boloney, confetti (hard candy), *cash, carnival, cartoon, studio, solo, opera.*

Spanish words include *alligator, banana, canoe, cocoa, hammock, hurricane, mosquito, potato, tobacco, rodeo, cockroach, cork, tornado, sombrero.* In western United States many towns, hills, rivers, are Spanish-named as a result of the early exploration and settlement in those states during the seventeenth and eighteenth centuries. The terms of ranch life and the cowboy and his vigilante equipment are usually Spanish in origin: *hacienda, mustang, corral, lasso, lariat.*

The Dutch are responsible for such words as *chapter, yacht, schooner, boor, drawl, deck, boom, cruiser, furlough, landscape, tub, scum, freight, jeer, snap, cookie, toy, switch, cole slaw,* and *yankee.*

The Arabic language gave us *candy, lemon, orange, spinach, sugar, algebra, alkali, alcohol, assassin, syrup, sofa, divan, mattress, magazine,* and *safari.*

From Hebrew, we find *camel, ebony, sapphire, seraph, cherub, cabal, rabbi.*

From India comes *loot, pundit, rajah, punch, coolie, bungalow, calico, cot, polo, thug, khaki.*

Kimono, samurai, and *kamikaze* are Japanese.

Malay gave us *caddy.*

The primitive tribes of Africa are responsible for *gorilla, voodoo, zebra,* and probably *jazz.*

The American Indians are the creators of many of our words; among these are *moccasin, raccoon, skunk, totem, woodchuck, hominy, caucus,* and *tomahawk.* Every state contains Indian place names: Chicago, which means "a place that smells like skunks," and Peoria, "a place of fat beasts," Manhattan, "the place where all got drunk."

New words come into our language almost daily. Some are changes in the word root: *edit* from *editor, peddle* from *peddler, jell* from *jelly.* Others are abbreviations such as *pub* for *public house, cad* from *cadet, pup* from *puppy.* Some imitate other words: *motorcade* and *aquacade* from *cavalcade, litterbug* from *jitterbug, telethon* from *marathon.* We combine words to

make new ones with *smoke* and *fog* becoming *smog; motor* and *hotel* becoming *motel; liquid oxygen* becomes *lox*—used for combustion of fuel in rockets.

Old words are used in new ways or as different parts of speech. A master of ceremonies is abbreviated *emcee;* this in turn becomes a verb in such usage as: "Allen may emcee the show." An example of one word used to serve different parts of a sentence in the newspaper headline that reads: "Police Police Police Show."

Words change in meaning. *Harlot* once was a servant, *wanton* and *lewd* meant "untaught" or "ignorant." *Notorious* was simply "well known." A *governor* was a "pilot," *rheumatism* meant a "head cold," and a *nice person* was a "foolish" person.

In the years since the war many words have been added to our language: *Cinerama, countdown, zoorama, fallout, readout,* and *sonic boom* are examples.

Modern slang is a source of new words. Often this is the private language of an age group. Expressions like "Twenty-three skiddoo" are now archaic, since they are no longer part of the living language. One recent coinage, however, seems to have found a permanent place in our speech. One sees it in headlines. The President uses it and it has found a place in literature. It is the term *to goof.* It means "to make a mistake, yet know better." When one word will say that much, it probably deserves a permanent place in our language. The third edition of Webster's *New International Dictionary* does not consider this term to be slang, although similar expressions are still held to be questionable usage.

Today the opportunities for vocabulary enrichment have been both extended and accelerated by the advent of such instruments of communication as radio, motion pictures and television. The number of radios in use has grown from about 15 million in 1950 to more than 80 million today. To this we might add the influence of almost 20 million television sets. The influence of the motion picture has been increased not only by the entertainment film in commercial theaters and drive-ins but also by those made especially for television or for instructional use in school.

San Diego State College Laboratory School

Listening to the taped recording of the first American astronaut's flight gives meaning to such new words as lox, countdown, pad, egress, gantry, drogue chute and re-entry. The class calls this equipment their "Listening Post."

The amount of reading material now being published is almost unbelievable. In 1900 the daily newspaper circulation was just over nine million copies; today it is more than 52 million. The average newspaper has increased almost fourfold in size; indeed, the Sunday edition in many cities contains over a hundred pages. In 1900 there were 266 magazines published with a circulation of 23 million; today over 5,000 magazines with more than 208 million copies circulate in this country. This circulation is larger than our population and equals six magazines per month for each family in America.

While the adults in the United States do not read books with as high a frequency as do readers of many other countries, the total production is significant; in 1947, there were 9,182 different books published with a total sale of 487 million copies. In 1962 the number of titles published was 16,448. The figures on paperbacks are not available, but their total circulation is vast. The surprising as well as satisfying fact is that such books as *Coming of Age in Samoa* by the anthropologist, Margaret Mead, and *The Pocket Book of American Verse* have each sold over a million copies.

The wealth of our public libraries should not go unnoticed. The attitude that books are to be used by all who desire to read them rather than treasures to be hoarded has influenced the language picture of our day. The English language is truly a many-splendored thing. We are the heirs of a language of tremendous vigor and force; its extraordinary growth both as to words and geographical range is only a partial witness of the value of our heritage. It is our task as teachers not only to help children to understand the wonderful power of this language, but to guide students so that its use will enrich their lives and those with whom they live.

1. Make a list of new words and slang expressions as you hear them or see them in print.

2. How should we explain the use of slang to children?

3. What influence do you think the paperback books have had on the reading habits of individuals your age?

4. Find examples of good and poor English used in comic books or in television programs. Do these have any influence on the children you teach?

5. A new word was coined by the press at the time this book was being written. The first monkey had been sent into space and recovered. Within three days children across our land were talking of the *chimpanaut*. Can you identify a recent word coined in current news events?

6. How could the story of a word's origin help a child remember its spelling?

7. A few of the long words of our language may add interest to a bulletin board or discussion. Here are some: *antidisestablishmentarianism* was used in 1869 by Prime Minister Gladstone to describe the principles of those opposed to the separation of Church and State. *Honorificabilitudinitatibus* appears in the fifth act of "Love's Labour's Lost" by Shakespeare. *Floccinaucinihilipilification* means estimation of worthless. *Pneumonoultramicroscopicsilicovolcanokoniosis* means a disease of the lungs. *Aqueosalinocalcalinocetaceoluminosocupreovitriolic* was used to describe the waters at Bristol, England.

8. Some of the language found in the Bible is no longer used. Why do we no longer use *thee, thou* and such verb forms as *maketh*?

9. Can you explain some of these inconsistencies?

An English Test

We'll begin with box, the plural is boxes,
But the plural of ox should be oxen, not oxes.
One fowl is a goose, but two are called geese,
Yet the plural of mouse is never meese.
You may find a lone mouse, or a whole nest of mice,
But the plural of house is houses, not hice.
If the plural of man is always men,
Why shouldn't the plural of pan be called pen?
The cow in the plural may be called cows or kine,
But a bow, if repeated, is never called bine;
And the plural of vow is vows, not vine.
If I speak of a foot and you show me two feet,
And I give you a boot, would a pair be called beet?
If one is a tooth and a whole set are teeth,
Why shouldn't the plural of booth be called beeth?
If the singular's this, and the plural these,
Should the plural of kiss ever be written keese?
We speak of a brother, and also of brethren,
But though we say mother, we never say mothren.
Then the masculine pronouns are he, his, and him,
But imagine the feminine, she, shis, and shim!
So the English, I think you all will agree,
Is the funniest language you ever did see.

—UNKNOWN

HOW DO CHILDREN LEARN LANGUAGE?

By the time we meet the child as his teacher, a tremendous amount of learning has already taken place. Because the language the child brings to school is so important, let us start by a brief survey of what has happened during those preschool years.

By the end of the first month of life a mother can often detect pain, rage, or mere exuberance in the vocalization of the baby. Just as the baby makes random movements with his arms and legs and is in general learning some control over his body, so does he exercise his voice mechanism. At the end of four months most infants have mastered fairly well the principles basic to effective use of the vocal mechanism. They blow bubbles, chuckle, gurgle, laugh, and experiment with the use of the tongue, larynx, and breath control. This might be called the babble stage of language growth. Through it the infant learns the modification in tension of vocal chords and the positions of tongue and lips necessary to the imitation of the sounds he hears. He has command of most of the vowels and a few consonant sounds at this time. By six or seven months some children are able to make all of the consonant and many of the diphthong sounds necessary for speech. By nine months the babble softens into the rhythm of the speech the child hears around him. Actual words begin to develop at eleven or twelve months when the child's active vocabulary consists of *mama, daddy,* and one or two other words.

It is difficult to decide when babblings cease and actual words are substituted. Since it is necessary to depend on parents for records, data is not always reliable. The first words are so anxiously awaited that word formation is likely to be more imagined than real.

The first words are usually monosyllables. As soon as parents notice the first *ma, da* or *by,* they encourage the child and soon some association of sound and situation is established. In the main the first words are interjections or nouns. Added by gestures the child is able to convey a variety of meanings with only one word. The single word *water* or *wa-wa* may mean "I want a drink," "see the bath," "it is raining," or "bottle," "glass."

First words have an emotional quality. They may express a wish or feeling. Or again, they may express a real personal need. Interestingly enough, it is believed by some authorities that speaking the word is secondary to the general emotional status of the child at the time of using the word. As words are learned they are used to supplement body movements, emotional expressions and other devices used to express wants. In time language becomes a substitute for certain aggressive behavior of children.

Imitation plays an important role in the child's linguistic development. Evidence of learning by imitation is shown by the fact that the child learns the language of his environment, and by the fact that the congenitally deaf child cannot learn normal speech, since he is unable to hear and therefore cannot imitate sound. Of equal importance to the imitation of others is the imitation by the child of those sounds which he himself has made. Nearly everyone is familiar with the continued repetition of a sound by an infant. It is thought that a desire to hear himself talk is what contributes to this activity. When the child is in the presence of adults and accidentally or purposely makes sounds, parents are likely to pronounce a word which approximates the sound made by the child. This is good training since it provides an auditory strengthening and stimulates the child to remake the sound he has produced.

Understanding the language of others is of great assistance to the child in learning to use language himself. Normally a child has considerable understanding of what others are saying before he uses words. Such understanding occurs at about the end of his first year. The infant's use of gestures before he can speak is evidence that he understands adults.

A method of studying children's vocabulary development is the direct observation procedure. The investigator records all of the child's utterances in a given situation. In a study of twenty-five babies during the first two years of life, Shirley noted some trends in oral vocabulary growth. The children were interviewed and tested at weekly intervals during the first year and at biweekly intervals during the second year of life.

Expressive Response	Median Age in Weeks
One syllable	8
Two syllables	13
Talk to person	25
Singing tones	32
Expressive sounds	37.5
Single consonants	35
First word	60
First imitative word (bow wow, etc.)	66
Name picture in book	
Dog	84
Baby	98
First pronoun	99
First phrase	101
First sentence	101

On the average, each baby had spoken approximately thirty-seven different words in the interview situation by two years of age. The range was from 6 to 126. There were a total of 274 different words used by the entire group.[4]

The tremendous amount of oral expressiveness indulged in by young children is illustrated in an unusual report. Every word uttered by a girl two and one-half years old was recorded for a full day, from seven in the morning until seven-thirty at night. Here is an example of this child's expression as she sat with her grandmother:

I'm sewing a button—I found a big button, too. That's the best one. Now it'll be all right. On this side. Now I make a nightgown. Is that a knot? Helen don't have a very large buttonhole either. Cut it now. Now the button is sewed on. Now I have to get another string. Here's a pad—didy to go underneath. Here's the woolen blanket. I found it. Helen has some more sewing to do. Helen wants to set a buttonhole on it. What kind of buttonhole? What kind of buttonhole? What kind of buttonhole? That's too little. That's not very large. I'm not ready.

Speech is often a social overture such as the asking of a question that requires no answer. Talking often accompanies action in other motor areas. The child appears bent on filling every waking moment with oral expression; indeed, it seems that talking is almost compulsive in nature.

One investigator found that in a single day his three-year-old child asked 376 questions and that his four-year-old child asked 397.[5] This is probably somewhat high for average children, but gives an idea of why this age is referred to as the question age. As early as three years language serves the purpose of simple narration, the incidents talked about usually are telescoped into a single simple sentence. "We went downtown," being used to cover all the exciting situations involved. Occasionally children of three can enlarge upon this, and some children of four can tell enough of an incident to hold the attention of other children. Imaginative elements often creep in, possibly as a reflection of the stories being read to children at that age. "Once there was a big engine. It came right up to the door and asked for breakfast."

The most complicated and advanced use of language is to express reasoning: "If I don't wear my mittens, I won't get them dirty," or "Where does my dinner go when I eat it?" As the child's experiences enlarge, and as his mastery of vocabulary increases, the form of reasoning he can do becomes increasingly complex.

In content of language we find a predominance of egocentricity in the speech of young children. The six year old's insistent: "Look at me—See me!" is familiar to every parent and teacher.

Almost all studies of children's language have noted the lateness with which pronouns are added to the child's vocabulary. It is not unusual to hear a three-year-old refer to himself as Jimmy rather than I, me or myself. Dr. Dorothea McCarthy of Fordham University conducted a study by recording responses from twenty children at each of seven age levels, from eighteen to fifty-four months.[6] She found that nouns constitute about 50 per cent of the total speech of very young children. Verbs increase from about 14 per cent of the total speech at eighteen months to about 25 per cent at fifty-four months. Adjectives increase over the same interval from about 10 to about 20 per cent. Connectives do not show up until about two years of age and then steadily increase in proportion. These developmental trends explain the peculiar flavor of the very young child's speech. He typically uses many nouns and verbs, very few pronouns, and practically no connectives. His speech is thus direct, unadorned, and essentially disconnected.[7]

The rapid speech of nursery school and kindergarten children has been studied with the aid of a mechanical hand tally and stop watch. The findings indicate that children of this age level have an average verbal output of about sixteen words per

---

[4] From *The First Two Years: A Study of Twenty-five Babies,* Vol. II by Mary M. Shirley, Child Welfare Monograph Series, No. 7. University of Minnesota Press, Minneapolis, Copyright 1933 by the University of Minnesota.

[5] *Ibid.,* p. 327.

[6] Leonard Carmichael, *Manual of Child Psychology* (New York: Wiley, 1951), p. 476.

[7] *Ibid.,* p. 530.

minute, and an average rate of 186 words per minute while speaking. When one considers the average rate of about 100 words per minute adapted by experienced lecturers, the young child's verbalization rate is indeed high. It was further found that the child who talked the most uttered approximately seven times as many words as the child who talked the least. Boys tended to speak less than girls in a given time interval, but spoke more rapidly when they did verbalize.[8]

Measuring the vocabulary of an individual presents many problems. Words used will be limited to the occasion or situation. Decisions must be made as to what constitutes a word. Should *chairs* be counted as a separate word from *chair,* should *moo-moo* be accepted as a word for *cow,* should one meaning of a word be counted as a separate vocabulary understanding from its other meanings?

Vocabulary studies have been made in a number of situations. Conversations have been recorded, the written material of an individual has been analyzed, children have been stimulated to write all the words they know by showing them pictures or giving them key words, lists have been used to check recognition.

One research study used a pocket dictionary of 18,000 words to check vocabulary. As a result it was concluded that a twelve-year-old knew 7,200 words. When another study used a dictionary of 371,000 words it was concluded that a child that age would know 55,000 words. With respect to the vocabulary of first-grade children, some studies indicate that a vocabulary of 2,500 words is normal when others indicate 24,000 words.[9]

Repeated tests with college undergraduates indicate that their vocabulary is over 100,000 words, probably over 200,000. It would be expected that such vocabulary development would be gradual through the individual's growth. The evidence would indicate that the vocabulary of children has probably been underestimated.

An additional consideration is the fact that an individual's speaking vocabulary will differ from his listening and reading vocabularies. Children understand many words spoken to them that they never use in their own speech. Adults read words that would not be used in their spoken vocabulary.

1. How might the parental use of "baby talk" such as "itsy bitsey bow wow" influence the speech habits of a child?

2. How may the "Southern dialect" of the United States have been started?

3. Should we seek uniformity in the speech habits of children?

4. Note any influence of television on the speech of children you know.

5. Listen to the questions of little children. How many seek an answer? How many are conversational openings?

6. Ask your parents to recall any words you invented and used which were understood by the family.

7. In later childhood there are many words with regard to games that are the inventions and sole property of childhood. In hide and seek we have "Allee-allee-otsen-free!" for "all in free." "Dibs" means "that's mine," or "Dibs on first base" means "I get to play first base." Can you think of others?

HOW DO WE WORK WITH THE VERY YOUNG CHILDREN IN SCHOOL?

At the age of five, each day is one of wonder and discovery. There are new things to see, new words to use, and new ideas to try. No day is long enough to see it all, and tomorrow seems so far away. As a teacher you will be amazed at children's energy and constant need for activity.

In order to work well with this age, a teacher must learn to use a very different technique from that suitable for an older group of young adults. In the Orient, a form of wrestling called "judo" has been

---

[8] *Ibid.*, p. 553.

[9] Nancy Larrick, "How Many Words Does a Child Know?" *The Reading Teacher,* (December 1953), pp. 100–104.

developed. It is a method of using the strength and energy of an opponent so that it reacts against him. When an opponent makes a rushing attack, the master of judo estimates his force and momentum and instead of meeting it with an opposite force, attempts to direct it against the opponent himself, so that he is thrown to the floor. Although the analogy is a bit strained, it suggests how the teacher can manage the energy of young children. She should not try to stop it or even keep up with it; but she should attempt to understand it, and provide ways for directing this energy so that the child's needs may be met.

A visit to a kindergarten will reveal the physical characteristics of the age. Children are active and must move their large muscles. There are room centers where movement is appropriate and which are equipped with play equipment suitable for children in this age group. Girls grow faster than boys and are frequently more mature in all respects. Because this is the age of chicken pox, measles, and mumps, there are frequent physical checkups and absences. Because vision is not yet mature, the child is protected from activities that call for frequent refocusing of the eyes. Rest periods and quiet times alternate with periods of activity because fatigue is a natural result of expending so much energy.

Intellectually these children are beginning to understand time patterns, can follow simple directions, see differences more readily than similarities, are not quite certain about the distinction between reality and fantasy, and are able to tell or retell simple stories. The teacher provides opportunities to talk about and distinguish between imaginary and real things. The group shares experiences in order to build a common background. There is freedom to ask questions. Perhaps most important of all, children have an opportunity to listen and to be aware of the things they have learned through listening.

Emotionally the five-year-old demands affection and attention. The desire to please is powerful and many ways are used to gain status. Some show evidence of fear of the unknown, and the wise teacher is careful about phobic response to punish-ment. At this age the threat of being sent to the principal's office can become in the imagination of a child almost equal to that of capital punishment for an adult. On the playground they become combative but are beginning to substitute language for force, using name-calling or verbal quarreling instead of hitting and kicking.

In the classroom there are outlets for emotions through dramatic plays, listening to verse, creative expression with paints, clay, and paper. There is freedom to express opinions without fear of criticism, freedom from pressure to work beyond abilities. Help is given the child to recognize himself as an individual and to respect the individuality of others. Limits to behavior are clearly defined so that the child is aware of how things are done inside while sitting on the rug, while tinkering with toys or equipment, or when playing outdoors or moving in single file through the halls.

Socially, children of this age are self-centered in contact with others. They have to learn how to work in a group, find sharing of prized objects a bit difficult, and look to adults for approval.

In the classroom the children are given an opportunity to participate in group activities and to be creative in social situations by dictating stories, poems, and experiences to the teacher, who records them. Opportunities to look at the work or behavior of the group, or of other small groups provide occasions to define limits and expectations.

The children are taught such specifics as what to reply when a visitor comes to our room and says, "Good morning, girls and boys." How may we show a visitor what we are doing? How can this block-house be made better? What might we do to improve the way we played at the swing today?

While much of what is done in school at this age is important to the immediate needs of the child, teachers must anticipate the future needs that must be satisfied as the child masters reading, writing, and the skills needed by educated persons in our society. The term used to describe this is "promotion of readiness." Among the many factors involved in language readiness are the following:

Children master the appropriate language for social living through purposeful play.

Broad, rich experience.
Vocabulary development.
Ability to attend (stories, completion of work, participation).
Seeing likeness and differences.
Hearing likeness and differences.
Organizing thought in sequence.
Being able to classify and generalize.
Ability to follow instructions.
Ability to speak clearly.
Interest in books and experience of others.
Ability to draw conclusions.
Ability to recall details.

A wise teacher looks at the language needs of children at the kindergarten level and asks herself two questions: What skill do they need now as they live and work together in this room? And what later needs will be influenced by what we do? These children are not taught to read, spell, or write, but nearly every activity will be related to later development of these skills. As children learn to identify their own clothes hangers, as they watch the teacher put labels on objects in the room or write the day of the week on the chalkboard, each child begins to understand the meaning of reading. When a particular sound appeals to a child and he repeats it in a song or verse, he is mastering the sounds of our language which will later help him in spelling. The pictures done with great concentration at the easel are expressive experiences almost identical with writing in that they express an idea or experience visually.

From the moment the child enters the room and is greeted in a friendly manner until he leaves with a satisfactory feeling about the day, he has many language experiences. As he makes an airplane, he enjoys using the words that he has heard: *jet, pilot, hostess, fuel,* and maybe *supersonic.* As he paints the plane, color words take on meaning. A feeling of orderliness, neatness, and appropriateness accompanies his activities throughout the day. In cleanup, he uses words like *over, under, behind, beside,* which have indefinite associations. Dramatic play in the home, store, and other interest centers calls for conversations which explain sentence structure, choice of words, and organization of ideas. On his walks he learns to see, listen to, and appreciate the sights and sounds of nature. When his sensory experiences are vivid, he bubbles over with ideas and loves to talk about what he saw, what he did, how things look, and how he feels.

Throughout the day the teacher finds the right moment to bring literature either to one child alone or to a group of children. As a child works with others to build a road, church, or bridge, the teacher may find an occasion to read to the group such poems as James Tippet's "Trains," "Trucks," "Tugs," and "The River Bridge." A teacher who can go to her file and find "My Dog" and read, "His nose is short and stubby, his ears hang rather low," ending with the thought "Oh, puppy, I love you so," has given the group an expression for their inner feeling. If she teaches them the action play or finger play that starts, "My dog, Duke, knows many tricks," and substitutes the name of Mary's dog, new experience is shared.

At times, the teacher is wisest who remains silent and waits for children to react. She realizes that truly educative experiences mean not only active presentation of ideas, questions, and materials, but also a quiet alertness to and observation of the child's responses to the environment and to her.

There is much "planned" listening for these children. While they close their eyes, they listen to the fire crackling, the sound of a truck passing, or an object being tapped. They listen to the teacher reading and to each other telling about the events at home. It has been said that "the child who listens is one who has been listened to." In order to serve the child's listening needs, we establish standards not only for what children will tell us but also for how they will listen. The group decides that today we will only tell about happy things, beautiful things, pets, or things that make sounds. The very shy may tell only the teacher, the very vocal must limit himself to only one incident of his trip.

The child leaves the kindergarten with the beginnings of many skills. Among those closely related to language, one should note these:

Ability to listen:
When a story is read aloud.
When a speaker is telling of an experience.
To different sounds and tones.
To directions.
To hear likenesses and differences.
To rhythms.
To gain ideas.

Ability to speak:
In complete thoughts rather than single words.
Repeating sounds.
Imitating good speech patterns.
In a pleasant voice.
Telling of his own experience.
Showing feeling in manner of expression.

Abilities related to future reading:
Recognizing simple sequence.
Recognizing likenesses and differences in shape and size.
Connecting symbols with ideas.
Care in handling picture books.
Interpreting the events in a picture.

Abilities related to future writing:
Learning to use paintbrush, chalk, pencil.
Putting teacher-made signs and labels on objects.
Expressing oral ideas which the teacher records.
Experimenting with paint, chalk, crayon, and pencil in imitating writing.

1. How may children who have not had kindergarten be helped at the beginning of first grade?

2. What does modern research indicate with respect to teaching some children to learn to read at the end of kindergarten?

3. Are the major purposes of kindergarten important enough to justify the expense of these institutions?

4. What tests should be used to check the sight of young children?

WHAT WILL CHILDREN IN THE GRADES BE LIKE?

As children progress through the first and second grades their standards often exceed their abilities. There is much dissatisfied crumpling of paper or erasing. One writer describes this as the "eraser" age. Teachers sometimes make it a rule that all erasing will be done by the teacher in order to keep children from rubbing holes through the paper. This behavior is only one aspect of the child's awareness of criticism from peers or age mates. The world is no longer made for him alone but for the group or gang with whom he identifies himself. What others think, the praise or punishment that others receive, other children's opinions about things, now have much greater influence on his conduct than previously.

There is a loss in personal freedom of expression in art and story. Where the child once wanted to paint simply what he felt or saw, he is now concerned about the effect his work will produce on others. Group judgment or practice will influence his clothes, eating habits, books read, language used, and personal conduct.

By the age of eight, definite speech patterns have developed. The eye is more adapted to the tasks of reading and writing. There is a sense of hurry and untidiness which is related to a tendency toward accidents. These accidents are also associated with curiosity and interests that outdistance caution. Exploring the unknown is a favorite activity.

Emotionally, primary children desire and seek prestige. The Cub Scout or Brownie uniform is worn with pride. Those who do not belong show jealousy, and because feelings are still near the surface, violent outbursts or sullen withdrawal can be expected at times. Boy-girl relationships are wholesome and are either at the companion level or ignored. These children look for recognition from adults through use of social courtesies and individual association, but at the same time seek independence through peer group approval. Most want adults to keep "hands off," literally and figuratively.

The older children of this age range are sometimes referred to as being in the latency period rather than preadolescence. Since they have already mastered the basic skills they can follow their interests in all directions. Teachers of these groups are true generalists from the educational point of view. One day they may be learning how humans can breathe in outer space, the next how the United Nations is organized, and on the third how the Aztec Indians told time.

In the sixth grade many of the girls have entered adolescence. They find emotions difficult to control. Trivial sights or events can cause a major crisis. Some overt emotional display may belie underlying causes. Sometimes these children cry when happy and show antagonism toward persons they admire. Ordinarily, the girls are taller and weigh more than the boys throughout the intermediate grades.

Intermediates like to plan and organize. Clubs are organized almost solely for the fun of organizing them, although such activity may express a yearning for great achievement. There is little regret when nothing of much significance happens in a club meeting. The important thing seems to be that the meeting took place. Close friends also constitute an aspect of this period and new friendships explain some of the changed classroom behavior. Elections are often little more than popularity contests. New students go through a period of popularity as individuals seek them as friends. Note-passing, and in a few cases, actual flaunting of boy or girl friend, are other common forms of social behavior at this time.

Working with these children requires a fine balance of permissiveness and control. At times free rein must be given to permit maximum use of abilities and extension of interest. At other times the control of the adult leader must be exercised to prevent immature judgments and emotional actions. This control requires both a knowledge of each individual and the nature of group interaction.

Beginning teachers are usually unprepared for the wide range in abilities encountered. A study in Ferndale, Michigan, showed a reading range among children aged seven of 32 months while among those aged twelve it was 107 months.[10] The range in mental age increased from 65 months at age seven to 107 months at age twelve. Excluded from this study were children who had been placed in special rooms, so in some classrooms teachers would expect a greater range than this. Ferndale is a suburban city near Detroit. The range is probably similar in most American communities. This means that we must expect great variability in the results of teaching effort. There are many common interests and needs toward which teaching energies are directed, but by no effort or magic can we produce common achievement or "fifth-grade work" or "sixth-grade norms" with a total class. We have not failed as teachers nor have some children failed as students. Although teaching and learning took place, the responses were influenced by the individual abilities of those with whom we work.

Previous studies of the growth patterns

[10] W. A. Ketcham and Rondeau G. Lafitte, "A Description and Analysis of Longitudinal Records of Development of Elementary School Children in Ferndale, Michigan," Ferndale Public Schools, 1960.

of individual children reveal that each child's pattern is uniquely his own. Some start early and continue to grow rapidly, while others start late and are always behind their age mates. Yet we cannot be certain that one who starts early will be always ahead of his group. The following case study reveals why teachers hesitate to make absolute predictions.

At 78 months of chronological age all of Mary's growth measurements but one were below her chronological age. Her mental age was 64 months, reading age 74 months, weight age 76 months, and height age 84 months. By 138 months of chronological age, all of her growth measurements were above her chronological age. The child's IQ was 100 when she was 78 months old and 131 when she was 137 months old. By age twelve she had a reading age of fifteen although her reading did not equal her chronological age until age 8.

Such children are not unusual. Parents will sometimes say, "My boy did not like reading until he had Miss Nelson in the fifth grade." With all due credit to Miss Nelson, it is safe to assume that the child was probably like the girl described above. However, it may have been the efforts of a Miss Nelson that prevented this child from accepting a self-image of being slow to learn or poor in scholarship.

Children move through this sequence of language growth in the elementary school—no two at the same rate or in the same way.[11]

[11] Tulare County Schools: *Tulare County Cooperative Language Arts Guide* (Visalia, Calif., 1949).

Kindergarten (4½–6 years)

Listening: Listen to peers in play groups. Develop an increasingly long attention span to stories. Can remember simple directions and messages.

Speaking: A few will still be developing speech sounds, using them correctly in some words and not in others. Use simple direct sentences. The vocabulary ranges from 2,000 to over 10,000 words.

Reading: Interpret pictures, explore books, can identify some signs such as STOP or displayed words on television. About 1 in 600 can read children's books.

Writing: Likes to watch adults write. Experiments with crayola and paints.

Grade One (5½–7 years)

Listening: Listen to clarify thinking or for answers to questions. Can repeat accurately what is heard. Listen for specific sounds in words and the environment.

Speaking: Can share experiences before the group in an established way. Use compound and complex sentences. Use the grammar patterns of the home. Some speech repetition takes place as they try to remember words for ideas they wish to express.

Reading: Read charts, preprimers and primers, and master a vocabulary of 300 to 600 words. Understand the use of many consonant sounds.

Writing: Write names, labels for pictures and stories to illustrate art work. The spelling applies the phonics of reading.

Grade Two (6½–8)

Listening: Listen with increasing discrimination. Making suggestions and asking questions to check their understanding. Are aware of situations when it is best not to listen.

Speaking: Have mastered all sounds of speech and use them correctly. Use some of the "shock" words of our language without complete understanding.

Reading: Read with increasing attention to meaning, enjoy selecting their own stories, read their own writing. Usually start the year in a first reader of a commercial reading series.

Writing: Write well with print script. Use dictionary books or notebooks as references for spelling. Seek to correct misspellings.

Third to Fourth Grade (7½–10)

Listening: Are increasingly aware of the value of listening as a source of information and enjoyment. Listen to the reports of others, tapes of their own reports, and radio broadcasts with purpose and pertinent questions. Display arrogance with words or expressions they do not understand.

Speaking: Re-enact and interpret creatively radio, movie and story situations as they play. Speak fairly well to adults and can make themselves understood. Are praised in most school associated social situations. Vocabulary of some children may be as high as 60,000 words.

Reading: Read with interpretive expression. Grown in reading speed as they read silently. Most children succeed in using reading as a study skill.

Writing: Cursive writing is learned. Reports are written in all subject areas. Creative stories and poems are written. Write rough copies with a willingness to recopy to improve legibility, ideas, and punctuation.

Fifth to Sixth Grade (9½–12)

Listening: Listen critically for errors, propaganda, false claims. Listen to a wide variety of stories, poetry, rhyme, find pleasure in exploring new types.

Speaking: Show an increasing awareness of the social value of conversation and try to get what they want through persuasion. Become increasingly competent in the use of inflections, modulation and other methods of voice control employing singing, yelling, whispering, and talking. Can conduct club meetings and present organized talks or dramatic recitations.

Reading: Show increased interest in factual material and how to do it books. Many read independent of instruction. Use reading with greater purpose such as getting information for a trip, checking references, or following a personal interest. Adapt method and speed of reading to the content and purpose.

Writing: Make between 1½ to 2 errors in each sentence at first. Find new uses for writing as they answer advertisements and do creative work. Are interested in the writing techniques of others and will note good and poor composition in the newspapers. Like to see their writing in print. Use the dictionary as a spelling aid.

The chapters that follow present many of the specific techniques used to achieve their results.

1. What events or incidents remain in your memories of the school years between ages nine to twelve? Were you in a program? Can you recall a favorite book? Did you write any letters?

2. In light of what we know about child growth would it be possible to group children of similar ability at the beginning of a school year and keep them similar throughout the year?

HOW DO SCHOOLS MEET THE SPECIAL NEEDS OF INDIVIDUAL STUDENTS?

The classroom teacher does two things to meet the extreme ranges of talent and abilities encountered in some classrooms. One is to modify the requirements of the regular curriculum; the other is to enrich the content of the curriculum. Usually we modify the requirements for children who are slow in maturing or handicapped, and enrich for those who are above average or gifted. In a sense, the modification for the slow child is an enrichment for him.

With respect to the gifted, the term "enrichment" describes two types of practices. One is to give these children more advanced work. This can be done by promoting the child to a class where he works with students much older than himself, but where he finds the contest a stimulating challenge. Or the child may be kept with children his own age and yet work in books that are more difficult than those read by the other children. Thus, an eleven year old gifted child might be reading Shakespeare either in a fifth-grade class or with a high school group. This method is usually called vertical enrichment, since the child moves upward toward more difficult material. The other type of enrichment would be to have able children remain with their age mates but explore areas that all the other children do not share. The gifted child might study a foreign language, astronomy or geology, or read avidly as he solves research problems, sharing the results with his classmates. This type of practice is called horizontal enrichment.

We do not know which method is best. The answer may be a combination of the two, or it may depend upon the child. With respect to language arts the horizontal type is more apt to meet the needs of most children. Our mission is not achieved by treating children as adults. In spite of an individual's brilliance, the adult world will seldom have a place for a fifteen- or sixteen-year-old as an equal. The years of youth are precious and brief. We seek to enrich the world of able children while they are living in it, not when they have become adults. Their needs to belong, to be accepted, and to be wanted are shared by all other young people. It would hardly be enrichment to put them in a world where neither children their own age nor adults satisfied these needs.

Many schools follow a practice of "clustering" a group of above-average children in classrooms with normal students. This provides some mutual stimulation yet affords opportunities for leadership and sharing with age mates who have similar social and physical interests. Others provide "seminar classes" where small groups of gifted children work together all day. It is a growing practice to provide an enrichment program in a summer school where foreign languages, typewriting, and advance science courses are taught.

Children are usually considered intellectually gifted if they have an IQ of more than 148. In order to provide special classes many schools lower this requirement to 130. But identification of gifted students is not just a matter of high intelligence. The tests we use seem to measure abilities in mathematics, reasoning, and the use of words. Other abilities such as talent in art, music or social leadership are not measured. Neither are such personality factors as interest, steadfastness, and emotional stability. Frequently outstanding students in science have quite normal IQ ranges.

Terman's great study of very bright children did indicate that many were equally superior in physical and social adjustment.[12] However, teachers who have worked with these children insist that things are not always well with those who have a mind with adult power despite their child's body. The very insight these children possess makes for sensitivity. The high goals they set make them extremely critical. Their abilities tend to set them apart socially, and frustrations use up some of their

energy. Many are lonely as a result of isolated or adult interests. Some become bored and resentful with regimented class drill. Others suffer from overenrichment that leaves little time to live and play as normal children.

There are many activities for these children in the language program. Guided reading in the world of literature, research reports from encyclopedias, creative expression in original stories, plays and poems, and surveys relating to a personal interest are but a few of these activities. But procedures will differ when working with this type of ability. Larger block of subject matter and longer periods of time are needed to permit the expression of the abilities these students possess. A vast amount of material must be made available that is beyond the needs of a regular classroom. Evaluation with these children to establish desired goals and quality of work takes considerable time and individual counseling.

There are some special problems to consider. The books these children are able to read frequently contain an emphasis upon sex or abnormal personalities that are beyond the social maturity of these children. In the areas of religion and politics comparable problems exist. These children are seriously concerned about philosophy, social questions, religion and economics, and their interests are not to be taken lightly.

There may be a difference between highly creative individuals and those with high intelligence quotients. One study reports that creative talents do not seek conformity with teacher approved models nor do they seek to possess now the qualities that will lead to adult success. The investigators report, "It is as if the high-IQ children seek and like safety and security of the known while the highly creative seem to enjoy the risk and uncertainty of the unknown." These creatively gifted individuals consider high marks, IQ, pep and energy, character, and goal-directedness, less important than do the high-IQ group. They do rate a wide range of interests and a sense of humor higher than the high-IQ group. Indeed, humor is marked among

---

12 L. M. Terman and M. H. Oden, *Genetic Studies of Genius* (Palo Alto, Calif.: Stanford, 1947).

the creatively talented. Apparently these children do not find a comfortable place in many classrooms, yet they possess a gift more rare than intelligence.[13]

At the other extreme there are the slow learners and the handicapped. There is one special group that a beginning teacher needs to understand well to avoid serious errors in judgment and practice. These are the children who come from homes where English is not spoken. Common sense tells us that their primary need is a knowledge of the English language. They are not necessarily slow learners and should not be treated as such. Of course, they appear slow in a world where the printed books and all instruction are in a foreign language.

The following chart will help identify some of the expected achievements of the slow learner. It is important to note that these children are learning. The child with an IQ of 75 may be working at the kindergarten level through Grade 2 but by the age of thirteen he can do beginning reading. It is important that this experience be as pleasant for him as it is for the normal child who masters the beginning reading at the age of seven or eight. The two great needs of these children are a feeling of acceptance and a sense of growth or academic achievement.

Potential Academic Achievement of Children with Various IQ Levels

| Chrono-logical Age | Slow Learning Range | | | | Slow Normal Range | | | Average |
	50 IQ	60 IQ	70 IQ	75 IQ	80 IQ	85 IQ	90 IQ	100 IQ
6	Pre-K	Pre-K	K	K	K	K	K	K & 1
7	Pre-K	K	K	K	K	K	K & 1	1 & 2
8	K	K	K	K – 1	K & 1	1	1 & 2	2 & 3
9	K	K	K & 1	1	1 & 2	2	2 & 3	3 & 4
10	K	K & 1	1 & 2	2	2 & 3	3	3 & 4	4 & 5
11	K	1	2	2 & 3	3	3 & 4	4	5 & 6
12	K & 1	1 & 2	2 & 3	3 & 4	4	4 & 5	5	6 & 7
13	1	2	3 & 4	4	4 & 5	5 & 6	6	7 & 8
14	1 & 2	2 & 3	4	5	5 & 6	6	7	8 & 9

From *Design for Teaching*, Elementary Curriculum Bulletin No. 2, Dade County Public Schools, Miami, Fla., 1947.

In the language program there will be a greater emphasis upon oral speech experiences based upon actually shared experiences of the group. These children need a lot of directed "doing" of the type associated with kindergarten activities. They need to handle things. Early reading will be limited to basic signs such as "Stop" and "Go." Much of the learning is situational—what we do and say when we visit the principal's office, when we go to the cafeteria, when we watch a program.

The slow learner cannot compete with children who operate in a more rapid way. They want praise and honor as much as any individual. It should be given to them when they achieve growth or improvement.

[13] J. P. Guilford, "Convergent and Divergent Aspects of Behavior," Lecture, San Diego County, October 1960. See also his *Personality* (New York: McGraw-Hill, 1959), chaps. 15 and 17.

Just as the gifted need to be challenged, so do the slow. It is sometimes difficult to think of a challenge for a gifted ability. It is equally difficult to appreciate what may be a challenge for these children. One student of this type in the sixth grade was using all of his ability when he wrote his name correctly.

With an understanding teacher the children become steady, stable, dependable workers in situations where the routines and tasks give them security. The three R's for these children are repetition, relaxation, and routine.

1. How can we explain the needs of a slow learning child to a parent who is an average or above average learner?
2. Why do schools sometimes hesitate to publicize the work they do with slow learners? With the gifted?
3. Does it take a gifted teacher to work with gifted children?

WHAT PRINCIPLES OF LEARNING GUIDE THE TEACHER OF LANGUAGE?

Learning has been described in many ways. For our purposes it might be described as a change of behavior which persists and which is not due to maturation alone. This rules out those changes associated with the physical growing-up that do influence behavior. When a child learns to substitute a carefully drawn letter in the first grade for the scribbling he did before coming to school, and uses this acquired learning as the beginning of his writing skills, he has changed his behavior in a manner that will persist.

Behavior involves more than acquired skills. It is a combination of knowledge and skill with a goal, supported by an attitude of confidence. As we influence the behavior of children in a learning situation we are aware of these three factors. Often our task is not to teach a skill but to establish a goal for the learner so that he will employ knowledge he already has; or it may be encouragement to instill the confidence needed by the child in directing his skills toward a goal.

To a college student it is quite possible that learning seems to mean the gathering of information and facts. A history or literature course might be thought of as examples of this kind of learning. Why did you take the history course? Your goal, frankly, may have been to learn more about the United States. Did it change your behavior in any way? Will it influence your actions as a citizen? Will it influence your interests as you select recreational reading? Is your attitude the same with respect to political decisions you are asked to make? Your answers may be negative to all of these questions, yet the fact remains that you chose to take the course because of some personal motivation. Usually a college instructor attempts to make his classes interesting and to motivate your participation. In the back of his mind there is the comforting thought that you are there to learn from him because he knows more than you do about that particular subject. In addition, he does not face any special problems of communication. If you do not understand his language you can review the subject matter in books or other reference materials on your own. If you fail to understand or compete unsuccessfully, you are notified about this in the form of a low grade.

The teacher of grade-school children faces a different situation. Many a well-informed adult has failed completely as an elementary teacher because he or she could not guide the learning of immature individuals. The child is in your classroom because of cultural pressure rather than any specific decision of his own. As a matter of fact, he had no alternative but to go to school as required by law. Fortunately, he has two culturally important goals that make school an attractive place. First, the little child wants to learn to read and write and, second, he desires to be accepted and loved. Because of this he strives to please the adults who are his associates. A child does many things through no other motivation than to please his parents or other family members and his teachers. One of the tragedies of childhood is to be in a situation where the tasks assigned cannot be accomplished in a way that wins approval.

Modern psychology has much to offer the teacher of language arts. The following five principles will emphasize some results of the work in that field which make learning more effective.

1. *The first principle is that teaching effort is most effective when the learner has basic understanding of established goals and sees the relationship between what is taught and those goals.* A visit to an elementary classroom will reveal that the teacher knows a great deal about each child. One of her concerns is interest. As she plans she asks, "What will interest John?" Or she will remember, "Mary is very interested in insects." She also knows that children follow patterns of interests as they develop. Home, mother, baby, and fun are universal interests of the beginners. As their environment expands the interest will include neighbors, children far away, foods of different countries. Schools often plan their curriculum units around these known common interests. Such interests establish purposes for reading, writing, and research; they therefore provide goals for the child in undertaking certain tasks.

When children have rather limited interests the good elementary teacher plans situations that will arouse curiosity and questions. Sometimes a film will awaken interest in volcanos or animals. An exhibit of pioneer objects which can be handled may lead to the study of history as the teacher desired. When this is accomplished, the teacher has motivated an interest. Sometimes a teacher is criticized for forcing interests on children rather than developing interests that already exist. The problem faced by most teachers is one of working with a large group of children rather than just one or two. With one or two, a teacher could teach language well in association with the emerging interests of each child. With a total class a teacher faces such practical problems as meeting certain expected achievement standards and having enough material on hand to gain certain objectives, as well as the social responsibility of controlling youthful energy so that learning can receive some direction. But motivation that results only in acceptance by children of teacher-determined goals will never be as effective as goals mutually felt and accepted by both teacher and pupil. At times during the day motivation can come from each individual child; at other times it must be group-determined.

The word *attainable* with respect to goals is a significant one. The child who is constantly asked to do more than he can accomplish with success is in a difficult position. The adult can simply walk away from the situation by resigning from a job, changing courses, or moving to another town. The child cannot meet these frustrating conditions in the same way. He may misbehave or move into a dream world and ignore what is happening to him. Some will put forth extra effort to master a task for a time if they feel the pressure from home or the teacher. Eventually, for the sake of relieving tension, these children create an acceptable self-image which does not place great value on the specific skill. It is safe to say that few children are motivated for any length of time by continuous failure. Of equal importance in considering the word *attainable* is the child who achieves without effort. For some children the tasks of education present little challenge. Proficiency with the yo-yo is not an especially satisfying skill for a college student. In almost any classroom there is one child who is completely bored by the situation. Frequently we exploit these children by making little teachers out of them. This action at least recognizes their superior knowledge although it seldom helps them toward greater educational growth. The most effective effort is put forth by children when they attempt tasks which fall into the "range of challenge"—not too easy and not too hard—where success seems quite possible but not certain.

2. *A second basic understanding about directing learning of children is that a teacher must consider individual differences.* A college classroom of future teachers study-

ing the language arts present a very homogeneous group. Not only have they passed through a number of educational filters so that their ability is that of rapid learners, but they have made a common vocational choice. No elementary classroom can be made as homogeneous. Yet there are great differences within the college classroom; some students are married and have children, others have traveled widely; some belong to campus organizations, others do not. Although they may have a common interest in teaching, their other interests may vary widely.

A classroom of children will reveal differences in rate of learning, interests, social and economic backgrounds, and dozens of other factors that must be recognized. The teacher knows that the *whole* child comes to school—not just a mind to be taught. Some of the differences that the teacher considers would be the child without a breakfast, the child who is worried because he heard his parents quarreling the night before, and the child who had night terrors after seeing a late-late TV movie. The differences have a direct influence on the goals established for each child.

It should not be assumed that all instruction must be individualized because of these differences. There are common needs that the teacher considers with respect to the group. There are many similar interests based on their ages and years in school that form the basis for group instruction. The important thing to remember is that a competitive rating, which is felt to be fair in a college class, is not appropriate in many elementary classrooms. To let a child who reads very well set the expected standard for the class would be as foolish as to let the one who sings the best establish the only acceptable vocal standard for all. Yet we sometimes act as if we were saying that unless you read as well as Mary you cannot get an A in reading. A more common way of ignoring the significance of individual differences is to use an average score as the means of measurement. This is simply a mathematical manipulation that seems to have an authority far beyond any defendable reason. If we give a spelling test and add the scores made and divide by the total number of students, we can find the average score. If all those taking the test were of equal ability and aptitude, the results might indicate those who put forth the greatest effort and least effort to study the words. But if those taking the test represented the normal range in ability, the average tells us nothing. It is only as we consider the work exhibited by each child in terms of his personal idiosyncrasies that we can make any judgment worthy of a professional teacher.

It is especially important that a teacher accept individual differences as well as recognize them. Some teachers spend a career trying to make people alike in the area of reading and writing. One hears them say, "If John would only try!" the inference being that with only more effort John could be like Jane. As children advance through the school years the differences in the skills taught at school will become greater. The span of reading ability in a first grade will be small, usually ranging from six months to three years. The span of reading ability in a sixth grade will range from the second-grade level to the adult reading level. The device most frequently used to make dissimilar groups alike is to hold the top ones back by limiting material to sixth-grade books while providing special training for those "below grade level," with the assumption that through some teaching magic those who read second-grade material can be brought to the sixth-grade level.

A modern teacher is also careful as to predictions about children based upon present performance or potential level of achievement. Some "late bloomers" may eventually surpass pupils who seem far ahead of them in grade school. It is well to remember that it is only in school that success is limited to success in reading.

3. *A third basic principle of teaching children is to present the skills or understanding in situations similar to those in which they will be used.* Language is functional when it is used in conversation, reports, letter writing, listening to the radio, viewing television, telling a story, or any of the communicative acts of daily life. Effective expression, legibility in writing, correctness in usage, or thoughtfulness in

listening and reading will develop only to the extent that children discover these skills to be of value in the daily, functional use of language. To isolate instruction on any aspect of language without this understanding on the part of the learner produces very limited results.

This does not mean that drill is entirely out of place in the language arts program. But to be effective the drill must be self-assigned by the learner in terms of a specific goal he desires to achieve. Drill on a specific word in spelling may involve writing the word many times, just as drill in basketball may involve shooting toward the basket over and over again.

The same is true of worksheets which involve selection of such correct usage items as *set* and *sit* or *lie* and *lay*. They are true learning devices only when the student does them with an understanding of the possible error and the desire to correct an error he has made. Some children in filling in blanks on worksheets have made the same errors year after year. The teachers have carefully recorded scores made on these assignments. Some had them corrected by the students and thought they were doing a good job of teaching. In some schools teachers will defend this procedure by saying that all judgments by their principals concerning the language arts are based on the standardized test results. The teachers feel that they are preparing the children for this measurement by such drills and in that they are correct. But it should be recognized that they are teaching for testing rather than for any functional use of the language.

An example of intelligent application of this learning principle can be found in association with letter writing. During the year the need to write a business letter will develop in connection with the work of the students. At that time instruction should be given concerning the form of such letters as well as paying careful attention to their content. If the letter is actually to be mailed, children will welcome and remember the information taught.

Related to this is the care that must be taken to assure that something once taught will be used when needed. As a new language skill is introduced it becomes a standard to be applied in all work. Throughout the year students will add to the list of standards which they expect to maintain as they write and speak. As new knowledge is employed, habits are established.

4. *A fourth basic principle of teaching is that concepts are best established by using many first-hand perceptual experiences.* How easy our task would be if it were only a matter of "telling" the child. If concepts were built by lectures, an oral reading of the law would make good citizens of all of us. Children can learn only what they have experienced. All meanings are limited by the experiences of the learner. The understanding of democracy may start from such basic behaviors as taking turns, participating in a group decision, acting as chairman of a group, or being on the Safety Patrol of a school. Eventually we hope that it will develop into an explanation of our way of life.

Fortunately the imagination of a child is so vivid that some concepts will develop as he identifies himself with characters in a story or with great men in history. Some children can do this as they read, others as they participate in role-playing dramatizations, and still others through discussion of problems and situations.

Some of the concepts are developed in association with other learning. The teacher may think she is doing a fine job teaching speech by means of a verse choir, yet the child may actually be learning to like or dislike poetry rather than how to enunciate correctly. All learning situations have an emotional content. Often the feeling about a learning situation remains long after the facts taught are forgotten. One teacher reports remembering a composition he had written on Italy in the fifth grade. The contents are forgotten except that for his cover he drew a flag of Italy. He does remember vividly a mental picture of the teacher mounting his composition on the bulletin board. He also reports that since that time Italy and things Italian have always held a special attraction for him.

5. A fifth basic principle has been implied in the other four but for the purpose

of emphasis should be noted by itself. It is simply that *learning to be retained must be used.* Learning for a specific situation— such as memorizing a part in a play or studying Japanese while visiting Japan— disappears in a very few years if not used. Nearly every college student reading this page once knew how to solve a problem involving square root. Now if they try to obtain the square root of any four-figure number without referring to tables, they will probably find they have completely forgotten how to do it, simply because the knowledge has not been used recently. Usually we plan instruction with respect to specific learning in what might be called a spiral organization. We start with the known, go to the new, then return to the known. We call this reteaching, reinforcing knowledge, integration of knowledge, or simply review. Seldom do we attempt to move toward the new by climbing stairs where each step represents new knowledge.

This reteaching principle places a responsibility upon the teacher. The teacher as the mature individual in the teaching-learning situation is expected to plan and select experiences that are useful to the child at his present stage of development. In the language arts curriculum of today this can be illustrated by the way phonics is taught. A few years ago the school day provided a separate period for phonics. Children were drilled in the sounds of the English language. Some were able to transfer this knowledge so that it could be used in reading and spelling. Others failed to make the transfer. In order to render this knowledge more useful, teachers were told to teach the specific phonics needed to meet a specific reading or spelling need. As soon as the child knew two words that started with the same sound he was taught to note the beginning letter and to apply its sound in a new word. Thus the immediate usefulness of phonics was apparent to the learner.

Later, when we discuss the parts of speech, we will see that this problem has relevance to teaching sentence analysis. No matter how sincerely we drill children in identification of nouns, verbs, adjectives, and other parts of speech few children remember this information. For some reason we have not taught this knowledge in a way useful to the learner in the elementary grades. Application of this principle means that teachers must first find a way in which the language skills we teach children can be of immediate service to them and, second, see that it is used with frequency to prevent forgetting.

Modern psychology has taught us much more with respect to the way children learn, but the preceding five principles will help solve many of the immediate problems of a beginning teacher planning instruction for children.

1. State to what extent the five principles of learning discussed in this chapter are repeated in the following statements:

Principles That Influence Learning [14]

a. Learning takes place more readily if the child accepts as useful and important to him the activities in which he is expected to engage.

b. A child's learning is both richer and easier if he shares in selecting and setting the goals of learning, in planning ways to gain them, and in measuring his own progress toward them.

c. A child learns to solve his life problems, some of which he cannot now anticipate, only to the degree that he is capable of understanding and directing his own actions.

d. Learning is more efficient if it has satisfying emotional content, if feeling is supportive of thinking.

e. Firsthand experience makes a deeper impression upon a person than vicarious experience.

f. Learning is facilitated and reinforced when more than one sensory approach is used.

g. A child learns best when he is relieved of too great pressure to compete and when he feels reasonably confident that he can accomplish what is expected of him.

h. A child learns best when his failures are viewed constructively by a teacher who likes and respects him and when appropriate

[14] Camilla M. Low, "Selecting and Evaluating Learning Experiences," *Guidance in the Curriculum,* Ch. 4, 1955 Yearbook (Washington, D.C.: ASCD, 1955), pp. 52–65.

remedial or corrective measures are worked out with him.

i. Attitudes, feelings, values, and appreciations are learned. Every experience involves a constellation of such learnings.

j. A child learns best when his efforts are appreciated by his teacher and his classmates.

k. A child learns best when he is freed from the distractions of personal problems.

l. A child learns best when the rhythm of mental activity, physical activity, and relaxation is appropriate for him.

m. Learning opportunities are richer for children when they are not restricted to the things which the teacher already knows.

2. Carl Rogers feels that no man can teach another. At best we present situations and questions that cause the learner to teach himself. Is this what the poet Kahlil Gibran is saying in this situation from his book, *The Prophet?*

SPEAK TO US OF TEACHING [15]

And he said: No man can reveal to you aught but that which already lies half asleep in the dawning of your knowledge.

The teacher who walks in the shadow of the temple, among his followers, gives not of his wisdom but rather of his faith and his lovingness.

If he is indeed wise he does not bid you enter the house of his wisdom, but rather leads you to the threshold of your own mind.

The astronomer may speak to you of his understanding of space, but he cannot give you his understanding.

The musician may sing to you of the rhythm which is in all space, but he cannot give you the ear which arrests the rhythm nor the voice that echoes it.

And he who is versed in the science of numbers can tell of the regions of weight and measure, but he cannot conduct you thither.

For the vision of one man lends not its wings to another man.

And even as each one of you stands alone in God's knowledge, so must each one of you be alone in his knowledge of God and in his understanding of the earth.

HOW DO THE LANGUAGE ARTS FIT INTO THE SCHOOL DAY?

In the experiences of life, language skills are seldom used separately. In the classroom close interrelation exists even when we break the day into periods of emphasis on one skill at a time. The exercises in a workbook for a reader are often identical with the exercises in a spelling lesson. In spelling, we are as concerned with handwriting as a cause of error as we are with the correct order of letters in a word. One finds children working on problems of sentence structure, punctuation, word meanings, and pronunciation in nearly every period of the school day.

As beginning teachers, you will be interested in the way the language arts classes fit into the school day. The following report of a day's work by a teacher

represents one school organization; in the first schedule there is no specific provision that takes advantage of the close relationship between the language arts.

Normal School Day (Grade 4)

7:30	Leave for school
8:00	Arrive
8:00–8:55	Work in room, prepare worksheets, get ready for day
8:55	School begins
9:00–9:55	Opening, flag salute, news, social studies
9:55–10:00	Relief
10:00–10:40	Arithmetic in two groups
10:40–11:00	Music and rhythms
11:00–11:15	Recess, rotating yard duty
11:15–12:20	Reading in three groups
12:20–1:20	Lunch, rotating duty

(contd.)

[15] Reprinted from *The Prophet* by Kahlil Gibran with permission of the publisher, Alfred A. Knopf, Inc. Copyright 1923 by Kahlil Gibran; renewal copyright 1951 by Administrators C.T.A. of Kahlil Gibran estate, and Mary G. Gibran.

Normal School Day (Grade 4)

1:20–2:00	Spelling and handwriting in two groups
2:00–2:20	Physical Education
2:20–2:25	Relief
2:25–3:05	Language and art, Mondays excepted—on that day I take class of another teacher while she teaches school chorus
3:05–5:00	Faculty meeting on Mondays, sometimes other called meetings, sometimes go to pick up teaching materials, rest of time work in room and in teachers' room preparing for future needs

5:00   Leave for home—sometimes a little earlier, sometimes a little later!

In contrast to the apparent rigidity of this schedule—and it is never quite as rigid as it appears—other schools divide the day into large blocks of time.

Block plans are devised for the purpose of outlining a sequence of teaching activities and experiences to be followed over a reasonably long period of time. In these plans the role of the other language arts and reading is indicated. It may be that as a teacher you would prefer to make separate plans for reading. As you read the suggested plans, see if you can determine which group is more advanced in the skills of reading.

Children of Foreign Lands, Grade 4 [16]

First Week	Linda's Group	Ralph's Group	Minutes
Monday	Teacher introduces unit, showing pictures of Eskimos, Lapps, and Dutch children. Children are invited to name countries from which their parents or grandparents came. Teacher shows selected library books, indicating exciting parts and illustrations. Children comment about books they know on unit.		45
	Children and teacher build up board list of topics they would like to know more about.		45
	Children read library books on unit, for pleasure.	Teacher introduces section, "Cut of the Wind and the Rain," *Faraway Ports*, p. 61. Children read silently to see what story has to do with children of foreign lands.	30
Tuesday	Teacher introduces lesson in spelling text.		20
	Teacher introduces story, "Lapp Boy of Lapland," *Good Times Tomorrow*, p. 184, giving special attention to such words as "Arctic Circle," and "Northern Lights."	Children choose and read library books on unit, for pleasure.	30

[16] From *A Guide to Instruction in the Language Arts, Grades 4, 5, and 6*, copyright by Detroit Public Schools, 1959, pp. 28–37. Used by permission of the publisher.

First Week	Linda's Group	Ralph's Group	Minutes
	Children read story silently to find out (1) what Ormar did in winter, (2) what he did in summer.	Teacher and children discuss how to write sentence, referring to textbook to see whether their ideas are correct.	30
	Teacher guides children in discussing two points they were looking for.	Children glance through story read yesterday, then answer four questions on it, using short, written sentences.	30
	Teacher reads aloud poem, "In Holland." Children open books and join in on second reading. They begin preparing to give poem as verse-speaking choir.		10
Wednesday	Children study spelling lesson about Holland.		20
	Children form small groups according to interests in particular countries and sections of the world—lands within the Arctic Circle, South Seas, etc. Teacher lists on board names of children in each group.		30
	Teacher guides discussion of proper procedure for meeting in small groups. Teacher and children decide upon standards for listening politely and attentively, and the standards are written on board.		45
	Small groups meet for purpose of organization; teacher moves from group to group, helping pupils observe standards and challenging superior pupils.		15
	Each chairman of group comments briefly on group topic to class. Class offers suggestions.		10
Thursday	Children learn extra words chosen from unit given on board and "Additional List" given in spelling book. Teacher gives individual help with both spelling and handwriting.		20
	Children read silently riddle teacher has written on board and try to name country described. They write it on slips of paper, then engage in free reading.	Teacher introduces stories, "A Cave in Spain," and "A Houseboat in China," Faraway Ports, p. 67 and p. 72.	20
	Teacher and children talk about ways of telling riddles. They build standards on board. Children decide to write one good riddle each in their spare time.	Children read silently to see the advantages and disadvantages of living: (1) in caves and (2) on houseboats.	30

First Week	Linda's Group	Ralph's Group	Minutes
	story, "Taktu, an Eskimo Boy," *Good Times Tomorrow*, p. 195.		
	Children read silently to compare life of Taktu with that of Ormar, the Lapp boy.	Teacher guides discussion of story to report, first, advantages mentioned in story, and, second, other points that children have thought of.	30
	Teacher gives special help to the few retarded readers. Other children work on their special handwriting problems.		20
Friday	Practice test on spelling lesson.		20
	Children discuss story, "Taktu, on Eskimo Boy." Teacher builds on board list of Eskimos and Lapps. Children give riddles on other countries. Listeners evaluate in terms of standards.	Children draw pictures of different types of homes which they have read about so far. They write sentences describing each picture. After evaluation by group, the best will be posted on bulletin board.	40
	Teacher reads aloud book, *The Five Chinese Brothers*, by Bishop.		20
	Small groups meet to discuss what has been learned about countries so far and to decide on how it will be presented later.	Teacher introduces stories, "An Eskimo House," and "A Grass House in Africa," *Faraway Ports*, p. 74 and p. 76.	20
	Small groups report on plans to entire group.	Children read silently to find out about two very different kinds of houses: where each is built; of what it is built; and what the inside is like.	20

Second Week	Linda's Group	Ralph's Group	Minutes
Monday	Children carry out word practice activities in spelling lesson.		20
	Teacher introduces story, "Kah-da Captures a Pet," *People and Places*, p. 56.	Each small group meets to examine books and pictures on its country.	30

Second Week	Linda's Group	Ralph's Group	Minutes
	Children read silently for purposes of finding out how Eskimos get food.	Teacher consults with each small group to hear report of its findings so far. Teacher gives special help to few retarded readers.	30
	Children discuss story, "Kah-da Captures a Pet." They talk about animals mentioned in story, how Eskimos travel, and how they hunt bears and musk oxen.	Children read library books to find answers to questions brought up in small group meetings. Books have been selected for each group with help of teacher.	30
	Teacher reads poem, "Foreign Lands," by Robert Louis Stevenson. Children give reactions.		10
Tuesday	Teacher gives children final test on spelling words about Holland.		10
	Children discuss and plan murals to be drawn on Arctic countries in art class. Child leads discussion. Children check information with books. Teacher comments as needed.	Teacher introduces stories, "A Mud House in Africa," and "A Stone House in Ireland," *Faraway Ports*, p. 79.	35
	Teacher introduces story, "Abdul Lives in Egypt," *Good Times Tomorrow*, p. 204. New words taught are: "cliffs," "camel," "canal," "dam," "wheat," "Nile River."	Children read silently to find out about two other kinds of houses.	25
	Children read silently to discover how Abdul lives in desert land, noting: (1) how he and his family get water, (2) what kind of a house they live in, and (3) what work each member of the family does.	Children discuss houses described in stories, and begin plans for constructing display of different types of houses which they have read about.	25
	Children discuss story in terms of three points given above. They plan to prepare outline maps showing various countries.	Children write sentences to explain each type of house they will place on display.	25

Second Week	Linda's Group	Ralph's Group	Minutes
Wednesday	Children begin working on outline maps.	Teacher has examined yesterday's written work. She now discusses the best sentences with group. She gives help on common errors found in English, spelling, and handwriting.	20
	Children select and write, with teacher's guidance, several unit words to be learned for spelling.		20
	Children and teacher discuss capitalization, referring to language textbook.	Children write sentences about foreign lands, using new unit words. They try to give important idea in each sentence.	30
	Children write sentences using new spelling words to tell about foreign lands. Children read library books for pleasure.	Teacher introduces story, "Pelle's New Suit," *Fun With Story Friends*, p. 47, and shows library book from which it was taken.	25
	Each small group meets to look over stack of books provided by teacher on given topic. Each child chooses book to read for further background.	Children read story silently to learn what Pelle did to get his new suit. Teacher works with few retarded readers.	25
Thursday	Teacher introduces lesson on homonyms in speller.		20
	Teacher introduces story, "One Morning with Manu," *Good Times Tomorrow*, p. 212.	Children copy from board short poem for their collection. When finished, they read library books.	30
	Children read silently to find out what Manu does instead of going to school.	Children and teacher begin working on dramatization of "Pelle's New Suit."	30
	Children and teacher discuss story. As children make their suggestions, teacher lists on board work which Manu does.	Children meet in small groups, and look over books to find background material.	30
	Teacher reads aloud story, "Master of Boats," *The Rabbit Lantern*, by Dorothy Rowe.		10
Friday	Children see films, "Children of China," and "Children of Holland."		20

Second Week	Linda's Group	Ralph's Group	Minutes
Friday (contd.)	Children and teacher discuss films. Emphasis is placed on similarities in children's lives from country to country.		15
	Children, meeting in small groups, read library books to find answers to questions brought up during group discussions.	Teacher introduces story, "Little Pear," in reader, showing, and referring to, book from which story is taken, *Little Pear*, by Lattimore.	30
	Each small group reports to teacher on progress. Teacher advises group, offering challenging suggestions to superior pupils.	Children read silently to find out what things Little Pear sees on adventure on big road: "rickshas," "Chinese carts," "beggars," etc.	30
	Children make picture dictionaries to clarify meanings of words in spelling lesson on homonyms. They refer to handwriting manual as needed.		25

State departments of education offer suggested schedules for rural schools, combined classes, and a variety of weekly plans.[17]

Throughout the nation there are many variations with respect to the organization of the elementary curriculum. In the self-contained classroom one teacher directs all the learning that takes place. This program assumes that the teacher is competent in all areas. The main advantage of such programs is that the teacher gets to know the children almost as members of a family. The ideal class size for such groups is 25–30. In contrast to this organization are departmental curriculums which use specialists in such areas as art, music, and science. Ordinarily the reading, writing and spelling aspects of the language arts are taught by one teacher. Frequently the language arts teacher is the "homeroom" teacher, who assumes the responsibilities for some of the guidance aspects of learning which are found in the self-contained classroom. Class size may average 40 in such departmental organizations.

[17] *Resource Ideas for Planning Classroom Programs* (Des Moines: Iowa State Department of Public Instruction, 1955).

In an effort to provide for individual differences some cities have a nongraded primary school. Children in these schools move from level to level (usually reading) until ready for an intermediate school. One system has 26 levels which were completed by the able group in 2½ years, the average group completed 20 levels in three years, and the slow, 15 levels in four years. In the plan known as "little rural school" organization, each classroom contains several grades. The age differences are used to enrich the learning experiences of the group.

In an effort to individualize instruction there are plans which attempt to combine some of the values of these curriculum organizations. In team teaching two or more teachers may work with a group. This may be as simple as having one teacher instruct two classes in art while the other supervises the music period in the two classes, each teacher handling the other subjects in her own classroom. Or it may mean developing a unit of work as a cooperative effort of two or more teachers. Sometimes the children are divided according to ability for the skill subjects. If there are three fifth-grade teachers, one will take the very able, another the average, and the third those with special needs. One successful plan is based on the principles of the self-contained classroom for all subjects except the language arts. When the time scheduled for reading, spelling, and compositions arrives the children leave the self-contained room with its heterogeneous ability grouping and regroup for the language arts according to homogeneous needs.[18]

There are many local variations in school schedules. Some allow an hour and a half for lunch so that all children may go home. Where children are transported by bus, one part of a class may be in attendance in the classroom for a half-hour before the others arrive, then at the close of the day leave a half-hour before the others. Some schools schedule a weekly visit to a public library while others combine the school and public libraries.

It is natural for a beginning teac[ ] to ask which organization is best. There[ ] evidence that favors each one of these [ ] well as others that have not been men[ ]tioned. Such factors as differences with [ ] respect to finances, buildings, teachers, leadership, and even the climate where the school is located have guided each school system in its choice of organization used.

1. What is the daily schedule in the classroom where you are teaching or observing?

2. Who determines the classroom schedule?

3. How may a language period be a work period for social studies or science?

4. Are we justified in using time allocated to other subjects when we prepare for a program or celebrate a holiday?

INDIVIDUAL PROJECTS OR AREAS OF SPECIALIZATION

Provision for the differences between individual students is as important at the college level as it is in the elementary school; however, it is seldom possible for a teacher at that level to know the students as well as the teacher does during the beginning years of school. As a result, individual needs must in part be met by the college students themselves. In a methods course, this can be done by having each student select a problem or area which he will study with some intensity and share with the others.

At the end of each chapter there are suggested projects that you may want to select as an area of specialization, or these may suggest others to you that have occurred in your teaching. During the first weeks of the course, glance ahead at these suggestions and select one that interests you, one in which you feel you need greater understanding and competency.

One characteristic of the teaching

profession is the sharing of ideas that will help others. Our educational magazines are full of such experiences contributed by teachers. Classroom teachers welcome visiting students and will pass on material that has taken them months to develop. Few other groups are so cooperative with regard to the "secrets" of the trade. Your entire class can profit from the presentation of these individual studies; instead of one area of ideas, each student gains those of as many as there are in the class.

Some projects can best be presented by a paper which is a short summary of information learned; others require a demonstration with a puppet, a story, or other device. A third type represents collections of materials and the major value of sharing is that others may learn of sources.

Your class should decide if these should be a part of your grade. Up until now you have often worked for a high grade. Perhaps this is the time to change your objective to working for professional competence. Like the good teachers you have known you will be guided by the question, "Will this help me be a better

---

[18] The town of Escondido, Calif., has used this plan for many years. The schools of Joplin, Mo., have received considerable publicity for a plan similar to this.

teacher?" rather than "Will this get a good grade for me?" The chances are that the reputation you build as a professional person will be far more important than a grade.

The material in this chapter would be related to projects like these:

1. Make a study of local place names. What was the original source and meaning?

2. Review some of the chapters in *Essays on Language and Usage* by Leonard F. Dean and Kenneth G. Wilson, published by the Oxford Press in 1959.

3. Compile a list of contemporary slang. Attempt to separate that which may last from that which is only "in-group" language of the present.

4. In the book by Helen and Carlton Laird, *The Tree of Language* (Cleveland: World, 1957), there is much that will interest children with respect to the story of names and common words. Adapt some of this material for classroom use. Why do so many unpleasant word meanings start with *sn?* What words can have opposite meanings such as *fast?*

5. Review current practices with relationship to the gifted or slow learning child as reported in course of study publications or periodicals.

BIBLIOGRAPHY

BOOKS

Anderson, Edna. *Round the Clock in the Classroom.* Minneapolis: Denison, 1959.

Applegate, Mauree. *Everybody's Business: Our Children.* Evanston, Ill.: Row, 1952, Chap. III.

Bensen, Minnie P. *Kindergarten, Your Child's Big Step.* New York: Dutton, 1959.

Breckenridge, Marian, and Vincent, E. Lee. *Child Development.* Philadelphia: Saunders, 1955, Chap. 11, pp. 321–343.

Burton, W. H. *The Guidance of Learning Activities* 3rd ed. New York: Appleton, 1962, Ch. 2–4.

Claremont College Reading Conference, Fifteenth Yearbook. Claremont, Calif.: Claremont College Curriculum Laboratory, 1950.

Cronbach, Lee J. *Educational Psychology.* New York: Harcourt, 1963.

Davis, Allison, and R. J. Havighurst. *Father of the Man.* Boston: Houghton, 1947.

Dawson, Mildred, and Marion Zollinger. *Guiding Language Learning.* New York: Harcourt, 1957, Chapter III, p. 49.

Eels, Kenneth, *et al., Intelligence and Cultural Differences.* Chicago: U. of Chicago, 1951.

Ernst, Margaret D. *Words.* New York: Knopf, 1941.

Fisk, Charles E. *Heavens to Betsy.* New York: Harper, 1955.

Garrison, Karl C., and Dewey Force, Jr.: *Psychology of Exceptional Child.* New York: Ronald, 1959.

Gesell, A., and Francis Ilg. *The Child from Five to Ten.* New York: Harper, 1946, pp. 376–387.

Havighurst, Robert J., and Bernice L. Neugarten. *Society and Education.* Boston: Allyn, 1957, Parts I and II.

Heffernan, Helen. *The Kindergarten Child.* Boston: Heath, 1960.

Hutt, Max, and R. G. Gibby. *The Mentally Retarded Child.* Boston: Allyn, 1957.

Laird, Charlton. *The Miracle of Language.* Cleveland: World, 1953.

Lambert, Eloise. *Our Language.* New York: Lothrop, 1955.

Lambert, Hazel. *Teaching the Kindergarten Child.* New York: Harcourt, 1958.

Lee, J. Murray, and Dorris Mae Lee. *The Child and His Curriculum.* New York: Appleton, 1960, Chap. X, pp. 274–289.

Lendesmith, Alfred R., and Anselm L. Strauss. *Social Psychology.* New York: Holt, 1949.

Pei, Mario. *All About Language.* Philadelphia: Lippincott, 1954.

———. *Language for Everybody.* New York: Scribner, 1957.

———. *The Story of English.* Philadelphia: Lippincott, 1952.

Piaget, Jean. *The Language and Thought of the Child.* New York: Harcourt, 1932.

Prescott, Daniel. *The Child in the Educative Process.* New York: McGraw-Hill, 1957.

Scheifle, M. *Gifted Child in Regular Classroom.* New York: Bureau of Publications, Teachers College, Columbia U., 1953.

Schlauch, Margaret. *The Gift of Language.* New York: Dover, 1955, Chapter VIII.

Shepley, Joseph T. *Dictionary of Word Origins.* Ames, Iowa: Littlefield, 1959.

Templin, Mildred C. *Certain Language Skills in Children.* Minneapolis: U. Minnesota Press, 1957.

Ward, M. *Young Minds Need Something to Grow On.* New York, Ill.: Harper, 1957.

Webster's New International Dictionary. 2nd ed., Springfield, Mass.: Merriam, 1960.

PERIODICALS AND CURRICULUM GUIDES

California Elementary Administrators Association: *The Gifted Child—Another Look.* Palo Alto, Calif.: National Press, 1958.

Children's Bureau. *Your Gifted Child.* Children's Bureau (Pub. 371), U. S. Dept. of Health, Education and Welfare, 1958.

Children's Bureau. *Curriculum Adjustment for the Mentally Retarded.* U. S. Dept. of Health, Education and Welfare, 1950.

Chamberlin, Naomi, and D. Moss: *The Three R's for the Retarded.* National Association for Retarded Children, New York, 1956.

Cincinnati Public Schools. *Challenging the Gifted.* Cincinnati: Primary Bulletin 301, 1958.

Denver Public Schools. *Helpful Hints for Teachers of the Less Able Children.* K–12 (N. 93139). Denver, Colo., 1956.

Houser, L. J. *Curriculum Enrichment for Gifted and Able Learners.* K–6. Riverside, Ill.: Riverside Public Schols, 1958.

Ketcham, W. A., and R. G. Lafitte. *A Description and Analysis of Longitudinal Records of Development of Elementary School Children in Ferndale, Michigan,* Washington: U. S. Office of Education, 1961.

Loban, W. *Language Ability in the Middle Grades of the Elementary School,* Washington: U. S. Office of Education, 1961.

Miami, Florida Department of Special Education. *Program Planning for Special Adjustment Classes.* Dade County Supt. of Schools, 1958.

Montebello Public Schools. *Enrichment Activities for More Capable Learners.* Curriculum Bulletin G 103. Montebello, Calif., 1955.

Oklahoma State Department of Education. *Curriculum Guide for Teachers of Educable Mentally Handicapped Children.* Oklahoma City, 1959.

Olson, W. C., and B. O. Hughes. "Concepts of Growth—Their Significance to Teachers," *Childhood Education,* 1944, pp. 53–63.

Portland Public Schools. *127 Ideas for Classroom Teachers to Use With Gifted Children.* Portland, Oreg., 1955.

San Bernardino County Schools. *Arts and Skills of Communication for Democracy's Children.* San Bernardino, Calif., 1956.

Tulare County Board of Education. *Tulare County Cooperative Language Guide.* Visalia, Calif., 1949.

Watson, Goodwin. "What Psychology Can We Feel Sure About?" *Teachers College Record,* February, 1960.

Witty, P. *Current Practices in Educating the Gifted Child.* The Packet. Boston: Heath, Fall, 1959.

Chapter 2

Speaking and Listening

WHAT VOICE QUALITIES SHOULD A CLASSROOM TEACHER POSSESS?

Speech instruction in the elementary classroom starts with the voice of the teacher. The tone used, the manner of speaking, and the vocabulary employed all influence the quality of instruction. A voice that is too low to be heard or has a high irritating quality produces classroom tension and behavior problems. A monotonous voice robs literature of the emotional content that makes it interesting. Voice is a major aspect of personality. When we think of someone as gracious or poised, our judgment is partly based on that person's voice and vocal expression.

The teacher's words carry meaning not only because she conceives and expresses her thoughts accurately, but also because her voice is properly attuned and controlled to convey this meaning. The tonal quality of her voice may make the difference between interested and inattentive children. A thin voice gives an impression of weakness, causing the listener to shift his attention. Clarity of enunciation, combined with resonance quality or timbre, determine whether or not a teacher's directions and suggestions will be followed. The teacher's voice is of greatest value when it

is calm yet firm, well modulated yet sufficiently loud to be heard in a busy classroom, and suitably inflected to convey the varied feelings and emotions encountered in oral reading.

There are two ways to discover how you sound to others. One is to make a tape recording and then to listen critically to yourself. The other is to cup your hands behind your ears and read aloud either a paragraph of a story or a verse of poetry. If the results are not pleasing, there are a number of things you can do about it.

Start by learning to control your breathing and posture. Standing "tall," head up, shoulders back, and breathing deeply will do much to improve the sound of your voice. Creative listening to people whose voices you find attractive while consciously imitating some of their patterns of speech, will also help. Speaking with relaxed throat and lips well apart helps to produce full, rounded tones, as does proper sitting and standing. Barring a physical deformity in the throat or mouth, anyone can learn to speak distinctly and agreeably.

Voice modulation means a "toning-down" or tempering of the voice to avoid nasal twang, harshness, stridency, shrillness, or shouting. A man with a high-pitched voice sounds feminine; conversely, a woman with a hoarse or low-pitched voice sounds masculine. Speech exercises can help remove these defects by providing a pattern of speech to imitate that will modify the disturbing qualities. At first one may feel a bit self-conscious saying "How now, brown cow" over and over again, but this exercise is just as therapeutic as those used in a gym class to correct posture.

Relaxation is fundamental in all speech training. Not only the muscles used for speech but all other parts of the body as well should be free from tension in order to produce relaxed, clear voice tones and harmonious coordination of the many elements comprising the speech mechanism. Relaxation may be gained by perusing a quiet story, a short poem, or by gazing upon a restful scene or painting.

Flexibility and control of the lips are important in the projection of correct "labial" sounds. Proper placement of the tongue is essential to the production of well-rounded vowels and to the formation of distinct, clear consonants and other "velar" and "glottal" sounds. This type of exercise is best done at home. The object is to "throw" the sounds toward the back of the room and to imagine that they are bouncing off the wall. The sounds should be thrown with an explosive breath effort.

> ba,
> ba, be;
> ba, be, bi;
> ba, be, bi, bo;
> ba, be, bi, bo, boo.

The same exercise may be used with *p*, *m*, *v* and *f* as well. The poem below provides practice in lip movement.

ANTONIO

Antonio, Antonio
Was tired of living alonio.
He thought he would woo
Miss Lissamy Lu,
Miss Lissamy Lucy Malonio.

Antonio, Antonio
Rode off on his polo-ponio.
He found the fair maid
In a bowery shade,
Sitting and knitting alonio.

"Oh, nonio, Antonio!
You're far too bleak and bonio!
And all that I wish,
You singular fish,
Is that you would quickly begonio."

Antonio, Antonio,
He uttered a dismal moanio;
Then ran off and hid
(Or I'm told that he did)
In the Antarctictal Zonio.

—LAURA E. RICHARDS

Flexible tongue practice can be obtained by the same type of exercise used for the lips:

> ta,
> ta, te;
> ta, te, ti;
> ta, te, ti, to;
> ta, te, ti, to, too.

These letters may also be used: *l*, *n*, *d*, *k*, *g*.

Insufficient breath and lack of volume are often the speech characteristics of timid, insecure individuals. With a group or alone, the timid can be reassured through the device of projecting himself into a character. Have these children pretend to be newsboys crying, "Extra! Extra! Read all about it." Or peddlers selling fruit, "Big, ripe bananas. Buy your bananas here!" Or cheerleaders, "Team! Team! Team! Fight! Fight! Fight!"

The roof of the mouth or hard palate is a cavity that amplifies sound vibrations in addition to giving them a strong and more pleasing quality. Voice resonance can be cultivated by the way the oral cavity is used. Dull voices are frequently associated with dull faces. A smile and a happy state of mind will help increase resonance. Humming is also good for this purpose.

Intonation and emphasis give variety to the voice. It may come down emphatically at the end of an important idea, or go up in suspense and wonderment. Parts

of words, entire words, or complete phrases may be lowered or raised.

Practice in Raising or Lowering the Voice [1]

Read the following sentences up and down as they are written:

```
                          hear me?
            do        you        Stop
1. Don't   that! Do                    I say.
   Put          not
     it   here,        there.
2.      up        down
                          I'll
     you         here        there.
3. If     don't come        come
                   do?    help you? Thank
   How   you   May
4.       do       I              you.
   That's           What is      rodent?
5.        an unusual animal.    it? A
```

Make the voice go up or down as the lines indicate:

1. Police horses are trained by encouragement, not by punishment.
2. He was a bully, not a hero—a cheat, not a conqueror.
3. You would vote for that stupid, that hateful, that impossible beast?
4. Here were strangers to face, tasks to conquer, opportunities to grasp.
5. The game was almost a landslide for our boys.

Emphasize the underlined word and note the change in meaning of the sentence:

1. I am going to the show.
2. I am going to the show.
3. I am going to the show.
4. I am going to the show.

Read the different interpretations of this sentence:

1. Naturally he'd like some cake. (of course he would)
2. Naturally he'd like some cake. (whether anyone else does or not)
3. Naturally he'd like some cake. (but he can't have any)
4. Naturally he'd like some cake. (he wouldn't need much)

5. Naturally he'd like some cake. (he wouldn't like bread)

Carrie Rasmussen suggests that teachers use the following questions to decide how qualified they are in the speech area of the language arts: [2]

Do my visible actions add meaning to my words?
Does my facial expression reinforce my words?
Is my whole body alive?
Do I appear free physically?

Do I talk loud enough to be heard easily?
Do I pronounce my words carefully?
Is my voice pleasant?
Is my tone quality (pitch) good?
Does my voice have variety?
Do I speak clearly?

Do I know what I am talking about; is my information accurate?
Is my vocabulary good?
Do I understand my audience—one, four or forty in number?
Do I make clear what I am saying? Is my choice of words good?

Do I try to understand others?
Do I talk too much?
Do I know how to listen?
Do I know how to make things interesting?
Do I have a sense of humor?
Do I get the other person's point of view?

Do I have ideas?
Do I know how to create things?
Do I know how important creating is in the life of man?
What do I know about Creative Dramatics?
Am I teaching poetry in my class and are they enjoying it?
What do I know about discussion, storytelling, giving a talk?
Can I direct a play?
Can I integrate one subject with several others and make it fun?

You can tell from this that Rasmussen considers speech far more inclusive than voice. Her definition is an interesting one:

Speech is the blending of those elements: thought—mental processes; language—the molding of thought and feelings into words; voice—carrying thought and words through vocal sound to someone else; action—bodily

---

[1] Agnes Frye, "Syllabus for Speech," mimeographed (Sacramento, Calif.: California State Department of Instruction, 1956).

[2] Carrie Rasmussen, *Speech Methods in the Elementary School.* Copyright 1949 The Ronald Press Company.

bearing and response and listening. Speech is designed to transmit belief, emotion, or attitude on the part of the speaker, and our chief reason for speaking is to arouse corresponding ideas, meanings, and actions in others. It is sometimes called a code; but whatever we call it, we use it almost constantly; it is one of our most necessary tools.[3]

1. Should a teacher who moves from Georgia to California attempt to change her speech pattern to conform to her new classroom?

2. Should college students with speech faults, such as lisping or high-pitched voices, be admitted to a teacher-training program?

3. Observe a classroom. Note the different tones of voice the teacher uses as she explains material to the total class, talks with an individual child, or gains attention of a group.

4. Do you have a speech habit that you would not wish children to imitate?

5. Can you tell from a person's voice if he is tired or emotionally disturbed?

WHAT SPEECH ACTIVITIES ARE PRESENTED IN THE PRIMARY GRADES?

Some children come to school who have not yet mastered all the sounds of our language. Studies indicate that we can expect this development of speech sounds: [4]

Age	Consonants
3½	p, b, m, h, w (lip sounds)
4½	d, n (tip-of-the-tongue sounds)
5–5½	f, j, w, h, s, z
6–6½	v, th, sh, zh, l
7–7½	ch, r, th (voiceless)
8	such blends as pl, br, st, sk, str

The sounds most frequently defective are: s, z, sh, zh (as in pleasure), ch, j, th, l, r, wh and the -ing ending which is shortened to -en.

With young children the following letters have more than names—they are given a personality to focus attention on the sound they represent. In order to do this, key words or sounds are used as the children practice the sounds. Naming objects in pictures, talking for dolls or animals, aid sound identification.

Lip sounds	p	the *pop* sound (not *puh*)
	b	the *bubble* sound (not *buh*)
	m	the *humming* sound
	w	the *soft wind* sound
	y	the *smile* sound
Lip-breath sounds	h	the *little puff* sound
	wh	the *big puff* sound
Tip-of-the-tongue sounds	t	the *ticking watch* sound
	d	the *tapping* sound
	n	the *spinning* sound
Back-of-the-tongue sounds	k	the *little cough* sound
	g	the *gurgle* sound
	ng	the *ring* sound (*ding-a-ling, ting-a-ling*)
Lip-teeth sounds	f	the *cross kitty* sound
	v	the *airplane* sound
Tongue-teeth sounds	th	(as in *this*) the *flat tire* sound
	th	(as in *the*) the *motor* sound
Teeth sounds	s	the *steam* sound
	z	the *buzz* sound

[3] *Ibid.*, p. 8.
[4] Irene Poole, "The Genetic Development of the Articulation of Consonant Sounds" (doctoral dissertation, University of Michigan, 1934), p. 60.

	sh	the *baby's asleep* sound
	zh	the *vacuum cleaner* sound
	ch	the *train* sound
	j	the *jump* sound
Tongue and voice sounds	*l*	the *bell* sound
	r	the *rooster* sound

Some sounds are twins. They look the same when we make them but some sounds whisper in words and some talk out loud: *p-b; t-d; k-g; f-v; th-th; s-z; sh-zh; ch-j.* The second is the "talker" because it adds the vibration of vocal chords.

Ear training is important if the children are to improve speech habits. Until they hear the difference between the way they are pronouncing a word or producing a voice sound and the way it should be pronounced or produced, they will not change their pattern of speech. Ear training to develop auditory discrimination for the sounds of speech is the first step in speech correction and improvement.

Do not try to correct an *s* or *r* before easier sounds have been mastered. Instead, give much ear training on these sounds. Of course, there is no sense working on blends if the *l* and *r* have not been perfected.

A picture test can be made by the teacher to check the child's ability to say the initial consonants. Frequently, an alphabet book or picture dictionary will provide the pictures needed. These are suggestions that might be used: *h*, hat; *m*, man; *wh*, whistle; *w*, wagon; *p*, pig; *b*, ball; *n*, nail; *y*, yellow; *t*, table; *d*, day; *k*, kite; *g*, gun; *ng*, ring; *f*, fish; *v*, valentine; *l*, lamp; *th*, thumb; *th*, feather; *sh*, shoe; *zh*, tape measure; *s*, sun; *z*, zebra; *r*, rabbit; *ch*, chair; *j*, jar.

A still more comprehensive test uses separate pictures for each sound in all three positions—initial, medial, and final. As the teacher points to the picture, the child names it, with the teacher recording all errors. Teachers may make this test themselves with pictures cut from magazines, or they may purchase any of the commercial tests that are available. Many authorities feel that at the kindergarten level testing for errors in the initial position only is sufficient.

An individual test that is interesting for the child is a story using the rebus method of picture insertion. The tester reads the words and the child "fills in" by giving the words for the pictures. One in the Los Angeles City Speech Course of Study goes like this: "Jimmy sat up in (picture of bed). He looked through the (window) at the bright (sun). It was time to get up. He put on his (coat) and (pants) his (stockings) and (shoes). He put his magic (ring) on his (finger) and went downstairs." The story continues until all sounds have been tested.

Speech activities are involved in all phases of the curriculum. Singing, dramatic play, storytelling, finger plays, sharing time, and puppet plays and poetry reading stimulate and provide practice for speech improvement.

The following games are speech-centered and may be used with positive results in the primary grades.

Treasure Chest

Place several small objects in an attractive box. The names of these objects contain specific sounds. For the development of the sound of *k* the chest might contain a car, comb, kite, cane. Children take objects from the chest and say their names correctly.

I See Something You May See

A child makes three statements to describe something he sees. Children guess what it is by saying, "Do you see_____?"

Lip Reading Game

Teacher: "I am going to say names of children in the class but I am not going to use my voice. Watch for your name. Stand when your name is said on my lips."

CH Guessing Game

Guess the answer. Example: Two sides of the face (cheeks). Where you go on Sunday (church).

I Have Something in My Sack

In a large box put many small paper bags in each of which is a small toy.

The names of the toys may contain specific sounds for improvement. A child chooses a sack from the box, peeks in, and discovers his toy. He then describes the toy without naming it. The child who guesses correctly then chooses a sack from the box and the game continues.

Telephone Games

One child orders from a list of toys and telephones order to Toy Store. He then goes to the storekeeper and asks if his package is ready. Storekeeper answers, "What is your name?" "My name is_____." "Yes, your package is ready," etc.

Fishing Game

Select pictures representing words which contain sounds you have been working on. Put paper clips on each picture, then put pictures in a pail or box. Attach a magnet to a string hanging from a pole. After lifting the picture out of the pail, the child tries to say the name of the picture. If he does, he keeps the picture; if he does not, he must put picture back (after having practiced it a little) and try again.

Sound Ladder or Word Ladder

Draw an outline ladder on paper or on the blackboard. Place syllables you are practicing or words on each rung of the ladder. Child begins at bottom and climbs ladder by pronouncing each of the words or syllables correctly. The game is to see if he can climb to the top and back down again without "falling off." If he misses he must start at the bottom again.

Animal Talk

The sounds: *quack-quack, moo-moo, baa-baa, oink-oink* and *peep-peep,* are good for lip movement. Pictures of animals may be shown and the children imitate that animal. A story may be told about a farmer and when an animal is mentioned the children make the proper sounds.

Noisy Cards

Make picture cards that suggest sound effects. The pictures are face-down in a stack. A child takes the top card. Questions and answers should be in sentences.

    Child: "My picture says_____. What do I have?"

    Answer: "Do you have a_____?"

    Child: "Yes, (or no) I have a_____."

A Listening Story

Negative practice is important in checking the child's knowledge of sounds. Ask children to raise their hands when they hear a sound error as you read. Have them identify the error, and then give the correct sound.

Sound Boxes

Collect and place in boxes small objects starting with easily confused sounds; example *s-z, th-s, th-f, w-r.* Review the contents of the boxes periodically letting children use names of objects in sentences.

I See Something

Use sound boxes mentioned above. Teacher says, "I see something in this box that starts with_____." Child chooses object and says, "Is it a_____?"

Mailman

Pictures of objects containing sound being worked on are placed in envelopes.

    Child: "Mr. Mailman, please look and see if you have a letter for me."

    Mailman: (Gives child envelope) "Yes, I have a letter for you."

    Child: (Opens envelope) "My letter has a_____in it."

Balloons

(especially good when working on "L")

Make colored paper balloons about six inches in diameter with a string fastened to each one.

    First child: "I am the balloon man. Balloons! Balloons for sale! Who will buy my balloons?"

Second child: "I will buy a balloon."
First child: "What color would you like?"
Second child: "I would like a_____ balloon."

(Continue game until all balloons have been chosen) After all balloons have been chosen, ask for them to be returned by colors, using only the lips to form the words without a voice. Do not exaggerate lip movements when forming the words.

1. Should a child be expected to read a word containing a sound that is not present in his speech?

2. Should a child be expected to read a word containing a sound that he cannot or does not hear?

3. What games would you suggest that a child play at home who has not mastered the major speech sounds?

4. Why are you no longer aware of the difference between such sounds as *th* in *this* and *throw*?

5. How might singing games help in the development of a child's speech?

HOW MAY THE CLASSROOM TEACHER HELP CHILDREN WITH SPEECH DEFECTS?

"Speech is defective when it deviates so far from the speech of other people in the group that it calls attention to itself, interferes with communication, or causes the possessor to be maladjusted to his environment." [5]

About one of every ten children in the public schools has a speech defect as defined above. About half of these defects are relatively simple problems, such as substituting *wun* for *run* or saying *pay* for *play*. The remaining are more serious. These include hearing impairment, physical defects such as cleft palate, stuttering, and delayed speech due to psychological causes. The first group can be cared for by a classroom teacher, the second needs the help of a specialist. However, many of those receiving special training will be in regular classrooms and in all other respects their education is the responsibility of the regular teacher.

In all cases, early recognition and treatment of the defect will help the child. Even if some of these defects cannot be corrected, the child, like other handicapped individuals, can be shown how to adjust to his limitations. The teacher can aid in this recognition, but in so doing she must also recognize and be able to distinguish between those defects that can be corrected and those that cannot. It is as unprofessional to attempt to remove some of these speech defects without special training as it would be to treat serious illnesses without medical training.

Parents and regular teachers can assist the child in correcting simple articulation errors. The process is one of changing a speech habit by re-education, and involves letting the child hear the word pronounced correctly while seeing it formed by the lips of the speaker.

When Ricky says, "shire crackers" for fire crackers, don't make the mistake of mimicking his incorrect pronunciation. Simply let him (1) hear the word pronounced correctly; (2) see your lips as you say it; and (3) try to say it himself. "Ricky, the word is *fire* crackers. See my lips and teeth—*fire* crackers, *fire* crackers. Now you say it." At first he will repeat it exactly as before, but be patient. The next time he mispronounces the word, try again. Note how he says the *f* sound in other words. Let him practice a word that he says correctly and then have him contrast that word with "fire crackers." Have a group of children say a verse that uses this sound, and make Ricky a part of this group. Invent sentences for him to practice, such as "First Frank built a fire." Here are some common speech errors of early childhood:

[5] Charles Van Riper and Katherine G. Butler, *Speech in the Elementary Classroom* (New York: Harper, 1955).

Child	Teacher
fank you	*thank you*—See my tongue peek between my teeth.
wed ball	*red ball*—See how I say it.
thee me	*see me*—See my teeth together.
I wike you	*I like you*—See my tongue jump high.
muvver	*mother*—See my tongue touch my teeth.
seben	*seven*—See my lips and teeth.
sherry pie	*cherry pie*—See my lips and hear me say it.

Probably the most frequent defect of all is the s sound. It is commonly called a lisp and is sometimes difficult to correct. The teacher might say, "I am going to say a sound. Listen while I say it and make believe you are saying it to yourself as I say it." Say the sound softly three times. "Now you say it with me." After the child can say the sound practice on these words:

Initial Position	Medial Position	Final Position
say	messy	yes
sell	basket	pass
soap	listen	rice
silk	beside	guess

Tell the child to raise his tongue to a position directly behind but not touching the upper front teeth and expel a sharp s sound. Many times a child fails to make this sound because his tongue touches the teeth, as in the th sound. If he can keep his tongue back and up he should be able to produce the correct, pure sound.

Actually, correction involves the efforts of all concerned. The school day is only a small segment of a child's speaking experience. What is started at school must be continued at home. One caution should be understood by both teachers and parents. The child's recitation or conversation should *not* be interrupted to correct a speech error. The speech drill is a separate activity. When the child is talking, notice what ideas he is expressing without embarrassing him by attention to a fault. Failure to do this can result in social withdrawal and extreme self-consciousness that will be a greater problem than the lisp. The following type of guidance is sent to the child's parents in a handbook by the San Diego City Schools.[6]

[6] Helen Loree Ogg, *A Manual of Speech Therapy for Parents' Use.* (San Diego, Calif.: San Diego City Schools, 1950).

Sounds: S–Z

How the Sounds are Made

The most common minor speech problem is the lisp. Generally speaking, a lisp is the substitution of th for s. Probably the reason for such widespread substitution is that for a long period of time in a child's life the front teeth are in the process of replacement. During this time there is nothing in the front of the mouth to restrain the tongue tip and so out it comes beyond the line of the teeth and the th sound results. This tooth-growing period is so long that the tongue habit becomes well established and is, therefore, quite difficult to break. Nevertheless, it can be done if parents and teachers work together to remind the child of the new speech pattern. The s sound pattern is an easy one to understand and to make.

1. Place the teeth together either as they meet on edge or as they meet in chewing.
2. Then force the air out through the spaces between the teeth.

It is as simple as that in most cases. S is an AIR sound.

For the z sound, follow the directions for making s, but voice the outflow of air making a buzzing sound. Place the finger tips against the hard ridge on the front of the throat and feel the vibration or buzz as you say z. Z is a VOICE sound.

How to Help the Child

If the air flows through the teeth easily, then the child needs only a reminder to close his teeth when he says a word with an s or z sound. Help the child learn a few of the more common words first—the ones he uses every day such as SHOES (z), PANTS, BREAKFAST, SUPPER, ICE (s) CREAM, CEREAL (s), ZIPPER, POTATOES (z), CARROTS, SOAP.

If the air doesn't flow through freely it

may be necessary to train the tongue to a flatter position in the mouth. Suggest touching the lower teeth with the tongue tip. Or with a tongue depressor (also called a tongue blade—the kind the doctor uses when he examines the throat), press the tongue gently to the floor of the mouth. Then when it is in a more relaxed position use the edge of the depressor to stimulate a groove down the center. Quickly close the teeth while the tongue is still relaxed, force the air out, and the s, or hissing sound, is made. Time and practice will establish the new pattern.

In words that begin with an s blend (that is, with two or three consonant sounds, the first of which is s) such as STAND, SWING, SNOW, and STRING, separate the s from the rest of the word: s—tand, s—wing, s—now, and s—tring. Don't hurry the speech. Give the child ample time to put his teeth together, to force the air through, and to make a good strong s sound before saying the rest of the word.

It will be observed that every child who lisps is a rapid speaker. The trouble is that time is not taken to close the teeth for the s and z sounds (maybe also for some others). So slower speaking and an attempt to speak all words more carefully and more clearly are worth striving for, together with the stimulation for closing the teeth.

Another type of incorrect s sound is the lateral s. In this case, the tip of the tongue is high, touching the upper teeth ridge, or even farther back on the roof of the mouth, and the teeth are always separated. The high tongue position blocks the straight outflow of air. Instead, the air escapes laterally, over the sides of the tongue, and with this outflow there is always a more or less unpleasant sound, as if there were too much saliva in the mouth. To correct the lateral lisp follow the procedure already explained: relax and flatten the tongue, close the teeth, and direct the air straight out over the tip of the tongue and through the front teeth.

The greatest difficulty with the production of the z sound is that far too many people never say it, except as it occurs at the beginning of the word. At the ends of plural words (meaning more than one object) such as *doors, tables,* and *beds,* the s should be pronounced as z. The general rule for pronouncing s as z is this: whenever s follows a VOICE sound, the s is changed to z. To explain further let us examine the words given above.

DOORS	*r* is the sound before the *s*, it is a voice sound, therefore, the *s* is a z sound.
TABLES	*l* is the sound before the *s*, it is a voice sound, therefore, the *s* is a z sound.
BEDS	*d* is the sound before the *s*, it is a voice sound, therefore, the *s* is a z sound.

Here is a complete list of VOICED and AIR sounds. At the end of a word

S Becomes Z Following

1.	A	as in	BANANAS	9.	M	as in ROOMS
2.	B	" "	BIBS	10.	N	" " PENS
3.	D	" "	BEADS	11.	NG	" " SINGS
4.	E	" "	TREES	12.	O	" " TOES
5.	G	" "	PIGS	13.	OO	" " SHOES
6.	I	" "	EYES	14.	R	" " BEARS
7.	J	" "	BRIDGES	15.	V	" " WAVES
8.	L	" "	BELLS			

S Remains S Following

1.	P	as in	TOPS
2.	T	" "	TENTS
3.	F	" "	DWARFS
4.	TH	(air) as in	MONTHS
5.	K	" "	BOOKS

Practice Material

		pussy	lazy	yes	pencils
		inside	buzzing	guess	tapers
say	zoo	answer	easy	pass	trees
see	zipper	myself	busy	us	apples
soap	zebra	must	visit	dress	teachers

Other sounds that cause trouble are the *k-g* sounds and the *r*. These letters are not visible on the lips of a speaker and so present special problems in teaching.

K and *g* are formed in the back of the mouth. The organs of speech principally con-

cerned are the back of the tongue and the soft palate. These two must meet.

1. Raise the back of the tongue.
2. Touch the soft palate (as it lowers to meet the tongue).
3. They meet for a moment and then

separate with a slight explosive sound as the air rushes out. This air explosion is the sound of *k*. It is, therefore, an AIR sound.

When the air is voiced, or we might say when the *k* is said aloud, the *g* sound is made. *G* is a VOICE sound.

In the production of some of our sounds there is a kind of two-fold process. For *s* and *z*, as explained previously, the teeth and tongue are placed in their proper positions and they are not moved when the sound is made. But for *k* and *g*, and certain other sounds, the organs of speech used (the back of the tongue and the soft palate for *k* and *g*) take their positions for the sound production, but as the sound is made they move back to their normal positions. We call these the "make" and "break" positions. Furthermore, it is not the "make" movement alone that produces the sound—that is only preparation for the sound. It is the "break" movement that gives the sound. So in helping children learn these sounds, *k* and *g*, be sure there is a "break" movement.

It is a little easier to stimulate production if the lower jaw is in a somewhat relaxed position, the mouth thus being partly open.

If *t* is substituted for either the *k* or *g* sound (*tum* for *come*), or if *d* is used for *g* (*dame* for *game*), the *tip* of the tongue is in a raised position instead of the *back*. There are several ways to correct this. Suggest that the tip touch the back of the lower teeth and stick to them as tightly as if the tip were chewing gum. This centers attention on the tip and builds up tension there so that the back of the tongue may be freer for use. If this is not successful, use a tongue depressor over the tip to hold it down. As soon as it is held down the back will rise. Also using a depressor, the tip may not only be held down but a slight backward pressure exerted on the depressor will aid in pushing the back up to its proper position. As the tongue moves upward the soft palate automatically moves down to meet it.

Still another aid is the use of two finger-tips placed on either side of the trachea (the hard ridges felt on the front of the throat) just under the chin. From this position push up gently. This stimulates the muscles of the back of the tongue to move upward.

Sometimes the *k* sound may be secured through the suggestion of "coughing." An excellent bit of verse to be used in this connection may be found in the practice materials below. A mirror may be used to show the relaxed lowered position of the tongue tip. And a feather or piece of paper held in front of the mouth will indicate the amount of air being expelled. The paper will move quite jerkily when the sound is made correctly.

Practice Material

		cookie	begin	look	egg
		pumpkin	forgot	stick	flag
come	go	pocket	hungry	talk	frog
can	give	basket	tiger	thank	dog
kite	girl	monkey	wagon	milk	bag

BIG PIG

"Where are you going, big pig, big pig?"
    "Out in the garden to dig, dig, dig."
"Into the garden to dig, dig, dig, dig,
    Shame on you big pig, big pig."
"I'm sorry, Madam, but I'm only a pig
    And all I know is to dig, dig, dig."
                    —AUTHOR UNKNOWN

THE CLOCK

    Tick, tock,
    Tick, tock,
    Tick, tock,
Hickory dickory dock.
The mouse ran up the clock.
The clock struck one
The mouse ran down
Hickory dickory dock.
    Tick, tock,
    Tick, tock,
    Tick, tock,
Merrily sings the clock.
There is time for work
There is time for play
And so it sings through all the day,
    Tick, tock,
    Tick, tock,
    Tick, tock.
                    —MOTHER GOOSE

THE CAT

The black cat yawns,
Opens her paws,
Stretches her legs,
And shows her claws.

    Then she gets up
    And yawns once more.
    Lifting herself
    On her delicate toes,

She arches her back
As high as it goes.

Then she lets herself down
With particular care
And pads away
With her tail in the air.

—MARY B. MILLER

The r is one of the most difficult sounds to produce, possibly because the parts of the tongue used for r are used in much the same way in the production of several other sounds. There are three basic ways to make an r sound, but in all three some part of the tongue must touch or almost touch the roof of the mouth. The tip may contact the roof of the mouth (the hard palate) any place from the ridges back of the upper teeth to about midway to the back. Or the middle of the tongue may approach the middle of the hard palate, or the back of the tongue may almost touch the back of the hard palate.

1. The easiest for a child to learn is the tip of the tongue position. He can see this position in a mirror and usually it is easy to raise the tip of the tongue to the roof of the mouth.

2. Then give the sound of the r (er) and ask the child to try to imitate the sound. Sometimes moving the tip back a bit will help. Also, the suggestion that the sound is made in the throat, and that it is rather like a lion's growl, helps. R is a VOICE sound.

If the child has difficulty lifting the tip of the tongue use a tongue depressor and lift it for him. Occasionally, it is easier to place the depressor against the tip of the tongue and gently push the tongue back into the mouth at the same time raising it to near contact with the roof.

Sometimes it helps to use the name of the letter, R, instead of the r sound. The name of the letter starts with the ah sound, then er. Say the ah with a fairly wide open mouth and keep the mouth open for the tongue position for er, ah—er.

Words beginning with r, such as red and read, should be practiced er—ed and er—eed in very slow tempo at first. This gives the tongue time to find its place on the roof of the mouth. Words ending in the r sound, as mother and father should be said muth—er, fath—er. When r is in the middle of a word, as in three, bird, bright and horse, say th—er—ee, buh—er—d, buh—er—i—t, and haw—er—s, working up the timing to that of normal speech.

When the r sound is practiced with the l sound, the r may be more easily learned. The l is made with the tip in a forward position on the upper teeth ridge. With this position for l, use the back of the tongue position for r. Alternating from l to r, giving the tongue a sort of rocking back and forth movement may bring the desired r sound.

Some children say ah for r, as kah for car, in what we call Eastern or Southern dialect. In this case, follow the directions given for the name of the letter r, ah—er, adding the er to the ah that they already say.

Also, a child may substitute w for r, saying wed for red. This calls for elimination of the lip movement for w, first of all. There are several ways to do this. Show the child your own nonuse of lips for r and use instead, the tongue tip. Let him use a mirror to help avoid the unnecessary movement. One may use the first and second fingers horizontally, to hold the lips against the teeth. From there on work as suggested above.

Practice Material

		very	story	door	bear
		carry	every	car	floor
ran	rabbit	carrot	fairy	hair	for
red	run	orange	horse	four	near
rain	right	squirrel	around	color	chair

RAIN

The rain is raining all around
    It falls on you
    It falls on me
Don't you love to hear its sound?

Pitter, patter, pitter, patter
That's the raining sound.

The rain is raining on the ground,
    It falls on field
    It falls on tree
It falls on all the ships at sea.

Pitter, patter, pitter, patter
That's the raining sound.

—Adapted from R. L. STEVENSON

"Cleft palate" means the pathological condition in which the roof of the mouth has failed to grow together before the child was born. Surgery can correct this, but sometimes the condition is neglected until after the child has developed speech, when correction requires relearning breath control. Ordinarily a classroom teacher is not trained to meet this problem but she may have such a child in her class. The sounds made by these children are distorted, since they have no sounding board except the throat and nose chambers. A film is available called "The Wisconsin Cleft Palate Story" which might be used to help a child's parents understand this problem or to enlist the aid of others. During the long period of re-education that follows a cleft-palate operation these children need patient understanding by teachers, parents, and their peer groups.

A malocclusion is a failure of the teeth to mesh—usually at the front of the mouth. During the intermediate grades this is a frequent condition of new teeth in the as yet undeveloped jaw. A large number of these situations adjust themselves with growth. It is a frequent (and expensive) practice to correct malocclusion during the junior high school years. Mrs. Eleanor Roosevelt, one of the most beloved women in American public life, who for years had protruding front teeth which affected her speech, had the condition corrected late in life.

Probably the most misunderstood of all speech defects is stuttering. In this situation the speech is only a symptom of a deeper psychological cause. Correction is not a matter of speech alone. The most important thing for all teachers to remember about stuttering is that it is caused by pressure and tension at some critical moment in a child's life. The tragedy is that stuttering is sometimes caused by the school itself. Strange to say, in our culture it is more frequent among boys than among girls. Equally strange is the fact that stuttering does not exist at all in some cultures. At times when the child is facing considerable speech development, as at the age of three or in the first grade, ideas sometimes come faster than the sounds or words can be recalled and produced. Nearly every child "clutters" or says "ah-ah-ah" while seeking the word. Concern by parents or teachers during this period seems to cause some to stutter. These children are so robust that we may forget their inner sensi-

tivity. A remark of concern, such as "I am afraid John is going to stutter," overheard at this time may actually cause stuttering. Even an attempt by the parent to correct the speech by saying "Stop and start again" may cause damage.

Because stuttering is misunderstood, parents of older children frequently think they are clinging to a childish habit and can stop stuttering if they want to. Stutterers can usually sing, speak or read in a group, take part in a memorized play that involves them physically (such as sweeping with a broom) and talk while dancing without stuttering. Increased language facility that is the result of much writing and a growth in psychic confidence and security usually helps a person who stutters.

The most important thing a classroom teacher can do for a stutterer is to help him accept this defect without embarrassment. The child who can accept this speech pattern as one accepts being left-handed is a long way toward satisfactory educational and social adjustment. These suggestions may be shared with the child's parents:

1. Do not provide words, finish a sentence, or act impatient when listening to a stuttering child.
2. Do see that the child is not subject to physical or emotional strain. "Stuttering is the weak and weary nervous system protecting itself from complete exhaustion."
3. Do praise the child's efforts and make him feel both worthy and loved.
4. Do not put the stuttering child in an exciting and highly competitive position. Overly ambitious parents or those who expect high behavior standards sometimes create ulcers for themselves at the same time they make a stutterer of their child. Far too many stutterers are the sons of highly ambitious professional men.
5. Do not correct or reprimand the child for stuttering or call attention to it. He is already building up fears in meeting speech situations and is extremely conscious of his trouble. Anticipate some speech situations, such as telephoning, meeting strangers, answering questions, and provide confidence building practice.
6. Help him accept himself as a stut-

terer. "Sure I stutter sometimes but I'm trying to get over it" is a healthy attitude. All of us on occasion do what the stutterer does more frequently.

There are some publications containing information about speech development in children and suggestions for parents in dealing with these speech problems. If the teacher has some of this material available she can give it to the parents to read or she may suggest that parents avail themselves of this material. A suggested list follows:

Beasley, Jane. *Slow to Talk, A Guide for Teachers and Parents of Children with Delayed Language Development.* New York: Teachers College, Columbia U.P. 1956.

Chapin, Amy Bishop. *A Child Doesn't Talk.* Cleveland: Junior Chamber of Commerce, 1947.

Chapin, Amy Bishop, and Ruth Lundin. *Your Child's Speech and How to Improve It.* Cleveland: Western Reserve U.P., 1949.

Cleveland Public Schools. *Let's Grow with Good Speech.* Cleveland: Cleveland Public Schools, 1953.

Hejna, Robert. *Your Child's Speech. A Handbook for Parents.* Madison, Wisconsin: College Typing Company, 1955.

Holland, Dorothy. *Development and Correction: Suggestions for Parents and Teachers.* Lincoln, Nebr.: Nebraska Department of Education, 1955.

Minneapolis Public Schools. *Speech Correction in Practice.* Minneapolis: Minneapolis Public Schools, 1948.

Sanderson, V. S. *What Should I Know About Speech Defects.* Columbus: Ohio State U.P., 1946.

Ogg, Helen Loree. *A Manual on Speech Therapy for Parents' Use.* San Diego, Calif.: San Diego City Schools, 1950.

Schreiber, F. R. *Your Child's Speech—A Practical Guide for Parents for the First Five Years.* New York: Putnam, 1956.

Trombly, Thelma. *Helping Ted Improve His Speech.* Columbia, Mo.: University of Missouri Speech and Hearing Clinic.

Van Riper, Charles. *Helping Children Talk Better.* Chicago: Science Research Associates, Inc., 1953.

1. There are other speech defects than those described here. Can you describe some of them?

2. Would you advise a parent to send a child with a speech defect to some of the special speech camps held during the summer months? What would you want to know before doing anything?

3. Would there be any advantage in clustering all children with speech defects in a few rooms?

4. A child with a speech defect in your classroom has been accepted by the other children as a humorous clown. The speech-defective child likes this role and plays it well. What actions would you take?

HOW DOES A TEACHER WORK WITH CHILDREN WHO DO NOT SPEAK ENGLISH?

Some schools place children who do not speak English in special orientation classes regardless of grade until language is mastered. For little children a year of "prefirst" following kindergarten is considered essential. When the problem concerns only a single child, a buddy system usually works well—changing the buddy at times. This is an excellent learning experience for the English-speaking child in that he is forced to note the structure of his language.

While the great stress will be upon listening and reproduction of oral language, there will be some reading. Anyone who has traveled in a foreign country knows that it is easier to read some of the basic signs than it is to speak the language.

The very first day of school the foreign-speaking child has one word in common in both languages—his name. His experience with language should begin with this one word. First the teacher must make sure that the child recognizes his name orally. Some parents use a different name or an abbreviation but give the school the full formal name. This results in difficulty for the child. Frequently the teacher pronounces the name differently from the way the parents do.

The teacher presents the name cards by attaching one set to the child's table or chair or coat hook, and teaches the child to find his own place. Then she gathers them in small groups and presents the cards, holding one up, saying the name, and handing it to the child. The following games provide needed practice. Although designed for Spanish-speaking children these activities are appropriate for any child learning the English language.[7]

Mailman—(Tests the "mailman.") A child who is chosen to be mailman tries to pass out the name cards of his group, giving each one his own card. If a recipient gets the wrong card and does not realize it, the teacher may call for an inspector to check on the mail delivery. The game is good because it involves no competition.

Going to the store—(Tests each participant.) The teacher places all the name cards of the group in the pocket chart. She then calls a child to "go to the store" and get his name. This is especially valuable when there are names which begin alike, as it calls for careful discrimination. It can be varied by telling the child to get another child's name.

Storekeeper—(Tests the storekeeper.) The teacher places all the names in the pocket chart. One child is the storekeeper. The others go up one by one, say their names, and the storekeeper tries to give out the correct card. If he misses, the one to whom he gave the wrong card is the new storekeeper. This game provides opportunity to teach new English phrases orally, such as "Good morning," "What do you want?" "I want," and "Thank you."

Find the stranger—(Tests discrimination of each participant.) The teacher uses a double set of name cards. She arranges each line in the pocket chart so that it

contains two identical names and one different name. The children in turn study one line and point out the stranger.

Find the twins—(Tests discrimination of each participant.) Using a double set of name cards, the teacher arranges the pocket chart so that each line contains three different names, one of which is repeated. The children in turn study one line and point out the twins.

It is usual for most first grades to have many labels around the room, such as *window, door, books,* etc. If the class will contain many non-English-speaking children it is better not to put up these labels at the beginning of the term, for the child may associate the label with the language they know. The words should be used in every possible classroom situation before being presented in written form. The first word chosen might be a *chair.* When the teacher can say the word "chair" and get a satisfactory response from the child, such as touching the chair or pointing at it, she is ready to present the word. She presents a card to the child with the word chair on it and attaches a duplicate card to the chair. The child then takes the card to the chair to prove that it is identical, saying the words as he does this. This is called *matching* and will be used in many other lessons.

In presenting the nouns, it is best to present the singular form first, and avoid the plural as much as possible. In Spanish, the final s is usually preceded by a vowel, and it is difficult for the child to pronounce the plurals which have a consonant preceding the s. There is also another difficulty because the final s sometimes has a z sound. When the plural form is used in the course of schoolroom activities, the teacher should try to establish the correct pronunciation as soon as possible.

The following list of words is divided according to the number of pronunciation difficulties. They should be presented slowly and practiced in enjoyable situations. They provide the Spanish-speaking child with the satisfaction of reading achievement while he is learning speech.

---

[7] Margaret E. Gott, "Teaching Reading to Spanish Speaking Children" (Unpublished thesis, San Diego State College, 1955).

A. *Few Pronunciation Difficulties:*

ball   game   chair   toy   crayola
clay   house   nail   clock playhouse

B. *One Pronunciation Difficulty:*

table—*bl*   paper—final *r*
door—final *r*   saw—*aw*
window—short *i*   box—short *o*
book—short *oo*   car—final *r*
paint—final *nt*   airplane—no vowel
pencil—short *i*   between *rp*
rug—short *u*   top—short *o*
                     crayon—*on*

C. *Two Pronunciation Difficulties:*

hammer—short *a*, final *r*
sharpener—*sh*, final *r*

D. *Three or More Pronunciation Difficulties:*

blackboard—short *a*, final *d*, no vowel
   between syllables
puzzles—short *u*, *z*, final *s*
playthings—*th*, short *i*, *ng*, final *s*
scissors—short *i*, *zr*, final *s*
picture—short *i*, *tu*, final *r*, no vowel between *ct*
drawing—*aw*, short *i*, *ng*, no consonant
   sound between syllables

Games

Matching (Tests discrimination of each participant)—This should be played with no competition and in the slow group should involve much bodily movement. Each child is handed a card and tries to match it with the label on the object before the teacher rings her bell. When he finds the correct object he stands quietly until his turn to read his word to the group.

Where Are You Going?—(Tests recognition of words by each participant.) In this game the teacher holds up a card and asks a child, "Where are you going?" He tries to remember the word on the card and points to the place where he is going to try to match it up. Then he is given the card and goes to prove the correctness of his recognition, matching the word with the proper label and reading it aloud. If he is in error, he is allowed to go about the room and hunt for the correct label. This game teaches silent reading with comprehension.

Picture Match—The teacher prepares a set of small pictures mounted on cards about 3×4 inches and places the pictures in the pocket chart. The children try to place the word cards under the correct pictures. A card incorrectly placed is checked against the labeled object in the room. The children may place one card in each turn, or one child may try to place them all. If this game is used at the stage where the child has been taught only two words, and then each new word added to the set, there will be no confusion.

After the words *door* and *window* have been taught, the teacher may play an oral language game of "Open the Door. Open the Window." This may be done first in the group with a cardboard house and later in the room. The words *open* and *shut* need not be presented in printed form, for they seldom occur below primer or first-reader level. The child hears the word *the* in the complete sentence first. Later the teacher uses it just with the noun. She shows the cardboard house and says, "The door." The child points to the door. After the child has shown that he is familiar with the article in oral language, the time has come to present it in written form.

For the first presentation the teacher says the words "the door" while showing the phrase on a card, and a child responds by indicating the door. The label on the classroom door has only the noun. Some bright child sees this at once and calls the teacher's attention to it. Her card is different! The teacher then holds up the card with the noun only, saying "door," then holds up the other saying "the door." Ask children to add "the" to other words.

Pictures drawn by the children supply a good medium for the first sentences. The child brings his picture to his small group to show. If he knows no English he can quickly learn to hold it up and say, "See." The children will quickly learn to express appreciation for the picture by saying, "Oh! Oh!" These words are easy for the child to say. The teacher can employ them many times daily. She should use only a simple paraphrase of the meaning of *pleasure* and *approval* at first; later on she can add *excitement, dismay,* and *disapproval.*

A number of pictures are now placed in the chalkrail or hung along the chalkboard. Then the children learn to indicate their own by saying, "my boat" or "my airplane." The teacher can very easily facilitate this by having all the children or all the group draw the same thing. The word *my* is also easily taught, as soon as the children know the word *chair,* by having each child indicate his chair with his name on it and say, "My chair."

On the wall or on a bulletin board the teacher arranges an ever-changing display of children's pictures. As the child shows his drawing he says, "See my boat." The teacher selects, with the children voting, a picture of the day, and puts it up, writing on the tagboard label what the child said, "See my boat." The child goes to the bulletin board, points to the picture and says, "See my boat." The teacher then indicates the label, and moving her whole arm under the line of words in a horizontal position from left to right, repeats the phrase. Some pictures are left up for several days and the children play matching games with the duplicate labels. Two or three pictures may be mounted on large sheets of tagboard or paper and hung on the chart rack with the labels printed below. These are the first experience charts used by the children.

HOW MAY ORAL READING SKILLS BE IMPROVED?

A good oral reader is eager to share with his listeners something that seems important. It may be new information, an experience, a vivid description, an interesting character, a bit of humor or a poetic phrase. Without a motive of this kind, oral reading is impersonal and lifeless. The reader should know his audience's interests and needs and interpret the material accordingly. To read aloud well, the reader must have mastered the skills of perception so that he recognizes words quickly and accurately. Equally important is ability to group words together in thought units and to read smoothly. To help his listeners grasp the author's meaning, the reader uses various devices. He highlights new ideas through the use of emphasis, makes clear the transition from one idea to another; indicates by proper phrasing the units of thought within a sentence; relates the ideas of a series by keeping his voice up until the end is reached; and indicates climax by force and vigor of expression.

Most teachers will grasp at this point and ask, "Does such reading take place in the elementary school?" They are thinking of the slow, halting oral reading of the reading circle. Day by day teachers have urged children to read as if they were talking, to read to find the answer to a question, or to read the part of a story they liked best. But seldom has such reading produced anything like that described above. It was usually thought good if the child knew all the words. Nor was anyone in the listening group charmed by what was read. After all, they had read the same material.

Unfortunately, most oral reading in a classroom has been for the single purpose of evaluation. In addition, there has been an emphasis on speed as an indication of growth. Children have sat before machines to increase eye movement, have taken timed tests, have been taught how to skim, and have been given vast amounts of materials to read for information. Little wonder then that few read well orally.

The skills of oral reading are most naturally developed in the reading of plays. The reading of plays adds many values to

La Mesa-Spring Valley Public Schools, Calif.

It is easier to hold the book in the "oral-reading chair." Careful selection of material and preparation by the reader assures that this honor will be a valued listening experience for the class.

reading; it enlists the delight in dramatization which appears in the everyday make-believe of all children; it enriches imagery in the reading of fiction; it provides disciplines not found in other types of reading; it enhances comprehension, vocabulary development, phrase reading, expression, and general speech skills.

Children of all reading levels may be cast in a play. Undiscovered personality qualities are often brought out in play reading. When a child is "someone else" while reading a play, new and delightful aspects of his personality are revealed. Plays are good for reducing shyness in timid children, and for finding sympathetic qualities in aggressive ones. Plays allow discussion of personal qualities, manners, habits, and ethical choices without self-consciousness on the part of pupils or moralizing by the teacher. The children can talk objectively about the actions of the characters knowing that the roles they have played are only "make-believe."

Play reading requires disciplines not encountered in other reading. Alertness to timing of speeches, coming in on cue, keeping one's place on the page, reading words and phrases correctly, expressing oneself well—these and other factors are recognized by the child as important in the success of the play.

The motivating power of the true audience situation is always found in play reading. Comprehension is assured; the child cannot interpret his lines unless he understands them. Phrase reading is improved by play reading. The child who is inclined to read a word at a time or to ignore commas and periods in oral reading will strive for complete phrases and attend to punctuation when he interprets his role. Improvement of expression through emphasis, pauses, and interpretation of mood and feeling is the main outcome of play reading.

Modern elementary readers contain plays designed to achieve these goals. But children need more experience with this form of literature than that provided in a reading series. Those in the format of radio plays provide excellent practice in oral skills. The radio format is modern and appeals to the children. It also has great appeal for the teacher, since costumes and scenery are not needed.

College students enjoy reading this one although it is planned for the intermediate grades.[8]

Read the following play to yourself in order to get the meaning and *feeling* of it.

There is nothing difficult about the words or the lines.

As soon as you have read the play decide who will take the different parts.

Now practice reading aloud together. Your big job is to see that each person comes in on time.

Betsy, Clem, and the Wise Woman all get impatient with Noodle at some time or other. *Be sure you show this impatience in your voice.*

Noodle is not very bright. His speech is slow and hesitant. *Try to sound stupid as you read his lines.*

After you have read the play over two or three times, decide together how well you are doing these things:

1. Does Noodle sound stupid?
2. Does Betsy sound quick, alert and confident?
3. Are your voices clear and loud enough to be heard?
4. Are you pronouncing every word carefully?
5. Is each person ready to come in "on cue" with his lines?
6. Are you paying attention to the punctuation?

If you cannot truly say yes to these things, get busy and practice again.

Don't read the whole play. Work on the parts that are not coming right.

When you are sure you are ready to read the play for others, let your teacher know. You can then decide with her when it is best to read to the class.

----
[8] Donald D. Durrell and B. Alice Crossley, *Thirty Plays for Classroom Reading* (Boston: Plays, Inc., 1957).

A KETTLE OF BRAINS
adapted from an old folk tale by
Gweneira M. Williams

Characters

(2 boys, 1 girl, 1 woman, and the narrator)

NARRATOR

NOODLE, a stupid boy who wants a kettleful of brains.

CLEM, Noodle's friend who is trying to help him to get some brains.

THE WISE WOMAN, who is old and a little impatient with Noodle. She is really poking fun at him.

BETSY, a smart girl who decides Noodle needs her care.

NARRATOR: Noodle, a stupid boy, is being brought to the hut of the Wise Woman. His friend, Clem, is showing him the way. Noodle is hanging back.

NOODLE (*fearfully*): But I'm afraid.

CLEM: You want brains, don't you?

NOODLE: I need a whole kettleful, I do.

CLEM: Well, then, go to the Wise Woman's hut there and knock at the door. Maybe she knows a way to get you some brains.

NOODLE: Aw, Clem, I'm scared.

CLEM: Noodle, don't be more of a fool than you can help, will you? Go on!

NOODLE: Hello, in there!

WISE WOMAN: What do you want, fool?

NOODLE (*hesitantly*): Well . . . well . . . well . . .

CLEM: Noodle, you're a fool.

NOODLE (*hopefully*): It's a fine day, isn't it?

WISE WOMAN: Maybe.

NOODLE: Maybe it'll rain, though.

WISE WOMAN: Maybe.

NOODLE (*gulping*): Or on the other hand, maybe it won't.

WISE WOMAN: Maybe.

NOODLE: Well, I can't think of anything else to say about the weather. But, but . . .

WISE WOMAN: Maybe.

NOODLE (*in a rush*): The crops are getting on fine, aren't they?

WISE WOMAN: Maybe.

NOODLE: The cows are getting fat.

WISE WOMAN: Maybe.

NOODLE: Wise Woman, I thought maybe you could help me.

WISE WOMAN: Maybe.

NOODLE (*desperately*): I need brains. Do you have any to sell?

WISE WOMAN: Maybe.

NOODLE: What d'you mean, maybe?

WISE WOMAN: Maybe I have and maybe I haven't. It depends on what kind of brains you want. Do you want a king's brains?

NOODLE (*astonished*): Ooh, no!

WISE WOMAN: Or a teacher's brains?

NOODLE (*startled*): Lawkamercy, no!

WISE WOMAN: Or a wizard's brains?

NOODLE: Heavens to Betsy, no!

WISE WOMAN: Well, what kind do you want?

NOODLE: Just ordinary brains. You see, I don't have any at all!

WISE WOMAN: Maybe I can help you.

NOODLE: Maybe? How?

WISE WOMAN: You'll have to help yourself first.

NOODLE (*eagerly*): Oh, if I can, I will.

WISE WOMAN: You'll have to bring me the thing you love best.

NOODLE: How can I do that?

WISE WOMAN: That's not for me to say. But when you bring it here, you must answer a riddle for me, so I'll be sure you can use the brains.

NOODLE: Oh, gosh to goodness!

NARRATOR: Noodle hurried home and now we see him dragging a big bag toward the Wise Woman's hut.

NOODLE (*eagerly*): Here it is, Wise Woman.

WISE WOMAN: Here's what?

NOODLE: The thing I love best.

WISE WOMAN: What is it?

NOODLE: My pig!

WISE WOMAN: Well, now that you're here, can you answer this riddle?

NOODLE: I'll try.

WISE WOMAN: Tell me, what runs without feet?

NOODLE (*stupidly*): Maybe . . . caterpillars?

WISE WOMAN (*angrily*): Idiot! You're not ready for brains! Come back again

when you've decided what you love next best!

NOODLE (*thoughtfully*): What runs without feet? . . . Gosh I loved my pig best. What do I love best after him? . . . I know! My hen, my little hen! Wait a minute, hey, wait! Just wait a minute! I'll be back in a jiffy! Wait!

WISE WOMAN: Burn, fire, burn,
    Burn to a turn,
    One thing's sure as sky and fire,
    Fools never learn!

NOODLE: Here it is! Wait, here it is! Gosh, my goodness, heavens to Betsy, wait! Don't sell that kettle of brains! Here it is!

WISE WOMAN: Here's what?

NOODLE: Here's the thing I love best next to my pig!

WISE WOMAN: What is it?

NOODLE: My hen!

WISE WOMAN: Are you ready to answer me another riddle?

NOODLE (*bravely*): I'll try!

WISE WOMAN: Well, tell me this. What is yellow, and shining, and isn't gold?

NOODLE (*hopefully*): Cheese, maybe?

WISE WOMAN: Fool! . . . What do you love best next to your hen?

NOODLE (*crying*): What'll I do? What'll I do? I've lost the two things I love best! And I still haven't any brains! Whatever will I do now? They were the only two things I loved in the whole world! . . . Who are you?

NARRATOR: As Noodle looks around helplessly a girl comes in. When she sees him, this is what she says.

BETSY: Well, for heaven's sake!

NOODLE (*still crying*): Who are you?

BETSY: My name's Betsy. What's the matter with you?

NOODLE: Oh, I wanted some brains.

BETSY: Why?

NOODLE: I don't have any.

BETSY: Well, where did you think you could get some?

NOODLE (*sobbing*): The Wise Woman in there said she'd give me some if I brought her the things I loved best in the world.

BETSY: Well, did she?

NOODLE: No-o-o!

BETSY: You poor fool, why not?

NOODLE: I c-c-c-couldn't answer the r-r-riddles sh-sh-she asked m-me!

BETSY (*kindly*): There, there, don't cry. Don't you have anyone to take care of you, silly?

NOODLE: No.

BETSY: No one?

NOODLE: No one.

BETSY: Well, I wouldn't mind taking care of you myself!

NOODLE: Lawkamercy!

BETSY: Well?

NOODLE: You mean . . . (Hesitating) *marry* me?

BETSY: Well, yes.

NOODLE: Can you cook?

BETSY: Yes.

NOODLE: Can you sew?

BETSY: Yes.

NOODLE: Can you scrub?

BETSY: Yes, I can. Will you have me? I'd be a good wife.

NOODLE: Well, I guess you'd do as well as anyone else.

BETSY: That's fine.

NOODLE: But, but . . .

BETSY: But what?

NOODLE: What shall I do about the Wise Woman?

BETSY: Let *me* talk to her!

NOODLE: Oh, no, no!

BETSY: Why not?

NOODLE: I'm afraid!

BETSY: I'm not! Don't you need brains?

NOODLE: Well, yes.

BETSY: Come on, then, come on!

WISE WOMAN: What do you want, young woman?

BETSY: Brains for my husband here!

WISE WOMAN: Your husband, eh?

BETSY: We're going to be married.

WISE WOMAN: Does he love you the best of anything in the world?

BETSY: Go on, tell her!

NOODLE: I reckon I do.

BETSY: There, now give him the brains!

WISE WOMAN: Not so fast, not so fast. He'll have to answer the riddles first.

NOODLE (*sadly*): Oh, the riddles.

BETSY (*unafraid*): What are they?

WISE WOMAN: What runs without feet?

NARRATOR: Betsy nudges him and whispers something. Noodle speaks.

NOODLE: Well, my goodness, water!

WISE WOMAN: H'm.

BETSY: Give him the next riddle.

WISE WOMAN: What's yellow and shining and isn't gold?

NARRATOR: Betsy whispers something to Noodle. He answers again.

NOODLE: Well, heavens to Betsy, the sun!

WISE WOMAN: H'm. Here's the third riddle. What has first no legs, then two legs, then four legs?

NARRATOR: Noodle looks at Betsy. Betsy makes swimming motions with her hands. Then she whispers something.

NOODLE (*happily*): A tadpole!

WISE WOMAN (*crossly*): That's right. Now go away!

NOODLE: But where is the kettleful of brains?

WISE WOMAN: You already have them.

NOODLE: Where? I can't see them.

WISE WOMAN: In your wife's head, silly. The only cure for a fool is a good wife. And you have one . . . or will have one. I can't help you any more. Be off with you! Good day!

NOODLE: Maybe she's right . . . You'll marry me, lass? I won't have any brains if you don't.

BETSY: Of course I will! I have brains enough for two, anyway! Come on!

THE END

There are other ways of practicing oral reading. One very good practice in many schools is that of having children in the intermediate grades prepare a library book which they read to a small group in the kindergarten or first grade. One fourth grade motivates this by keeping a record of "Books I Have Read to Others."

Some selections in great literature especially lend themselves to oral reading. The whitewashing of the fence in *The Adventures of Tom Sawyer* is written as if it were a play. Some of the scenes in *Freddie the Pig* by Walter R. Brooks consist almost exclusively of conversation that makes delightful oral reading.

1. It is reported that high school and college students dislike reading aloud in class. Can you explain why?

2. In his book, *Trippingly on the Tongue,* Harry Hiltman uses a system started by the Fred Waring singers of enunciating tone syllables. In this system *nights* becomes "nigh-tiz." This transposition of the final consonant is practiced in speech. *Bee-duh-vice* (bead of ice), *fee-dit-two-me* (feed it to me). Would such material interest children in enunciation?

3. Since reading ahead of the voice with the eyes is necessary in oral reading, do you think oral reading can be done by children having reading difficulty?

4. Give reasons for agreeing or disagree-

ing with this statement: "Oral reading at sight of new material is the most difficult of all reading tasks."

BOOKS OF PLAYS DESIGNED FOR ORAL READING

Durrell, Donald D., and B. Alice Crossley. *Thirty Plays for Classroom Reading.* Boston: Plays, Inc., 1957.

Kissen, Fran. *Bag of Fire, The Straw Ox, The Four Winds.* Boston: Houghton, 1941–52.

Schneideman, Rose. *Radio Plays for Young People to Act.* New York: Dutton, 1960.

Stevenson, Augusta. *Dramatic Readers.* Boston: Houghton, 1930–54.

Ward, Winifred. *Stories to Dramatize.* Anchorage, Ken. Children's Theater Press, 1952.

WHAT IS THE PLACE OF DRAMATICS IN THE CLASSROOM?

Creative dramatics starts with the simple, natural play of the preschool or kindergarten. Here the children play house in the roles of father, mother, child, and the lady next door. In these roles the children try out the vocabulary they hear spoken in the situations of the adult world around them. There is no better way to teach children the social amenities of greeting and farewell. Teacher suggestion as to what should be said is usually welcomed and frequently sought. Some of the more imaginative children will provide patterns that others will imitate.

Children will observe the storekeeper, bus driver, and waiter with new interest after playing any of these roles in the classroom. While the teacher is seldom imitated in the classroom, playing school is a favorite home activity. Parents frequently know many of the teacher's mannerisms and practices as a result of this. However, most children seem to invest the role of teacher with a crossness and severity that is more a part of childhood's folklore than actuality. The influence of television will reveal itself in the children's acting. Where once children saw a movie once a week, they now see one daily. It is only natural

that free play will reflect some of the behavior they observe. To avoid some of the noise and violence it is well to establish through discussion and practice the "acting" techniques that are appropriate to the classroom.

As the children get older the influence of television can be converted to an asset. No generation of children has had wider experience with dramatic form. Many children by the age of twelve have seen more of the great dramatic personalities and literature than past generations have known in a lifetime. The attention-getting exposition, the involvement of the main character with a problem, the gradual working out of that problem and the final resolution become almost second nature after so much familiarity with this form. Many of the favorite children's programs, such as those of some TV comedians, usually follow a theme as simple and obvious as that of old folk stories so that the concept of unity, which once seemed such a difficult idea, can be easily understood. Unfortunately, some of these comedy shows have a degree of sophistication of theme and action that is inappropriate for the classroom.

A few items to use as props (proper-

La Mesa-Spring Valley Public Schools, Calif.

With simple equipment these children have created a sensitive dramatic presentation of a much loved story.

ties) help children give realism to a role. An apron establishes a grandmother, just as a cane identifies a grandfather. A hat makes a boy a man and nothing gives a girl more maturity than a long skirt.

Creative dramatics in the school has no concern that children become "actors," nor that story plays be produced for a guest audience. In some situations the presence of an audience may make the children self-conscious of their roles as actors, rather than assisting the process of creating the play. The stage may be the front of the classroom but the whole room may be involved, in order to indicate a change of scene. Aisles are used as roads, scenery is drawn on the chalkboard, and tables become bridges, mountain tops, or castle towers.

In the primary grades the attitude is one of creative play. "Let's play that story,"

the teacher will suggest. "Who wants to be the mother bear?" Some children are quite content to be a tree in the forest, others will need suggestions as to what to say, but the values of released imagination, language practice and dramatic interest are always there.

In the intermediate grades children imagine that they are the Pilgrims or pioneers. Such dramatics frequently become organized to the extent that the main ideas are outlined, children experiment with different scenes, select the ones that seem most effective and actually write a script which is later presented as a formal production.

One of the most serious uses of dramatic play is to help children with personality problems. A boy with effeminate traits may develop more "manliness" by playing the role of a cowboy or Santa

Claus. A girl lacking grace or poise may gain a measure of these when cast as a beautiful princess. A shy child may find vent for repressed feelings as a wicked witch.

Ordinarily the group decides who will take the various roles in a play. After discussing what a character should be like, it is wise to have different individuals "try out" for the part. The king should walk with lordly mien, speak deliberately and quite loud because of his vast authority, and perhaps flourish a wooden sword. After such a character is established in the minds of the children, let them take turns feeling like a king or whatever character is being developed. At the beginning most teachers cast parts by type. This means using the child whose personality most nearly fits the part. But after children have had some experience with dramatics there will be opportunity to use the story to help a child with a social or personality problem. All the parts, however, should not be assigned on a "problem" basis or children will lose interest. One case of "play therapy" at a time is enough for most teachers to handle.

Sociodrama is closely related to group dramatics as an aid to personality adjustment. Its main purpose is to assist children in being aware of the feelings and problems of others. "How does it feel to be the only child in a room not asked to a party? Let's act it out in a story." The situation may be centered in any problem; the child who acts as a bully and mistreats little children, the child who does not speak English, the lonely lady who complains about the noise children make.

Puppets are used as a vehicle for dramatic work in all grades. Some shy children find it easier to project their language through a puppet actor. Certain dramatic effects can be achieved with puppets that make the productions much more satisfying. Animal actors, folklore characters, magic changes and exotic areas (such as the bottom of the sea) are much easier to manage with puppets than with human actors. Somehow the simple plays written by children seem more spirited when given with puppets.

Puppets should be kept simple. Figures on a stick, sacks on the fist, and even the toy hand puppets that can be purchased are better than elaborate string marionettes. Marionette-making is an art rather than a language project. The time taken to make and manipulate these figures does not stimulate enough language activity to warrant the effort.

Formal dramatics, involving the memorization of a well-written play, have many values for children able to participate in them. The discipline of memorization, the work on characterization, the team spirit developed in presenting the material and the gratifying applause of a truly appreciative audience are valuable experiences. The beginning teacher is often tempted to start with a play that is too difficult. The professional children's theaters with well-equipped stages and trained staffs can produce elaborate plays with such apparent ease that a teacher is tempted to try the same in the classroom. Don't do it unless you are willing to spend hours rehearsing after school, devote week ends painting scenery and making costumes, and act as a military policeman during rehearsal and the performance. Perhaps in a summer school or with a special talented group you can realize your ambitions. In the meantime, be content with less professional material. By all means avoid plays that require large casts or run more than an hour.

Plays such as *Why the Chimes Ring, Strawberry Red, King of Nomania, Knights of the Silver Shield, Elmer, Cabbages* are favorites for the junior high school age group. The little plays published in the magazines *Grade Teacher, Instructor,* and *Plays* are widely used in the lower grades and relatively simple to prepare. Most children will learn their parts in six or eight readings. By the time of the production most of the children will know all the lines. Get mothers involved in making costumes, and on the day of the show have at least one adult to supervise children backstage who are not performing. If make-up is used, keep it simple. A little rouge on the cheeks, a dab of lipstick and a stroke or two with the grease pencil will

Combine paper-sack puppets with some cardboard boxes and the class has a theater which will stimulate the use of all the language skills.

sufficiently transform most child actors. No matter how well it is put on, a beard never looks right on a child. Crepe hair applied with spirit gum, available at all theatrical supply stores, is about as satisfactory a method of "aging" as any.

Most scenery problems can be solved by using sets of folding screens on which the outline of a forest, window, or fireplace has been drawn in colored chalk or water colors. Children's imaginations are so vivid that anything more than this is lost effort. Various sound effects are available on records or they can be put on a tape and amplified at the proper time.

Children are usually excited after a performance. If possible, plan to have a postperformance period with refreshments and general relaxation while costumes are put away and other details attended to. Children are seldom ready for a scheduled class after a play, and the wise teacher will recognize this fact in making plans. Avoid

showing concern over forgotten lines or things that did not go just right, but instead find much to praise.

Radio and television scripts offer excellent possibilities at the elementary level for group composition and speech. The definite pattern in which action and dialogue must be cast gives pupils a needed support as they plan what scenes the cameras should focus on, or what sounds the microphone can pick up. In a television script the scenes for the cameras ("video") are placed on the left-hand side of the page; the words spoken, music and sound effects ("audio") are placed on the right, opposite the scenes they will accompany.

"The First Thanksgiving" below was first produced in the school auditorium by a fifth grade and then on local television.[9]

---

[9] Minneapolis Public School Board of Education, *Communications*, 1953.

VIDEO	AUDIO
1. Announcer.	1. Opening announcement.
2. Pupils stage left.	2. Short reports on pilgrims settling in Massachusetts.
3. Play given stage right and center; scenes as follows:	3. (Dialogue from play.)
4. The Lullaby: Mistress Hopkins at home, taking care of her baby when Squanto arrives.	4. Squanto tells Mistress Hopkins that Governor Bradford and Chief Massasoit have agreed upon a feast of Thanksgiving.
5. Squanto exits. Mother and baby at home.	5. Mother sings Old Lullaby.
6. Other pilgrim mothers and children come to visit Mistress Hopkins.	6. Women discuss the coming feast.
7. Priscilla enters. Priscilla and children begin preparations for the feast.	7. Priscilla directs the children in preparation for the feast.
8. Priscilla sends two boys on an errand.	8. Priscilla sends boys out to get corn.

(The script continues through ten more scenes and ends as follows):

21. Governor Bradford advances and holds out hand to Massasoit.	21. *Gov. Bradford:* Welcome, Massasoit! Welcome to the great Sachem! Welcome to all your braves. The palefaces (gestures toward Pilgrims) welcome the Red Men. We are happy to be here.
22. Massasoit shakes Governor's hand, nodding head solemnly. Then waves his hand toward distance, as if game had been laid down there.	22. *Massasoit:* Massasoit brings heap buck, turkey, rabbit for white man's feast.

VIDEO	AUDIO
23. Governor Bradford exits followed by Standish, Massasoit, braves, Squanto and pilgrims.	23. *Gov. Bradford:* We thank you. And now follow me (BECKONS) I will show you to your tents till the feasting begins.
24. Pilgrims and Indians worship, Elder Brewster leading meeting. Tithing man has a stick with rabbit's foot on one end and hard ball on the other. Pilgrims seated on benches. Taller pilgrim men stand in rear. During service the tithing man quietly touches a small girl who has fallen asleep with her head on her neighbor's shoulder.	24. Elder Brewster offers prayer. "Lord, we come before Thee, now, At thy feet we humbly bow, Oh do not our suit disdain, Shall we seek Thee, Lord, in vain? May the Lord abide with us till our next meeting."
25. All stand and sing.	25. Song ("O God, Beneath Thy Guiding Hand") 26. SIGN OFF

The script is actually a continuity sheet.

Children should be told to speak in a clear and natural voice, without "rushing" their lines yet moving along as though they were talking normally to other students. They should not try to imitate or exaggerate. This does not mean, however, they should not strive to get some feeling into their voices.

On most educational television shows, all colors are seen as shades from black to white. Blacks, grays, and light grays give good contrasts. Pure white is not good since it produces a halation effect and configuration is lost. However, this does not exclude murals and drawings done in color, but if you are preparing "props" for the show, use blacks, grays, and light grays in order

San Diego County Schools, Calif.

to obtain contrasts that are desirable. Values are easier to control with these colors rather than with yellows, reds, blues and greens.

Lettering on posters should be large and simple—not less than one inch in height. Remember that lower case is more legible than capitals. Do not use "fancy" lettering. Try to use black letters when possible.

Prints or photographs can be used to show specific objects, scenery, or people. They should be mounted on 11 in. × 14 in. board and preferably a horizontal shot.

Normally, there are at least two TV cameras on each show—one takes all "placement" or long shots and the other the close-ups. This is important to know, for if you want to show something you have made you must hold it a little above waist height, tilted slightly forward to prevent glare— very steady for about 10 to 15 seconds in the direction of the close-up camera.

Children will be interested in the following television terms and signals:

Placement Shot—Camera is back 10 to 15 feet from the subject and shows the setting of the scene, including persons and props.

Close-up—A close shot, 18 inches to 4 feet from the camera. Shows some item or object in detail.

Pan—This means that the camera is going to swing to the right or left to cover some action (a person walking) or to show several objects in succession or one big object like a mural.

Cut—Means to stop what you are doing. The hand signal for "cut" is to draw your index finger across your throat.

Stretch—Means to lengthen it out, you are covering the material too rapidly. The hand signal for this is to place the fingers of the left and right hands together and slowly pull them apart.

Faster—Means to speed it up, you are running out of time. The hand signal is: rotate your right hand in a clockwise direction very rapidly with the index finger extended.

Softer—Means the audio—your voice or some other sound—is too loud. Hand signal is: spread the thumb and the index finger of the right hand; move your hand away and to the right and gradually bring the index finger and the thumb together.

Louder—Means you are not being heard. Hand signal is: place the thumb and the index finger of your right hand together. Move your hand away to the right and gradually open the thumb and the index finger wide open.

Perfect—Hand signal is: form a circle with your right thumb and index finger.

1. Do you feel that every child in a classroom should have a part in a program presented for an audience?
2. You work in a school where assembly programs and PTA programs are assigned to teachers a year in advance. As a result the teachers put on elaborate productions and compete with each other. This year you have drawn the Christmas assembly. What would you do?
3. You have a class with many emotionally disturbed children. These children come from broken homes, attend clinics, etc. Should you attempt creative dramatics?

PUBLISHERS OF DRAMATIC MATERIAL

Banner Play Bureau, 619 Post Street, San Francisco 9, Calif.

Bakers Plays, 569 Boylston Street, Boston, Mass.

Children's Theatre Press Coverlot, Anchorage, Ky.

Eldridge Publishing Company, Franklin, Ohio.

Samuel French, 25 West 45th Street, New York 36, N.Y.

Lancaster Marionettes, Stratford-upon-Avon, Warwickshire, England.

Plays, 8 Arlington Street, Boston 16, Mass.

Harper & Row, 2500 Crawford Avenue, Evanston, Ill.

Wetmore Declamation Bureau, 1631 S. Paxton St., Sioux City 6, Iowa.

T. S. Denison & Company, 321 Fifth Avenue, S. Minneapolis 4, Minn.

HOW IS COURTESY TAUGHT IN THE LANGUAGE ARTS PROGRAM?

The first lesson in the first book published in the Korean language after the close of World War II had to do with the way a child should greet his parents and grandparents. While Orientals may have a greater regard for the social amenities of family life than Americans who still think of themselves as hardy pioneers, there is nevertheless a growing concern for courtesy in our country. Some states have laws requiring that manners and morals be taught in the schools. Other courses of study list courtesy as one of the values to be sought as an objective. Because certain aspects of courtesy depend on a proper use of language, most textbooks in the language arts include lessons on this topic.

A part of the awkwardness of children in a social situation arises from not knowing the proper thing to say. Greetings, introductions, apologies, interruptions, and expressions of appreciation involve established patterns of language. At first these may be taught as examples to be imitated. "Say bye-bye," a mother urges the infant. Or the parent will, by asking the child, "What do we say when someone gives us something?" eventually elicit a "thank you."

A student teacher working with a group of small children knows that it is a disturbance when an adult enters the classroom. Naturally, children are curious about the stranger. The teacher can maintain control, keep the class moving ahead, and teach some courtesy by stopping a minute and saying, "Girls and boys. This is Mr. Jones from the college. He is here to watch me teach. What do we say when we have a visitor in the room?" The children chorus, "Good morning, Mr. Jones," then return to their work. In upper grades a monitor will go to the visitor, show him where to sit and hand him a copy of the book in use. Then at a convenient time the teacher greets the visitor. Many states require that a record of all visitors be maintained. Even if this is not required it provides an interesting way to greet a visitor. Prepare a "Visitor's Register." Have a child make an attractive cover for it. After the visitor has registered, it is sometimes good to have the courtesy monitor introduce him to the class.

Courtesy instruction will seem a bit silly to children unless it is presented in terms of situations. These situations should reveal the need for some type of social convention. At the time when the school is having an open house or a parents' evening, present the problem of just how we should introduce a parent to the teacher, a parent to a classmate, or one child's parents to other parents.

In a social studies class there will be times when opposing opinions must be expressed. Just how do we express disagreement without offending people or starting an argument? And if we should offend a person, how can we express our apologies? It will interest children to learn how these problems have been solved in other lands. Many of our concepts of courtesy reflect our democratic belief that everyone has certain rights and freedoms. We do not avoid direct contests in athletics even though we know someone will lose, whereas the Oriental feels that "loss of face" is tantamount to personal ruin. His only choice is to avoid direct contests and find indirect ways of expressing his ideas.

There is no better place to discuss table manners than in a health class. Start with problems like this: "Do you like to sit at a table where someone is messy with food? Talks with his mouth full? Shouts and plays at the table?" Lessons about the use of knife and fork, setting the table, refusing food you don't like, discussing certain topics at the table, and even ordering food at the restaurant all involve language skills in this area.

In the third grade, children are growing in social awareness and are anxious to know ways of behaving. Etiquette that requires girls to precede boys through door-

Contrast between the table manners of Japan and the customs of the United States
has added to the appreciation of both cultures by these sixth-grade students.

ways, to walk "on the inside," and to make the initial greeting does not seem quite so trivial at this age as it may later. A party at Halloween or Valentine's Day can be rich in lessons in courtesy. Some classes make little guidebooks on good manners.

Basic to all courtesy are two concepts, respect and kindness. Respect is shown to our parents and to older people, to our country and its flag, to those who serve us, and to our friends and neighbors. Much of courtesy consists in the application of the Golden Rule in an awkward situation. Kindness covers a broad area of human virtue and includes good will, compassion, generosity and love for one's fellow man. Rudeness is the opposite of kindness in that it makes another person suffer. Even following the rules of etiquette can be unkind if it causes others to be embarrassed. The story of Queen Victoria blowing on her soup to cover up a guest's bad manners can be told as a true act of courtesy. Merely following the accepted forms can make us appear as if we considered ourselves superior to all others—or, as children say, "high-toned" or "uppity."

Both respect and kindness are expressed when we speak of consideration of others. This must go much deeper than the language aspect, but knowing the language is a way of establishing the behavior desired as well as the inner sensitivity that is true courtesy. There is no more courtesy in a curt or thoughtless "thank you" than in the thoughtless salute of a new recruit in the army. But a salute that reflects respect, alertness, and a dedication to service is the heart of military courtesy.

Again the importance of example must not be forgotten. The teacher's everyday manners will provide many object lessons in this area. It might be well for the children to know more about the teacher's prerogatives and responsibilities. While it is usually not courteous for a child to criticize his schoolmates, it is quite another thing for a teacher to overlook their shortcomings. Consistency is the key to success.

Some teachers, too, need to "mind their manners." The hasty lunch hour, eating alone, or being too much apart from social activities can develop poor table manners. A friend who works for the F.B.I.

says he can always identify teachers by the way they eat. Teachers may also reflect ungraciousness in accepting favors. Hundreds of requested letters of recommendation have been received by teachers without a word of thanks to those who wrote them. Teachers sometimes accept dinner invitations as though these were a part of their salary. There is no reason why a teacher should not do something in return. If anyone else in our society is invited out to dinner, appreciation is expressed by a reciprocal invitation, a little gift of flowers or candy, or at least a pleasant thank-you note. Even a bachelor can invite people to dinner at a restaurant.

Boorish behavior is always offensive because it betrays callous disregard for the feelings of others. Men in education who depend on profanity, salty anecdotes, and expansive exuberance at conventions to prove they are "regular fellows" may succeed in proving quite the opposite. The woman teacher who overdresses, overspends or overeats may in fact be disclosing a sense of insecurity. Unless they take steps to correct these personality disorders, such teachers cannot be very successful in teaching courtesy. Even the young child can see the type of persons they really are.

The following plan was used successfully in teaching good manners in a third grade. Start by helping children to know that the real basis of good manners is sincerity; that merely being familiar with the "rules" won't tell us what to do in every situation. Sometimes we simply don't know the precise rule to apply, but as long as we are sincere our behavior will be appropriate.

Concepts to Discuss

People use good manners and courtesy because they make living and working together more enjoyable.

What things can we do to make our classroom more enjoyable?
1. Hang up clothes on hangers.
2. Clean up spilled paint and water.
3. Leave the easel clean and ready for the next person.
4. Keep desks clean and neat.
5. Respect the rights of others. Try to help other people.
6. Equipment in the room belongs to all of us. We each have the privilege of using it, and the responsibility of taking care of it.

Learning Activities

The children can be asked to speculate on what the room would be like if no one used manners and courtesy.

Why Have Good Manners, filmstrip (Eyegate House), gives many ideas on why people use good manners.

Children will mention most of these specifics and probably add many more.

The song, "It's Good to Share" (*New Music Horizons, Book III,* p. 70) fits in nicely.

Young America Films' *We Plan Together* is an excellent filmstrip to use prior to committee work.

The group will profit from planning and executing a "model" work and clean-up period. Afterwards, the values of all working to achieve a common purpose can be pointed out.

Flag Courtesy

Why do we show respect for our country's flag?
1. To show that we are thankful for our country.

The film *The Flag Speaks* will make an especially valuable contribution. It discusses our national pride for the flag, and demonstrates correct flag courtesy.

Flag Courtesy

How do we show respect for the flag?

1. When giving the pledge, stand and face the flag, place right hand over heart.
2. When the flag is brought into a room, stand and remain standing until the flag is in place in its holder.
3. When the flag is raised or lowered on the flagpole, stand still, face the flag, and place hand over heart.
4. When the "National Anthem" is played, face the flag and salute. If the flag is not displayed, face the music, but do not salute. (This holds true only for "live" music, and is generally not done if the music is recorded.)
5. Cubs and Brownies, when inside a room, salute instead of placing hand over heart, only if they are in full uniform.

Members of the class who are Cub Scouts or Brownies can be called upon to share what they know about flag courtesy.

The filmstrip *Flag Etiquette* (Young America Films) will provide an excellent summary of what has been learned.

A committee can be formed to learn and demonstrate these rules for the class. This might also be shared at an assembly.

This is a good time to learn or relearn "The Star-Spangled Banner," and "America, the Beautiful."

As the children's outlook begins to widen, the transfer to situations outside the room can be made. The playground is a real testing ground for social amenities. Here the conflict between serving one's own desires as opposed to being considerate to others is especially marked. Even though children know the correct thing to do, they cannot always bring themselves to do it. The very child who contributes the best ideas in the classroom is often the one who fails most to "practice what he preaches." It is obvious that boys and girls will need understanding guidance in utilizing what they learn during this phase.

Concepts to Discuss

What are some things a good citizen tries to do on the playground?

1. Learn the rules of the game, and play according to the rules.
2. Observe safety rules for the swings, slide, and other equipment.
3. Avoid picking fights.
4. Try to include new children in games. Do not tease.
5. Take care of school equipment.
6. The equipment belongs to everyone at our school, therefore all must share it.

Learning Activities

The filmstrip *Good Manners at Play* (Eyegate House) is a helpful aid to introduce playground manners.

Have a problem-solving discussion centered around difficulties that can be prevented by learning and knowing rules.

A small committee can undertake the writing down of game rules. These could be put on a hektograph master and reproduced.

Another group might prepare a bulletin-board display on playground manners.

Dramatic play to demonstrate several ways of handling a "touchy" situation.

Role playing might be used in regard to the "new child" on the playground.

Use filmstrip *New Classmate* (Popular Science Films).

Having given consideration to the social amenities that come into use in the classroom and on the playground, the children can now be guided into a study of

manners and courtesy on a broader scope that includes the whole school, and the school's personnel.

Concepts to Discuss

Why do we need to use courtesy and manners, in other places, at school?

1. Use of good manners will make our school a more enjoyable place.

Besides the teacher, who are some of the people at school who need our help in order to do their jobs?

1. The principal.

2. The school secretary.

3. The custodian.

4. Patrol boys and school safeties.

What can we do to help these people help us?

1. Be courteous to and remember that what they say is to help us.
2. Follow the rules because rules are like manners in that they help everyone get along better.

Learning Activities

Some of the ideas that were developed in answer to this same question for the room and playground can be reviewed and enlarged upon.

This will be a good opportunity to invite resource people to the classroom.

The principal may be asked to explain the "whys and wherefores" of the various school rules. She might also help develop a cooperative attitude toward these.

She can tell of her job, and its complexities. The need for manners in the school office should be emphasized, as her job is often complicated by children who forget to use good manners.

The school custodian will appreciate the opportunity of talking to the group. He can help them in many ways by stressing the need for conservation of paper and soap in lavatories, explaining the need for respecting property, etc. He may also wish to express his appreciation to those who help him keep the school clean.

Since the patrol boys and safeties make such a valuable contribution to the school, they should be given a chance to speak to the group.

Children are naturally grateful for things done for them. They may want to discuss ways of expressing their gratitude to the people who have come to the room and helped them learn. This can lead to a consideration of *ways* of saying "thank you."

The language period can be used to study the mechanics of letter writing. Emphasis should be placed upon individuality.

Expressing Gratitude

When someone has done something nice for you, what can you do to show you appreciate it? (Children need to be introduced to other ways besides verbal thanks.)

1. Write "thank-you" notes.
2. Make things to show our appreciation.
3. Do something.

Are there other times and places at school when we need to use good manners and courtesy?
1. The cafeteria:

Wait in line patiently.
Use good table manners.

(Table manners are fully discussed under "Manners at Home.")

2. Auditorium.
Find seat and sit down quietly.
Give attention to the program.
Applaud politely.

3. Corridors.
Walk on the right side.
Say "excuse me" when necessary.
Keep voices low.
Look where you are going, or go where you are looking.

4. The school bus.

(The school bus deserves special consideration, since difficulties often arise in such situations where children are without close supervision. Children need to know that certain behavior is very dangerous on the bus. Riding the bus is a privilege which, if not respected, may be lost.)

Why do we *especially need* to use courtesy and manners on the school bus?

1. Safety factors.
2. Buses are usually crowded. Consideration for others helps make it a pleasant trip.

Learning Activities

Children should see this as a pleasurable activity rather than a disagreeable task.

Committees can be organized so that each child is given the chance to say "thank you" in his own way. Some groups may write "thank-you" notes, while others express their gratitude by making things such as clay paperweights, calendars or pictures.

The filmstrip *Good Manners at School* (Eyegate House) discusses many situations at school calling for the use of good manners.

This will provide an opportunity for small-group work. Each group may choose a specific situation such as the auditorium, etc. They can find out what manners and courtesies are in order at these places. A report can be prepared and a presentation given to the class such as: a puppet play, illustrated talk, etc.

See instructional material section for appropriate verse.

A good lead-in discussion might be centered around what the bus driver does for us.

An excursion will provide the best learning opportunity for this concept.

Expressing Gratitude

What are some of the ways to use good manners on the bus?

1. Let people off the bus before getting on.
2. Sit where the bus driver asks you to sit.
3. Keep arms and hands inside the bus.
4. Keep feet out of the aisle.
5. If you accidentally bump someone, excuse yourself.
6. Take up only your share of the seat.

Learning Activities

Children may enjoy acting out a bus ride in the classroom. The audience can be given the chance to guess what is being done correctly and incorrectly.

A committee can do some research to find out if these rules are applicable to a public bus, and if there are other rules for city buses.

A review of the preceding material may be covered at this point. Some of the evaluation techniques might be given.

Good manners and courtesy are for the home, too. Children aware of this make a valuable and appreciated contribution to the family unit. In using social amenities at home, children find a way of showing appreciation and expressing their gratitude for a good home, for father and mother, and for the other members of the family.

Concepts to Discuss

Why do we need good manners and courtesy at home?

1. They are ways of showing appreciation.
2. Helps the family get along better.
3. Helps us to make a contribution to the family.

What are some of the good manners a person can use at home?

1. Being cheerful, and ready to help.
2. Showing the family that they can depend upon you.
3. Try not to ask for special favors that the other members of the family do not get.
4. Try to keep your belongings in a definite place and put things away.

What is a courteous thing to do when you bring home a new friend? How do you introduce people?

1. Say the name clearly.
2. Usually say, "Father, may I present (or may I introduce)?"
3. If you are being introduced to a lady or an older person, it is polite to stand.

Learning Activities

Role playing will help to dramatize these ideas, and to gain insight into parent's ways of looking at things.

The concept of introducing a younger person to an older person, or woman, may come slowly. The children can remember it more easily if they will say the woman's or older person's name first. For example, "*Mother,* may I present George?"

Children will enjoy practicing introductions in the classroom. They should also be encouraged to practice at home.

The filmstrip *When We Have Guests* (Evegate House) gives pointers on how children can help make visitors feel at home.

There are a great many specifics for the pupils to learn here. Providing many situations for them to *use* these concepts will help reinforce learning.

One such situation can be dramatizing a dinner party.

Concepts to Discuss

Can you think of a very important time to use good manners at home?

What are some good table manners?

1. Come to dinner with clean hands.
2. Say "please" and "thank you" often.
3. Use knife and fork to cut large pieces of meat.
4. Break bread and then spread butter. Chew with mouth closed.
5. When finished put knife and fork across plate.
6. Use napkin to wipe mouth.
7. Ask to be excused if you must leave the table before the others.
8. Boys may help seat women by pushing in their chairs.

How can a person use good manners with the family telephone? (Children need to be shown the correct way to use a telephone.)

1. By answering courteously.
2. Find out who is calling.
3. If the person being called is not able to come to the phone, take a message from the caller.
4. If you are on a party line, never listen or interrupt someone else's conversation.
5. Make sure that the telephone is free before starting to dial.
6. Do not prolong telephone conversations.

Learning Activities

Show filmstrip *Good Table Manners* (Eyegate House).

The World Book Encyclopedia, Volume V, has clever illustrations of these ideas. Children can get suggestions from this page and then create their own visual aids on good table manners.

The school cafeteria provides another good learning situation for good table manners.

Many telephone companies make available a complete kit on the use of the telephone. This kit is used in conjunction with the 16-mm sound film, *Adventures in Telezonia.*

A committee can find out how to take a telephone message and report to the class. The language arts period could be used to practice writing them.

The class may be interested in producing their own telephone directory. This is a valuable experience because it helps teach alphabetical order. Also familiarizes the children with the real telephone book.

The last part of this suggested sequence concerns itself with applying courtesy and manners while on the street, at the movies, or on public or private property. This is very important learning, since children (and the school) are not infrequently judged by their behavior in public.

Concepts to Discuss

Suppose that you and a friend were downtown on your way to the movies. What are some of the considerate things you would do?

1. Walk on the right side of the street.
2. Obey traffic lights and use the crosswalk.
3. Throw paper in trash cans instead of just dropping it on the sidewalk.

Learning Activities

The filmstrip *Manners on the Street* (Eyegate House) will be helpful in presenting this concept.

Children may enjoy representing these ideas humorously in a style similar to Munro Leaf. Simple drawings could be made for use on the opaque projector.

Concepts to Discuss

Learning Activities

When you go to the movies what could you do to be courteous?

A committee may like to visit the local theater manager and discuss children's movie behavior with him. A tape recording could later be made and sent to the student council.

1. Wait your turn at the box office.
2. Find seat quickly and as quietly as possible.
3. Rise to allow others to pass.
4. Avoid running in the aisles.
5. Keep feet off the chair in front.
6. Try not to make noise with paper wrappers.
7. Applaud politely but never boo or whistle.

The filmstrip *Good Manners at the Movies* (Eyegate House) will need some adaptation to this level but will be good to summarize.

How can we show respect for public and private property?

Teacher share the "Golden Rule," or similar object story.

1. By treating it as if it were ours.
2. Public property is just like school equipment. We all have a share in maintaining it.
3. You may be trespassing if you are on someone's private property without the owner's permission. (Teacher may explain that the property owner is entitled to certain legal protection from trespassers.)

Role playing in a given meaningful situation such as this: Several children are picking flowers as they wait for the bus. What would you do if you were the person who planted these flowers and how would you feel about this?

If you find something which you think someone has lost, what is the right thing to do?

A spontaneous puppet play can be used in connection with lost-and-found concepts. This can demonstrate how the loser feels and how the finder reacts.

1. Do everything you can to find the owner.
2. The more valuable a thing is, the more reason a person has to try to find the owner.

   1. Do you think that a "courtesy week" would be effective in a school? What would you suggest as activities?

   2. What understandings should children have concerning telephone courtesy?

   3. Who had the greatest influence on your own habits of courtesy? Your mother? Father? Scout leader? Teacher?

   4. In the primary grades it is sometimes effective to have a "boy of the day" and "girl of the day." Sometimes these children wear a special badge or crown. This is an honor which is given as a reward for desirable behavior. Would such a device work with intermediate grade children?

WHAT SHOULD BE TAUGHT ABOUT LISTENING?

The prophet Jeremiah (5:21) laments that his people "have ears but hear not." In a less strenuous vein a teacher once complained to me, "The children all have that tuned-out look." A marriage counselor reports that the most frequent complaint by either spouse is, "You're not listening to a thing I say!" Nonlistening may be a natural defense against the bombardment of partially useless information and sound that assaults the ear in our mechanized society. Or nonlistening may be the result of limited auditory perception and understanding on the part of an audience. For some people, listening to music may be only a pleasant physical experience comparable at best to basking idly in the sunshine, while for others the music may have a deep intellectual and spiritual significance, involving perception of inner harmonies and complex rhythmical patterns.

No one questions the importance of listening as a means of learning for boys and girls. Paul Rankin's pioneering study showed that high school students in Detroit spent 30 per cent of the time they devote to language each day in speaking, 16 per cent in reading, 9 per cent in writing and 45 per cent in listening.[10] Dr. Miriam Wilt more recently found that elementary school children spent about 2½ hours of the five-hour school day in listening.[11] This was nearly twice as much time as their teachers estimate the children spent in listening. Some feel that in the usual classroom the chances are about 60 to 1 against any given pupil speaking, compared to the possibility of others speaking and a pupil listening.

Undoubtedly, there is as wide an individual difference in the area of listening as in other skills. We speak of some people as

[10] Paul T. Rankin: "The Importance of Listening Ability," *English Journal* 17, October 1928, pp. 623–630.
[14] Miriam E. Wilt: "A Study of Teacher Awareness of Listening as a Factor in Elementary Education," *Jour. Educ.* **43**, April 1950, pp. 626–636.

being auditory-minded in contrast to others who are visual-minded. Speech and music teachers have long been aware of the differences among children in hearing specific sounds.

It has been suggested that some of these differences are culturally directed. Some sociologists explained the fact that boys in the elementary school are apt to have more reading problems than girls by the observation that in many families the mother talks more frequently with the little girl than with the little boy. The result of such "preferential" talking according to the theory is that girls are more advanced in language than boys of the same age, especially in the primary grades. In Japan, just the opposite has been noticed. Little girls were long considered academically "inferior" until it was realized that the boy child was getting much more attention at home and at school. In some classrooms over 80 per cent of the questions were being directed to the boys until the inequity was brought to the attention of the teachers.

Another cultural influence upon listening is provided by radio and television. Kindergarten teachers are reporting that children come to school with a much wider knowledge than the curriculum assumes. In India, where there is a high degree of illiteracy, one might assume that the population would be relatively uninformed about world events. This, however, is not the case. The availability of free radios in many community teahouses has resulted in a surprisingly well-informed adult population.

Don Brown suggests that the terms *learning* and *listening* are both limited in meaning, and that the gerund *auding*, based on the neologic verb "to aud" more accurately describes the skill that concerns teachers. "Auding is to the ears what reading is to the eyes." If reading is the gross process of looking at, recognizing, and interpreting written symbols, auding may be defined as the gross process of listening to, recognizing, and interpreting spoken symbols.[12]

David Russell uses the following formula to further contrast reading and auding.[13]

Seeing is to Hearing
as
Observing is to Listening
as
Reading is to Auding

"To aud," then, would mean to listen with comprehension and appreciation.

Children *hear* the whistle of a train, the chirp of a bird, or the noise of traffic. They *listen* either passively or actively to a popular song or news broadcast. But when they listen attentively to a teacher to follow directions, or to get facts from a classmate's report, or to understand two sides of a debate, they may be said to be *auding,* for they are listening to verbal symbols with comprehension and interpretation. Throughout this discussion, however, the term *listening* will be used in referring to the response that Brown describes as "auding."

Different levels of listening are really different degrees of involvement. Some activities to be as satisfying call for much less involvement than others that demand a high degree of dedication. The following situations are examples of listening levels in terms of different purposes.

1. Hearing sounds of words but not reacting to the ideas expressed: a mother knows that Joey is speaking.
2. Intermittent listening—turning the speaker on and off: hearing one idea in a sermon but none of the rest of it.
3. Half listening—following the discussion only well enough to find an opportunity to express your own idea: listening to a conversation to find a place to tell how you handled a child.
4. Listening passively with little observable response: the child knows the

[12] Don Brown, "Auding as the Primary Language Ability" (Unpublished dissertation, Stanford University, 1954).

[13] D. H. Russell, and E. F. Russell, "Listening Aids Through the Grades" (New York: Bureau of Publications, Teachers College, Columbia University, 1959).

teacher is telling them once again how to walk in the hall.
5. Narrow listening in which the main significance or emphasis is lost as the listener selects details which are familiar or agreeable to him: a good Republican listening to candidate from another party.
6. Listening and forming associations with related items from one's own experiences: a first-grade child hears the beginning sound of Sally, says and said, and relating it to the letter *s*.
7. Listening to a report to get main ideas and supporting details or follow directions: listening to the rules and descriptions of a new spelling game.
8. Listening critically: a listener notices the emotional appeal of words in a radio advertisement.
9. Appreciative and creative listening with genuine mental and emotional response: a child listens to the teacher read *Miracles on Maple Hill* and shares the excitement of sugar making.

These levels overlap, but they do describe listening with respect to situations that teachers know. In the classroom it is possible to guide a child's listening so that his auding may be selective, purposeful, accurate, critical and creative, just as we guide growth in the skills of reading.

Listening in some respects is more difficult than reading. In the process of reading, a strange word may be the signal to stop, look at other words in the sentence or pictures on the page, or refer to the glossary. In listening this is not possible. One must make a hasty guess as the speaker continues, rethink what the speaker has said while keeping up with the current ideas being spoken. Most college students know the experience expressed by a freshman when he commented, "I was with him until he mentioned the macrocephalic measurement, then he lost me." Children too have their "frustration level" in listening. The "tuned-out look" familiar to teachers is a signal with respect to either the interest or difficulty of spoken content.

The fact that we listen from six to ten times faster than a person can talk means that dedicated concentration must be practiced in some listening situations to avoid distractions. The printed page demands attention and can be read at a rate of speed equal to that of our mental reactions. In listening this happens only if the listener disciplines himself to attend to what the speaker is saying. Interruptions to an oral explanation by a classroom visitor, outside noises, or any disruptive incident mean the explanation must be repeated. Once listening is accepted as important the learner must accept the responsibility to put forth an active listening effort to learn. This activity should equal the effort to gain information from reading.

One element that makes listening more difficult than reading is that a person usually listens for the main idea rather than specific parts. In reading, one has a record of the specifics and usually remembers where they may be located. In listening, the speaker has designed the material to highlight a major idea which he wants the audience to remember. To do this he uses facts, stories, and emotional appeals. These are recalled only if the listener relates them to the total effect of the talk. Church sermons and college lectures are good examples; a person may tell a friend that he heard a good sermon or lecture, but when asked what was said may be able to recall only that it was "about brotherhood."

Related to this is the problem of listening to a discussion or conversation. Such speech is frequently disorganized as the speakers explore various ideas or aspects of a topic. Strange to say, people seem to remember as much or more from such situations as from a well-organized lecture. Apparently the careful organization and fixed pattern lulls some listeners into a comfortable enjoyment which is less involving than the disorganized rambling that permits or requires involvement with random changes of topic or subject matter.

Many bad habits develop in the listening area. Both children and adults have a way of avoiding difficult or unpleasant listening. Every parent knows the "Surely, he is not talking about me!" attitude of a child who is being corrected. Emotions interfere with listening to ideas. "Who is he to be saying that?" "They will never convince me that those ugly things are art," and "How would she know, she's never been a mother!" are emotional statements that reveal limited reception.

It is interesting to note the wide variation of response to a distraction in a classroom. A lawn mower operating outside the window or music being played in the next room will command the complete attention of some and be ignored by others. Some individuals have a habit of seeking distraction even though they may be interested in the speaker or topic.

The expression of ego is as obvious in listening as it is in the constant use of "I" in speech. This is especially obvious in little children. A teacher or speaker will be telling about a trip to Europe or showing a cowboy lariat. A hand will pop up and a child will volunteer, "Tomorrow is my birthday," or "We have some baby chickens at our house." For some this is an innocent way to "say something, too." Usually it is an indication of lack of interest in others. Adults will be listening or participating in a conversation about a topic, then suddenly say, "I think I'll have my hair done tomorrow," or "When do we eat?" Or there may be a subtle attempt to impress, as in "When I was in Mexico," or "The President said to my cousin."

Teachers are frequently poor listeners. For some, teaching limits their interests to such an extent that they dismiss many subjects prematurely as "uninteresting." At one University Club the matron said she felt sorry for many of the people who lived there. "They are such specialists they cannot listen to each other." Some teachers develop the habit of not listening for ideas but are always judging the manner of expression or organization of speech. They are actually evaluating or grading the manners of those they hear.

Good listening habits involve not only thinking with the speaker but anticipating the direction of his thoughts, objectively evaluating the verbal evidence offered in terms of the speaker's purpose (rather than arguing with it item by item as it is presented) and reviewing mentally some of the facts presented. Taking notes of ideas or phrases helps many people. There are others who find note taking a distraction. Some report that they find the ideas in their notes rather than in their heads. Brief summaries are probably better than detailed stenographic reports.

There is no more attentive listener than the child who asks a question that truly concerns him. These are probably the most "teachable moments" in any classroom. Choosing the question to ask a visitor or the principal or when planning material before a unit sets the stage for careful listening. Before oral reading, attention is assured if children are listening in order to answer a question. A good story writer builds this interest or suspense into his plots. The reason the reader gets involved in a story is usually because he wants to know how a problem will be solved.

In the classroom, the language arts teacher wants to be sure that the listening experience will be worth the children's time and effort. The sharing period can be improved by having each child think first of his audience and how he wants them to respond. At one time this period was considered valuable simply as a spontaneous period of free expression. At the beginning that may be its purpose. But such items as, "I have a new petticoat," or "our cat had kittens" belong in the free conversational exchange of children rather than the crowded school curriculum. The following suggestions provide the same practice in language but add a concern for the listeners.

1. Share the signs of the change of a season noted while going to and from school.
2. Share things that happened at home or play that were pleasant or humorous.
3. Share the most important thing that happened on a trip.
4. Share one toy by telling about it or demonstrating its use.
5. Share something good or kind that a person has done.
6. Share the local or national news. Some classrooms have a television committee, a radio committee and a picture committee. These children report events they have learned from these sources. In the intermediate grades some teachers provide the clippings from which children select their reports. Others give a little quiz at the end of the week on the news reported. Sometimes better preparation will result if the listeners may ask one question about a report. Two standards should apply —the news must be told rather than being read orally, and it must not concern crime.
7. Share something an individual has made.
8. Share a riddle or joke (after first checking with the teacher).
9. Share a fact or interesting bit of knowledge about a bird, a rock, a stamp, a coin, insect, star, airplane, sea shell, object from a foreign land, a book, or "believe it or not" item.
10. Share a new word and its meaning or history. This might be a word in a foreign language if there are children from foreign-speaking homes.

Material shared is better if children have to plan ahead a bit. Children might sign on the chalkboard today for sharing tomorrow, or each row may have a day which is their sharing day. The teacher is responsible for the quality of material shared in literature. If children are to listen to material read, it should be material that offers true enrichment. Poetry appropriate to the child's interests that is read well will reveal the beauty of words. Stories that add stature to the child's value concepts should be told and read.

The responsibility of the listener should be discussed. There is the point of courtesy to a speaker that all children understand. It is only the Golden Rule applied to speech—"you listen to me and I will listen to you." Listening for meaning is just as important as reading for meaning. A listener may *disagree* but should not *misinterpret*. Causes of misinterpretation might be discussed with benefit to both speaker and listener.

The attitude of the teacher toward listening will influence children. Teaching is as much listening as telling. We listen to discover interest and needs. Those trained

Burbank Public Schools, Calif.

Material prepared with the listener in mind adds to the educational result in all curriculum areas.

in nondirective guidance know how important it is for the therapist to listen. The psychologist listens a great deal as the patient talks. A good salesman listens to discover what customers want. The wise teacher listens to encourage the expression of children. At times a teacher listens because a child, or parent, needs an audience for a personal concern. The following suggestions will help in such situations.[14]

1. Take time to listen. When someone is troubled or needs to talk, give him the time if at all possible. It will help clarify communication between you.
2. Be attentive. Let tirades flow uninterrupted. Try to indicate that you want to understand.
3. Employ three kinds of verbal reactions only—"H-m-mm," "Oh," or "I see." Remain silent, nodding to show understanding. (College professors frequently work with a pipe at this time, cleaning it, etc.) If the talker is unreasonable, restate what he said, putting it in the form of a question.
4. Never probe for additional facts. There is a difference between willingness to listen and curiosity. Your purpose in therapeutic listening is seldom to obtain information.
5. Avoid evaluating what has been said. Avoid moral judgments and the temptation to advise. The talker is getting his problem clear through talking and then must define alternative solutions.
6. Never lose faith in the ability of the talker to solve his own problems. The talker is really talking things over with himself as he talks with you.

Start instruction in listening by establishing standards. The discussion might be centered about situations where listening is important: You are a waiter taking an order; you are to go to the principal's office with a message and return with his; you are to interview a famous person; you are to report on a news broadcast. These imaginative exercises could lead to an inventory of listening habits. A check list like the following may be used: Do I get ready to listen? Do I give the speaker my attention?

[14] R. G. Nichols and Leonard A. Stevens, *Are You Listening?* (New York: McGraw-Hill, 1957).

Do I think with the speaker? Can I select the main idea? Can I recall things in order? Can I follow directions? Can I retell what I hear?

Children learn from discussions of this nature that a good listener is polite, gets the facts, listens thoughtfully, listens for a reason, and makes intelligent use of what he hears.

These classroom activities emphasize the skills of listening:

1. Develop a routine of giving directions only once in a lesson. Select one subject, introduce the challenge of a "One-Time Club" or "First-Time Club" with respect to assignments or directions. If a child misses the first time, he is not a club member but may get the information from a member. For some groups the teacher might say, "I will give the assignment only once, then I will ask some of those in the 'First-Time Club' to repeat what I have said."

2. Use oral tests frequently that require more than one-word answers. Dramatize the test if the group responds to that type of motivation by imitating the pattern of a television quiz program.

3. Ask children to review the work of the previous day in a subject for a child who was absent.

4. Practice oral summarization of the information presented in a film.

5. Read a descriptive paragraph, have children paint or draw the picture presented, then read the story again as a check.

6. Play a listening game by giving increasingly difficult instructions to one child and then another. To the first child you might say, "Peter, take the apple from the desk and place it on the chair." To the next child, "Fred, take the apple from the chair, show it to Mary and return it to the desk." The game increases in difficulty until someone fails to follow directions correctly.

7. Ask the pupils, in pairs, to interview each other on hobbies or special interests. After the interviews talk about the

possibilities of learning by this method. Discuss the advantages and disadvantages of interviewing as compared to reading.

8. A game called "Efficient Secretary" is designed to challenge children to write entire sentences from dictation. The sentences are read only once. At first the sentences are short but they are increased in length as the child's ability increases. This exercise has a natural correlation with spelling.

9. Second-chance listening is valuable in the social studies. The teacher reads an informative article which is followed by questions. After this the article is read again and children check their answers or answer the questions a second time.

10. The game "Lost Child" is good for both oral description and listening. One player is the policeman. Another player describes someone in the room who is his "lost child." If a class member can guess who it is before the policeman does, the two exchange places.

David H. Russell and his wife have collected a group of listening activities called *Listening Aids Through the Grades,* published by the Bureau of Publications, Teachers College, Columbia University, New York, N.Y.

1. A visual-minded individual is one who remembers things that he sees. An auditory-minded person would be one who remembers what he hears. Which of your memories are most vivid—things you hear or see?

2. Do you know of any way of measuring individual differences in this respect?

WHAT IS THE RELATIONSHIP BETWEEN LISTENING AND READING?

Both reading and listening require the learner to have a readiness for accomplishment. This includes his mental maturity, vocabulary, ability to follow sequence of ideas, and his interest in language.

In general, the purposes of reading and auding are both functional and appreciative. In functional reading and auding, children are concerned with finding facts, getting a general idea, following directions, or putting the material to work in some way. In appreciative reading and auding, children are ready to enjoy a selection for its own sake—a story for its humor, or a poem for its expression. Or they may combine function and appreciation in reading or listening with a view to creating a dramatization.

In both reading and auding, the word is not usually the unit of comprehension but it affects comprehension of the phrase, the sentence, and the paragraph. Children must hear certain key words clearly (e.g., "world" vs. "whirled") if they are to understand an oral passage, and they must see them clearly ("bond" vs. "board") if they are to read them exactly. But along with exact perception in both activities must go understanding of word meaning. The grasp and interpretation of both oral and written paragraphs depend upon understanding the meaning of individual words in their context and in varied relationships.

In both reading and auding, the unit of comprehension is either the phrase, the sentence, or the paragraph—rather than the single word. Comprehension is aided if the speaker or writer avoids common errors of pronunciation, spelling, and usage. Both reading and auding make use of "signals" in the form of written or oral punctuation.

In addition to an exact, literal understanding of a sentence or passage, both reading and auding may involve critical or creative interpretation of the material. In both situations the receiver may critically question the reliability of the source, the relevancy of the argument, or the emotive power of the language employed. In both cases the receiver may utilize his previous experiences to combine the materials into some fresh, original, and personal interpretation.

Reading and auding may take place

in either individual or social situatiòns. Critical, analytical activities often flourish best in the individual situation; creative and appreciative reactions under the stimulus of the group situation. Analysis of the propaganda devices in a political speech is easier reading the printed version of the speech in a quiet room than listening to the speaker deliver it in a crowded hall. Conversely, appreciation of the choral reading of a poem may be heightened by an enthusiastic group response.

Some modern readers provide listening exercises in the teacher's manual: [15]

"Sue's big brother, Jerry, has made a model airplane. He is going to fly it in the contest Saturday. The contest is going to be at White Park. Prizes will be given there for the best made airplane, the airplane that flies the longest, and the airplane that makes the best take-off and landing. One of the prizes is a motor for a model airplane. Jerry hopes he can win that.

"Here are the questions: What I read said, 'Sue's brother, Jerry, has made a model airplane. He is going to fly it in the contest Saturday.' Who is meant by the word *he* in those lines, John? . . . Yes, the word *he* means Jerry. What is meant by the word *it* in those lines, Carl? . . . Yes, the model airplane.

"Then what I read said, 'The contest is going to be at White Park. Prizes will be given there for the best made airplane, the airplane that flies the longest, and the airplane that makes the best take-off and landing.' What did I mean by the word *there* in those lines, Jim? . . . Yes, I meant White Park.

"The last two sentences said, 'One of the prizes is a motor for a model airplane. Jerry hopes he can win that.' What does the word *that* mean in those lines, Ann? . . . Yes, it means the motor for a model airplane."

Deciding which of Several Meanings a Word Has in Statements

"When Harry said, 'It's a long way to our house from here,' the word *way* meant distance. When Paul asked, 'Which way do we go from here?' the word *way* meant direction. When I say, 'I like the way in which

you are fixing your hair,' the word *way* means manner.

"Listen while I read three sentences to you. Decide what the word *way* means in each sentence.

"Here is the first sentence. 'John swims in the same way that Bob swims.' What did I mean by the word *way* in that sentence, Ben? . . . Yes, I meant manner.

"Here is the second sentence. 'Which way is the zoo from here?' What did the word *way* mean in that sentence, Ruth? . . . That's right. It meant direction.

"Here is the third sentence. 'It's not a very long way from our house to Betty's house.' What did the word *way* mean in that sentence, Carl? . . . Yes, it meant distance.

"You can see that one word can have many different meanings. To decide what a word means each time it is used, you have to think of the meaning of the words that are used with it."

The SRA Reading Laboratory includes a number of listening-skill exercises.[16]

Listening is something like reading. It brings you things that are useful or entertaining. The more useful or entertaining you think something is, the harder you listen to it. Have you ever stayed "glued to your radio" as a mystery thriller came to life before you? Of course you have. Even with television you would hardly turn off the sound while watching a play. Listening brings you as much as seeing.

Have you ever listened to someone give directions, an explanation, or a talk and found yourself asking, "What was he talking about?" Of course you have, and so have most of us at one time or another. You do not feel good when this happens. Poor listening causes you to make mistakes in doing things, thereby creating trouble for yourself and for those around you.

Can we overcome poor listening? Fortunately, yes. By using methods worked out by scientists who have studied the listening process, you can improve your listening in much the same way you can improve your reading. And it is worth the effort, too. The average person spends about 45 per cent of his waking time in listening.

Scientists have found, too, that when

[15] Paul McKee, *Reading for Meaning; Come Along*, Teacher's Manual (Boston: Houghton, 1957).

[16] Science Research Associates, *SRA Reading Laboratory—Instructor's Handbook* (Chicago: Science Research Associates, Inc., 1959), pp. 36–37.

When we listen
1 We sit quietly.
2 We look at the
Reader.
3 We try to remember
the story.
4 We ask politely
about anything we
want to know

The chart of listening standards acts as a reminder until habits are established. The children participate in developing the chart and understand its meaning.

you are listening carefully to directions, explanations, or classroom talks by teachers, you are doing the same things as when you listen to a mystery thriller. And there is a tested listening formula somewhat like the SQ3R reading and study formula. We call it TQLR: Tune-in, Question, Listen, Review.

Now let's think about the first part, the "T" for Tune-in. In listening to a radio program, you not only tune in a station, but you tune in your own mind to what you are hearing. You begin to think of the time, the place, and the people in the radio or television play. This is like your Survey when you begin to read. Next, as in your reading, Questions will come popping into your mind. "What is it going to be about? What usually happens in a program like this? What will be the outcome? What can I learn from it? What will it mean to me?" You are becoming *interested*.

All of this probably happens in a matter of seconds and makes you ready for just what you would expect . . . the L, or listening, step. Now you are listening for main points; you are getting certain details. You will try to "think ahead" of what you hear and to think about what you have already heard. You will relate one thing to another. You will see things beginning to add up. The plot or main idea will begin to take shape. And the more carefully you listen, the more your interest will build up and, as a result, the keener your listening will become.

Then, suddenly, the play is over and you are saying to your friend beside you, "That surely was a good play, but I wonder how the man found out about the black mark on the horse?" Now you are doing the last part of the TQLR, the "R" step, Review. You are going back over parts about which you were not quite certain, and, in doing this, you have to think back over, or Review, the whole play. This helps you remember all the main points better.

Whether you know it or not, this is the same process your mind has probably been going through every time you have listened to a radio play. Can you see how this same process can be used to get the most out of anything you listen to?

Comprehension Check for Listening Skill Builder No. 1

Directions: Draw a circle around the letter standing before the phrase that *best* completes each statement.

1. If you were listening to a teacher give a short talk on the history of your state, you would
(*a*) use SQ3R (*b*) use a radio (*c*) use TQLR (*d*) talk to your neighbor

2. Listening can be improved by
(*a*) listening to mystery thrillers (*b*) using correct methods (*c*) reading more (*d*) scientists

3. Learning to listen better is important because
(*a*) it protects your hearing (*b*) people listen 100 per cent of the time (*c*) then you can talk more (*d*) we spend a lot of our waking hours listening

4. Listening to classroom talks and radio mystery thrillers are alike in that (*a*) they are both on the radio (*b*) you hear them every day (*c*) they are always entertaining (*d*) you use the same skills in listening to them

5. The "T" part of TQLR helps you
(*a*) to hear more clearly (*b*) to know everything the speaker will say (*c*) to become interested in what the speaker will say (*d*) to survey your reading

6. During the "L" or listening stage you are
(*a*) thinking ahead of what the speaker says (*b*) think about what he has said before (*c*) asking questions out loud (*d*) both (*a*) and (*b*)

Suggestions for Projects

1. Evaluate parliamentary procedure as a speech activity and illustrate its use.

2. Show how certain radio and television program ideas or techniques might be adapted to classroom use.

3. Evaluate educational television and illustrate how a class might prepare a program for broadcast.

4. Plan a way to use puppets to gain better speech habits.

5. Discuss and illustrate how the sharing time may be made an effective language learning experience.

6. Evaluate some of the listening tests. Examine the Brown-Carlsen Listen-

ing Test, World Book Company (9–12) California Auding Test, Council on Auding Research, 146 Columbia Avenue, Redwood City, California (9–12), Listening Test, Educational Testing Service, Princeton, New Jersey, four levels.

7. Make a courtesy handbook to use in an intermediate classroom.

8. Make a collection of speech drills and verse to use with children who have articulation problems.

9. Some school systems have "listening posts" in some rooms. These consist

of sets of earphones which the child uses while a recording is played. Investigate the literature relating to these or evaluate one in use.

10. The platoon school program provided for a daily speech period in the auditorium. Courses of study for auditorium published in Denver, Dallas and Detroit, contain many speech suggestions. One pattern suggested is that the program be assigned long in advance so that children could plan and prepare for the experience. What do you think of this plan?

Date _____
Chairman _____
News _____
Music _____
Humor _____
Science _____
Art _____
Poetry _____
Story _____

Evaluate such a device as it might be used to give direction to the sharing period or an occasional talent period.

BIBLIOGRAPHY

BOOKS

Allstrom, Elizabeth. *Let's Play a Story*. New York: Friendship, 1957.

Anderson, Virgil A. *Improving the Child's Speech*. New York: Oxford U.P., 1953.

Axline, Virginia Mae. *Play Therapy*. Boston: Houghton, 1947.

Batcheller, Marjorie Hope. *Hand and Rod Puppets*. Columbus, Ohio: Ohio State U. P., 1947.

Batcheller, Marjorie Hope. *The Puppet Theatre Handbook*. New York: Harper, 1947.

Board of Education of the City of New York: *Toward Better Speech*. Curriculum Bulletin No. 5, 1955.

Bryngelson, Bryng, and Elaine Mikalson. *Speech Correction through Listening*. Chicago: Scott, 1959.

Carlson, B. W. *The Right Play for You*. New York: Abingdon, 1960.

Crow, L. D., and Alice Crow. *Teaching in the Elementary School*. New York: Longmans, 1961.

Durland, Frances Caldwell. *Creative Dramatics for Children*. Yellow Springs, Ohio: Antioch, 1952.

*Eisenson, Jon, and Mardel Ogilvie. *Speech Correction in the School*. 2nd ed. New York: Macmillan, 1963.

Heltman, H. J. *Trippingly on the Tongue*. New York & Ill.: Harper, 1955.

Kase, Robert. *Stories for Creative Acting*. New York: French, 1961.

Miel, Alice (ed.). *Helping Children in Oral Communication*. New York: Bureau of Publications, Teacher's College, Columbia University, 1959.

Nichols, Ralph G., and Leonard A. Stevens. *Are You Listening?* New York: McGraw-Hill, 1957.

Ogilvie, Mardel. *Speech in the Elementary School*. New York: McGraw-Hill, 1954.

Penn, Erta V. *A Handbook for the Remedial Speech and Phonics Program*. Avenal, Calif., Reef-Sunset Schools, 1957.

Pronovost, Wilbert, and Louise Kingman. *The Teaching of Speaking and Listening in the Elementary School*. New York: Longmans, 1959.

Rasmussen, Carrie. *Speech Methods in the Elementary School*. New York: Ronald, 1949.

Robinson, Helen M. *Oral Aspects of Reading*. Chicago: U. of Chicago, Supplementary Educational Monographs, 1955.

Russell, David H., and Elizabeth F. Russell.

Listening Aids through the Grades. New York: Bureau of Publications, Teacher's College, Columbia University, 1959.

Scott, Louise B., and J. J. Thompson. *Speech Ways.* St. Louis, Mo.: Webster, 1955.

Van Riper, Charles, and Katherine G. Butler. *Speech in the Elementary Classroom.* New York: Harper, 1955.

Ward, Winifred. *Playmaking with Children.* 2nd ed. New York: Appleton, 1947.

Werner, Lorna Shogren. *Speech in the Elementary School.* New York & Ill.: Harper, 1947.

PERIODICALS, PAMPHLETS AND CURRICULUM GUIDES

Ball, Rachel S., and Elsie H. Campbell, "Manners and Courtesy." *Childcraft,* Volume X, Field Enterprises, Inc., Chicago, 1949.

Berry, Althea, "Experience in Listening." *Elementary English,* (March 1951), pp. 130–132.

Brown, Don, "And Having Ears, They Hear Not." *National Education Association Journal,* (November 1950), pp. 586–587.

Brown, James J., "The Construction of a Diagnostic Test of Listening Comprehension." *Journal of Experimental Education,* (December 1949), pp. 139–146.

Bursten, Frieda J., "Creative Dramatics for the Mentally Retarded." Unpublished Masters Project, San Diego State College, San Diego, Calif., 1955.

Hatfield, W. W., "Parallels in Teaching Students to Listen and Read." *English Journal,* (December 1946), pp. 553–558.

Indianapolis, Indiana, Public Schools: *Character Building.* 1952.

La Mesa-Spring Valley School District: *I am a Citizen in an American School.* La Mesa, Calif., 1954.

Montague, A., *Helping Children Develop Moral Values.* Chicago: Science Research Associates, Inc., 1953.

National Dairy Council: *Who, Me?* National Dairy Council, Chicago, 1948.

Philadelphia Public Schools: *Social Behavior.* Philadelphia, Pa., 1948.

San Diego, Calif., City Schools: *A Guide to Moral and Spiritual Values, Part I,* 1950.

Subcommittee of the Social Studies Committee, Southern Section of the California Supervisor's Association. Dr. Hilda Taba, Consultant, *Skills in Human Relationships,* Office of the Superintendent of Schools, San Diego County, Calif., 1954.

Ward, Winifred, and Mayo Bryce, *Drama with and for Children,* Washington, D.C., U.S. Dept. of Health, Education and Welfare, Bulletin No. 30, 1960.

Whelan, Marjorie Loomis, "A Speech Improvement Handbook for Kindergarten, First and Second Grades." Unpublished Masters Project, San Diego State College, San Diego, Calif., 1958.

Wilt, Miriam E., "A Study of Teacher Awareness of Listening as a Factor in Elementary Education." *Journal of Educational Research* (April 1950), pp. 626–636.

Chapter 3

Handwriting

WHY DO WE WRITE THE WAY WE DO?

We do not know when writing first began. At the time the pyramids were built in 3000 B.C., the Egyptians were already using a form of picture writing called hieroglyphics, employing the reed pen and paper made of papyrus. Even then the pictures had become so stylized that it was considered an ancient art; "hieroglyphics" means "sacred writing."

The hieroglyphic writing was more difficult to master than ours. It demanded the recognition and accurate reproduction of hundreds of different signs and required long practice to attain skill. The first great step in the direction of the development of an alphabet was the use of pictures of certain objects to represent the *sound* of a word rather than its *meaning*. Thus, the picture for water, which was a simple design of waves resembling a series of printed letter *n*'s was pronounced "nu," began to be used for that sound in other words ordinarily represented by a picture. At first this was a kind of shorthand using about 600 signs. Then these were reduced to twenty-four symbols representing the common consonants.

Today when one reads the ancient Egyptian writing one must guess as to the vowel sounds that connected the written consonants. However, it may have actually been the lack of a vowel system that made the alphabet adaptable to many languages, since each could follow its own dialect.

The earliest phonetic alphabet is of Semitic origin, dating from approximately 1500 B.C. This North Semitic "syllabary" developed into the consonantal alphabet of the Phoenicians, who in turn passed it on to the Greeks and Romans and eventually to us.

The letter *a* may have started with the Egyptian word for ox, which they pronounced *apis* and wrote by drawing the head. This became modified by the Cretans and Phoenicians to *aleph,* represented by a drawing which is very similar to our letter for capital A, written upside-down. The letter was taken by the Greeks as *alpha* and turned upright.

When the Greeks accepted the alphabet they kept the letters *b, g, d, z, k, l, m, n, p, r, t,* since these expressed common sounds in Greek and Semitic.

The Greeks used some of the letters of the alphabet to express the vowel sounds; thus the letters *a, e, i, o, u* were pronounced in ways unrelated to their original meaning or sound.

Later when the Romans developed the

93

Latin alphabet, they discarded three Greek letters since there were no sounds in their language similar to them. These extra letters were used to represent numbers; C became 100, M, 1,000 and L, 50.

Some letters changed sound values for other reasons. At one time the Romans used C for both g and k. Later a bar was added to the lower end of c to show the sound of g and thus our capital letter G came into existence.

In Cicero's time (106–43 B.C.) when many Greek words came into Roman use, the letters y and z were added to the later alphabet. This explains why they are placed at the end of our alphabet. At times other letters have been added but are no longer in use. A reverse C (Ɔ) once represented the ps combination, an upside-down F (Ⅎ) was used for w to distinguish it from u. In the Middle Ages the letter J was added to express the consonantal i.

In ancient times all writing was done with what we term the capital letters. These letters were designed to be written with a chisel in hard stone. As the writing tools changed, the small or "lower-case" letters developed, the latter term deriving from the invention of printing, when small letters began to be kept in the "lower" case of the type cabinet. Among the ruins of Pompeii examples have been found of a type of cursive writing done on wax with an incisive tool called a stylus, or painted on walls with brushes.

Beginning in the sixth century A.D., the pen made from a bird's feather became the major writing tool for hundreds of years. It was this pen with its preference for curved lines that eliminated the angular forms of early letters. Papyrus, and later parchment or vellum, provided a smooth writing surface which made these curves easier to form. Some details in such letters as d, g, f, b, are due to writing on sheets of wax.

The pattern of our writing is normally from left to right. The Egyptians and Hebrews, however, wrote from right to left. The Greeks wrote "as the ox plows," which means a line from right to left, then one from left to right. We do not know why this was later changed to left-to-right; the change may have been influenced by the inscriptions on columns, which spiralled from bottom to top.

During the ninth century the main form of handwriting used in manuscripts was called the Caroline Hand. This was brought about by a reform decreed by Charlemagne and taught by an English Abbot, Alcuin of York, in a monastic school at Tours, France. Here for the first time we see the prototype of our modern letters: capitals, small letters, word spacing and punctuation.

By the twelfth century, a too-liberal use of the slanted quill brought about a lateral compression of writing. Curves gave way to the angular broken lines of the style of writing which was later termed Gothic. This in turn was condemned by the poet Petrarch (1304–1374) as being barely legible. Petrarch produced a clear, simple script that spread rapidly among the humanistic scholars.

Fortunately, the beginning of printing coincided with the new writing. The presses set up in Rome and Venice used the writing forms of the humanists. The printing of our books today reflects the forms devised at that time.

In 1522, at the request of the educated classes, Lodovico Vicentino produced in Venice the first copybook for teaching handwriting. Other writing masters followed with similar books.

As the art of printing improved, the process of engraving on copper plates with a fine-pointed steel instrument replaced the early wood engravings. The instruments used permitted considerable artistic freedom. Printing handwriting examples from engraved copper plates marked the beginning of a new form of writing.

As engraved copybooks were developed, students set themselves to the difficult tasks of imitating the engraved line with pen and paper. Pens were cut narrow with a deep slit so that shading could be achieved only by pressure of the hand instead of by the automatic action of a broad-pointed quill. Dutch writing masters provided copybooks with ingenious flourishes and masses of extravagant decoration. English writing masters fought each other with competing styles, all composed of drawn, rather than written, forms.

In school, writing was usually the first subject of the day. For each writer the master set a copy at the top of a page in the pupil's copybook. This copy, for a beginner, would be simply straight lines, but a little practice on these sufficed. Then the master changed the copy to "hooks and trammels"—that is, to curved lines which received their names from their resemblance to the fireplace "pothooks" or hooks on which pots and kettles were hung from the crane. For the more advanced pupils the master wrote in a large, round hand, "Contentment is a virtue," or some other gem of wisdom. Every writer was expected to fill out a page daily in emulation of the master's copy. Occasionally, a master had narrow slips of engraved copy that he would distribute among the pupils. The first series of these copyslips put forth in this country was prepared and published in 1796 by the celebrated Boston schoolmaster and textbook writer, Caleb Bingham (1757–1817).

If the end of the term were near, the writing schools made exhibition pieces to pass around among the visitors on the last day. The sheet would contain a sentence or a short essay on such subjects as "Happiness," "How to Get Rich," "Spring," "Resignation," and there would be a decoration border of flourishes and often drawings of birds, flowers, ships or other objects.

The quill pen was still in use and great skill was required to cut the nibs to the fine point needed to imitate engraving. But with the invention of the steel pen the chore of pen-mending ceased. Exactly who was the inventor is uncertain. In 1820, Joseph Gillott conceived the idea that the press used in the buckle and button trade could be adapted to produce metal pens. In a short time these pens became inexpensive and widely accepted.

In the United States as in England the "copperplate" writing was extensively used. Business schools taught the Spencerian Script, which was a beautiful, ornate writing, closely related to that devised by the Dutch teachers. Systems based on "arm movement" became popular in the schools. These consisted of a carefully organized series of exercises designed to train the individual to write rhythmically. The writing arm rested on the forearm muscle, and finger movement was avoided. One of the reasons for the wide acceptance of this method is that much of the fatigue associated with long periods of writing was avoided. The exercises consisted of a series of continuous ovals and "push-pulls," or were designed to give practice in writing individual letters and their parts. Students were encouraged to complete sets of exercises of high enough quality to receive certificates of merit and pins awarded by the publishers.

Some have criticized exercises of this type as being so unrelated to actual writing as to be isolated skills; one may learn how to make ovals but not necessarily how to write. A discouraged teacher is apt to accept such criticism and justify neglect of writing practice. On the other hand, there is a great deal of evidence that writing drills did produce excellent and even beautiful handwriting or calligraphy. Many students were actually self-taught by the manuals because their teachers were not masters of the system. While all students did not become calligraphers, it should be noted that neither did all become excellent readers, mathematicians, musicians or artists.

Nearly all systems used today involve a modification of those in the past. At the end of this chapter you will find listed the materials available for penmanship instruction.

The reform movement in penmanship instruction that was started in England by William Morris (1834–1896) is still growing. This is an effort to return to the forms used at the time of the Renaissance. In the schools of England one finds systems based on this influence. That of Marion Richardson is an extension of the use of "print-script" writing in the primary grades, while that of Alfred Fairbanks seems more closely associated with historic letter patterns. It

Sing a song of sixpence,
Pocket full of rye;
Four & twenty blackbirds
Baked in a pie.
When the pie was opened
The birds began to sing
Wasn't it a dainty dish
To set before a King?

Marion Richardson, Good Writing

is called Italic writing. This is a form of print which was first used by Aldo Manuzio in Italy during the Renaissance; Virgil was the first author printed in this type (1501). The current revival is based upon the desire to find a script that is both beautiful and legible, yet expresses individuality. No claim is made concerning speed. Italic writing uses a flat pen held at a 45-degree angle which gives a thick descending line and thin ascending line. The oval, rather than the circle, is its basic movement. Many of the letters appear connected and may be if the writer wishes.

Manuscript or print-script writing which is now widely used in the primary grades of the United States started in England. In 1919 Miss S. A. Golds of St. George the Martyr School, London, published a copybook called, "A Guide to the Teaching of Manuscript Writing."

In 1922 a course taught by Marjorie Wise of England at Columbia University introduced print script to the American schools. Since that time the use of this simple form of lettering has been accepted in nearly all the schools of the United States.

The term cursive means "running" or "connected," while the terms "print script" and "manuscript" refer to writing in which each letter is separately formed, as in printer's type.

The major differences are contrasted below:

Manuscript	*Cursive*
Letters are made separately.	Letters are joined.
Pencil is lifted at the end of each letter or stroke.	Pencil is lifted at the end of each word.
Letters are made with circles, parts of circles and straight lines.	Letters are made with overstrokes, understrokes, connected strokes and ovals.

Manuscript

Letters are spaced to form words. Space between letters is controlled by the shape of the letter. The *i* and the *j* are dotted and the *t* crossed immediately after the vertical stroke is made.

Letters closely resemble print and are, therefore, legible and easy to read.

Small letters and capitals are different except for *c, o, s, p, v, w, x* and *z*.

Cursive

Spacing between letters is controlled by the slant and manner of making connective strokes. The letters *i* and *j* are dotted and the *t* crossed after the completion of the word.

Letters are unlike those on the printed page.

Small letters and capitals are different.

Virgil Herrick, et al., *"Handwriting in Wisconsin," University of Wisconsin*

Virgil Herrick, et al., *"Handwriting in Wisconsin," University of Wisconsin*

The use of print script in the primary grades has been accepted because of the following reasons: Primary children learn only one alphabet for reading and writing. With its three basic strokes, i.e., circles, arcs, and straight lines, print script is easier for the young child to learn. Print script is more legible than cursive and with time may be written rapidly. Children who master print script do a great deal more writing of a creative nature than children who must master the cursive form. The major disadvantage of using print script would be the fact that a transfer to cursive writing must be taught later.

Recent surveys indicate that some schools do not require children to change from this script to cursive writing in the upper grades unless they desire to do so. The majority make the change in the third grade. In others the change is made in the second grade. Those favoring no change give these reasons: Print script is a legible, easily produced form of writing that with practice can be written as rapidly as cursive writing. Those who change do so primarily because children indicate a desire to write like grown-up people do and because of the greater speed possible with the cursive form.

About ninety minutes a week are spent on direct practice of writing in the primary grades. In the upper grades sixty minutes a week, divided into three twenty-minute periods, is a common practice. Some schools have thirty minutes each day for handwriting. This period is used for the writing of school reports as well as practice on handwriting techniques. Other schools combine handwriting and spelling in an alternating schedule.

Experiments with the typewriter in the elementary school date back to at least 1927. All such studies have indicated that children enjoy the experience and achieve some skill in the use of the machines. Kindergarten teachers report that as a prewriting experience it is an effective way to teach letter names and aspects of visual discrimination. Gifted children in the upper grades profit from summer schools that have courses in typing. The typewriter appears to provide a bridge between their advanced ideas and the lack of physical maturity for a large amount of handwriting.

It would be impractical to assume that typewriting skill would replace the need for learning to write either print script or cursive writing. The ability to write a neat, legible hand with reasonable speed and without strain is an essential learning in the modern curriculum.

Modern trends in handwriting instruction reflect current understanding of factors in child growth and recent study. None can be said to be universally acceptable or based on such absolute information that future change would be impossible. In comparison with the past, these changes may be observed:

1. Cursive writing is losing its place as a recognized part of the early primary program. The simpler forms of manuscript or print-script writing are preferred. Print script is being accepted as desirable writing in all grades.

2. Children no longer trace letter forms except under critical circumstances. Writing in the air is considered inappropriate and wasteful.

3. Children who show a strong preference for writing with the left hand are no longer required to learn to write with the right hand.

4. The use of the rhythmical aids is discouraged. The size and shape of the various letters are so different that an absolute conformity to set rhythm is unnatural.

5. Accessory drills that presumably contribute rhythm and freedom in muscular movement are minimized. The use of ovals and related exercises are used much less than in the past.

6. There is less emphasis on speed in writing.

7. Fountain pens and ballpoint pens are used in classroom practices.

8. Such incentives as penmanship certificates and pens are not widely used, although still available.

1. How can children be led to appreciate the significance of the skill to write?

2. What information do you find in children's encyclopedias that might be used for classroom research on the alphabet?

3. Find an example of Spencerian writing, or, if possible, one who can write this script. Defend the modern point of view that such art is not needed in writing.

4. What is the basis for objections to the use of colored ink or ballpoint pens in adult writing?

5. How would a school use a special penmanship teacher?

WHAT ARE OUR OBJECTIVES IN HANDWRITING INSTRUCTION?

The purpose behind the statement that handwriting should be viewed as a means of expression and not an end in itself is to focus the attention of teachers and learners on the context rather than on penmanship. This is a proper emphasis.

Unfortunately, some have interpreted the statement as a justification for neglecting instruction in the mechanics of writing. The inconsistency of this thinking is revealed when we look at typewriting. Here, too, the skill is a means of expression. But for a period when the skill is being mastered it becomes a legitimate end to study the habit-forming routines that constitute the skill.

The psychology of habit formation in teaching handwriting is similar to that used in a sport like golf or tennis or in a skill like piano playing. The learner must first decide to seek mastery of the skill area. After that each specific movement receives critical attention and drill. In tennis the coach will first illustrate a stroke, then repeat it in slow motion and finally have the class perform each movement that he has demonstrated. He may even take the learner's arm and guide it through the movements if a correction is needed. The stroke will be practiced separately and in connection with other movements previously taught. In the same way the piano teacher will have the child play simple melodies and then do specific scale exercises to gain the finger control desired. This psychology is different from that involved in the usual concern of teachers with meaning and understanding. Watching an athletic coach at work would be of great help to a handwriting teacher. One would observe that the coach is enthusiastic about the game and concerned about the actions of each player. He praises good plays, but also points out errors. Both are analyzed to make the players aware of their actions, using demonstrations by the coach and selected players. Rewards or trophies are given to the winners. Above all, it should be noted that athletic skills are perfected through a great deal of individual practice, as well as by actually playing the game.

Because we are concerned with muscular development and physical maturity in handwriting, there are some factors in the growth patterns of children that should be considered in our teaching. The primary child frequently lacks the muscular coordination needed for writing. The powers that are developed are in the big muscles and nerve centers rather than the small ones of the fingers. We accept the dominant handedness of little children which is usually observable at the age of three but may not be fully developed until the age of eight. Because farsightedness is the nor-

mal vision of young children we avoid long periods requiring close work with small details. Patterns of progress will differ widely during the primary grades, but girls will usually be more mature than boys.

Instructional implications based upon these factors would include the following practices: The little child is encouraged to work with clay, finger paint, or other materials that require finger coordination. Large muscles are used by using chalkboard letters about three inches high. The paper used has one-half inch spaces between lines. The width used corresponds to the sidewise span of the forearm of the child. Soft chalk and thick, soft lead pencils are used. Speed is never emphasized. Careful attention is given to the physical comfort of each child. Copy work, which forces constant refocusing of the eye, is avoided. This especially applies to work on the board which the child copies on paper. No effort is made to keep the entire class together for instruction. Each child sets his own progress pattern. The aptitudes or skills of boys and girls should not be compared. Early writing efforts are usually characterized by great deliberateness.

In the intermediate grades the children gain greater control over both large-muscle activities and eye-hand coordination involving the small muscles. These are the years that influence lifetime habits with regard to musical instrument, skill with tools, and handwriting. The longer attention span results in a willingness to accept drill and repetition if the children understand the final goal. As the boys approach adolescence the rapid growth of the hands may cause a deterioration in their handwriting. At this stage handwriting can be improved by exercises involving ovals, push-pulls, and writing exercises to music. Older children sometimes express their egos through highly individualized writing such as ringing the i's instead of dotting them, making triangles of loops below the lines, or crossing the t's in unconventional ways. Insistence on standard practices in school papers is not unreasonable.

As children mature, their handwriting becomes smaller. In grade four it becomes standardized according to the system used, with concern for exact proportioning of letters being a part of the instructional program. Ballpoint pens or fine-point fountain pens are introduced. Much of the drill is self-assigned as the result of comparing work with a standardized writing scale, which reveals various types of handwriting

defects. Speed is gradually encouraged. To secure peer-group approval, writers' clubs are organized; good writing is displayed and rewarded. Children with severe handwriting problems are usually encouraged to use print script rather than to continue with cursive writing.

WHAT ARE THE EXPECTANCIES OF HANDWRITING INSTRUCTION?

As with all skills there will be great personal variation, but in general, most schools attempt to meet these goals at the following grade levels:

By the end of kindergarten, most children may be expected to possess the following knowledge concerning handwriting:

1. Writing is a form of communication. It is language shared through signs. Signs, names, and other written symbols have meaning.
2. In some cases, a child will be able to write his first name.
3. Some familiarity with the forms of print-script writing as the teacher uses it in recording children's stories, labeling pictures, or writing names.

By the end of grade one, most children may be expected to:

1. Write in print-script form all letters —both capitals and lower case.
2. Write his name and address.
3. Write simple original stories.
4 Understand and practice proper spacing between letters of a word and between words of a sentence.

By the end of the second grade, a child should:

1. Be able to do good print-script writing in daily lessons.
2. Know about margins, heading of paper, and spacing.
3. Write a friendly letter.
4. Know the correct use of the terms: capital letters, period, question mark, comma as used between city and state and in dates.
5. Write print script with apparent ease.

By the end of the third grade, a child should be able to:

1. Use both print script and cursive writing to meet his daily needs.
2. Write his own name, his school, city, and state in cursive style.
3. Analyze and improve his own written work.
4. Write with reasonable speed.

During grade four, the child should be able to:

1. Write correctly, friendly letters (one or two good paragraphs).
2. Write notes to friends and classmates.
3. Write original stories, poems, plays, and programs.
4. Show evidence of retaining manuscript writing as a supplementary tool.
5. Meet the grade standards as indicated on a handwriting scale.
6. Recognize and correct his errors in letter formation.

By the end of grade five, the child should be able to:

1. Write a business letter.
2. Take notes in class.
3. Plan and present written reports.
4. Use pen and ink neatly.
5. Attempt writing on stationery without lines.
6. Meet grade standards with regard to legibility and speed (50–60 words per minute).

By the end of grade six, the child should be able to:

1. Proofread and rewrite many first writing efforts.

2. Take pride in submitting neat, orderly papers in all class work.
3. Meet grade standards of legibility and speed.

In grades seven and eight, the language teacher should devote some time to writing instruction each week. Teachers of *all* subjects should check and grade papers for neatness and legibility in handwriting. Ideas and the willingness to express them are more important than mechanics, but a carelessly written paper should be handed back to a student to be done over and a grade withheld until the second paper is handed to the teacher. The second effort is accepted if it is an improvement.

1. Compare the child learning to master handwriting with a child learning to type. Which is the simpler task?
2. The terms print script and manuscript are used interchangeably to describe primary printing. Which do you prefer? Why?
3. Why is it difficult to explain to parents that a child who prints is writing?
4. Can you recall a time when you experimented to develop a personal writing style? What were your motivations?

HOW IS WRITING INSTRUCTION STARTED?

There are three kinds of experiences which lead to writing readiness. The first group can be described as manipulative experiences. These are designed to strengthen muscles needed for writing and to gain control over tools used in writing. Children develop the small muscles of the hands through playing with toys, dialing the telephone, setting the table, changing a doll's clothes, putting puzzles together, cutting with scissors, finger painting, and clay modeling. They draw or scribble with chalk at the chalkboard or with crayons on large sheets of paper. It is well to remember that scribbling is writing, and that it is the child's first means of identifying himself with the writing process until he is ready to be taught the letter forms. Years ago Johann Pestalozzi (1746–1827) had children draw geometric forms on slates as he told stories. These were actually exercises in writing readiness.

The second group of experiences is designed to increase the child's ability in the use of language. It is futile for children to learn to write before they can express their ideas orally. Beginners must have many experiences that stimulate the desire for self-expression. As they listen to stories and poems, look at pictures, dictate stories and letters, or make up songs they should be encouraged to comment freely. As children see their ideas written by the teacher in a letter or invitation, writing becomes a magic tool for extending speech. With this recognition comes not only an understanding of the usefulness of writing but a strong personal desire to perform the writing task.

The third group are those experiences designed to give practice to the basic movements of writing itself. These are usually started at the chalkboard, where only large muscles are involved. The purpose is to understand certain letter forms and how they are created. Circles are first drawn by the children. They are given directions as to the starting place. Following this, the children are asked to look at the number "2" on the clock. When a circle is made it is best to start where the "2" would be if you were making a clock. Children draw clocks, doughnuts, balls, soap bubbles, and Halloween faces, or "set" a table with a circle for the plate and lines for the knife, fork and spoon. Some like to attempt such advanced circles as a string of beads, a bunch of grapes, a Christmas tree with ornaments, an umbrella, or a cat.

Combination of circles and straight lines can be made by drawing a square wagon with wheels, making a turkey with tail feathers, or stick figures with round heads.

As children transfer this activity to paper, some supervision is necessary to establish certain habits. All lines are made from top to bottom and left to right. All circles are started at the two o'clock position or where one would start to make the letter *c* and move toward the left.

As soon as possible—even at the readiness period—writing should say something. Children should be encouraged to label their picture of a cat with the word; the letters *c a t* might be copied from a teacher-made example. The child should know the names of these letters before writing them, and realize that he has made a word when he finishes. Thus, knowing the letter names and the ability to read what is written are a part of writing readiness.

One teacher introduced writing to a small group at the chalkboard in this manner: She first placed her chair close to the board and sat as she wrote, in order to make it more convenient for the children to watch as they stood about her. She was writing at their eye level. The teacher said, "Today we are going to write. We must first learn to hold the chalk so that it will make a soft, white line. If it squeaks, it is trying to tell you that you are not holding it right."

The teacher then demonstrated how to hold the chalk, first in the right hand and then in the left. "Good writers do it this way. I put my pointer (index) fingertip at the end of the chalk, the middle fingertip next to it, and my thumb underneath. Now let's see if you can do this." After each child had held the chalk, the teacher continued: "I am going to write the name of one of the children in our reader. Watch and see where I start each letter." The teacher wrote each letter slowly, calling attention to the letters that start at the top line and the letters that start in between the lines. "Now I will do it again," the teacher told them. "You will tell me everything I must do." The children, with teacher prompting, directed the action through a second writing of the word. The original word remained on the board as a guide and reminder. "Let's see how well we have written," the teacher remarked. "Bobby, draw your fingers along the bottom of the letters to see if they sit tight on the line. Are they all right? Mary, draw your finger along the tops of the low letters to see if they are even. And now, Jack,

check the tall letters to see if they start at the top line."

After these checks to sharpen visual discrimination had been made the teacher continued. "I want each of you to find a place at the chalkboard. I have written the lines on the board. Find the line that is even with your eyes. That is the one you will write on. Find your place and then write the same word that I did." The teacher gave individual help as needed. With some groups it would be better to have one child demonstrate what is to be done before the others try. After each child had appraised his work the teacher had them write the word a second time.

Other similar lessons teaching spacing between words, as well as other words and letters, should be done at the board before writing on paper is started at the desk.

If a section of the board can be reserved, writing practice during free time will be a popular activity. The teacher can put an assignment at the top of the space such as "Write the names of three boys," or "Write three words that start with B."

When making the transition from chalkboard to paper—and until the child is able to write correctly from memory—he must have a copy from which to write. The copy should be made on the same kind of paper that the child uses. The letters should be well formed. The amount of work will be controlled by the amount of time free for supervision, as well as by the fatigue factor. Most children tire after writing for about ten minutes.

Various systems of print script form the letters in different ways. Usually a school system selects one program and attempts to have a common form throughout all grades. Spacing is a problem in all systems. The instruction to leave the space of the letter *o* between words, and of one hump of the *n* between letters means little to beginners. Teachers frequently say "one finger between letters and two fingers between words." The problem is that letters made of straight lines should be closer together than those with curves, in order to give the illusion of uniform spacing throughout.

All writing that is made available to

San Diego City Schools Calif.

These second-grade children are evaluating their writing. Note the effort to keep the writing at the natural eye level.

the child for observation or for copy should be properly spaced and aligned. Occasional comments by the teacher may be used to strengthen the child's impression of well-spaced letters and perfectly straight lines. But in the early stage of writing instruction, the child needs to concentrate chiefly on getting a clear visual image of the letters he writes and in learning the correct order of making the strokes. After the child has learned to form the letters properly, there will be plenty of time for him to master the art of letter arrangement.

The paper should be placed directly in front of the child parallel with the lines of desk or table, rather than at a slant. The paper is moved as the child writes. Soft lead pencils or crayons are used. Ordinarily, a child can write easily while seated in a properly fitted chair and desk. Some small children write better if they can stand while writing. This is especially true if they are writing on large or oversize easel paper.

Early handwriting instruction should use whole words that have real meaning for the children—words they are interested in and that are easy to write. It will probably be necessary to contrive ways to bring in words like *queen, quiet, quail, fox, fix, box, excuse, zebra, zoo, buzz* and *dozen*, in order to teach the letters *q, x,* and *z,* which are not frequently used. The entire alphabet must be taught.

As the teacher writes, she should call attention to details, naming the letters and commenting on the size, shape, and direction of strokes. She should watch the child write the word, comment favorably on letters well formed, and give additional instruction when it is needed. If a particular letter proves difficult, the child should give it additional practice. When introducing letters in a word for the first time, or isolating a difficult letter for study, the teacher may give more time to demonstration and discussion, thus:

"The *t* is a tall letter. We start at the top, go down, and try to make it very straight. We cross it near the top from left to right. The *t* is not quite so tall as an *l*, but it is taller than *i*, or *m*, or *n* [depending on which letter the children already know]."

At this point it is well for the teacher to bear in mind that when a child begins to write he cannot remember everything he has been told. Only two things are essential: he must form the letters in fair approximation to the copy, and he must make every stroke in the right direction as he forms his letters. If he cannot do both, he probably is not ready to write and would profit more from nonwriting activities at this time.

The practice of tracing, except in special problem cases, may do more harm than good. If the child cannot make the strokes without the tedious, time-consuming muscular drill involved in tracing, he is hardly ready for handwriting instruction. And if the child, in tracing, puts all his attention on the segment of line that he is attempting to follow at the moment, he loses sight of the letter or word as a whole, and so at the end of the lesson may be able to write no better than at the beginning.

In learning to write, as in other kinds of growth, children pass through the same general stages of development. But the rate of progress and the time at which each level of achievement is reached will vary according to the individual differences of the children themselves. The rate of learning among the children in any one class may range from slow to normal or fast. It is not uncommon for a child to start slowly and then pick up speed as he matures, or for another to start rapidly and then "slow down" later. Nevertheless, at any given time there will be enough children with similar needs to make some group instruction possible. In writing as in reading, groups must be small enough to permit close personal supervision of each child's work by the teacher. This is true whether the writing is done on the board or on paper.

A good lesson in handwriting contains five elements: (1) visualization, (2) analysis, (3) practice, (4) comparison or evaluation, and (5) correction.

Note the following in teaching the child to write his name.

1. *Visualization.* The teacher has prepared a card (3 × 5) with the name of each child. "I wonder how many can read each other's names. As I go through the cards, the person whose name it is will call on another child to read it. After all have been read, I will give you your name cards."

2. *Analysis.* "How many have an *e* in their name? Jane, show us how to make an *e*. This is one letter that does not start

at the top. Does anyone have a *g* in his name? Gregory, show us how to make a *g*. That is another letter that does not start at the top. Look at each letter in your name. Are there any you think we should practice?"

3. *Practice.* "Now go to the board and put an *x* at the eye-level line where you will start. Write your name once. When you have finished, go over your name card and see if each letter is correct."

4. *Evaluation.* "How many have all the letters on the line? How many have all the letters right? How many have the space between letters right?"

5. *Correction.* "Now let us write our names once more and make them better. You are to keep the name card at your desk and use it whenever you wish to write your name."

In the first grade, many lessons in handwriting will require the teacher to prepare a worksheet. Normally, these worksheets should meet the following standards:

The learner's attention will be focused on a few handwriting difficulties.

The worksheet will contain enough guidance so that possible errors will not be practiced.

While the drill is on a single element, the practice should result in the feeling that something has been written.

There should be enough practice to give a sense of purpose to the lesson, but not so much that there is physical strain.

The first thing on the worksheet should be the letters or word demonstrated by the teacher. There may be arrows or other markers to show where the writer starts each letter, and the direction of the strokes. The first stroke might be in red, the second in yellow and the third in blue.

The second part of the worksheet may consist of practice on one or two letters. An example should be given and spaces should be made indicating how many "copies" of each letter are required.

Finally, these letters should be put together to form a word or sentence. Sometimes only part of a word is given, with blanks left for the missing letters. Other worksheets may indicate by a picture what word is to be written. As soon as the child is ready the writing should become personal. The worksheet may start a letter by having printed on it: "Dear Santa, please bring me . . ."

The next step is to have the children do a great deal of personal writing, using model alphabet charts to guide the writing. "Home-made" greeting cards provide writing practice. These cards may then be sent to a child who is ill or used for birthdays, Christmas greetings, Mother's Day remembrance or for Valentine's Day. Labeling also provides excellent writing practice. Children can make flash cards for reading drill. But best of all are the stories written to illustrate a picture or to entertain the group. We will discuss such stories later under creative writing.

There are standardized scales to evaluate print-script writing. However, few children can use them. A chart that asks the child to check the following elements will serve for most evaluation needed at this grade:

Did you make each letter the way it is on the chart?

Are your letters on the line?

Are your down strokes straight?

Are your round letters like a circle?

Did you leave enough space between words?

There are a number of devices that teachers use during this period to add interest to the writing practice. Here are some of them:

writes it on the board. The teacher then describes another letter.

The teacher asks, "Who can find the letter that comes before *m*? What is its name? The child who identifies the letter may write it on the board. A variation is to ask, "What letter comes after *m*?

Each child in turn goes to the front of the room and gives his name and initials. "My name is Robert Smith. My initials are R. S." Then he writes them on the board. Or a child may write a classmate's initials on the board and have the class identify the person.

A magic slate can be made with transparent acetate sheets from a novelty store. Insert a sheet of paper with the letters, words or numbers you wish the child to practice. The children trace over these with a crayon —or better, write under the examples. These can be used many times since the crayon marks can be wiped off.

One teacher starts her group by saying, "We are going to make pumpkins today. Watch how I make one." The teacher uses the guide words "One around." After the children have made a row of pumpkins, the teacher says, "Let's put our pumpkins beside a fence post. Now look again," the teacher says, "because you have made the letter *a*."

Another teacher talks about the letters that are done only on one floor such as *a, c, e, m*. Other letters are upstairs letters like *b, d, h,* and *l*. Basement letters are *g, j, p, y*.

Sometimes children do a better job of alignment if they are told, "Let's see if we can keep our letters sitting straight on a shelf."

PEANUTS ®   **By Charles M. Schulz**

United Features Syndicate

Ask the children to listen carefully to a word description to see if they can identify a letter which is on the alphabet chart. The teacher says, "I am thinking of a small letter that is made with a circle and then a tall stick." The child who identifies *d* goes and

After the children have spent several lessons on lines, circles, their names and single words, one teacher starts with a sentence such as "I am a boy." After the unlined paper is distributed the children are asked to fold the paper in half lengthwise, then fold the bottom half to the center fold. This provides folded lines to follow. The children write the sentence on the bottom fold and then draw a picture in the top half to illustrate their sentence.

1. Why is it important that early writing practice result in a word?

2. Primary pencils do not have erasers. Children are told to put a line through an error and write it again. Do you think erasers should be available? Give reasons for your answer.

3. Do all children need readiness experiences before receiving writing instruction?

4. Are some children ready for cursive writing in the first grade?

5. Plan a worksheet that will provide for the steps in a writing lesson suggested in this chapter.

HOW DO TEACHERS GUIDE THE CHILD'S LEARNING AS HE TRANSFERS FROM PRINT SCRIPT TO CURSIVE WRITING?

While there are some school systems that make no effort to teach any form of writing but print script, the majority do introduce cursive writing in either the late second grade or third grade. This change is more the result of response to cultural tradition than to educational merit. We have enough evidence to indicate that with practice, print-script writing can be written as rapidly as cursive writing. It remains a legible and easy form of writing. It also assumes enough personality so that signatures in print script are now legal. There are usually two reasons given for the change. One is that children are attempting to imitate the cursive writing they see and need direction to do it correctly. The second is that parents disapprove of older children's use of print script. There are no studies known to this writer that indicate if either of these arguments is valid.

A strong traditional force is within the teaching group. Upper-grade teachers use cursive writing. They seem unwilling to change. Thus the child must change to conform to the teacher's writing pattern. Another factor in this situation is that it represents a teaching specific which seems to indicate educational growth. Teachers often like to introduce something new; the home reaction is generally that "children in Miss Smith's class are certainly making progress."

Certainly it makes sense for the child to use print script as often as possible after having mastered this skill. Children will more readily express their ideas in the written form throughout the second and third grade if they use print script. Rather than start the transfer late in the second grade—which means that children will be subject to unsupervised practice during the summer months—it seems wisest to start the transition in the third grade. Even then total transfer should not be rushed in the third grade. Children should continue to write spelling words and answers to test questions in the form of writing that is easiest for the individual. Even after cursive has been mastered there will be occasions throughout all grade levels to use print-script skills in such exercises as filling out forms, writing invitations and designing greeting cards or posters.

The major aspect of readiness for training in cursive writing is the ability to read words written in this script. Members of the family will frequently teach a child to "write" rather than "print" his name. Teachers will start using cursive to present assignments and words in the spelling lessons. Children play games with their sight vocabulary in both printed and cursive forms. Other factors—such as desire to write, adequate physical development, and the ability to use print script—should be considered. Slower children who are just beginning to understand how to read should not face the additional problem of learning a new way to write.

A few children will make the transfer in imitation of the writing of parents or older children. The change is made with very little guidance and penmanship instruction is only a matter of perfecting the new forms. These children do not need to follow any of the instructional patterns suggested here.

The transfer to cursive should conform to the principle of moving from the simple to the complex. Experience indicates that the small or lower-case letters should be introduced first, in the following order: *l, e, i, t, u, n, m, h, k, w, o, b, v, x, y, j, f, s, p, r, c, a, d, g, q, z.*

Capital letters with the exception of "I" should be taught in association with the children's names. Rather than drill on all of them in grade three, it is best to practice them in usage with an example and teacher guidance.

The best equipment to use is an ordinary lead pencil at least six inches long, with soft lead (No. 2). The paper should be ruled. Because some children have a tendency to write too small, wide-ruled paper is usually used. Space lines such as two faint lines dividing the space into thirds between the regular lines of the paper aid most children. Usually the lines are closer together than that used for beginning manuscript writing. This sequence is followed in many schools:

"Many of you have noticed that your mothers and fathers do not use print-script writing. Some of you have written your name or a few words in this writing. You will see how this writing differs from the writing we have been doing. I will write the name of our town on the board in this new writing. You will see that the letters are slanted and joined. We have been writing with our papers directly in front of us. It will be easier to write this new way if you slant your paper. For those who are right-handed, the paper should slant to the left with the bottom corner pointing toward your heart. If you are left-handed, the paper should slant to the right."

The exact position for each person will differ according to arm length. These variations may be suggested to the individual as the teacher observes his writing.

The first step is to make guidelines to use in letter formation. The teacher might say, "Watch while I make some lines on the board. Notice how each line slants the same as the other lines. I want them to slant only a little. I am going to leave a space between each pair of lines. Now you may make three pairs of slanted lines."

Grade 1	At first unruled paper (without lines), 12-in. × 18-in., folded.
	Later, 1-in. ruled paper.
	Later, ruled ½-in. light and heavy, long way.
Grade 2	9-in. × 12-in., ruled ½-in. alternating light and heavy lines.
	Ruled 1-in. light, long way.
Grade 3	At first ½-in. alternating light and heavy lines.
	Later, ⅝-in. one space for tall letters.
	Reduce to ½-in. as children are ready.
Grade 4	Ruled ½-in., reducing to ⅜-in.
Grade 5, 6	⅜-in. spacing.

It is good classroom management to have a jar of sharpened pencils ready (having been prepared by a monitor) so that a pencil with a broken point can be exchanged for a new one without class interruption.

Slanted cursive writing is best introduced as a completely new form of writing. Before distributing paper to the class, the teacher might make remarks like this:

"The first letter we make will be the letter *l*. I will start on the bottom line, cross the bottom of the slanted line, make a curved line to the top and then come down the guideline and finish with a small curve. Now, you try it. Make an *l* with each guideline."

"Now, make three more pairs of guidelines and this time we will make two letter *l*'s that join. We might say, "Up,

San Diego City Schools, Calif.

The hand movement of some children needs the direct guidance of the teacher in much the same manner as a golfer needs the guidance of a professional coach.

around, straight down; up, around, straight down."

Observe to see that the letters are neither too wide nor too thin. In the second lesson, demonstrate the letter *e*, using only half of a slanted line as a guide. Use the same three steps. Follow this with the letter *i*.

The third lesson introduces the letter *t*. Start by making guidelines on two-thirds of the writing space. The cross on the *t* is one-half the distance between the top and bottom writing lines.

The children should now start to use these letters in words.

The teacher might say, "I am thinking of some words that use the letters we have practiced. If I put the guidelines for the words on the board, I wonder how many of you will be able to write the word. Copy the guidelines on your paper before you write the word."

"Yes, the words are *ill* and *tell*. Can you think of another word that we can write with these letters? Yes, we could write *tile*. What guidelines will we need? See how many other words you can think of, using *i, e, l,* and *t*. We'll compare lists after

I have helped some children with their writing."

Some children will think of only two or three. Possible words include *little, let, lie, lit, tie, title, tell, it, ill, tilt, eel,* and *tee*.

The fourth lesson introduces the letter *u*. Start by making two short guidelines in groups of three. Use guide phrases such as "up, down, around; up, down, around."

The letter *n* is made with groups of two small guidelines. This letter begins with a hump that starts a space before the first guideline. Guide words such as, "hump, down, hump, down, up" may be used.

The letter *m* is made with groups of three guidelines. The first stroke is the hump, a space before the first guideline.

Now a number of words may be written. "Instead of starting with guidelines, write the word, then put in the slanted guidelines to see if you have the proper slant. I wonder how many words you can make using *i, l, t, e, m, n* and *u*." Practice on these letters should continue several days.

The fifth lesson introduces the letter *h*. This is a combination of *l* and *n*. As a guide one needs a long line and a short line.

Write words: *hit, hen, hill, him, the, then, them.*

The letter *s* presents a special problem. Some prefer a square as a guide rather than a slanted line. The upstroke goes to the corner of the square and the downstroke follows straight down before making the curve.

The sixth lesson introduces the term *bridge* or *bow*. The new letter is *w*. Start by making groups of three lines as for *m*. The teacher might say, "We will make the letter *w* by starting as if we were making the letter *u*. At the end, we go up once more, then make a bridge. This bridge sags a little. The letter *o* does not need a guideline but the bridge should be stressed. For the letter *b* we need only a long line as a guide. We first make the letter *l* then close the ending by coming around as one would make an *o* and end with a bridge."

Words to write: *will, bill, we, be, wet, bet, tub, new, bum.* Practice several days on words with the *bridge*. Note that when *e* and *i* are after a letter with a bridge, they start in a different way. The letter *r* is a bridge with a point. Difficult combinations at this point are: *os, or, ox, ve, br.*

The next letter to study is *k*. This letter is like *h*. It starts as if one were writing *l*, then instead of a letter like *n*, one goes around and makes a little circle, then comes down to finish the letter.

If one covers a part of the letters *k* and *h*, one should see *l*.

The letters *a, g, d,* and *q*, contain the oval which is the most difficult aspect of transfer from manuscript to cursive. One reason for insisting that when learning manuscript the child starts his circles at the two o'clock position is to aid in this transfer.

Start by having the child make a series of "eggs that tip or leaves on a stem." If short slanted lines are used, start at the top of these guidelines, make the oval by returning to the starting point, then follow the guideline down to make the connecting stroke.

Another method that might be described as "connected print script" would be handled in the following manner:

Have the child print a word like *good.* Then have the child trace the word he has printed, without raising his pencil. This, of course, means that he will connect the letters. As the child retraces give him directions such as: "Around, down, make the tail on the *g*; now, without raising your pencil, go up and over to the top of the letter *o*, around the *o*, and without raising your pencil, slide over to the other *o* and around the *o*; without raising your pencil, slide over to the round part of the letter *d*; go around and up on the stick stroke, down again, and add a tail stroke." Next, let the child try to write the word *good* without retracing the print script.

Only letters which connect almost automatically should be taught by this connective method. The following primary words have letters which are easy for children to connect:

in	in	in
it	it	it
call	call	call
put	put	put

1. act	21. goat	41. hut	61. pail
2. add	22. gold	42. it	62. pat
3. all	23. good	43. lad	63. path
4. at	24. got	44. laid	64. pig
5. auto	25. ha	45. lap	65. pool
6. call	26. had	46. late	66. pop
7. cloth	27. hail	47. laugh	67. pot
8. cloud	28. hall	48. lip	68. pull
9. cold	29. hat	49. little	69. put
10. cup	30. hill	50. load	70. tag
11. cut	31. hid	51. log	71. tail
12. dad	32. hit	52. lot	72. tall
13. did	33. hog	53. oat	73. tap
14. dig	34. hold	54. o'clock	74. till
15. do	35. hole	55. oh	75. to
16. dog	36. hood	56. old	76. too
17. dot	37. hop	57. out	77. tool
18. dug	38. hot	58. pa	78. tooth
19. glad	39. hug	59. pad	79. up
20. go	40. hunt	60. paid	

The letters *b, e, f, r, k, s, z* must be taught as specific difficulties. The cursive that results from the method is vertical. Slant is obtained by turning the paper. Some teachers prefer to introduce this method by using dotted lines to show the cursive form on top of the print script. Children trace over these dotted lines as they master the new form.

The teacher starts with words containing letters that are alike in cursive and print script. These would contain the small letters *i, t, o, n, m, e, h, l, u, d, c* and the capital letters B, C, K, L, O, P, R, U. A word is written in print script on the board as an example for the children to observe. The word *it* would be printed at a slant. The teacher then adds a "reach stroke," going to the first letter and from the first to the second. An ending stroke for the word is added. Then the teacher says, "Now I am going to do it without patching (guiding dots). Reach for the *i*. Now make the *i* lean right back against the reach line. Reach high for the *t*. Lean the *t* right back against the reach line. Reach up as high as the *i* to end the word. Now cross the *t* in the middle and dot the *i*. Let's do it again but this time you tell me what to do. First we will put in patch lines then we will do it without patching." After this each child practices at the board.

This type of lesson is repeated with *in, me, he, let, nut, do, cut, ice, mud, hut, den, cent, nice, home, mile, come, then, did*. Each lesson contains these steps: the word is written first in slanted print script, reach strokes are patched in, the word is written without patching and children steer the teacher's chalk through the word before writing it under supervision. Practice cards are provided which illustrate these steps for all the other letters. In the independent writing of the children during this period both cursive and print script appear. Both are expected—and permitted.

In the past, music was used a great deal as students practiced penmanship exercises. Experience with music as an aid to manuscript writing indicates some serious limitations. The music puts a premium on speed that is unnecessary and frustrating. The major practice should be with words, and since each letter has a different rhythm, no music is of the proper beat for words. Little children respond to music with total body movement that interferes with writing.

When parents ask about teaching their children to write at home the teacher may explain thus:

If a child writes before he is ready, he frequently develops a feeling of tension, grips his pencil too tightly, and builds up a dislike a c d g h i j l m

a c d g h i j l m

a c d g h i j l m

n o p q t u v w x y

n o p q t u v w x y

n o p q t u v w x y

b e f r k s z

b e f r k s z

a clown doll

a clown doll

a clown doll

New York City Schools, Brooklyn, N. Y.

for writing. Then too, a young child's muscles are not developed enough for successful writing. Therefore he should use large pencils and crayons. These are provided in school. Writing at school is supervised to avoid poor habits, such as gripping the pencil too tightly, incorrect letter formations, and poor position.

If, however, the child is eager to write and seems ready, parents might give the child a large, soft pencil or crayon and unlined paper, and teach manuscript letters using capitals only at the beginning of proper names. (Send a copy of the specimen alphabet to the child's home.)

1. Do you consider the second, third or fourth grade the best place to make the transfer to cursive writing?

2. Which method of transfer do you prefer? Why?

3. Make a worksheet to be used during this period of writing instruction.

4. Try writing to music. Do you feel that it would aid instruction?

5. Write a letter to parents explaining the handwriting program in your school.

HOW MAY GOOD CURSIVE WRITING BE ACHIEVED AND MAINTAINED?

There are a number of well-planned, modern handwriting programs available for use in schools. Some school systems like those of Minneapolis, Detroit, and Philadelphia have prepared programs for their own use. The first step toward achieving good cursive writing is to select or devise a system of handwriting and then follow it with determination and consistency.

Determination is needed because so often the short time allowed for handwriting practice gets crowded out of the school day. In most intermediate grades only about sixty minutes a week divided into three twenty-minute sessions on Monday, Wednesday, and Friday are available for handwriting drill. This is enough time if the practices stressed are consistently followed in all the writing of the child. These short sessions are usually planned to provide practice on a single element in writing. It may concern the formation of a letter, spacing, alignment, slant, connecting strokes or ending stroke. After the teacher has demonstrated the element and the group discussed the writing problem presented, the students usually follow an exercise in a copybook. After this is completed a comparison is made between the students' work and the example for the purpose of evaluation. The motivation is usually based on the student's desire to gain recognition through excellence or to improve a weakness.

Frequently only those who have special handwriting problems participate in the classwork, while those who have no special needs use the time for independent writing. One disadvantage of many programs is that they use as examples a higher quality of writing than is normally achieved. Indeed, the same examples serve for the sixth grade that are used in the third. The Minneapolis Schools have solved the latter problem by selecting examples for each grade from children in that grade. These have been reproduced in a handwriting scale for each grade. Sample One is of the very best and is labeled "You have reached your goal. Your writing is very good." Below the example attention is called to the word shapes, spacing, and letter formation with the teacher's suggestion on how to score a writing sample that is similar to it. Sample Two says, "You are on the right track. Your writing is satisfactory." Sample Three says, "You are on the right track. You need to improve." Attention is called to some of the errors in the samples as well as the good qualities. Number four says, "You are on the wrong track. You need help." Again the errors are noted. Each child has an individual Handwriting Record which is based on the above scale and other charts. Each grade level has a series of lessons—sometimes described as writing tricks—designed to improve items checked in the record.

There are handwriting scales available with nearly all commercial programs. Children find these difficult to use in analyzing their own writing. There is no reason why any class or school cannot collect enough writing samples to develop its own standards or expectancies for each grade. The standardized scales can be used by teachers as they make judgments concerning the samples selected. Probably the most scientifically constructed scale is that devised by Leonard P. Ayres and published by the Educational Testing Service of Princeton, N. J. A major consideration is general quality of writing rather than specific style. This is difficult to determine if the writing being judged is vertical or backhand. Most individuals making such appraisals are also influenced by the formation of certain letters, such as capital R or small *r*. Noble and Noble and the Palmer Company have scales that diagnose specific writing problems of children practicing the methods published by these firms. The Zaner-Bloser Company makes available a small dictionary of letter forms which each child uses. This dictionary presents the letters of their system with a space for the child to make his own examples. These can be used as a record of a child's progress. As the child compares his present writing with his past work he can note progress or weakness. This comparison serves much the same purpose as a standardized scale.

Writing samples should be collected from each child at least four times during the year and kept in a collection of other examples of his work. Some teachers ask the child to write, "This is a sample of my writing on October 1." This inscription is folded back so that it is not visible when the child later writes, "This is a sample of my writing on January 1." Direct comparison can be made to see if skills are being maintained or improvement made. Both examples of writing are folded back when the child writes a third or fourth time on the same paper. Such a sample is especially helpful when talking with a parent about a child's work.

The following lesson is an example of an individual diagnostic device. It is designed to help children establish goals for their work in handwriting as well as establish meaningful standards.[1]

---

[1] *My Handwriting Quotient,* Madison Iowa, W. A. Sheaffer Pen Company, 1960.

Pupil Self-Analysis Sheet

A. Here is how I write when I am in a hurry:
   (Write: "This is a sample of my writing")

_____

_____

B. Here is how I write when I do my best writing:
   (Write: "This is a sample of my best writing")

_____

_____

C. I would mark my fast writing: (circle one grade) Excellent   Good   Fair   Poor
   I would mark my best writing: Excellent   Good   Fair   Poor

‖‖

D. Here is my analysis of my handwriting: EXCELLENT   GOOD   FAIR   POOR

   1. SLANT . . . .
      Do all my letters lean the same way?   ____   ____   ____   ____

   2. SPACING . . . .
      Are the spaces between letters and words even?   ____   ____   ____   ____

   3. SIZE . . . .
      Are all small letters evenly small and tall letters evenly tall?   ____   ____   ____   ____

4. ALIGNMENT ....
Do all my letters touch the line?

——   —— —— ——

5. LOOPS ....
Are l, f, h, g, y, k, b well formed?

——   —— —— ——

6. STEMS ....
Are all my downstrokes really straight?

——   —— —— ——

7. CLOSINGS ....
Are a, d, g, o, p, s closed?

——   —— —— ——

8. ROUNDNESS ....
Are m, n, h, u, v, w, y rounded?

——   —— —— ——

9. RETRACES ....
Are t, i, d, m, n retraced?

——   —— —— ——

10. ENDINGS ....
Do my words have good ending strokes without fancy swinging strokes?

——   —— —— ——

In the handwriting period there will be times when the entire group will be working on the same problem—perhaps that of word endings or alignment. Since all have a like purpose, group diagnosis is effective. Project samples of the writing on a screen by means of an opaque projector. Since the purpose is to seek means of improvement rather than being graded, most children will welcome the attention and suggestions concerning the next step they should take to improve. At first, attention should be directed toward one or two specific points. After using this type of diagnosis for some time, any aspect of the child's writing may be the basis for suggestion. A plastic transparent overlay will help some children examine specific letters. These are available with most handwriting systems. Another device is to cut a small hole in a piece of paper and examine the child's writing one letter at a time.

Those who write well should receive recognition. There should be a place to exhibit "our best work." Some teachers have rubber stamps made so that they can place EXCELLENT or from one to four stars on a paper. We know that intermediate children respond to such praise and that all learners work better if they know the work will be evaluated.

Regardless of the system used, the following five elements enter into the handwriting program; a chart of these made for the classroom can act as a constant reminder:

1. *Formation*—Each letter should be made and joined correctly according to whatever penmanship system is followed. Examples of letters that cause trouble can be shown on this chart.

2. *Size*—This is to remind them of the need for uniformity in size regardless of the type of letter.

3. *Slant*—The problem here is usually one of consistency.

4. *Alignment*—Letters that go above or below the line get mixed with other writing and thus are very difficult to read.

5. *Spacing*—Even spacing is necessary for rhythmic reading. This chart, based on the program of the New York City Schools, emphasizes these ideas.

Guiding Rules for Cursive Writing of the Small Alphabet [2]

1. In the lower-case alphabet, every letter, except *c* and *o*, must have a *straight* down stroke, slanting from right to left.

    The downstrokes are straight.

    The downstrokes are not straight.

2. The *space* between two letters should be wide enough to hold an *n* without the up-stroke:

    "n spaces" between letters

    Spaces are too narrow.

    Spaces are too wide.

3. All downstrokes must be parallel.

    Downstrokes are parallel.

    Downstrokes are not parallel.

4. All letters must rest ON the line.
    Letters rest ON the line.

    Letters do not rest on the line.

5. Letters must be of uniform and proportionate size.

6. The TOTAL slant of the writing should be parallel to the diagonal of the paper, whether by right-handed or left-handed writers.

The final judgment concerning handwriting should be based upon the child's daily written work. Occasionally, before and after children complete a written assignment, make a class inventory of writing needs. Have the students look at their papers while you record by number (not name) the results on the chalkboard. Use the following inventory of writing habits:

Alignment
    How many had
        correct top alignment?
        uneven top alignment?
        correct bottom alignment?
        uneven bottom alignment?
        writing under the line?
        writing over the line?

Letter Spacing
    How many had
        correct letter spacing?
        uneven letter spacing?
        letter spacing too close together?
        letter spacing too far apart?
Word Spacing
    How many had
        correct word spacing?
        uneven word spacing?
        word spacing too close together?
        word spacing too far apart?

The secret of continuous improvement is to establish a feeling of achieve-

[2] Max Rosenhaus, "You Can Teach Handwriting with Only Six Rules," *The Instructor*, March 1957, p. 60.

ment. This can be done by setting specific attainable goals. When a goal is achieved, celebrate it fittingly. (While one can hardly recommend leading a snakedance through the halls whenever the whole class learns to make a good capital A, it is no less of an achievement than winning a basketball game.) Examples of such objectives which the entire group can eventually achieve are:

Write the small letters of the alphabet correctly four times, joining the letters to each other. The teacher (or a committee) can be the judge until an acceptable exercise is received from each member of the class.

Write sentences using words with difficult letter-joinings such as *bring, arrows, written, following, uncommon, bewitched, disturbance, suited* and *delighted.*

Write sentences using these words: *there, their, they're; here's, hears; were, we're, wear; your, you're.*

Copy a short poem.

Write a good thank-you letter.

Write the alphabet in capital letters.

Write the addresses of three friends as they would appear on an envelope.

Write five quotations.

Make a directory of the class showing names, addresses, and telephone numbers.

Keep the minutes as a secretary of a meeting.

One third-grade classroom had a G and Y week. For this week all *g*'s and *y*'s in the spelling and other written work were to be checked. Each child wore a paper badge announcing "G & Y Week." This naturally aroused the curiosity of other classes. So the group decided to make it a secret and added an air of mystery to the situation by putting this sign on the hall bulletin board and in some classrooms: "What Will Happen During G & Y Week?"

Each day the class had a short lesson on these letters working on formation, slant and ending. All *g*'s and *y*'s written were subject to careful examination. When they thought that each was an expert on these letters they planned to visit another class to check on the way the letters were written there. To prepare this class for the situation, a tape recording was played, explaining that the visitors were detectives who were searching for bad *g*'s and *y*'s.

Each child made a paper magnifying glass à la Sherlock Holmes to use in the search for *g*'s and *y*'s.

Through advance arrangements with the teacher, another third grade was visited. The president announced that they were doing some investigating and that the tape recording would explain their visit. At the end of the tape each child was asked to show his spelling workbook and a visiting child examined it for bad *g*'s and *y*'s. Later they were invited to visit a fourth and sixth grade.

In turn they started receiving mysterious messages and the other third grade came in to check their *d*'s and *t*'s. Thus, with a bit of imagination, handwriting came alive and took on importance for the entire school.

Many schools purchase an alphabet strip which they place over a chalkboard to act as a constant point of reference for children as they write. This technique can be effective if it is made significant to the children. Some teachers have pictures drawn to go with each letter. In the lower grades the drawing may be an apple for *a*, but the upper grades may require something more challenging to illustrate such words as *avocado* or *astronaut*. Unfortunately, the space over the chalkboard is an awkward point of reference. For some children the details of the letters are lost because of vision problems. Some programs provide individual desk cards which are used by the children when they need to recall how a letter is made. In practice these are more effective than the alphabet strip.

There are two types of children who must be provided with such individual references. One is the left-handed child who needs examples that apply to his pattern of writing. The other is the transfer student who has mastered a system other than the one being taught in the new school. To require that such children change to the system taught in the new situation is an example of educational inefficiency.

The following three lessons were designed as part of a rapid review program with intermediate grade children:[3]

---

[3] Nathan Naiman. *A Blitz Handwriting Program* (San Diego, Calif.: Oak Park School, 1960).

Finishing Strokes

Ending the last letter of each word with a good finishing stroke makes our handwriting look much better. Most of these strokes swing up with a slight upward curve to the height of the letter *a*. The curve of the final stroke is downward on the letters *g, j, y* and *z*.

PART 1

Look at yesterday's sample of your best handwriting. Look for the final stroke or "tails" on every word that you wrote on this sample. Put the number of tails that you left off here: _____ Count every tail that is poorly shaped or that reaches above or below the height of the letter *a*.

PART 2

Now put you name on the right of the top line of your paper. Put the date just below your name. On the third line just to the left of the center, put the title, "Handwriting." Skip the next line. Using good finishing strokes, write the following sentence three times:

Paul said, "The big brown fox quickly and slyly jumped over the lazy dog.

Skip a line and then write the following words, ending them with good tails:

month	because	windy	high	kite	string	west	held	fell
oak	broke	away	will	where	an	hold	east	air

PART 3

Again, look at yesterday's sample of your handwriting. Copy those words needing tails and put good tails or finishing strokes on them. Look closely at the ending of each word to see that you are improving your final strokes.

Using Good Slant in Handwriting—Lower Loop Letters

Proper slant in handwriting is very important in the making of lower loop letters. Be sure the slanted part of these letters is straight. The lower loop letters are: *g, j, p, y* and *z*.

PART 1

Take the written work. Put the guide sheet under it. See if the lower loop letters have the correct angle of slant. How would you grade your slant? Is it excellent, good, fair or poor? _____

Now look at the finishing strokes. Put a check by those that do not reach as high as the letter *a*.

PART 2

Today we will practice good slant on the lower loop letters. Put your name on the upper right on the top line of your paper. Put the date just below your name. On the third line just to the left of the center, put the title "Handwriting." Skip the next line.

Carefully write a line of each of these lower loop letters:

g, j, p, y, z

Here are some words that have lower loop letters. Write each two times:

gag   pipe   gang   jig   pig

Write this sentence two times: "The big pig danced a jig."

PART 3

Now look at all of the writing you have done today. See if all of your lower loop letters reach half way below the line. See if they have straight backs. Circle those which are poorly formed. Practice writing those words that you circled. How would you grade today's work? Is it excellent, good, fair, poor? _____

Spacing in Handwriting

After one word has been finished, a space is left before the next word is written. This space is just about as wide as the small letter *a*. This space should never be larger or smaller than this.

PART 1

Look back at the sentences you wrote in earlier lessons. See if the spacing between words is about as wide as the letter *a*. Are you leaving too much space or not enough? How would you grade your spacing on these sentences? Is it excellent, good, fair, or poor?

_____

PART 2

Put the heading on your paper.

Now here are some sentences for you to write. Be careful to leave a uniform space between your words. Write each sentence twice:

> The quick brown fox jumps over the lazy dog.
> Whatever is worth doing at all is worth doing well.
> Well begun is half done.

Here is a sample of good spacing:

_____

_____

PART 3

Skip a line and write the following:

> "Here is another sample of my best handwriting. I am careful with finishing strokes, slant, letter size, and the spacing between letters."

Compare this writing with the writing in the first lesson. Is it better, just as good as, or poorer than this first lesson? _____

These are other suggestions with respect to handwriting instruction in the intermediate grades which come from experienced teachers.

Make the paper on which the final writing will appear have special significance. Make mimeograph copies of a flag, holiday picture, or school letterhead on good-quality "mimeo" bond paper. Explain that the number of copies is limited and that the paper should not be used for the exercise until each person feels that he is prepared. Sometimes attractive stationery will serve the same purpose.

Hold a writing clinic with one or two of the best writers acting as "doctors" for specific letters.

Exchange handwriting samples with other schools, both in the United States and other countries.

Suggest to parents the value of a good writing instrument as a birthday or Christmas gift.

Make art designs formed of alphabet letters.

Have an "Each One Teach One" week, during which each child teaches one letter and its formation to another child or small group. Let the children devise worksheets or lessons for this. One fifth grade produced a textbook titled, "How to Write Well."

Add novelty to the copy material as illustrated by the following worksheets:

Zillions of zephers floated over the trees
Zany zebras zipped along the plains
Zooming airplanes filled the sky
Zealous fifth-graders learned z's with zeal!

Copy this "poem," being very careful of your z's.

_____

_____

_____

_____

_____

Are your z's zippy or zero?
On the back of this paper try to make an example we could use for another letter.

Squacky, the squirrel scrambled down from her tree
Squacky sat down and along came a bee,
Suzy, the bee, was filled with dread
But when the creatures spied her, they all fled!

Copy the above "poem" on the lines below being very careful of your s's.

_____

_____

_____

_____

_____

Are your s's snappy?
On the back of this paper try to make an example we could use for this or another letter.

The most important handwriting problem is that of illegibility. The Veterans Administration is so concerned that they have issued a pamphlet, "How to Improve Your Handwriting, a Practical Guide to Legibility," to its employees. Beginning teachers may wish to secure a copy by sending 15 cents to the U. S. Government Printing Office, Washington 25, D. C., and requesting VA Pamphlet 03-2 or Number 1960-0-552101. Another inexpensive pamphlet designed for businessmen (and sometimes sent free) is "Write it Right," published by Birk and Company, 22 East 60th Street, New York 22, N. Y.

Illegible handwriting is due to seven errors: (1) faulty endings, (2) incorrectly made undercurves, (3) mixed slant, (4) failure to give letters in the *a* group proper slant, (5) incorrect formation of the initial stroke of such letters as the capitals W, H, K, (6) incorrect endings in final *h, m, n,* and (7) failure to make the downstroke of *t* and *d.*

End strokes as spacers between words improve the legibility of writing more than any other single device. One writer claims that attention to this factor can improve legibility by 25 per cent.

Ability to make the undercurve of the letter *l* alone improves the shape of many related letters and brings about the orderly appearance of written paragraphs.

The letters that extend below the line should show the same slant as those above the line. The principle of parallel slants brings about harmony in handwriting.

Many letters exhibit an initial stroke shaped like a cane. The stroke consists of two parts, a loop and a downstroke. These should be made so as to conform to the slant of the other letters. There are eleven letters to which this principle applies.

When *h, m* or *n* appears at the end of a word, there is a tendency to slur the last two strokes. Emphasis upon precision in making the last downstroke in writing these letters and in the final upstroke re-

San Diego City Schools, Calif.

This class is working on the "cane" stroke in the cursive alphabet. The handwriting copybooks are placed so that there is adequate desk space for writing.

moves a common fault. The letters *t* and *d* constitute a special application of the *l* principle. Once the relationship of these letters to the *l* principle is recognized, errors in letter formation are eliminated.

The letters *e, a, r* and *t* cause the most confusion. Such combinations as *be, bi, br, by, bo, oe, oi, os, oc, oa, ve, va, vo, vu, we, wi, wa, ws* and *wr* also cause trouble. The demons of handwriting are: *a* that looks like *o, u,* or *ci; l* that becomes *li; d* that appears as *cl; e* like *i* or the reverse; *m* and *n* like *w* and *u; t* like *l* or *i;* and *r* like *e* or *n.*

Some writing habits must be changed to increase legibility. Children who write *gt, ot,* or *ju* with short connecting strokes should be told to "swing between each letter," or "spread your letters out like an accordion." At first the distance should be exaggerated, then modified to proper spacing. If a child continues to write all letters close together, let him practice his spelling words on a regular sheet of ruled tablet paper but with the lines vertical rather than horizontal. There should be one letter between each line.

Speed is the great enemy of legibility. We can think as fast as 250 words a minute and write about twenty-five. This is one reason why all writing must be reread to correct errors.

If a child persists in poor writing, it may reflect an emotional problem. In such cases it is wise to forget about handwriting instructions until the basic problems of the child are cared for.

When the writing problem is due to a bad habit of holding the pen, the interesting and inexpensive plastic writing frame available from Zaner-Bloser may prove helpful. This device positions the writing instrument and aids the necessary retraining.

The basic cause of illegible handwriting is carelessness. The solution is, of course, to make handwriting so important that the learner will care enough to do it well.

1. How can a bulletin board be used to motivate good writing?
2. What should be the attitude of a teacher whose handwriting is not a good example for the children?
3. How can a "Good Writers' Club" or a "Pen Pal Club" motivate good handwriting?
4. Give arguments for and against awarding handwriting certificates.

WHAT PROVISIONS SHOULD BE MADE FOR THE LEFT-HANDED CHILD?

It is seldom very satisfying to be a member of a small minority or to be considered "different" from other people. The left-handed person faces both these problems. In our population the left-handed number from 4 to 11 per cent of the population. The range of these figures may be explained by the extent of tolerance of left-handedness in the segment of the population surveyed. Where no effort has been made to convert the left-handed individual to right-handed writing we have higher percentages than in those places subject to more pressure to change. (In a society where table manners, writing tools, and student desks conform to the assumption that everyone is right-handed, the left-handed individual certainly is at a disadvantage.)

To expect or require a left-handed person to become right-handed makes no more sense than expecting a right-handed person to develop left-handedness. There are many outstanding left-handed persons, ranging from Leonardo da Vinci to former President Harry S. Truman. The term "sinistral" used to describe a left-handed person comes from Latin and simply means left-handed. (Unfortunately, the term "sinister" is closely related and has an unpleasant connotation.) Sinistrals in school should have the same individual respect that we advocate for all children in a democracy.

Once we acknowledge the right of a child to write with his left hand, we then have the task of finding ways to help him do this task well. The usual ways that left-handedness is revealed is through the individual's activities. Observation of a child while using a pair of scissors, bouncing and catching a ball, putting marbles into a jar one at a time, eating with a spoon, or using a hammer and saw will reveal the dominant hand. If a child uses both hands with equal ease we say that he is ambidextrous. Because of the general convenience that it will provide, these children are taught to write with the right hand.

It is not easy to determine true dominance for some children. They may have a left-eye dominance and still be right-handed. Some children should be referred to trained clinicians to determine true dominance.

A number of simple tests have been suggested to help determine mixed dominance, left-eye preference with right-hand preference, or right-eye preference with left-hand preference. Cases of mixed dominance are evidenced in the problem some children have in keeping their paper in the "arm track." They seem to be maneuvering their paper constantly to try to keep it in place.

The preferred eye can be determined by having the pupil sight a coin on the floor through a cardboard cylinder held at arm's length. The coin is sighted with both eyes open. First one eye and then the other is covered as he looks at the coin. When the dominant eye is covered, the coin can no longer be seen through the cylinder.

A more elaborate device to determine motor-visual preference and to stimulate the development of controlled vision in the eye on the same side of the body as that of the dominant hand is the Leavill Hand-Eye Coordinator produced by the Keystone View Company, Meadville, Pa.

At one time it was felt that forcing children to change from left- to right-handedness would cause stuttering and other psychological tensions. Some experiments seem to indicate that it is not so much the change as the way the change is directed. While there is no clear-cut evidence that cerebral nerve damage does take place when a child's natural handedness is tampered with, there is equally little evidence that it does not. As teachers we must ask ourselves this question: Is right-handed writing so important that we are willing to risk creating speech trouble, neuroses, or other evidence of emotional disturbance? The answer is usually "no."

Some of the difficulties faced by the left-handed person learning to write a system devised by right-handed individuals can be experienced by a right-handed person who attempts a few left-handed exercises. Draw a series of squares, first with the right hand and then with the left. Note that the "pull strokes" with the right hand are "pushing strokes" with the left. These strokes involve different muscles according to the hand used. Then observe a right-handed individual writing. He starts at a mid-body position and writes in a natural left-to-right movement, away from the body. An attempt to imitate this will reveal why a left-handed child copying a right-handed teacher will write moving away from his mid-body position toward his natural direction, or right to left. The result is mirror writing—which is completely legible to the writer but can be read by the rest of us only when held up to a mirror. Correction is the result of explaining to the child that he must conform to the left-to-right pattern so that others can read what he writes. Have him copy individual words and letters, always starting at the left side of the paper. This will take considerable time because he is being asked to learn to write words that seem "backwards" to him. Eventually, as these children master reading, the problem disappears. Sometimes it is wise to postpone writing instruction temporarily until reading is well established.

Another result of imitating right-hand writing is that the child develops an awkward writing position. In order to hold a pencil or pen in exactly the way a right-handed person does, a left-handed child may twist his hand around to a backward or upside-down position. Some actually write upside down.

It is very difficult to help these children once such awkward writing positions are well established. The first requirement is that both the child and his parents want to correct it. Without this desire the results of any teaching effort will be limited. For the child it is almost a punishment. Some will write quite well in the "backward" position, but for many it will mean uncomfortable writing for a lifetime.

Start by adjusting the position of the paper and arm. Place two tape markers on the desk or writing table. Have the child rest his left arm between these two tapes. This will prevent the arm from swinging out. Another tape can be used to indicate the proper position for the paper. Provide a long pencil or ballpoint pen as the writing instrument. Have the child hold this about an inch and a half from the point. The first exercises should be tracing over letters and words written by a left-handed individual. A considerable amount of writing should be done at the chalkboard; it is practically impossible to use the upside-down position there. The teacher might guide the hand movements to assure the correct response. These children should have a card of letters written by a left-handed person for personal reference at their desks. If the child who has reached the fifth grade is using an awkward position, it is sometimes best to let him continue. Urge instead that he learn to use the typewriter as soon as possible. Some school systems have special summer classes in typing for such left-handed children. Here the left-handed have an advantage over right-handed people; the standard typewriter keyboard was designed by a left-handed person.

There is little experimental evidence to guide a teacher in developing a writing program for the left-handed child. Teachers with experience suggest the following procedures.

Group the left-handed together. This makes it easier to supervise instruction and prevents a tendency to imitate right-handed individuals.

Begin instruction at the chalkboard where close supervision can be given. An error caught early can prevent the formation of a bad habit. Stress left-to-right movement and the starting place when writing each letter. Circles should be made from left to right in manuscript, even though this may seem awkward at first.

When the left-handed child starts writing on paper, it may be wise to have him place an arrow as a "traffic signal" at the beginning of his writing to assure the teacher that he is starting at the correct place and proceeding in the correct left-to-right direction. A left-handed child may be a good helper to another left hander.

The child learning to write manuscript with his left hand places the paper directly in front of him just as the right-handed individual does. It will be necessary for him to move the paper frequently as he writes; this is the task of the right hand. Accordingly the writer should be seated at the left-hand side of a table—or alone at an individual desk rather than sharing a table with a right-handed child. Once these first steps have been mastered, the left-handed child should continue writing print script throughout the grades. Otherwise, he should be started on cursive immediately. Why should he be required to learn two different systems developed for right-handed people?

The natural arc of the left hand as it rests on the desk should determine the position of the paper for cursive writing. The upper right corner of the paper will be in line with the centerline of the body. Children can be told that the bottom corner should point "toward their heart." In shifting the paper the right hand presses down on it, holding it firmly until one line is finished, and then moves it up for the next line. The left hand slides lightly along the line of writing while the paper is kept stationary.

The pen or pencil is held with the thumb, index, and middle fingers. It should slant toward the writer's left shoulder. The pen should be held a little higher than for a right-handed writer, so that the child can see what he writes and avoid running the left hand over the written material. Some teachers place a small rubber band around the pen to indicate where to grip the instrument.

A good ballpoint pen is a better writing instrument for the left-handed person than a pen with a steel nib. The ballpoint does not dig into the paper with the up-strokes, and the ink dries immediately. Avoid cheap ballpoints that are too short, or those that must be held in a tight grip because the sides are too smooth. A strip of adhesive tape on the barrel helps to keep a pen from slipping.

Copy for the left-handed writing exercises should be directly in front of the writer, not on the chalkboard. At first some children need to have their hands guided through the proper movements. If a single letter is reversed in any writing, take time to work on that letter alone.

Let the child determine his own letter slant after you have established the proper position of the paper for him. Most left-handed children seem to prefer a vertical form of writing. A few find a backhand more natural. Since our objective is legibility and ease of writing, slant should not be predetermined for the left-handed.

Special attention may need to be given to the letters O, T, F, and H to prevent the use of sinistral strokes. Since upward strokes are difficult for some left-handed writers, they may be eliminated on the letters a, c, d, g, o, q when they begin a word.

A complete set of writing exercises is available for left-handed children learning cursive writing. These exercises were written by Dr. Warren Gardner and are available from the Interstate Press, 19 North Jackson Street, Danville, Ill.

A special meeting with parents of left-handed children is of value. Stress at this meeting the normalness of being left-handed, the problems relating to changing handedness, and a demonstration of proper left-handed writing. The pamphlet, "For Lefties Only," published by the Handwriting Foundation, provides a good foundation for such a discussion.

With normal teaching effort the left-handed child will write as well as right-handed individuals. Many left-handed individuals resent as much discussion as provided here with respect to their writing. "What is the problem?" they ask. And we can truthfully answer, "For many left-handed individuals, there is no problem."

1. Luella B. Cole in her material concerning the left-handed child is opposed to the use of ballpoint pens for these children. Do you agree with her? Give reasons for your answer.

2. What advantages and disadvantages does a left-handed teacher have?

3. Would it be wise to have all left-handed children in the intermediate grades meet together for handwriting instruction?

Suggestions for Projects

1. Assemble enough samples from one classroom or school to construct a handwriting scale. This might be a scale for judging the manuscript writing of children in the third grade, the writing of left-handed individuals of the same age, or one for boys in the sixth grade.

2. Investigate the materials used in England to teach "italic" writing. That published by Ginn and Company (London) is widely used. Dillons University Book Store, 1 Mallet St., London, is another source of such materials.

3. Investigate the use of the typewriter by elementary school students. When is typing taught? How is the skill used by a child in the regular classroom? What special teaching programs are available?

4. Plan a display that will explain the handwriting program of your school to the public.

5. Make a comparison of the various handwriting programs now on the market. What are the essential differences with regard to philosophy, equipment, letter-formation drills, and special features?

6. Make a case study of an individual with a handwriting problem.

BIBLIOGRAPHY

BOOKS AND PAMPHLETS

Burgoyne, Philip A. *Cursive Handwriting.* Leicester, England: Dryad, 1955.

Cole, Luella. *A History of Education, Socrates to Montessori.* New York: Holt, 1950.

————. *Handwriting for Left-Handed Children.* Bloomington, Ill.: Public School Publishing Co., 1955.

Diringer, D. *The Alphabet.* New York: Philosophical, 1948.

Forrer, Jan. *Enseignement de l'écriture.* Geneva: Département d'Instruction Publique, 1956.

Freeman, Frank N. *What Research Says to the Teacher. No. 4—Teaching Handwriting.* Washington, D. C.: National Education Association, 1954.

Gardner, Warren H. *Left-Handed Writing Instruction Manual.* Danville, Ill.: Interstate, 1945.

Gillingham, A., and B. W. Slettman. *Remedial Training for Children with Specific Disability in Reading, Spelling and Penmanship.* New York: Sackett and Wilhelms, 1956.

Gourdie, Tom. *Italic Handwriting.* London: Studio, 1955.

Gray, W. S. *The Teaching of Reading and Writing.* UNESCO. Chicago: Scott, 1956.

Handwriting Committee. *Manuscript Writing in the Primary Grades.* Madison, Wis.: Madison Public Schools, 1951.

Herrick, Virgil, et al. *Handwriting in Wisconsin,* School of Education. Madison, Wis.: U. of Wisconsin, 1957.

Hunnicutt, C. W., and W. J. Iverson. *Research in the Three R's.* New York: Harper, 1958, Part 2, chap. 9.

Mercuse, Irene. *A Study of Children's Handwriting as a Guide to Emotionally Disturbed Children.* New York: Noble, 1957.

Rudland, Peter. *From Scribble to Script.* London: Allen and Unwin, 1955.

Tarr, John C. *Good Handwriting and How to Acquire It.* London: Phoenix, 1954.

West, Paul. *Better Handwriting.* New York: Barnes & Noble, 1958.

PERIODICALS

Anonymous. "Poor Penmanship Costs Money," *Nation's Business,* **43** (April 1955), 101.

Arnold, Esther. "The Transfer from Manuscript to Cursive Writing," *Elem. School Jour.* (April 1933), 616–620.

Capehart, B. E., and Maynard McNesh. "The Typewriter as an Educational Tool—What Research Says," *National Elementary Principal,* **38** (February 1959), 23–27.

Cole, L. W. "Reflections on the Teaching of Handwriting," *Elem. School Jour.* (November 1956), 95–99.

Sister Mary Elmira. "From Manuscript to Cursive Writing," *Catholic School Journal,* (January 1960), 29–30.

Freeman, Frank N. "An Evaluation of Manuscript Writing," *Elem. School Jour.* (February 1936).

————. "On Italic Handwriting," *Elem. School Jour.* (February 1960), 258–64.

Furness, E. S. "Diagnosis and Remediation of Handwriting Defects," *Elementary English,* (April 1955), 224–8.

Harrigan, Lewis B., and Grace Hildebrand. "Handwriting in the Primary Program," *National Elementary Principal,* **38** (February 1959), 8–12.

Hildreth, Gertrude. "Should Manuscript Writing be Continued in the Upper Grades?" *Elem. School Jour.* (October 1944), 85–93.

————. "Manuscript Writing After Sixty Years," *Elementary English* (January 1960), 3–13.

Irwin, Theodore. "Why Our Kids Can't Write," *Saturday Evening Post,* **228** (September 10, 1955), 24–28.

Kravitz, Ida. "The Philadelphia Handwriting Story," *National Elementary Principal* **38** (February 1959), 27–31.

Mellon, O. A. "Lesson Plan for Manuscript Practice," *Grade Teacher* (March 1950), 34.

Mock, R. "Ye Olde Italic." London: *Jour. of Educ.* (May 1956), 214.

O'Brien, R. "Moving Finger Writes but Who Can Read It?" *Saturday Review* (July 18, 1959), 8–10.

Perlson, P. "Board Writing Problems of New Teachers." *Education* (March 1960), 402–404.

Phelps, Grace. "Handwriting Today." *Parents Magazine,* **22** (March 1947).

Rosenhaus, Max. "You Can Teach Handwriting with Six Rules." *Instructor,* (March 1957), 60–66.

Stauffer, Russell G. "Research in Spelling and Handwriting." *Rev. of Educ. Res.,* No. 2 (April 1949), 29.

Templin, Eloise. "Handwriting—The Neglected 'R." *Elementary English* (October 1960), 386–389.

CURRICULUM BULLETINS

Aberdeen Public Schools. *Handwriting*. Aberdeen, Wash., 1957.

Baltimore, Md., Public Schools. *Resources for Developing Functional Handwriting*.

Houston Public Schools. *Cursive Writing Handbook, Curriculum Bulletin* No. 58CBM23 (1958).

Leavett, J., and H. Johnson. *Curriculum Bulletin No. 124* (January 1956). Eugene, Oreg. School of Education, U. of Oregon, 1956.

Minneapolis Public Schools. *A Guide to Teaching Handwriting*. Minneapolis: 1956.

Philadelphia Public Schools. *Handwriting Suggestions*. Philadelphia: Curriculum Office, 1959.

SPECIAL AIDS

A clearing house for the exchange of letters from classroom to classroom is maintained by the Parker Pen Company in Janesville, Wis.

The W. A. Scheafer Pen Company at Fort Madison, Iowa, has a number of aids including "My Handwriting Quotient."

The Joseph Dixon Crucible Co., Handwriting Research Department, Jersey City 3, N. J., has a number of aids, including handwriting improvement certificates.

The Esterbrook Pen Company, Camden 1, N. J., has a special italic pen point for use with that form of writing.

HANDWRITING TEXTBOOKS PROGRAMS

Each of these programs has teacher's manuals, special evaluation devices such as plastic overlays or standardized scales. Each company will send information describing its programs upon inquiry.

Billington, Lillian E., and E. H. Staffelback. *Our Handwriting Series*. San Francisco: Harr Wagner, 1957.

Boone, L. P., and George Spache. *Writing Elements*. Birmingham, Ala.: Colonial, 1957.

Davidson, Ethelyn, and Rosa C. Veal. *The New I Learn to Write*. Indianapolis: Seale, 1961.

Dunn, Joseph, C. E. Strothers, J. W. Trusler, and Earnest A. Jones. *Legible Handwriting Series*. Chicago: Benefic, 1957.

Freeman, Frank N. *Guiding Growth in Handwriting*. Columbus: Zaner-Bloser, 1959.

Hackman, I. Z. *Hackman's Coordinated Manuscript-Cursive*. Elizabethtown, Pa.: I. Z. Hackman, 1960.

Haines, N. and N. Vashte. *It's Fun to Write*. Wichita, Kans.: McCormick-Mathers, 1951.

Kettles Penmanship Series. Chicago: American, 1956.

Lewry, Marion E., Avis Herbert, and Oscar Miller. *Noble's Handwriting for Everyday Use*. New York: Noble, 1957.

Monroe, M., et al. *We Talk, Write, and Spell*. Chicago: Scott, 1961.

Norwick, Terese D. *Now I Learn to Write*. Indianapolis: Seale, 1961.

Palmer Method for Better Writing. Chicago: Palmer, 1957.

Stone, Ala, and Ethel Smalley. *Manuscript and Cursive Basic Handwriting*. New York: Scribner, 1952.

Townsend, R. *Imaginary Line Handwriting Series*. Austin, Tex.: Streck, 1953.

A total of nineteen programs are carefully analyzed in *Comparison of Practices in Handwriting* by Virgil Herrick et al. (Madison, Wis.: U. of Wisconsin Press, 1960).

Chapter 4

Phonics

WHAT IS THE PLACE OF PHONICS IN THE LANGUAGE ARTS PROGRAM?

If our language were as phonetic as Italian or Finnish, the teaching of phonics would be quite simple. In those countries many schools do not need a speller. The language is so pure phonetically that if an individual can say the word and knows the letters for the sounds in the word, he can pronounce or spell it. Each letter has only one sound and each sound is represented always by one letter.

Phonetics and phonics are terms which are often confused in meaning. Phonetics is the science of speech sounds in actual use. Phonics is the application of phonetics in the teaching of reading and spelling. The phonetic symbol in speech for the _s_ sound would be the same in all these words: bu_s_, ki_ss_, _sc_ene, va_s_e, fa_c_e, _ps_alm, li_s_ten, _sch_ism, _s_ix, an_s_wer, _c_ity. Yet in the use of phonics a child must remember that the sound is made by different letter combinations. The sound element is called a phoneme. In the words listed above the sound _s_ is a phoneme.

There are forty-two sounds frequently used in the words we speak. Twenty-four of these sounds are consonants; eighteen of these come in pairs. A true consonant can be pronounced only in a whisper; as soon as it is voiced, a vowel sound has been added.

_p_ and _b_	as in _pet_ and _bad_
_t_ and _d_	as in _tan_ and _do_
_k_ and _g_	as in _kite_ and _go_
_f_ and _v_	as in _folder_ and _visit_
_s_ and _z_	as in _say_ and _zip_
_th_ voiced	as in _they_
_th_ voiceless	as in _think_
_wh_ and _w_	as in _whistle_ and _way_
_ch_ and _j_	as in _church_ and _jam_
_sh_ and _zh_	as in _shoe_ and treasure

There are five other consonants that are usually voiced:

_l_	as in _lull_
_m_	as in _man_
_n_	as in _none_
_r_	as in _roar_
_y_	as in _you_

The twenty-fourth sound is a voiceless consonant:

_h_	as in _his_ and _hers_ (voiceless because it takes the position of the following vowel)

128

The other eighteen vowel sounds are:

Five short
vowel sounds: *at, pet, if, doll, up*
Five long
vowel sounds: *ate, be, ice, no, use*

There are combinations of two sounds (diphthongs) and each have two spellings: *au* as in *auto* and *saw*, *ow* as in *our* and *cow*, *oi* as in *oil* and *boy*.

Two more are the "hard" and "soft" *oo*:

oo (hard) as in *food, rude*
oo (soft) as in *good* and *bush*

Two different sounds combine with the r:

air   as in *pair, heir, rare, tear*
er   as in *her, learn, sir, worse, fur*

One vowel sound, the *ah*, stands alone:

ah   as in *pa, ma*

Also to consider are the all-purpose vowel sounds which are represented by the schwa in some school dictionaries:

a   as in *drama*
e   as in *item*
i   as in *devil*
o   as in *button*
u   as in *circus*

The long vowel sounds have different spellings:

ai   as in *paid*
ie   as in *pie*
ow   as in *row*
ay   as in *day*
y   as in *sky*
ew   as in *sew*
ee   as in *sleep*
oa   as in *boat*
ue   as in *hue*
ea   as in *eat*
oe   as in *toe*

The consonants *l, m, n, ng, r, w* and *y* closely resemble vowels and have sometimes been considered vowels, since they can all be made with no other audible sound than unobstructed voice. *W* and *y* are consonant before a vowel as in *wall* or *yard* but as vowels in words like *cow, say* and *lonely*.

One point must be understood from the beginning of any discussion of phonics. Communication involves an exchange of meaning. It is quite possible for a child to learn to sound out the letters of a word like *d-a-w-k-i-n*, but unless the sounder then associates the word with its meaning (stupid) he is not reading. Similarly the child may spell a word without meaning. In such a case all that he has done is written a design with letters of the alphabet. Although phonic skills can be used in such meaningless ways, it does not follow that they are valueless skills. Indeed, the skill to use the sounds of our language as it is written, combined with a demand for meaning, is basic to both reading and spelling.

Phonics instruction starts in the area of speech. With immature children, any speech fault such as the confusion of sounds in some words as *wed* for *red* when the child does say the *r* sound in *road* correctly, requires corrective instruction. With older children, careless habits of pronunciation such as "gimme" for give me, "negstor" for next door, or "put nearly" for pretty nearly, must be corrected before phonics knowledge can function in spelling. In addition to these corrective measures, the child must be helped to identify individual letter sounds in different positions of the word. It is not necessary for a child to be able to pronounce all the sounds of the language before he can start learning the symbols of the sounds he does make correctly.

The teacher must understand how this knowledge will be used before attempting to teach sound and letter association to children. In reading, children use phonics to do these major reading tasks:

1. To identify the initial sound of a word.
2. To divide a word into syllables in pronunciation.
3. To check a guess when a strange word is identified from context.
4. To identify prefixes and common endings.
5. To identify the word root.

In spelling the child uses phonics to accomplish these results:

1. To identify the letter symbols of the sounds he hears in a word.
2. To interpret the pronunciation key in the dictionary.
3. To interpret the phonetic respelling of words used in some dictionaries.
4. To divide a word into syllables as the word is written.

Since the words must first be written in order to be read, let us consider some of the problems related to the use of phonics in spelling. The first and most serious one is that we have so many phonetic inconsistencies in the way our language is written. Ernest Horn analyzed the word circumference by syllables and by letter in order to determine the possibilities for spelling the word by sound. He discovered 288 possible combinations when the word is broken by syllables and 396,-900,000 possible combinations when each letter is analyzed. In summarizing this study, Horn states: [1]

It is no wonder that a few months after a word has been temporarily learned in a spelling lesson, and subsequently used only occasionally in writing, the child is sometimes confused by the conflicting elements which his pronunciation of the word may call out of his past experience. With so little of the rational character to guide him the wonder is that the child fixes as easily as he does upon the one arbitrary combination which constitutes the correct spelling.

This point can be illustrated in its most extreme form by spelling *potato* as "gh-ough-pt-eigh-bt-eau" by using these sounds: *gh* in hiccough, *ough* in though, *pt* in ptomaine, *eigh* in weigh, *bt* in debt, *eau* in beau.

Everyone knows the uncertainty of the English graphic form *ough* in such words as *though, through, plough, cough, hiccough, rough.* Only slightly less troublesome to the learner are such ambiguities as:

doll:roll, home:come, sword:word, few:sew, break:squeak, paid:plaid.

When the child meets the letter a in a word, it may have one of these sounds: *all, allow, nation, want;* e is different in *legend, legal;* i in *fin* and *final;* o in *pot, post, come;* u in *cub, cubic;* y in *cyst* and *tyrant.* The combinations of vowels are still more perplexing: ea has such variations as clean, bread, hearth; ei in receive, in addition to being a variety for ie in siege, has a different sound in neigh, weight and still another in height. The o combinations give forms like: *blood:bloom, cow:crow, shout:should, shoulder:though, thought:rough, couple:court, cough:enough, plough:rough.* Final e is generally mute and is supposed to affect the preceding vowel as in *van, vane; rob, robe;* but in *change* and *sleeve* it has no effect and there is a series—*come, dove, love, some, have*—in which the vowel is shortened rather than lengthened.

In our writing of the language, the letter a has forty-seven different sound associates. There are 300 different combinations which express the seventeen vowel sounds.

The short i sound is especially difficult. It is spelled at least fifteen ways in common words and only in a little more than half the time with the letter i alone. Examples are i (*bit*), e, y (*pretty*), ie (*mischief*), ui (*build*), ey (*money*), a (*character*) ay (*Monday*), us (*busy*), ee (*been*), ei (*foreign*), ia (*marriage*), o (*women*), and ea (*forehead*). There are other spellings in less common words. In these words one would expect the long vowel sound: furnace, mountain, favorite, minute, and coffee.

Another sound, the schwa (ə), is found in half of the multisyllabic words in the ten thousand commonest words. It is spelled 30 ways with almost any vowel or vowel digraph: about, taken, pencil, lemon, circus, teacher, picture, dollar, nation. While the use of the schwa may simplify the pronunciation of the unstressed syllables, the implication for spelling is quite different.

Good auditory perception and careful listening habits are a part of spelling study procedure. If children use common pronunciation as a guide for spelling they

---

[1] Ernest Horn, "Phonics and Spelling," *Journal of Education,* May 1954. See also E. Betts, "Phonics: Practical Considerations Based on Research," *Elementary English,* October 1956.

face many difficulties. If the pronunciation of a word is somewhat blurred in reading, the sound is still near enough to carry the meaning. In spelling the word must be exact. Any word with a schwa calls for careful visual discrimination in order to learn the pattern used to spell the sound.

Silent letters are especially perplexing in spelling. If one includes letters not pronounced in digraphs as in please or boat and double letters where only one is pronounced, nearly all letters of the alphabet are silent in some words. In reading we can call them ghosts or use them to identify words that may be confused with others, but in spelling, all these silent letters must be remembered. There is no phonetic clue to their presence in a word.

But it is wrong to conclude that no phonetic aids exist in the spelling of the language. An analysis of the 3,381 monosyllables in our language and the separate syllables of 2,396 polysyllables in words from the Jones spelling list shows that the English language is 86.9 per cent phonetic. James T. Moore reports that our system of writing is basically alphabetic and that for almost every sound there is a highly regular spelling. He states: [2]

Eighty per cent of all the speech sounds contained in words used by elementary school children were spelled regularly. Single consonants are represented by regular spellings about 90 per cent of the time.

The vowel sounds cause the most spelling difficulty but even here the short _a_ is spelled with an _a_ about 99 per cent of the time as is the short _i_ at the beginning of a word. Short _e_ is spelled with an _e_ about 89 per cent of the time, short _o_ with an _o_ 92 per cent, and short _u_ with the letter _u_ 72 per cent of the time.

The long vowel sounds cause much more trouble in spelling than short vowel sounds. All the long vowels may be written in a variety of ways.

Other studies have indicated that some of the frequently used words of our language do have phonetic consistency.[3] Of

the first thousand words on the Rinsland spelling list we find the sound _a_ is spelled as follows, the figures in parenthesis representing percentages:

a = _able_(57)	ei = _reindeer_(3)
ay = _lay_(23)	ea = _break_(3)
ai = _laid_(13)	ey = _they_(1)

The sounds of the consonants are more consistent:

b = _bad_(100)	s = _sit_(67.3)
p = _pin_(100)	s = _city_(25.1)
j = _age_(58.4)	m = _me_(100)
j = _jump_(31.5)	t = _time_(99.8)
f = _fun_(85.3)	z = _his_(75.5)
f = _phone_(10.5)	l = _lit_(89.7)
d = _dog_(99.5)	l = _ball_(10.3)
r = _run_(100)	n = _no_(99.8)
k = _came_(60)	v = _vine_(99.4)
k = _keys_(15.9)	z = _zero_(17.4)

The letters that seem so consistent such as _b_, present spelling problems in words where it is silent as in _bomb_, _debt_, _doubt_, or _subtle_. The letter _d_ is silent in _handkerchief_, _handsome_, _Wednesday_, and in _soldier_ has a _j_ sound. _P_ is silent in _raspberry_, _receipt_, _cupboard_, _corps_ and in words like _psalm_, _pneumonia_, and _psychology_.

An analysis made by Sister Roberta Wolfe of spelling errors in a fifth grade indicated that 36.3 per cent were phonetic mistakes.[4] Vowel substitution formed 8.1 per cent; _sence_ for _since_, _togather_ for _together_, _eny_ for _any_, _lissen_ for _lesson_. Vowel omissions formed 6 per cent; _busness_ for _business_. Doubling or nondoubling caused 5 per cent; _currant_ for _current_, _refuell_ for _refuel_. Consonant substitution, endings, and diphthongs caused the remaining errors: _pance_ for _pants_, _feels_ for _fields_. Vowel and consonant insertions were not grouped with phonetic errors but are related; _pagun_ for _pagan_, _leater_ for _later_, _stolden_ for _stolen_, _finely_ for _finally_.

Phonetic errors seem to indicate a need for emphasis on visual and auditory imagery, but it is apparent that there are

[2] Paul R. Hanna and James T. Moore, Jr., "Spelling—From Spoken Word to Written Symbol," _Elementary School Journal_, February 1953; republished as a pamphlet by Houghton Mifflin Company, Boston.

[3] Unpublished study by R. Madden, San Diego State College, San Diego, Calif.

[4] Sr. Roberta Wolfe "A Study of Spelling Errors," _Elementary School Journal_, April 1952.

elements of unreasonableness in the way our language is spelled.

It would only confuse the child more if this problem were presented to him as he started to learn to spell, but as teachers we need to understand the phonetic complexity of the task we seek to have mastered.

Spelling permits a word to be separated into its various letters and sounds much more easily than ordinary reading because there is no problem of meaning involved. If a child has the word in his language and desires to write it down, it must be done letter by letter, sound by sound. When the beginner writes about his birthday cake and spells it *kake* or *kacke*, we know the sounds he is expressing. This is a great step forward in written communication. The next step is to modify his choice of symbols for the sounds, simply as a matter of social convention. It is important for the child to know that he is phonetically correct. The modification is a relatively simple one. Wide reading of the word in its conventional form, combined with an awareness of the error, will usually be enough.

The phonics problem in reading is that of changing printed letters to sound and then giving meaning to that combination of sounds which makes a word. Without a meaning clue this process is difficult; if the word is completely unknown to the child it is almost impossible. Simple words like *adage* and *adobe*, *table* and *tablet*, or *tamable* and *tamale* require distinctions of pronunciation that are not easily discoverable by phonetic analyses.

On the market today there are programs which teach sounds independently and then apply them to words. Some start with vowels, others with consonants, and still others with consonant-vowel combinations such as *fe, fi, fo, fu*. When this material is well taught, children memorize many of the sounds and alphabet letter associations of our language.

In application of the sounds, this material usually ignores the many nonphonetic words which are common in our language, such as *was, been, have, come,* and *you* and does use those that can be built phonetically, such as *gun, sun, fin, mold, ill, dill,* and *kill,* which are not very useful in the reading material of the primary grades.

A more serious problem is that the skills learned do not apply to the analysis of longer words. The ability to sound *pat* simply does not apply to *patriot, pathetic,* and *patience.*

In the classroom one observes wrong teaching practices concerning phonics. Some teachers confuse visual similarity with sound similarity. Words like *grow, snow, low,* and *grown* are included with exercises on the *ow* sounds in *owl, cow,* and *clown.*

Finding little words in big words gives a sound clue less than half the time, yet teachers persist in telling children to look for the little word. There is no sound like *an* in thanks, *fat* in father, *is* in island, *of* in often, or *all* in shall. Finding the little word may give a false sound value as *bat* in *bathe, am* in *blame, doze* in *dozen,* and *row* in *trowel,* or prevent proper syllable identification as *am* in *among, even* in *eleven,* and *beg* in *began.* Finding the base or root word is quite another matter. Finding *father* in *fatherly* or *forget* in *unforgettable* is quite different from attempting to find *fat* in *father* or *table* in *unforgettable.* Take any page of material and note the little words in the big ones. In the previous sentence a child might find *an* (any), *age* (page), *at, ate, mat* (material), *an* (and), *no, not* (note), *he* (the), *it, lit* (little), *or* (words), *on* (ones). In none of these is the meaning of the small word a clue to the meaning of the large word. If a child considers *no* as a meaning, the meaning of the little words read into the larger word could create confusion or establish a habit of not seeking meaning.

An observation of a class in first and second grades will reveal that the teachers do a great deal of prompting with phonetic clues. Suppose the child is trying to read the word *mumps.* After getting the initial sound the teacher will say, "It rhymes with *jumps.*" With that help the child says the word. It should be noted that alone he would never have been able to provide the clue, "It rhymes with *jumps.*" If he could do that, he could have read the word. We do not know if such figuring out with teacher clues helps the child remember the word. Some evidence indicates that the beginning sound and meaning are all some children need. If they cannot identify the word, it should be told to them and be taught as a sight word along with some nonphonetic words as *laugh, each,* and most proper names or place-names.

Basic reading series differ considerably with respect to their use of phonic material. Some use any device that will work with specific new words as they are introduced. One new word will be remembered by the shape, another by the fact that it starts with the *m* sound, still another because it rhymes with a known word. Other programs attempt to teach patterns of attack that the child should use with each new word.

At present the following sequence of learning is commonly followed:

Kindergarten or Preparatory Period

Listening to and understanding oral language.

Recognizing names that begin alike.

Recognizing the beginning sound of a word.

Recognizing letters and word differences.

Matching letter and word forms.

Ability to express speech sounds and use language.

Grade One

Ability to hear and recognize in words the following single consonants in the initial position *b, c* (hard sound only), *d, f, g* (hard sound only), *h, j, l, m, n, p, r, s, t,* and *w.* Omit *k, v, x, y* and *z.*

Ability to hear and recognize in words the speech consonants *ch, sh, th* and *wh;* the consonant blends such as *sk, sm, sn, sp, st, sw, tw, br, bl, gl, pl, fr, tr* in initial positions.

Any one of the initial sound items may be introduced as soon as the pupil knows two or more words which begin with that item.

Grade Two

Introduce *v* and *y* in addition to reviewing the initial consonants presented in first grade and later present *q* and *k.*

Continue learning of blends *gr, fr, cr, dr, bl, cl, gl, sw, tw, scr* and *thr.*

Emphasize the short vowel sounds.

Introduce the long vowels (the terms *vowel, long* and *short* are used).

Teach the speech consonants in final position.

Introduce the vowel blends *ow, ou, oi, oy, ew, au, aw, oo.*

Teach the double vowels *ai, ea, oa, ee, ie, ay, oe.*

Grade Three

Maintain single consonants and consonant blends.

Silent letters in *kn, gh, wr.*

Variant consonant sounds *c, g, s, z, ed* and *t.*

Continue work on double vowels.

Influence of final *e.*

Vowels followed by *r.*

Prefixes *a-, be-,* and *un-.*

Suffixes *-y, -ly, -er, -est, -less, -ful, -en.*

Dividing words into syllables.

Alphabetizing.

Three-letter blends: *str.*

Contractions.

Grades Four, Five, and Six

Maintain all previously taught and add appropriate difficulties.

Prefixes *dis-, ex-, in-, out-, re-, trans-, un-.*

Suffixes *-eenth, -ese, -ical, -ion, -ous, -ship, -sun, -ty.*

Marking accent on words divided into syllables.

Using key words for pronunciation in dictionary.

Use diacritical marks.

The foregoing is only a suggestion of the placement of specific phonic elements. Each reading and spelling series presents a detailed program in the teacher's manuals for the primary grades.

1. Do you think spelling reform will ever be accepted in this country? What major forces would oppose such a step?
2. Does a child who knows how to read before starting to school need to be taught phonics?
3. Should a child who speaks a foreign language at home, and is learning English at school, be taught the same phonic skills as the other children?
4. What skills do you use to get the meaning of a foreign word in a book you are reading? Do you usually pronounce these words or do you "read around them?"

HOW ARE CHILDREN TAUGHT TO USE THE CONSONANT SOUNDS?

To use a consonant sound in reading requires the child to do two things. First he must identify the sound of the letter, then he must use that sound in combination with the other letters to make a word.

In order to identify the sound of *b*, this type of exercise or combination of them may be used. There are others used in workbooks and suggested in teacher's manuals.

1. The teacher says, "Listen to find in what way these words are alike: ball, bell, bent, bill, book. Yes, they all have the same sound at the beginning."
2. "Now look at these words while I say them: ball, box, beg. In what two ways are they alike? Yes, they sound alike at the beginning and start with the same letter. The letter is *b*."
3. "I am thinking of a girl in class whose name begins with B. Who is she?"
4. Here are some pictures of toys. Which one's start with the letter *b*? (ball, bed, bat, bus)"
5. "Listen while I say a sentence. Name the words that start with *b*. The big ball is baby's. Bobby will buy a book."
6. Put a marker on each picture that starts with *b*.

button	box	cane
cat	basket	book
banana	duck	bonnet

7. "I am thinking of something that is good to eat that starts with *b*. Can you name it?"
8. "Say Little Boy Blue and Baa Baa Black Sheep. When you hear a B hold up a finger."
9. Mark *b* on four letter cards. Do the same for some of the other letters. Put them all together. Show the letter *b*, have the children find others like it. Or place all letters that are like it in a row.
10. The teacher says, "I am thinking of a *b* word that rhymes with *fall, cone, maybe, cat*."

Once the sound is identified in words and associated with the letter, then the task is to substitute the sound into a word in a way that helps identify the word. This type of substitution exercise is widely used. The teacher reviews the sound. "You know these words on the board: *ball* and *big*. I have put a line under the new word in the sentence:

The apples are in the <u>box</u>.

With what letter does it start? Yes, it is a *b*. What sound does it have? What is the sentence talking about? What words do you know that will make sense that start with a *b*?"

Sometimes the substitution must be made in other parts of the word. "What letter does the new word start with in this sentence? Daddy has a new *job*. Yes, it is a *j*. What word do you know that would make sense? No, it is not *jet*. Look at the last letter in the new word. What sounds does it have? Does jet have the sound of *b* at the end? Can you think of a word that would make sense that starts the way jet does but has a *b* sound at the end?"

On the chalkboard:

Which words begin alike?

baby   dog
farm   barn
           look
           birth
           ball

On the reading chart:

Puff wanted to play.
"Mew, mew," she said
Puff wanted to sa
"Please play with m
She did not say th
She said "Mew, mew

Group phonics practice may be done with words drawn from the reading chart, the lesson in a reader, or as a result of needs noticed by the teacher in an individualized reading program.

Or the sentence may be *Mary has a red ribbon.* "No, the word is not raincoat. What letters are in the middle of the word? What words do you know that start with an r? Use that sound and the other words to read the new word."

Special practice in substitution should be done with exercises like this: "You know these words: *ball, big.* You also know these words: *get, look.* What new word do we make when we take away the g in *get* and put a b in its place? What new word do we make when we take away the l in *look* and put a b in its place?"

In order to construct this type of exercise follow these steps:

Start with words that contain the letter on which the children are to practice. In the above example start with *book* and *bet.* Then change them to words such as *look, took, cook* and *get, jet, let.* Select the one that is best known by the children. These words can be used in substitution exercises for the letters indicated:

c	not, ball, now, look
f	ball, box, can
l	dog, tip, not
n	cap, hot
p	will, not, get, can, big
w	bent, hill, lake
s	get, funny, no, Jack
t	Jack, ball, down, can, look
r	can, make, fun
j	will, big, may
k	will, sick, deep
wh	tip, kite
st	sand, make, may, jump, sick, keep
str	may, feet, like
sh	take, not, look, my, mine, make
bl	bed, show, came
pr	hide, mint
cr	sleep, show, back, thank, down, just
cl	down, hear, Dick
i	(short) but, better, fast, had, let, lamb, lock, pull
	(long) none, done, rope
e	(short) but, ball, band, follow, bunch, full, hold, not, sat, shall
ea	bad, but, fast, hit, not, sat
ee	but, choose, did, said, stop
a	(short) ten, pet, trick, dish, fun
a	(long) time, while
o	red, put, cut, let

o	mist, ride, wire
oo	feet, head
u	big, bad, cap, dog, hit, not, pop
oa	get, cut, bet
th	first, jump, tick
tr	may, got, cap, just, made, by
tw	dig, fine, girl

Another form of substitution exercise asks the child to choose between two words in a sentence.

Write the word live on the board. "Who can read this word? Tell me what happens to the word live when the first letter is changed." Write give under live. Have the new word pronounced. Then ask the children to select the proper word in these sentences:

John and Paul $\frac{give}{live}$ on High Street.

John will $\frac{give}{live}$ Paul a cake.

"Can you tell these new words that are made from words you know?" Write the words *dog, get, night,* and *cake* on the board. Substitute l for the first letter in each of these words. Follow this by having the children select the proper word in a sentence using these words.

Consonant blends present some difficulties. The major error to avoid is that of adding an extra vowel sound at the end of the blend. Clear would become "cul-ear," blue becomes "bul-oo," scream becomes "sker-eam" and stream becomes "struh-eam" or "stur-eam."

In presenting the consonant blends through many listening experiences, William S. Gray believes that there is an advantage in presenting all the possible blends involving an identical consonant letter in a group, as *bl, cl, fl, gl, pl* and *sl.* In this way children will become aware that the consonant l is often used as a blender. This is true as well of the letters r and s.[5]

In some words a trigraph, or three consonants blended together, can be sounded before the vowel sound, as in *scratch, stream, splash, sprint, scream.* At the end of words there are many possible combina-

[5] W. Gray, *On Your Own in Reading* (Chicago: Scott, 1961).

tions of two or more consonants which form blends in words such as *bulb, self, held, hard, large, earth, spark.*

To develop skill in attacking new words through the visual and auditory recognition of consonant blends, proceed as follows:

1. Write *bring* and *bread* on the chalkboard. Have the words pronounced and the letters *br* underlined in each word. Say: "Listen as I say *bring, bread* again. Do the letters *br* have one sound or two?" Call attention to the sound of *b* in *ball* and *r* in *ride*. "Let me hear both sounds when you say *bread, bring.*" Have several children in turn repeat the words.

"Listen as I read some sentences to hear other words that begin with the same two sounds as *bring*." Read the following sentences, pausing after each for a child to repeat the *br* words.

Throw the *broken branch* in the *brook.*
The *bridge* over the *brook* is not *broad.*

Write the following sentences on the chalkboard and have them read silently and orally. Help the group to identify *brook* by comparison with *bring* and *book.*

Bring this *book* to the *brook.*
Go *down* to the store and get some *brown bread.*

2. Use the method given in the preceding activity to develop recognition of the consonant blend *tr*. Use the known words *train, tree, truck* and the following sentences on the chalkboard:

Will you *try* to make my *train* go?
Dick can do a *trick* with his *truck.*

3. Provide each child with a pair of cards 1 × 4 inches on which has been written *br* or *tr*. Ask the children to listen as you pronounce the following word groups and to hold up the card that has the two letters with which all the words begin.

tr: traffic, trick, traveler, trip, tractor
br: break, brothers, breakfast, brook

Drill on consonants and blending can be done with a "word wheel." Two circles are cut from heavy paper or oak tag. One is larger than the other. The upper circle has a consonant or consonant blend aligned with a slot which exposes the remainder of the word on the other disk. As the top disk is revolved, the words are formed for the pupil to call. The *Webster Word Wheels*, published by Webster Publishing Company of St. Louis, Missouri, provide practice on fourteen common beginning blends. The *Phono Word Wheel* available from the Steck Company of Austin, Texas, provides a number of sets for different purposes. *Phonics Flip-its* is a variation of the "word wheel" available from Primary Playhouse, Sherwood, Oregon.

Picture dictionaries or student-made charts are helpful. The children may gather pictures, bring them to school, and paste them on the page in the dictionary where the appropriate beginning consonant sound is printed, or on the chart labeled with that consonant. This should be a group activity because children usually tire of making individual sound dictionaries.

An initial consonant game based on "word families" provides a check on a child's understanding. The student has a card on which an entire word is written or printed. Used with this card are a number of single-consonant cards which may be placed one at a time over the initial consonant to make another word. For example, if one used the word-card with the word *man* on it, the consonants *p, r, t, f, b, c,* and *v,* may be written on the smaller cards. By superimposing each small card on the first letter of *man,* the child may form the words *pan, ran, fan, ban, can,* and *van.* When not in use, the small cards may be clipped to the larger one.

Exercises in which the child writes an initial consonant to complete a word, and then says the word, give him the opportunity for *seeing, saying, hearing,* and *doing* activities. These are effective in all phonics work and are particularly good in corrective work. Such an exercise appears here:

Directions: Write the initial consonants indicated in each of these words. Then say the words.

m	*c*	*b*
_____ad	_____at	_____all
_____other	_____ome	_____ig
_____ud	_____old	_____oy
_____ay	_____up	_____ack
_____eat	_____ar	_____ox
_____op	_____all	_____ell
_____ill	_____ap	_____ut
_____it	_____an	_____ook

In studying individual consonant sounds, there are many word-card devices that can be used. A card is made so that the initial consonant shows only when the card is folded. When the card is unfolded, a key picture replaces the initial consonant. For example, with the word *cat*, when the card is not folded, the child sees the key picture of a cat and the element *at*; when it is folded, the *c* appears, making the word *cat*.

One of the card devices resembles the first one mentioned for use with initial single consonants. It differs only in that there is a consonant blend which may be superimposed on the initial letter of a *known* word to make a *new* word. For example, the known word may be *black*. On separate cards, the consonant teams *tr, st,* and *cr* are printed. By manipulating these cards, the child can make *track, stack,* and *crack.*

Children may easily make their own individual consonant key cards by using heavy folded paper. One side of the card contains the consonant. When the card is opened, the picture and key word appear. These cards serve as excellent helps when children are still learning the initial consonant sounds and need frequent help with them. On the back of the folded card a simple sentence is written to help the child to see the word in context.

There are some groups that need extra practice and explanation. It is for these children that the following "games" or activities were devised:

1. *Listening for the Beginning Sound*

Before the children know the letters or words, it is a part of their readiness preparation to hear the sound in parts of words. Many reading-readiness books do this with pictures. On some long strips of construction paper the teacher pastes five pictures. Four have the same initial sound —one is different. These are folded so there is a "book feeling" and some practice in looking at the pictures from left to right.

A bed	A leaf	A banana	A baby	A bear

The children say the words and answer the question, "Which one does not start with the same sound?" Some of the charts are designed to give practice in speech sounds such as the *th* or *wh*. Others enlarge the vocabulary of the children by using the pictures of tools, kitchen utensils and furniture, that are not in common use in some of the homes.

A special value of the device is that children can practice in pairs or alone. When a child works alone he stacks those he knows in one pile and those he does not know in another. For some exercises a star is placed on the back of the card to indicate the correct response so that the child may check his selection.

2. *Learning to Reconcile B, D and P*

When one teacher discovered that the manuscript letters *b, d* and *p* confused some

Phonic drill material may be used as an independent study activity while the teacher works with other children. Teachers make most of these games, although many are available from school-supply stores.

of the children, she drew upon the children's familiarity with the game of horseshoes. A stake was made of cardboard and backed with flannel or sandpaper so it would stick to the flannel board. A cardboard horseshoe about half as tall as the stake was made and prepared in the same way. By placing the horseshoe against the stake in different positions the letters *p, d* or *b* can be simulated. The game may be played for points. The leader may place the horseshoe and stake in any of the three positions and ask a child to give the sound, name of the letter, or a word that starts with that sound. Since the letter *p* looks like a ringer, its identification is worth two points, and *d* and *b* are leaners worth only one point. (This gives a little practice in counting or adding.)

3. *Sound Picture Cards*

After a child has the ability to hear the beginning sound, cards may be used to help him associate the sound with a letter. After the letter *b* is introduced the children locate pictures of words that start with that sound such as *box, boy, baby*. These are mounted with the letter. She is careful to get words in which the sound is not part of a blend. For example, the picture of a shoe would not be used for *s*. Instead words like *soap* or *sun* might be used. When the vowels are used, the pictures are limited to the short form since that will be of more help during the beginning period for reading. In time this can be arranged in alphabetical order. The children use the cards as a reference when practicing sounds on new words. To practice on the sounds themselves, the children look at the card, say the letter, pronounce the names of the pictures, then try to add a word from their language that starts with the same sound. This is a good partner- or small-group game in which one child shows the cards and each player is timed, keeping the card he successfully identifies. Later, the beginning and ending sounds may be matched. To start, put such letter combinations as b____d, s____l or c____l, and

have the children place the picture of a bird, seal or camel, in the proper blank.

4. *Word Families*

While this game is essentially a drill on the recognition of initial consonants, it also emphasizes some of the structural similarity of words. There are many variations. For the group the teacher arranges in a pocket chart some word-endings as the following:

-an	-ag	-as
-ab	-at	-am
-ax	-ad	-ap

Words that end with these parts are written on some cards. Such words as *can, man, pan, cab, tab, tax, wax, bag, lag, rag, hat, bat, cat, had, mad, sad, ham, jam, gas, tap, lap, map,* may be used. When a player draws a word he pronounces it and then puts it in the chart behind the word ending. Each card may count a point—some may count more than a point if they cause difficulty and need special attention.

5. *Desk Lotto*

This game is similar to the above except more endings are put on the large card usually emphasizing one vowel sound. The following is good for the long *a* sound. It is better for more advanced reading students.

-ame	-ale
-aid	-ake
-ase	-ate
-ane	-ail
	-ade
-ace	-ay
-ain	-are
-air	-age

Word-cards can be used but some are ready for the more complex skill of using only letter-cards and adding them to the ending to make a word. The children take turns drawing letters from a box. For example, a child may draw a letter *c*. He can add it to *-ame* to make *came*, *-are* to make *care*, *-ake* to make *cake*, etc. If he cannot make a word he puts his letter back and waits for another turn. One variation is to give each child the same number and kind of letter cards and see who can use all of them. While all letters do not lend themselves to these games, it should be noted that a child learns by identifying those letter sounds that do not make words as well as using those that do. Children can play this alone as a table game when the word endings are written on a large tag board and the child tries to cover each ending or square with a word-card. If a small group is playing, each player draws a word-card in turn and covers a square. The first to make a line of words, either horizontally, vertically or diagonally, wins.

While it is possible to put more than nine endings on a card, it is more manageable to have different tag boards and sets of word-cards. Then one group can exchange game sets with another or play different games if it is an individual activity. Other endings that might be used are:

-ill	-un	-in
-ome	-oy	-it
-eat	-en	-et
-ame	-ack	-all
-ake	-are	-and
-ade	-ar	-end

Word-cards would include:

fill, hill, come, some
beat, seat, fun, run
toy, boy, hen, men
tin, fin, sit, hit
get, net
came, same, bake, cake
made, wade, pack, rack
care, dare, far, car
ball, fall, wall, hand
sand, bend, lend

6. *Labeling*

Large letter-cards are used. A child draws a card from the stack such as *M* or *H*. He then must place the card on some-

thing in the room that starts with that sound. For *M* it might be *mirror, mitten, muffler, mouth, money*, or even *Mildred, Mary* or *Max*. This game permits some movement and also focuses the attention of the entire class on the sound while they watch to see if it is correctly placed.

A knowledge of the consonant sounds is one of the most helpful ways phonics can be used in reading. Teachers frequently ask the children to ignore the vowels but to use only the consonants in sounding a word. A sentence in which all vowel letters have been omitted can be read by most children. For example: Th_ m_ther w_s s_ h_pp_ t_ f_nd h_r ch_ld wh_ h_d b_ _n l_st th_t sh_ cr_ _d.

Simple tests can be made by the teacher to check the understanding of phonics by the children. The teacher might name five or ten objects and have the children write the letter that they hear as the beginning sound. Each child may have a set of pictures and identify objects named by the teacher.

1. George Bernard Shaw claimed he could spell *fish* in this way—"ghote." The *gh* has the sound as in *rough*. Can you think of the source of the other sounds?
2. Do you think that reading material written phonetically in dialect as the Joel Chandler Harris stories or some of the stories in quaint rural language, would help a child master the sounds of our language? What influence would it have on the child's spelling?
3. The dictionaries often respell a word phonetically as *gin* (jin), *ginger* (jinger), *plight* (plit), *people* (pepl). Why do they do this? Should the spelling lesson contain this aid?

7. *Matching Sounds*

Sets of cards are used on which the pictures of objects that start alike are shown. The following sets are examples:

As an individual game the child first mixes all the cards, then sorts them out, stacking the four that start with the same sound together. For a group game, six cards

boy	box	balloon	baby
dog	Daddy	donkey	doll
store	stove	stand	straw
monkey	moon	money	milk
house	hand	horse	hose
shoe	ship	sheep	shore
coat	can	candy	cane
fan	fig	fur	fox
rabbit	radio	radiator	refrigerator
pony	policeman	pan	pick
slide	sled	sleep	slipper
train	truck	trunk	track
wagon	waffle	watch	window
girl	gas	goat	gun

are given each player and six are placed face up on the table. A player may claim any card in the center by placing one of his cards that starts with the same sound on top of it. As the cards in the center are claimed, new ones are added. The child wins who first plays all of the cards in his possession. Only one card may be claimed at each turn. If the child cannot match one of the center cards he loses his turn.

HOW DO CHILDREN LEARN TO USE THE VOWEL SOUNDS?

The first step in use of vowels is obviously the ability to recognize *a, e, i, o,* and *u,* as being the letters that represent vowel sounds. As recognition is being mastered the children should also understand that when these letters make the same sound as their names we call them long vowels and put a straight line over them. The letters *a* and *I* are little words that children know. The *e* in *be* and *o* in *no* are long because we hear the letter names in them. The long *u* as in *use* (verb) and *Utah* is quite rare in the basic reading vocabulary.

One authority suggests the following pattern of instruction with respect to the short *a.*[6]

Step 1 (see)—Print *bad, can,* and *hat* on the board. "Here are three words we have learned to read. Look at the middle letter in each word. Do all these words have the same letter in the middle? What is that letter? Is it a vowel?"

[6] Paul McKee, *Come Along,* Teacher's Manual (Boston: Houghton, 1957).

Step 2 (hear)—"Now I am going to say six words. Listen for the sound you hear in the middle of each word. Say *map, bad, rag, can, last,* and *hat.*" (Slightly elongate but do not isolate the sound of the vowel *a.* Do not print these words or try to teach pupils to read them.) "Did all those words have the same sound in the middle?"

Step 3 (associate)—Point to the words on the board. "Let's all look at these three words and say them together. In what two ways are all three words alike?" (They all have the same letter and the same sound in the middle.) "That sound is the same as the sound we hear at the beginning of *and, am,* and *at.* It is one of the sounds that the vowel *a* very often has in a word. It is called the short *a* sound."

Step 4 (apply)—"We have now learned the short sound that the vowel *a* often has in words. Let's see if we can use that vowel and its short sound to decide what some new words are." (Print *but* on the board.)

"What is this word? Now watch while I take out the vowel *u* and put the vowel *a* in its place." (Erase the *u* and print *a* in its place to make *bat*.) "Who can tell us what this new word is?" (Follow the same procedure to change *cut* to *cat*, *him* to *ham*, *put* to *pat*, and *top* to *tap*.)

The short *e* is one of the most difficult phonetic elements a child is asked to master. Here is one way of presenting it:

(Print *men, bed, get, let, red,* and *neck* on the board.) "Let's look at these words and say them together." (Point to *men*.) "What is the vowel in this word?" (*e*.) "Do you hear the long *e* sound or the short *e* sound in *men*?" (The short *e* sound. Continue in the same way with the remaining five words.) "What did you notice about the *e* in each of these six words? (Each *e* has the short sound.) "When *e* is the only vowel in a word and it is followed by one or more letters, the *e* usually has the short sound.". . ."Let's use what we have learned about the short *e* sound to help us read some words that we may not know." (Print the following short sentences on the board:)

Ben had a pet dog named Shep.
Shep sat up to beg for his bones.
Ben put a bell in Shep's pen.
Shep could make Ben hear the bell
    when he wanted to be fed.

Then say: "In the sentences on the board, some words are underlined. Read the sentences to yourself. Use what you know about the short sound of *e* to help you decide what the underlined words are. Be sure the word you decide on makes sense in the sentence. Will you read the first sentence aloud? (Have two or more pupils read each sentence aloud. Then have one or two pupils read all four sentences aloud.)

Ea presents a special problem because it may be either long or short. Print the words *ready, head,* and *breakfast* on the board. "Let's look at these words and say them together. What two vowels are used together in these words?" (*ea*.) "Do you hear the long *e* sound or the short *e* sound in these words?" (The short *e* sound. Print *clean, cream,* and *read* on the board. Point to *clean*.) "What is this word?" (*clean*.) "Do you hear the short *e* sound or the long *e* sound in *clean*?" (The long *e* sound. Treat *cream* and *read* in the same way as *clean* was treated.) "The vowels *ea* usually stand for the long *e* sound. When you see the vowels *ea* in a word you don't know, try the long *e* sound first for those vowels. If that doesn't give a word you know, try the short *e* sound.

"Let's see whether we can use what we know about the sounds of the vowels *ea* to help us read some words that we may not know." (Print the following sentences on the board:)

Ann went to one store for some *beans,*
    some *bread,* and some *meat.*
She went to another store for some white
    thread.

Read the sentences on the board to yourself. Use what you have learned about the sounds that the vowels *ea* can stand for to help you decide what the underlined words are. "Will you read the first sentence aloud?" (Have two or three pupils read each sentence aloud.)

With upper-grade students the first step is to discover the nature and extent of the child's knowledge of vowels. Write four or more familiar words on the board and ask the students to identify a vowel sound that may appear in only one or two of them. For example, write on the board the words *cake, man, ran,* and *made*. Ask the child to say the words to himself. Then ask in which he hears the short form of the sound *a*. Below are listed some of the vowel elements and some suggested words that may be used in the exercise.

Short sound of	
a	cake, man, ran, made
e	bed, deep, feet, bread
i	give, light, mind, twin
o	lot, hop, joke, hope
u	jump, music, mumps, use

Long sound of	
a	late, band, mail, catch
e	fresh, green, neat, left
i	city, did, find, hide
o	both, toast, cloth, chop
u	puppy, puff, use, mule

There are some rules that will help a few children. Rather than ask them to remember these rules, it is wiser to place them for reference somewhere in the room. Of course, this is after they have been made meaningful.

variations of the vowels before he has the help of a dictionary.

Rule 2—When a word has only two vowels and one of them is *e* at the end of the word, the first vowel is usually long.

This is the old "silent *e*" rule. It is

This third-grade group continues to work on phonic understanding. This review of information concerning vowels which have been taught in lower grades is needed by many children.

Rule 1—If you do not know what sound to give to a vowel, try first the short sound. If you do not get a word that makes sense, try the long sound of the vowel.

This rule is most useful with the short words of our language and does have considerable consistency in books that follow a controlled vocabulary. There will be some vowels that will be neither long nor short. When the child discovers one, the teacher might explain this. There is no reason why the child needs to learn all the

least helpful when most needed. Such exceptions as gone, have, love, and come, are introduced early in primary reading. One teacher called this *e* "company that had come for a visit." Then she would say, "Once there was a little girl named Elizabeth but at school people called her Betty. But whenever her name was on a program or the minister came to visit, her friends called her Elizabeth. That is the way with some vowels. When they are alone they have one name but when they have company they have another." I suspect this satisfies the teacher more than the children, but it might help some who need a reason.

Rule 3—When a word has only one vowel and it is the last letter in the word, the vowel is usually long.

Such a rule would only help with the little words such as *me, be, go, no, so,* but there are also *to, ha, ma,* etc.

When a child does not recognize one of the vowel sounds, the same steps that were used in teaching the consonants may be followed. The *first step* is to help the child hear the sound. Print on the board the words: *an, and, am, at.* Say, "We know these four words. Let's say them together. Now listen while I say them again. What did you notice about the way these words begin? What other words do you know that begin with the same sound?" (With some vowels it is wise to use the medial position such as *bad, can, bat.* In this case the children are asked to note that the words sound alike in the middle. Other words they might recall are *had, ran, sat, fat, cat.*)

The *second step* is to see the letter and associate it with the sound heard.

The *third step* is to substitute the letter and sound to make new words. Use the words *fed, miss.* Substitute the *a* as heard in *an, am* to make *fad, mass.*

The following words may be used for this step:

long *a*	bone, hole, glide, woke
short *a*	bread, quick, fed, hitch
ai	boat, bread, get
aw	drown, flew, down
short *e*	beat, pack, flash, him
ee	boat, did, stood, had
long *i*	bend, spoke, race, grape
short *i*	bud, butter, fast, wet
long *o*	clever, grape, mile, sale
short *o*	bag, rid, map, left
long *u*	late, done, care, fame
short *u*	back, hill, dance, desk

Many combinations of two vowels are used to represent vowel sounds. Teachers often use a rule, "When two vowels go a-walking, the first one does the talking."

This is to help the child use a long *e* sound in words like meat and bead. Overdependence on this generalization can lead to mispronunciation of many words. A better warning might be, "When two vowels go a-walking, there's danger a-stalking."

The danger is that the two vowels are blended together in a diphthong or that two vowels may form a digraph in which one vowel sound is made. The last vowel rather than the first may be the sound made. Vowel combinations which form diphthongs are *oi* as in *boil, oy* as in *boy, ou* as in *mouse, ow* as in *crowd.* Two vowels together which make a digraph may have the sound of the first or the second vowel. *Ai* as in *mail* and *aisle, ea* as in *beam* and *steak, ie* as in *pie* or *believe, ui* as in *suit* or *guide.* The digraph may not present the long sound of either vowel as in *head, foot, fruit, canoe, would* and *could.*

A basic generalization that children need to make about vowels in both reading and spelling is that they have a variety of pronunciations but that outside of certain exceptions there are patterns of pronunciation and spelling that will help them.

The following activities (1 through 9) are practical for drill with vowel sounds.[7]

1. When introducing the long and short sound of vowels, write the word *dim* on the blackboard, and ask the children to tell you the word. Then add an *e* and ask the children to tell you the word. Do this with several words until the children notice that a final *e,* although silent, makes the long *i* sound. Divide the class into two groups. One group looks in books for words with short sounds. The other group finds words where the final *e* makes the other vowel long.

2. For a long-and-short-vowel game, collect pictures of objects with long and short vowel sounds as bell, shoe, cat, cone, and glass. Paste these on 3- × 5-in. cards

---

[7] Selma E. Herr, "Phonics Clinic," *The Instructor,* May 1957, pp. 35–39. (Available as a reprint.)

and place in a box. Paste a picture of a short-sound vowel word in the lid and one of a long-sound vowel word in the bottom. The children sort the cards and put them in the right places. Later use words instead of pictures. Provide a key for self-checking.

3. Play a detective game to find the silent letters. Prepare a list of words from reading or spelling lessons. The children circle the letters that are silent; *before, coat, high, blue, leaves.*

4. List several words on the black-board. The children rewrite them substi-tuting another vowel for the one given; *went, want; wish, wash; dish, dash,* and so forth.

5. Give the group a duplicated list of words. They add another vowel to make a new word; *mad, made, maid; led, lead; din, dine.*

6. Everyone numbers his paper. The teacher says, "I am going to say some words that have either a long or a short sound of *a* in them. When I say the word, write S on your paper beside the number of the word if the *a* has a short sound. Write an L if the word has a long *a* sound in it." Be sure that the words are short and, of course, familiar.

7. Eight words (*bow, brow, cow, how, now, plow, sow,* and *allow*) are the only words primary children need with the *ow* sound. They meet these words in which *ow* has the sound of long *o—blow, crow, flow, glow, grow, know, low, mow, row, show, slow, snow, throw, tow, sow,* and *below.* Once their meaning is clearly understood, have several activities to provide further study. Put them on flash cards and show. Have the children stand up if they have an *ow* sound, sit down if they have an *o* sound. (Notice that *bow* and *sow* are in both groups.)

8. Make separate flash cards for prac-tice on phonic irregularities. Have a bulle-tin board with pictures and words that have unexpected sounds. Let children pair off and show the cards to each other. For variation show them in the opaque projec-tor. Avoid words with many irregularities.

Duplicate a list of common words in-volving the hard and soft *c*. Read over the list with the group, then have the children write the words in two separate columns. Do the same with *g*.

9. Present *ar, er, ir,* and *ur* separately, rather than treating the vowels alone. Use groups of words such as *sir, were,* and *blur* to show that *ir, ur,* and *er* have the same sound. Point out that with *ar*, the *r* usually says its own name.

In spelling, the vowels cause a great deal of trouble. The short sound of *o* may be written by *a* as in *wander, watch, want, waddle, wallet, wallow, wan, wash.* The short sound of *i* may be written by such letter combinations as *women, build, scene, been,* and *pretty.* In unaccented syllables the short *i* is spelled in even greater variety as in *senate, mischief, lettuce, college, bushes, smallest.* The short sound of *u* is spelled with *ou* or *o* as in *done, son, couple.* The short *e* may be spelled by *ie* in *friend, ea* in *feather, bread, death; us* in *busy, an* in *many, any; ai* in *said; ay* in *says.* The long sound of *a* may be represented by *ea* in *break, steak; ey* in *obey, prey, grey; et* in *bouquet; au* in *gauge;* and *ei* in *veil.* Long *u* found with *y* as in *you, yule* and *yew,* and in other combinations in *view, few, cue, beauty, lieu, pew, feud, queue.* Some unusual ways of representing the long sound of *i* are found in *buy, aisle, choir* and *height.*

Homonyms represent a special prob-lem in spelling. The words are pronounced alike but spelled differently to reveal differ-ent meanings. *Too* appears on many "demon lists" for this reason. A few homo-nyms that deserve special attention are: *made-maid, sale-sail, tale-tail, break-brake, meet-meat, steal-steel, beat-beet, peel-peal.* All homonyms require special instruction to prevent error.

The following type of exercise is a good check on spelling and understanding of vowel variation. It would not be a good way to teach all these words if they were new to the student.

Spelling the Long ū Sound

Add u, ui, *or* ew

tr__e	gr____	d____
t__ne	s____t	t__be
bl____	__se	fl____
ch____	dr____	J__ne
c__pid	__nited	n____
d__ty	f____	fr____t
st__dent	r__le	m__le
bl__e	d__e	gl__e
__sing	st__pid	J__ly
cl____	st____	cr____

Spelling the Long ā Sound

Add an ā, ai *or* ay

c__me	br____n	l__te
d____	g____n	p__te
b____ke	t____l	m__ke
p____d	pl____	r__n
g____te	s__me	n____
p____	p____n	v__se
m____l	tr__n	c__ke
g__me	b__se	b____
ch__se	w____t	gr____
pr____	m__de	t__me

Spelling the Long O Sound

Add o, oa, oe, ow, ough

c____t	gr____n	gr____
wr__te	b____	b__ne
thr____t	g__	g__es
sl____	fl____t	g____t
al__ne	s__	thr____
t____	s____	bl__t
c__mb	wh____	st__ne
r____d	thr__ne	h____
r____	b____t	d_____
l____n	h__me	m____n

1. When a child sounds each letter of a word does it help him establish the total word sound? Try this on some of the common words of our language. Does spelling the word out loud provide any clues?

2. At one time books were written with a line drawn through the silent letters and the long and short vowels marked. What would be the advantages and disadvantages of such print in primary readers?

3. Notice a group of spelling errors made by a class in a test. How many errors were

phonetic errors? How many of these were because of the vowel sound?

4. These are words usually listed as spelling demons. What would you consider the cause of the difficulty in each word: ache, friend, business, separate, Wednesday, women, doctor, sugar, minute, once, forty.

5. Identify a common vowel sound in these words: *fur, fir, mother, cellar, myrrh, word, journal, search, cupboard, colonel, acre, avoirdupois, were.*

HOW ARE CHILDREN TAUGHT TO DIVIDE WORDS INTO SIGNIFICANT PARTS?

In the reading experiences of the third grade and beyond there are situations which require the ability to find the syllables in a word. Normally, while the child is in the fourth grade, he learns how to use the dictionary. In the development of such skills he learns how to find the pronunciation and meaning of new words. Teaching the child to find the syllables in a word earlier than that assumes that the child uses the word correctly in his language and that his concern is to change the printed form of the word back into his familiar language. The exercises listed below also assume that the student has already mastered the ability to associate a language sound with individual letters. It should be apparent to both the teacher and the child that the reason for dividing long words into syllables is to make the phonetic analysis easier.

With most of the short words of our language, a clue as to the beginning sound combined with the context is enough to discover the word used. In a similar manner, the first syllable provides a significant clue: Mary watered the gar_____. Many compound words involve a knowledge of language structure in addition to meaning. To read: "He was eat_____ candy," or "Mary had for_____ her money"; correct oral habits are essential.

The first understanding that will help the child is to develop the fact that usually the number of syllables in a word is the same as the number of vowel sounds. Print

a familiar word on the board such as *moment.* Ask a child to pronounce the word.[8] Then say, "Listen while I say the word again. Listen to decide how many parts it has." Explain that each part is called a syllable and print them separately. Do the same with such words as *behave, picnic, elephant, different, land.*

The second understanding that is helpful is that if two consonants come right after the first vowel in a word, the first syllable usually ends with the first of those consonants.

Print on the board such words as *window, carpet, important,* which the children already know in print. Again, divide the words orally and print the separate parts. Call attention to the fact that each part is a syllable. Then say, "What is the first vowel in window? How many consonants follow right after the *i?* With what letter does the first syllable end? That letter is the first of the two consonants that follow the first vowel in the word." (Repeat with the other words.) "Usually, when the first vowel of a word is followed by two consonants, the first syllable of that word ends with the first consonant."

"Now let's use what we have learned to find the first syllable in the following words." (*Dinner* and *mistake* are usually familiar words.)

------

[8] Paul McKee, *Bright Peaks* (Teacher's Manual). (Boston: Houghton, 1954), pp. 207–211.

"Next, let's see if we can use this rule to help us figure out some new words." (In the following sentences I have assumed that all the words are familiar to the child except the ones underlined.)

First read the sentence to get the meaning. Then use the rule to help find the sound of the first part of the strange word.

> There was a splash as an <u>alligator</u> slid off the bank.
> Tom did not know what the alligator <u>intended</u> to do.
> He had no <u>experience</u> with such animals.
> He decided that the <u>intelligent</u> thing to do was to leave, and he did.

The third understanding is the rule that if the first vowel in a word is followed by only one consonant, the first syllable may end either with the vowel or with the following consonant.

Use such words as *lemonade, tomorrow,* and *color.* Say the words, divide them into syllables and note the nature of the first syllable. Then say, "Here is a rule that may help you: When you need to find the first syllable in a word which has only one consonant that follows right after the first vowel, say the syllable as though it ended with the first vowel. If that syllable does not help you get the word, say the syllable as though it ended with the consonant that follows the vowel. Now let us see if the rule will help on some new words:

"In these sentences, the underlined words may be new to you. Read the sentences to yourself. When you come to an underlined word, use the meaning of the other words in the sentence, the first syllable, and other parts you know to help you decide what the word is."

> Jack lives in an <u>apartment</u> in the city.
> He has a job and is paid a <u>salary</u>.
> <u>Frequently</u> he has to work late.
> His job is a <u>peculiar</u> one.
> He washes dogs for a pet store on <u>Liberty</u> Street.

The fourth understanding is the result of noting common syllables in words. Use

such words as *attention* and *vacation.* Pronounce them, note the similar sound at the end, note the letters which represent the sound. Write the words in syllables and compare the final ones. Then print other words such as action, adoption, connection, construction, protection. Divide them into syllables and note the nature of *tion.*

A fifth understanding is that in words ending with a consonant and *le,* that consonant usually begins the last syllable. Examples would be *able* and *jungle.*

Of the 20,000 commonest words in English, 4,992 or 25 per cent have prefixes.[9] Fourteen prefixes make up 82 per cent of the total number. Some 4,043 words in the 20,000 have the prefixes *ab-* (from), *ad-* (to), *be-* (by), *com-* (with), *de-* (from), *dis-* (apart), *en-* (in), *ex-* (out), *in-* (into), *pre-* (before), *pro-* (in front of), *re-* (back), *sub-* (under), *un-* (not). Prefix meaning can best be taught with familiar root or base words.

Words like *subway, submarine,* and *suburban* are more interesting and easier to read and spell if the meaning of the prefix is noted.

Com- means with or together. Sometimes *com-* is changed to *con-* or *co-*. It is simple then to see why *compassion* means *pity; commotion* means *disturbance; cooperate,* to *act jointly;* and *copilot* means *assistant pilot.*

Dictionaries help by listing the prefix and its meaning separately. Of course, the words that follow this definition use the prefix so it is easy for children to make lists of words they know using the prefix.

Unless children have had instruction in the use of prefixes and suffixes, it is impossible for them to identify word roots or as some call them, the base word.

Some common suffixes are used to make nouns out of other words. Adjectives are made into nouns by adding *ness, ence, ance,* such as: *blackness, difference, resistance, attendance.* It is easy to change these words to nouns in this manner—*sad,*

---

[9] R. G. Stauffer, "Study of Prefixes in the Thorndike List to Establish a List of Prefixes That Should Be Taught in the Elementary School," *Journal of Education Research,* February 1942, pp. 453–458.

humane, kind, clever, distant, happy, soft, assure.

In spelling, the forming of plurals sometimes adds a syllable or alters the form of the base word. Children learn to read these forms before spelling them. Reading manuals present these as structural changes in the word. The same is true for various forms of a verb. The *-ing* and *-ed* ending are among the structural differences presented in the first grade.

The best approach in spelling is through the left-to-right progression stressed in all reading. The root word is the meaning clue for which the child is searching. Children soon understand that the meaning is modified by the addition of a suffix. The time (tense of verbs) is changed in *jump, jumped, jumping.* The number is changed in the plural forms: *horses, babies, knives.* Comparison of adjectives is indicated in *long, longer, longest,* and possession is indicated by an *'s* as in *Dick's.*

Sometimes the familiar root word changes in appearance and spelling. If the root word ends in a single consonant, that consonant may be doubled before the ending is added. The double consonant becomes a visual clue to pronunciation and meaning as in *hop, hopping, hopped; hot, hotter, hottest.* Another familiar visual clue is the effect of the silent final *e.* By examining words in a reader children can discover that the final *e* is dropped before the suffix is added. Children who know *bake* will have little trouble with *baking* in "Mary was baking some cookies." By learning the likenesses and differences between words that might be confused, children can note the importance of doubling the final consonant or dropping the final *e.* Words such as *hop, hopped,* and *hope, hoped;* or *scrap, scrapping; scrape, scraping,* will serve as examples.

The meaning clue is more difficult in words which end in *y.* After meeting such words as *fairy, fairies; carry, carries; fly, flies; cry, cries;* the generalization can be made that when base words end in *y,* the *y* may be changed to *i* before an ending or suffix is added. A collection of words will reveal that the consonant before the *y* influences when it is changed to *i.*

Ease in speech determines the pronunciation of some word patterns. The changing of *f* to *v* can be explained in the plural of knife and wolf simply by the fact that it sounds awkward to add the *s* for the plural to the *f* ending.

It should be noted that in reading a child seldom needs to divide a word into *all* of its syllables. However, in spelling this is not only required but is one of the ways a word is studied in order to remember its parts. It is not unreasonable to have intermediate grade children write their spelling lessons in syllables or to underline base or root meanings.

1. What meaning is implied in these suffixes: *-er, -est, -ly, -y, -ness, -less?* To help you, try to match them with the meaning of these words: *most, more, manner of, like, less, in that way* and *one who.*

2. What meaning is suggested by these suffixes: *-ate, -ic, -ant, -ment, -age, -able, -let, -ine, -ory?* (Look them up in a dictionary of suffixes.)

3. How do you recognize a compound word? Which compound words are in this list: *overshoe, biology, altogether, padlock, painless, pantry, parson, passport, seashore, season, sundown, target, toward, touchstone?*

Suggestions for Projects

1. Evaluate the phonics program in an intermediate-grade spelling book.
2. What place does the accent have in word-attack skills?
3. What are some of the words ordinarily taught in the first grade which do not lend themselves to phonetic attack?
4. Devise a group of games to help the child practice phonic skills.
5. Examine the reading series at the first grade level and note the extent of material on phonics.
6. Evaluate two of the series of phonics instructional materials.
7. Make a set of drill sheets to use in teaching phonetic elements in a specific grade.
8. Plan a set of individual games which might be used to teach phonetic elements.
9. Evaluate some of the film strips which present phonics lessons.

BIBLIOGRAPHY

BOOKS

Boyce, E. R. *Learning to Read*. London: Macmillan, 1956.

Gray, W. S. *On Their Own In Reading*. Chicago: Scott, 1960.

Herr, Selma. *Phonics Handbook for Teachers*. Los Angeles, Calif.: E. R. A. Publishers Inc., 1961.

Kottmeyer, William. *Teacher's Guide for Remedial Reading*. St. Louis, Mo.: Webster, 1959.

Russell, D. H., and Etta Karp. *Reading Aids through the Grades*. New York: Bureau of Publications, Columbia University, 1955.

CURRICULUM GUIDES

Anderson, Ind., Elementary Schools: *Phonics Guide*, Anderson, Ind., 1953.

Grand Rapids Board of Education: Grand Rapids, Mich., *Suggested Study Guide for the Language Arts*, K–6, 1960.

Shoreline Public Schools: *Phonics*, Seattle, 1955.

PERIODICALS

Agnew, Donald. "The Effects of Varied Amounts of Phonetic Training on Primary Reading," Duke University Research Studies in Education, No. 5. Durham, N.C.: Duke U. P., 1939. pp. 8–50

Betts, E. A. "Phonics: Practical Considerations Based on Research." *Elementary English,* October 1956. Reprint available from National Council of Teachers of English, 704 S. Sixth Street, Champaign, Ill.

Burrows, Alvina T. "What About Phonics." Bulletin No. 57 of the Association for Childhood Educational International, 1200 Fifteenth Street, N. W., Washington 5, D.C.

———. "The Conflict Over Phonics is Still Raging," *The Reading Teacher,* May 1953, pp. 12–17.

Dolch, E., and M. Bloomster. "Phonics Readiness," *Elementary School Journal,* November 1937, pp. 201–204.

Garrison, H. C., and H. T. Heard: "An Experimental Study of the Value of Phonics." Peabody *Journal of Education,* July 1931, pp. 9–14.

Hanna, P. R., and J. T. Moore. "Spelling—From Spoken Word to Written Symbol," *Elementary School Journal,* February 1953, pp. 329–337.

Horn, E. "Phonetics and Spelling," *Elementary School Journal,* May 1957, pp. 424–432.

Maney, Ethel. "The Reading Workshop—How to Get Children to Sound Out New Words They Meet in Reading." *Reading Teacher,* October 1953, pp. 42–46.

Pronovost, Wilbert. "Teaching Consonant Sounds in the Primary Grades," *Journal of Education,* May 1954.

Russell, David H. "A Diagnostic Study of Spelling Readiness." *Journal of Education Research,* December 1943, pp. 276–283.

Spache, George D. "Limitation of the Phonetic Approach to Developmental and Remedial Reading." (International Reading Association Proceedings.) *New Frontiers in Reading,* **5,** 1960, pp. 105–108.

Tate, Harry, Theresa Herbert, and Josephine Zeman. "Non Phonetic Primary Reading." *Elementary School Journal,* March 1940, pp. 529–537.

Witty, Paul. "Phonics Study and Word Analysis." *Elementary English* **30,** (May 1935), October 1953, Part II.

PHONICS PROGRAMS FOR STUDENTS

Armstrong, Loila, and Rowena Hargrave. *Building Reading Skills*. Wichita, Kan.: McCormick-Mathers, 1960.

Cooke, Dorothy E. *A to Z Phonics*. Darien, Conn.: Educational Pub. Corp., 1960.

Fillmore, Nadine. *Read More—Spell More*. Benton Harbor, Mich.: Sound Chart Educational Service, Inc., 1956.

Hay, Julie, and Charles E. Wingo. *Reading with Phonics*. Philadelphia: Lippincott, 1959.

Herr, Selma. *Improve Your Reading Through Phonics*. Los Angeles 7, Calif.: Educational Research Associates, 1961.

Kottmeyer, William. *Eye and Ear Fun*. St. Louis, Mo.: Webster, 1946.

McCrary, Mae, and Pearl Watts. *Phonics Skilltext*. Columbus, Ohio: Merrill, 1955.

Meighen, Mary, Marjorie Pratt, and Mabel Halvorson. *Phonics We Use*. Chicago: Lyons & Carnahan, 1959.

Scott, L. B. *Time for Phonics*. St. Louis, Mo.: Webster, 1962.

Sloop, Cornelia, Harrell Garrison and Mildred Creekmore. *Phonetic Keys to Reading*. Oklahoma City: Economy, 1960.

Thompson, L. M. *Happy Times with Sounds*. Boston: Allyn, 1960.

Chapter 5

Spelling

WHAT IS THE PLACE OF SPELLING IN THE LANGUAGE ARTS PROGRAM?

A person who wants to spell a word starts with a concept, or idea of a thing, which he wishes to express in writing, such as "pain" or "cake." The idea must be associated with its speech symbol, or word. After the word is selected, the speller thinks of the separate sounds in that word (or words). These sounds are identified with the letters of the alphabet which represent them. The next step requires the speller to reproduce those letters in the sequence that will spell the word in an approved form, so that the letters c-a-k-e rather than k-a-k, c-a-k or k-a-k-e are used, normally in their written form.

After one has mastered the spelling of a word, parts of this sequence are performed without conscious effort. If you learned to use the typewriter, you will recall how you progressed from a conscious effort involved in striking each letter to an automatic "cluster" of whole words and phrases. Similarly, the fluent writer expresses abstract ideas or involved concepts without having to grope for words letter by letter—and without resorting to the dictionary or thesaurus, except when an unusual word or its spelling eludes him.

It may help to clarify the steps in the spelling process to note that they are the opposite of the steps in the oral reading process. In reading, one starts by seeing the printed word. If the reader is not completely familiar with the word the letters are examined. These are associated with the sounds they represent in the oral *vocabulary* of the reader. This oral word is next connected with the meaning which it represents in the *experience* of the reader.

The process used to read and spell differs with individuals. The present analysis may not be descriptive of what *you* do. Some will use sound association much less than others, substituting visual associations. "Seeing" the word for spelling involves a problem that is not present in "seeing" the word for reading. In spelling, the word form must be supplemented by a clear impression of different letter elements in correct sequence. This impression requires not only a longer period of time to see the word for spelling than reading, but also better visual memory and discrimination.

Classroom practices involve spelling in all subjects throughout the school day.

Spelling activities which are a part of the reading program would include ability to:

Recognize the letters of the alphabet.

Hear and see parts of words and isolated letter sounds.

Hear and see similarities between words.

Pronounce words correctly.

Use the dictionary.

Identify the syllables in a word.

Use phonetic aids to pronounce a word.

Alphabetize words.

Listening skills which will influence spelling include a child's ability to:

Recognize related verb forms.

Recognize rhyme patterns.

Recognize meaningful words from nonsense sounds.

Associate emotional meanings based on word emphasis.

Supply unspoken parts of language to complete normal structural patterns.

Recognize common patterns of sentence structure.

Speech skills which also influence spelling would be the ability to:

Pronounce words accurately.

Enunciate properly.

Interpret the key in the dictionary.

Relate the sound of words to their spelling.

Note common sound substitutes, omissions, and distortions.

Writing skills which contribute to spelling proficiency include the ability to:

Write all letters legibly and with reasonable speed.

Select the most meaningful vocabulary to express the writer's ideas.

Report, summarize, and organize information in writing.

Proofread.

Write from dictation.

Express original ideas in letters, stories, and poems.

Use the skills of composition such as capitalization and punctuation as they apply to spelling.

There are three ways in which spelling textbooks are used. The larger cities favor a hard-bound book of one of the series recently published. They feel that this assures them of a modern word list, some purposeful activities, and a standard program throughout the system at a reasonable cost. Of equal popularity are workbooks which contain all of the material in the hard-bound book but also include space for the student to write the tests and exercises. Since these are consumed each year, the administrative costs are more expensive than a program using the hard-bound textbook. A third type of program is built on the words children need in writing at the time they wish to use them. Los Angeles, New York, and Portland (Oreg.) have modified this slightly by providing notebooks or personal workbooks which contain prescribed words in addition to those the children add as they use spelling in other written expression.

1. How may an awareness of the spelling process used by an individual help the teacher in giving remedial help?

2. What major difficulties does a primary child face when spelling a word that an older individual does not know?

3. Are there any words toward which you have any unpleasant feelings as a result of spelling difficulties?

4. Why would a child write "great" rather than "enormous" if too much emphasis were placed upon correct spelling in creative writing?

WHAT WORDS SHOULD A CHILD STUDY IN THE SPELLING PERIOD?

You should know how the words were selected for the book you are using. In the teacher's manual you will find a discussion of this with reference to some of the research studies done in the field of spelling.

Two highly significant studies are the basis for most spelling word lists. One

made by Ernest Horn of the University of
Iowa examined correspondence of business
firms to learn what words were most frequently used by adults.[1] The second was
a nationwide study of children's written
material directed by H. D. Rinsland of the
University of Oklahoma.[2]

In addition to these research efforts,
other scholars have examined the words most
frequently misspelled at each grade level,
words that are of frequent usage in both
adult and children's word lists, words common to reading lists, and words that contain special difficulties.

When a group of authors start to write
a spelling textbook, they consult all these
studies and make a list of their own that
reflects their personal philosophy as to what
should be done with respect to spelling
instruction. Those who feel that success
motivates students will usually have a
rather short list. Those who stress phonics
may include words that are not used very
often yet provide phonetics practice. Those
who feel that children learn to spell many
common words outside of school will emphasize the words in the language that
cause misspelling. Usually they include
about 4,000 words. A survey of twenty-four
of the most popular spelling textbook series
revealed that there were just short of
10,000 different words to be found in all
these texts.[3]

All studies reveal the interesting fact
that a few words of our language are used
over and over again. Over one-half of our
writing consists of a repetition of the following one hundred words:

a	and	baby	my
all	are	ball	name
am	at	be	not
		big	now
		boy	of
		but	on
		can	one
		Christmas	our
		come	out
		did	over
		do	play
		dog	pretty
		doll	put
		down	red
		eat	run
		for	said
		girl	saw
		go	school
		going	see
		good	she
		got	so
		had	some
		has	take
		have	that
		he	the
		her	then
		here	them
		him	there
		his	they
		home	this
		house	time
		how	to
		I	too
		I'm	tree
		in	two
		is	up
		it	want
		just	was
		know	we
		like	went
		little	what
		look	when
		made	will
		make	with
		man	would
		me	you
		mother	your

[1] Ernest Horn, *The Basic Writing Vo-cabulary* (Iowa City, Iowa: University of Iowa, 1927).
[2] H. D. Rinsland, *A Basic Writing Vo-cabulary of Elementary School Children* (New York: Macmillan, 1945).
[3] E. A. Betts, *Spelling Vocabulary Study: Grade Placement of Words in Seventeen Spellers* (New York: American, 1940), p. 143; *Grade Placement of Words in Eight Recent Spellers* (New York: American, 1949).

Horn noted that after the first thousand words the addition of the next 1,000
added a very small percentage of the words
used by writers.

TABLE I

Frequency of Word Usage in Percentages
of the Word Count Derived from
the Horn Basic Writing Vocabulary *

Different Words	Percentage of Total Word Count
100	58.83
500	82.05
1,000	89.61
1,500	93.24
2,000	95.38
2,500	96.76
3,000	97.66
3,500	98.30
4,000	98.73

* Reprinted by permission of E. Horn from the Twenty-third Yearbook of the National Society for the Study of Education.

A person who learns 2,800 words knows 97 per cent of the words in common use. If he learns the 1,200 words next in frequency he increases his writing vocabulary only 1.1 per cent or up to 98.3 of all the words he will write, which are found among the frequently used words of our language.

Henry D. Rinsland discovered similar facts, as illustrated in Table II.

TABLE II

Frequency of Word Usage in the Rinsland Vocabulary †

(*e.g.*, 10 words comprise about 25 per cent of all children's word usage.)

Different Words	Percentage of Total Word Count
25	36
50	40
100	60
200	71
300	76
500	82
1,000	89
1,500	93
2,000	95

† Reprinted by permission of Henry D. Rinsland and The Macmillan Company from *A Basic Vocabulary of Elementary School Children,* copyright 1945 by The Macmillan Company, New York.

Gertrude Hildreth explains,[4]

The richness of the English language results in infrequency of use for the majority of words. Beyond the short list of words learned in the elementary school years is a tremendous store of thousands of words from which people may wish to select. There are relatively few words used as frequently as *girl* or *get,* but a word such as *gigantic* can be matched by 5,000 other words that are used with about equal frequency in English writing. Ten thousand words is a conservative estimate of a person's life writing needs. It is practically certain what 2,500 of these words will be, but not the remaining 7,500. Some persons will use two or three times ten thousand words in a lifetime of writing.

Because of the differences which do exist in the thinking of those who write textbooks, the teachers who favor the third program where words are drawn from chil-dren's writing feel that the word list each child builds for himself is about as good as one built upon past research. The studies mentioned are old in terms of the generation now in school. Horn's was published in 1925 and Rinsland started his study in 1936. Teachers use a certain amount of judgment and guide the children, placing words of a temporary nature on a chart for reference as needed, without spelling mastery. Usually the school determines a basic list for each grade, and the teacher refers to it often enough to ascertain whether children are mastering the words in their notebooks. Rather than learning the list in order, the words are checked as they appear in writing.

A good list for teacher's use is the core vocabulary of the 350 most useful spelling words.[5]

Second Grade

all	ball	run				
dog	he	his	is			
big	doll	play	her	has		
after	box	way	saw			
baby	went	did	him	how		
car	ride	you	horse	like		
hand	head	man				
best	help	house	make	made	over	
eat	there	fire	got	I		
an	tree	from	bring	live	set	
letter	next	they	walk			
first	seen	ten	when			
well	name	will	been	does	goes	
dress	gave	now	some	milk		
table	rain	snow	food	ice	nice	take
cold	come	end	wanted			
what	glad	here	mother	our	dinner	
every	fish	five	home	three	too	
happy	have	little	most	new	store	put
as	blue	red	six	who	your	
if	more	much	took	than	said	
were	read	school	told	candy	game	
bad	could	kind	left	men	know	
about	sister	say	that	girl	let	long
away	but	by	please	far	into	

---

[4] G. Hildreth, *Teaching Spelling* (New York: Holt, 1955), p. 141.

[5] James A. Fitzgerald, *A Basic Life Spelling Vocabulary* (Milwaukee: Bruce, 1951).

Second Grade

came	other	would				
very	tell	smell	down	of	off	water
love	one	out	think	right		
again	back	boy	father	wish	once	
dear	each	egg	four	today	near	where
find	them	send				
any	good	last	lot	with	thing	why	sent	show
try	this	keep	or	black	brother	feet	just	soon
bed	time	room	daddy	night	story	write		

Third Grade

before			lesson		better	Easter	pair
buy	hope	use			Sunday	writing	
corn	good-by	I'm	town				
birthday		children	party		afternoon		April
around	these				clean	fourth	third
across	along				second	paper	
yesterday							
used							
coming	miss	train	which				
close	outside						
another	friend	swimming	Christmas		found	morning	
their	place	both	isn't	class	grade	lesson	sometime
may	Mr.	Mrs.	aunt	hurt	street	people	money
played	thank	upon	because	high	stayed		

Fourth Grade

answer	wash	brought	should	easy	getting	winter	spring
everybody		didn't	awhile	summer	together		never
cousin	Halloween		handkerchief		can't	fifth	Friday
o'clock	teacher	picture	sometimes		clothes	loving	something
bought	visit	always	anyway	quit	front	haven't	maybe
it's	quite	won't	hello				

Fifth Grade

remember	program	receive	enjoy	received		
Thanksgiving Day	address	written	hospital		I've	studying
interesting	jewel	already	all right			

Equal in importance to the problem of *what* words should be taught is the question of *when* a word should be taught. This problem might be emphasized by asking yourself, "At what grade level should the word *school* or *elephant* be taught?" Textbook authors have been guided by the answers to these two questions: "When do children want to use this word? How difficult is it to spell?"

It is a complex task to decide about the difficulty of a word. If we were to take a single word such as *elephant* and give it to ten children in each grade in school, we would learn that some children in each grade would spell it correctly and that others would misspell the word. If the following figures indicated those who spelled it correctly in each grade, we would have the beginning of a scale to measure how difficult the word is.

Grade	Number Spelling Word Correctly
2	2
3	4
4	7
5	9
6	9
7	10
8	10

On the basis of both need and possible error, it would seem that these students needed help on the word during the third and fourth grade. It may be that the word is too difficult for the second and would challenge no one in a seventh-grade class.

The first spelling scale was made in 1913. The most recent scale is the Iowa Spelling Scale by Harry A. Greene.[6]

The extent of the Iowa Spelling Scale indicates the amazing scope of modern research. Approximately 230,000 pupils in almost 8,800 classrooms in 645 different school systems were involved. Since each pupil undertook to spell one hundred words, a total of over 23 million spellings comprise the data for this scale. With respect to the words *elephant* and *school*

---

[6] Harry A. Greene, *The New Iowa Spelling Scale* (Iowa City, Iowa: Univ. of Iowa, 1955).

the scale provides the following information:

Per Cent of Class
Spelling Word Correctly

Grade	"elephant"	"school"
2	0	32
3	5	68
4	24	86
5	55	92
6	57	97
7	74	99
8	82	99

It is obvious from the above table that *school* is a much easier word than *elephant*. However, we still do not know how interested the child in your room is in using the word *elephant*. As a teacher you need a copy of this scale on your desk at all times to give you information about other words that grow out of classroom writing.

Although the Iowa Spelling Scale provides better information than we have had in the past concerning word difficulty, there will remain uncertainties about the grade placement of individual words. When we recognize that the linguistic maturity of each child differs, it is apparent that a formal graded list will be unrelated to the needs of certain children in a classroom.

The first lesson in a spelling textbook may be as difficult as the last. Thus if there are units designed for Halloween or Christmas, it is good judgment to skip to those units at the appropriate time. Similarly, the words in a fourth-grade speller may actually be more difficult for a specific child than those in a fifth-grade lesson. Individual needs cannot be met in spelling, as they often are in reading, by having a sixth-grade child use a fourth-grade book. Each spelling list must be examined and individual needs met by adjustment to the words to be studied.

1. Why do classroom teachers frequently favor a workbook in spelling? What advantages and what disadvantages exist in such a program?

2. Why is a word easy for one child and difficult for another in the same grade?

3. What words do you think will be in the adult needs of children now in school which are not included in the studies listed, such as *computer* and *transistor*.

4. How can you explain the frequent misspellings of such words as *going, Christmas, knew* and *hear*?

5. Since the basic list of one hundred words appears over and over again in the writing of children, do they need to be isolated for spelling instruction?

6. Think of the number of words you

spell correctly that were never in a spelling lesson. How did you learn to spell them?

7. Can you think of some words that would be used in the vocabulary of children in your locality that are not frequently used nationally?

8. Would it be necessary to put all the words in a spelling lesson that children want to use in a special report?

9. Can it be demonstrated that the words in the last lesson of the speller you use are more difficult than those in the first?

HOW SHOULD SPELLING BE TAUGHT?

We have noted the efforts that have been made to find *what* words should be taught, and *when* they should be taught. The problem of *how* words should be taught has been of equal concern. In 1897 J. M. Rice [7] suspected that the methods of spelling instruction were not very efficient. He conducted experiments which convinced many schools that they were spending too much time on the direct teaching of spelling. (To this day we have not been able to decide whether it is best to teach spelling in association with other school work or to have a specific period each day.) The amount of time spent in the spelling period has been reduced to about seventy-five minutes a week and the child who already knows the words is permitted to do something of greater value than learning to spell more words.

Ernest Horn demonstrated the efficiency of the test-study plan of organizing a week's work. In this plan, the students take a pretest of the weekly assignment the first day. This separates the words they know how to spell from those that need drill. Exercises and other activities to encourage writing of the words that were misspelled are used during the week; a final test of all the words is given at the end of the week. A chart of progress is kept by each student, words missed are added to the next week's lesson, and review lessons are given at intervals to assure a respelling of words studied.

A variation of the above is used under the *study-test* plans. In this program, fewer words are given each day but these words are known to be difficult for most of the class. There are daily tests as well as one at the end of the week on all words. The following plans for spelling instruction are typical of many school programs.

Plan A

First Day

1. Introduce the words in the new lesson in a meaningful way.
2. Discuss meanings of words.
3. Use words in sentences.
4. Note which words are phonetic.
5. Note likenesses to words previously learned.
6. Note any unusual spellings.
7. Form visual images and sequence of letters in each word.
8. Write the words.

Second Day

1. Use the words in a worksheet.
2. Do the exercises in the spelling book.
3. Write sentences using the words.
4. Write a story suggested by the words.

Third Day

1. Test and check words with the children.

---

[7] J. M. Rice, "The Futility of the Spelling Grind," *Forum* 23 (1897), pp. 169–172.

Fourth Day

1. Study the words missed on the test and words from individual card files.
2. Give additional words to children who have mastered the list by the third day. (This may be done earlier in the week.)
3. Teach additional words by making derivatives.
4. Work with individuals and small groups with special needs.

Fifth Day

1. Give the final test. It is advisable for each child to have a booklet in which to write the words.
2. Check the tests with each child.
3. Test children on additional words learned.

Plan B

In some cases, teachers may wish to (1) present the lesson on Monday, (2) test on Tuesday, giving additional words to children who need no further study on the regular lesson, (3) study the words and use them on Wednesday and Thursday, and (4) give the final test on Friday.

Plan C

Still another plan might be used with some groups. They might be given a pretest on Monday and then plan the following days according to the results of the test.

Tests can be made more interesting and valuable by variety in method. In addition to writing the words of the lesson, certain abilities may be tested. Among them are:

1. Circle or underline vowels in certain words.
2. Mark long or short vowels in certain words.
3. Select the words of more than one syllable.
4. Divide words into syllables and mark accents.
5. Write abbreviations of words.
6. Alphabetize the words.
7. Change all singular words to plurals.
8. Show contraction or possession.
9. Introduce words similar to those in the word list to apply generalizations.

While students sometimes may profit from grading each other's tests, this task is best done by teachers. Students should understand the standard for scoring a test. A word is marked wrong if the letters are not in correct order, or if a capital letter is omitted in a word always capitalized, or if either the apostrophe, period, or hyphen is omitted.

After the papers have been returned to the pupils, a short discussion of the common errors is valuable. Review the steps used in individual study by asking:

1. Did you pronounce and *hear* the word correctly?
2. Did you try to spell by sound when the sound does not agree with the letters?
3. Did you forget the letters in one part of the word?

Each misspelled word should be written correctly in the pupil's individual review list or workbook. Teachers should praise pupils who initiate their own review work. This is one of the habits of the good speller. He is concerned over his misspelling and makes an effort to correct it.

The learner and the teacher should recognize the fact that testing in spelling is done to guide learning. Errors should help the student to direct his study efforts. After the children have rewritten each misspelled word in the review list correctly, the class and teacher should analyze words to diagnose the nature of error. Common types of error are:

1. Omission: *the* for *they*
2. Carelessness: *surily* for *surely*
3. Phonetic spelling: *Wensday* for *Wednesday*

4. Repeating or adding a letter: *theeth* for *teeth*
5. Transposition: *esaily* for *easily*
6. Ignorance of the word: *parell* for *parallel*

7. Failure to hear or perceive words correctly: *bureau* for *mural*

As a teacher examines errors made by children she should analyze possible causes:

Error	Cause
acurate for *accurate*	faulty observation
docter for *doctor*	group pronunciation or faulty teacher pronunciation (break into syllables and point out difficult spots)
laffun for *laughing*	inaccurate auditory and visual perception
horse for *hoarse*	inaccurate visual perception
athalete for *athlete*	pronunciation error
ate for *eight*	incorrect meaning association
bying for *buying*	incorrect root word association
non for *none* *opn* for *open* *Wensday* for *Wednesday*	too dependent on phonics (children must be helped early in spelling to note orthographic irregularities of our language)
beyoutey for *beauty* *exampull* for *example*	overemphasized pronunciation (words should be spoken naturally)
cents for *sense* *except* for *accept*	incorrect meaning association (such words should be taught in pairs)
askt for *asked* *berrys* for *berries* *largist* for *largest*	unfamiliarity with common word endings (these should be taught as they apply to many common words)
dissturb for *disturb* *preevent* for *prevent* *bysect* for *bisect*	unfamiliarity with common prefixes
acke for *ache* *bucher* for *butcher* *juge* for *judge*	failure to note silent letters that appear in some words (help children to form correct mental images)
bill for *bell* *brin* for *brain* *alog* for *along*	lack of phonics or faulty writing habits
allright for *all right* *goodnight* for *good night* *airlines* for *air lines*	unfamiliarity with expressions that must be written as two words (specific teaching is required)

An analysis of the errors made by a class will reveal a wide variety of spelling of a single word. Usually one point of major difficulty can be located as indicated in the following chart. The word *almost* was spelled twenty-six different ways. The most frequent misspelling was a doubling of the *l*. Study exercises are planned to place emphasis upon such parts of words without identifying them as "hard spots." It is apparent that other spots caused spelling trouble as well.[8]

Word	No. of Misspellings III	IV	V	VI	Total	No. of Ways	Common Type	No. of Occurrences III	IV	V	VI	Total	Specific Errors	No. of Occurrences III	IV	V	VI	Total
almost	21	23	28	15	87	26	allmost	6	14	19	8	47	ll for l	13	17	20	10	60
													n for m	4	4	6	4	18
already		46	45	25	116	44	allready		13	11	8	32	ll for l		28	19	12	59
													y omitted		11	12	7	30
													e for ea		10	8	4	22
													a for ea		•8	3	1	12
family		45	53	31	129	66	famly		10	7	7	24	i omitted		15	21	15	51
													ey for y		6	13	3	22
													n for m		8	10	4	22
													l misplaced		7	9	3	19
first	45	36	27	16	124	35	frist	12	4	18	9	43	ri for ir	14	8	19	9	50
lock	69	38	10	6	123	33	loke	17	14	2	1	34	e added	24	15	3	1	43
													c omitted	21	14	3	1	39
													a for o	10	3	2	1	16
makes	55	33	25	16	129	32	maks	24	15	8	3	50	e omitted	45	21	11	3	80
passed	52	48	58	47	205	22	past	28	44	38	34	144	t for sed	34	44	39	35	152
													st for ss	5	3	18	4	30
vacation		58	51	37	146	86	vaction		9	20	23	52	2nd a omitted		30	26	30	86
													c omitted		10	6	1	17
													ca omitted		6	6	4	16
													k for c		10	2	0	12
while	33	25	22	23	103	54	wile	9	9	5	9	32	h omitted	24	17	12	19	72
													ll for le	6	2	2	6	16

A popular remedial practice is to concentrate on the spelling of a few words, maybe four or five at a time. If a student actually masters five words a week for several months, he will probably become a good speller.

Spelling is a field in which there is little systematic relationship between growth and the amount of time spent in teaching. It appears probable that growth in ability to spell is related to extensive reading, maturational factors, and the specific needs for oral or written communication. A successively larger number of children spell a given word correctly in each grade. However, the progress does not appear to be closely related to the presence or absence of the word in the formal curriculum. In one study a spurt caused by using a sixth-grade book in the fifth grade was followed by a decline to normal rate. Apparently substantial gains made in special drives, as in spelling contests, prove ephemeral. Perhaps the results are to be expected because of the significance of total maturation in individual spelling abilities when all children have adequate opportunity for learning.

A teacher can build a good spelling program that is consistent with modern psychology and gain additional time in the curriculum with the following program:

1. Be aware of the words used frequently in everyday speech as revealed by a word list, and make occasional checks to see if these are being mastered. The *Iowa Spelling Scale* would serve as a guide in judging the appropriateness of specific words for the children in a class.
2. Have the children keep a notebook of words they misspell and once a week have a lesson pertaining to these words. A class list may serve as well.
3. Have planned worksheets available for use by those who are not able to make letter-sound association; divide words into syllables, identify base words, use use abbreviations, apply generalizations, etc. These should be ungraded and are appropriate to some children's needs in each of the intermediate grades.
4. Base spelling grades on spelling pro-

[8] G. C. Kyte, "Errors in Commonly Misspelled Words in the Intermediate Grades," *Phi Delta Kappan* (May 1958), pp. 367–371.

ficiency as evidenced in written work. (Papers retained in the writing portfolio of each student are a good source of material.)

For such a program to be practical, more individual planning and work are required than most teachers can give to this one subject of the many in the curriculum. Modern textbooks reflect the careful thinking and planning of many individuals. Used as a means for teaching spelling rather than the end of spelling instruction, these textbooks will serve the teacher well. The teacher should feel free to change the words in the assignment to meet the needs of her students. The fact that grade placement of words follows no absolute rules should encourage her to select the lessons in any sequence that seems wise. Above all, she must remember that the average textbook presents the minimum needs of children. Only the teacher can meet the spelling needs represented by each child's desire to express his ideas in words that are uniquely his own.

1. Classroom management of testing procedures needs to be planned. How would you distribute workbooks and collect them? Should children check their own papers or exchange them? How do you handle individual words in a test? (Each child will have different errors.)

2. Should one have a "hundred per cent" club for those who always achieve a hundred? Should some who are perfect in an early test be excused from the final? Should a student who is assigned only five words and gets them correct receive the same grade as one who is assigned ten and spells them correctly?

HOW SHOULD SPELLING BE TAUGHT IN THE PRIMARY GRADES?

In the first three grades, the child's individual development in relation to the school objectives strongly influences his spelling needs. It must be remembered that the child is attempting to master the physical skill of writing and that the major teaching objective during these years is to establish sound reading habits.

The peculiar phonetic nature of our language has created a teaching dilemma. We want the child to establish some competence in the use of sounding so that he can learn how to pronounce new words. Reading programs have been designed to help the child do this by means of a carefully selected group of words on which he can practice. As long as the spelling and reading involve the same vocabulary, conflicts are limited. But the primary grades' reading vocabulary is also the speaking vocabulary of the normal three-year-old. The six-year-old child of today has a relatively large vocabulary. When he writes, it is normal for him to use the words in his oral language, some of which contain the spelling irregularities peculiar to the English language. Any demand for conformity to accepted spelling places a serious limitation on the child's willingness to write his ideas. For this reason we accept the application of phonetic spelling to a primary child's writing. The primary child writes to express his ideas. He uses the letters that will make the proper word sound. The teacher who has been trained to expect it will not be confused when she sees *elephant* spelled *lefant* or *once* spelled *wants*. The acceptance by the teacher of such unconventional spelling seems to give the child confidence in writing.

If the teacher wishes to introduce a spelling period late in the first grade, the words should be related to reading words and should be phonetically simple. Thus spelling can be a successful experience and the child begins to think of himself as a *good* speller.

The close association of the skills of handwriting, reading, listening, and spelling at the primary level creates a number of factors that must be considered carefully. Nearly all that is done to achieve what is called "reading readiness" leads also to "spelling readiness." When the child notes sounds, makes his first phonetic associations, practices at the easel to coordinate hand and eye, or works with clay to develop small hand muscles, his growth in these areas will influence his subsequent development in spelling.

Spelling starts when the child first seeks to produce a written word in order to tell something. First-grade children do this as they label, do reading exercises, write at the chalkboard, or compose group charts.

Many schools do not have specific spelling books or a formal spelling period in the first three grades; instead, the work is directed by means of reading workbooks and writing instruction. When a textbook is used the following procedure is effective:

1. *Introduce the word* (recognition and meaning):
   Teacher writes the word on the board.
   Children point to it in their books.
   Children find it in the story.
   Children use the word orally in meaningful sentences.
2. *Identify letters* (visual and auditory imagery):
   "What letters are needed to write the word?"
   "Have we a new letter in this word?"
   If so, the teacher shows on the board how to write the new letter.
   Children practice the letter. (Teacher observes and helps where help is needed.)
   (*Again*) "What letters are needed to write the word?"
   "Betty, Joe, all the girls, all the boys, row two, row five, etc. say the letters needed, fingers pointed to the word and eyes taking a picture of it."
   "Who can tell the letters (spell the word) without looking at the book?"
3. *Write the word* (visual and motor imagery):
   Teacher writes the word on the board, calling attention to the details of letter formation. (Uses ruled lines to set example for height of letters.)
   Teacher writes the word again, and a third time if necessary to strengthen visual imagery and the "know how"

of writing the word. Children write the word once. (*Compare.*)
   Repeat until the word has been written four or five times, not more.
   Teacher in the meantime observes and helps where necessary.
4. Same procedure for the next word.
5. *Recall:*
   Children spell orally new words learned during a particular study lesson.
   Children recall and spell orally words learned the day before.
   If time permits, children may take a written trial test on words learned thus far (in a given week).

At the primary level the following drill procedures are suggested:

Teacher flashes a spelling card (written). Child identifies the word and spells it, or all children write the word. In the latter case, children check written words and write those misspelled in a notebook for further study.

"I am thinking of a word that rhymes with *cat* but begins with *h*." Child identifies the word *hat* and spells it orally or all the children write the word.

"I am thinking of a word that tells (means) the kind of weather it is when you need to bundle up to keep warm." (*Cold.*)

"I am thinking of the base word in *farmed*."

"I am thinking of a word that means the *opposite* of *high*." (Low.)

List a number of words on the board. Children put heads on desks while the teacher erases one word from the list. Child recalls word and spells it. Repeat until the entire list is erased. Everyone can participate in the game if all children *write* the words as they are erased.

Second-grade teachers in the Riverside, California City Schools organized the following word list into a series of lessons. Each lesson was planned to use only a few of the letters the children were mastering in handwriting. In this way handwriting problems were reduced to a minimum.

The list contains a total of 215 words. They have been organized in lessons for 24 weeks. The placement by weeks is indicated by the number before each word.

1	a			5	good	12	long	21	ran	6	to
15	about	19	clean	5	got	14	look	8	read	20	today
13	after	8	cold	24	grade			7	red	24	together
21	again	11	come	20	green	16	made	17	ride	12	too
10	all	22	could	20	grows	9	make	21	right	3	tree
19	always	20	cut			17	man	15	round	24	try
2	am			8	had	22	many	10	run	7	two
4	an	8	day	18	has	16	may				
1	and	18	dear	18	have	9	me	16	said	23	under
10	any	17	did	8	he	16	milk	10	saw	6	up
3	are	6	do	18	help	16	mother	22	say	10	us
20	around	19	doll	8	her	23	much	8	school	15	use
12	as	23	don't	13	here	11	must	3	see		
13	ask	18	down	17	him	9	my	8	she	9	very
3	at			11	his			24	show		
5	ate			13	home	2	name	16	sit	13	walk
12	away	16	eat	23	hot	18	never	23	six	12	want
		16	every	11	house	1	new	14	sleep	12	was
6	ball			13	how	14	no	21	small	1	we
7	be	10	fall			15	not	7	so	14	well
23	because	10	far	2	I	17	now	23	some	24	were
21	before	12	fast	11	if			15	soon	1	went
15	best	18	find	14	in	15	of	22	stop	14	what
22	better	20	first	3	is	24	old				
7	big	18	five	7	it	22	on	4	take	23	when
21	black	12	fly			19	once	9	tell	17	where
6	blue	13	for	10	jump	2	one	14	ten	24	which
15	both	20	found	20	just	21	open	4	thank	11	white
7	boy	15	four			13	or	21	that	13	who
19	bring	11	from	9	keep	11	our	4	the	17	why
19	brown	15	full	22	kind	6	out	21	their	20	will
21	but	10	funny	18	know	24	over	23	them	11	wish
19	buy							14	then	17	with
17	by	19	gave	22	laugh	5	pet	22	there	24	work
		7	get	8	let	9	pick	16	they	24	would
19	call	19	girl	22	lights	6	play	22	think		
17	came	9	give	9	like	22	play	11	this	20	yellow
12	can	7	go	16	likes	18	please	23	those	7	yes
5	cat	12	going	14	little	9	pretty	8	three	4	you
				13	live	10	pull	14	time	4	your
						5	put				

(1)

a
and
we
new

6 letters
new letters *
a n d   w e t

(2)

I
am
on
one

6 letters
I m o

(3)

are
at
see
is

7 letters
r i s

(4)

thank
you
your
an
take

10 letters
k y u h

(5)

pet
cat

(6)

to
blue

(7)

red
two

(8)

school
read

(5)	(6)	(7)	(8)
dog	ball	go	he
good	play	get	had
ate	out	boy	cold
put	do	yes	let
got	up	be	three
		so	she
		big	day
		it	her
9 letters	10 letters	11 letters	10 letters
pc g	b l		

(9)	(10)	(11)	(12)
pretty	jump	white	fly
make	all	wish	away
my	funny	house	want
pick	fall	must	fast
keep	any	this	as
give	saw	come	can
me	run	our	going
very	us	his	long
tell	pull	if	too
like	far	from	was
13 letters	12 letters	12 letters	12 letters
v	j f		

(13)	(14)	(15)	(16)
walk	what	four	eat
ask	time	of	likes
who	ten	use	milk
after	little	round	mother
live	sleep	full	made
or	then	about	every
for	no	best	they
home	look	both	said
how	in	soon	sit
here	well	not	may
14 letters	13 letters	13 letters	14 letters

(17)	(18)	(19)	(20)
man	help	girl	out
ride	find	doll	green
where	five	brown	grows
by	dear	call	just
came	have	gave	will
now	please	buy	around
why	never	clean	found
did	down	always	yellow
with	know	bring	today
him	has	once	first
14 letters	15 letters	16 letters	17 letters

(21)	(22)	(23)	(24)
before	better	under	grade
black	could	because	would
open	laugh	hot	old
ran	lights	don't	together
right	many	much	over
small	say	them	were
that	kind	when	which
their	stop	some	show
but	there	six	work
again	think	those	try

18 letters   17 letters   17 letters
                                           x (new)

HOW ARE GENERALIZATIONS FORMED IN SPELLING?

In psychology, the word *generalization* describes the process of discovery in a learner as he notices identical elements in different situations. If one teaches generalizations made by others, these become the traditional spelling rules. Good spelling teachers plan situations in which the identical elements needed for a generalization may be discovered by the learner. For example:

Teacher: "Quick is an interesting word. The *qu* sounds like *k*. What other words do you know that start like quick?" (These words are listed on the board.) "Do you notice anything about these words? Yes, they start with *q*. Let's look in our dictionary and notice the words that start with *q*. What do you notice about spelling words that start with *q*? Yes, usually *q* is followed by *u*."

Follow these suggestions:

1. Before considering a generalization be certain that enough words are known to the child to form it.
2. Help the child to notice why there are exceptions, such as attempting to pronounce the plural of dress only by adding an *s* rather than *es*.
3. Consider only one generalization at a time.

The following two lessons will illustrate the development of generalizations with children: [9]

---

[9] Grosse Point Public Schools, *Thinking About Spelling* (Grosse Point, Mich.: 1948).

Type of Lesson: Simple Generalization

Generalization—"Many new words are developed from root words by simply adding *s*, *ed*, or *ing* to a root word, without any other change."

Aims

1. To show that by adding *-s*, *-ed*, and *-ing* to many words one can spell three or four more words after learning to spell the root word only.
2. To give pupils experience in spelling the derivatives of such base words through generalization.
3. To gradually extend the concept of generalization so that pupils can use it as an aid in discovering correct spellings.

Materials

The words were chosen from word lists for Grades Two and Three.

play	burn
rain	clean
help	need
spell	open
want	paint
garden	pull

This list was chosen for the simple meanings

at Grade Three level and because they are base words to which the suffixes -s, -ed, and -ing can be added to make new words without any other change. Thus, if the child learns to spell *play,* he should be able to generalize and spell *plays, played* and *playing.*

Procedure for the Week

Monday

1. Present root words somewhat as follows:
   "Here are the new words to be learned this week. Some of them you already know because you had them in the second grade. Who can point out one that we know?"
2. Have a child point out one and spell it. Continue somewhat as follows:
   "This week we have chosen some words that we already know how to spell because we are going to learn to use a spelling trick that will save us time and work. We will take the word *play.* Let us call this a root word. Root word means the simplest form of a word. In talking, writing, and in spelling, we use many forms of a root word by adding one or more letters to it to make new words that we need. Let us see what happens to *play* when we add an *s.* What word does this make?"
3. Use both in sentences and demonstrate on the board. "Barbara and Bill play with the dog." "Barbara plays with the dog," etc.
4. Have pupils demonstrate with other words in list, until you are sure they understand. Have pupil tell what he does as he changes word at the board. Have pupil spell new word without looking at the board.
5. Use remainder of the period for supervised study period. *Pronounce, use,* and *study* each word.
   Allow the best spellers to spell the root words and make a new word from each by adding *s.* Their work can be checked individually.

Tuesday—Review

1. Have the root words written on the board. Give ample opportunity for recall of the new spelling trick. Select several pupils to go to the board and change a word by adding *s,* spelling it as they do so.
2. Point out again that we only had to add one letter to make a whole new word, which we could spell without studying.
3. Suggest that there is another trick by which one can add another ending and get another word. (Perhaps some child will be able to show this step.)
4. One of these endings is *ing* with the sound, *ing.* Using *play,* add *ing* to show that the new word now becomes *playing.* Examples:
   "Bobby is *playing* with James."
5. Call for a volunteer at the board to change *help* to *helping.*
6. Go through the whole list, showing by pupil demonstration how each word may be changed and used.
7. In the same manner add -ed and get *played,* etc.
8. Have all pupils make a chart as follows. Pronounce several of the words. Have pupils spell the other forms.

	New Words Formed		
Base Word	+ s	+ ing	+ ed
1. play	plays	playing	played
2. rain	rains	etc.	etc.

9. Announce that there will be a test on Wednesday. Suggest that maybe only the root word will be given and they will be asked to build three new words from it.
10. How many new words should we be able to spell by Friday? (count) (36 new words) (48 words counting root words)

Wednesday

The trial test may be a game. Explain that different forms of the words will be given, such as play*ed,* jump*ing,* help*s,* etc. Each pupil must spell the word correctly and then write the root word following the form pronounced. Give children time to correct the mistakes and rewrite the words. (NOTE: Do not give words that end in *k* for examples of the -ed ending. The pronunciation is not clear enough. It sounds like *t.* Example: *bark, barked.* Explain this later to the pupils.)

Thursday

1. Reproduce chart on board.
2. Give only the root word. Have indi-

vidual children fill in the spaces under careful guidance. (Choose those who had errors on Wednesday.)

3. Have pupils spell orally all four forms.

4. To show a working knowledge, give about three new base words, such as *look, fill, hunt,* and have the children discover the derived forms from them.

5. Select only words to which the generalization will apply.

6. Caution the children that there are some words which have other changes before -s, -ed, or -ing are added. To explain an instance in which other changes in words are necessary, select the word *grow*. Try the generalization. Show pupils that they do not say grow—ed, but use gr___w. See if some child can supply the *e*. Such exercises develop *thought spelling*.

Friday—Final Test

1. At this time, as many of the derived words as desired may be used.

2. After the derived word is pronounced, the group could be asked to give orally, then write the root words beside the other as an aid to spelling.

3. Check papers. Make note of pupils who do not understand the process. Repeat this type of lesson soon for these pupils.

Individual needs may be met in these ways:

1. Pupils who are able to learn more words could be allowed to take their readers, find words with these endings, and write the root word, followed by other derived words. These should be checked individually.

2. A few extra words from the Grade Two or Three list could be given such as *add, hunt, wheel, seat.*

3. Those pupils who did not learn the trick should be given copies of the chart and several of the easy words to work on the following week for extra practice.

After a generalization is discovered it is important that a maintenance program be planned to use this knowledge.

1. Every subsequent list of words should be studied for new words, derivatives of which are formed by adding s, ed, and ing.

2. A number of words in the third grade list are formed with other generalizations which will be learned later. The teacher should explain this to the pupils as they discover them.

3. One group of words which may confuse them—such as *know, hear, grow, bring, buy, fall, find*—may be used to show how new words are formed by adding -s and -ing, but a different word is used to form the past, such as *knew, heard,* etc., instead of simply adding -ed.

4. Extending the pupils' experiences to include the spelling of derived forms as they learn the base words, will prepare them to write more fluently and with fewer errors in written English situations. Individual discovery of spellings creates an interest in the various forms of words they use and causes pupils to scrutinize more carefully the arrangement of letters in all words. The feeling of success in achievement (learning the spellings of 48 new words in a week) has a tonic effect on attitude toward learning to spell.

5. This generalization is a valuable one at this level for there are many words to which it applies.

Other words that can be used for this generalization are:

Second Grade List

ask	look
call	last
end	show
milk	snow

Third Grade List

add	land	park
count	learn	part
fill	light	pick
jump	nest	pull

The following lesson might be taught in grade four and above to establish the silent *e* generalization.

General Aims

1. To provide children with adequate methods of word study, so that they may grad-

ually solve their spelling difficulties individually.
2. To increase child's written vocabulary.
3. To stimulate pride in correct spelling in all written situations.

Specific Aims

1. To introduce the use of the generalization —"Many words ending in silent *e,* drop the *e* before adding *-ing* or *-ed.*"
2. To gradually extend the use of the silent *e* generalization to include the use of other common suffixes such as *-er, -est, -able,* etc., beginning with a vowel.
3. To emphasize the fact that in adding suffixes, such as *-ly, -ful, -ness, -less,* beginning with a consonant, do not drop the final *e.*
4. To develop the concept of learning to spell by the use of insight or transfer of training as well as automatic memory.
5. To emphasize the economy of time and effort in becoming a good speller when insight is used.

Materials

The following word list was selected from the Word List for Grades Three and Four:

skate	hope
dance	bake
close	chase
share	divide
vote	smoke
move	love
place	trade
line	

Approach

A very easy group of words ending in silent *e* was chosen from the third- and fourth-grade list so as to present as few spelling difficulties as possible in mastering the root words. Attention here should be focused on what hapepns to the root word ending in silent *e* when the endings *-ing* and *-ed* are added to make new words. When this is clearly understood, the fun of discovering new words and their spellings by adding these endings to other silent *e* words should follow.

Procedure for the Week

Monday

1. Teach or review meaning of *root word, syllable, vowel, consonant, silent letter, derived.* Illustrate and ask for examples to make sure pupils understand.
2. Begin the lesson in the following way: "Most of you already know how to spell some of these words, for several of them you learned in the Third Grade. The others are easy. Let us look carefully at these words. What final letters do you see in all of them? Yes, it is *e.* (Bring out the fact that it is silent by having words pronounced.) This week we are going to learn how to spell twenty-four or more new words without studying them. To do this, we will use a spelling trick on these root words. Before we are ready to learn the trick we must be sure we can spell the root words. Remember, they all end in a silent *e.*"
3. Study base words. Make sure pupils can spell them.

Tuesday

1. "Yesterday we noticed some things that were alike in all these root words. What are they? (Each ends in *e.* Final *e* is silent.)"
2. "You often learn to use new words by adding new endings to root words. (Illustrate with *skate-s.*) Each ending changes the meaning and the spelling of the word. Let us see what happens when we add the ending *-ing* to *skate.* This is the trick." Write *skate* on the chalkboard. Erase *e,* adding *-ing.* "What new word does this make? What happened to the final *e* when we added *-ing?*"
3. Write *skate* on the board and say, "Let us see what happens when we add the ending *ed.*" (Erase *e* and add *-ed,* calling attention to return of the *e* when we add *-ed.*) Illustrate on board the need for dropping final *e,* to avoid skat*eed.*
4. Repeat same procedures with *dance, close, share.*
5. Let pupils make new words with *vote, move, place,* by adding *-ing* and *-ed.* Carry on with pupils at chalkboard and in seats. Bring out the fact that the trick works for all words in the list.
6. Let pupils try phrasing the generalization for all of these words. A simple wording

is this: "Most words ending in silent *e* drop the *e* before adding *-ing* or *-ed*." Write this on the chalkboard and leave for further reference.

7. Let several pupils come to the board to illustrate by stating the rule, and spelling the word formed.

8. Address class somewhat as follows: "This week's spelling words should not be difficult. When you learn the base words you can easily spell the derived words by following the rule. How many words will we have in our final test?" (3 times the number of root words.)

Wednesday

1. Turn to the list of base words on the chalkboard. Have one child pronounce all the words. Review the application and statement of the generalization.

2. Pass out duplicated sheets (see sample) and say: "Complete this chart by adding *-ing* and *-ed* to the words you learned Monday. The new words are called derived words. The first one is done for you. Perhaps you will need to read the generalization before you start to work."

3. Call attention to the increase in pleasure and the decrease in work that comes from spelling by transfer.

4. Check work of poor spellers as they proceed.

Thursday

1. Pass out duplicated sheets again. Explain to children that you will pronounce the root words or their derivatives and they are to put them in the correct spaces. See that the children are following directions.

2. Be sure that the children think of the generalization as a way to increase their ability to spell without study.

Friday

1. Test on generalization: "dropping the final *e*." Have pupils prepare 3 columns on their papers.

2. Mastery test: spell root word and both derivatives for each as pronounced.

3. To give practice in recognizing word variants by identifying the base word, the following lesson might be used:
Write the following words on the chalkboard. Have pupils copy in a single line on paper. Then opposite these words write the word from which the derived word was formed. (Example: glancing—glance.)

faced	saving	smoking
sneezing	poked	graded
taking	prancing	stating
chased	loving	becoming
noticing	taken	blamed

4. Children may show that other derived words can be made by adding other suffixes such as *-er* or *-est*, or *able* to *love*, *notice*, *move*, etc. Continue to show how many new words they can spell by using this generalization.

5. In order to avoid the development of incorrect ideas concerning the addition of *-ed* to all base words when we wish to make them tell what happened yesterday rather than today, it is advisable to call attention to other ways of changing a root word We say *lost* not *losed*, *took* not *taked*, *drove* not *drived*, etc. These changes should be noted, not as exceptions to our present generalization ("Most words ending in silent *e* drop the *e* before adding *-ing* or *-ed*"), but rather as unusual changes in root words in order to change the meaning of the word.

6. There are a few exceptions which may well be noted. We do not drop the silent *e* in such words as *see*, *free*, *agree*, when we add *-ing*, although we do so when we add *-ed* in order to avoid *freeed*.

Lessons of the following type should follow in order to reinforce the learning.

1. Extension of the use of generalization— for words ending in silent *e* to include *all* common suffixes.

   a. Use small groups of words ending in silent *e* to which common endings or suffixes, such as *-er*, *-able*, or *-est* can be added. (Note that *-ed*, *-ing*, *-er*, *-est*, *-en*, and *-able*, all begin with vowels.)
   love   lov*ed*   lov*ing*   lov*er*   lov*able*
   use   us*ed*   us*ing*   us*er*   us*able*
   Pupils should be encouraged to note other words ending in final *e* which they use often in their writing to add to spelling lists.

   b. Use groups of words to show that final *e* is *not dropped* when adding common endings such as *-s*, *-ly*, *-ness*, *-ful*, *-less*, *-ment*, etc. (Note that these suffixes begin with consonants.) Use only the forms of words which pupils understand readily and can use in meaningful sentences. The following words are appropriate.

voice	voices	voice*less*	
care	cares	care*less*	care*ful*
love	loves	love*ly*	
bare	bare*ness*	bare*ly*	
brave	braves	brave*ly*	
case	cases	case*ment*	
sore	sores	sore*ness*	

Have pupils suggest others that they use.

c. Formulate a statement of the generalization for suffixes beginning with a consonant.

2. Maintaining and developing skill in the use of the generalization as a spelling aid.

   a. Pupils should be exposed to many new situations with root words in which they are asked to discover spellings of derived words. They should say orally the derived form for a given use of a base word, try to spell it by substituting other letters or adding syllables, then write it. "Checking guesses" is an important step in this procedure. This play with words combines ear, eye, and thought spelling so that pupils have several types of associations to aid in recall. Games based on such procedures can be devised. Emphasis on saving of effort, time, and having fun with words should be stressed.

   b. When selecting words for spelling lists in Grades Three, Four, Five, and Six, make sure that representative root words or their derivatives are used each week so that the new word list can be analyzed for the purpose of detecting words with which pupils have learned to deal through generalization, i.e., include a -*y* word, one ending in silent *e*, others to which -*s*, -*ed*, or -*ing* can be added without change, etc.

   c. Group root words included in grade list ending in silent *e* to which pupils are to add common endings beginning with vowel or consonant through using generalization, such as nic*er*, nic*est*, nic*ely*; care*ful*, car*ing*, care*less*, car*ed*; clos*er*, clos*est*, clos*ely*, clos*eness*.

Make hectograph chart as follows:

d. Other words in the list for Grade Four that can be used for the application of this rule should be noted.

e. Note important exceptions such as *tie, die, lie, tying, dying, lying*. (Final *e* preceded by *i* is dropped and the *i* changed to *y*.) Teach these individually as they are common words often used. See if children can think of others.

f. *Emphasize* the value of using generalizations by having pupils select certain derivatives or root words formed from words in list which they agree to add to list *without study*. Provide opportunity each week for pupils to practice use of generalization with these unlearned words. A limited number of such words should be pronounced and spelled in the *final* test each week.

g. A correlated lesson with reading will extend the use and understanding of this generalization dealing with the spelling of one-syllable words. Change the emphasis of the reading aid, "Words of one syllable containing two vowels, one of which is a final *e*, the first vowel is usually given long sound."
   Apply it as an aid in spelling one-syllable words when they are pronounced. Take such a word as *safe*—ear spelling would stop at saf, but applying the reading rule for final *e* spelling would help the children to remember to add the silent e—safe, also *side, shake, cave*, etc.

In the middle and upper grades, a number of generalizations may be drawn inductively from experience with words. Examples of such generalizations suggested as important are the following: [10]

1. Plurals of most nouns are formed by adding s to the singular: *cat, cats*, etc.
2. When the noun ends in *s, x, sh*, and *ch*, the plural generally is formed by adding *es: buses, foxes, bushes, churches*.
3. A noun ending in *y* preceded by a consonant forms its plural by changing the

[10] Board of Education of the City of New York, "Teaching Spelling" (Curriculum Bulletin, Series No. 6, 1953–54).

Base Word	Derived Words									
	-ing	-ed	-er	-est	-s	-able	-less	-ful	-ness	-ly

y to *i* and adding *-es*: *body, bodies*. Words ending in *y* preceded by a vowel do not change *y* to *i*: *boy, boys*.

4. Plurals of a few nouns are made by changing their form: *woman, women; mouse, mice; scarf, scarves*.
5. An apostrophe is used to show the omission of a letter or letters in a contraction: *aren't, we'll*.
6. An abbreviation is always followed by a period: *Mon., Feb.,* etc.
7. The possessive of a singular noun is formed by adding an apostrophe and *s*: *father, father's*.
8. The possessive of a plural noun ending in *s* is formed by adding an apostrophe: *girls, girls'*.
9. A word that ends in silent *e* usually keeps the *e* when a suffix beginning with a consonant is added: *nine, ninety; care, careful*.
10. A word that ends in silent *e* usually drops the *e* when a suffix beginning with a vowel is added: *breeze, breezing; live, living; move, movable*.
11. A one-syllable word that ends in one consonant following a short vowel usually doubles the consonant before a suffix that begins with a vowel: *fat, fattest; big, bigger, biggest*.
12. A word of more than one syllable that ends in one consonant following one short vowel usually doubles the final consonant before a suffix beginning with a vowel provided the accent is on the last syllable: *commit, committed, committing; forget, forgetting*.
13. A word ending in *y* and following a consonant usually changes the *y* to *i* before a suffix is added unless the suffix begins with *i*: *cry, crying*. A word that ends in a *y* and following a vowel usually keeps the *y* when a suffix is added: *buy, buys, buying*.
14. The letter *q* is usually followed by *u* in a word.
15. The letter *i* is usually used before *e* except after *c*, or when sounded like an *a* as in *neighbor* and *weigh*. Exceptions: *neither, either*.
16. Proper nouns and adjectives formed from proper nouns should always begin with capital letters: *America, American*.

Many old rules must be evaluated carefully not only as to their accuracy but also as to the child's ability to use the rule in practice. It was once taught that when two vowels are found together in a word as in *each*, the second is silent but helps the first to "say its own name" or have the long vowel sound. If you check the words in spellers, you will find more exceptions to this rule than applications of it.

It is not true that one can spell correctly by "spelling the word the way it sounds." In fact thiss staytmeant iz enuff to mayk won shreak. However, some phonetic generalizations should be mastered in the intermediate grades. The polysyllabic words in the Rinsland list contain 23,000 syllables. Of these, fifty are key syllables spelled consistently the same way. The fifty are listed on the page following.

United Features Syndicate

Initial Syllable	Medial Syllable	Final Syllable
<u>re</u> ceive	an <u>i</u> mals	go <u>ing</u>
<u>in</u> to	Jan <u>u</u> ar y	start <u>ed</u>
<u>a</u> round	sev <u>er</u> al	mat <u>ter</u>
<u>de</u> cided	dec <u>o</u> rated	on <u>ly</u>
<u>con</u> tains	af <u>ter</u> noon	hous <u>es</u>
<u>ex</u> cept	el <u>e</u> phant	va ca <u>tion</u>
<u>un</u> til	pe <u>ri</u> od	ver <u>y</u>
<u>com</u> mon	reg <u>u</u> lar	pret <u>ty</u>
<u>dis</u> covered	In <u>di</u> an	re <u>al</u>
<u>en</u> joy	won <u>der</u> ful	ta <u>ble</u>
<u>an</u> other	car <u>ni</u> val	af <u>ter</u>
<u>o</u> pen	gym <u>na</u> si um	base <u>ment</u>
<u>e</u> ven	ar <u>ti</u> cle	sto <u>ry</u>
<u>pro</u> gram	ear <u>li</u> est	long <u>est</u>
<u>ac</u> ci dent	o <u>ver</u> alls	sev <u>en</u>

The syllable which occurs most frequently is -*ing* which is found in 881 words. Thus a child who has learned to spell the -*ing* syllable in one word will know it in 880 more. A test might be given asking that only the first syllable heard be spelled, as the words in the first column are pronounced, the second syllable as the next column is heard, etc.

When the regular spelling test is given check the ability to transfer phonetic knowledge in this manner:

Word in Spelling Lesson	Pronounce this Word and Use in a Sentence
stop	stopping
<u>blow</u>	<u>black</u>
shrill	drill
nation	vaca<u>tion</u>

There are some learners who do not form generalizations with ease and thus need special help in spelling. If you have a poor speller who is an able student capable of doing better work and who *wants* to spell correctly, suggest that the following steps be followed in learning to spell a word: [11]

Step 1. Look at the word very carefully and say it over to yourself. If you are not sure of the pronunciation, ask the

---

[11] From *Remedial Techniques in Basic School Subjects*, by Grace M. Fernald. Copyright 1943, McGraw-Hill Book Company, Inc. Used by permission.

teacher to say it for you, or look it up in the dictionary yourself.

Step 2. See if the word can be written just the way you say it. Mark any part of the word that cannot be written the way you say it.

Step 3. Shut your eyes and see if you can get a picture of the word in your mind. If you cannot get a clear picture of the word, you can remember the parts that are written the way you say them by pronouncing the word over to yourself or feeling your hand make the movements of writing the word. If you are learning the word *separate,* all you need to do is to say the word to yourself very carefully and then write what you say. If there are any parts of the word that you cannot write the way you say them, you will probably have to remember them by saying something you can write. Say the letters, if necessary, for these syllables of the word, but not for the rest of the word.

Step 4. When you are sure of every part of the word, shut your book or cover the word and write it, saying each syllable to yourself as you write it.

Step 5. If you cannot write the word correctly after you have looked at it and said it, ask the teacher to write it for you in crayon on a strip of paper. Trace the word with your fingers. Say each part of the word as you trace it. Trace the word carefully as many times as you need to until you can write it correctly. Say each part of the word to yourself as you write it. After you have learned words in this way for a while you will find you can learn them as easily as the other children do without tracing them. (Some teachers have the child trace the word in sand or on fine sandpaper in order to achieve a greater touch impression.)

Step 6. If the word is difficult, turn the paper over and write it again. Never copy the word directly from the book or from the one you have just written, but always write it from your memory of it.

Step 7. Later in the day, try writing the word from memory. If you are not sure of it, look it up again before you try to write it.

Step 8. Make your own dictionary. Make a

little book with the letters of the alphabet fastened to the margin so that it is easy to see them. Write any new words you learn, or any words that seem especially difficult for you, in this book. Get this book out often and look these words over, writing again, from time to time, those that seem difficult. When you write these words by yourself, do just as you did when you learned them the first time. Say them, looking at them while you say them, and then write them without looking at the word in your book.

1. Do you recall a student who was bright in other school work but was unable to spell? Was attitude a part of the problem? What other explanations might be given?

2. Do you recall cheating in a spelling test? What pressures cause children to cheat in a test?

3. Are students motivated by continuous failure?

4. Are there some words you habitually misspell? What remedial action would you suggest?

5. Make a tabulation of errors from one final test of a class. Can you detect common needs suggested by the errors?

6. Why is it more difficult to change the habit of misspelling than to teach the correct spelling of a new word?

7. Do you recall an association you have used to help remember the spelling of a word? These are called mnemonic devices. Sometimes the more absurd they are the easier they are remembered. Dessert has ss while desert has only one s because you would rather have more of it. Remember the stationery you write on has er just the same as letter. Make a collection of those used in your class.

8. For some groups, such simple generalizations as adding s making more than one, or that each syllable has a vowel, are quite an achievement. Tell how you would teach one of these.

9. Can you recall ever using any spelling rule to help you spell a word?

HOW MAY SPELLING GAMES BE USED TO MOTIVATE THE LEARNING OF SPELLING?

Games provide extra motivation for some of the drill that children need to master spelling.[12] While it is unlikely that spelling will ever have the fascination of baseball for some children or golf for some adults, interest in words and their spelling can be heightened by using a game involving spelling. The spelling bee of our frontier traditions and the daily crossword puzzles of the newspapers are examples.[13]

Games call for considerable planning to be successful. In introducing the game, first give the name, then have some children "walk through" each step as you describe it. After that, have a trial run to be certain that everyone understands. Establish a few rules during the practice period. Choosing partners or teams can create considerable social tension. This can be avoided by using row against row or counting and having "odds" versus "evens." Since the girls as a group are usually superior in spelling, a "boys-against-girls" contest is unfair. It may brand the ability to spell as a feminine skill.

The timing of a game is important. Just before recess is usually a good time, since it avoids the necessity of a difficult transition from an exciting game to an uninspiring page in a history book. Do not make a game last too long unless it is a special privilege. Ten to fifteen minutes should be the maximum.

12 Unless otherwise noted this material is adapted from Paul S. Anderson, *Resource Materials for Teachers of Spelling* (Minneapolis, Minn.: Burgess, 1958).

13 A strong case is made for games as teaching devices by Delwin G. Schubert, "Reading Games: Why, How, When." *Elementary English*, October 1959, and "The Smartest English Class," *Life*, Vol. 34, 1953.

Games for Primary Grades

1. Puzzle Elements

a. I am in *see, sing,* and *say.* What sound am I?

b. I am in *took,* but I am not in *look.* I am ___.

c. *Baby, book, ball.* The *b* is at the _____.

2. *Making New Words by Changing a Vowel*

bat	fur
bet	far
bit	ham
but	hum
cat	him
cot	pen
cut	pan
bug	pin
big	pot
beg	pat
for	pit

3. *Writing Alliterative Sentences*

Bob bought big, blue balloons.

This might be a team affair with two or three working together to produce the sentence. Older children like to make advertising slogans:

Buy Billie's Best Boston Beans;
Can Charlie's Canaries Comfort Charlie's Comrades?

4. *Making New Words by Adding Letters*

all (call, ball, tall, fall, hall, stall, wall)
and (sand, band, hand, land)
old (cold, bold, fold, gold, hold)
an (fan, can, man, pan, ran)
in (tin, bin, fin, pin)
ike (bike, dike, like, hike, Mike)
ate (bate, crate, date, fate, gate)
ill (bill, dill, fill, hill, pill)

5. *Treasure Box*

Words are written on separate slips of paper which are then folded and put into a box called the treasure box. Each child in turn draws out a slip which he hands to the teacher without opening. The teacher pronounces the word and the child attempts to spell it. Any misspelled words are handed back to the children who had difficulty with them. The object is for the pupil to end the game with no slips of paper. Those who do have slips learn to spell the words that are on them. Two children can thus provide extra practice for each other as they play this game in the quiet corner.

6. *Endless Chain*

A player starts this game by spelling any word he chooses. The next player spells a word that begins with the last letter of the word spelled by the first player. The game continues in this way with each player spelling a word which begins with the final letter of the word last spelled. This game may be played as a relay race with two groups competing at the chalkboard, or it may be used as a timed exercise in which each child writes as many words (makes as long a chain) as possible in a given length of time.

7. *Turn Up Letters*

For this game the players are seated at a table. Before them on the table face down are a number of alphabet cards. The players decide on some object for the game—animals, birds, cities, flowers, etc. Then each player in turn picks up a card and exhibits the letter.

The first child to write a word beginning with that letter, belonging to the category decided upon and spelled correctly, gets the card. The player to the right of the first one who writes the word may challenge the spelling. If it is incorrect, the challenger gets the card.

When all the cards have been turned up, the player having the most cards wins. Letters which appear infrequently at the beginning of a word such as *j, u, x, y,* and *z,* should be omitted.

8. Alphabet Jumble

Two sets of the alphabet are placed in a long chalk tray. Two children compete to see which one can be first to arrange one set in correct alphabetical order.

9. Find It

Words are listed on the chalkboard. The teacher or a student gives the definition of the word and the children in turn spell the word defined.

10. Hear It

The words are listed on the board. The leader says, "I am thinking of a word that starts with the same sound as one hears at the beginning of _____," or "one that rhymes with _____." The children write the words indicated and gain a point for their own score for each correct selection.

11. Guess and Spell

"It" selects an object that is in plain sight in the room. The other children start guessing the first letter of that object. When the first letter is guessed, they start working on the second, then the third, until the word is spelled. The correct letters may be put on the chalkboard as they are spelled by the one who is "it." When any student thinks that he may be able to spell the total word after the first few letters have been guessed, he may challenge the leader and complete the word. He then becomes "it."

12. Novelty Spelling

Instead of calling words from a spell-

ing list, the teacher asks such questions as "Spell a word that rhymes with *joint.*" "Spell a word containing *ph* which sounds like *f.*" "Spell a word that means _____." Have the class in turn read their lists. The variety adds interest as well as influencing vocabulary.

13. Chalkboard Spelling

Primary children feel it is a privilege to write on the chalkboard. Reserve a place at the board where a child may go during his free time just as he might go to the library corner. Put a different exercise on the board for each child, such as:

> What children in our room have names that start with B?
> What do you want for Christmas?
> What do you like to eat?
> Where would you like to visit?
> How many words do you know that start with *wh?*

14. Find the Missing Letters

Identical lists of words, each with a missing letter, are placed on the chalkboard. There should be as many words as there are children in each of the teams. At a signal, each child in turn goes to the board and writes in the missing letter in a word. The first side to complete all words correctly wins. Examples of words that may be used: -ice, -long, ba-, -and, -ant, -are, pat-, -hat, -ate, -ale, -is, -it, -eel. The meaning element is introduced if the words are part of a sentence.

15. Use the Word

The words of the spelling lesson are placed on the board and left during the day. Each time one of the words is used in a child's writing during the day counts one point for his side. This can be row-against-row competition. The word does not count unless the one who writes the word reports it for the count.

16. Balloons

Draw balloons on the chalkboard. Write the first letter of spelling words in each balloon. You are to sell them. Each child who can say and spell the word which starts with a beginning letter buys a balloon. Let the child select the balloon he wants. If he spells the word correctly write on the balloon the word and his name.

17. Sliding

Let's play we are going sliding. To take your sled uphill, you must say a word that begins with each letter and be able to spell it. If you make no mistakes, you may slide down. Use letters of words from their spelling lesson.

18. Pear Tree

How many pear (pair) trees can you develop with your class? Synonyms and antonyms? But how about such pears (pairs) as *horse, colt; cow, calf?* Or *hands, gloves; feet, shoes?* Or *swimming, swimmer; archer, archery?* Divide your class into committees to develop these trees. Each committee draws a large tree and puts pairs of words on yellow or light green pears. Add leaves for effect.

19. Scrambled Words

Here's an idea for spelling review. Duplicate the list of review words with the letters scrambled. Give the list to each child and then give a direction for each word. For the first word, rearrange the letters to spell a word that means "all the time." For the second, rearrange the letters to spell "something to ride in," etc.

20. Pop the Balloons

Draw a bunch of balloons, using the spelling words from the lesson as shown. The teacher or a student gives the definition of the word and another child spells the word defined. Each correct answer "pops" a balloon. The child may erase his balloon until all are gone.

Spelling Games for Upper Grades

1. Dictionary Games

One child opens the dictionary at random saying, "I have opened the dictionary to an *sp-* page." Each child then writes as many words starting with *sp-* as he can. Two teams may compete, each child in turn adding a word. To prevent careless or poor writing, each team may have a "recorder" who writes the words suggested by the team. Have three to five on a team. The winning team may be challenged by another team.

2. Memory Game

Several picture cards, each portraying a single object, are shown to pupils (or it might be the objects themselves). The pictures or objects are then concealed and the children are asked to write the names of all the objects they remember. To vary this game, expose a list of words and then have pupils write as many as they can recall. It is more difficult if the words must be written in alphabetical order. For some children a test of listening is valuable. Start by having them listen to three words, then write them. Keep increasing the number of words.

3. Baseball

One form uses word cards and is especially good for practice on words frequently misspelled. Each card contains a word, a value such as one base hit, home run, etc., and the name of the position who is to catch the ball if it is misspelled. The cards would look like this:

all right	separate	February
2-base hit	home run	3-base hit
3rd baseman	pitcher	right field

Sometimes children take positions in the classroom as if it were a baseball diamond. It is equally interesting to use a chalkboard diagram with players remaining at their seats while the team captain indicates their movement on the diagram.

In another form, four diamonds are drawn on the chalkboard. The first member of the team at bat goes to the first diamond. The first word is given by the pitcher. The pitcher may be the teacher or a member of the opposing team. The child at the board writes the word. Those at their seats write the word for practice. If the word is spelled successfully by the batter he moves to the second diamond (first base) and a new player goes to the first diamond. Again the teacher pronounces a word to be spelled. Both players at the board write the word. If both spell the word correctly each player moves to another diamond and a third player goes to the first diamond. If either player misspells the word he is out. Thus it is possible for two or more players to be put out by one word. When a player advances through all four diamonds a score is made for the team he represents.

4. The Maiden and the Dragon

At one chalkboard area a "maiden" is drawn, tied to a rock by five ropes. On the other side a dragon is drawn facing five waves. (Flannelboard figures make this easier.) One group represents the maiden, the other the dragon. The game proceeds in the manner of a traditional spelldown. Each time a member of the team of the maiden misspells a word one of the waves is erased. The waves are protecting the maiden from the dragon. Each time a member of the dragon team misspells a word one of the ropes is erased. When the five waves are gone the dragon will be released to devour the maiden. But if the five ropes are cut the maiden is freed and the dragon dies. Suspense develops although no player leaves the game.

5. Roots and Branches

This game is intended to develop awareness of parts of words. Make four cards for each of several root words— for example: *march, marched, marching, marcher; fear, feared, fearing, fearful;* etc.

Make enough copies of each set of words for four "books." Shuffle the cards and deal six cards at a time to each player. Players sort their cards as in playing "Authors." If a player holds four cards of words from the same root, he can make a "book." Each player in turn may call for a card by naming the card he holds and may continue to call as long as other players hold wanted cards. When there are no more available cards of the kind he calls, he discards, and the next player takes his turn. The objective is to get as many books as possible. Care should be taken in preparing the cards for this game not to introduce different elements too fast for retarded readers; for example: doubling the final consonant of a root, or changing the sound, as *lose* and *lost,* etc.

6. Word Addition

To facilitate the use of word endings and prefixes, words are listed on the board. Each child uses that list of words to see how many new words can be made by adding beginnings and endings. Plural forms, *-ing, -er, -est, -ed, -r, pre-,* and *im-* are syllables that may be used. Words that may be used are: *run, occupy, view, prove, write, large, build, hear, stand, call, part, play.*

7. Ghost

One child starts with a letter that is also a word, as *I* or *a*. The next child adds another letter to make still another word, as *in*. The next child might spell *tin*, the next *into*. The letters may be rearranged, but each previous letter must be included and just one new letter added. The child who cannot make a new word in this way is a "ghost," the object of the game being to avoid becoming one. A good game for a large number of players.

8. Spelling Jingles

When the children come across a new word, they can help establish its spelling in their minds by writing jingles using the word in rhyme. The children enjoy composing the jingles and, at the same time, learn to spell the new word and other similar words. When the word *night* was learned, for example, the following was written:

> When it is night
> We need a light.

9. What's My Word?

Each child has a different word. One stands in front of the group. Each student in turn may ask one question, then spell the word he thinks is the word of the one in front. The questions may concern the meaning, the beginning sound, a rhyming word, or the word root. The student who identifies the word takes the leader's position.

10. Travel

Ticket salesmen are appointed for various points such as "Airplane ride to New York," "Bus ride to Los Angeles," etc. Each has a group of words. Stu-

dents in turn apply for tickets and are given them after spelling all the words on the salesmen's list. A variation might be a county fair or a circus with the ticket admitting the speller to special events.

11. Correct the Mistake

Students alternate writing spelling words on the board. The first misspells the word but must use all the letters in the word when correctly spelled. The second corrects the word. The third writes a misspelled word, and so on. The list of words used is limited to those in a lesson. It is all right for the misspelled word to spell another correctly, but it still must be changed to one of the words on the spelling list.

12. Individual Challenge

The player takes a word or name and writes it vertically. The object is to write a word containing each letter. To make it more difficult, try to make the words into a sentence or question. A variation is to see who can use the longest words.

May	May
plAy	fAther
aRt	Return
saY	todaY?

13. Smoked Bacon

Make two or more sets of cardboard letters with the letters of SMOKED BACON. Teams face each other with each child holding one letter. Teacher calls out a word which can be spelled by these letters. First team to get in correct positions gets a point. These letters form at least a hundred words.

This can be a chalkboard game. Write SMOKED BACON on the board. Let each team write a word in turn. The winner is the one who writes the longest list of words in a certain time limit. As a flannelboard game, this may be a group or individual activity.

14. *New Spelldown*

The 15–16 words of the week's lessons are put on the board. Each child is assigned one word, which becomes his "name." (Two or more may have the same word.) The leader goes to the front of the room and calls on one of the students. This child faces the rear of the room (since the words are still on the chalkboard) and is asked to spell the leader's word. If he is incorrect he sits down; if correct, he asks the leader to spell his word. The class, looking at the words on the chalkboard, acts as judges. When the leader misses, the challenger takes his place.

15. *Fourth-Grade Scramble*

Take any week's lesson and scramble the letters in each word. The teacher scrambles the letters of a word on the board and the children write the word correctly on their papers. If each letter of the word is on a separate card they may be placed on the chalkrail. One child unscrambles the word, writes it on the chalkboard and uses it in a sentence. The class watching this may write the words as each one is unscrambled.

16. *You Can't Catch Me*

As the teacher gives the first word, each child writes it on his paper. Then the papers are passed in a predetermined order (to left, etc.). The child receiving the paper checks the last word and writes the word correctly if necessary. Then the teacher gives the second word and the papers are passed. Every paper should be perfect if all errors are caught. While this may not always happen, those words needing review will have received attention in a different way.

17. *Rhyming Race*

The teacher gives a word which the children write and then write a word of their own to rhyme. A point is given for each rhyming word correctly spelled. (Example: *teach—reach; grew —flew.*)

Spelldowns

1. *Traditional*

In the traditional spelldowns, one team competes with another. If a child misspells a word and the person whose turn it is to spell on the opposite team spells it correctly, that child is "spelled down" and takes his seat. He can be saved if the opponents misspell the word and the next person on his team spells it successfully. A good P.T.A. feature is to have a group of girls spell against their fathers. Ordinarily, "boys-versus-girls" are not fair contests, but sometimes Boy Scouts will challenge Girl Scouts, or a fifth-grade team will challenge a sixth-grade team. (The National Education Association has a clever little play available which uses a spelldown dramatically. Write for "Command Performance," by Tom Erhard.)

2. *Checkers*

This is a spelldown in which the student who spells a word correctly "jumps" two persons in the direction of the end of the line. When he reaches the end, he goes to his seat. The advantage of such procedure is that those who need practice remain, while those who know the words have time for independent work. This may be called a spellup and the students may move from the end of the line to the top when they drop from the line.

3. *Spellup*

This is the traditional spelling bee with one exception—instead of the teams lining up, each team member remains seated until he misses a word; then he stands. When a player misses a word, one standing is given a chance to spell the word correctly. If he succeeds, he sits down.

4. Spelling Partners

This is an adaptation of a well-known TV program. Couples compete and must decide on a correct spelling during a time limit. (A watch with a second hand is needed.) Winners compete with the next couple. A couple who spells down another may be challenged by any two in the room, or another couple. Sometimes it is wise to combine a good and poor speller in each team.

5. O'Toole Bee

This is played as the traditional spell-down, except that a list is kept of the order each child goes down. When a word is missed by a child, those at their seats have a chance to try to spell it. The first downed child has first chance; if he gets it right, he is permitted to resume his place in line.

Simple Equipment Games

1. Spelling Tic-Tac-Toe

Two individuals compete, each in turn. No. one writes in a word on crossbars of the tic-tac-toe game. The object is to write three words in line or diagonally which contain a common element. This may be beginning, ending, prefix, word

bring		sleepy
ring	happy	
spring	lumpy	string

root, etc. The first player has written *bring* in a square. The second player writes *happy* in the middle square. The first player now writes *string* in a square.

The second player writes *sleepy* in a square. The first one writes *spring*, the second puts in *lumpy*. The first player then puts in *ring* (or any *-ing* word) and wins.

2. Word Bingo

Each child makes his own bingo board. In each square he places the first letter of the words in the spelling lesson. He puts these letters as he wishes and tries to make his card different from others. As the words are called, he spells each in the space where the initial letter may be found. The words are called at random. The child who first has five in a row shouts "Bingo" and thus wins. Others continue to play until all have a Bingo.

(Sample Card)

a	t heir	g	y	i
c	i	h	t	m
b	f	m	h	y
a	o	w	l	w
d	d	m other	l	e

3. Guggenheim

Each player has a chart as follows. The object is to fill the blanks with words of each category beginning with letters at the top of the column. The letters and categories may be changed. Each player scores a point for each word used. The game stops as soon as the first player completes all the blanks. This can be team versus team effort. The winner may be challenged and if an error is found, the one discerning the mistake is declared the winner.

	M	A	R	Y
fruit				
river				
boy's name				

4. Pencil Putts

Use prepared charts as below. Place a sheet of paper over all except the first three letters of the words on a printed page. Enter these three uncovered letters in the column marked "Play." Use as few letters as possible to make a word. Count a stroke for each letter used. Least number wins. A variation is to make the longest word possible with the highest score winning.

The chart shows the first four "putts" in the game, assuming the uncovered letters on the page were *mus,. to, the, sho, chi, veg, scr, fil,* and *mis.*

Hole	Play	Strokes
1	music	2
2	too	1
3	they	1
4	show	1
5	chi	
6	veg	
7	scr	
8	fil	
9	mis	

A player who added *-ic* to *mus-* to make *music* would have taken two strokes (letters) to make a word and thus scored two points. Little words like *to* and *the* must be added to, so a play might add *o* to *to* making *too,* scoring one stroke, and adding *y* to *the,* making another stroke, etc.

5. Two-Bit Words

A word is written up one side of a sheet of paper and in reverse order on the other. The word "parted" would appear thus:

p		d
a		e
r		t
t		r
e		a
d		p

The object is to fill the spaces with as many letters as possible to make a word. Give one point for each letter. Highest score wins. Beware of words with *c, j, i, v,* and *x.*

HOW MAY MNEMONIC DEVICES BE USED AS SPELLING AIDS?

A mnemonic device is one that aids the memory. Such devices are highly personal; although they may help some children, they may be merely an additional burden to others, since in order to remember one thing the individual must remember the association among several things.

Below are a few association ideas that may help some children who are having specific spelling difficulties:

all right	*All right* is like *all wrong.*
cemetery	Watch the *e's* in *cemetery.*
principal	The *principal* is a prince of a *pal.*
separate	There is a *rat* in *separate.*
balloon	A *balloon* is like a *ball.*
familiar	There is a *liar* in familiar.
parallel	*All* railroad tracks are pa*rall*el.
almost	*Almost always* spelled with one *l.*
capitol	There is a d*o*me on the capit*o*l.

bachelor	The *bachelor* does not like *tea*. (Common error is batchelor.)
yardstick	A *yardstick* is in one piece.
air-conditioned	*Reconditioned* is different from *air-conditioned*.
dictionary	Don't be contr*ary;* use the diction*ary*.
governor	To govern *or* not, the govern*or* will decide.
calendar	One *e* in the middle of calendar.
divided	The *v* divides two *i*'s.
intelligent	Always *tell* the in*tell*igent.

A mnemonic association that works for one person does not always work for another. The associations you think up for yourself are better than the proclaimed masterpieces of others. The more startling an association is, the better it will be remembered.

```
                          l
                          e
                          t
                          t                              station a ry
            station e ry                                  t
```

hear	You have to use your *ear* for this one.
indepen*dent*	We made quite a *dent* in England in 1776.
gram mar	Anyone can spell the first half. Copy the second part from the first, in reverse order.

```
            l
            i
            f
        exist e nce
```

curr*ant*	You wouldn't find an insect near an electric current, would you?
misspell	No wonder the girls don't have much trouble with this one. They're in league.
acco*mm*odate	This is best remembered together with the word *recommend*, another demon. *Accommodate* is the bigger word; no wonder it can accommodate a few more letters.
too	One pupil said he could remember this one because the sound of it is usually longer than the sound of *to;* it's about as long as the call of an owl and can be made to resemble one (if you draw a long *t* bar over the o's and put a dot inside the *o*).
angel	Think of the word *angelic* which comes from it. If misspelled, angelic could hardly be pronounced.
Jones' and James'	Do those who write it *Jone's* or *Jame's* know they have no right to change a person's name to Mr. Jone or Mr. James?

The hardest spelling rule concerns when to double a final consonant and when not to. Note how a single consonant favors a long sound and a double consonant a short sound. Examples will make it clear:

hated (hatted)   bated (batted)
mated (matted)   dined (dinned)
fated (fatted)   planed (planned)
rated (ratted)   writing (written)

1. Why are mnemonic devices better for adults than children?

2. What criteria would you use to evaluate the value of a spelling game for use with the group of children you teach?

OUR QUEER LANGUAGE

When the English tongue we speak
   Why is *break* not rhymed with *freak?*
Will you tell me why it's true
   We say *sew* but likewise *few;*
And the maker of a verse
   Cannot cap his *horse* with *worse?*
Beard sounds not the same as *heard;*
   Cord is different from *word.*

Cow is *cow* but *low* is low,
   Shoe is never rhymed with *foe;*
Think of *comb* and *tomb* and *bomb;*
   And think of *goose* and not of *choose;*
Think of *comb* and *tomb* and *bomb;*
   Doll and *roll,* *home* and *some;*
And since *pay* is rhymed with *say,*
   Why not *paid* with *said,* I pray?
We have *blood* and *food* and *good;*
   Mould is not pronounced like *could;*
Wherefore *done* but *gone* and *lone?*
   Is there any reason known?
And in short it seems to me
   Sounds and letters disagree.
                              —SOURCE UNKNOWN

HOW MAY THE SPELLING PROGRAM BE ENRICHED TO CHALLENGE THE ABLE STUDENTS?

In every intermediate classroom there are children who do not respond to formal spelling instruction or who are far beyond the spelling level of the class. The suggestions that follow may be used in light of the teacher's knowledge of the children's needs.

These may be assigned by the teacher or self-assigned by the student as is appropriate to the situation. The child who gets 100 per cent in the week's assignment in spelling instruction or who is far beyond the class might profit by doing one of these activities. The child who never succeeds with the words in a spelling assignment may find motivation for proper spelling through an interesting writing experience. Correct spelling is a refinement of writing, and a writing approach to spelling makes sense to many students.

Write a news report of an event in the school or classroom.

Find other meanings for words in the spelling list and write a sentence illustrating the meaning.

Write a paragraph about a secret wish, or a wish you make but do not really want such as being a baby again, or a dog.

Write a story of the first Thanksgiving (or any holiday) you remember.

How did people first learn to use fire, the wheel, or glass? Make up a story answer or find the material in a reference book.

Take an old story or fable and make it modern, such as "Christmas with The Three Bears."

What was the bravest thing your father or mother ever did?

Make up a story of a dog hero (or any pet).

Write a description of a bird or flower.

Make a list of first-aid suggestions that should be in every automobile.

Look up in an encyclopedia and report how long these animals usually live: dog, horse, bear, elephant.

Write a description of someone in the room; let the class guess who it is.

Try to write twenty compound words.

How many words can you list that end with -le (-age or any other common ending)?

Report on a radio and TV programs that you think your class would enjoy.

Make up a Paul Bunyan story.

Make a list of words that have *tele-* in them (or any other base Latin or Greek form).

Cut out a newspaper story and do one of the following: Underline each adjective (or noun, adverb, etc.). Underline each compound word. Underline the topic sentence. Make an outline of the story.

Correct the English used in a comic strip or book.

Discover different ways in which the same meaning is expressed in different parts of the English speaking world; e.g., in England: *lift* for *elevator; cinema* for *movie; petrol* for *gasoline; sweets* for *dessert* or *candy;* in Canada: *spool of cotton* for *spool of thread; tap* for *faucet; window blind* for *window shade;* in Australia: *sundowner* for *hobo.*

Report on the origin of some of the words we use.

Collect and discuss words that have come to us from other peoples. For example:

African	zebra, chimpanzee
American Indian	hominy, persimmon, squaw
Arabian	admiral, alfalfa, magazine
Australian	kangaroo, boomerang
Chinese	silk, pongee, tea, ketchup
Dutch	skipper, sleigh, waffle, boss
French	cafe, bouquet, aileron, dinner
German	hamburger, waltz, kindergarten
Greek	theater, botany
Hebrew	amen, hemp, shekel
Hindu	calico, jungle, chintz, dungaree
Hungarian	goulash, tokay
Irish	brogue, colleen, bog
Malay-Polynesian	gingham, bantam, tattoo
Persian	scarlet, caravan, lilac, seersucker
Portuguese	veranda, marmalade, yam
Scandanavian	ski, squall, smelt, keg
Scotch	clan, reel (dance)
Slavonic	sable, polka, robot
Spanish	barbecue, broncho
Turkish	tulip, coffee, fez
Welsh	flannel, crag

Collect and discuss words that have been derived from place names. For example:

Italics	Italy
cashmere	Cashmere (Kashmir, India)
morocco (leather)	Morocco
calico	Calcutta
milliner	Milan

Discuss new words invented to meet new needs; *e.g., airplane* (1870); *vitamin* (1930); and *jeep* and *radar,* in the last few years. Explore the new section of the dictionary.

Find out how the days of the week and the months of the year got their names.

Discuss and list the origin and meaning of the names of members of the class. (Example: John = Hebrew *Yohanan,* "God Is Gracious.") The following references will be helpful:

Ernst, Margaret. *Words* (New York: Knopf). 1954

Funk, Charles E. *Heavens to Betsy* (New York: Harper). 1955

Funk Charles E. *Thereby Hangs a Tale* (New York: Harper). 1950

Garrison, W. B. *Why You Say It* (Nashville: Abingdon). 1955

Laird, Helen & Carlton. *Tree of Language* (Cleveland: World Publishing). 1957

List slang expressions heard by the class and, using the following criteria, discuss the survival possibilities of each expression. Is there no other word that expresses exactly this meaning? Does this expression have a definite, single meaning? Slang that is vague in meaning and is overused as filler in conversation soon dies. Does it have originality, spontaneity, or genuine humor?

Discuss and list occasions for which slang is appropriate and those for which it is inappropriate.

Original writing may be used for spelling reviews. A story is written using as many review spelling words as the child wishes. The third-graders average about fifteen words. After the story is written with the spelling words underlined, the teacher makes duplicate copies of it. Blanks are put in to replace the spelling words. The child who wrote the story then gets to read it to the class. The class fills in the blanks as he reads. The writer of the story also enjoys checking the papers.

NAME _____

Barbara's Story

At school we made a house of _____. We asked _____ Leaverton to come to our _____ to see it. We asked her to please come _____. We will make some _____ _____ for the house. We used a _____ _____ to make them. You _____ look at everything we have made. Our _____ is about homes. We _____ it every day. Most of the children have a good _____ studying about homes. Sometimes we _____ the names of the houses. We have to write the names of the houses or _____ we will not get a _____ of 100. We asked _____ Leaverton to ask _____ Leaverton if he would come too.

The National Spelling Bee is sponsored by various newspapers across the country. These words may challenge some of the best spellers.

Famous Last Words

The following list consists of 30 of the words on which national championships have been won or lost since the National Spelling Bee began in 1925. Can you spell them?

brethren	semaphore
gladiolus	acquiesced
abrogate	sacrilegious
albumen	propitiatory
plebeian	chrysanthemum
interning	therapy
luxuriance	onerous
promiscuous	dulcimer
intelligible	canonical
deteriorating	stupefied
knack	sanitarium
fracas	oligarchy
foulard	abbacy
flaccid	psychiatry
asceticism	pronunciation

A Fateful Fifty

The fate of fifty contestants in National Spelling Bee championship finals in recent years was determined by the following fifty words. On each of them a boy or girl finalist missed—and a championship chance was lost. See if you know them.

pallor	medallion
minatory	aeriferous
catalyst	peripatetic
rue	coruscation
jocose	exacerbate
urbane	saponaceous
fission	effeminate
aggressor	disputatious
scintillate	requiem
insouciant	archetype
wainscot	guttural
assonance	yawl
consensus	vilify
herbaceous	foment
meretricious	glacial
pomegranate	ennoble
agglomeration	imitator
peroration	obloquy
manumit	impostor
febrile	homiletic
bier	mattock
aplomb	shellacked
elision	emendation
cuisine	indissoluble
quandary	efflorescence

1. Do you think it might be possible to omit a spelling period in some classes? Give reasons for your answer.

2. Are there words in your listening or reading vocabulary that are not in your speaking and writing vocabulary? Which vocabulary is largest?

WHAT DICTIONARY SKILLS DO CHILDREN NEED?

Children need to appreciate the tremendous effort that has gone into the production of the dictionary they use. Let them discuss what it must be like to live in a country that does not have a dictionary for reference. There are many such countries.

Yet the idea of a dictionary is not new. The Assyrians prepared a dictionary of their language nearly 2,600 years ago. Other people, notably the Greeks and Romans, prepared dictionaries, but these included only the rare and difficult words to be found in their language. With the coming of the Renaissance during the fourteenth and fifteenth centuries, a great deal of attention was turned to the early literature of the Greeks and Romans. This brought about the preparation of lexicons and glossaries containing the translated meanings of foreign words.

It was not until about the middle of the eighteenth century that any attempt was made to catalog the common words in the English language. The most complete work was done by Samuel Johnson, who brought out his famous dictionary in 1755. Johnson spent nearly eight years in getting his book ready and did make an effort to include the most accepted spelling and definition for each word that he used.

The first American dictionary of 70,000 words came from the pen of Noah Webster in 1806. The Merriam Brothers brought out their dictionary in 1864 with 114,000 words. The Second Edition (1934) contained over 600,000 entries. The most recent revision of the Second Edition contained a little more than 750,000 words, of which over 100,000 were new entries. In 1962 the radically new Third Edition appeared, causing considerable controversy among scholars because of its inclusion of many words and expressions previously considered to be substandard or slang. The Third Edition contains 100,000 "new" words, but the total number of entries is less than that of the Second Edition. The fact that many words are dropped explains the lack of a great increase in the number of entries.

The last twenty years have brought a newcomer to the dictionary field, the dictionary designed for elementary classroom use. Up until now each classroom, regardless of the age of the pupils, usually had a large Webster's Unabridged Dictionary on a stand or shelf for use by the entire class. A few of the more enterprising pupils might have small dictionaries of their own, but these were rather drab, uninviting books with diminutive type, few illustrations, perplexing definitions, and a selection of words ill-suited to the pupils' needs. The newer dictionaries had hundreds of illustrations of plants, animals, and objects, with their scale indicated by a numerical fraction. The point-size of the type has been increased, the format made more attractive, the definitions clarified, and illustrative sentences added. All words are carefully appraised before inclusion in an effort to eliminate rare, obsolete, or obsolescent words. A good modern dictionary is one of the most valuable books the pupil can have. It is as essential as any textbook.

Picture dictionaries have been developed for use in the primary grades. The picture-word association does help some children as they look up words for spelling. Picture dictionaries are subject to two serious limitations: they seldom provide new meanings, and the vocabulary is usually unrelated to other words the child is learning in his reading.

In all classroom work with the dictionary, the words to be alphabetized, located, or discussed should be carefully chosen to contribute some real purpose in the pupils' writing or reading. The children, as well as the teacher, should recognize the need or use.

Some fourth-graders will be ready to begin with more advanced work than will some sixth-graders. The teacher should determine each child's ability and then work with small groups having common needs. She should vary and repeat practice at intervals until the children achieve mastery of a given skill. Besides a list of words, the dictionaries for schools frequently contain other information: the story of language, flags of nations, foreign words, biographies, geographical names, pronunciation, syllabication, and even instructions on how to use the dictionary.

Steps in teaching the use of the dictionary are discussed below in an approximate sequence of difficulty, but teachers may vary the order of presentation and omit or add material to meet the needs of their classes.

The first dictionary skill to be taught is the location of a word. Some children may not know the alphabet sequence since it has not been used frequently prior to this time. Check to be sure that the children know the sequence of letters in the alphabet, and then practice until they can find words in the dictionary by their first letters. To avoid the necessity of having some children recite the alphabet before they can locate a word, discuss the relative placement of letters. Have the children discover that when the dictionary is opened in the center we find the words that start with l and m. If it is opened at the first quarter we find the words with d and e, and the third quarter we find the r and s words. Discuss how this will help them to locate a word more rapidly than if they just start at a and go through the alphabet.

Next, have the children suggest a word near the place the initial letter would be found without thumbing through the pages. Then have one pupil open the dictionary at random while the other members of the group guess the initial letter of words on that page.

To teach pupils how to arrange words in alphabetical order have them alphabetize brief lists in which no two words begin with the same letter. When this has been mastered, alphabetize by second letters (*sat* before *seven*); by third letters (*share* before *sheep*); etc. For additional practice, ask children who finish work early to arrange the books in the classroom library alphabetically according to titles, write an index page for a class book, make a card catalog for a collection of pictures, or find in a telephone directory the telephone numbers of absentees.

The second skill to be learned is the use of guide words. After discussing the advantages of being able to find a word quickly show the group that at the top of each page in the dictionary there are two words. The one at the left is the same as the first word on the page. The one at the right is the same as the last word on the page. These are called "guide words." For practice give a page number. Have the children turn to that page and read the guide words.

Then write on the board a word that the group wishes to find. Above this, write the guide words on the page at which you happen to open the dictionary. Have the group decide whether you must look nearer the front or nearer the back of the book. Continue the process in this manner until you find the right page and word. To check understanding write a word on the board. Have the pupils find the word without opening their dictionaries more than three times, (1) at the right beginning letter; (2) in the neighborhood of the word, and (3) at the exact page. This type of work should be repeated many times under supervision and then independently.

Chalkboard drills may be used to develop skill in the use of guide words. Start by writing on the board a pair of guide words taken from the dictionary. Below

them write a group of four words. Two should be words that are listed in the dictionary between the given guide words, and the other two should not. Have the children select and check the words that belong on the page of the dictionary. For example:

kent	khaki	kindred
	kennel	
	kine	
	kidnap	

This kind of work should be repeated on successive days. At first it should be done under teacher guidance at the board. Later the children may do it independently at their own desks. Individual children may create exercises of this nature for the class to do.

The following game is helpful as a review:

Divide the group into two teams. Write a word on the board. Ask children to find the word and hold up their hands when they have found it. First child to find the word scores one point for his team. First team to finish scores one point. (Check by page number.) The game should be limited by using a certain number of words (*e.g.*, ten), or by playing for a certain number of minutes.

Another exercise is built on word meanings. The teacher prepares a list of words that the children will need to know, locates each word in the dictionary, and for each word notes the guide words. When the game begins the teacher writes a pair of guide words on the board and gives a brief definition of the word which the group is to find. The pupils find the page and scan it for the right word. For example:

Guide words: springboard and *spurt*
Definition: a short run at full speed
Answer: sprint

The third major area of dictionary skills is that associated with the definitions. Whenever a word is found in reading or social studies which cannot be defined from context, use the dictionary. Many words have only vague meanings. Use the dictionary for more exact meaning. Explain

Burbank Public Schools, Calif.

Learning how to use the dictionary is important in the intermediate grades. The teacher is using the flannelboard as an effective teaching aid. The chart is a free service bulletin from the publishers of the *Thorndike-Barnhart Dictionary*.

the difference in meaning between these words: *climate* and *weather; less* and *fewer; hotel* and *restaurant.*

Some words get so overworked that we call them "tired" words. The dictionary can suggest other words to use for *said* or *grand.* Considerable thought is required in selecting the right meaning from several meanings given in the dictionary. For a few children it will be a discovery that words have more than one meaning. Introduce this work with the word *run.* Have the group think of several meanings before looking it up in the dictionary. Or use a sentence from some child's story. For example: "The initial expense was about thirty dollars." Have the children find *initial* in the dictionary. Discuss the meanings given, and choose the one most applicable. The children may be asked to select the best meaning for a word in a given sentence, and then to write another sentence in which the same word has a different meaning. Choose a word having several meanings such as *pack.* Write at least two sentences to illustrate each meaning. After placing the sentences on the chalkboard ask the children to define the meaning of the word.

This could be followed by having pupils select a common word like *safe, strike, husband,* or *signal* and discover how many different meanings for it they can find and illustrate.

Interesting lessons can be planned to show how the illustrations in the dictionary clarify meaning. The arithmetic in the ratio should be studied so that the phrase "one-sixth actual size" has meaning. An interesting discussion can be planned around the topic, "Which words can be illustrated and which cannot?"

An understanding of prefixes and suffixes is another aid to word meaning. When the children understand that *trans-* means "across" or "over" in *transportation, transfer, translate,* and *transcontinental* they have a meaning clue to other words with this prefix. They can discover that the dictionary gives the meanings of many prefixes. The following list of prefixes is for teacher reference. No group of children would be expected to study them all.

Select and teach one or two at a time as the opportunity presents itself:

a, ab-	without, as in *abate*
ad-	to or toward, as in *adjoin*
an-	not or without, as in *analgesic*
ante-	before, as in *anteroom*
anti-	against, as in *antiaircraft*
auto-	self, as in *autobiography*
bi-	twice or two, as in *bimonthly* or *bicycle*
circum-	around, as in *circumnavigate*
com-	with or together, as in *compress*
de-	reverse of, as in *decamp;* down, as in *depress*
equi-	equally, as in *equidistance*
ex-	out of, as in *exclude;* formerly or past, as in *ex-member*
il-	not, as in *illegible*
im-	not, as in *impossible*
in-	within, as in *indoors;* not, as in *inaccurate*
inter-	together, as in *intermixture;* among, as in *interchange*
ir-	not, as in *irregular*
mis-	wrong or bad, as in *misconduct*
mono-	one, as in *monotone*
over-	too much, as in *overexercise*
pre-	before, as in *prewar*
pro-	forth, as in *proclaim;* on the side of, as in *pro-British;* in place of, as in *pronoun*
re-	again, as in *rebuild*
sub-	under, as in *submarine;* again, as in *subdivide;* less, as in *substation*
super-	over, as in *superstructure;* in excess, as in *superabundance*
trans-	across or over, as in *transcontinental*
under-	below, as in *underline* (*understand* is a special case; see dictionary derivation)

Lessons on suffixes are helpful to some but too difficult for many in the elementary school. The following list is for teacher reference. No group of children would be expected to study all of the suffixes listed.

-ation	state of, as in *admiration;* process of, as in *addition*
-cy	position or rank of, as in *presidency*

-ed	denoting past time, as in *played;* possessed of, as in *cultured*
-en	cause to be, as in *blacken;* made of, as in *woolen*
-ence	state of, as in *dependence*
-ful	full of, as in *cheerful*
-fy	cause to be, as in *simplify*
-ic	pertaining to, as in *Icelandic;* having the nature of, as in *heroic*
-ish	somewhat, as in *oldish;* resembling as in *a childish man*
-ive	tending to, as in *active;* having the quality of, as in *pensive*
-kin	little, as in *lambkin*
-ment	act or state of, as in *enjoyment*
-ness	state of being, as in *blackness*
-ous	full of, as in joyous; like, as in *thunderous*

One of the basic clues to meaning is the ability to identify the root word. Start by supplying a root word and have pupils list other members of the same family: *kind* (kindly, kindness, unkind, kindliness). Discuss the fact that these words are similar in meaning as well as in appearance. Children need help in learning how the dictionary deals with word families. The root word is listed at the margin in heavy type and other members of the family are not listed marginally but are explained under the root word. In spelling and reading, root words should be identified and sometimes checked with the dictionary. This is important when the word is to be divided into syllables. Even though we divide the word as we pronounce it the basic root is seldom divided in writing. Some children will enjoy knowing about a few common Greek and Latin roots which will help them guess word meanings. These were used by a fifth grade:

Latin

annus (year)	annual perennial anniversary
aqua (water)	aqueduct aquaplane aquarium
audio (listen or hear)	auditorium audible audition

Latin (contd.)

avis (bird)	aviary aviation aviator
ducere (to lead)	conduct educate aqueduct
via (way)	viaduct trivial deviate

Greek

aster (star)	aster astronomy asterisk
cycle (ring or circus)	bicycle motorcycle cyclone
graphein (to write)	autograph telegraph graph
logos (word)	catalogue dialogue astrology
metron (measure)	meter thermometer speedometer
phone (sound)	phonics telephone phonograph

From a child's point of view the most valuable use of a dictionary is to locate the correct spelling of a word. This is not easy when it is a word that the child cannot spell. Take as an example a word that a child has asked you to spell for him, such as *usable.* The group will be sure of the first two letters. Have them look up the word as far as they are sure and then glance down the page until they find the word. Even after looking up a word it is possible to make a mistake. Before copying the spelling from the dictionary the definition must be read in order to prevent such errors as the use of *complement* for *compliment.*

Sometimes a word is located through the trial-and-error method. Words with difficult beginnings, such as *cistern,* when not located under *s* must be sought under other letters having the same sound. It takes real detective work to track down some words such as *light*.

Other spelling help in the dictionary concerns abbreviations, the use of capitals, and plural forms, but children must be shown how to locate each of these items.

Another area of dictionary skills concerns pronunciation. The first step involves dividing words into syllables. These rules are usually taught in third-grade reading. This is a good time for children to discover that the dictionary can act as a check on their syllabication. A few listening lessons in which children tell how many syllables they hear when words are pronounced will reveal the fact that the number of vowels we hear in a word tells us how many syllables there are in it. While dividing words into syllables, notice that we pronounce some syllables with more force or accent than others. Then show how the dictionary indicates this stress with the accent mark. Children will be interested in words where a change in accent may indicate a change in meaning, as in "Use the movie machine to *pro ject'* the picture," or "He found that building the dam was a difficult *proj' ect.*"

Some dictionaries indicate a secondary as well as a primary accent, as in *mul' ti pli - ca' tion.* To check understanding of accent, give the children sentences containing blanks and a choice of the same word syllabized and accented in two different ways. The pupils decide which form to use in the blank, and then write a sentence of their own using the other form. For example: The chairman will (*pre' sent* or *pre-sent'*) the speaker.

Another skill involves the use of diacritical marks as an aid to pronounciation. The pronunciation key at the bottom of each page (or on the end papers of the book) is a basic reference. While this key may differ according to the dictionary, its use remains the same. If the children can read the key words there is no great need to be able to identify all the markings. The sound association can be made between the key pronunciation word and the one in the dictionary.

Instruction needs to be given which involves marking long and short vowels and then discovering that vowels have other sounds as well as the long and short. Illustrate how these are indicated in the key words on each page in the dictionary.

Have available such assignments as the following as spare-time work for superior students.

Underline words which have the same vowel sound:

ă as in *at*	rattle, sale, athlete, clasp, gas
ā as in *age*	pale, name, display, radio, pat
â as in *care*	square, maple, fair, compare, dare
ä as in *art*	harvest, tame, star, depart, arm
à as in *ask*	grass, vast, grant, brave

Teach the children to use the phonetic respelling given in the dictionary as an aid to pronunciation. Have the group make a list of words in which:

ph or *gh* sound like *f* (*elephant, tough*)
ch or *ck* sound like hard *c* (*chorus, tack*)
d, dg, or soft *g* sound like *j* (*soldier, ridge, ages*)
c sounds like *s* (*cent*)
c sounds like *k* (*act*)
c, x, s sound like *sh* (*ocean, anxious, sugar*)
l, w, k, b are silent (*calf, wrong, comb*)

Teach the children that for some words there is more than one accepted pronunciation and that the preferred one is given first.

Although the dictionary is usually not introduced for the student's use until fourth grade, there are several good practices which will familiarize the students with dictionary procedure prior to the fourth year of school.

In grades two and three children should be encouraged to keep their own file of words they have learned in reading. A brightly painted shoe box makes an excellent file of this sort. Each divider cut from cardboard should be labeled with a letter of the alphabet in both small letters and capitals. Children write the words they want to keep on file on cards or construction paper, or they can find words in magazines to cut out and paste them on the cards. Then the words are filed behind the proper letter of the alphabet.

Another device is to make picture dictionaries either for individual or class use. Children choose a big scrapbook, label the pages with each letter of the alphabet, and write the words on the scrapbook pages, complete with accompanying pictures.

After the dictionary is introduced in either the third or fourth grades, the following exercises may be used to facilitate its use.

1. A dictionary is placed on the first desk of each row. The teacher writes any ten words on the board. At a given signal, the first pupil in each row looks up the first word. When he finds it, he jots down the page number and passes the dictionary to the person behind him who does the same for the second word, etc. The first row finished is the winner. If a mistake is made in a page number, the second row finished is the winner.

2. The same game is played with definitions or pronunciations.

3. The same game may be played with names of mythological characters.

4. Each student brings to class a sentence containing a difficult word. A dictionary is placed on each student's desk and the class is divided into two teams. A pupil reads his sentences and states the word he wants defined. The opposing team is given approximately half a minute to look up the word in the dictionary. At a signal from the teacher, dictionaries are closed and the one who presented the sentence calls a pupil from the opposing team to define the word. If the pupil misses he is eliminated and another is called. The game is continued until all of one team has been eliminated.

Worksheets like the following are sometimes used to practice dictionary skills:

Burbank Public Schools, Calif.

In the intermediate grades each child should have his own dictionary.

Dictionary Study in Grade 4

Rules of the game: A dictionary is a book that tells about words:

It tells how to spell words.
It tells how to pronounce words.
It tells what the words mean.

You cannot use a dictionary until you know the alphabet; that is, until you can name the letters in order. Can you do this? Here they are, just to help you: A, B, C, D, E, F, G, H, I, J, K, L, M, N, O, P, Q, R, S, T, U, V, W, X, Y, Z. If you do not know them very well, say them over and over until you do.

Try making a little dictionary of your own; that is, arrange these words in alphabetical order. There is one for each letter.

ball	fun	_____	_____
zero	hunt	_____	_____
play	ice	_____	_____
club	youth	_____	_____
swim	under	_____	_____
run	tag	_____	_____
jump	nap	_____	_____
win	laugh	_____	_____
knot	mop	_____	_____
arch	open	_____	_____
game	x-ray	_____	_____
dive	queer	_____	_____
eat	vote	_____	_____

Write three sentences explaining what the dictionary tells us about words:

1. _____
2. _____
3. _____

Dictionary Study in Grade 5

Write the letters of the alphabet: _____

There are _____ letters. The first half of the letters of the alphabet is composed of letters A to __. The last part of the alphabet is composed of letters __ to __.

Arrange the following words alphabetically. Write *F* before words found in the first half of the dictionary. Write *L* before words found in the last half.

| envelope | pencil | train | yellow | curtain | fruit |
| surprise | hurry | answer | velvet | umbrella | draw |

_F_ 1. e n v e l o p e   — 7. _____
  2. _____   — 8. _____
  3. _____   — 9. _____
  4. _____   —10. _____
  5. _____   —11. _____
  6. _____   —12. _____

Arrange these words the same way as above:

Henry   George   Robert   Albert   William   Thomas

  1. _____   —4. _____
  2. _____   —5. _____
  3. _____   —6. _____

Some Special Practice in Using the Dictionary in Grade 6

The dictionary is your chief help when you are in doubt as to the spelling of a word. Consult it if necessary to make sure of the correct spelling of each of the following words. Cross out the incorrect form. Then on the lines at the right show each word correctly spelled in your own handwriting.

1.	acqueduct	aqueduct	_____
2.	business	busness	_____
3.	calendar	calander	_____
4.	certainly	sertainly	_____
5.	comfortable	comfortible	_____
6.	desparate	desperate	_____
7.	elementery	elementary	_____
8.	guard	gaurd	_____
9.	gesture	jesture	_____
10.	immence	immense	_____
11.	khaki	kahki	_____
12.	nickle	nickel	_____
13.	ocassion	occasion	_____
14.	perfer	prefer	_____
15.	pidgon	pigeon	_____
16.	possessive	possesive	_____
17.	recognize	reckonize	_____
18.	spere	sphere	_____
19.	subscription	subscripsion	_____
20.	typewriter	typewriter	_____

When a word has to be divided at the right margin of a composition, the division must be made at the end of the syllable. Find the syllable division of the following words in your dictionary.

1. factory _____   5. radiator _____
2. invitation _____   6. statistics _____
3. journey _____   7. miscellaneous _____
4. knowledge _____   8. victory _____

Matching

From the endings in the right-hand column, pick out the endings that go with the beginnings in the left-hand column and write them in the spaces provided:

1. equip_____(ian)
2. fru_____(ary)
3. hydrau_____(tical)
4. jambo_____(fin)
5. imprac_____(gent)

6. negli_____(ment)
7. legend_____(ism)
8. guard_____(ree)
9. magnet_____(lic)
10. paraf_____(gal)

Plurals

In the blank space after each word, copy its plural form as you find it given in your dictionary.

1. library _____
2. oasis _____
3. motto _____
4. index _____
5. lath _____

6. ski _____
7. vertebra _____
8. basis _____
9. veto _____
10. fungus _____

Homonyms

In our language, we have a number of words that are pronounced alike but have different meanings. The words *to, too,* and *two* are homonyms. Try to find a homonym for each of the words given and write it on the line provided:

1. right _____
2. way _____
3. whole _____
4. very _____
5. air _____

6. rain _____
7. steal _____
8. won _____
9. cent _____
10. there _____

Synonyms

A synonym is a word that has the same meaning as another word; *big* means the same as *large. Big* is the word, *large* is the synonym. *A synonym is only one word.* Write synonyms for the following:

1. craven _____
2. robust _____
3. wrath _____
4. guilty _____
5. falsehood _____

6. liberal _____
7. adept _____
8. rebuke _____
9. soothe _____
10. torpid _____

Antonyms

There are many words in our language that have meanings that are directly opposite. The words *large* and *small* are antonyms. Write antonyms for each of the following:

1. far _____   6. expensive _____
2. victory _____   7. backward _____
3. before _____   8. idle _____
4. guilty _____   9. pure _____
5. dull _____   10. pleasant _____

Suggestions for Projects

1. Evaluate or create a series of spelling games designed to accomplish specific purposes with a group of children.
2. Report on the simplified spelling movement in the United States.
3. Compose three different spelling programs with respect to similarities and differences.
4. Analyze the spelling errors made by a specific class. Are there patterns of errors or common needs revealed?
5. Write a talk to give at the P.T.A. explaining the school's spelling program to parents.
6. If children study spelling words that are based on those that are quite certain to appear in their writing, why shouldn't these words be taught in the writing association and less frequently used words be taught in the spelling lessons?

BIBLIOGRAPHY

BOOKS

Dawson, Mildred, and Marian Zollinger. *Guiding Language Learning.* New York: Harcourt, 1957.

Dawson, Mildred, and Marian Zollinger. *Language Teaching in Grades 1 and 2.* New York: Harcourt, 1951.

Dolch, E. *Better Spelling.* Bloomington, Ill.: Garrard, 1943.

Fernald, Grace M. *Remedial Technique in Basic School Subjects.* New York: McGraw-Hill, 1943.

Foran, T. G. *The Psychology and Teaching of Spelling.* Washington, D. C.: Catholic Education Press, 1934.

Fitzgerald, J. A. *The Teaching of Spelling.* Milwaukee, Wis.: Bruce, 1951.

Gates, Arthur I. *A List of Spelling Difficulties in 3,876 Words.* New York: Bureau of Publications, Columbia University, 1937.

Gates, Arthur I. *Diagnostic and Remedial Spelling Manual.* New York: Columbia U. P., 1941.

Goldensen, R. M. *Helping Your Child to Read Better.* New York: Crowell, 1958.

Herrick, Virgil. *Children and the Language Arts.* Englewood Cliffs, N.J.: Prentice-Hall, 1955.

Hildreth, Gertrude. *Teaching Spelling.* New York: Harcourt, 1955.

Horn, Ernest. *A Basic Writing Vocabulary.* Iowa City: University of Iowa, 1927.

Horn, Thomas. *Spelling Instruction—A Curriculum-Wide Approach.* Austin, Tex.: University of Texas, 1954.

Rinsland, H. D. *A Basic Vocabulary of Elementary School Children.* New York: Macmillan, 1945.

Strickland, Ruth G. *Language Arts in Elementary School.* Boston: Heath, 1951.

Tidyman, W. F., and M. Butterfield. *Teaching the Language Arts.* New York: McGraw-Hill, 1951.

Wijk, Axel. *Regularized Spelling.* Uppsala, Sweden: Almquest and Wiksell, 1959.

Zyve, Claire T. *An Experimental Study of Spelling Methods.* Teacher's College Contributions to Education, No. 466. New York: Bureau of Publications, Teacher's College, Columbia University, 1941.

PAMPHLETS AND COURSES OF STUDY MATERIALS

City of New York Board of Education: "A Manual to Guide Experimentation with Spelling, List A, B, and C." Division of Curriculum, Bureau of Curriculum Research, 1951.

Grosse Point, Mich., Public Schools: "Spelling Course of Study." 1948.

Madison, Wis., Public Schools: "Improvement of Spelling." 1949.

New York State Education Department: "Learning to Spell." Bulletin No. 1368, 1949. University of State of New York.

Oakland, Calif., Public Schools: "Course of Study." 1957.

San Diego County, Calif., Schools: "Spelling Course of Study." 1955.

Tulsa, Oklahoma, Public Schools: "A Guide to the Teaching of Spelling." 1952.

Washington, D. C.: "How Children Learn to Write." Bulletin No. 2, U. S. Office of Education, 1953.

Washington, D. C.: "Research Helps in Teaching the Language Arts." Harold Shane, ASCD, Department of NEA, 1201–16th Street, N. W. Washington 6, D. C., 1956.

PERIODICALS

Cook, R. C. "Evaluation of Two Methods of Teaching Spelling." *Elementary School Journal,* 58 (October 1957), pp. 51–57.

Furness, E. L. "Sputnik Science and Spelling." *American School Board Journal* (May 1958), pp. 36–37.

Howell, M. "Spelling Through Written Expression." *Elementary School Journal,* 52 (December 1951), pp. 207–214.

Kottmeyer, W. "On the Relation of Word Perception Skills in Reading and in Spelling." *Education* (May 1952), pp. 600–603.

Sister Mary Josephine. "Spelling, the Responsibility of Every Teacher." *Clearing House* (March 1958), pp. 393–394.

Wells, D. P. "Today's Children Can Spell." *Elementary English* (March 1958), pp. 182–184.

Wolff, M. R. "Study of Spelling Errors and Implications Concerning Pertinent Teaching Methods." *Elementary School Journal,* 52 (April 1952), pp. 458–466.

In the book *Research in the Three R's* by C. W. Hunnicutt and W. J. Iversen (Harper, 1958), the following are found:

Dupee, C. W. "Self Study in Spelling," pp. 301–303.

Gates, Arthur I. "Generalizations in Spelling," pp. 296–301.

Hanna, Paul R. "Spelling from Spoken Word to Written Symbol," pp. 309–315.

Russell, David H. "Some Factors in Spelling Readiness," pp. 293–296.

Russell, David H. "Why Are Some Children Poor Spellers?" p. 287.

Tonn, T. D. "Do They Learn from Tests?" pp. 304–306.

Zyve, C. "What Methods Are Better?" pp. 306–309.

Popular spelling textbook series include the following:

Betts, E. A., and P. A. Killgallon. *Language Arts Spellers.* New York: American, 1959.

Billington, Lillian E. *Spelling and Using Words.* New York: Silver Burdette, 1957.

Breed, Frederick, and Don C. Rogers. *My Word Book Spellers.* Chicago: Lyons & Carnahan, 1962.

Fitzgerald, James A. *Learning Spelling.* Milwaukee: Bruce, 1960.

Glin, T. E., and Frank S. Manchester. *Basic Keys to Spelling.* Philadelphia: Lippincott, 1962.

Hanna, Paul R., and Jean S. Hanna. *Building Spelling Power.* Boston: Houghton Mifflin, 1961.

Keller, Helen Bass, Mary N. Forster, and May V. Seagoe. *A to Z Spellers.* San Francisco: Harr Wagner, 1957.

Kottmeyer, William, and Kay Ware. *Basic Goals in Spelling.* St. Louis: Webster, 1960.

Madden, Richard and T. Carlson. *Success in Spelling.* Chicago: Harcourt, 1956.

O'Donnell, Mabel. *Reading Road to Spelling.* New York: Harper, 1962.

Yoakam, G. A. and Seward E. Daw. *Learning to Spell.* Boston: Ginn, 1956.

Chapter 6

*R*eading

WHAT READING SKILLS ARE TAUGHT IN THE LANGUAGE ARTS PROGRAM?

The Eskimo language has many different words for "snow." Because of their culture and environment, the Eskimos need to distinguish between soft light snow, an icy, wind-driven snow, a dry snow, a wet snow, and other types. Such vocabulary makes for a more exact form of communication. A part of our problem in the language arts is that the term *reading* can be used with many meanings. Some of these have to do with purpose such as *oral* reading, when a writer's ideas are projected through speech; reading that describes an *area* in the curriculum; reading that means *action* and may refer to anything from a child's telling what he sees in a picture to a judge's interpretation of a point of law. A child may read a word by changing it to sounds which he recognizes in his language, or he may change it to sounds and discover that it is still meaningless. Another might get the meaning from a word without being able to pronounce it. In terms of response the word means different things. Sometimes the response is careful and profound thought, at others it is an imaginative fantasy. There may be a great emotional feeling in the response, or only a light and casual notice of the material that is soon forgotten.

Eventually all these aspects of reading are mastered by most students. But to the beginner the problem is one of looking at words in their printed or written form and discovering the meaning intended by the one who wrote them. Reading is the method by which we communicate to ourselves—and sometimes to others—the meaning contained in printed symbols.

In some literature the authors seem to assume that "reading" is the ability to look at printed symbols and change those symbols through phonics to oral reading. One author boasted of his ability to do this with the Czech printed material although he admitted that he had no idea what the sounds meant. It is possible for reading to be so taught that attention is called to the words themselves rather than to the meaning they should convey.

Reading may be thought of as looking *through* words to the fields of thought *behind* them. The degree of relationship between the meaning of the writer and the interpretation of the reader determines the accuracy of the reading. The meaning is not on the printed page, but in the mind of the reader. Thus meaning will differ, since each reader possesses different experiences in terms of which he interprets the words.

To the beginner each word represents a puzzle to be solved. A word like *mother* or *baby* presents little or no difficulty since the meaning is definite, the words are familiar in language, and the feelings associated with the words are usually pleasant. A word like *fruit*, however, which can mean *apples, bananas, oranges, grapes, lemons,* or *peaches,* is a different problem. A word like *here* which may mean *at school, by the teacher, where to stand, on the desk* or almost any place, is a puzzle indeed. Then there are words like *at*, which even the teacher cannot define without talking a long time. Some printed words are interesting visually, such as *look*, which has a pair of eyeglasses in the middle, and *Oh*, the first letter of which is the shape of the mouth when you say it. Each new word that is recognized and remembered is a satisfying experience when one is six and learning to read.

From the teacher's point of view the process is one of repetition, encouragement, reteaching, searching for material, making special material, being pleased by the success of some and being concerned about the failure of others. Teachers do not expect beginners to identify words that are strange in meaning or new to their oral language. Effort is directed toward the establishment of word recognition skills that will help a child change the printed words to their proper sounds and meanings which are already part of his oral vocabulary. The focus of teaching effort is on the individual child. Reading is not taught to a child but rather a child is taught to read.

A beginner probably remembers each word through the same kind of association process that an adult uses in recalling the identity of people. Such factors as age, hair color, size, profession, place of meeting, and topic of conversation serve as memory aids. If we are seeking to recall a person's name we use these factors as clues. In much the same ways a child learns to look for certain clues that will help him to recognize the message of the printed word. Five types of reading clues are taught as a part of a child's word attack skills.

Context clues are found in the picture, in the meaning of known words in the sentence, or in the oral discussion of the class. It is always wise to discuss the pictures in a story first or children have a habit of moving their eyes away from the new word to look at the picture for help. If the oral discussion has set the story in Africa, the child may use that clue to understand a new word when he comes to it.

Phonetic clues have been discussed in the chapter on phonics. None of the reading programs widely used today neglect the importance of this knowledge.

Word form clues are sometimes called configuration clues. These are the forms of the word that give it some identity. *Christmas* and *grandmother* are relatively easy words because of their meaning and length. *Elephant*, with its silhouette or shadow of tall and long letters, may be recognized because of its form. For some words these configuration clues render little assistance. Words like *such, said,* and *word* have similar silhouettes or, as some teachers say, have like shadows.

Structural clues are those noticed in common endings such as *-ing, -ed* or *-tion.* Compound words contain structural clues when children recognize the two combined words. The ability to use prefix and suffix meanings or to recognize the root word represents an advanced use of this clue.

Sight words are those that must be memorized through repetition. Words with indefinite meanings, such as *of*, those with difficult phonetic combinations such as *one*, and some proper names are examples of sight words. Children with keen visual memories will usually learn almost all primary words by sight. Certain words need many repetitions before they are mastered. Words like *here, there, who, what,* and *where* are especially difficult. Others will be remembered after only a few repetitions.

Dictionary skills are sometimes referred to as a reading clue. Certainly for older students it is a way of determining the meaning of a word.

In practice, clues are combined. Word

form and phonics are combined in locating the base word and the ending in a plural like *birds*. Even sight words will often contain a structural or phonetic clue that an individual child will use to remember the word.

In addition to these word-attack skills, there are skills that relate to the thinking side of reading that are of equal concern. The word-attack skills enable the reader to examine a printed word and determine its language sound and meaning. The *skills of response* help the child organize and interpret what the writer has said. These refer to understanding the main idea expressed, noticing details that add meaning, determining if the idea is true, and the personal responses of appreciation. Another group of skills are usually called the *study skills*. These include the ability to locate information, read maps and charts, and select pertinent information.

Meaning is closely related to purpose or incentive in reading.

The following are some of the purposes or goals which lead to meaningful reading experiences.

Reading for Details or Facts

Read to find out what discovery the character made, what the character did, what happened to a particular character in the pictures of the story, or to answer the questions the group had (about Indian life or space flight).

Reading for Main Ideas

Read to find out why it was a good title, what the problem is in the story, what the character learned, and to summarize what the character did to achieve his purpose.

Reading for Sequence or Organization

Read to find out what happened in each of the parts of the story, what happened first, second, and third—each step

taken to solve a problem, scenes and events for dramatization.

Reading for Inference

Read to find out why the characters feel the way they do, what the author is trying to show us, why the characters changed, what qualities the characters had that helped them succeed or caused them to fail.

Reading to Classify

Read to find what was unusual about a character, what was funny in the story, or if the story were true.

Reading to Compare or Contrast

Read to find out how the character changed, how life is different from life we know, how two stories are alike, how the character is like the reader.

Reading to Evaluate

Read to find out if the character was successful or lived by certain standards, whether you would like to do what the character did or work the way he did in the story.

A modern reading program seeks a content so interesting and so related to what is known about children that it serves as the instrument for the mastery of the reading process. This process involves a number of specific skills, such as the use of word-analysis clues. At times the mastery of process is the focus of instruction, but it is not the end purpose of a reading program—which is to help the child attain a level of reading that will enable him to acquire, organize, and share ideas as an intelligent member of society.

1. What sight words might a child learn from watching television? Should such words be used in beginning reading instruction?

2. In what sense would the term *reading* be synonymous with *thinking*? Are there thinking skills that should be taught?

WHAT MATERIALS ARE USED IN THE "BASIC READER" APPROACH TO READING INSTRUCTION?

The term *basic reading* is usually applied to a planned program of instruction presented in a series of books written by an author or group of authors and presented by a single publisher. Since the publisher has the missionary task of spreading the author's ideas about reading instruction, there is a tendency to stress one or two ideas in order to gain distinction. In order to teach reading, competing series in basic reading contain much that is similar. However, each series will have methods as well as content that differs from others. One will stress a carefully selected vocabulary or phonetic controls. Another will emphasize the teacher aids in the manual or workbooks that will make the task "easier." Still another will emphasize content of stories, which may correlate with social studies or be selections from children's literature.

Basic reading series usually have one or two reading-readiness books, three or four preprimers, a primer, a first reader, and two books for each grade up to grade four. Each book has its own workbook. Some series use the workbook to present the new words before reading in the textbook. Others use the workbook for additional practice, testing, and independent reading. A few series introduce some words in the readiness books. Between 45 and 60 words are used in the preprimers. All of these are used in the primer. A primer usually adds 90 to 100 words, the first reader 140–160 to complete a total of about 300 words in the first grade. Second readers will add from 350 to 600 words and the third readers from 600 to 900. The total number of words used in the primary readers of different authors varies from about 1,100 to 1,800. A number of additional words are derived from these basic words lists. The actual number of different words the child will see in print in the first three grades would range from 2,500 to 4,000.

There are two reasons for the careful control of vocabulary in a modern series. First, a small sight vocabulary can become the foundation for development of phonetic and structural analysis skills. Second, the child reads something that satisfies him without too much difficulty. Piano lessons are planned in much the same way. Simple melodies provide a feeling of accomplishment and the reading of notes can be limited to simple techniques.

Each reading series contains a different vocabulary, but a large percentage of words in all series will be from the first 1,000 of the Thorndike Word List. This is a study of 20,000 frequently used words in children's books and is referred to by all publishers.

Words that are taught in one series and used in another are called "overlap" words. If *come* has been taught in one preprimer, the child will be able to read it in another. Notice the overlap words in five first preprimers listed at the top of p. 204.

The following facts should be noted. No two series use exactly the same vocabulary. Words such as *come, look, and,* and *here* do overlap. While no single book contains more than 21 words, the number of different words in these first preprimers is 65.

Because of these facts teachers find it best to go through the preprimers of one series first, then the preprimers of other series may be used for free reading while a child is studying in the primer.

The question of vocabulary control is of concern to teachers with respect to all materials available for classroom use. Simple library books with controlled vocabulary are being produced in great numbers. It is obvious that if this vocabulary does not have considerable overlap with the basic readers, it may be difficult. However, word count alone cannot determine the interest a child has in certain material. A book that is of great interest to a particular child may not

Overlap of Vocabulary in Five Preprimers

A	B	C	D	E
Tom	go	Tip	Ted	Bill
ride	Dick	no	run	come
Betty	help	here	jump	see
fast	look	come	Sally	and
Susan	Jane	Jack	Boots	Linda
Bunny	Sally	is	Mother	Ricky
see	Puff	not	to	here
Flip	here	with	come	Rags
and	Spot	me	look	run
Mother	run	Janet	at	fast
come	oh	find	and	to
airplane	at	home	Father	midnight
the	me	go	play	me
can	Tim	the	splash	look
Pony	get	ball		work
Father	down	will		at
apple	jump	you		home
get	come	I		can
Toys		and		
		play		

be as difficult as a vocabulary study indicates.

Schools sometimes adopt one basic series and then use books from other series as supplementary readers. This usually means that equipment such as flash cards and workbooks for the basic series is available. A common practice is to use three basic series in some grades to take care of differences in ability. The major advantage gained is in the area of content. Children in each group have their own stories. Then, too, some series may be better adapted to a slow group than to a fast group. However, attempting to follow three different manuals and plan three different types of lessons is a burdensome way for a beginning teacher to start.

From the child's point of view a reader is interesting or "good" according to its content. But the teacher looks upon the stories as the vehicle whereby certain skills are developed. The writers of a basic series first determine the method of teaching, which they build into the teacher's manual. Stories and vocabulary are selected that will best support the method employed. The manual is the key to the teacher's success. A student beginning to teach starts with the manual of the series used,

adjusts the suggestions in terms of what is known about the children, and adds material when needed. Although the manual is not a teaching plan, it does make suggestions for use as such. Basic reading instruction is a carefully organized activity designed to develop specific reading skills as well as an intensive consideration of the writer's ideas. Reading instruction is not a race to get to the end of a book or to cover a great mass of material in a short time.

Efforts have been made to organize the reading skills into levels of development. A textbook series often considers the reading readiness and preprimer books as being level one. The primer would be level two. Since modern series have divided the second and third grades into two levels, there are seven levels of skill development in the first three grades. Charts showing the plan of skill development may be secured from the textbook publishers. In practice the reading skills do not develop in such an orderly fashion. Unlike arithmetic with an orderly sequence, the language we use has a less apparent order of difficulty. The following chart indicates five levels of development in reading. While the first two are considered primary, some children will go beyond these levels in the second grade.

The Developmental Stages in Learning to Read [1]

V

THE STAGE OF REFINEMENT IN READING ABILITIES, ATTITUDES, AND TASTES

This stage may continue from the upper elementary grades well into adult life. In it the individual develops a differentiated attack on reading problems in line with his varied purposes for reading. He extends his reading interests and develops tastes for more worthwhile materials in current publications and recognized literature.

IV

THE STAGE OF EXTENDED READING EXPERIENCE AND RAPIDLY INCREASING EFFICIENCY

Children at this stage are no longer restricted to simple content because of limited vocabulary and are able to read material of such quality that interest motivates effort and increases power and independence. Children are capable of using a variety of texts in solving problems if they are trained in the techniques of setting up the problem, searching for authoritative answers, and of pooling, evaluating, and summarizing their findings.

III

THE STAGE OF RAPID PROGRESS IN BASIC READING SKILLS, HABITS, AND ATTITUDES

During this stage a child increases his sight vocabulary and develops ability to recognize new words by context, by association, by known parts, or by more detailed analysis. He begins to read with understanding a greater variety of materials. He forms the habit of reading independently for information and for pleasure. He develops the desire to share pleasant reading experiences with others and sees some of the possibilities of using reading in problem-solving activities.

II

THE INITIAL READING STAGE

This is the stage in which the children are taught to read material based on their current group experiences. The simple content involved may be that of science or events of daily living. Charts or booklets made by the teacher are used. It is important at this stage that children come to realize that their reading yields information useful to them in their activities and to feel that reading is fun. Habits of reading from left to right and from line to line are begun. Some practice in locating sentences is provided. Children are encouraged to note the distinctive configuration of words of special interest or of unique form and to compare words with like beginnings. At this stage, a basic reading vocabulary is established upon which to build as progress is made.

I

THE PREREADING STAGE

This is the stage during which the children engage in a program of experiences designed to develop mental, physical, emotional, and social readiness for reading.

---

[1] *The Elementary School Program in California XXVI*, No. 2 (Sacramento: State Department of Education, April 1957), p. 19.

1. What factors make a book easy or difficult for a child?

2. If there were no reading textbooks what material might be used to teach a child to read?

3. Why is the comic book format avoided in reading instructional material?

4. How many different words would be taught if the three preprimers of three different reading programs were used?

5. Why would a third grade teacher want to use a first reader that had not previously been used? Should there be certain books of simple reading difficulty reserved for use in the upper grades?

6. If a new series of readers were to be purchased in a system why would it be an efficient use of such material to use them in grades above that for which they had been written as well as at the level for which they were intended?

7. Is supplementary reading instruction the same as recreational reading?

HOW HAS THE READINESS CONCEPT INFLUENCED INSTRUCTIONAL PRACTICE IN READING?

In the development of each child there is a time when his language facility, experience, or social development would indicate that the child is ready for an aspect of reading instruction. The following check list indicates the aspects of readiness that a teacher would consider in the first grade. Some of these factors are developmental and cannot be influenced directly by instruction, while others, of course, may be influenced by the work of the kindergarten.

Check List for Reading Readiness [2]

Physical Readiness

	Yes	No
1. Eyes:		
a. Do the child's eyes seem comfortable? (Does he squint, rub eyes, hold material too close or too far away from eyes?)	____	____
b. Are the results of clinical test or an oculist's examination favorable?	____	____
2. Ears:		
a. Does he respond to questions or directions, and is he apparently able to hear what is said in class?	____	____
b. Does he respond to low-voice test of twenty feet, a whisper test of fifteen inches?	____	____
c. Is his audiometer test normal?	____	____
3. Speech:		
a. Does he speak clearly and well?	____	____
b. Does he respond to correction readily?	____	____
4. Hand-eye coordination:		
a. Does he make his hands work together well in cutting, using tools, or bouncing a ball?	____	____

----

[2] David Russell, et al., *Manual for Teaching the Reading Readiness Program* (rev. ed., Boston: Ginn, 1961), pp. 55–57.

	Yes	No

5. General health:
   a. Does he give an impression of good health? _____ _____

   b. Does he seem well nourished? _____ _____

   c. Does the school physical examination reveal good health? _____ _____

Social Readiness

1. Cooperation:
   a. Does he work well with a group, taking his share of the responsibility? _____ _____

   b. Does he cooperate with the other children in playing games? _____ _____

2. Sharing:
   a. Does he share materials without monopolizing their use? _____ _____

   b. Does he share his home toys with others? _____ _____

   c. Does he wait his turn in play or games? _____ _____

   d. Does he await his turn when classwork is being checked by the teacher? _____ _____

3. Self-reliance:
   a. Does he work things through for himself? _____ _____

   b. Does he work without asking teacher about the next step? _____ _____

   c. Does he take care of his clothing and materials? _____ _____

   d. Does he find anything to do when he finishes an assigned task? _____ _____

4. Good listening:
   a. Is he attentive? _____ _____

   b. Does he listen rather than interrupt? _____ _____

   c. Does he listen to all of a story with evident enjoyment so that he can re-tell all or part of it? _____ _____

   d. Can he follow simple directions? _____ _____

5. General:
   a. Does he take good care of materials assigned to him? _____ _____

   b. Does he follow adult leadership without objection or show of resentment? _____ _____

   c. Does he alter his own methods to profit by an example set by another child? _____ _____

Emotional Readiness

1. Adjustment to task:
   a. Does the child see a task (such as drawing, preparing for an activity, or cleaning up) through to completion? _____ _____

   b. Does he accept changes in school routine calmly? _____ _____

   c. Does he appear to be happy and well adjusted in school work, as evidenced by good attendance, relaxed attitude, pride in work, eagerness for a new task? _____ _____

	Yes	*No*

2. Poise:
   a. Does he accept a certain amount of opposition without crying or sulking?

   b. Can he meet strangers without unusual shyness?

Psychological Readiness

1. Mind set for reading:

   a. Does the child appear interested in books and reading?

   b. Does he ask the meanings of words or signs?

   c. Is he interested in the shapes of unusual words?

2. Mental maturity:
   a. Does the child's mental test show him sufficiently mature to begin reading?

   b. Can he give reason for his opinions about work of others or his work?

   c. Can he draw something to demonstrate an idea as well as children of his own age?

   d. Is his memory span sufficient to allow memorization of a short poem or song?

   e. Can he tell a story without confusing the order of events?

   f. Can he listen or work an average length of time without restlessness?

   g. Can he dramatize a story imaginatively?

3. Mental habits:
   a. Has the child established the habit of looking at a succession of items from left to right?

   b. Does he interpret pictures?

   c. Does he grasp the fact that symbols may be associated with pictures or subjects?

   d. Can he anticipate what may happen in a story or poem?

   e. Can he remember the central thought as well as important details?

4. Language:
   a. Does he speak clearly?

   b. Does he speak correctly after being helped with a difficulty by the teacher?

   c. Does he speak in sentences?

   d. Does he know the meanings of words that occur in pre-primers and primers?

   e. Does he know certain related words such as *up* and *down*, *top* and *bottom*, *big* and *little*?

The readiness books of a reading series are designed to present certain aspects of reading which the child will need for primer instruction.

Pictures of a mitten, man, monkey, and mouse are shown. After naming these pictures the child is led to notice that they start with the same sound. And he learns what the teacher means by "beginning of the word."

Context and sound clues are combined through pictures and listening exercises. A picture of a sweater, a mitten, and a mouse are shown. The teacher says, "Max went into the house to get something to keep him warm. What he got starts with the same sound as his name." [3]

Readiness tests measure some of these abilities. While limited in many ways, the readiness test helps the teacher check her own judgment of a child. A teacher inventory like the following will help her make judgments with respect to beginning reading.

Does the child have basic information about color and number?
Can the child carry out a sequence of directions?
Can the child tell what he sees in a picture?
Is the child interested when a story is being told?
Can the child listen to part of a story and provide an ending?
Can the child relate an experience in sequence?

At all levels of reading there is a readiness factor that concerns meaning.

Are you as a teacher ready to read the following selection and understand its meaning?

While the doctrine of the Trinity remains a mystery over which subtleties may be endlessly poured out as intellectual libations, in its total tangible effect it is an admonition that pure monotheism is not enough, whereas tri-theism is too much; the true idea of God lies between them; it must at least contain a procession out of the infinite reserve into the life of the universe of men, and without abandoning its absolute selfhood.[4]

Readiness is determined by interest in the topic, familiarity with the vocabulary and the intellectual ability to respond to the ideas.

Concepts such as the following from fourth- and fifth-grade books will cause reading difficulty unless the teacher anticipates the language background of the students and helps provide meaning for these terms:

Most of the *infectious* and *contagious* diseases are caused by *bacteria*.
Birds help to keep the *balance of nature*.
The *red corpuscles are racing through the capillaries*.
Business and industry were *paralyzed*.
Science has *unlocked the greatest force in nature*.

While such figures of speech and strange terms often cause trouble, the child may have the wrong meanings for the words. If the term *stag* means a boy without a date, imagine the meaning that might be read into Scott's line, "The stag at eve had drunk his fill."

Often it is the thought, rather than the words, that requires a readiness to understand. Even a beginning reader can recite Hamlet's "To be or not to be," but to understand these words requires a psychological orientation far beyond the child's mental capacity.

The clarification of concepts after reading reveals the need for teacher planning prior to reading. However, such clarification is also a part of long-range readiness training in that the children form a habit of demanding meanings that make sense as they read. Other long-range readiness practice may be illustrated by the way primary grades provide readiness for the work study skills of the intermediate years. Getting the main idea essential for the study of social studies and math, as well as outlining in language, can be started in the

[3] Lucille Harrison, *Getting Ready* (Boston: Houghton, 1960).

[4] Hocking Hibbert Lectures, "Living Religion and a World Faith" (London: G. Allen, 1940), p. 273.

primary grades by listening to decide what is the best title for a selection. Drawing conclusions can be presented in terms of listening to decide what will happen; the important skill of understanding association between ideas can be presented in terms of noticing the meaning of such words as *it, there, they,* which are referents to persons or things in preceding sentences.

As the children mature, the responsibility with respect to readiness for meaningful reading is shared with them by the teacher. In all areas of the curriculum the teacher accept responsibility for these tasks:

Help students construct the concepts which are needed to understand what is read. Express the assignment in questions that are stated and organized cooperatively by the teacher and the pupils. Such cooperative activity focalizes the assignment, sets purposes which motivate the reading, and provides opportunities for the pupil to evaluate and organize ideas read.

Provide for individual differences in reading by supplying some books that can be read by the poorest readers and other books which satisfy the best readers.

Set purposes for the discussion and additional activities which give the pupil opportunities to evaluate, organize, and plan for the retention of ideas gained through reading.

Give attention to each pupil's deficiencies in the reading-thinking jobs. The point of breakdown in locating information, arranging ideas, etc., must be diagnosed for each student.

In classroom practice the readiness concept has led to some specific ways to handle individual differences. These include (1) dividing the class into groups of children with similar needs, (2) creating reading material that will interest older children yet will not be too difficult in terms of word-attack skills, (3) planning so that children will learn from each other, (4) providing special rooms for those who need additional instruction, (5) individual-

Typical Group Organization

		GROUP III (6–10 pupils)	GROUP II (10–14 pupils)	GROUP I (10–14 pupils)
Characteristics		These pupils tend to cluster below grade level in achievement. They often have major reading difficulties. If they are below average in intelligence, they may be working at capacity. They lack interest in reading and seldom participate willingly in independent reading activities.	These pupils tend to be average achievers in reading. They progress steadily. They usually enjoy reading, but may not participate actively in personal interest reading. They have a good span of attention.	These pupils tend to exceed grade level expectancies. They are alert, curious, usually rapid readers, and complete assignments quickly. They can work on long assignments, engage in problem solving, enjoy reading, possess language facility, and have broad interests in reading.
Needs		These pupils require more oral reading, much work with easy material to gain fluency, review of word-attack skills, and assignments that are short, specific, and varied. Frequent encouragement and much motovation is needed. A diagnosis of cause of difficulty should be made if possible.	The needs of these pupils are similar to those in Group I, but with fewer extended assignments and somewhat less difficult work. They may need considerable encouragement in independent reading activities. They need careful and consistent skill development.	These pupils need more silent reading, less oral reading, challenging assignments, much supplementary and enrichment work, high level vocabulary activities, and thought-provoking comprehensive questions.

Pupils are changed from one group to another as their needs change.

Three groups are at work in this room. The teacher has made specific provisions on the chart to guide the work of one group while she is working at the reading circle. The third group studies independently.

izing all reading instruction in a single classroom, (6) organizing the curriculum as a nongraded primary school, (7) planning summer school programs that are both remedial and enriching.

Since the normal distribution of reading ability will present an achievement range of three to five years, three groups are a common pattern of classroom reading instruction (see p. 210).

1. Readiness is used in the sense of judging the maturity of a learner and in the sense of preparing the learner. Give an example of each practice.

2. In what situations do you feel it justified to delay instruction for a child who is ready to read until more in the class are at the same stage of development?

3. In Sweden, Denmark, and Norway children do not start to school until the age of seven. What could be the reasons for such practice?

4. Some children come to school who have taught themselves to read. What explanation can be given for such achievement?

5. Under what circumstances might it be better for a child to spend a summer on a farm than to attend a summer school?

HOW ARE READING SKILLS TAUGHT AT THE PRIMARY LEVEL?

The first step in word recognition is to help the child realize that the printed letters represent language. In the pre-primers the story is told through the pictures. The children discuss what is happening, and at first the teacher reads what the book characters are saying. As the story progresses and one of the characters is calling to his mother (or dog or baby) the teacher asks, "What would you say if you were the boy in the story?" Eventually a child will say, "Come here, Mother." "That is exactly what the story says," explains the teacher. "Now you read the words that tell us what the boy says."

The clue used here is the context or meaning clue. Through repetition of the words the child eventually remembers what the word says whenever he sees it. Some words cannot be developed from the meaning alone. Such words as *said, at, was, am, is,* and *blue* must be learned through planned repetition.

The beginner seldom depends upon sound clues alone to recognize a word but uses the sound represented by a letter in combination with meaning or word form. As soon as the child knows by sight two or more words that start the same way, he has a clue as to the sound of all words beginning with that letter. Some letter-sound associations seem to be used by most

children. The consonants *m, s, b, t, n,* and *j* appear to be quite easy as sound clues.

The first reading level would correspond to the time children are reading in the preprimers of a basic series. Programs that use other introductory procedures, such as writing, would postpone some of these activities until later.

Primary sight vocabulary is based upon words that the children use frequently and with meaning in their oral language. Familiar objects in the room are labeled. Words to be presented emerge from the discussion and are written on the board or on the chart. "This is what Dick said," the teacher comments as she writes *Come Jane. Come here.* "Who will read these words for us?" Then the word will be used in other situations until it is repeated many times and the children recognize it without prompting. Small cards with words printed on them are used. The children place the words on the proper article in a picture. Or the words are distributed and in turn each child puts his label on the proper article in the room. A box of variety-store items may provide the models. Names of the articles are pasted on a large cardboard designed to lie flat on the table. The children in turn place their article on the correct word. Color names are learned by matching two cards— one with only the name, the other with the name and color. The children in turn place their article on the correct word.

Word form clues are indicated in a number of ways. Have the children notice the form of a word, its general length, shape, size and configuration, without reference to individual letters. This is always done with a left-to-right motion of the hand under the word. After a short sentence, phrase, or word is read to the children, the word or words are displayed. The children are then asked to choose one of several pictures that illustrates what the word says. After a word is shown to the children, it is taken away. Children then close their eyes and try to "see" the word. Check by showing two words and have the children select the one they saw first. During this period words of unlike appearance are used such as: *name, bed, funny.* Attempting to distinguish between words that look alike, *this* and *that* or *funny* and *bunny,* will only cause confusion at this time.

Structural analysis starts with the *-s, -ing,* and *-ed* endings on words. Emphasis is placed on the part of the word that helps a child to remember which is the base or root word. Too great an emphasis on these endings will cause children to start looking at the wrong end of the word. The left-to-right habit of observing words can be stressed by presenting some words for drill in this fashion:

$$\text{help} + \text{s} = \text{helps}$$
$$\text{or} \quad \text{help} + \text{ed} = \text{helped}$$

or by direct contrast:

help	help
helps	helped

Phonetic analysis at this time is directed toward auditory discrimination. Speech jingles that repeat sounds should be used. If two or more words start with the same sound, the fact should be noted. Names that start the way words do provide a personal association with a sound. The emphasis is still on hearing parts of words, hearing the beginning of a word, or hearing the ending of a word. Names of letters are still being learned by some children during this period.

In preprimers the story is told with the pictures, while the reading is usually what the characters in the book say. Some stories are more easily reviewed if the pages are mounted in sequence like a cartoon strip. Have the children tell the story, then have them read what the story people are saying. Many series have the first preprimer in the form of a big book. This can be used for group instruction without the physical handling of the reading material during the initial introduction periods. When the child does get his own book it is a tremendous psychological experience for him to be able to read the first story independently.

The preprimer level will be completed by many children during the first half of the year. Some children will remain at this level throughout the first grade, a few need to start at the preprimer level in the second grade.

Most children arrive at primer level after reading the preprimers of the basic series. Children are ready to read a primer story when their interest has been aroused, their previous experiences have been keyed in with the story, and their speaking vocabularies have become adequate to deal with the concepts. Guided discussion and sharing of experiences pertinent to the story to be read give the children experience in talking and listening and develop readiness. A motivating question before silent reading helps children to read for meaning. Good reading and study habits are developed during the silent reading of the story. The children learn to identify their own problems of word recognition and comprehension and ask for help when needed. In the beginning, a lesson may consist of only one page of a story. As reading skills are developed, the children can manage larger units.

Discussion following silent reading helps the children to clear up comprehension problems. They can enjoy the humor of the story together and discuss relationships of characters. The teacher is able to check comprehension further by asking questions.

Rereading may be done after the silent reading of each page or after the reading of the entire story. The motivation of rereading should be to find the answer to a question, to find out how the characters felt, to enjoy the story, or to find the most interesting parts.

With respect to phonics, the children and teacher start to build a chart of "key" words to use in working out new words. This chart is built slowly, adding words as they are met in reading.[5]

The following single-consonant chart is a typical example. Words used on the chart should be words in the reading series being used. One series would use *work* instead of *wagon;* another, *look* instead of *little.*

Bb	baby	*Nn*	not
Cc	come	*Pp*	pet
Dd	dog	*Qq*	quack
Ff	father	*Rr*	run
Gg	go	*Ss*	something
Hh	house	*Tt*	toy
Jj	jump	*Vv*	valentine
Kk	kite	*Ww*	wagon
Ll	little	*Xx*	

---

[5] Devices presented here are from many sources, the major one being the 1960 Language Arts Course of Study of Grand Rapids, Mich. Other suggestions came from teachers in classes taught by the author.

Mm	mother	*Yy*	yellow
		Zz	zoo

(The word after *x* is omitted because the children will encounter *x* mostly at the end of words, as in *box*.)

From the very beginning, children should be taught how to skip over a word and then think it out from context, since they must necessarily do a great deal of this in later independent reading. After the student becomes familiar with the sounds of initial consonants he should be taught to check his guessed word with the beginning sound of its printed form. The following procedure is suggested as one means of helping him acquire this skill:

In the sentence "Tom saw a bird fly to the ground," we assume that *fly* is the only word which the child does not know.

TEACHER: Look at the word. What is another word that starts with the same sound?

CHILD: "Fun."

TEACHER: What does a bird do that starts like *"fun?"*

CHILD: "Fly."

TEACHER: Now read the sentence again to see if the word fits.

The following purposes and exercises are appropriate at the primer level:

Purpose

To develop greater comprehension emphasize reading for meaning.

Exercise

From a pack of cards with words on them, choose the ones that fit in each of the following sentences:

See the _____ red car.
  (little)
Find _____ big cars for me.
  (two)
Find a big _____ ball.
  (red)

Draw a picture illustrating a riddle. Copy the riddle and paste it below the picture.

To develop auditory and visual discrimination, encourage meaningful associations of sight words through the use of picture clues.

Make cards with a picture on one side and the word on the other side. Say the word and then turn the card over to see if it is correct.

Purpose

To develop the use of structural analysis as a means to better word recognition by providing opportunities to recognize the variant *s*.

Exercise

Provide pictures of two boats with the words boat and boats. Have the children look at the pictures and put a circle around the correct word. Repeat with many different pictures.

The same words beginning with a capital and small letter are like two completely different words to first graders. You can put two lists on the board:

come	not
do	Do
Not	will
Will	Come
Go	go

Touch two children and say a word. The children go to board, frame the word and say it. Have a child touch and say the word in the first column and another child finds it again and says it in the second. Direct a child to draw lines between the two words that say the same. Ask a child to erase the words he can say. Later these same words may be used in sentences on the board. This should give further meaning to words and provide an added reading situation.

* * *

At the first-reader level the children show more independence in reading. They are able to read and grasp the meaning of longer and more involved stories, to use context clues, to predict outcomes and draw conclusions in stories, to feel success and joy because they have a substantial reading vocabulary. Many children are at this level at the beginning of their second year in school, others will have mastered this material by the end of the first year.

In auditory and visual discrimination the children begin to recognize initial consonant blends such as: *bl*—black, *fr*—friend, *sp*—spell, and *dr, gr, pl, st, tr*. Words are added to a chart of consonant blends as they are met in reading. Some will not be met until second reader level. The consonant

blend and digraph chart would appear like this:

bl	black		*sh*	she
br	brown		*sk*	skate
ch	children		*sm*	small
cl	clown		*sn*	snow
cr	cry		*sp*	spell
dr	dress		*st*	stop
fl	flag		*sw*	swing
fr	friend		*th*	this
gl	glad		*tr*	train
gr	green		*tw*	twin
pr	pretty		*wh*	white
sc	scat			

Children at the first-reader level begin to learn the following final consonant sounds:

d	red	*g*	pig	*k*	book
l	wheel	*m*	him	*n*	hen
p	up	*s*	us	*t*	bat

Picture dictionaries made by the children will reinforce most of the consonant sounds as well as establish a dictionary concept. Such an activity might be an early homework assignment. Use a notebook or single sheets that may later be assembled. At the top of each quarter space the child may paste a picture of some familiar object. Each object picture must start with a different sound. He then cuts words from old magazines starting with those sounds and pastes them in the correct column.

With respect to word structure children begin to recognize the *-ed, -d, -ing* and *s* ending. After the children have studied a story with the teacher, sentences such as the following may be written on the board:

The man stopped at the house.
The big black bear walked in.
The baby climbed on his back.
The children marched around the room.
The door opened.

The teacher then gives the following directions:

Draw a line under the word that tells what the man did when he came to the house.

Draw a line under the word that tells how the bear came in.

Draw a line under the word that tells how the baby got on the bear's back.

Draw a line under the word that tells what the children did.

Draw a line under the word that tells what the door did.

The teacher will then call attention to the way all of the words underlined on the board end.

TEACHER: Very often we come to a word that looks like a new word to us when it is really an old word with *-ed* on the end of it. I'll write a word on the blackboard and then I'll ask one of you to write *-ed* on the end of the word and tell what it is after you have changed it. (*Writes such words as* help, look, call, walk, *etc. Individuals write* ed *on the end and pronounce the word.*)

. . . .

The following exercises may be used at the first reader level:

Purpose

To check the children's understanding.

Exercise

Write the best word on each line:

1. A rabbit _____ in a hole under a tree.
      live lived
2. The rabbit said, "I _____ I had red wings."
         wish wished
3. He _____ in the Wishing Pond.
      look looked
4. The rabbit _____ around three times.
            turn turned
5. He _____ home to show his wings to his mother.
      start started

To develop the ability to comprehend more involved stories provide opportunities for answering questions about a story. Children may be urged to make inferences with exercises like this.

Draw a circle around the correct word.

Dick liked Spot.   Yes   No
Sally was happy.   Yes   No

Purpose

Comprehension of words may be checked in a game of this nature.

Exercise

Play "Going Places":
A pack of cards placed upside down at the front of the room. Two or three players are chosen. A starting line and finish line are designated. Each in turn takes a card from the top of the pack. One may read, "Take two steps." "Take one big step." Another, "Go back one step." "Jump." "Stay where you are." A "Run" card allows the child to go to the good line at once and win.

Classification exercises will also check comprehension.

Put these words under the correct heading:

Things to Wear   *Things to Ride*

coat	train	cap
boat	horse	mitten
airplane	dress	hat

The Reading Lesson

During the period of reading instruction there are details with respect to the attention span of individuals in the group, the need for physical movement, the handling of material, the thought given to the remaining members of the classroom, which are in addition to the immediate aspects of the lesson. These are indicated in the following lesson. A group of students in a class of Dr. Constance McCullough created this material. The story being read is "Little Red Riding Hood." [6]

The teacher and pupil activities are indicated first; then an explanation of the points remembered by the teacher is given as the class proceeds throughout the lesson.

The first aspect of the lesson is to build a common background for the group and to build the forms and meaning of the vocabulary used in the story.

1. The children are in a circle in the front of the room. The teacher starts by asking, "How many of you have ever been to the woods?" "What is it like in the woods?" "Are there woods near here?"

"How is it different from the town or city?"

Set the mood for reading. Develop unfamiliar concepts. Find out what is known; have children inform each other; determine what, if anything, you must explain to them. Contrast is an effective teacher.

2. "Our story today is about a girl who lives near the woods. Read this silently as I write it and be ready to read it aloud." Write: The little girl lives near the woods. As you start to write the *w* for woods, say "woods," for this is the one word the children do not know. (If the word were polysyllabic, like *hunter,* you would say "hunt" as you wrote the *h* and say "er" as you wrote the *er.*)

Silent reading before oral encourages efficient reading unimpeded by lip movements. Stand to one side as you write, so that *all* can see. Seat children so that this is possible. Say new words as you write them, so that children may have *simultaneous* impressions of the word from ear and eye. Write the word in a phrase or sentence so that it appears in a normal setting, making normal demands upon the reading eye and providing clues for later identification.

[6] Constance McCullough, *Handbook for Teaching the Language Arts* (San Francisco: Paragon Publications, 1958).

3. "Let's all read it together." Run hand under the sentence as the children read, to stress left-to-right observation.

All children thus experience seeing, hearing, saying—of the new word in a setting that emphasizes its meaning as well as its form. Unison activity tends to keep all children involved, watching and thinking.

4. "The little girl's name was Little Red Riding Hood." Write, and say as you write, Little Red Riding Hood. "Let's all say it." "Who can find the new word in this name and frame it and say it for us?" Child comes up, puts hand on either side of "Hood" and says "Hood." "Is he right?" "Let's read that word together." Pass hand under word as they read.

Children watch you write the words and are forced to observe them from left-to-right. Their first impression, at least, cannot be reversed or confused about which word says what. Have children take special notice of the new word. Framing of the words focusses the attention of the group and shows clearly which word child thinks he is "reading." "Is he right?" makes whole group think and react rather than being silent and passive spectators. "Who can find" rather than "John, show us" puts all children on their toes.

5. "Red Riding Hood met someone in this story. You can solve the word for yourselves. Watch carefully as I write and be ready to read the phrase." Write: met a hunter. The children know *hunt* and *-er* from word analysis training. Pause to give children time to read. "Who will read it for us; Bill?" Bill comes up, frames phrase and reads. "Is he right?" "How do you know? Jane?" Jane explains that the word contains *hunt* and *-er*. She comes up, frames separate parts and says them as she does this. "Let's read the phrase together." Have children discuss what a hunter does, what he might be hunting, etc. Show picture if necessary to clarify idea.

Have children solve for themselves the words that follow principles of word analysis they have learned. All children should engage in word analysis which they have been taught. Those who don't understand can learn from another child's explanation. All experience multisensory approach to the word in a meaningful setting. Develop concept of *hunter*.

6. Suppose that all words that are new in the story have been introduced as above. On the chalkboard now are the sentences and phrases: The little girl lives near the woods, Little Red Riding Hood, met a hunter, carried a basket, a big wolf. The teacher says, "Let's read together now the phrases and sentences on the chalkboard." Some children will need much repetition of the words, others very little. For extremely slow readers (learners), the teacher may not even introduce the story itself that day, but invent a story of her own on chalkboard and pocket chart which gives additional practice with new words and phrases.

7. *Comprehension check:* "Who can find, frame, and read the line that tells where someone lives? Jerry?" "Who can find the phrase that tells whom she saw in the woods? Janet?" "Who can find the name of our little girl? Buster?" "Who can find the phrase that tells about a man? Dick?" "Who can find what Little Red Riding Hood took with her? Jo?"

Recognition of the word should stress its meaning as well as its form. Here, you are not just testing one child; you are giving others a chance to see and hear the words again. Make sure that all are watching, not tying shoestrings.

8. *Word recognition check:* "Stand when you think you can find, frame, and read to us one of our new words. Pat?" Do this for all the words. "We read our words from left to right. Underline the new word from left to right as you say it." (Pat doesn't know what to do.) "Janet will you help him?"

Change of position relieves physical fatigue and keeps children with you. Young children needs these changes more frequently than older. Chair-scraping, wiggling and inattention are your signals. Stress left-to-right direction. Give children experiences in helping each other. Encourage them to feel that being shown the way is help rather than negative criticism or a cause for embarrassment.

9. *Flash-card exercise:* Have flash cards containing words they know and the new words, so that you can build phrases and sentences with them. Sit to the right of the pocket chart so that you will not cover the cards as you set them in from left to right. "I am going to make a story; but, instead of telling it to you, I am going to have you read it to me. Watch carefully and be ready to read my first sentence."

Maintain the left-to-right observation of print by the order in which you insert the cards. Give children a purpose for watching before you start. Children who know what is expected of them are more apt to do it.

10. Put into the pocket chart the cards: I went into the woods one day. Have a child read the sentence. Have all stand who agree that this is right. Add other sentences similarly. Finally, have whole story read, then new words identified.

Do not summarize here the story they will read in the book; make a different story. Physical relief through movement is provided again if needed.

11. "Now, I am going to show you some words. If you recognize the word I show, stand." Show *hunter.* Children stand. "Jim, will you read it for us?" "Let's all say it together: *hunter.* Be seated. Are you ready for the next word?" Etc.

Test of word recognition without context fosters careful study of the word. Speed is not nearly so important as care, here. Call on one child; otherwise, children who don't know the word will stand for the honor of looking smart and get away with it.

12. *Chalkboard exercise:* This can be similar to the pocket chart exercise or a variation such as: Trees grow in the woods; A hunter shoots animals. "I shall write a sentence on the chalkboard. If you can read it, stand." Have a child read it. "Is this a true statement? Do trees grow in the woods? Can you prove it?" Have the child show the picture you used for the concept of woods earlier, showing the trees in the woods.

These sentences make children think of the meanings of the new words. Have an established signal such as standing, raising hand, to reduce chaos. When true-false statements are given, always require proof. Otherwise, you are teaching guessing, not reading or thinking.

13. *Chart or newsprint exercise:* Prepare a story on a chart, using the new words. Have the children read it to you and reread parts in response to your comprehension clues. Or have children make up their own cooperative story using the new words. Draw stick figures on the chalkboard and have child read the sentence your picture refers to. Have child pantomime a meaning and have another child read the word or sentence so illustrated.

Words are best learned in meaningful settings of known words. Repeated exposures to the new words in varied settings finally cause learning. Creative expression is an effective way of cementing impressions. The drawings provide interest of guessing and variety for the same old purpose; getting the child to read the sentence. Pantomime also lends variety and gets the wiggliest temporarily off the squeaky chair.

The second aspect of the lesson concerns the directed reading of the story.

14. "Who would be a good person to pass books today? Petunia?" "Let's open our books to the table of contents. How many have found the page with the table of contents on it? George, you could find it faster with the book right-side up. There; that's right." "Look down the page, now, for the name of our new story, *Little Red Riding Hood.* Let's read the name of our story and the page it is on aloud, together: *Little Red Riding Hood,* page forty-five."

Keep the books safely tethered until you need them. Make passing the books an honor—incidentally, another reason for good behavior and attention. Some children get D in reading because they get A in horseplay. Much better than drawing attention to George would be a quiet signal to him or turning his book. Give him credit when he does it right.

15. "Who will write our page number on the chalkboard? Angus?" "In which half of our book will we find page forty-five?

Esther?" "When you have found the page, study the picture at the top of it and be ready to tell me what you see."

Do this if writing numbers is still difficult for the children. Help children judge how far back into the book to look for a page. Reading the table of contents is learned by using every opportunity to read it. Even primers have tables of contents.

16. "What is happening in the picture?" (Little Red Riding Hood is talking to a lady—must be her mother. Little Red Riding Hood must be ready to go to the woods—she has her basket her mother is just filling with cookies and she has her little red riding hood on.) "Who is talking in the picture?" (her mother) "Read the first page and be ready to tell what her mother said." "Look up when you are ready." Aside to Everett: "Are you sure you read it carefully and know the answer?" "What did Mother say? Alec?" (Take this here baskit to gramma's and doan say nuttin to strangers and come straight ta home.)

This general question brings out main idea and some details, whereas "Who is in the picture?" gives you just one detail. In guiding the reading of young readers, give them something to look for in a paragraph, a page, or in two pages. Older readers (such as high third or fourth grade average readers) may have a purpose set for reading an entire story alone. In all cases, however, a purpose is set. Children need to learn to read for a variety of purposes. Therefore, try to vary the objective of the reading throughout the lesson.

17. "Why do you think she wanted Grandmother to have the cookies?" "Why did she warn Little Red Riding Hood about strangers and coming straight home?" "Who will read what she said and make it sound the way she must have said it?" "Let's look at Joe and listen while he reads, to hear how she sounded." "What do you think Little Red Riding Hood will say? Let's read the next page to find out." Proceed through the story, asking questions and discussing points, until the end.

Make children aware of the human relationships and feelings, reasons behind behavior. Oral reading should have a listening audience. Oral reading is optional here, depending upon how much is needed for practice. Oral reading here serves the purpose of increasing children's awareness of mother's feeling and concern. Have children predict events. Here, again, a purpose is set for silent reading. The third aspect of the instruction is to provide purposeful rereading of the material.

18. "We talked yesterday about how Little Red Riding Hood's mother felt about her going into the woods alone. How do you think Little Red Riding Hood herself felt? Find the place that makes you think that, and read it aloud to us."

A single reading of a basal reader story does justice neither to the story nor to the learning of the new words. Basal reading experience should give the child more insight into the story meaning than he would have derived alone or in one reading. "Intensive reading" is the term.

19. "Let's listen carefully while Harry reads and decide whether that part does show that Little Red Riding Hood was happy and excited as Harry said . . . " (Harry reads.) "Do you think Harry is right? Does any other place in the story make you think that she was glad? Billy?" Etc. "Why do you think she was happy and excited? Any other reasons?" "Did Little Red Riding Hood remember everything her mother said? How many of you think she did? No one? Find the place that makes you think she didn't. . . . What should Little Red Riding Hood have done instead of stopping to talk?" (Children can act this out if you wish, to get the feeling for situation.) "What kind of person do you think Little Red Riding Hood was?" Various answers here will lead to reading various parts for proof. Put the adjectives used by the children on the chalkboard. "What words describe your idea of the wolf?" Put these in parallel column.

Oral reading should have an audience that listens for meanings. Children should not always watch the page as a child reads aloud, for this practice puts the children's attention on the accuracy of the reading rather than on the ideas expressed. Have the audience either look at the speaker, "breast" their books, or hold their fingers in the partly closed book. In any case, impress the children with the fact that this is a *listening* time.

Purposeful rereading time is a time for asking questions which require a variety of types of comprehension, skimming to find answers, and oral reading activities.

20. As children discuss wolf's characteristics, have them notice these points of plot in relation to him: "Why did the wolf use a special voice, as Esther said, when he talked to Little Red Riding Hood? Why did he tell her to pick a bouquet? Why didn't he eat her then instead of going for her grandmother? Pretend you are the wolf talking to himself about what he did and what he is going to do. Who would like to do that? Did the wolf succeed in fooling Little Red Riding Hood when he sat in bed dressed like Grandmother? No? Find the place that makes you think she began to doubt."

Make children aware of cause and effect, motives and results, effect of certain choices upon plot. Have children grasp the point of view of each important character. Give children the experience of skimming for evidence.

21. "Do you think this story could really have happened? Why or why not? What in the story seems real? What seems untrue to life? What do we call a story like this?" "If your grandmother were in trouble in her home, would a hunter come to rescue her? Who would? Who protects us? Who could give her the best help?" Have the children observe that the kind of helper would depend on grandmother's trouble: illness, burglary, fire, etc.

Have the children judge the real as opposed to the fanciful. Have them learn the terms applied to fanciful tales of this kind. Feature the relationship of the story to the child's own living.

22. "We can take better care of our grandmothers than Little Red Riding Hood could in the woods." "Do you think this story is a story of today or of long ago? Do you get any clues in the pictures or the story that make you think this? What are

they?" "Why do you think this story was called Little Red Riding Hood? Can you think of a better name for it? What if this story appeared in a newspaper. . . . What would the headline be?" (Hunter De-Grandmothers Wolf.)

Protect the children from nightmares! Study the illustrations for a purpose. Have children express the main ideas in a variety of ways.

The fourth aspect of the lesson provides practice and application of skills taught.

23. "The author of this story had a good way of telling how things looked and acted and felt and tasted. How did he say Little Red Riding Hood skipped down the path? (like a bouncing ball) How did he say the wolf's eyes looked when he saw the cookies?" (like two ripe plums) Write these expressions on the chalkboard, under one another. "What do you notice about these two lines?" (They both begin with "like." They both liken something to something else to make it clear.)

Skill-building of various types (word recognition, word analysis, comprehension, interpretation, study skills) is done in five or ten-minute exercise periods. Preferably they are done at the end of a period (group meeting), so that you may assign individual follow-up work at the children's desks to prove individual grasp of the work done. Usually reader manuals suggest from two to five such exercises. You should use all of them at some time during the days involved in the story, unless you are sure that the children can do them well enough without practice. Each exercise is a link in a chain of learnings. To leave one out is to risk worse performance later on, or forgetfulness of the technique. Reading skills rust out from disuse.

24. "As I pass out these sheets of paper to you, read the directions at the top to see what authors can do with words. Will you read the directions to us, Henry?" "What does that mean we should do? Yes, we are to read each sentence, find it in our story, and complete it. Read the first one to us, Bill." (Little Red Riding Hood skipped down the path like a ____ ____.) "What should we write in the blanks? . . . Yes. Now you are to do the others in the same

way. At the bottom of the page you are to write your own endings to sentences. You are to tell how YOU think Little Red Riding Hood looked as she skipped down the path. What could you say she looked like when she skipped?" "These expressions are called similes." Write *similes* on the chalkboard. Have the children repeat the word with you. Face them so that they can see your lips.

Help children read directions. Have one child read aloud, or all in unison. Don't assume they know what is meant. Ask them to tell what is meant. Go through the sample with them. This is creative work. Each lesson desirably has some imitative activity and some creative; something that takes a short time, something that takes time, thought. Use the technical term the children will have to become accustomed to in later work. Strange words are better grasped when the lips of the speaker can be seen.

25. "Now, who will tell us what he is going to do on this page? Douglas?"

Have a child tell what the job is, in summary, so that no question remains.

26. "Does everyone understand? If you finish early, what can you do?" Have a list of activities somewhere on a chart or on the chalkboard, which are legitimate uses of reading time if a child finishes early.

Waiting for the class causes restlessness if a child finishes early. Use reading time for reading activities, not bead stringing, sawing, unrelated to reading.

27. Later, either that day or at the next meeting with the group, go over the papers with the children, either individually or as a group. "Who will read the first sentence? Do you all agree with his answer? No? What do you have, Jerry? How can we find out who is right? Let's look in our books and find the place. Now, read it aloud, please, to us, Jerry."

Rereading of the papers provides another reading experience. Proofreading to find one's own rights and wrongs is more effective for learning than teacher-marked papers. Teach the children to refer to author-ity rather than languish on a "tis-taint" basis.

28. The following exercise was designed to make children aware of author's style, to give them a new language tool of their own, and to reexperience the words of the story. As you read this story of life in the woods many years ago, was there anything you wondered about that the story did not tell? List the questions the children ask. Decide where they might find the answers. This may lead to a visit to the library, the reading of books you have collected on woodland animals, etc., the seeing of a film, the listening to a story you read—then having the children tell what they found out. Perhaps, then, having collected this information, they will wish to express it in pictures or in a scrapbook as well as in discussion. Other creative activities might be such as these: to have the children pretend they had been Little Red Riding Hood and write or tell the story as it would have happened to them; to write the story cooperatively as a news story; to write a story about another wolf, etc.; to make illustrations for the story the child makes up.

Enrichment activities are of two kinds: informal and creative. Informational activities are those which add to the child's knowledge. Creative are those in which he expresses his own ideas regarding the story. Both are important and desirably we should have both in a lesson plan for a story. Children should have the incentive of being read to as well as the work of reading for themselves. Creative work can be a natural outcome of research activities. Telling a story involves the use of concepts being learned; sometimes reveals misconceptions which must be straightened out. Writing a similar story means writing the new words the children are still trying to master—an effective left-to-right experience with the new symbols. Drawings or other artistic expression related to reading not only give children a pleasant association with reading but crystallize impressions for the child and reveal any misconceptions to the teacher.

1. Observe a first grade teacher at work. Note the similarities between what she does and what was described above.

2. Would it confuse a beginning teacher to attempt to explain all aspects of a lesson that she has taught?

3. How much of these activities could be imitative of those of an experienced teacher without knowing the reason why they are done and still be a part of a good teaching performance?

4. Do you agree that vocabulary is best developed in situations that require its use, or would you plan lessons involving lists of new words for lessons similar to spelling lessons for vocabulary development?

5. Would you defend the use of special-skill textbooks in addition to the readers being used?

6. Do you think that primary children should make greater progress in reading than we now expect? How might this be done? What factors other than reading skill should be considered in instruction?

7. Defend or criticize this statement: "The teacher should spend as much time finding the right reading material for a child as instructing him in reading."

8. Would it be possible for two different children to use different clues to recognize a word? If possible, illustrate different ways of recognizing a word.

9. Children may recognize a word that is familiar in their language but they must identify a word that is strange in meaning as well as form. What skills are more associated with identification than recognition? At what grade levels are identification skills used?

10. While some children will have mastered much of the reading process by the end of six months, we know that it is quite normal for others of equal mental ability to reach the fourth grade before this happens. How can we explain this to parents? How can we give these children praise and recognition in a nonreading activity? What are the children learning that is as important as learning to read?

11. Studies of highly gifted children (150 IQ and above) reveal that a common pattern for them to follow in reading development is to be average or below until the late third grade. How can this be explained?

12. What special problems does a child face in learning to read when he comes from a home where English is not spoken? What are his major educational needs? Should such children be grouped with slow learning children from English speaking homes?

HOW ARE CHARTS USED IN READING INSTRUCTION? [7]

Many children enter first grade with great enthusiasm for learning to read. Some fully expect to read the first day. We know that the best quality of learning takes place when there is thirst for it. If a class "has its mind set" on wanting to read, there is a simple way to begin that not only satisfies the eager child but also paves the way for the more formal type of reading. The first group experience to be recorded and read may be as simple as a brief record of play. It might look like this:

We played dodge ball.
It was fun.

The teacher may need to create the brief statements of the very first recorded experiences. Very soon, however, children

catch on to the idea and there is ready response to: "What might we say about what we did?"

Interest span of first graders at the beginning of the year is very brief so care must be taken to get a few brief statements on the blackboard rather rapidly. Then with the teacher using pointer to help scan the line from left to right, the group repeats what has been written. Then the pointer moves to the beginning of the next line and moves smoothly to the end of the sentence as it is read with the teacher. There is no stopping at words. It is saying what had been said with attention to two lines of symbols that are as unfamiliar to the children as the scratchings on the Dead Sea Scrolls would be to most adults. After it has been read once or twice the teacher might say, "That is reading and you can do it." Her enthusiasm and pleasure reassures

[7] This section developed by Verna Dieckman Anderson, formerly professor at Wayne University, Detroit, Mich.

the children that reading is fun and they anticipate a next experience. That would be enough for one time and the group would proceed to other types of activities. During the day the teacher might copy the sentences on a sheet of newsprint and bring it out just before the children go home. Again they would read it together with the teacher and go home with the feeling that they had learned to read, just what they had expected to do, and parents are convinced from the first day's report that the children are off to a good start.

Each day new experiences are recorded. The teacher gives guidance in getting variety into the sentences, in keeping them simple, and in supplying appropriate words or phrases as needed. Sometimes charts are reread from day to day as long as interest is maintained. They are discarded as they lose significance.

This classroom example will illustrate a part of the teacher planning that takes place as an experience chart is developed.

The children have completed the construction of a barn. The teacher considered possibilities for stories which would include words from the reading list such as:

Look, look.	See, see.
Look at our barn.	See our barn.
It is big.	It is green.
Hay, horses, and	It is white.
feed are in it.	Animals live in the barn.

These two stories, thought out by the teacher, should be compared with the story finally composed by the group. The teacher guided the children to make up their story and accepted their contributions, even though she had several ideas as to how it might develop. The pre-planning helped her to control vocabulary and length, even though the resulting story dictated by the children was different.

With this preparation the teacher guides the children's discussion:

TEACHER: What are some of the things we could write about our barn?

CHILD 1: Bobby, John, and Mary helped to make it.

CHILD 2: It is big.

CHILD 3: It is painted.

CHILD 4: I helped.

CHILD 5: I saw one. It was red.

TEACHER: What color is ours?

CHILD 1: White and green.

TEACHER: What is in a barn?

CHILD 1: Horses.

CHILD 2: Food for the animals.

CHILD 3: Cows to be milked.

TEACHER: You've told many interesting things about our barn. Do you think we could tell in a story the things which are most important?

CHILD 4: You mean a story like we did about the trucks?

TEACHER: Yes.

CHILD 3: Yes, a story like the truck story.

As the teacher asks questions in logical order and the children respond, their sentences are written on the chalkboard by the teacher.

TEACHER: You've made a fine barn. What could you say to make others look at the barn?

CHILD 2: See our barn. (Teacher records.)

TEACHER: That would make us look, wouldn't it?

TEACHER: What color is it?

CHILD 1: White and green.

TEACHER: What can you tell about the colors in a sentence?

CHILD 3: It is white and green. (Teacher records.)

TEACHER: What is kept in the barn?

CHILD 4: The farmer goes in there.

TEACHER: That's right. Is that where he lives?

CHILD 4: No, but the horse does.

TEACHER: Yes, and what else would we find in the barn?

CHILD 2: Hay.

CHILD 3: Feed.

TEACHER: Who can give us a sentence with the things you mentioned in it?

CHILD 1: The farmer stays in the barn sometimes; the horse, the feed, and hay are in the barn.

TEACHER: You've included everything that was said. Would it be all right if I left the farmer out since he doesn't live there,

Gg Hh Ii Jj Kk Ll Mm Nn Oo Pp Qq Rr Ss Tt Uu Vv Ww Xx Yy Zz 1234567890

Oh see.
See Puff.
See funny Puff.
Funny funny Puff.

Lyneal's Pet

Lyneal has a pet.
It is a dog.
It is called Pancho.
It is brown and white.

See the red ball.
See the ball go up.
See the ball go down.
Up and down.
Up and down.
See the red ball.

See Puff.
See Puff jump.
See Puff jump up.
Up, up, up.
See funny Puff.

San Diego County Schools, Calif.

The initial reading instruction in this classroom is with reading charts. The class is reviewing charts made during previous sessions. The teacher has planned the vocabulary so that the children will be able to read preprimers independently.

and say, "Hay, feed, and horses are in the barn"? (*Teacher records.*)

CHILD 1: Yes.

TEACHER: We've said many good things about the barn. Let's read the story together, and as we are reading, maybe you can think of a title for the story. (*Class reads together.*)

CHILDREN: (*In unison.*) See our barn. It is white and green. Hay, feed, and horses are in the barn.

TEACHER: Does someone have any idea for our title?

Titles are not necessary for all stories. When they are used the teacher will guide children to select a title quickly.

CHILD 1: See Our Barn.

CHILD 2: The Green and White Barn.

CHILD 3: Our Barn.

TEACHER: Shall we use that one?

CHILDREN: (*In unison.*) Yes. (*Teacher records "Our Barn" above the story.*)

Follow-up activities may include such things as drawing a picture to illustrate the story; work on such basic words as look, at, our, it, big, see; writing one sentence or word, and of course, rereading the story the next day.

In making charts, keep the printed matter well centered so there is a balance of space around the story. The print must be large enough so that it can be easily read by all the children. It is a good idea to draw very light lines if newsprint is used, or scratch lines with a pin if oaktag is used. Tall letters should be about three inches high and small letters about an inch and a half. An inch should be allowed between lines. Use a medium-size felt pen to do the lettering and be sure to make correct letter forms with proper spacing between letters and between words.

In addition to group-experience charts other types of charts are needed.

Picture Charts—For variety a large colorful picture may be introduced and short sentences written about the picture. Sometimes the class will dictate short sentences telling about the picture; later, when a sizable sight vocabulary has been estab-

lished, the teacher may bring in a surprise illustrated story using words the children know.

Weather Charts—The first type of recording might be: This is a sunny day; or, Today is cloudy. Children might advance to: Today is December 4. It is cloudy and cold. We saw snowflakes this morning. It may snow tonight.

Sometimes symbols for clouds, wind, sun, rain, etc., are inserted in slots on a chart. If turnover pages are kept, at the end of the month children may count the number of cloudy days, etc. The days of the week may be added to such a chart as time goes on. The months of the year as well as temperature readings may be added as children are ready for such experiences. Third grade children might have a rather complete weather record including the direction of the wind and barometric readings.

News Item Charts—As children share news with the class a teacher might record such items as:

Linda has a baby brother.
Paul's father went to Chicago.
Barbara has new shoes.
Jim has a birthday today.

As the year advances the news might extend to what is happening in the community and in faraway places.

Planning Charts—These may start with something as simple as:

We will listen to a story.
Next we will play a game.
Then we will sing.
Our work period comes next.

As time goes on such charts could include specific directions the group will follow such as:

Tomorrow we will make butter.
We will need:

— — —

etc.

A listing of names of those responsible for bringing certain things or doing each of the tasks involved may be included.

Directions for a new game, social studies procedures, choice of work experiences, household duties, and rules for fair and safe play may go into various charts in which children play a part in the planning.

Record Charts—Such charts would indicate progress or growth. There might be a height and weight chart. One might indicate the changes that take place as children observe bulbs or plants grow and bloom. Another might keep the scores of games that are played from time to time. Still another might record the names of stories the teacher reads so it can be referred to for later choices of favorites. Later in the year records can be kept of books the children read, of achievements in other learning activities, and of items they might wish to include in a "First Grade Yearbook."

Reference Charts—A color chart to which children may refer when they are learning their colors; a number chart; a picture dictionary type chart for word recognition; a phonics chart; a bird or flower chart are all examples of this type of chart.

In summary, the use of charts with young children serve the following purposes:

Classroom-created charts give the reading process real meaning and significance, since the children's own experiences are the basis for them.

The mechanics of reading are practiced. These include:

Left-to-right eye movement.
The sweep from the end of one line to the beginning of the next.
The significance of words and sentences.
Observation of the use of simple punctuation.

Children are helped to see that reading serves many purposes.

Much language development takes place (producing clear, simple sentences; expansion of vocabulary; thought organization; proper sequence of events).

Charts can serve as a beginning in the development of perceptual clues:

As certain words are used repeatedly, they can be identified and used on flash cards to become fixed as sight vocabulary.
Whole sentences can be printed on oaktag strips so children can match them on the chart to note likenesses and differences.
Children note that many words start alike. As these words are said they hear the likenesses in beginning sounds and you have an introduction to phonics.
As the beginning of a sentence is read, children anticipate what follows and this becomes groundwork for use of the context clue in later reading.
Children understand that the picture at the top of the chart is a clue as to what the printed matter relates.

There are limitations in the use of charts. Charts seldom accomplish within themselves all that we hope to do in the area of reading. The range of words used on charts is very broad. No attempt is made to teach all the words used. Only those that are used commonly are pulled out and used on cards to become sight words and a part of each child's reading vocabulary. Of course, some children will learn many words simply by seeing them used on the various charts—which is to be encouraged. Charts do not provide for all the development of perceptual clues. Charts merely serve to introduce, to reinforce, or to make use of such clues that are developed in the reading program.

1. Some authorities feel that one weakness in a chart story is that no new meaning is revealed to the child as he reads such material. "It is as if the child has written a letter to himself." Do you agree or disagree with this point of view?

2. Some teachers construct the chart story with the children then cut up the story to create flash cards. What would be their purpose in such a procedure?

3. Some teachers have created chart stories which they use year after year. This saves the time taken to create a story and provides simple reading material for practice. What weakness would you see in such a program? What strength?

4. Could adequate charts be made by putting words in a pocket chart so that sentences were formed? What would the children miss in a chart so constructed?

WHAT PLANS MUST BE MADE FOR INDEPENDENT WORK IN THE PRIMARY GRADES?

With any type of individualized instruction the teacher has the responsibility of planning work that will keep the rest of the class busy while the teacher works with a small group. The basic reading series provides in the workbook purposeful individual activities. When the basic workbook is not available, it is a growing practice to employ outstanding teachers during the summer months to produce this type of material for a district. If the material created meets a local need with special content, the time is well spent. If, however, the material is merely a copy or adaptation of existing published work, the effort may be questionable professional conduct. There are companies that provide master copies of worksheets printed with a special ink so that they can be reproduced. While these may not be directly related to the material being taught, a busy teacher will often find them better than those she might hurriedly produce. Some manuals for basic readers now recognize this problem and suggest work that is designed for reproduction.

When worksheets are used, demonstrate to the children how to mark each activity when the work is first presented. The vocabulary of the directions sometimes must be taught. Later only brief directional sentences need to be addressed to the pupils until they are able to read and carry out the directions independently. There are often general directions or questions at the beginning of a page. They are there for the purpose of motivating pupil reading of the text. They require thought and oral responses are expected, the pupils write on the lines provided or on lined paper. Enrichment suggestions may require children to use books and materials other than their reading textbooks. A teacher's daily reading plans should include the reminder to provide all needed materials.

In order to establish standards with children on how to obtain the materials necessary to complete enrichment activities, discuss the location of books, desirable traffic patterns as children move about the room, the way items are returned to the proper places. Some work-type activities may be too varied for the slow groups. If so, use only the portions that are suitable. Use the remainder at another time when the teacher is able to be with the groups.

Independent activities should be checked by the teacher to give children a feeling of security in accomplishment and to know the day-by-day effectiveness of pupil work. The teacher will then know what to review and when to provide additional independent work. A quick check may be sufficient on some days, but a detailed evaluation should be made at least twice a week. Papers sent home should be carefully checked; errors should be marked.

A sample and an analysis of a good reading worksheet:

Analysis of a Good Reading Worksheet

BOOK: *Finding New Neighbors*   "Baby Bears," 110–117   Adequate space should be provided when writing is required.

NAME_____

Read pages 110–127 carefully so that you can discuss these questions:
  1. How did the bears feel about Iva?
  2. Why were the bears happy at the end of the story?
  3. Do you think this story could really have happened? Why or why not?

Guide questions should establish purpose for reading. Answers should be *oral,* not written.

Number the following sentences in the order they came in the story:

_____ The bears were given a home in the cottage.
_____ A man found two baby bears in the forest.
_____ The bears enjoyed doing their tricks for the children.
_____ The bears played tricks on people in the entire neighborhood.
_____ The man carried the bears in a hat.
_____ A hunter took the bears to the city.
_____ The hunter sold the bears to the circus.

> Activies should require thought. Writing should be kept to a minimum.

R usually gives a vowel a special sound if it comes after the vowel in the word, as *ir* in *stir*.
Say each word softly and circle each vowel-with-r sound that you hear.

her	for	herd	burn	river
girl	acorn	circle	turtle	squirt
barn	story	far	purple	cart

> Word study skills should be practiced after they are taught at the circle.

Usually you can tell how many syllables are in a word by softly clapping the rhythm as you say the word. Write on the line before each of the following words the number of syllables it has.
(Avoid excessive picture drawing.)

_____ only	_____ important	_____ shell	_____ promise
_____ village	_____ apron	_____ slowly	_____ which
_____ market	_____ molasses	_____ bananas	_____ curtains
_____ mind	_____ sneeze	_____ doctor	_____ swish

> Fast workers should be encouraged to make additional contributions to the class by finding and sharing interesting and pertinent information. For the "Early Birds": Can you find some interesting facts about bears? Look in your science books or in the dictionary.

To provide additional oral reading the independent reading circle has been established by some teachers. In late first grade the children who are in the top group are permitted to form an independent group that reads to each other without the teacher being present. The material provided is easy reading for the children involved. For children working in a basic first reader the group may read from a preprimer of a series not used in their previous work. The leader has a set of cards with the names of those in the group. These are rotated to determine who will read next. Should a child need help with a word, the leader calls on members of the group to help.

Since being a member of such a group is a special privilege, these children must assume responsibility for their own behavior. At the designated time the children form a circle in a secluded corner of the room. Monitors distribute the books which are stored in that area. Each child has a marker which is left at the page where the reading will start. In turn, the students read aloud. At times the teacher may visit the group or ask them to tell the class about the story they are reading. The period lasts for fifteen to twenty minutes. In second grade, all groups may participate limited only by available material and in the third the low group. The other third grade groups profit more by individual reading of library books.

Individual games which provide drill are needed to supplement worksheets. Each game must be taught at the circle, then placed on a shelf to be chosen by the child when he is given that opportunity. Any worksheet that involves drawing lines to match a picture and a word, a singular and plural form, a contraction and the two words that form it, words that start alike, or words that rhyme may be put on a shoestring board. This is a heavy piece of cardboard with the two parallel lines of words written on it. A shoestring is attached to the words in the first column and a brad

These children have chosen to work with phonics drill games during a work period. Some games are self correcting; others will be checked by the teacher.

or a hole put near the word in the second column. Instead of drawing a line the child connects the shoestring between the appropriate words. After the board is checked the strings are disconnected and the drill may be used by another child. Sometimes rubber bands can be used as well as shoestrings.

Another way of matching words is to use clothespins. The snap type clothespin is used. On a card one list of words is presented. The words to be matched are written on the clothespins. The child snaps the pins opposite the appropriate words. Each cardboard should have a cloth bag attached, which contain the pins to be used in that drill. Clothespins can be used in many exercises which would require the child to fill in a blank. Prefixes or suffixes might be on the clothespins while the base word is on the card. Beginning consonants may be on the clothespins and the remaining part of the word on the card. Sentences may be on the card with the word omitted. The proper words would be selected by the child as he reads these on the clothespins

and snapped next to the sentence that it completes.

Boxed drills have a game appeal. The most convenient boxes for these games are hosiery boxes. Stores will usually save them for a teacher if she requests them. The directions for the game are pasted in the top of the box. Sometimes the correction key can be included so that these will be self-correcting. The box may contain a picture with words on small cards to be placed on the object named. There may be a series of questions which the child answers yes or no by putting all the yes on one side and the no on the other. The sentences on the strips of cards may be reassembled to tell a story. Vowels may be put in their proper places in words. Old workbooks and readers may be cut up and put in these boxes in the form of dozens of interesting game-drills.

Manila folders with a pocket or envelope to contain the cards with the words, vowels, or sentences used in the exercise, is another convenient form. The following type of exercise is used:

Short *a*	Long *a*
_____ _____	_____ _____
_____ _____	_____ _____
_____ _____	_____ _____
_____ _____	_____ _____
POCKET	POCKET

A cardboard folder with space for short vowels on one side, for long vowels on the other. On small pieces of cardboard, words with both long and short vowels are written.

To Play: The pupil places the words on the right page. When not in use, the word cards may be placed in the pockets at the bottom. Folders for each vowel may be made, choosing words from pupil's needed vocabulary.

Sentences using words often substituted for one another are used.

_____time is it?	_____do you like to play?
_____is my book.	_____is the way
_____boy is eating my cake.	
POCKET	POCKET

That	What	That	What

To Play: Place word cards in proper places on blank lines. One pupil checks another. Pupil works game by putting prefix and suffix cards in proper blank and pronouncing words.

un	er

_____happy	farm_____
_____certain	work_____
_____equal	clean_____
_____clean	read_____
POCKET	**POCKET**

un	er

un	er

un	er

Make folder and cards. Choose card that makes a word for each blank. Say the new words.

tall

cover

dis_____	_____ly
un_____	_____ness
re_____	_____est
POCKET	**POCKET**

dark

cover

fill

kind

Some teachers make their own magic slates out of a sheet of heavy cardboard (9 × 12 in.) and a sheet of clear acetate but the same size in breadth. The acetate is taped to the board at both sides but left open at top and bottom. A skill-building exercise slipped between the board and the acetate sheet can be marked with a china-marking pencil. The pencil marks rub off easily with a cloth, leaving the slate ready for another child to use. Both the acetate and china-marking pencils can be purchased at art supply stores.

Acetate envelopes made of two trans-

parent sheet fused together, are obtainable at most stationery stores. These envelopes will accommodate two exercise pages placed in the envelope back to back, with perhaps a thin sheet of cardboard between them for stiffening.

Worksheets which present a word over and over again in context is better drill practice than flash cards. It is quite possible for a child to recognize a word in isolation and not be able to read it in a sentence. The meaning in flash card drill is sometimes ignored. Thus it becomes important that teachers find ways of presenting work material that serves this purpose yet is easily evaluated and administrated.

1. How may parents be involved in the creation of some of the materials described?
2. There is much discussion of teaching machines at this time. In what sense is an independent work device a teaching machine?
3. Evaluate some of the following devices as independent reading equipment:

Garrard Press, 119 West Parke Avenue, Champaign, Ill.
Basic Sight Vocabulary Cards. Grades 1–3
Consonant Lotto. Grades 1–4
Group Sounding Game. Grades 1–8
Picture Word Cards. Grades K–1
Group Word Teaching Game.
Syllable Game. Grades 2–4
Vowel Lotto. Grades 1–4
Sight Phrase Cards. Grades 1–4

Kenworthy Educational Service, Buffalo, N.Y.
Doghouse Game. Grades 2–4
Steck Company, Box 16, Austin 61, Texas
Reading Essentials Reading Aids. Grades 1–3
4. Examine "Independent Activities" by R. Van Allen and Helen Darrow, published by the Bureau of Publications, Teacher's College, Columbia University, 1961. Check activities that might be used with your children.
5. Construct the necessary materials and work out one of the following drill games, demonstrating its use with children.*

---

* These are the suggestions of Marie Lovell, formerly Supervisor of Elementary Education of the San Diego Unified School District.

What Happened Next?

Grade Level: Kindergarten (second semester)
First Grade (first semester)

Purpose:

Reading Readiness. To help develop the concept of logical sequence of events in stories, as shown by a series of pictures. To increase ability to classify pictures that are alike in general ways (content) or that belong together.

Materials:

A box. As pictures are to be pasted along the left side of the inside of the box, the size of the box will depend on the size of the pictures obtainable. If using very small pictures cut from reading readiness discarded books, the box might be as small as a hosiery box. A larger box is preferable if pictures are used from discarded preprimers, as the pictures in this case will be about the size of half a page in the preprimers. (Suggest a shirt box.)

Select three or four illustrated stories. Only the pictures are to be used. *Each* story should provide 3 to 5 pictures about that one story. Each picture should illustrate the action of the story in sequence. Paste the *first* picture (first in logical sequence of action) of each story inside the box in a vertical column, along the left side. Then rule heavy horizontal lines between the pictures. Mount the remaining pictures on separate cards of tagboard or chipboard, one picture on each card.

Procedure for Use:

With the first picture for each story already pasted inside the box, the child using this work box proceeds to select the cards that belong to each story, and to arrange these cards horizontally in the box, in a left-to-right progression, thereby reinforcing left-to-right eye movements. For the child, the problem involves two phases:

1. Selecting the correct cards that depict any one story, such

selection being made from several cards involving illustrations of three or four stories.

2. Deciding on logical sequence and interpreting each picture within the framework and boundaries of each story.

Note:

When presenting this work box to the class, it is desirable that the teacher briefly *tell* each story, and place the cards in their correct position while she tells it. Thereafter, replace the cards in the box, making sure the cards are well mixed.

Make A Story   Grade Level: First Grade

Purpose:

To provide additional reading experience at the preprimer level. To provide practice in reading whole sentences, whole phrases, as they appear in complete lines as in preprimers.

Materials:

Two discarded preprimers from which four or five complete stories have been taken. From one preprimer cut out the pictures illustrating these stories, and mount on tagboard cards. Half-page or full-page pictures are suitable. Then cut out the pages of text and mount each page on tagboard cards. The child will be matching the picture cards with the corresponding cards that tell the story accompanying the illustrations. From the other preprimer, cut out only the text of the same stories, mount these pages on tagboard, and then cut into strips, each strip showing one line of the story text. A box in which to keep all parts of this reading device.

Procedure
for Use:

The child using this work box first lays the pictures belonging to one story in a horizontal row. Under each picture he then places the story or text that tells about the pictures. Thereafter he finds the appropriate matching strips that repeat the story text, and builds the same story with strips, matching the story text line for line, as frequently done in the reading circle with experience story charts and strips. When one story is completed, he rereads the complete story and then begins to assemble the next story in the same way. Perhaps it might be simpler to have only *one* story in the box when the device is first presented to the class or group. Then, as the children use it again and gain experience and are able to assemble or build the story rapidly, add one or two other stories. The problem of selection thereby becomes more complicated for the child, especially when selecting the story strips that accompany each story.

Something Is Missing   Grade Level: First Grade

Purpose:

To provide practice in word recognition (separate individual words), to use these words correctly in context, and finally to read a whole sentence containing these words.

Materials:	Tagboard or chipboard strips, at least 5 × 1-in. and 30 or more strips. Teacher prints simple sentences on strips, omitting one word in each sentence, and drawing a short line in the sentence in the place of the missing word. Sentences may be copied from preprimers or readers. Words omitted should be those that consistently need review and emphasis, such as *with, where, want,* etc.
	Small tagboard cards, about 1 in. square or smaller. On these cards the teacher prints the missing words, omitted from the sentences on the strips. A box in which to keep strips and cards.
Procedure for Use:	The child using this device places the sentence strips on desk or table surface or on floor. The small cards are then laid on the strips, in the correct spaces where words have been omitted. It is apparent, therefore, that in leaving spaces on the strips for the missing words, the blank spaces must be about as large as the cards that will be placed in these spaces. The child then reads the complete sentence.

Ring Around the Word   *Grade Level:* First Grade

Purpose:	Word matching to develop reading-readiness, and to build word recognition.
Materials:	Tagboard strips about 10 in. long by 2½ in. wide. Small pictures cut from discarded reading-readiness books or primers. Several 1 in. or smaller brass curtain rings. A box in which to keep the strips.
To Make Strips:	Each strip is divided into three sections. The first section has a picture pasted on it. The next section has a sentence printed on it, describing an object or action in the picture. The last section shows one word repeated from the sentence—a word that the teacher wishes to emphasize by providing this means of drill and self-help for the children. Two curtain rings are needed for each tagboard strip.
Procedure for Use:	Rings are placed on the tagboard strip to encircle the two words that match, one appearing in the sentence, and the other at the end of the strip, in an isolated position. Rings may be purchased at variety store or at notion counters in department stores.

All Kinds of Sounds   *Grade Level:* First Grade

Purpose:	Discrimination of Sounds, Phonics.
Materials:	1. Large cards with pictures of objects pasted on them, *e.g.,* sun, fish, bed, etc. Convenient size for cards is 4 × 4 in.

2. Many smaller cards, having smaller pictures of objects pasted on them. The names of the pictured objects should begin with the same sounds as the names of objects on the large cards, e.g., large card showing picture of a fish. Smaller cards could depict fairy, faucet, frog, etc. Convenient size for small cards is 2 × 2 in.
There should be at least five cards, and 30 or 40 small cards. Pictures can be cut from catalogues, or discarded reading-readiness books.

3. Box to hold cards.

Procedure for Use: Large cards are lined up horizontally, with a small space between each. Under each card the smaller cards are grouped in two vertical columns, to show that some of the pictured objects have the same sound as the picture on the large card.
Suggested consonants for beginning sounds: S, B, D, F, T.

Variations:
1. Substitute actual consonant letters for the pictures on the large cards. This can be done later in the year.

2. Because the large cards constitute some extra help or guidance, these cards can be eliminated later in the year, and the problem of classifying and grouping the smaller cards by sounds that match then becomes more difficult.

Word Endings

Grade Level: First Grade (second semester, or perhaps toward the end of the first semester.)

Purpose: To provide practice in recognizing and reading words that have similar endings.
To emphasize the similarities in sound (as well as in appearance) of such endings.
To increase word-attack skills.

Materials:
1. A standard form board (large cardboard divided into squares) or a box having the inside bottom divided into squares. There should be at least 30 squares.
2. At least 30 small cards have word-endings printed on them. (e.g., -oat, -ay, -all, -ed, etc.) These are "guide" vards. The other 20 or more cards have words printed on them, words that end with the same endings as the "guide" cards. These may be boat, goat, coat, say, way, day, ball, tall, wall, bed, fed, red.

Procedure for Use: The "guide" cards are laid on the squares first, in a vertical column along the left edge of the form board or box. Next, other word-cards are laid on squares beside the guide cards in horizontal rows, with only matching endings beside the corresponding guide cards.

Note: It is suggested that the word-endings in the guide cards be underlined in red, to increase possibility of correct matching, and to draw attention visually to these endings.

One and More Than One   *Grade Level:* Second Grade

Purpose:

To emphasize the plural forms of nouns, and the correct spelling. Specifically, to show that some plural forms are the same as the singular (*sheep, sheep*), that in others the suffix *es* is merely added to the singular (*dress, dresses*), that in some the plural is formed by adding *ies* to *part* of the singular form, (as in *cooky, cookies*) and that in others the plural form is quite unlike the singular (as in *mouse, mice*), etc.

Materials:

Two sets of cards, at least 15 cards in each set. One set has nouns printed on them. Words should be those in the reading vocabulary for second grade. Each noun is printed in its singular form. The other set of cards show the plural form for each noun. Plurals that are formed by adding *es* or *ies* require *two* cards; one would show the unchanged root or part identical with the root used in the singular form, and the second card would show the suffix *es* or *ies*. The example below clarifies this.

Procedure for Use:

The cards showing words which are singular nouns are laid down in a vertical column. Besides each card, horizontally, the child matches the singular word-card with the appropriately plural word.. Whenever two cards are required for the plural form (one card showing the unchanged root, and another card showing the plural suffix *-es* or *-ies*), the two plural cards are laid down in an overlapping position so that the plural word appears as one card.

Examples		*Explanation*
one	*more than one*	
mouse	mice	
woman	women	
city	cit ies	two cards overlapped
cooky	cook-ies	two cards overlapped
child	children	
tooth	teeth	
dress	dress es	two cards overlapped
story	stor ies	two cards overlapped
loaf	loaves	
man	men	

Make One Word from Two Words   *Grade Level:* Second Grade
                                                                        Third Grade

Purpose:

To teach contractions, their forms and derivation.

Materials:

Standard form board (cardboard, chipboard, ruled in squares the same size as the cards) if desired, but not essential. At least 15 cards on which are printed the words that are contractions, and an equal number of cards on which are printed the pairs of words from which the contractions are derived.

Examples:	don't	do not
	haven't	have not
	wouldn't	would not
	couldn't	could not
	shouldn't	should not
	didn't	did not

Procedure
for Use:

The pairs of words should be matched as they appear in the examples above. The cards may be laid on the formboard, in the squares, side by side; or one may dispense with the formboard, and lay the cards down on the desk, floor, or table.

Unscramble the Stories   Grade Level: Second Grade
                                                        Third Grade

Purpose:

To teach paragraph sequence, and the thought sequence in stories.

Materials:

Selected stories (three) from a discarded reader, including pictures that accompany the stories. Each paragraph from all the three stories is cut apart from others and each is pasted on a separate card. Each picture is also cut out and pasted on separate cards. This affords from 15 to 40 cards of pictures and text, depending on the number of paragraphs in the stories. The cards should each be about as large as one half-page of a reader, so that the half-page illustrations will fit on to the cards. (Cut tagboard for cards.)

A box is needed in which to keep the cards.

Procedure
for Use:

Children must first sort out the three stories, deciding which pictures belong to each story. The pictures are placed in horizontal rows. Then the cards showing paragraphs are placed in sequence under the appropriate illustrations, and the completed stories are read.

A B C   Grade Level: First Grade (second semester)
                                          Second Grade
                                          Third Grade

Purpose:

To teach the letters of the alphabet in sequence, and recognition of the letter forms for capitals and lower case.

Materials:

Fifty-two small cards, half of these having the capital letters, and half having the lower case letters printed on them. (Use felt pen or black crayon.) Box to hold cards.

Procedure
for Use:

Using the manuscript strips that are posted in the classroom as a guide, the children arrange the cards in pairs to show correct alphabetical sequence. The capital letters can be placed in horizontal rows, with the corresponding lower-case letters just below the capitals.

Variation:	In third grade, a set can be made to show the cursive forms of the letters. For first grade, a third set of cards can be made, having pictures of objects whose names begin with the letters on the alphabet cards, e.g., A, a, apple.
Caution:	The small or lower-case letters should be the correct size *in relation* to the capitals. Generally speaking, this is half the size of the capitals. Both sets of *cards,* however, should be the same size. Because so many cards are required, it is suggested that each card be about 1 × 1 in., or 2 × 2 in.

Words that Mean the Same   Grade Level: Second Grade
                                                                                              Third Grade

Purpose:	To develop an understanding of synonyms, to increase vocabulary; and this work box might be labeled, "Find the words that mean the same thing."
Materials:	Two sets of cards on which words are printed. One set shows simple words, and the other set shows matching synonyms for the words selected for the first set of cards.
Procedure for Use:	Each card in set 1 (simple words such as sad, brave) is laid down in a vertical column, and then the synonyms from set 2 are laid beside the words that have the same meaning.

sad	unhappy
brave	unafraid

Use vocabulary from grade level readers, also from words used for spelling lessons. A few unfamiliar words may have to be used for the synonyms, but these should be such that the children can use word-attack skills which have already been taught, in trying to read the new words.

How Many Syllables?   Grade Level: Second Grade
                                                                                              Third Grade

Purpose:	To provide practice in division of words into syllables, especially to differentiate between one-syllable and two-syllable words.
Materials:	*At least* 40 cards, on which are printed one-syllable words (20 cards) and two-syllable words (20 cards). Two tagboard strips printed as follows: One-syllable words, two-syllable words. A box is needed to hold cards and the two strips.
Procedure for Use:	Under the strip "one-syllable words" place the cards that show one-syllable words, arranging in a vertical column. Do the same in a column for two-syllable words.

The Months of the Year   *Grade Level:* Second Grade
                                                      Third Grade

Purpose: To provide practice in reading the words for the months of the
                  year. To teach the sequence of the months. To aid recall of
                  some of our special American holidays, and the months in
                  which these appear.

Materials: A shallow box. (Suggest hosiery box because of convenient size
                  and shallowness.)
                  A card of tagboard the size of the inside of the box.
                  Tagboard strips on which are typed the names of the months,
                  each month being typed twice on two separate strips, to provide
                  24 strips.

Directions   Rule off 24 lines on the large tagboard card (which is the size
for Making: of the box). On each line type a clue, the answer to which will
                  be the name of a month of the year. Two different clues should
                  be given for each month, as there are duplicate strips for each
                  month. So there are 24 clues on the card. If this crowds the
                  card unduly, make two cards, with 12 clues on each, in which
                  case, of course, only 12 lines would be ruled on each card.
                  Make the clues short, so that there is sufficiently long space
                  left at the end of each line on which the strip can be laid by
                  the child using this box. Paste the card inside the box. If two
                  cards are typed, paste the second card inside the lid of the box.

Procedure   The child reads a line of typing which gives a clue. The an-
for Use: swer to the clue is the name of a month. The correct strip show-
                  ing the name of a month is then selected and placed at the end
                  of the same line as the corresponding clue. Examples:

1. The month school is over _____ June
2. The eighth month of the year _____ August
   (These answers are the answer strips placed at the end of
   the line by the child.)
   Other suggested clues are:
3. The month that has a Fools Day _____
4. The month we have Halloween _____
5. The third month of the year _____
6. The month we have Christmas _____
7. The month we have Thanksgiving Day _____
8. The month after June _____
9. The month that starts the year _____
10. The fifth month of the year _____
11. The month we have Valentine's Day _____
12. The month school starts _____

Adaptation for upper grades: Include more clues which denote numerical sequence of the
months, *e.g.,* the fourth month, the sixth month, the eleventh month, etc. This knowledge is used by the older children in filling in the date (current date and date of birth)
on many application forms, test forms, census cards, health forms, and whenever the
date is to be written as 6-9-58, etc.

Sounds that Blend   *Grade Level:* Second Semester, Second Grade
                                           Third Grade

Purpose: To provide practice in reading and using consonant blends
                  that appear at the beginning of words.

Materials: A shallow box (such as a hosiery box, or a larger box) having
                  the inside lined off into squares. Each square should be roughly
                  1½ in. The inner side of the box lid is covered with squares
                  as well as the inside of the lower part of the box. This affords
                  approximately 60 squares. In each square is printed a consonant
                  blend. (Use felt pen.) Examples:

bl	sp	tr	gr	pl	sh	br	dr	sn	tw	sk	ch	
st	cl	th	wh	fl	cr	fr	st	sc	cl	sl	gl	cl

                  Note that many of these blends can be used more than once
                  in squares.

                  A set of cards is needed, corresponding in size and number
                  with the squares as drawn in the box. These cards can be used
                  with the box, and are also kept in the box when not in use.
                  On each card is pasted a small picture of an object whose name
                  begins with one of the consonant blends printed in the box
                  squares. Examples of such pictures might be, <u>dr</u>um, <u>cl</u>othes,
                  <u>fr</u>og, <u>sn</u>ow, <u>sk</u>ates, <u>ch</u>urch, etc. Sources for pictures are cata-
                  logues, and discarded readers and reading readiness books.

Procedure   A card is placed in each square, placing the frog picture-card
for Use: on the square marked <u>fr</u>, and the drum picture-card on the
                  square marked <u>dr</u>. The box and its lid are set side by side
                  when in use to expose all the squares to view.

HOW IS READING TAUGHT AS CHILDREN ADVANCE IN PRIMARY READING SKILLS?

Children at second grade level are beginning to develop an independence in word recognition, a realization of the many happy experiences that they get from books, and an understanding that reading can help them to solve problems and to satisfy their curiosities. Growth in reading skill continues through exercises of the following nature to achieve the purpose stated. The exercises are illustrative. Similar ones constructed for drill purposes would be longer and at a difficulty level that challenges the student.

Purpose

To develop comprehension skills and knowledges provide opportunities for children to make judgments.

Exercise

Read and choose the correct reason:

Jane liked to read books about birds. One morning she saw a book about birds in Mr. Brown's store. Jane wanted the book. She went home for money because _____.

Purpose	*Exercise*
	She had to pay for the book.
	She wanted to buy candy.
Provide opportunities for children to find the main idea of a story.	Choose a sentence which tells what a story is about.
	What would be a good name for this story? What did we learn by reading the story?
Provide opportunities for children to remember logical sequence.	Review the action in a story using such words as *first, then, next, after that,* and *finally* in brief sentences. Then skim the story to note words or phrases that cue the reader to the time when certain events occurred and how long a period of time the events covered.
	Number events in correct sequence:
	_____ Bill went to school.
	_____ Bill got out of bed.
	_____ Bill ate his breakfast.
Provide opportunities for children to make inferences.	Underline the best answer to the question:
	Mr. Hill put a dish of food outside his back door. He called his dog, but the dog did not come. So Mr. Hill left the food near the door and went into the house.
	Soon a big brown dog came by. When the Hills' dog came home, he did not find any dinner.
	Why didn't the Hills' dog find his dinner?
	Mr. Hill did not feed him. A cat ate the dinner. A big brown dog ate it.
Provide opportunities for children to perceive relationships of time and place, manner, sequence, cause and effect.	After reading a story, underline the correct phrase.
	When did Tom hide?
	during the night before breakfast at noon
	Where was father working?
	in the yard near the tree near the river

Purpose

Exercise

Provide opportunities for children to experience sensory images.

Choose the words to use when talking about the weather:

branch	voice	penny
cloudy	cold	stormy
mother	sunny	rainy

To develop vocabulary through the understanding of fundamental concepts; provide opportunities for children to understand related values.

Fill in the blanks in the following sentences:

Apple pies are _____ than apples.
Mother's pies are _____ than apples.
Jane liked applie pies the _____ of all.

good   better   best

Provide opportunities for children to use chronological sequence.

Fill in the blanks:

Wednesday is the _____ day of the
  week.   (fourth)
Jane is the _____ child in the row.
                    (third)

Provide opportunities for children to understand complementary concepts.

Supply the proper word:

Pies are made by a baker; clothes are made
  by a _____.
A cat runs on its legs, but a car runs
  on _____.

Provide opportunities for children to strengthen the ability to perceive analogous relationships.

Cross out the word which does not belong:

house	door	road	roof
eight	dress	ten	four
lunch	dinner	nail	breakfast

Provide opportunities for children to develop the ability to anticipate meaning.

Write a word on the line which makes the sentence true:

The color of the grass is _____.
The name of the dog is _____.

Write a word on the line which makes the sentence true:

Jerry wanted a _____.
Tom _____ home.
Mother gave _____ a new doll.

Mary   went   boat

Provide opportunities for children to develop an understanding that a word may represent more than one meaning.

Notice that some words have more than one meaning:

  a bank of snow
  money in the bank

Purpose	Exercise
	post a letter a fence post an Indian trading post
Provide opportunities for children to identify sounds and the meanings of homonyms.	Insert the correct homonym cards in the blank spaces on a large chart:

A _____ has horns.
Betty is a _____ little girl.
Do you like a _____ sandwich?
I will _____ you at the corner.
I _____ my dinner at twelve o'clock.
Jane has _____ pennies.
This book is _____ my brother.
Two and two are _____.

deer	dear	meat	meet
ate	eight	for	four

Draw a line from the word in the first column that sounds the same as the word in the second column.

bear	mail
male	blew
sail	bare
blue	sale

* * *

The first two weeks of the second school year should be spent in reviewing the subject matter outlined for the work of the first grade. At the end of this period the teacher would have discovered those children who are not yet able to make use of these skills in attacking unknown words. Such children may be grouped together and given the type of instruction suited to their needs.

The remainder of the class can begin their work with the short and long sounds of the vowels. The ability to make intelligent use of the long and short sounds of vowels in attacking unknown words has been acquired with difficulty by the average and below-average child. Therefore, these sounds should be developed with particular care.

The order of development of the word elements and phonograms depends upon the difficulties which the children encounter in their reading and upon words used for study in drill or practice periods. For example, one group working in a practice period with such words as *harder, start, sharp* and *arms* would profit from a study of the phonogram *ar*, while another group who finds words such as *mouth, shout* and *loud* difficult, should study the phonogram *ou*.

To Develop the short sound of a

(1) Introducing the short sound of *a*

TEACHER: What sound do you hear first in these words? (*Points to such familiar words as* at, am, apple, and, *while the children pronounce them.*) See if you can hear that sound in these words. (*Points to such words as* cat, ran, sat, fat, back, *as different children pronounce them.*) What sound do you hear first in these words? (*Points to* at, am, *etc.*) Which letter in these words has the same sound? (*Points to* cat, ran, sat, *etc.*) Think of another word in which you hear that same sound. (*Write words on the blackboard as they are given.*)

Burbank City Schools, Calif.

Review is an essential step in every lesson. These second-grade children are working on final consonant sounds.

(2) At another period such a list as the following may be written on the board:

bag	tap	bad
pan	sad	lap

TEACHER: Yesterday we found out the sound of this letter. (*Write a on the blackboard.*) What was it? Find that letter in these words. (*Individual children point out the letter a in the different words.*) That letter has the same sound in these words that it had in *apple* and *at*. See if you can think of all of the sounds in the first word and tell us the word.

Have various children respond as the different words are indicated. If a child calls the word *bag, bad*, have him give the sound of the final letter *g* and then say the word as a whole. The child should never be allowed to pronounce the word as *ba-aa-gu* or *baa-gu*, but should *think* the separate sounds and pronounce the word as *bag*.

(3) The following exercise will help children differentiate between the long and the short sounds of *a* in words with which they are familiar. In arranging work of this type, the teacher must include *only known words*.

Write on the blackboard a list of words such as the following:

can	play
had	sang
baby	fat
last	place
stand	bank
name	stay
ran	apples
ate	that

Individual children should take turns pronouncing these words and drawing a ring around those words where the *a* sounds like the *a* in *at*. Such an exercise may later be hectographed and used for independent seat work. The short sounds of the remaining vowels may be developed similarly.

(4) To develop the long sound of *a* review the words in which *a* has a short sound.

TEACHER: Sometimes the letter *a* has another sound. Listen for the sound of *a* in these words. (*The teacher will point to and pronounce such familiar words as* ate, make, came.) What was the sound which you heard in every word? What is this word? (*Write* at *on the board*.) Now what is it? (*Change* at *to* ate.) What did I do to change the sound of *a*? (*Do the same with* mad *and* made.) What is the difference between these words? (*Write* cap *and* cape *on the board*.) What is this word? (*Point to* cap.) What is this one? (*Point to* cape.) What have we found out?

A child should be able to state the generalization in words such as these: When there is an *e* on the end of a word with *a* in it, the *a* says its own name.

(5) To develop the long sound of *e*.

Review the short sound of *e* in such known words as *pet, left, held, went, nest, get, hen, tell*, etc.

TEACHER: Here are some other words with e in them. (*Points to the following list of familiar words on the chalkboard:* wee, three, weeks, sleep, feet.) Find a word that means very small. (*Child points to* wee *and pronounces it*.) Find a word that is the name of a number, and so forth. The other day when we studied words like pet and hen we found one sound that e has. Sometimes it has a different sound. Listen for the sound of e in these words. (*The teacher pronounces* wee, three, *and so forth, very distinctly*.) What sound do you hear? When e changed the sound of a where did we find the a? Instead of coming at the end of the word, where does the second e sometimes come in these words? That is another thing we must remember when we are working out new words for ourselves. (*Follow this by changing* met *to* meet, step *to* steep, fed *to* feed, *etc*.)

(6) To develop the phonogram ay

Words such as the following, which the children have already encountered in reading, should be written on the board.

play   stay   gray   away

TEACHER: Find the word that tells the color of the squirrel. Find the word that tells what the squirrel liked to do. Find the word that tells what Sally wanted the squirrel to do. Find the letters that are the same in all four words. (*Individually children may frame* ay *in each of the four words*.) See if you can find out for yourselves what these words are. The following words are written on the blackboard and the children are helped to work them out independently as already described above:

gate	sale	fade
lame	tame	fake

An exercise such as the following will be of value in helping the children discriminate independently between long and short vowels, and at the same time, grow in the skill to use contextual help effectively. The following exercise would not be used until the long and short sounds of the letters a, e and i have been developed.

Read each sentence. Look for the word which belongs on each line. Write the word on the line.

One morning Tom _____ up.
                wake woke
He _____ out of bed.
   got goat
"I _____ I am not late," he said.
  hop hope

Listen while Billy pronounces the words and see if you can hear the sound of those letters.

TEACHER: What is it? Here is another word with that same sound in it. (*Writes* say *on the board*.) What is it? I'm going to change say into a new word. Watch and see if you can read the new word. (*Erases* s and *writes* m.)

Continue to change the initial consonants, using d, h, l, p, r, w.

To provide opportunities for discriminating between words containing the phonogram ay. After a phonogram has been developed by procedures such as one above, a seat work exercise of the following type may be added practice in word discrimination.

Write the word that makes the sentence true.

1. One _____ Tom went to the farm.
   pay way day hay
2. He rode all the _____ in a car
   day say may way
3. He saw the cows eat _____ .
   lay hay pay ray
4. One cow _____ down in the barn.
   lay hay pay ray
5. Tom said, " _____ I try to milk a cow?" way say may ray

Application of word attack skills is achieved through the following activities:

Purpose

To develop the ability to perceive visual and auditory differences, provide opportunities for children to hear the sounds of letters.

Exercise

Listen to the teacher pronounce a series of words, most of which rhyme. Clap hands when a nonrhyming word is heard.

Complete orally very short rhymes begun by the teacher.

> The funny clown
> Jumped (*down*)
> How much does a farmer pay
> For a wagon load of (*hay*)

Listen to and imitate the sounds of animals, birds or machines.

> tick-tock of the clock
> ch-ch-choo of the train
> peep-peep of a chicken

Provide opportunities for children to recognize the letters and combinations of letters.

Use rhyming words to fit content.

lunch-punch

> Soon it will be time for _____.
> He made a hole with a _____.

matter-fatter

> Do you think it will _____.
> If you are a little _____.

Provide opportunities for children to blend sounds in order to pronounce unknown words.

Complete the rhyming word at the left. Then write the correct word in each sentence.

(*clown*) Billy had a little br_____ puppy.
The king wore a gold cr_____.
The bright sun made Sally fr_____.

Purpose	*Exercise*
Provide opportunities for children to recognize vowel sounds and identify them.	Underline the vowels in each word:

<table>
<tr><td>thing</td><td>find</td></tr>
<tr><td>red</td><td>let</td></tr>
<tr><td>solo</td><td>long</td></tr>
<tr><td>sang</td><td>sun</td></tr>
<tr><td>ball</td><td>day</td></tr>
<tr><td>he</td><td>she</td></tr>
<tr><td>hop</td><td>wing</td></tr>
<tr><td>mind</td><td>hat</td></tr>
</table>

To develop the ability to analyze the structure of words give the children opportunities to become aware of endings such as -er, -est, -s, -ed, -ing, and -es.	Add *s, ed,* and *ing* to the end of the word *shout* to make new words to fit in the blanks.

Fisherman Bill heard some _____.
It was Jack. He _____ again and again.
"Who can be _____?" asked Fisherman
   Bill.

Give the children opportunities to learn the structure of compound words.	Combine the words in the first column with those in the second column to make compound words.

<table>
<tr><td>after</td><td>way</td></tr>
<tr><td>door</td><td>ball</td></tr>
<tr><td>air</td><td>noon</td></tr>
<tr><td>gold</td><td>fish</td></tr>
<tr><td>class</td><td>room</td></tr>
<tr><td>base</td><td>plane</td></tr>
</table>

Make a list of the compound words in a paragraph in a reader.

Give the children opportunities to learn to identify contractions.	Match contractions with the words from which each was contracted.

<table>
<tr><td>she'll</td><td>it is</td></tr>
<tr><td>it's</td><td>she will</td></tr>
<tr><td>won't</td><td>cannot</td></tr>
<tr><td>can't</td><td>will not</td></tr>
</table>

Give the children opportunities to learn possessive forms.	Write the name of the person who owns these things:

                  Jane
Jane's dog   _____
The girl's doll   _____
My mother's dress   _____
Tom's cat   _____
Father's car   _____

Purpose

To develop the ability to alphabetize provide opportunities for children to alphabetize words by the first letter.

Exercise

Write the correct word in each blank.

A pilot flies in it.	a_____
We read it.	b_____
It is a baby bear.	c_____
It can bark.	d_____

Children may be challenged to go on as far as they can with other clues.

The Third-Reader Level

When children come to the third-reader level, they have already met many words of more than one syllable, some of which they have learned as sight words. They have had experiences in listening to spoken words to identify the number of parts in each. At the third-reader level the term *syllable* is introduced. The children are beginning to develop skill in noting the number of syllables and whether the vowel is long or short.

At the third-reader level they have a directed reading class daily—a time when they work with the teacher in reading groups or individually for basic reading instruction. During the silent reading, they receive help when needed in attacking new words.

By the end of the third-reader level, the children have gained much skill in attacking words independently. They should use and apply these skills in all school work. Periodic checks must be made to be sure previous learnings are not forgotten.

Purpose

To develop the ability to interpret the written page give children the opportunity to follow written directions.

Exercise

Follow simple directions written on slips of paper or on the chalkboard.

Walk to the window.

Perform several written directions in the order given:

Write *go* on the chalkboard.
Tap Teddy on the head.
Walk around a table.
Open the door.
Sit down.

Give children the opportunity to arrange words into sentences.

Unscramble a jumbled sentence written on the board. Choose teams. Unscramble several jumbled words. The team unscrambling them first wins.

Play "Grab Bag":

Choose an envelope containing words which will make a sentence. Arrange the words in order.

Purpose	Exercise

Purpose

Exercise

Give children the opportunity to interpret ideas by planning riddles.

Compose riddles:

> I start with w.
> I live in a frame.
> I am in schools, homes, and stores.
> What am I?
>
> (A window.)

Give children the opportunity to skim to find something quickly.

After reading orally in class, take turns pantomiming a part of the story for others to find in the book. The first one finding it may read it aloud.

Find the one element that is not right in each paragraph.

Sam's mother was getting dinner. She cooked beans, potatoes, meat, and rubber, and she made a cake.

Tom and Betty were playing in the snow. They both wore warm clothes. Betty had on her winter coat, mittens, woolen scarf, pajamas, and a cap.

Tom had on a warm sweater, his sister's dress, his mittens, cap and boots.

Give children the opportunity to interpret a story and follow the sequence of events.

Interpret through dramatization a story studied and read during a directed reading class.

Choose a chairman to lead the discussion and to direct the play. Discuss what should be done to make the story into a play. List important events in proper sequence. Discuss what the characters would do and say. Draw pictures of each main event in a story. Arrange them in sequence. Write a sentence about each.

Give children the opportunity to form sensory images.

Answer questions such as the following:

What would *smell* this way?
>   spicy_____   sweet_____
>   strong_____   unpleasant_____

What would *feel* this way?
>   furry_____   soft_____
>   smooth_____   prickly_____

What would *taste* this way?
>   sweet_____   bitter_____
>   sour_____   salty_____

Purpose	*Exercise*
To develop the ability to clarify and learn new meanings provide opportunities to enrich vocabulary.	List all the words possible which describe a familiar object.

Draw a circle around the word that means the same as the underlined word.

My brother <u>hurt</u> his hand.
     repaired   injured
I listened to his <u>tale</u>.
      story music

To develop functional understanding of word relationships provide opportunities for children to organize and classify types of things.

Draw a line under the family name of a group of words.

lamb   beef   <u>meat</u>   pork

Draw a line through the word that does not belong in each group.

book   <u>girl</u>   page   word

Arrange a list of words in categories:

Animals	*Food*	*Clothing*
bear	coat	antelope
milk	shoes	trousers

Provide opportunities for children to perceive relationships of time, place, manner, and sequence.

Arrange the following words and phrases in the proper column:

Where?	*When?*	*How?*
in the car	under the tree	
later	into the school	
one day	in his room	
with a bang	every night	
everywhere	at the window	
that morning	as fast as he could	
fast		
this noon		

Provide opportunities for children to strengthen meaning associations.

Respond with the opposite of a word given.

forget (remember) laugh (cry)
tired (rested)   cross (happy)
top (bottom)   hot (cold)

Provide opportunities for children to discriminate in multiple meanings.

Choose the right word to have each sentence make sense:

wraps   patch   change

See the pretty strawberries in the _____.
Did your mother _____ your dress?
Put your _____ in the cloakroom.
My sister _____ her Christmas presents.
_____ your shoes.
The clerk gave me the right _____.

Purpose	*Exercise*

Purpose

To develop an awareness of phonetic elements provide opportunities for children to discriminate between hard and soft sounds of g.

Exercise

In each sentence fill in the blank with the word which has the soft sound of g.

The _____ was eating the seeds.
      goose   pigeon

The _____ came from Sue's aunt.
     message   gift

Fill in the blank with the word which has the hard sound of g:

We could see the beautiful _____.
              bridge   gate

The _____ animals crowded close together.
    strange   greedy

Provide opportunities for children to discriminate between hard and soft sounds of c.

List these words in the proper column:

	Soft c	*Hard* c
take	cellar	dancing
circus	cups	package
count	cabbage	ice
lettuce	city	cap

Provide opportunities for children to organize and develop phonics rules.

The Phonics Express: Write a phonics rule on each car. Add new cars as new rules are learned.

To develop an awareness of the meaning and sound of prefixes and suffixes, and skill in identifying root words and structural changes give the children the opportunity to learn how new words are formed by adding suffixes or prefixes to known root words.

Form known root words with alphabet blocks or scrabble tiles. Add a prefix or suffix to the root word and discuss the change in the meaning of the word:

	kind			fair	
un	kind		un	fair	
	kind	ly		fair	ly
	kind	ness		fair	ness

The children in a word study period have worked with a group of words such as the following which have been written on the board by the teacher:

raccoon	enough
waddles	hardly
several	perhaps
hollow	special

TEACHER: I am going to write some things for you to do on the board. (*After the teacher writes each of the following directions she calls upon a child to respond. The other children check the response.*)

Purpose

Exercise

Opportunities should frequently be provided which will necessitate careful attention in detail in following written directions. These procedures offer suggestions for work of this kind and at the same time calls attention to the prefix *be*.

Put a cross before *waddles*.
Draw a line between *several* and *perhaps*.
Draw a line below *enough*.
Draw a ring beside *special*.

In each sentence there is a group of words which told you exactly *where* to put your mark. Look at the first sentence. Draw a line under the words which told you where to put the cross. (*Continue in this way with the remaining sentences.*)

Read the first word that is underlined in each of those sentences. What do you notice particularly about those words?

Very often we find *be* at the beginning of words just as it is here. Think of some words you know which begin that way. (*Write on the board such words as* because, begin, become, behind, *etc., given by the children.*)

This may be followed at a later period by an exercise in which the children must discriminate between words with the prefix *be* and so give careful attention to meaning. Such an exercise as this, must of course be based upon the actual experiences of the group working with it:

Write the right word on each line:

1. Tom sits _____ Joe.
            because   behind   belong
2. Mary sits _____ Sally and Jane.
        between   began   become
3. The table is _____ the
   clock.   between begin below
4. The Indian dolls _____ to Dick
            become belong beside
5. Tom is at home _____
                between
   _____ he has a cold.
        beneath   because

The ending *-ful* as it changes the form of known words may be presented in this manner.

Choose phrases from the child's reading such as: *very kind and faithful, a very useful work animal, a wonderful sight.*

TEACHER: In the first phrase find a word which tells you that the elephant was trustworthy. What is it, Ellen?

Purpose	*Exercise*
	In the second phrase find a word which tells you what kind of a work animal the elephant was. What is it, Jim?
	In the third phrase find a word which tells you that it is a marvelous sight to see elephants at work. What is it, Dick?
	What interesting thing do you notice about those three words? Underline the part that is the same in all three.
	Read the word that you have left if you leave that ending off each word, Clara.
	Very often in our reading we will find words that end in -*ful*. Let's make a list here on the blackboard of words which you know that end in -*ful*. (*Such words as* thankful, thoughtful, careful, *as they are given by the children*.) What meaning is added by the ending *ful* to the root words?
To identify root words and structural changes which may be necessary for adding suffixes.	An exercise like this one may be used:
	Place many cards on a table with root words that have been changed when suffixes were added.

circling	smoky
happily	racing
noisy	writing

Ask the children to identify the root word in each and tell what happened when the suffix was added. If the right response is given, the child takes the card. The child who has identified the most words wins.

Purpose	*Exercise*
To develop skill in recognizing syllables and learning to apply rules provide practice in applying known rules of syllabication as an aid in the pronunciation of words.	Make fish-shaped cards (2½- × 4½-in.). On each write a one, two, or three syllable word. Attach a paper clip to the tail. Place mixed-up cards, word down, on a table. With a magnet pick up a fish. Look at the word, say it applying known rules, and tap out the syllables, with a louder tap for the accented ones.
	Place words on large cards. Use colored string as dividers between the syllables of the words.

fur/ni/ture	au/to/mo/bile
ta/ble	ap/ple

Purpose

Exercise

To develop skill in alphabetizing provide experiences for children to associate first-letter word position in the alphabet.

Place the words listed below in the proper column:

abcdefg	*hijklmnop*	*qrstuvwxyz*
happy	when	
little	Judy	
ladder	cried	
apple	Tim	
girl	inch	
sorry	tall	

Provide experiences for children to alphabetize by the first and second letters.

Write a set of cards by having each child write his first name on one. Spread the cards on a table and pick them up in alphabetical order. At first alphabetize by only the first letter, later the second.

Choose a card on which three words beginning with the same letter have been written. While holding it so that others can see it, read the words in alphabetical order. If it is done correctly, keep the card until the end of the period.

slipped	chasing
strong	company
splash	carpenter

Number in ABC order the three words on each line below:

_____people	_____outdoors
_____window	_____almost
_____look	_____close

Exercises such as those that have been described are used as a step in a reading lesson. The teacher's plan will be based upon the materials read by the children. This plan outline is suggested for *groups reading at or above third grade level.*

Third Grade Lesson Plan

Date_____ Group_____

Book_____ Pages_____

MOTIVATE FOR CIRCLE ACTIVITIES.

_____

CHECK COMPENSATION. (Use guide questions as a basis for discussion.)

_____

_____

_____

PURPOSEFUL ORAL READING. (To support a point, to share an exciting portion, and so forth.)

_____

_____

_____

DEVELOP OR REVIEW SOME WORD-ATTACK OR COMPREHENSION SKILLS

_____

_____

_____

MOTIVATION OF NEW MATERIAL. (*Arouse interest.* Tie the story to children's own experiences and extend by using children's experiences to relate or contrast.)

_____

Select words from the new vocabulary that should be presented to the group. (Words are prewritten on board or chart. Introduce the words in sentence or phrase form.)

_____ _____ _____ _____

_____ _____ _____ _____

Ask questions to guide silent reading. (Have these listed on the chalkboard, a chart, or a worksheet. These questions usually determine the purpose for which children read. See "Guiding Group Activities" for examples.)

_____

_____

_____

Explain independent reading activity. (See "Guiding Group Activities.")

_____

_____

Indicate activities for early finishers.

_____

This plan outline is suggested for *slow reading groups*.

Date_____   Group_____

Book_____   Pages_____

MOTIVATION (brief)
   Arouse interest. (Relate the story to children's own experiences.)

_____

   Present the new vocabulary in sentence or phrase form. (Write on board.)

_____

_____

   Emphasize new words. (Move quickly into the reading of the book while interest is high.)

GUIDED READING FROM THE BOOK
   Interpret the pictures.

_____

   Ask questions to guide silent reading. Encourage good study habits. Try to avoid pointing and lip reading.

_____

_____

_____

_____

_____

   Tell the answer to the question.
   Read orally with good expression.
   Conclude the book lesson by anticipating, or rereading for fun, the ending of a story and look forward to the next day's lesson.

WORD-ATTACK SKILLS
   Conduct snappy review of new or difficult words met in story. (Use game technique.)

_____

_____

   Develop or review some word-recognition activities *every day*. (Write on board.)

_____

_____

_____

INDEPENDENT STUDY
   Explain the independent reading activity.

_____

_____

Supplementary Reading

Since the supplementary reading books reinforce rather than introduce the basic reading skills, pacing in the supplementary books should be accelerated. Approximately four to six weeks will be required to complete a reader depending upon the length of the book and the ability of the pupils.

It is a good plan to progress systematically through the book. In planning supplementary reading, the teacher gives less attention to detailed presentation of the new vocabulary and skills. Reading assignments should be considerably longer than in the basic program. It may be necessary to use several supplementary books before the group is ready to move up to the basic reader at the next level of difficulty. Caution should be exercised in moving a child into the basic reader before he is ready.

The period of supplementary reading affords an excellent time for a child with changing needs to move to a group where his needs can be better met. For example, if the child consistently misses three or four words on a page, his needs will probably be met by moving him to a level where he can succeed. If the material presents little or no challenge to a child, he should probably be moved to a more difficult level. It is usually advisable to make a gradual move by letting him work for a time in both the old and the new groups.

The elements of a lesson taught from a supplementary reader involve added emphasis on comprehension and interpretation of what has been studied. A maximum of silent reading and a minimum of writing exercises should be included in periods of independent study. If study-type exercises are provided in the reader, they should be carefully selected to serve the purpose of the lesson. Note how this is done in this third-grade lesson:

Text: Charles E. Merrill, *Treat Shop*
Purposes:

To build comprehension skills, to build oral reading skills, to review skills of structural analysis, to increase vocabu-lary, and to appreciate the author's ability to create feeling.

Assignment (at previous circle period):

Pages 56–71 were to be read silently. Pupils were instructed to be prepared to answer these questions orally:

1. What problem did the Tollivers have? How did they solve the problem?
2. Why did Joey appreciate his job more at the end of the story than at the beginning?

Children were given the following written assignment:
Reread the selections to find the page number and the paragraph number that tell:

1. Why the Tollivers decided to get rid of the cats.
2. How the Tollivers' house seemed with no cats around.
3. Why the cats caused no more trouble at mealtime in the Tolliver house.
4. Why Joey was discontented in the city.
5. How Joey felt when he first reached the farm.
6. Why Joey changed his mind about life on the farm.

Procedure (at the reading circle):

1. Check on work prepared independently.

   Build interest: "In what ways were the two stories you read yesterday alike? Have you ever felt like Joey?"

   Discuss guide questions.

2. Do purposeful oral reading.
   Set a standard: "Today, let's try to make our reading sound just like we're talking."
   Check assignment that was prepared independently by having pupils read to prove a point.
   Evaluate in terms of standards.

3. Build word-study skills.
Review the meaning of *un* as a prefix.
Write the following words on the
chalkboard:

unnecessary   unsuccessful
uncomfortable   unpack

Identify the root word and the prefix
in each of the four words.

4. Motivate the new story.
Read the introductory poem on page
73 aloud. Ask, "Did you ever see a
fairy? Why is it fun to read about
elves and giants today?" Discuss pictures briefly in the first two stories.
Show a book of *Grimms' Fairy Tales.*
Suggest that pupils who enjoy the
stories in the reader will probably enjoy other fairy tales.
Introduce key words of vocabulary
(prewritten on the board.)

better weather   powerful *crow*
beautiful *bray*   *goblins* screamed
fine *mouser*   The *Bremen* Town
                          Musicans

Present guide questions (list on chalk-
board, chart, or worksheet.)
Why do you think the shoemaker
and his wife were good people?
Tell why the title "Bremen Town
Musicians" does not fit the story.

5. Make assignment.
Read pages 74–85. Be able to discuss
the guide questions.
Reread the stories. As you do, list the
page number and the paragraph number for each story that has:

A sad part.
An exciting part.
A funny part.

WHAT ACTIVITIES MAY THE TEACHER USE IN THE CIRCLE TO PROMOTE INTEREST AND PRACTICE?

There are usually five steps in a primary basic reading lesson. This first is a
preparatory or readiness phase in which
the concepts needed to read the material
are developed and new words introduced.
A part of this period is to arouse the interest of the student.

The second phase involves a guided
reading of the material. This is usually
silent and then oral, followed by a discussion. The manuals provide well-planned
questions which establish purposes for the
reading and check on comprehension.

After the total story is completed there
is a discussion which involves additional
comprehensive check and interpretation of
the story.

The fourth step is drill on word recognition skills.

The fifth is an application of what
has been learned, an enrichment or a creative application of the information or
skills mastered.

Although the manuals are rich in suggestions, teachers need resource materials
to review the vocabulary of the previous

day, to provide interesting drill on new
words, and to meet special needs of children.

The following suggestions were made
by a group of experienced teachers in a
summer school class. Select only a few that
seem to appeal to the group you teach.
While children like a little variety, too
much may be overstimulation.

1. List words that may be causing difficulties on the chalkboard. Give meaning clues and challenge the children
to find the correct word, as, "Can you
find a word that means something we
do with our eyes?" (look or see). "Can
you find a word that joins other
words?" (and). "Can you find a word
that means a color?" (brown, etc.).
When children get the idea of clues
relating to the meaning of words, each
child who guesses the correct word may
give the clue for a next word for the
others to guess. This may be done with
phrases, too. In this way the children
are not merely calling out words but

are associating them with meanings, which is fundamental in reading.

2. One child is asked to leave the room momentarily. The others agree on a word from a list on the chalkboard. The first child returns and is given a pointer. He points to one of the words and says, "Is it 'wagon'?" The children respond with, "No, it is not 'wagon' or yes, it is wagon" as the case may be. In this way all children's attention is focused on the words and all maintain interest in the repetition that takes place.

3. Divide the class into two, three or four groups with a balance of fast and slow learners in each group. Present a pack of troublesome words to each group and challenge them to help one another until all members of the group can be checked individually on the entire pack. Those who know all the words are eager to help the slow learners during free time or whenever there is time before school starts or during bad-weather recesses. Group records may be kept and the competition continued as more words and phrases are presented in other packs.

4. Troublesome words during a reading class period are recorded on the chalkboard. Allow five to eight minutes at the end of the class time, check each child prior to dismissing them from the group. Those who are most likely to know the words are checked first and the slow learners remain for more help. If there are words of which some children are not sure, they may be put on flash cards and given to the respective children so they can work on them at home or during free moments with other children.

5. The children sit on the floor in front of their chairs. Each child in turn is asked to recognize a flash-card word or phrase. If he identifies it correctly he sits up on his chair and the teacher proceeds around the circle of children on the floor. This gives slow learners more chances for help. If a child does not know the word or phrase, a child who is seated on a chair is challenged.

This keeps all children attentive as those seated in chairs do not know when they may be called upon; if they cannot give immediate response they are again seated on the floor.

6. Place four or five difficult words along the chalk tray. Have the children repeat the words with you several times. Then have all children close their eyes while you remove one word. Mix up the remaining words. Then the children are to open their eyes and determine which word is missing.

7. Give each child a flash card with a word that has been especially difficult for that child. Have him take a good look at it. Then call out three words and the children having those words are to place them on the chalk tray. All the children then say the words after which the teacher mixes them up and the original children are to go up and get their own words and identify them.

8. Each child is given several flash cards. The teacher calls out an initial sound and children having words starting with that sound will place them on the chalk tray. Errors are detected and children helped who do not respond correctly.

9. Each child stands behind his chair. A flash card is placed on each chair. A child who needs help with the words is chosen to identify them. He picks up each card he can identify correctly. These are handed to the teacher. The children standing behind the chairs on which words appear that the child does not know may go with the child to a corner of the room and help him learn them. The game is repeated with the remaining words and another slow learner is helped.

10. A word is printed on the chalkboard beside the child's name who has been having difficulty with that word. It is his "word for the day." Frequently during the day at odd moments the teacher challenges him to identify it.

11. The semicircle of chairs on which the children are seated is referred to as the street car. One child is chosen as the

conductor. He stands behind the first chair. A word is flashed and if the conductor can identify it before the child on the chair he moves on behind the next chair and another word is flashed. If he is first to identify each word all around the class he goes to his seat for other activity. If a child on the chair is first to identify a word that child becomes the conductor and exchanges places.

12. Children are given one or two flash cards. The teacher calls for words that rhyme with a given word, or words that are action words, or words that are foods, or number words, or people's names, etc.

13. At the end of the reading class period the difficult words from the lesson are printed on the chalkboard. A child is given an eraser and asked to identify one of the words. If he says it correctly he may erase it and go to his seat. Another child is asked to identify another word, and so on until all words have been erased.

14. A list of ten difficult words is printed on the chalkboard. Each child starts at the bottom of the list and sees how far up he can go identifying the words. When he misses a word, his initials are placed beside that word and the next child starts at the bottom. If a child can identify them all, his initials are placed at the top of the list. The second time the children who missed a word are asked to identify the word they missed and then proceed up the list until they reach the top.

1. Would any of the foregoing devices be useful in a tutorial situation in which the children worked in teams of two to drill each other?

2. Would any of the foregoing devices be useful in the home where a parent wanted to help a child in reading?

3. Additional instructional games are available in these publications:

"Let's Play a Game" (Ginn)

"Independent Reading Activities" (Ginn)

"Such Interesting Things to Do #564" (Scott)

"100 Good Ways to Strengthen Reading Games #514" (Scott)

"Learning Activities for Reading" (Wm. C. Brown)

"Strengthening Fundamental Skills with Instructional Games" (J. S. Latta, Cedar Falls, Iowa)

WHAT READING PROBLEMS MAY A BEGINNING TEACHER ANTICIPATE?

A number of problems may surprise and dismay the beginning teacher. Space does not permit a discussion of all the special and remedial techniques used. These situations, which are accepted as normal by the experienced teacher, include the following:

Children frequently lose the place while they are reading.

Children continue to move their lips during silent reading.

Children reverse words such as *on* and *no* or *stop* and *spot*.

Children finish the worksheets too soon or not at all.

The books seem too difficult for a child.

Children will not read loudly enough to be heard.

Children say the words but do not understand what is being read.

Children doing seatwork keep interrupting the teacher when she is working with a group.

A child fails to recognize a word in a story even though he always knows it when used on a flash card.

The mother wishes to teach the child out of the basic reader.

Children continue to lose their place for three reasons. (1) The width of the line of type (or "measure") may be too great in proportion to the point size so that the eye cannot follow the line without "wandering" to the beginning of the next line. Newspaper columns are designed to permit rapid reverse eye movements for adults. Adults frequently lose the place when the reading lines of small type extend longer than five or six inches. In all cases, however, the *size* of the type is a factor, as well as the *measure* or length. Reading textbooks are usually designed with these factors in mind but the library books that children read aloud are sometimes difficult typographically. The otherwise excellent books of Holling C. Holling such as *Paddle to the Sea* and *Magoo* illustrate this problem. A related physical factor is the placement of illustrations on the page so that they tend to draw the eyes away from the beginning and ending of the line. (2) The second situation that causes children to lose the place is related to interruptions in reading. The interruption may be a difficult word. The reader may look at the picture on the page or in the previous paragraph in order to find help and then be unable to scan rapidly to the place where is he reading. A question from the teacher or a correction that causes the reader to look away from his material to the chalkboard or a chart is a common occurrence. (3) The third situation is boredom of the child in the teaching situation, sometimes resulting from waiting his turn to read in a large group of slow readers or because the story has no real interest for the reader. Books seem to grow heavier when held for a long period of time, and merely following the page while others read aloud is not a highly motivating situation.

Teachers sometimes have students use strips of heavy paper as place markers. These are held under the line the child is reading to guide his eyes. This can be done comfortably only when the child is at a table or desk. In a circle children must rest their books on their laps, steady them with one hand, guide the marker with the other and bend their bodies into unnatural shapes in order to read. Place markers are a great help when kept clean and used in situations where the children are physically comfortable. Sometimes it is better for the teacher to go to the child's desk or table rather than have him come to the circle.

Oral reading of unfamiliar material is usually difficult. Beyond the primary level a child should not be asked to read orally unless the material has first been read silently. The skilled oral reader actually scans ahead of the material he is voicing. This is a specific skill developed in the middle grades.

Lip movement or vocalization is natural for a beginner in the reading of any language. Adults studying a foreign language can be observed moving their lips as they silently pronounce the words they read. Many adults do not move their lips, but according to physiologists vocal cords are unconsciously activated by the speech center in the brain and take on all of the necessary configurations as in actual audible speech. College students complain of "tired throats" after a night of study without realizing that this silent reading may actually be the cause. Silent voicing all words results in slow, plodding reading.

At first, all silent reading means "saying the words to yourself." In the third grade and beyond, children are encouraged to scan material for the ideas presented rather than the sounds written on the page. While many are taught to do this before this grade, it is at this level that the child usually has mastered the basic reading skills and faces the need for such a skill in extensive reading situations.

To remind children that their lips are moving, teachers sometimes have them hold a pencil on the upper lip as they read. This will make them conscious of any lip movement. An extended reading of simple material for the enjoyment of the ideas, usually develops adequate speed of reading that causes the vocalization to be reduced or to disappear.

The problem of deciding which books are easy or difficult is a puzzle indeed. The use of various readability formulas is discussed in connection with children's literature. The concept of frustration levels of reading refers to the number of new words a child must be told as he reads. If there are more than three in any sequence of nineteen words, the books are considered difficult. Intermediate children face one new word in every ten due to the rapidly expanding vocabulary of the textbooks used. Such factors as print size or type and leading (from the "lead metal" used to make spaces between lines) cause printed material to look either easy or difficult. The attitude of the reader is important. When children say that a book is "too easy" their judgment may be influenced wholly by this factor of typographic appearance. The subject matter is also a factor in a child's judgment of a book. A book about "Cowboy Sam" may be accepted by a fourth-grade reader while an animal fable in a more difficult vocabulary will be rejected.

Each child has a level at which he can succeed and grow. To find this instructional level the teacher should:

1. Estimate the child's reading level from his previous records and tests.
2. Choose a book one level lower than the estimated level.
3. Choose a page approximately one-third from the front of the book.
4. Have the child read orally without preparation 100 running words. (Use a shorter passage if testing at a low reading level.)
5. Record as errors the following:
   substitutions
   mispronunciations
   words pronounced by the teacher
   repetition of more than one word
   insertions
   omissions
6. Test at the next lower level if the child misses more than one out of twenty running words.
7. Test at a higher level if he reads fluently.

The child's instructional level has been found when he averages no more than five errors out of one hundred running words. This method does not check comprehension, but it is an easy device for grouping. When groups are formed, the teacher can check comprehension. If a child consistently fails to comprehend 75

per cent of the material read, he should be moved to a less difficult book.

Modern reading programs provide plateau reading experiences or absorption periods during which no new vocabulary difficulties are added. These periods are designed to fix skills previously taught or to provide opportunity to increase reading speed. Frequently neither the teacher nor the child, strange to say, recognize these periods as easier than others.

In some cities kits of materials relating to a unit topic are prepared for a class. In theory, these books are selected to care for the wide reading range of the normal classroom. While the extremes of very simple and difficult are relatively obvious, the intermediate range is difficult for both teachers and children to distinguish. Intermediate readers are especially confusing. Some fourth-grade books seem more difficult to certain children than others designed for the sixth grade.

The child who reads was for saw is obviously starting at the wrong end of a word. A clear understanding at the start of reading instruction as to where to start to look at a word, will prevent this. Noticing which words are alike at the beginning is a readiness exercise that is widely used. Too much emphasis on rhyming will cause children to look at the wrong end of a word for a reading clue. The tendency to reverse a word, which is revealed when a word like no is read as on, may apply to other words, even though the child pronounces the misread word correctly. A great emphasis upon phonetic formulas like will, dill, sill may cause the child to look at the -ill first, then the beginning. When he does this to all words it is natural that confusion as to the word meaning and pronunciation results.

Worksheets provide extra drill, simple tests and independent activity. Certain types are unpopular with teachers. The most undesirable are those that require the child to cut and paste. This type of activity can seldom be done without supervision. Probably the most difficult are those that have a story cut into parts which the child is asked to rearrange in logical order.

(This is a good activity but should be done as a boxed individual game.) Nearly all worksheets provide an opportunity for children to add a colored sketch when they complete the work. This may be an effort to keep children busy while the teacher works with others.

Routines that provide the child with a place to put his work when finished and something to do while others complete the work, are established by wise teachers. One teacher has three folders, one for each group. As soon as a child completes his work it is placed in this folder. The work is corrected that evening and returned to the children in the reading circle the next day. Those who finish their papers are permitted to read a library book, go to an interest center in the room (usually with established rules as to how many may be in one place) or select an individual game. When workbooks are used, the drill sheets for the day are removed. The child cannot be expected to care for all the material that he does not use or need in these books. Normally they are an awkward size for desks and difficult for little hands to handle. Individual cardboard folders in which worksheets are inserted are especially helpful when some of the work is done in the circle where there is no adequate support to mark worksheets.

It is well to anticipate the reasons children come to the teacher for help. Perhaps there is a child who makes a practice of not listening to directions, or one who does not easily comprehend them when given. This child might be asked to repeat the directions after you have given them so everyone will be sure they know what to do (and you will know that he understands). Then a check must be made to see that everyone has a pencil or other needed materials. Seating the children far enough apart will eliminate complaints of copying or annoyances. Then it can be explained to the children that, since they know how annoying it is when someone interrupts their group procedures, it will be a good policy to rule out interruptions except for extreme emergencies. When interruptions do take place the teacher needs to be firm in her judgment as to whether the interruption is a real emergency. Especially at the beginning of first grade the interruptions are often merely to get attention and such interruptions should be discouraged at the outset. Be sure that after a group has finished reading you recognize good independent workmanship. Children need attention and praise but help them to understand that there are occasions when the needs of the group are more important than the needs of individuals.

The soft-voiced child has many desirable qualities, but he may be a source of distraction to other children if he cannot be heard beyond the first row. Low-voiced tones may be based on shyness or fear of making an error. Some beginners have been so frightened by wild rumors of school disciplinary methods that they practically refuse to talk.

Teachers put these shy children in small groups, sometimes bolstering their confidence by giving them a reading partner or letting them sit next to the teacher. Dramatic play, use of flannelboard characters, verse choir, and singing help this type of child.

More of a problem for a beginning teacher is the loud child with a short attention span. Each one of this type is different. Some are the center of attention at home and expect to be accorded the same status at school; some get no attention at home and therefore demand it at school. The "grasshopper" interests and activities of such children can disturb an entire classroom and create extreme tension for the teacher. No child should be permitted to interfere with the learning of others or take the satisfactions out of teaching. Some of these children belong in private schools. Establish a few patterns of behavior and insist that they be followed consistently. Some of these patterns will be of a negative nature. The more effective will be those that suggest alternate activities for the undesirable ones. It is not a teaching weakness to permit these children to act as leaders in the few classroom practices which they like. If activity is an essential, such errands that must be made to the principal's office may be assigned to this type of child. Chores like wrapping or un-wrapping books from the central office or serving as playground monitors use up some of the boundless energy of these children. Peer judgment has some influence, but don't place the responsibility for disciplinary decisions upon the other children.

There are some children who in the second or third grade develop the ability to verbalize the words of the reader without any clear understanding of what is being said. Sometimes these are children with a foreign-language background. They apparently have mastered all the word-attack skills except that of understanding word meaning. These children are sometimes good spellers as well. Each word is an interesting design in type rather than a thought symbol. Rather than more reading and writing these students need a great deal of speaking and listening with meaning. Word-calling happens at all levels of education. As the attitude of demanding meaning is developed—not just meaning in the abstract, but the specific meaning of the speaker or writer—this type of verbalizing disappears. Too great an emphasis on scope or speed of reading may develop an attitude of "covering ground" rather than assimilating thoughts or comprehending ideas. Exercises that require rephrasing or finding words of similar or opposite meaning focus attention on what the words mean rather than how they are pronounced.

I once asked a child how he knew the word was "the" on the flash card and he said, "I always remember that the card with 'the' on it has a bent corner." Such a remark may indicate that flash-card drills often become too detached from word meanings. As each word is presented it is well to give the children a chance to use it in their own sentences. Attention is then drawn to the first letter of the word and to any peculiarities in the word form such as preponderance of tall letters, length of the word, etc. If several copies of the flash card are available it is best to mix them with other words and call upon children to find all the cards that have the word "the." Then give each child a book and

ask him to find the word, put his finger under it, and raise his other hand. After you have checked to see if it is correct, the children of one group can be looking for another "the" while you are busy with a second group. Another form of drill is achieved by placing cards along the chalk tray and giving such clues as "find the card that has a girl's name on it," "find the word that joins other words together," "find a color word," or "find an action word," etc., so that children think about word meanings as they recognize them.

More and more schools are adopting the policy of not sending home the book used for basic reading instruction until the child has completed this book at school. A child attempting to follow the suggestions of two authorities, his teacher and his mother, can become a confused student. Some mothers are excellent teachers but there are many who in their zeal "push" children too much and take the joy from the reading experience. Coercion or prolonged sessions of reading when the child wishes to do something else tend to destroy the best teaching efforts at school. Belittling remarks or sarcasm from older children exaggerate a beginner's errors and lower the self-esteem of a sensitive child. The child who needs the most help with reading at school seldom benefits from home instruction. The careful diagnosis of individual problems is a professional task not to be attempted by a well-meaning parent. Supplementary readers and library books which provide practice on reading skills taught at school are designed to be read at home. Since these will contain some words that do not follow phonetic principles, parents might be informed that they can be of most help to their child by listening to the stories he reads, praising his efforts as he struggles with new words, and prompting him occasionally so as to avoid long pauses. Shared reading experiences, in which parent and child alternately read parts of bedtime stories from newspapers or books, are among the most precious memories of childhood.

1. The content of much primary reading consists of stories about children with a pony,

Daddy's new car, or grandmother's big farm-house. Children of lower socioeconomic groups seldom read about situations similar to their own. In what way may this influence reading instruction? Detroit is experimenting with reading materials for racial groups. Write

to Follett Publishing Company in Chicago for information.

2. Do you think that television has influenced children's interest in reading? How might the teacher influence home television habits?

HOW MAY READING INSTRUCTION BE INDIVIDUALIZED?

The reason teachers have turned to a program of individualized reading instruction is because of the range in abilities found in the normal classroom. It is not uncommon for the thirty-five children in a fifth-grade room to have a range that extends from below that of average third-grade readers to above that of average ninth-grade students. In such situations the teacher divides the class into groups for instruction. The books or assignments for each group will be determined by the reading achievement of the individuals in that segment of the class. In a small rural school that has one teacher for all the grades, similar grouping practices are followed. It is customary for an able second-grade child to read with those in the third or fourth grade. The term "personalized reading" is sometimes used to describe such practices.[8]

Two special methods of individualizing instruction within a classroom have been identified by the terms "self-selection" and "language approach." The "self-selection" program allows each child to seek whatever reading material stimulates him and work at his own rate with what he has chosen. The major points of a self-selection reading program as a method include the following:

1. Children themselves select their own reading materials.
2. Children read at their own rate.
3. Teachers work almost entirely with individuals.

4. The best elements of recreational reading and the one-to-one skill teaching are combined.
5. Groups are organized not on ability but upon purpose or goals.

Individualized reading is not a single method of instruction but rather a plan of organization. Nor does the individualized reading eliminate the use of groups. Instead, it changes the way groups are organized, how long they exist, and what their purposes are.

The child does not prescribe whether or not he will participate in developing skills, what materials will be supplied, what skills he will work on, or any other matter that pertains to professional competence. This is the teacher's role. An individualized reading program is planned, designed, and organized into an instructional program. Individualized reading is not recreational reading. Recreational reading does not usually involve reading instruction. In individualized reading, definite provision is made for the teacher to teach, the children to read aloud to the teacher at reasonable intervals, and for reading-instruction to take place daily.

Materials are a basic consideration of individualized reading. If children are to have any degree of self-selection, then materials in large quantities must be available. It typically means that a hundred or more titles might be found at any one time in the classroom. Material for individualized reading includes, of course, all book varieties: basal texts, supplementary readers, library books, texts in the various subject fields, trade books, pamphlets, brochures, teacher-made and pupil-made materials, magazines, and newspapers.

[8] See Willard C. Olson's, "Seeking, Self-selection, and Pacing in the Use of Books by Children," The Packet (Boston: D. C. Heath Co., 1952), for an interesting projection of the expected range of abilities to be found in a classroom. Copies are free upon request.

Management procedures and arrangements in individualized reading are flexible. The teacher does have well-defined purposes; goals are firmly fixed in mind, and an organization and structure are provided which releases children to learn. But materials, time allotments, and procedures are used and developed in terms of the individual learner's growth in reading and self-development.

Usually teachers plan scheduled periods to meet the following objectives:

1. To make selection of reading materials.
2. For individual reading conferences between teacher and pupil.
3. For independent activities for individuals not reading independently with the teacher.
4. For class or small group discussion and sharing.
5. For children in pairs or small groups to engage in creative work growing out of common reading.
6. For small groups or the whole class either with the teacher or independently to develop needed skills and to work on confusion and common difficulties in reading.
7. For children to read independently.

Time allotments vary. No two teachers work exactly the same way. Not all of these activities are provided each day. Some teachers set aside special days for certain activities; other teachers have such periods for short times throughout the day.

The typical daily program follows a routine of this nature:

The teacher gives some direction to the class as a whole before starting other activities. During this time the children have opportunity to raise questions about their work, to clarify committee work assignments, to decide reading plans, and to get a clear understanding of the day's plans.

Depending upon the day's purpose, activities needed, the needs and interest revealed, the teacher would work in one or more of the following ways:

1. Hold individual reading conferences while others work on independent activities.
2. Work with the small special group on a particular skill while others read independently.
3. Hold individual reading conferences while some children read independently, others work in pairs or small groups on creative activities.
4. Circulate to provide help as children read independently, carry on independent activities or work in groups.

Balance in the program is maintained by looking at the daily activities for a period of time. Some teachers keep a diary to record past activities and plan future programs. In this way they soon discover that a fixed daily routine is not necessary to achieve desired results with each pupil contact.

Grouping is flexible in time span and in composition. Some groups work only a day together, others longer. Depending on their needs, some children may participate in several groups at a time or perhaps none at all. After reviewing her notes the teacher recognizes a common need and plans a group activity; or after four or five reading conferences, volunteers are designated to form a group, the test results may indicate good possibilities for group work. Groups are formed in different ways but always for a specific task at a particular time. When the purpose is accomplished the group is disbanded. Grouping frequently occurs in individualized reading, but it is organized so as to focus on the individual learner.

Direct attention is paid to skills in individualized reading. The skills are no different from those found valuable in any basic reading program. The emphasis is on determining which skills are to be developed in individual children, and how much practice each should have.

Procedures used for skill development vary from day to day, but teachers generally find these basic steps helpful:

1. Provide individual guidance during the reading conference.
2. Perform group work with children who share a common need.

3. Encourage pupils to assist each other—working in small groups.
4. Divide the class into groups for practice with groups alternating teacher guidance and self-responsibility.
5. Make plans for the entire class.

Any program which encourages children to read in many areas for a variety of purposes at different speeds demands some kinds of records. In individualized reading many types of records are useful:

> Running diaries of reading activities.
> Individual plans for reading, sharing, or activity.
> Records of reading difficulties—new words met, meanings of words, development and completion of comprehension worksheets, etc.
> Kinds and amount of reading.

The teacher keeps individual cards or a notebook for each pupil, recording dates when books were started and finished, difficulties encountered, strengths noted, attitudes, and personal observations.

In the direct "language approach" the children dictate or write the material used for reading instruction. One report describes the experience of a group of teachers starting such a program.[9]

In the case of teaching reading to children in the first grade, we are prone to follow rather rigid practices. Before we ever see the children we are to teach, we have been given the materials for reading. In these, everything important has been *pre*pared, *pre*determined, and *pre*patterned—selection, order or presentation and frequency of repetition of words; which context clues to use; what consonant and vowel sounds to teach and when; and other matters of teaching method. Most of the materials were prepared by someone in a distant city even before the children we teach were born.

"We can't begin with prepared readiness sheets, because they don't represent the ideas of the children we teach," was the first point made by teachers thus challenged.

"We can't begin with a list of basic sight

words, because those may not be the words that represent the thinking and the interests of the children during the early days of first grade," was an additional agreement.

"We can't begin with group stories dictated by the children, because only a few participate at first, and we want participation on the part of every child from the beginning," was the further conclusion.

From their pooled experiences, the teachers decided to try using the children's earliest self-expression in "writing" as a beginning point in teaching reading. "Writing? Children don't *really* write in the first grade." But when a child makes a picture with crayons, he is "expressing" an idea that has meaning to him, and to him it is his way of *really* writing. In this sense, it is writing except that he doesn't yet know how to record his thinking in words. Crayon drawing is an activity that most children do with ease as a result of kindergarten experiences. The difference in using this as a starting point in language teaching was going to be in the treatment of the ideas that the children represented with crayons. Beginning with the first day of school, these teachers would give each child repeated opportunities to come to the threshold of reading without forcing an entrance.

In each of these classrooms, children were asked to bring the pictures of their own choosing and own making to the "reading group." There the teacher invited comment about each picture and together she and the child decided on a story to be written on the picture. The rest of the children watched eagerly as they saw the speech of one child take form on his picture. They participated by helping the teacher decide about initial sounds, capital letters, punctuation.

Although the reproduction of the story by reading it was not a requirement, the teacher found that each succeeding day additional children would try to "step across the threshold" by reading something which they had said for their picture story.

The children were so proud of their stories that they wanted to keep them. With the help of the teacher, they bound them into books for the reading table. When these books took their place alongside the other printed books, every child had a desire to read them because they were what he and his classmates had written.

Interest in the reading-writing process became so great that children needed more space and time for this self-expression. The teachers began to use all available space in the room to carry on the activity. They equipped

---

[9] R. Van Allen, "Initiating Reading Through Creative Writing," *Twenty-second Yearbook*, Claremont College Reading Conference, Claremont College, Calif., 1957.

easels to hold the children's stories and cleared spaces on the floor for the children to work with large pieces of paper. They developed writing centers with helps for children who were writing on their own.

To keep the reading-writing program going week by week, the teachers had to maintain an environment rich in ideas and receptive to the products of children in the form that they were produced. Since children do not create in a vacuum, the teachers constantly "devacuumized" their classrooms by reading to the children, telling stories, showing films and pictures, playing records, and having songs, field trips, dramatizations, and games. As the children gave pictorial and verbal (oral and written) expression to this interesting and rich environment, the teacher was available to write new words, write part or all of a story, help children clarify statements. The child's part was to keep on putting his ideas into pictorial and written form with gradually developing attention to correct use of language and to expansion of vocabulary.

Just one example will illustrate the abundance of raw material for reading which a teacher received from a group of beginning first graders who brought their pictures to the "reading circle." This is what they asked the teacher to write on the pictures which represented their thinking:

I wish I had a dog. (Dona)
This is my house and flowers. (Ida)
Here is my pretty sun. (Becky)
See my fish. (Michael)
Here is my bird and my big tree. (Chris)
See my big red apple tree. (Candy)
I'm moving into my new house. (Zoe)
Look at my house and flowers. (Sandra)
I plant my flowers. (Lana)

Contrast the "raw material" of these nine children with the usual material found in a first readiness worksheet. Of course, the children were not expected to read the captions on the pictures at first, but they did read them soon after the picture stories were fastened together into books for the reading table. Books from other groups also made popular reading material, and before long the classroom became filled with materials which the children could read—the books they had made as well as textbooks and library books.

The limitations imposed by the use of the highly controlled vocabulary found in any basic reading series was not present to restrict the reading development of the fast learners in these groups. Their selection of words for

writing and reading was limited only by their individual vocabularies. Neither were the slow learners frustrated by trying to remember words for which they had no real need in their expression; at the same time, they were stimulated to keep trying to use new words for their stories.

Reading skills were developed informally, but word counts made of such independent writing (which children can read because they wrote it) indicate that the reading vocabulary is from three to four times as great as that introduced in any standard basic reading series at the preprimer level. Children who had the experience of reading and writing from their own experiences and ideas *prior* to reading from basic readers could then read the textbooks with ease. Because they had watched their teacher record their speech and had learned to write some of their own, they had developed among other skills such important ones in reading as:

Left-to-right eye movement
Line-to-line progression
Awareness of sentence structure
Increased power of sustained attention
Ability to organize ideas
Ability to sound out words, beginning with the recognition of sounds of initial consonants and progressing to more complex phonic situations
Ability to hear and recognize endings such as -s, -ed, -ing
Use of context clues to recognize a word in their own stories
Use of picture clues to recognize words in the stories of their friends
A sight vocabulary of those words which naturally recur in children's writing

With basic skills such as the ones described above indicated in the reading-writing situation, the prepared materials in the basic readers were used to give the reading program some plus factors. For example, basic skills began to be habituated through the successful reading of numerous books. The sense of achievement from reading books successfully established a confidence conducive to rapid progress. Basic vocabulary words which were not recognized by sight were checked for further study and used in written expression. The elements of phonics which were learned in the letter-by-letter recording of language in writing were used in a functional situation in reading. The teacher always made sure that the minimum phonics program of the basic reading series had been accomplished by every child.

A serious limitation of the writing approach to reading is the fact that beginners have limited writing ability. At first the stories are written by the teacher but dictated by children. In some classrooms the children are encouraged to write without reference to correct form. This does mean practice of writing habits that must be changed later. The problem is solved in some schools by having the parents or teachers type the corrected stories. In practice, writing and reading are frequently parallel learnings.

Although some teachers prefer an individualized reading program, it is a growing practice to combine group and individualized programs. A part of such classes may follow a basic reader as it was planned by those who created the series, while others follow an individualized program guided by the teacher.

1. Would any material be used in an individualized program that the teacher had not read?

2. Would it be possible for certain skills to be neglected in an individualized program?

3. Individualized reading is noncompetitive. Does this mean that the poor reader might be a poor reader in an individualized program and not recognize the fact? What would be gained in such a learning situation?

4. Would it be possible for a teacher to direct her major effort toward the needs of the lower third of a class and neglect the upper third in an individualized program?

HOW IS READING INSTRUCTION DIRECTED IN THE INTERMEDIATE GRADES?

Teachers seek to achieve the following purposes in the reading program of the intermediate grades:

1. Continue development of word-recognition skills started in the primary grade. There will be many at this level

San Diego City Schools, Calif.

Some children in the intermediate grades need to read from books that are at a third grade level of difficulty. Success with this material will establish skills needed for more advanced work.

that are operating at second and third grade levels of reading. Some of normal ability follow a delayed pattern of achievement in reading. For a number of reasons about one boy in ten does not read comfortably until late in his tenth or eleventh year of age. A part of this is lack of purpose. Apparently the reading materials of previous years did not appear worth the effort to read them. But now that he needs to read directions to make model airplanes or is exploring vocational interests, reading assumes a new importance.

2. Develop a discrimination with respect to reading material. This involves elements of critical judgment, appreciation of literary quality in writing, and the ability to select material needed to solve a problem from material less important.

3. Teach the reading skills needed in association with the school program. Intermediate children need to practice increasing reading speed, skimming, using the index or other aids with respect to locating material and interpreting new concepts, terms and representation of ideas such as graphs. The dictionary is studied in detail.

4. Help the child integrate all the language art skills so that they act in a way to reinforce each other. The close association of these skills may be noted in these parellel columns of skills:

Listening—Reading Skills	*Speaking—Writing Skills*
Getting the Main Idea	Finding the Topic Sentence Paragraphing Note Taking
Reading for Details	Outlining Giving Directions Organizing Ideas in Sequence Summarizing
Determining Author's Meaning of a Word	Vocabulary Development Use of Dictionary Dramatic Interpretation
Using Context Skills	Understanding Sentence Structure and Paragraphing
Word Analysis Skills	Spelling
Oral Reading	Pronunciation Enunciation Dramatic Interpretation
Interpreting Poetry	Choral Reading, Creative Writing
Visualization	Descriptions
Understanding Modifiers and Referents	Use of Pronouns, Adverbs, Adjectives, Clauses, and Phrases
Drawing Conclusions	Logical Organization of Material
Social Sensitivity to Ideas Presented	Expressing Emotional Feelings

In the classroom the teacher uses sets of basic readers, library books, weekly and monthly magazines, and daily newspapers to teach reading. At the beginning of the year it is wise to use a reader at least one grade below the level of the children as a review reader. This gives the teacher a chance to know the students without discouraging those below grade level. It is normal that from one-fourth to one-third of an average fifth-grade classroom will be able to read only third- or fourth-grade material. Social studies books and some science books will be difficult for many to read until concepts are established through experience that provides meaning and language experience.

Intermediate teachers soon learn that many of the study skills such as drawing conclusions, reading for detail, getting the main idea and locating information are developed in materials other than the reading textbook. Intermediate readers are a source for some of these skills, but the major contribution made is in the area of literature.

Since a great range of ability exists in any intermediate class, lesson planning is usually done in terms of groups with similar needs. These steps in a reading lesson are suggested in most basic programs.

1. Motivate the silent reading of the new story. Pictures, questions, and the experience of the child or teacher are used to arouse interest. At this time teachers anticipate and present some of the language and vocabulary needed to read the story.
2. A few of the key concepts and words are introduced. Seldom is it necessary to present all new words, since the children need to practice the word-attack skills they know. Some of these skills may be used in the presentation of the new words as review or re-teaching.
3. Any related work in the form of workbooks, chalkboard work, or follow-up assignment is presented and explained.
4. The activities at the circle or with the group are developed. These may start by checking previously assigned work. This work may remain with the student for further practice or be collected for checking. The story that has been read silently is then discussed. This discussion will involve questions concerning the main idea, evaluating characters and conduct, drawing conclusions, enjoying humor or literary style. Oral reading is

often a part of this period as children clarify points, read dialogue for expression, choose parts or check understanding. Interest and purpose in the next lesson are established. Some of the new words may be analyzed or checked for meaning. Nearly every lesson provides some opportunity to strengthen phonetic and research skills.

Before leaving the group, the teacher asks some child to repeat the assignment as a means of reinforcing the memories of others. Circle procedures need variations to avoid monotony. One device that seems to appeal to intermediate children is to create problem-solving situations rather than always providing answers and directions by the teacher.

Certain activities of the class must follow established routines. These involve handling papers, distribution of books, and movement within the room. After a group has left the circle, the teacher will require a few minutes of time to check the work of those who remained at their desks.

In order to encourage and guide recreational reading, at least one period a week should be devoted to this type of activity. This may involve the entire class or only a single interest group, depending on the type of books being read or the level of reading. Those reading at an easier level often hesitate to talk freely about books that other children have already read.

Other special needs may be provided for in weekly one-hour periods. Those who are working in a skill-text which is below grade level or in special editions of the *Reader's Digest* may meet several times during a week for special instruction.

In order to free the teacher's time to meet the individual and group needs, purposeful work must be found for those at their desks. Some able children like to prepare challenging materials for others to read. These may be a series of questions concerning an article from a magazine or newspaper. If mounted in a manila folder, the article on one side and questions on the other, they may be used many times or sent to another room. The circulars children receive when they write to firms or communities are also interesting reading experiences when prepared in this fashion. There are well-planned workbooks for all the intermediate grades. While few classes would use one of these for all students, small sets of this material will save hours of teacher time as she helps children who have been absent, who need special help, or are above average and need challenging material.

The following activities have been found to be of value as seatwork practices:

Reread the first paragraph of the story. Answer the following questions:

Who are the characters introduced?
Where does the beginning of the story take place?
When does the beginning of the story take place?
What problem is being introduced?

Make a list of the leading characters in the story and skim story to find descriptive phrases of each.

Appearance   Characteristics
Action   Expressions
Feelings   Attitudes

Write a description in your own words, one for each character.

Choose your favorite character. Pretend you meet this person some place. Write a conversation you might like to have with this person.

Choose two characters in the story. Write a conversation between them.

Choose a character from this story and one from another story your class has recently read and write a conversation between them.

Choose one location mentioned in the story. Make a list of all descriptive words and phrases used in the text about this location.

Write in your own words a description of this place.

Read the ending of your story. Make a picture as you see the scene.

Choose a title for the picture. Write a short paragraph to go with the picture.

Read the first three paragraphs of the story and make an outline of them:

a. What is the first paragraph about?
1. People
2. Places
3. Action
b. What is the second paragraph about?
1.
2.
3.
c. What is the third paragraph about?
1.
2.
3.

Skim the story and make lists of words ending with *ing, ed, s, es.* Decide if any words are examples of the following rules, and if so, list the examples under the rule number.

Rule 1. If a word of one syllable ends with a single consonant by a single vowel, the final consonant is usually doubled before adding a suffix beginning with a vowel.

Examples: run, running; fun, funny; hop, hopping

Rule 2. When a word of more than one syllable ends with a single consonant preceded by a single vowel, the consonant is usually doubled before adding a suffix beginning with a vowel when the accent is on the last syllable.

Examples: omit, omitted

Rule 3. If a word ends with a single consonant immediately preceded by more than one vowel, the final consonant is not usually double when adding a suffix.

Examples: weed, weeded; dream, dreaming

Rule 4. If a word ends with two or more consonants or a double consonant, the consonants are usually retained when adding the suffix.

Examples: jump, jumped; dress, dresses

Rule 5. If a word ends with silent *e,* the *e* is usually dropped before adding a suffix beginning with a vowel.

Examples: hope, hoped

Rule 6. In words ending with *y* immediately preceded by a consonant, the *y* is usually changed to an *i* before adding a suffix.

Examples: cry, cries

Rule 7. Words ending with *y* retain the *y* when adding a suffix beginning with *i*.

Examples: hurry, hurrying

Rule 8. If a word ends in *y* immediately preceded by a vowel, the *y* is usually retained when adding a suffix.

Examples: play, played

Choose words from the story that will go with the following:

Words telling how high.
Words telling how low.
Words telling how fast.
Words telling how slow.
Words telling when.
Words telling where.

Look through the story and study all illustrations. Skim the story and choose one or two sentences as titles which you feel are appropriate.

Read the story again. Choose a scene as a subject for a peep-box. Make a peep-box for this scene.

Reread the story. List the scenes presented. Make characters for each scene to use on flannelboard. Practice the story using the pictures to illustrate.

Work with a committee to choose one scene from the story which can be told in pantomime. Plan for one pupil to read from text while others pantomime what happens.

Choose one character from today's story and one from another story you have read. Plan a meeting of these two characters. Decide what you would have them doing at this meeting. Paint a picture of this scene. Choose an appropriate title. Write conversation.

Choose an experience one of the characters had in the story. Write about an experience you have had similar to this.

Choose a situation as described in the story. Write a myth or a "whopper" about this situation.

Write a personal, newsy letter to one of the characters in the story telling about your activities and inquiring about something the character has been doing.

Write a personal letter as from one character to another. Write an answer to the letter as from the other character.

Make up a limerick about a person, place, or thing mentioned in the story.

Make a sequence chart of things that happened. You may want to make illustrations to go with the chart.

Choose a scene in the story. Make stick puppets to go with this scene and plan to put on a show for the class.

Choose a character. Pretend something he owns that has been mentioned in the story has been lost. Write an advertisement for the "lost and found" column of the daily paper.

Write riddles using characters, places, or objects from your story.

Pretend you are the news editor of the daily paper published in the city where the characters of the story live. Write articles which may appear in this paper mentioning the doings of these characters. Plan some headlines, etc.

Choose one of the characters who is in trouble. Write a short play for the class to act out, using the other characters as needed.

Look for words in the story and list them under the following headings:

dr	tr	fr	fl	bl	cl	sl	st	sw
st	sw	sn	sm	cr	gr	pr	br	qu
pl	sp	spr	str	thr	ch	sh	wh	th

Look for words ending with *ck, ng.*

Look for words ending with: *al, aw, ái, ay, oa, oi, oy; ow* as in *slow; ow* as in *cow; ar, er, ir, ur.*

Find words starting with soft *g*, hard *g*, soft *c*, hard *c*.

Find words illustrating the following:

Silent *e* at the end of the one syllable word.

Silent vowel in a word in which two vowels come together.

Silent letter in double consonants.

When *c* or *g* is followed by *e, i,* or *y,* it usually has the soft sound.

When there is only one vowel in a one syllable word it is usually short unless it is at the end.

Find words that have root words within them.

Find compound words.

Find hyphenated words.

Find words to which you can add *-y, -ly, -er, -est, -ful, -en, -able.* Make the new words by adding these endings.

Find words that start with *re-, un-, be-.* Find other words to which these prefixes may be added. How are they related in meaning?

Find contractions in the story such as *I'm, what's, we're, that's, haven't, there's, aren't.*

Find words that end in *e* to which *-ing, -ed, -er, -est,* or *-y* may be added to form new words. Make new words by adding these endings. Note that the *e* must be dropped in adding these.

Look for figures of speech in the story. Explain the meaning.

Choose single words that describe each character. In a column to the side of these lists, write words that are opposite in meaning. For example: happy, sad; laugh, cry.

List all the words on a certain page that express action; things a character did.

Tell briefly why you think each character did the things he did in the story.

Use the table of contents in the reader and find other stories that you think are similar to this one and tell why you chose that particular one.

Read in some source book in the room more information about something mentioned in the story.

List all the words of which meanings you are not sure. Find them in the dictionary or glossary if the book has one. Choose the meaning which you think best applies to the use made of the word in the story.

Write statements from the story for others in the class to decide if true or false. Be sure you know the correct answer.

Write sentences for others in the class to complete.

Find passages in the story that make you feel sad, happy, drowsy, excited.

Find parts of the story which you feel are humorous.

Write a fable, legend, or fairy tale about some incident or character in the story.

Look back through the book. List the stories which you have read under the following headings: fanciful tale, biography, true story, realistic.

Find words that begin with *dis-, en-, in-, un-, re-.* Words that end with *-ion, -ist, -ment, -ant, -er, -ance, -ish, -able, -ful, -less.* Note the influence of these elements on meaning.

Select an advertisement or news story and note the words that have emotional appeal in them.

Take a circular of a city or park and make a series of questions that a visitor might find answered in this circular. Clip a week's TV schedule from the Sunday paper. Make a series of questions that might be answered by reading this schedule. Read an advertisement of something you would like to buy—a bicycle, toy, car. What questions are *not* answered in the material?

1. When should children be permitted to read library books in the classroom?

2. Should a child in the sixth grade who reads as well as an adult be expected to participate in the reading class?

3. Do you feel a teacher is justified, at the beginning of the year, in having the better readers do a great deal of oral reading in the social studies and science classes?

4. Why are some more likely to enjoy reading circulars they have received in the mail, or a Scout Manual, or an item in *Popular Science Magazine,* than a story in the reader?

5. Examine some of the study skills such as reading for details, drawing conclusions, and getting the main idea in association with the content subjects. Find examples of reading details in a mathematics problem, in a science experiment and in a geography book. Would it be possible for a child to use the skill in one area and not in the other? What factors are operating to make these situations similar or different?

Suggestions for Projects

1. The Science Research Associates, 57 W. Grand Avenue, Chicago 10, Ill., publish a kit of reading materials for the primary, intermediate and junior high school grades. Evaluate one of these kits.
2. A number of companies publish books of simple vocabulary but with stories that interest older children. Evaluate one of these series. These are suggestions:

   American Adventure Series. Wheeley Publishing Company, 161 E. Grand Avenue, Chicago 11, Ill.
   Basic Vocabulary Series. Garrard Press, 119 West Parke Avenue, Champaign, Ill.
   Cowboy Sam Series. Beckley-Cardy, 1900 North Narragansett, Chicago 39, Ill.
   Pleasure Reading Series. Garrard Press.
   American Heroes. The Bobbs-Merrill Company, Inc., 730 N. Meridan Street, Indianapolis 7, Ind.
   I Want to Be Series. Children's Press, Jackson Blvd., Chicago 7, Ill.

3. The following companies publish special bulletins, magazines or monthly magazines that act as service material to teachers who use their publications. Make a collection of this material. Evaluate one article in each.

   Allyn and Bacon, Inc., Englewood Cliffs, N.J.: "Language Arts Bulletin" and "The Reading Bulletin."
   Scott, Foresman and Company, 433 East Erie St., Chicago 11, Ill.: "Supervisor's Notebook."
   D. C. Heath and Company, 285 Columbus Avenue, Boston 16, Mass.: "The Packet."
   Ginn and Company, Statler Building, Boston 17, Mass.: "Elementary School Notes."

   Harper & Row, Publishers, 49 East 33rd Street, New York 16, N.Y.: "Educational Monographs."
   Charles E. Merrill, Inc., Education Center, Columbus 16, Ohio: Frequent bulletins, excellent pamphlet each year on "How to Get Best Results in Reading."

4. The *Reader's Digest,* Pleasantville, N.Y., publishes special editions of material with a controlled reading vocabulary. Examine a set of these and suggest ways they may be effectively used in the classroom.
5. The American Education Press, Columbus, Ohio, publishes weekly newspapers for children. Scholastic Publications, 351 Fourth Avenue, New York 10, N.Y., also publishes weekly material. Examine copies of these publications and write a letter to your principal telling him why you would like them for your classroom.
6. Make a bibliography for any grade level of books published in the past five years that would be easy reading for that grade.
7. Select one of the standardized reading tests for your class. Explain why you selected it in preference to others.
8. Evaluate a set of filmstrips that have been designed for reading readiness purposes. Harper & Row, Laidlaw, and Houghton Mifflin are among the publishers that have such material designed for their reading series.
9. Compare a modern reading program with one used prior to 1920.
10. Since the teaching of reading presents similar teaching problems throughout the English-speaking world, examine professional publications and textbooks to learn of the reading program in Canada, Australia, England, or South Africa.
11. Compare the workbook programs of three reading programs for one grade.
12. Prepare a lesson for the intermediate grades to develop critical thinking with respect to reading advertisements, propaganda, editorials, or newspaper accounts.

BIBLIOGRAPHY

BOOKS

Anderson, Paul S., et al. *Readings in the Language Arts.* New York: Macmillan, 1963.

Barbe, W. B. *Education Guide to Personalized Reading Instruction.* Englewood Cliffs, N.J.: Prentice-Hall, Inc., 1962.

Betts, E. A. *Foundations of Reading Instruction.* New York: American, 1954.

Bond, Guy and Eva Wagner. *Teaching the Child to Read.* 3rd ed. New York: Macmillan, 1960.

Carter, Homer L. J. and Dorothy McGinnis. *Teaching Individuals to Read.* Boston: D. C. Heath, 1962.

Causey, Oscar S. *The Reading Teacher's Reader.* New York: Ronald, 1958.

Dawson, Mildred and Henry Bammen. *Fundamentals of Basic Reading Instruction.* New York: Longmans, 1959.

DeBoer, John J. and Martha Dallman. *The Teaching of Reading.* New York: Holt, 1960.

Durrell, Donald. *Improving Reading Instruction.* New York: Harcourt, 1956.

Fernald, G. M. *Remedial Techniques in Basic School Subjects.* New York: McGraw-Hill, 1943.

Gray, W. S. *The Teaching of Reading and Writing.* Chicago: Scott, 1956.

———. *On Their Own in Reading.* Chicago: Scott, 1960.

Goddard, Nora L. *Reading in the Modern Infant's School.* London: U. London P., 1958.

Herr, Selma E. *Learning Activities for Reading,* Dubuque: W. C. Brown, 1961.

Hester, Kathleen B. *Teaching Every Child to Read.* New York: Harper, 1955.

Hildreth, Gertrude. *Teaching Reading.* New York: Holt, 1958.

Horn, Ernest. *Methods of Instruction in the Social Studies.* New York: Scribner, 1937.

Hymes, James L. *Before the Child Reads.* New York: Harper, 1958.

McKee, Paul. *The Teaching of Reading in the Elementary School.* Boston: Houghton, 1948.

McKim Margaret G. and Helen C. Caskey. *Guiding Growth in Reading,* 2/e. New York: Macmillan, 1963.

Monroe, Marion. *Growing into Reading.* Rev. Chicago: Scott, 1960.

Murry, W., and L. W. Downes. *Children Learn to Read.* London: Harrap, 1955.

National Education Association. *Reading for Today's Children.* 34th Yearbook of the Department of Elementary Principals. Washington, D.C. National Education Association, 1955.

Sheldon, W. D., et al. *Sheldon Basic Reading Series.* Boston: Allyn, 1957.

Stauffer, R., et al. *Winston Basic Readers.* Philadelphia: Winston, 1960.

Thompson, Helen M. *SWIERL. A Plan for Better Reading.* New York: Vantage, 1956.

Veatch, Jeannette. *Individualizing Your Reading Program.* New York: Putnam, 1959.

PAMPHLETS

Clearmont Reading Conference Proceedings. Published annually. Clearmont College, Clearmont, Calif.

Darrow, H. F., and Virgil Howes. Approaches to Individual Reading. New York: Appleton, 1960.

———, and R. Van Allen. Independent Activities for Creative Learning. New York: Teachers College, Columbia University Bureau of Publications, 1961.

Gates, Arthur I. Teaching Reading. Department of Classroom Teachers, National Education Association, Washington, D.C., 1957.

Jewett, Arno. Improving Reading in the Junior High School. Bulletin No. 10, U.S. Department of Health, Education and Welfare, Washington, D.C., 1957.

Laubach, Frank C. Reading Readiness Charts and Stories. Baltimore, Md.: Koinonia Foundation Press, 1955.

Meeker, Alice M. Teaching Beginners to Read. New York: Holt, 1958.

Russell, David H., and Etta E. Karp. Reading Aids through the Grades. Bureau of Publications, Teacher's College, Columbia University, 1955.

Spache, George. Good Reading for Poor Readers. Reading Laboratory and Clinic, University of Florida, Gainesville, Fla., 1958.

———. Resources in Teaching Reading. Reading Laboratory, University of Florida, Gainesville, Fla., 1960.

Popular basic reading textbooks are listed below:

Betts, E., et al. *Betts Basic Readers.* New York: American, 1958.

Bond, Guy, et al. *The Developmental Reading Series*. Chicago: Meredith, 1954.

Gates, Arthur, et al. *The Macmillan Readers*. New York: Macmillan, 1957.

Gray, W. C., et al. *The New Basic Readers*. Curriculum Foundation Series. Chicago: Scott, 1957.

Harris, Albert J. and Mae Knight Clark. The Macmillan Reading Program. New York: Macmillan, 1964.

Hildreth, Gertrude, et al. *Easy Growth in Reading*. New York: Holt, 1960.

McKee, Paul, et al. *The McKee Reading for Meaning Series*. Boston: Houghton, 1957.

O'Donnell, M., et al. *The Alice and Jerry Books*. New York: Harper, 1957.

Russell, David H., et al. *Ginn Basic Readers*, Rev. Boston: Ginn, 1961.

Witty, Paul, et al. *Reading for Interest*. Boston: Heath, 1955.

Chapter 7

*R*ediscovering Children's Literature

WHAT RESOURCES ARE AVAILABLE FOR TEACHERS OF CHILDREN'S LITERATURE?

In recent years one of the great changes in publishing emphasis has taken place in the area of children's literature. Today nearly every major publishing house has a children's editor who selects or develops manuscripts for books suited to the interests and abilities of modern children. There are some publishers who specialize in books for young readers. In 1960 over fifteen hundred titles were published for children and youth in the United States.

This new interest in publishing for children is not limited to our country. In 1959 over 530 titles for children were published in Sweden. In the same year over 800 were published in England. Many of these books are read by children all over the world. Some Swedish books have been translated into as many as eight foreign languages. The adventures of *Snip, Snap,* and *Snur* and of *Pippi Longstocking* belong to the heritage of American children as well as to Sweden. From England we not

only have the older books of *Peter Rabbit* and *Winnie the Pooh,* but the modern adventure stories of Enid Blyton and Captain W. E. Johns. In turn, children of other lands are enjoying the books of American writers.

In all of this material there is much that is of only temporary importance, as is true for the many volumes published for adults. But it is quite possible that many books of real worth go undiscovered because busy teachers and parents do not have the time to keep informed in this rapidly expanding field.

An early task for one preparing to teach is to explore this segment of the children's world. At first, read at all grade levels in order to note the type of material available, and the quality of writing and illustrations. Later, concentrate on the grade levels that most concern you.

A source of information is the *Children's Catalog* published by The H. W. Wilson Company, New York. This is pri-

Burbank Public Schools, Calif.

Children find in books materials that will enrich the most limited and uneventful environment. It is the teacher's responsibility to provide publications whose quality is worthy of these precious years.

marily a reference work for use in libraries. In it are listed the books considered of highest merit published recently as well as those of enduring value of the past. If you are establishing a library for the first time, you will find in it a special list recommended for initial purchase as a nucleus for future growth. The *Children's Catalog* is too expensive for individual purchase by a teacher but should be available in a school district that spends funds for library books.

In order to recognize merit and to direct the attention of the public toward children's literature, a number of awards are made each year. The John Newbery Medal is awarded for a book which is considered the most distinguished contribution to American literature for children.

The Caldecott Medal honors the best illustrated book for children.

There are other awards which call attention to books of merit. These include The New York Herald Tribune Awards, The Laura Ingalls Wilder Award, and The Regina Medal. In Canada there are two Book-of-the-Year-for-Children Medals. The Hans Christian Andersen Award is an in-

ternational children's book award. In England the Carnegie Medal and Kate Greenway Medal correspond to the Newbery and Caldecott Awards in the United States. There are awards given in France, Germany, Norway, Sweden, and Switzerland, for outstanding children's books published each year in these countries.

In Munich, Germany, one finds an International Children's Library which frequently displays books of merit from all countries. It is especially interesting to visit the room where books that appear in several languages are displayed. *The Adventures of Tom Sawyer* is available in seven languages, *Pippi Longstocking* in five, and *Peter Rabbit* in eleven.

Another aid to teachers in the selection of books for children are the book reviews that appear in *The Horn Book, Saturday Review, Childhood Education, Elementary English, The New York Times, The New York Herald Tribune,* and *The Christian Science Monitor.*

The Children's Book Council, located at 50 West 53rd Street, New York 19, N.Y., promotes the nationwide Book Week. Posters, book jackets, wall charts, and other materials are available for school use at very low cost.

With all this emphasis upon the new it must not be forgotten that we share a great cultural heritage from the past. There are constant references in our language which assume that we know the meaning of such expressions as, "my man Friday," "the golden touch," "the patience of Job," and "whitewashing the fence."

Anthologies of children's literature contain collections of old and new verse, the fairy and folktales, short selections from modern writers, notes on authors and illustrators of children's books, and excellent suggestions for classroom use. In time, most elementary teachers will want to purchase one of these anthologies to keep on their desks, as a constant source of classroom material. A book of this nature is as basic to good instruction as chalkboard and chalk, but some districts hesitate to spend funds for individual teacher references. In that case the teacher has no choice but to purchase such a book as a basic tool of the profession.

The *Anthology of Children's Literature* by Edna Johnson, Evelyn R. Sickels, and Frances Clark Sayers, published by Houghton Mifflin Company, and *Story and Verse for Children* by Miriam Blanton Huber, published by Macmillan, are outstanding single-volume collections. Miss May Hill Arbuthnot has several books: *Time for True Tales; Time for Fairy Tales; Time for Poetry;* and *Children and Books,* all published by Scott, Foresman and Company.

In the area of children's literature we are endowed with great riches. Our problem is to spend it with wisdom.

1. What sources of information concerning new books for children are available in your teaching community? What responsibility must a teacher assume in order that this information is used?

2. Would you consider such old favorites as *Mrs. Wiggs of the Cabbage Patch* or *Black Beauty* appropriate for modern children?

3. How do you explain the popularity of series books with young readers?

4. The comic books are a favorite form of leisure reading for some children. Are they of literary merit? How should such material be handled in school?

WHAT IS BIBLIOTHERAPY?

When a book is intentionally used to improve the attitudes of a reader toward himself and his own problems or those of others, it provides a type of therapy or "healing." When books are used in this way, we are applying what may be called "bibliotherapy." Bibliotherapy is used most frequently in two situations. In the first, a child reads a book in which the hero or heroine suffers from trials very closely allied to the present problem of the child. In so doing, the reader lives out the hero's emotions. He gives vent to his own pent-up feelings and obtains in this way a certain amount of psychological relief. In the second, the child gains insight and absorbs general principles governing conduct, ideals, and mental attitudes which enable him to see his own difficulties from an objective point of view.

Edith Cahoe, who works with the blind in the Detroit schools, suggests that carefully chosen books might be used with the handicapped child to improve his attitude toward his handicap and to help him accept objectively the attitudes of others—attitudes that may range from over protective to neglectful or even derisive.[1]

In such reading the child may see his counterpart in a story and identify himself with individuals or groups who have similar problems. The reader follows the characters, observes ways in which they arrive at solutions, and notes how they resolve inner conflicts to make a happy adjustment. The teacher reads aloud Margaret Vance's *Windows for Rosemary* to a group of blind children. The children rejoice with the

---

[1] Edith Cahoe, "Bibliotherapy for Handicapped Children," *National Educ. Journal,* May 1960, pp. 34–35.

blind child in the story when she receives a Braille typewriter which enables her to write so others might read.

Bibliotherapy may be preventive as well as corrective. The presence of one or two foreign children in an Anglo-Saxon community can present a problem. One teacher read aloud to her class Eleanor Estes' *The Hundred Dresses*. The pupils quickly recognized that the little Polish girl with the strange name was worth knowing, and that she had been cruelly treated. One child said, "I wish she were in our class. We'd be nice to her." But the test did not come until three foreign children did appear in the classroom. There was a moment of silence, then smiles of welcome appeared on the pupils' faces and the three new, frightened children smiled back.

Many schools have the problem of the children of migrant workers who stay a week or a month in a school and then move on. Doris Gates in *Blue Willow* helps children understand this way of life. Related to this is the role of a Negro child in a recently integrated school. *Mary Jane* by Dorothy Sterling, provides a nonsentimental but sensitive study of a twelve-year-old Negro girl spending the first year in a school which had formerly been segregated. The problems of children in a country that lost a war become real and vital as the reader becomes part of the German family in *The Ark*, by Margot Benary-Isbert.

Bibliotherapy is most frequently considered in association with the children's individual personal problems. Marie's family has had to go on relief. John's parents are getting a divorce. Ellen is an adopted child, Ted is fat and awkward, Bob has no father in his home, Paul has a stepmother. Over a period of time such problems can cause personality disorders in a child. Situations like these must be treated individually. Here it is the teacher who is the key factor in any effort of bibliotherapy. It takes a dedicated concern for children's problems to start the search for the right book. Sometimes the right book does not exist. But even after the right one is found there are further problems. Sometimes children resent this interest in their private lives, or pride causes them to mask their difficulties. It is usually best for the child to "discover" the book. Then when he does want to discuss the story or character there must be a sympathetic listener. Listening is more important than suggesting ways of acting or feeling. A teacher may try to refer the story to herself and her own problems in the discussion, thus providing an indirect method of application to the child.

As in all therapy there are failures. Walter Loban made a study of the influences of stories on the attitudes of high school students.[2] Those who were sensitive to the feelings of others were responsive to problems presented in the stories. But some that lacked empathy or awareness of the feelings of others remained callous and indifferent to the story situations.

The following books are only a few that have been suggested for use in this area. In addition to their value for individual therapy, most of them would also serve as stimulators of group discussion. Miss Elvajean Hall, Coordinator of School Library Services of the Newton, Mass., Public Schools, maintains a current list of such books which is free upon request to Campbell and Hall, P.O. Box 350, Boston 17, Massachusetts.

BOOKS FOR BIBLIOTHERAPY

KEY:
E   Easy reading or picture books for primary grades.
M   Books which will be enjoyed primarily by the middle grades.
U   Books which will appeal to the upper grades and junior high.

THE PROBLEM OF APPEARANCE

Beim. *Smallest Boy in the Class*. Morrow (size) E
Engebretson. *What Happened to George*. Rand (fat) E

[2] Walter Loban, "Study of Social Sensitivity Among Adolescents," *J. Educ. Psychol.*, February 1955, pp. 102–112.

Evers. *Plump Pig*. Rand (fat) E

Felson. *Bertie Comes Through*. Dutton (fat) U

Felson. *Bertie Takes Care*. Dutton (fat) U

Field. *Hepatica Hawks*. Macmillan (size) U

Friedman, F. *Dot for Short*. Morrow (size) M

Gates. *Sensible Kate*. Viking (plain) U

Harris. *Big Lonely Dog*. Houghton (size) E

McGinley. *Plain Princess*. Lippincott (plain) M

Reyher. *My Mother Is the Most Beautiful Woman in the World*. Howell-Soskind (plain) E

PHYSICAL HANDICAPS

Angelo. *Hill of Little Miracles*. Viking (cripples) U

Beim. *Triumph Clear*. Harcourt (paralyzed) U

Burnett. *Secret Garden*. Lippincott (crippled) U

Dodge. *Hans Brinker*. Morrow (mental illness) M

Hatch. *Bridle-wise*. Messner (paralyzed) M

Henny. *King of the Wind*. Rand McNally (mute) M

Johnson. *Vicki, A Guide Dog*. Harcourt (blind) U

Knight. *Brave Companions*. Doubleday (blind) U

Lenski. *Corn Farm Boy*. Lippincott (health) M

Teilhet. *Avion My Uncle Flew*. Appleton (lame) U

Van Stockum. *Francie on the Run*. Viking (crippled) U

Vance. *Windows for Rosemary*. Dutton (blind) M

Webb. *Precious Bane*. Dutton (speech) M

THE NEW BABY

Flack. *New Pet*. Doubleday. E.

McKean. *David's Bad Day*. Shady Hill Press. E

Scott. *Judy's Baby*. Harcourt. E and M

CHARACTER AND PERSONALITY ADJUSTMENT

Burleson. *Toughey*. Steck (girl bully) M and U

Cutler. *Peg-a-leg*. Knopf (greediness) E

Daringer. *Adopted Jane*. Harcourt (adopted child) M

Flood. *Fighting Southpaw*. Houghton (music students considered sissies) M and U

Garner. *Little Cat Lost*. Messner (loneliness) E

Gates. *My Brother Mike*. Viking (court ward) M

Glenn. *Dumblebum*. Macrea Smith (loneliness) E

Haywood. *Here's a Penny*. Harcourt (adopted boy) M

Haywood. *Penny and Peter*. Harcourt (adopted boy) M

Haywood. *Primrose Day*. Harcourt (orphan with aunt) M

Henry. *Geraldine Belinda*. Platt (selfishness) E

Jackson. *Shorty Makes First Team*. Wilcox (extreme aggressiveness) U

Johnson. *Cowgirl Kate*. Messner (stepmother) U

Jones. *Peggy's Wish*. Abingdon (orphan) U

Moore. *Lucky Orphan*. Scribner (rejected child) M

Porter. *Footprints on the Sand*. Macmillan (orphan) U

Scott. *Silly Billy*. Harcourt (craving affection) E

Sigsgaard. *Nils All Alone*. Oxford (selfishness) E

Silliman. *Daredevil*. Holt (conceit) U

Sperry. *Call It Courage*. Holt (fear) U

Tunis. *Highpockets*. Morrow (conceit) U

Williams. *Timid Timothy*. Scott (timidity) E

Woolley. *David's Railroad*. Morrow (naughtiness) E and M

UNSETTLED LIVING

Agnew. *Sandy and Mr. Jalopy*. Friendship (migratory worker's family) E

Beim, J. *With Dad Alone*. Harcourt (divorce) E

Clymer. *Latch Key Club*. McKay (family retrenchment) M

Clymer. *Trolley Car Family*. McKay (peculiar dwelling) M

Gates. *Blue Willow*. Viking (migratory worker's family) M and U

Hager. *Canvas Castle*. Messner (adjustment to new environment) M and U

Harris. *Little Boy Brown*. Lippincott ("overprotected" city living) E

Lawrence. *Sand in Her Shoes*. Harcourt (adjustment to new environment) M and U

Lenski. *Judy's Journey*. Lippincott (sharecropper's family) M

Simon. *Robin on the Mountain*. Dutton (sharecropper's family) M

Sorrensen. *Miracle on Maple Hill*. Harcourt (family move) M

A "FOREIGN" BACKGROUND

Allee. *The House.* (several nationalities) U

Benary-Isbert. *The Ark.* (German) and *Rowen Farm.* Harcourt U

Clark. *In My Mother's House.* Viking (Indian) E and M

Clark. *Little Navajo Bluebird.* Viking (Indian) M

DeAngeli. *Bright April.* Doubleday (Negro) M

DeAngeli. *Up the Hill.* Doubleday (Polish) M

DeAngeli. *Yonie Wondernose.* Doubleday (Pennsylvania Dutch) E

Eberle. *Very Good Neighbors.* Lippincott (Mexican) M

Estes. *Hundred Dresses.* Harcourt (Polish) M

Evans. *All About Us.* Capitol (several nationalities) M and U

Eyre. *Star in the Willows.* Oxford (Mexican) M

Gerber. *Gooseberry Jones.* Putnam (Negro) M

Hader. *Mighty Hunter.* Macmillan (Indian) E

Lattimore. *Bayou Boy.* Morrow (Negro) M

Lattimore. *Indigo Hill.* Morrow (Negro) E and M

Lowe. *Somebody Else's Shoes.* Holt (Portuguese) U

McLelland. *Ten Beaver Road.* Holt (Scotch) M

Means. *Assorted Sisters.* Houghton (several nationalities) U

Means. *Great Day in the Morning.* Houghton (Negro) U

Means. *House Under the Hill.* Houghton (Mexican) U

Means. *Moved Outers.* Houghton (Japanese) U

Means. *Shuttered Windows.* Houghton (Negro) U

Means. *Tangled Waters.* Houghton (Indian) U

Noon. *Daughter of Thunder.* Macmillan (Indian) M and U

Politi. *Juanita.* Scribner (Mexican) E

Politi. *Angel of Olivera Street.* Scribner (Mexican) E

Shapiro. *Joe Magarac and His USA Citizen Papers.* Messner (Slavic) M

Seredy, Kate. *Chestry Oak.* Viking (Hungarian) U

Sterling, Dorothy. *Mary Jane.* Doubleday (Negro) M

Sze. *Echo of a Cry.* Harcourt. (Chinese) U

Tunis. *All American.* Harcourt (Negro) U

Tunis. *Keystone Kids.* Harcourt (Jewish) U

1. Can you recall reading any book that influenced your beliefs or attitudes?

2. How concerned should parents and teachers be when they discover children reading books that are vulgar or suggestive? What countermeasures would you suggest?

3. Should certain subjects such as death, union labor, working mothers, deceitful bankers and businessmen, be taboo in children's literature?

SHOULD A TEACHER READ TO CHILDREN?

There are many books that children enjoy and need to know before they have achieved the ability to read them independently. The "ear literacy" is far ahead of reading literacy throughout the elementary school. But more than the child's lack of ability to read justifies reading aloud to children. Shared experiences act as bridges between those involved. The quiet moments with a parent while Huckleberry Finn drifts down the Mississippi, or with an entire class as the teacher leads them through Alice in Wonderland or Dorothy's Wonderful Land of Oz, establish kindred spirits and high morale.

Another factor in reading difficulty is dialect. Many stories written for children are almost impossible for them to read aloud because of this. The Mary Poppin books by Travers contain English dialects and The Uncle Remus Stories by Joel Chandler Harris are written in the dialect of the deep South.

In many schools throughout the nation, teachers read selected books to children. In the intermediate grades the first fifteen minutes after lunch is usually set aside for this purpose. While the pupils relax after strenuous play, the teachers read from old and new classics. Favorites include Lewis Carroll's *Alice in Wonderland,* Joel Chandler Harris' *Uncle Remus*

San Diego County Schools, Calif.

Reading aloud is not to be undertaken casually, for it is merciless in its exposure of one's comprehension and appreciation of the passages read. It is a test of the book as well. Real values emerge both in style and content. Few skills are as important for an elementary teacher to cultivate.

Stories, Virginia Sorensen's Miracles on Maple Hill, L. Frank Baum's The Wonderful Wizard of Oz, E. B. White's Charlotte's Web, Betty MacDonald's Mrs. Piggle Wiggle's Magic, Kenneth Graham's The Wind in the Willows, Walter Edmond's The Matchlock Gun, Glen Round's Blind Colt, Lucretia Hale's The Peterkin Papers, Armstrong Sperry's Call It Courage, Kate Douglas Wiggin's The Birds' Christmas Carol, Hildegarde Swift's Railroad to Freedom, Alfred Olivant's Bob, Son of Battle, Rudyard Kipling's The Jungle Book, Howard Pyle's Otto of the Silver Hand, Glen Round's Ol Paul the Mighty Logger, Valenti Angelo's The Marble Fountain, Margot Benary-Isbert's The Ark, Mark Twain's The Adventures of Tom Sawyer, and the many books about space travel.

There are only a few hints that the teacher needs to remember to be a good oral reader. First, enjoy the story yourself. If it is a book that you do not mind rereading as each new group of children comes to your room, you can be certain not only that the book is worthy of your efforts but that your appreciation will be sensed by the children. Second, interpret the mood and differentiate between the principal characters in dialogues; be a bit dramatic when the plot is exciting, but don't explain the action while reading. Let some of the new words be interesting enough for the children to discover their meaning from the context; if there is a moral, let the listener discover that too. Third, because of time limitations, scan a new book and note the good stopping places. Sometimes it spoils a story just as it does a movie to come in late or to have the film break in the middle of a scene. Finally, always keep in mind that your purpose is to guide the children toward an appreciation of good literature and excellent writing. This period is not a time to spend with material of only passing interest or mass-production quality. Let the children read the detective series or The Scouts on Patrol, but don't use these precious periods for such material.

Reading a picture book to little children requires special preparation. The books for kindergarten and primary children must be selected with care. While little children will respond to almost any material presented by a teacher whom they love and respect, it should always be kept in mind that the materials read establish the standards the children will form for later reading. A book such as *Petunia* by Roger Duvoisin presents animals with childlike characters with which the child easily identifies. Humanized machines such as *Mike Mulligan and His Steam Shovel* or *The Little Engine That Could* tie together the worlds of fancy and realism. The humanized animals of the old, old favorite *Peter Rabbit* continue to charm children because of their intimacy with all living things. Rhyme adds charm but is not necessary. To be avoided at this level are stories with dialect; fairy tales of giants, dragons, and cruel stepmothers; and stories that are overemotional or exciting in tone.

The story should be short or in episodes that cover easily divided parts. Establish standards as to behavior during story reading. Routines should be known to all so that stories are expected at certain times or at a certain signal. Children should not be expected to stop an especially interesting activity without a "getting ready" or "finishing up time." At the beginning, some teachers prefer to start the story hour with only a part of the group.

To regain a wandering child's attention, call him softly by name, or smile directly at him to bring his attention back to your voice. In some groups, the more mature may need to work together. This may be the beginning group for the story hour while others rest or color. The teacher usually does as much telling as reading, using the pictures in the book to guide the questions and interest of the listeners.

While it may be handled well by some teachers, the retelling of the stories read by a child seldom holds the attention of other children. A story book brought from home should be identified as "Billy's book." After the teacher has examined the material, she may feel that the stories are appropriate for the group. Otherwise, a chance to see and talk about the pictures usually satisfies everyone.

To help some develop better habits, two children may be chosen to sit on each side of the teacher. These children in turn help show the pictures in the book. A special honor on a birthday or when there is

a new baby at home might be to select an old favorite for the teacher to read that day. It is well to remember that some children have never listened to a story read to them before coming to school.

One of the major purposes of presenting a book to a child of this age is to enable him to select the book to peruse with pleasure by himself. Watch children as they thumb through a new set of library books. They will pick one up, glance through a few pages, then discard it for another. In many classrooms it is wisest to put books on the library table only after they have been read to the children. With this experience, the child can make a meaningful selection. Here are nine suggestions for reading a picture book.

Gather the children closely around you either on low chairs or on the floor.

Sit in a low chair yourself.

Perform unhurriedly.

Handle the book so that children can see the pages at close range.

Know the story well enough so that you do not need to keep your eyes on the page at all times.

Point out all kinds of minute details in pictures so that pupils will look for them each time they handle the book later on.

Encourage laughter and spontaneous remarks.

Make illustrations as personal as possible by relating them to the pupils' own experiences.

Impart your own enjoyment of the book.

Here is the way one teacher did all these things in introducing *Wag Tail Bess* by Marjorie Flack.

"Boys and girls, the name of our story today is, 'Wag Tail Bess.' (*Run fingers under the title from left to right.*) Can anyone tell me what kind of a dog this is on the cover? (*Accept all suggestions.*) Maybe the story will tell us. (*Open the book.*) This is an envelope that shows that this book belongs to the library. This little card in the envelope says our class has the book and this slip of paper tells us when the book must go back to the library. This is done to remind us that other children would like to read the book when we have finished it. That is why children should not tear out such things. Sometimes inside the cover of a book there are very interesting pictures that tell us what the book is about. What do you see on these end papers? Yes, there is the dog again. There is an old friend of ours. Do you remember Angus? Do you think those are ducks or geese? Maybe the story will tell us. There is one other little animal on this page. Yes, there is a little kitten. You can just see his tail. (*Turn the page.*) This is the title page. There again is the title, 'Wag Tail Bess.' And this is the name of the person who wrote the story, Marjorie Flack. At the bottom it tells the name of the company that published the book." (*Turn the page and read.*)

"Once there was an Airedale puppy." (*Aside:* "Yes, you were right, John, the dog is an Airedale.") "Once there was an Airedale puppy and she was named Wag Tail Bess because her mother's name was Bess and her father's name was Wags. But Wag Tail Bess never wagged her tail or stuck up her ears or smiled as an Airedale should, so she was called plain Bess.

"Bess was so shy she was afraid of almost everything although she was big enough to know better." (*Look at the pictures of Bess.*) "See how afraid she looks." (*Continue reading.*) "When Bess was outdoors she was afraid to come indoors, and when she was indoors she was afraid to go outdoors. When Bess was taken walking she was afraid to walk forward, so she would try to walk backward, and when she couldn't go backward—she would lie down." (*Show the pictures.*) "See how Bess would pull back. Notice the other dogs looking at Bess. What do you suppose they were thinking?" (*Continue reading.*) "Bess was even afraid to eat her dinner. She would sniff at it on this side and sniff at it on that side, until at last she would get so hungry she would gulp down her dinner without chewing it at all." (*When you reach the words* "get so hungry," *read them slowly and show them to the children.*) "Then Bess would be afraid because her tummy ached." (*Look at Bess.*) "This is the way she would eat. This is the way she felt when her tummy ached." (*Continue reading.*) "At nighttime Bess was afraid of a strange, black creature. Some-

times it was small and sometimes it was large, but always it would stay with Bess wherever she went; crawling on the floor and climbing up the stairs and down the stairs, and sometimes on the wall. What do you think it was?" (*Show the picture.*) "Yes, it was her shadow. How do you feel about Bess? Don't you feel a little sorry for her?"

"One day when Bess was outdoors because she was afraid to go indoors, she heard these sounds come from the yard next door: 'Meowww! Quack, Quack! Wooof-Wooof!' (*Show the picture and repeat the sounds as you point at the words. Turn the page while the children are still watching the page. Read while they look.*) Then up in the tree jumped a cat! (*Again while they are looking at the book turn the page and while they look, read.*) Through the hedge came scuttling a duck, then came (*again read while they watch the action of the story in the pictures*) another duck! And then came (*turn the page*) Angus!" ("See the ducks and the cat and Angus. What will happen now? Well let's read and see.")

The foregoing excerpt is enough to show how the teacher should conduct a typical reading session. Such procedures take time but it is effort well invested. A teacher who takes such pains to ensure her pupils a pleasant first acquaintance with a picture book is providing those pupils with many later periods of recurring pleasure. They will relive in imagination all the activities she described, enjoy again the color and detail of the pictures, and rediscover familiar details in the scenes she has pointed out. The book will become a familiar friend which they will enjoy again and again.

1. Can you recall the names of any of the books your teachers read aloud to your class in school?

2. Do parents still read aloud to children at home?

3. What other sources are available for read-aloud stories?

4. How would you handle the criticism that reading aloud to a class is just entertaining the children when you should be teaching them?

HOW CAN A TEACHER TELL WHETHER A BOOK WILL BE EASY OR DIFFICULT FOR A CHILD?

There are more than forty different predictors that have been considered in an effort to measure readability. These include the number of familiar words, the number of unfamiliar words, the length of sentences, number of sentences, type of sentences, number of pronouns, number of abstract words and percentage of polysyllabic words.[3]

All have been directed toward the problem of matching the ability of the reader with the material to be read. While this is of concern to teachers it is of equal concern to businessmen who must write pamphlets telling how to use articles they sell or to persuade individuals to buy.

The Dale-Chall formula is widely used for books to be used in the intermediate and upper grades.[4] It is based upon a list of three thousand words which were found to be known or easy for children in the fourth grade. A sample of one hundred words is taken from the material to be evaluated. The number of sentences are counted, the average number of words in the sentences determined, and the number of words not in the list of three thousand counted. With this information the formula provides a grade placement of the reading sample. The Spache formula is an adaptation of the Dale-Chall formula which can be applied to primary material.[5]

In general, librarians and publishers are more inclined to rate books as "easy" than teachers. Many books suggested by publishers for third- or fourth-grade children are really read with ease by children in grades five and six.

The Reader's Digest publishes material that will interest older children in vocabularies graded at third- or fourth-grade reading levels. A number of companies now specialize in books that are of interest to fifth- and sixth-grade children, yet are easy to read.

Only the teacher working with an individual child can determine if a book is too difficult. The sentence, "The big, fat boy fell into the roaring river." may actually communicate better than, "The boy fell into the water." If so, the control for readability conflicts with the major purpose of language. It may even be true that added details clarify meaning and thus make the more complex material easier to understand.

1. What would happen if all reading material for children were controlled by formulas?
2. If you were an editor of children's books which value would you place first—story merit or vocabulary control?

HOW CAN WE INVOLVE PARENTS IN THE LITERATURE PROGRAM?

Our objectives in the teaching of literature will never be realized if our efforts are limited to what can be accomplished in the school day. Appreciation of literature as a personal enrichment takes time. The rhythm of the school day with its schedules and demands is not right for some literature. It is when the reader is alone, unscheduled and undisturbed, that a story can truly live. But children will complain that they do not have time to read at home. There is so much time needed for music lessons, homework, chores—and television.

---

[3] Jeanne S. Chall, *Readability* (Columbus: Ohio State U. P., 1958).

[4] Edgar Dale and Jeanne S. Chall, "A Formula for Predicting Readability," *Education Res. Bull.*, January 21, 1948, pp. 11–20, February 12, 1948, pp. 37–54. Also available in pamphlet from Bureau of Publications, Ohio State U., 1950.

[5] George Spache, "A New Readability Formula for Primary Materials." Gainesville: U. of Florida), n.d., mimeographed. Both the Dale-Chall and Spache formulas are available in C. W. Hunnicutt, and William J. Iverson, *Research in the Three R's* (New York: Harper, 1958).

Once the "rhythm of the night" was the inspiration of storytelling. Parents shared the stories of their youth and children discovered the world of imaginative writers. Today, the rhythm of the night has come to mean the sound of ricocheting bullets on television, the wearisome exhortations of announcers, and the tasteless prolixity of commercials. Somehow we must work with parents to find time for children to read. Our first task is to show parents the values of literature in contrast to the thirty-minute exercises in violence of TV drama. Annis Duff's book, *Bequest of Wings*, tells of the joys shared by a family as modern books were used in the home. If a teacher cannot get parents to read this book, it might be wise to discuss it with them at a Parent-Teacher meeting or conference.

Most parents will respond to the teacher's appeal for their help in providing good books for their children. Explain to them why we need so many children's books and how difficult it is to secure the right ones. Suggest that at Christmas or on a birthday they buy a book for their child which might be shared with the class. A group of parents and teachers might suggest a list of books to be purchased or the criteria to be followed when buying books for children.

Ownership of a book means a great deal to a child. A recent study asked the members of a sixth-grade class to list their three favorite books. The final list failed to correspond to any bibliography of children's books but one element was noted. If a child owned a book it was listed as a favorite.

Another way of making parents aware of the material available for children is a planned summer reading program. As summer approaches, a fifth-grade class might ask the sixth grade to suggest books that they would enjoy. The fifth-graders should also note the books their class has enjoyed but which some members have not had time to read. From these two sources each child might select six or eight books which he plans to read during the summer. A simple folder or notebook can be made and used for an early report at the beginning of the next school year.

When parents sponsor a book fair they discover the modern world of children's literature. Material for such an enterprise can be secured from the magazine *Scholastic Teacher* (33 West 42nd Street, New York 36, N.Y.).

Parents are sometimes concerned about the expenses of children's books. It does seem like an extravagance to pay three dollars for a picture book that only takes twenty minutes to read. Nancy Larrick, in *A Parent's Guide to Children's Reading*, makes an important point by comparing the costs of good books with toys, and then pointing out that long after the toys are broken or discarded the books are still available for rereading. This is one criteria to use in buying a book. Will it be worthy of rereading? If not, don't buy it. There are other sources for books of only temporary interest.

There are good, inexpensive books available. *Scholastic Magazines* publishes a series of paper back books for children. These are reprints of the finest modern books available. The E. M. Hale Company of Eau Claire, Wisconsin, also publishes reprints of outstanding children's books. Some of the "grocery-store" or "supermarket" books are worthy materials. A committee of the P.T.A. might evaluate some of these and suggest a few for purchase.

" 'Tis a strange sort of poverty to be finding in a rich country." are the words spoken by an immigrant lad in Ruth Sawyer's *The Enchanted Schoolhouse*. Though his words refer to the inadequate and dilapidated school facilities to be found in a wealthy and thriving city in America, they can well apply to America today—a land wealthy with a multitude of fine books that children and parents have not discovered.

1. What influence would this poem have on the parents of the children you teach?

MY MOTHER READ TO ME
Long ago on winter evenings,
I recall, my mother read;
There beside our old base-burner
Just before my prayers were said.

Here she gave me friends aplenty,
Friends to fill my life for years;
Meg and Jo and Sister Amy
For little Beth I shed my tears.

Scrooge and Tim and Mrs. Wiggs
Robin Hood and Heidi too,
Young Jim Hawkins and his treasure
Saved from Silver's pirate crew.

Can it be that one small lady
Could, just by her magic voice,
Change a room so, in a twinkling
To the scenes from books so choice?

Poor we were, as some might count us,
No fine house, our clothes threadbare

But my mother read me riches
From the books she chose with care.

Now in times of fear and struggle
When woe and want about me crowd,
I can use reserves of courage
From the books she read aloud.

—E. H. FRIERWOOD *

2. Why is involvement through concern for the reading of all children a better approach than one of concern for a specific child?

HOW MAY BOOK REPORTS BE EFFECTIVELY USED IN THE CLASSROOM?

Surveys of the school subject preferences of children usually reveal that language class is rated the favorite by one in ten, but as the least liked by about three in ten. Within the specifics of the language course the item most frequently listed as the least preferred is book reporting. It is probably safe to assume that book reporting has not been a very popular activity with many children.

There are a number of reasons why this may be so. At one time children were required to read a prescribed number of books from a specific list each month or report-card period. The books were frequently not appropriate to the readers and the motivation was one of coercion. It may not have been so distasteful to read the books, but to be required to review them in prescribed uniform style was an artificial writing assignment. Frequently, whole classes would cheat as they shared reviews or copied from book summaries found in libraries.

Dr. Charles Boehm, State Superintendent of Public Schools in Pennsylvania, expresses a concern of many teachers when he wrote:

Why don't more students seek . . . out [good books]? Because we discourage them. We make reading a penalty. We insist that our pupils write book reviews, naming the principal characters and important events in a format unchanging for a hundred years. So our youngsters read the short, the concise, the easily remembered books. And teachers should be the last to criticize them. The challenging, the thought-provoking books are to be shunned because teachers want only dates and names.[6]

A related reason for the unpopularity of this activity is what has been described as the "F.B.I. approach" to literature. The teacher's purpose might be stated: "Has the child really read the book? Has he just leafed through or looked at the pictures? He must answer certain questions so I'll be sure that he read it."

Another approach is that of account-keeping. This listing of books often incorporates a competitive spirit. The slow reader is naturally going to feel embarrassed if others read ten books while he reads only two.

In a third grade one teacher reports stimulating a high interest in books which the children were to select independently. A rule accepted by the group was that once a book selection was made, that book was to be completed. One child selected an excellent but long and difficult book. She was still reading this while other children were on a second or third book. Since a public record was kept, this had an effect. The next book she selected was short and had many pictures. Because the element of competition is difficult to eliminate, this factor can be corrected by allowing a number of points for each book so

---

* Recreation, February 1950, p. 532.
6 C. Boehm, "What You Don't Know About Your Schools," Saturday Evening Post (May 14, 1960), p. 37.

that the more difficult ones will be allotted more points and will thus not be avoided.

There are many worthy purposes for book reports. First, reports are a way of learning from the reading of others. When a child has had a reading adventure or learned some interesting information, others like to share it with him. Second, reading can be motivated by a report. One child's stamp of approval on a book will encourage others to want to read it. "Even the boys will like Laura," exclaimed one child after reading *Little House on the Prairie*. Third, reports meet a social need. Sharing the fun of *Freddie, the Detective* is as important in the conversation of fourth-graders as discussing the current best seller is among adults. Fourth, specifics need to be noticed for complete appreciation. Such specifics can include an author's use of words, descriptive passages, or illustrations. Fifth, reports give recognition to children. For many children reading a book is an achievement. Each one is a trophy that attests to greater mastery of a complex skill that has been put to use. Sixth, reports tell the teacher about the child's interests and needs. Misinterpretation or confusion revealed in a report indicate special needs that guide the teacher in planning work with the child. While literature is largely for enjoyment and appreciation, the reading process can be observed and help can be given in its improvement so that further experiences in literature will prove more satisfying and rewarding.

In all grades, both oral and written reports are used. Oral reports require careful direction and planning to be worthy of the attention of the class. Time required to prepare peep shows, cartoon strips, dioramas, dressed characters, flannelboard figures and other such accessories for book reports is often questioned. Some children have both the time and interest needed to make such comment and such visual de-

San Diego County Schools, Calif.

The library corner where books may be shared should be a part of every classroom. Children learn about authors, basic library organization, and the care of books by participating in the management of "The Library."

vices add to the effectiveness of a presentation. A balanced approach in terms of the overall needs of a child must play a part in any consideration by the teacher.

Primary children may give book reports as a part of the sharing period. Or an opening exercise one morning a week might emphasize books they find interesting. At such times, teachers make suggestions like the following: Show only the cover of a book and tell why the reader liked it. Show one picture and incite curiosity as to what is happening in the story. Show a sea shell, leaf, model airplane, space ship, or rock, that some books explain. Show a flannelboard figure or a picture for a part of a story read by a child. Form a book club and follow a simple outline in making reports. Such an outline might include:

1. What kind of a story is it? Is it true?
2. What is it about?
3. Is it about this country or some other? When did it happen?
4. What are the pictures like?
5. Is the book easy to read?
6. Who wrote the story? Do we know any other stories by that person?

These items are only suggestive. Certainly every book does not fit into the use of each question. Any item by item checking can become monotonous. We merely want to help children become conscious of the many qualities that books have and the substance that develops real appreciation of literature.

The following forms have been used by teachers:

READ FOR FUN

Name _____ Date _____
Book title _____
_____

Main character _____
_____

People who like
_____ animal stories
_____ stories about children
_____ stories about _____
_____

_____ adventure stories
_____ funny stories
_____ exciting stories
_____

will like this book.

Did you enjoy this book? _____

It was
_____ easy to read.
_____ hard to read.
_____ just right.

(Used in Grade 2)

(Grades 3 and 4)

Book Report

Name of book _____

Author _____

Illustrator (if any) _____

Name some of the characters: _____

_____

Tell which character you liked best _____

_____

The part of the book I liked best was _____

_____

_____

_____

_____

Do *one* of these things:
1. Tell your class part of the story.
2. Make a picture.
3. Make something suggested by book.

My name is _____ Room No. _____

Intermediate children have a wider range of possibilities with respect to book reports, both because of greater maturity in oral language and in writing facility, and also greater breadth of reading interests. The purposes of reporting are to interest others in expanded reading, to share information, pleasure of ideas from reading, and to emphasize the achievement of having read a book that was significant for one reason or another to the reader. Often, children themselves have significant suggestions for accomplishing these purposes. The person who read the book pretends to be one of the characters. The audience is to guess the name of the book from what he says or does. A series of clues may be given and the listeners and observers may write down the name of the book opposite the number of the clue. This guessing-games gives all children a chance to participate. Or a group of children may present a panel. They may discuss a book they have all read, or the subject, "Dog or Horse Stories I Have Liked."

A good way to emphasize authorship is to have a "Lois Lenski Day" or a "Newbery Award Day (or Week)." Students may be curious to find the qualities that made certain books worthy of awards. Such qualities as characterization, picturesque words, descriptive passages, ingenious plot, appropriate illustrations, imaginative humor, and range of experiences take on meaning and importance as children learn to recognize them. The group might create an award for a favorite book.

An oral synopsis of a story is good practice in arranging events in sequence and learning how a story progresses to a climax. It also helps children who are interested in writing stories of their own.

Broadcasting a book review over the public-address system or radio is a challenge for careful preparation and ingenuity in planning sound effects, background music, or dramatic reading. Clear enunciation and good voice modulation will also be important.

Telling a story, telling about a new book, or reading a small excerpt to another class may be good for the child who wants to share the experience, and it may stimulate the audience to learn more about the book or others by the same author.

During an informal "book club" session the students meet in small groups and talk about books they have read. The object is to whet the book appetites of the group.

An oral comparison of two books related in theme is a good exercise in critical evaluation. The problems of the Negro girls in *Shuttered Windows* by Florence Means and *Mary Jane* by Dorothy Sterling might be compared; so, too, the humor in the *Paul Bunyan Stories* might be compared with that in *Pippi Longstocking*.

Such projects as constructing a miniature stage, making preparations for a television show, planning and decorating a bulletin board, dressing dolls as book characters, impersonating book characters, and planning quiz programs about books may all on occasion stimulate interest in both oral and written reports. Displaying related objects such as a cowbell for Heidi, wooden shoes for Hans Brinker, a Japanese doll, travel pictures, or pioneer relics, are good devices for variation in vitalizing both reading and reporting. In social studies the study of a country can be personalized through a story character, thus providing broader understanding of both the literature and the geography of the country.

Written reports may take many forms. Letters of appreciation may be written to authors or librarians. A letter to a friend or relative recommending a book should actually be mailed. Advertisements may be written for the school paper, a bulletin board or a book jacket. Short reviews may be written for "We Recommend" bulletin boards or for "Before You Read" or "My Opinion" scrapbooks. Sometimes the local paper will publish well-written book reviews. Some classes keep a file of brief summaries which is consulted when a child wants a certain type of book. These are usually limited to a few sentences. Some children like to keep a "Personal Reading Notebook" in the form of a diary, like the following:

Personal Reading Notebook

Here are some ways in which information about the things in my book have helped people:

_____

_____

_____

Below are some unsolved problems or questions (about things in my book) which scientists are still working on:

_____

_____

_____

I recommend this book because _____

_____

Name _____ Date _____

My Book Report

Title _____

Author _____ Number of pages _____

Illustrator _____

The biographer (one who writes about a real person) tells the following childhood incident in the life of his subject:

_____

_____

_____

The subject of the biography is:

_____

The following people were important in helping this real person to grow into a famous adult:

_____

_____

_____

A problem which this person had to overcome was:

_____

This person overcame his problem in this way:

_____

_____

This person had the following characteristics which I admire:

_____

_____

I think the most exciting adventure which this person had was:

_____

_____

_____

Teachers have developed many techniques to encourage children to read widely. A bulletin board on which each child has a small book in which to record the titles and authors of each book read is quite popular. Sometimes this is done on a bookshelf and each child has a cardboard bound book cover in which to do his recording so that the bulletin boards are not occupied for such a long period of time. One class used the space idea by putting the name of each new book read on a small paper satellite. The caption was, "We Are Really Orbiting."

Children sometimes are inclined to limit their reading to a single interest.

MY OWN READING BOOKCASE

Name_____   Grade _____

Date started_____
Date finished_____

Adventure and Mystery

Science: Trees, Insects, Machines, etc.

Fairy Tales, Folk Tales, Fables, Myths

Animal Stories: Dogs, Horses, Cats, Other

Children of Other Lands

Fiction

Poetry and Plays

Factual Books: Everyday Affairs

Other

Books I have read more than once
1._____
2._____
3._____

My favorite authors
1._____
2._____
3._____

San Diego City Schools, Calif.

Mary will read only horse stories while John reads only about space. To encourage a more balanced reading program, teachers sometimes use a reading wheel which is divided into areas of: biography, foreign lands, animals, science, adventure, or folklore. As each child reads a book his name is placed in the proper area on the wheel. The object is to have one's name in each area. Scott, Foresman and Company, Chicago, provides a free wall chart designed to encourage a well-rounded program in reading. The *News-Journal* of North Manchester, Indiana, has several forms of "My

Reading Design" which also serve this purpose.

Another plan to widen the reading interest involves the use of a map. The object is to "Take A World Cruise" or "See America First." Books appropriate to each region are suggested. Sweden might be represented by *The Sauce Pan Journey,* France by *The Big Loop.* After a book is read about one country or area the child moves on to the next until the tour is completed.

Bulletin boards or charts frequently motivate the reading of a book. The teacher might make a list under the title, "These Are Miss Smith's Favorites." A group of children might list others under such titles, "Books Every Boy Should Know," "We Recommend for First Purchase," "Interesting Travel Books," "Girl's Favorites," "Books to Grow On," "Books About this Area."

In most situations the reading is more important than the reporting. The teacher needs to know the quality of the child's reading to be sure he is getting the most from each reading adventure. This can be done in class situations through observances of a child reading independently, in teacher-pupil conferences, and in some of the discussions and reporting that he does. There is no need for a report on every book. Some children need more of these reporting experiences than other children. In the final analysis the best reports may be a child's heartfelt spontaneous statement, "Miss Jenkins, do you know another like that?"

1. If your state has a Reading Circle try to learn these things about it. How are books selected? What motives are given the children for reading these books?
2. Do you feel the criticism of book reports is justified in terms of your own experience?
3. How can we prevent embarrassment for a child who must read books much below the reading level of others in the class?

HOW DO TEACHERS BECOME EFFECTIVE STORYTELLERS?

There are no basic rules to insure the proper telling of a story. Some of the greatest story craftsmen cannot agree as to best methods to use. Storytelling is as individual an art as acting or playing a musical instrument. Each person must develop his own techniques, style and selection of stories to suit his taste and abilities.

There are a few basic considerations, however, upon which most storytellers agree. First, the story must be appropriate to the audience. The very young child likes simple folk tales, but he does not respond to stories that are completely make-believe with goblins, elves and fairies. He does not understand the completely abstract. There must be some elements in the story that relate to his personal experiences. In the story of *The Three Bears* we have chairs, beds, bowls of soup and activities which are familiar. Having them associated with bears adds mystery and adventure but the events are familiar, everyday experiences. The child accepts the unreal because it is close enough to the real world he knows.

Little children love rhymes and jingles and many old story favorites have a marked rhythmic quality. In stories this rhythm is the result of repetition of words and phrases in a set pattern. Such phrases as "Not by the hair of your chinny-chin-chin," or "Then I'll huff and I'll puff and I'll blow your house in," always bring delighted responses.

Children like to play with words. That is the way words become more meaningful and a lasting part of their vocabulary. Children cannot keep from repeating "a lovely, light, luscious, delectable cake" as the teacher reads *The Duchess Bakes a Cake.* In telling some stories the teller prepares the listeners by saying, "This story contains some wonderful new words. One of them is _____ which means _____; another is _____ which means _____, etc. Listen for them."

Make-believe is most important to children in the years from six to ten since it helps them understand the world about them and increases their imaginative powers. In the stories that they read and hear the youngsters are the heroes—at least for the time being. They know they are pretending, but as the story unfolds each boy is Jack the Giant Killer and each girl is Cinderella.

Second, the storyteller knows that some stories are good to tell—other stories are better to read. A story for telling must be simple and direct. The plot must be strong and develop rapidly. In storytelling there is no place for long analyses of characters or situations. The mental pictures must be supplied by a few words or a phrase. Each incident must be vivid and clear-cut in the listener's mind. The climax must be emotionally satisfying. This can be a surprise, the solution of a problem, or something achieved.

The charm of simplicity can best be learned through experience. We know that children respond to cumulative repetition such as one finds in *The Gingerbread Boy*. They want the characters to talk. Descriptions are simple because children supply so much with their own imaginations. Good must triumph, but it is all right for the bad people to be very bad as long as in the end they are punished. Some prefer stories of animals to those with people in them. For many, the gentle stories about raindrops, flowers, and insects are a new discovery in contrast to the rapid pace of television and movie cartoons. A story that lasts six or eight minutes is quite long enough and many favorites take less time than that.

The Three Little Pigs is an example of a good story for telling little children. Each step is an event. No time is spent in explanation or unnecessary description. The story tells what the characters did and said and the events are linked in the closest kind of sequence. There are no breaks and no complexities of plot. Each event presents a clear, distinct picture to the imagination.

Ordinarily it is wisest not to change traditional stories. If you question any element in a story it is usually best to select another story. There is a trend in the direction of removing much of the horror aspects of the old folk material. The Three Bears are now friendly bears. They are provoked by Goldilocks because she enters their home without permission. The Wolf now chases Red Riding Hood's grandmother into a closet instead of devouring her. In the original version of the *Three Billy Goats Gruff* the troll had his eyes gouged out and was crushed to death. In the modern version he is merely butted into the river and swims away unscathed, never to return. The first two of the Three Little Pigs are no longer eaten by the wolf but make an exciting escape to the house of the wise pig.

Any idea that may cause the young child to lie awake at night is best omitted from the program. It is well to discuss make-believe with children. Let them be assured that there are really no dragons and that wolves are unlikely visitors in the suburbs. Even such innocent stories as *Little Black Sambo* have caused nightmares of being chased by a tiger. Much depends, of course, on how seriously the story is read.

Another common theme in many of the old tales is the cruelty of stepparents and other kin related by remarriage. Stereotypes which stigmatize kin, old age, or social groups have no place in the story hour.

A discussion before reading some of these stories can take care of such questionable elements. The story of a good stepmother like Abraham Lincoln's provides a balance to *Cinderella*. There are many good and kind old ladies to offset the cruel old hag in Hansel and Gretel. Teachers should remember that the horror that an adult senses in a story such as *Snow White*, is quite different from a child's point of view. Torture, and even death, have only incidental significance for many children. Death is frequently an acceptable solution to a problem. Children play Cowboys and Indians, "good guys" and "bad guys" with violent shouts, agonizing mock deaths and melodramatic hardships one moment and listen with rapt attention to a poem of delicate beauty the next.

Sometimes children themselves will suggest changes in these stories. This frequently happens as they dramatize a story. Another interesting variation on the traditional material is to put the characters in a new situation. Make up a story of visiting the Three Bears for Christmas or let Cinderella go to school.

Third, a storyteller knows that preparation is needed to make a story vivid to listeners. After a careful reading, put the story aside and think about it until you can picture the story to yourself—clearly in all details. Check any doubts by reading the story again. It is better for a beginning storyteller to know a few stories well than to attempt so many that none can be told with complete confidence. The "tell it again" quality of stories is a great safeguard for beginners. Any storyteller is almost sure to tell a story better each additional time he tells it.

And fourth, a storyteller knows that the audience must be comfortable and free from interruptions during the story, and that the story must end before the audience becomes weary or bored. Wait a few moments before starting a story so that

there is a hush of expectancy in the room. If some children are inattentive or noisy, pause until quiet is restored. If many grow restless it is quite obvious that you have the wrong story. Don't blame the children. Just say, "I guess this isn't the right story so let's stand up and stretch." Then go on with some other group activity such as marching, singing, or finger play. Start another story only when there is expectancy and readiness for wholehearted listening.

Certain devices can be used to hold the attention of listeners. When Hans Christian Andersen entertained the children of Denmark with his stories, he used to cut out silhouettes in order to make his characters more vivid. In ancient China the storyteller would cast shadows to illustrate the characters in his tales of magic and ancient ways. The modern movie cartoon favorites use a combination of silhouette figures and movement to hold attention. In the modern classroom, the flannelboard provides the storyteller with the means of achieving similar types of movement, magic and characterization.

As the child listens to the storyteller, his visual attention is focused on characters and movement as figures are moved

Burbank Public Schools, Calif.

The teacher is seated while telling this flannelgraph story in order to be at the eye level of the children.

about on the flannelboard. These figures are cutouts representing the main characters. On the back of each item used, the storyteller pastes a bit of flannel or sandpaper so that it will adhere to the flannelboard.

Flannelboard stories should be looked upon as a means of stimulating the imagination and improving the quality of oral language of children. Many teachers find that permitting children to make their own flannelboard stories and telling them helps children to expand their language power, self-confidence and creative talents. Another prospect is the emotional release that can be observed in some children as they plan, cut out and manipulate figures to illustrate some story they especially like or that they create.

Although the term flannelboard is used here, the device may be made with felt or coat lining. Those made for children's games are sometimes sprayed with "flocking." A store that specializes in window-display materials will have this for sale. If flannel is used, get the heaviest available. Coat lining is usually obtainable from a dry goods store. If you have a large bulletin board which you wish to cover, use felt or coat lining. This will cost about ten or twelve dollars. Each figure needs to have a large piece of flannel or felt glued to the reverse side. Then as it is placed on the board the teller should run his fingers over the figure, causing it to adhere to the board. Some use rough sandpaper or flocking on the figure. For some figures bits of flannel about an inch square in three or four places serves to hold better than one large piece.

Children seem to respond better to cutouts made of bright and heavy construction paper than to drawn figures. Apparently cutouts allow more scope for the imagination. However, illustrations cut from books and made into figures for the flannelboard also appeal to them. In a sense this type simply transfers the book illustrations to the flannelboard. Faces and clothes can be drawn with ink or wax crayon, or made of bits of construction paper pasted to the figure.

Some stories need scenic backgrounds —a big woods, a lake, a castle. Rather than make these of paper it is easier to draw them with crayon on a large piece of flannel. Then the figures will stick to the scenery as the story is told. Regular outing flannel that costs about forty-nine cents a yard is good for this purpose.

Most flannelboards are made of plywood or heavy composition cardboard about two feet wide and three feet long. The felt or flannel should be about three feet by four feet in order to allow adequate overlap on the back of the plywood. Staples from a regular paper stapler will hold it well. Do not glue the flannel to the board, as the glue reduces the static charge that causes the figures to adhere. The size should be large enough to hold the figures, but not so large that it is uncomfortable to carry or awkward to store away. Some teachers like to have handles on the board, others hinge them so they will fold. It costs about as much to make a board as to buy one. The only advantage to a homemade one is that you have exactly what you want.

The following story is a flannelboard favorite:

QUEER COMPANY [7]

A little old woman lived all alone in a little old house in the woods. One Halloween she sat in the corner, and as she sat, she spun.

Still she sat and
Still she spun and
Still she wished for company.

Then she saw her door open a little way, and in came

A pair of big, big feet
And sat down by the fireside.
"That is very strange," thought the little
old woman, but—

Still she sat and
Still she spun and
Still she wished for company.

[7] Paul Anderson, *Flannelboard Stories for the Primary Grades* (Minneapolis: Denison, 1962).

Then in came

A pair of small, small legs,
And sat down on the big, big feet
"Now that is very strange," thought the old
woman, but—

Still she sat and
Still she spun and
Still she wished for company.

Then in came

A wee, wee waist,
And sat down on the small, small legs.
"Now that is very strange," thought the
old woman, but—

Still she sat and
Still she spun and
Still she wished for company.

Then in came

A pair of broad, broad shoulders,
And sat down on the wee, wee waist.
But—

Still she sat and
Still she spun and
Still she wished for company.

Then in through the door came

A pair of long, long arms,
And sat down on the broad, broad shoulders.
"Now that is very strange," thought the
little old woman, but—

Still she sat and
Still she spun and
Still she wished for company.

Then in came

A pair of fat, fat hands,
And sat down on the long, long, arms.
But—

Still she sat and
Still she spun and
Still she wished for company.

Then in came

A round, round head
And sat down on top of all
That sat by the fireside.

The little old woman stopped her spinning
and asked

"Where did you get such big feet?"
"By much tramping, by much tramping,"
said Somebody.

"Where did you get such small, small legs?"
"By much running, by much running," said
Somebody.

"Where did you get such a wee, wee waist?"
"Nobody knows, nobody knows," said Somebody.

"Where did you get such broad, broad shoulders?"
"From carrying brooms," said Somebody.

"Where did you get such long, long arms?"
"Swinging the scythe, swinging the scythe,"
said Somebody.

"Where did you get such fat, fat hands?"
"By working, by working,"
said Somebody.

"How did you get such a huge, huge head?"
"Of a pumpkin I made it," said Somebody.

Then said the little old woman,

"What did you come for?"
"YOU!" said Somebody.

Here is an original story that contains
the simple repetitive element that lends
itself to flannelboard presentation.

WHAT DO YOU WANT FOR CHRISTMAS?
"What do you want for Christmas?" Mother
asked.
"I do not know," said Bill.
"I do not know what I want for Christmas."

"What do you want for Christmas?" asked
Bill.
The mailman said,
"I want some new shoes for Christmas."
"I do not want new shoes," said Bill.
"I do not know what I want for Christmas."

"What do you want for Christmas?" asked
Bill.
The milkman said,
"I want a new truck.
I want a new truck for Christmas."

"I do not want a truck," said Bill.
"I do not know what I want for Christmas."

"What do you want for Christmas?" asked Bill.
The baker said,
"I want a new apron.
I want a new apron for Christmas."
"I do not want an apron.
I do not know what I want for Christmas."

"What do you want for Christmas?" asked Bill.
The little girl said,
"I want a doll.
I want a doll that talks for Christmas."
"I do not want a doll," said Bill.
"I do not know what I want for Christmas."

"What do you want for Christmas?" asked Santa.
"I do not know what I want for Christmas," said Bill.
"But the mailman wants some shoes.
The milkman wants a truck.
The baker wants an apron.
The little girl wants a doll that talks."

"I know what you want for Christmas," said Santa.
"You want to be Santa Claus at Christmas.
You want to give things at Christmas."
"That's right," said Bill. "I want to be like Santa Claus."

So his mother made him a red suit.
The mailman let him have a mail bag.
The milkman let him have some bells.
The baker let him have some cookies.

So Bill went to the little girl's house in his red suit.
He rang the bells, opened his bag, took out a cookie
And gave it to the little girl.

The following techniques should be used as a story is told with the flannel-board:

1. Place the flannelboard where it will remain securely in a place that can be seen by all students. The chalkboard is good if the group is in a small circle seated before it. An easel is better if the board must be seen by an entire room. If children are seated on a rug they must be farther away from the teacher than when she uses a picture book.

Those in front will be under a strain looking up if too near the board.

2. Arrange the figures to be used in the sequence needed for telling the story. It is best to keep them in a folder away from the sight of the listeners. Otherwise, some of the surprise and suspense is lost as they are introduced. A manila folder used in file cabinets makes a good container. Staple a pocket on one side of the folder to hold the figures and staple the story to the other side.

3. There is a tendency to look away from the listeners to the figures as they are placed on the flannelboard. Of course, this is necessary. Try to use this movement to direct the listeners' eyes but turn back to the audience as you tell the story. Otherwise, you will find yourself talking to the flannelboard, thus creating a hearing problem for your audience.

4. Plan your follow-up before you tell the story. Are you going to evaluate the story? Are you going to have them retell parts of the story? Are you going to have the children create a favorite story? When a story ends in the classroom it is a bit different from the ending of a play in the theater or a television program. The audience is still with you. Instead of going home or turning on another station you must plan the transition to the next school task.

In the Orient there are still storytellers who earn a living walking along the street. They signal their approach by tapping two pieces of wood together. Each child offers a small coin and is given a piece of hard candy. While he eats the candy, the story-teller entertains with some of the famous folk stories of the land or the latest adventures of Mickey Mouse. As the story unfolds, the storyteller illustrates it by a series of color prints from books, or hand-drawn pictures. These *Kami-she-bai* or picture stories might well be used in our own country.[8]

Stick figures and simple puppets used as characters in a story or as the teller of the story will hold the attention of those children who need something to see as well as to hear. An important object in a story such as a lamp, old coffee mill, glass slipper, shaft of wheat, an apple, miniature rocker, spinning wheel, or toy sword may

---

[8] Sets of Kami-she-bai pictures may be obtained from the Tuttle Publishing Co., Rutland, Vt.

be used. Some stories depend for an explanation on the core of an apple, the way a seed or feather is formed, or the shape of a flower or leaf, since the fable was a means of explaining a fact of nature. And one should not neglect the chalkboard or simple stick figures to illustrate a scene or character.

In addition to a pleasant voice, clear speech, adequate vocabulary, and a relaxed appearance, today's storyteller needs the resources of inner grace which comes from sincerity and a respect both for the audience and for the art of storytelling. When you have a clear visual picture of each character and scene, know the plot thoroughly, can establish a mood for listening and are able to end the story so that your audience is satisfied, you are a good storyteller.

HOW IS POETRY PRESENTED IN THE MODERN CURRICULUM?

We teach at a time when rhyme and verse are almost as commonplace as the air we breathe. Singing commercials and jingles are heard too frequently on radio and TV. There is little wonder that a child of our times should chant "Pepsi Cola hits the spot" before he knows the rhymes of Mother Goose. The ballad singers and songwriters of today, unlike strolling entertainers of the past who sang for their supper, constitute a new breed of millionaires whose opinions are widely sought on such nonentertainment subjects as politics and religion.

We also teach at a time when people wish to express sentiments in verse. A major industry has developed around the production of greeting cards for every possible occasion. While some of this material can hardly be mistaken for literature, it is indicative of the desire, widespread in our culture, to express emotional feelings through words. The Greeting Card Association estimates that five and a quarter billion greeting cards were sold in 1959. Seven per cent of the total post-office revenue or two hundred million dollars was spent that year on postage to mail these cards. In the past few years another type of card has appeared that emphasizes a cynical or morbid humor such as: "Quick! Burn this card. Your postman is a carrier." Instead of lessening the sale of the traditional card, these seem to meet the need of many who never sent cards before. In the words of the Greeting Card Association, both serve to provide . . . emotional outlets and a sense of social well-being attainable by no other means.[9]

Our culture is rich in poetic tradition. In many communities there is a Longfellow School or one named for Lowell, Whitman, Field, or Stevenson. The respect for poetry was reflected in the curriculum of the recent past which frequently specified selections that were to be studied and memorized in each grade. Some schools had as many as a hundred "pieces" to be mastered in the seventh and eighth grades.

The purpose of this requirement was to ensure that each child would know this aspect of our cultural heritage. While it was recognized that some of this material was beyond the understanding of the students, and that memorization added a burdensome routine, teachers sincerely felt that eventually this material would enrich the lives of individuals. Many adults today get great satisfaction in reciting "Abou Ben Adhem" or "Snowbound." Some will say, "This poem did not mean much to me when I was in school but each year I seem to enjoy it more." On the other hand, some who were taught this way learned to detest poetry and still think of it as a disciplinary activity.

Poetry in the curriculum of the past was frequently associated with programs. One learned a piece to recite on Friday afternoon or at a parents' meeting. Grandparents especially were delighted with this

[9] C. Leedham, "Five Billion Greetings Yearly," *New York Times Magazine* (April 3, 1960), p. 44.

accomplishment and usually rewarded the speaker with an appropriate gift. Contests were held with all the participants reciting "The Highwayman." Audiences would spend an afternoon while ten or more elocutionists repeated the same selection.

Good poetry is sometimes found in popular magazines and daily papers. Although many of these are of transient value, some very good material undoubtedly goes unrecognized in the great mass of published verse. Some of the more talented poets of our day may turn to songwriting or prose because of the greater financial returns involved. Just as such poems as "Trees" and "America, the Beautiful" have been made into fine songs, the lyrics of popular songs such as "Love is a Many-Splendored Thing" have merit as verse.

In this environment, poetry in a modern classroom serves many purposes and needs. It is used to enrich all curriculum areas. Modern anthologies contain a great deal of verse appropriate to the age and reading level of the child for whom the book is intended, although this places a severe limitation on the choice of material. May Hill Arbuthnot has a useful collection in *Time for Poetry* which the teacher reads to children rather than having them read it aloud themselves.

Most teachers today start with the children with whom they work rather than with a collection of poetry which they feel must be mastered. They recognize the truth of Carl Sandburg's statement,

Poetry for any given individual depends on the individual and what his personality requires as poetry. Beauty depends on personal taste. What is beauty for one person is not for another. What is poetry for one person may be balderdash or hogwash for another.[10]

The teacher seeks to present material that will meet the immediate appreciation level of students as well as build sensitivity for growth in appreciation. Many teachers keep a file of poetry and draw from it when appropriate throughout the school

---

[10] Carl Sandburg, *Early Moon* (New York: Harcourt, Brace & World, Inc. 1930), p. 20.

day. As the seasons change, verses are used to express the children's feelings, or to call attention to the flight of birds or the budding of our pussywillow. Holidays are made special days through poems that may be used as the theme of a bulletin-board display. In social studies, the life of the Indian becomes personalized as the group recites a Navaho prayer or chant. On the playground the ideals of fair play and good sportsmanship are remembered because a verse suggests meaningful behavior. Throughout each day and year the child grows in perception and understanding through the planned use of poetry. He learns to listen to words for both meaning and sound. He finds that some words create an atmosphere that is sad or frightening, while others have a warm and lazy effect.

To accomplish this, the teacher starts with herself. Teachers who experience the most difficulty at the beginning are those who have a love for great poetry yet are unwilling to discover the appreciation level of the children with whom they work. Walt Whitman's "When Lilacs Last in the Dooryard Bloom'd" will not be accepted by a class that delights in "Little Orphan Annie" by Riley. The most important consideration in selection of material is to avoid any value judgment as to what children *should* like. Stated positively, the most important consideration is to discover what they do like.

Start by reading poetry to the children. First the teacher should read the verse aloud to herself, note the punctuation, the mood of the poem, and any unusual expression or words. Before reading, a few remarks help the listener orient himself. Introduce "Little Orphan Annie" in this manner: "Here is a poem your parents liked, and I think you will like it, too. There are a few words like *hearth* and *rafter* that you may not know; they mean . . . ," etc. Then the teacher might ask a few questions after the first reading. Appropriate ones would be "Why do you suppose the author repeats the words 'If you don't watch out'? Notice how they are written in the poem to show how they might be read." After showing the children the printed poem, another question would be, "How do you feel when you hear the words '. . . the lamp wick sputters and the wind goes whooo'? What was the writer trying to do?" If the children wish, the teacher might read the poem a second time, then place it on the reading table for those who wish to read it themselves.

Some children will bring poems they have found and offer to read them to the class. Others will respond to the invitation to bring poems for the teacher to read. Reading poetry aloud is difficult and many children do not do it well. As a result it is a deadly listening experience. We want to develop good listening habits, but there are better ways of doing it than forcing attention to poorly read poetry.

The poems found in children's readers are much more fun to read if they have first been heard with pleasure. These selections are the basis for instruction concerning the oral reading of poetry, but that instruction should follow an appreciative listening. Good oral reading is largely imitative and the example followed should be a worthy one. It is the poet who has to speak through the oral reader. It is not the reader speaking poetry.

WHAT VALUES ARE THERE IN A TEACHER'S POETRY FILE?

A poetry file assures the teacher of having interesting material available. Most teachers prefer to put in the file a few old favorites which they know will be used. Without a file it sometimes takes hours to locate such well-known verses as E. L. Thayer's "Casey at the Bat" or Joaquin Miller's "Columbus." I remember visiting a school where everyone was searching for the latter poem. The principal greeted me by asking, "Do you remember that poem about Columbus that has the words 'sail on —sail on' in it?" At the time none of us could think of the author.

After teaching the same grade for some time, some teachers prefer to put favorite verses in a notebook classified by the months. The beginning teacher usually finds a card file most convenient. Then as the teacher borrows and clips, she selects those that are most useful. Just a note about clippings—nothing is so discouraging as to remember that you saw a clever verse about a boy getting a crew haircut or some other timely happening which could be used in your class and not be able to locate it a second time. Clip and file until you have a collection that meets your needs.

There are many ways to organize such a collection. One heading might be *Holiday Poems*. Later these might be divided under the title *Halloween, Christmas, Valentine's Day*. While there are many poems related to this topic, it is sometimes difficult to find one appropriate to your group.

Another broad category for a poetry file would be that of *Curriculum Enrichment*. In time, this too, would be divided into the various subjects.

In the first grade one teacher used the following poem while studying the post-office:

A LETTER IS A GYPSY ELF

A letter is a gypsy elf
It goes where I would go myself;
East or West or North it goes;
Or South, past pretty bungalows,
Over mountain, over hill,
Any place it must and will,
It finds good friends that live so far
You cannot travel where they are.
—ANNETTE WYNNE

In science these three might be used. One is much more fanciful than the other two but all are worthy enrichment material.

CLOUDS

Over the hill the clouds race by
Playing tag in a blue, blue sky;
Some are fat and some are thin.
And one cloud has a double chin.

One is a girl with a turned up nose
And one wears slippers with pointed toes;

There's a puppy dog too, with a bumpity tail,
And a farmer boy with his milking pail.

Sometimes they jumble all in a mass
And get tangled up with others that pass.
And over the hill they go racing by
Playing tag in a blue, blue sky.
—HELEN WING, *The Christian Science
Monitor*

CLOUD NAMES

Cumulus clouds
Drift over the sky,
Fluffy as soapsuds
Bellowing by.

Along the horizon
In layers of light
The stratus clouds glow
In the sunset bright.

Cirrus clouds hang
So loosely together
Their cottony film
Means a change of weather.

Nimbus clouds threaten
With blackness of storm
Shut the door, light the fire
Be cozy and warm.
—LOS ANGELES CITY SCHOOLS

One of the major reasons for having
children write poetry is to act as a release
for strong feelings. Poems that express
these feelings for children probably act the
same way. There are some children who
will find these poems delightful "because
they say exactly how I feel." As a category
for a poetry file they might be listed under
Expression of Strong Feelings.

ONE DAY WHEN WE WENT WALKING

One day when we went walking,
    I found a dragon's tooth,
A dreadful dragon's tooth,
    "A locust thorn," said Ruth.

One day when we went walking,
    I found a brownie's shoe,
A brownie's button shoe,
    "A dry pea pod," said Sue.

One day when we went walking,
    I found a mermaid's fan,

A merry mermaid's fan,
    "A scallop shell," said Dan.

One day when we went walking,
    I found a fairy's dress,
A fairy's flannel dress,
    "A mullein leaf," said Bess.

Next time I go walking—
    Unless I meet an elf,
A funny, friendly elf—
    I'm going by myself!
—VALINE HOBBS

CHOOSING SHOES

New shoes, new shoes,
    Red and pink and blue shoes.
Tell me, what would you choose,
    If they'd let us buy?

Buckle shoes, bow shoes,
    Pretty, pointy-toe shoes,
Strappy, cappy low shoes,
    Let's have some to try.

Bright shoes, white shoes,
    Dandy-dance-by-night shoes,
Perhaps-a-little-tight shoes,
    Like some? So would I.

But

Flat shoes, fat shoes,
    Stump-along-like-that-shoes,
Wipe-them-on-the-mat shoes,
    That's the sort they'll buy.
—fRIDA WOLFE

PRESENTS

I wanted a rifle for Christmas,
I wanted a bat and a ball,
I wanted some skates and a bicycle,
But I didn't want mittens at all.

I wanted a whistle
And I wanted a kite,
I wanted a pocketknife
That shut up tight.
I wanted some boots
And I wanted a kit,
But I didn't want mittens one little bit!

I told them I didn't like mittens,
I told them as plain as plain.
I told them I didn't WANT mittens,
And they've given me mittens again!
—MARCHETTE CHUTE

Probably the most charming of all poetry for children is that which takes the commonplace and then because of some rare insight of an adult into the child's world we have a chance to rediscover the simple ways of life again. It is childlike rather than childish. In your poetry file you will want a section on *Enrichment of Daily Life*. Those who work with primary children will especially want material by Dorothy Aldis. Another author for this age is Aileen Fisher, who wrote this favorite:

COFFEEPOT FACE

I saw
my face
in the coffeepot.
Imagine
a *coffeepot face!*

My eyes
were small
but my nose was NOT
and my mouth
was—every place!
—AILEEN FISHER

Probably the best-known verse of this type is this by Annette Wynne:

INDIAN CHILDREN

Where we walk to school each day
Indian children used to play
All about our native land,
Where the shops and houses stand.

And the trees were very tall,
And there were no streets at all,
Not a church and not a steeple,
Only the woods and Indian people.

Only wigwams on the ground,
And at night bears prowling round—
What a different place today
Where we live and work and play.
—ANNETTE WYNNE

An example of poetry without rhyme that creates a mood is this poem by Beatrice Schenck de Regniers:

LITTLE SOUNDS

Underneath the big sounds
underneath the big silences
listen for the little secret sounds.

Listen.
ts   ts
That is the little sound of the sugar,
The little loaf of sugar
deep inside the cup of hot black coffee.
ts   ts
That is what the sugar says.

Listen for the little secret sounds.
Sh! be very quiet and listen.
tck tck tck tck tck tck tck tck
That is the little sound of your father's watch.
tck tck tck tck tck tck tck tck
It makes such a tiny hurrying scurrying sound.

Listen for the little sounds always.
When a pussycat licks her fur
can you hear a little sound?
When someone is licking an ice-cream cone
can you hear?

Did you ever hear
a rabbit biting a lettuce leaf?
a cow switching her tail?
a tiny baby breathing?

Listen
to the little sound of
a letter dropping into a letter box,
a pin falling to the floor,
a leaf falling from a tree,
dry leaves crunching under your feet.

Listen to the little secret sound
of a pencil writing on paper,
of a scissors snipping your fingernails,
of a flower stem breaking when you pick a flower.

Listen for the little sounds always—
Listen.
—BEATRICE SCHENCK DE REGNIERS

Primary teachers will want a special section for poems that can be told with the flannel graph. "Waiting at the Window" by A. A. Milne requires only three figures: two raindrops and a bright yellow sun. When the teacher first shares the poem, she guides the drops down. On the next telling, a child may do so. Eventually some children will learn this because it is so much fun to tell with these flannel figures.

Another that lends itself to a flannel-board presentation is "Mice," by Rose Fyleman.

MICE

I think mice are rather nice
Their tails are long,
Their faces small,
They haven't any chins at all,
Their eyes are pink
Their teeth are white
They run about the house at night
They nibble things they shouldn't touch
And no one seems to like them much,
But we think mice are nice.

—ROSE FYLEMAN

A category that will always be popular with teachers are those verses which suggest a way to act. Some of these suggest standards of conduct, others are gentle reminders, while a few use a bit of ridicule to guide behavior.

LITTLE CHARLIE CHIPMUNK

Little Charlie Chipmunk was a talker
Mercy me!
He chattered after breakfast
And he chattered after tea
He chattered to his sister
He chattered to his mother
He chattered to his father
And he chattered to his brother
He chattered till his family
Was almost driven wild
Oh, Little Charlie Chipmunk
Was a very tiresome child.

—HELEN COWLES LE CRON

THREE CHEERS FOR PETER

When Peter eats a lollylop
He doesn't walk or run or hop
He sits upon the bottom stair
Or in the kitchen on a chair
He doesn't try to chew or bite
Or swallow chunks; he just sits tight
And sucks. And he is careful not
To let it make a sticky spot
On furniture. Three cheers for Peter
He's a good safe candy eater.

—ALICE HARTICH

You will find many verses that are worthy of a poetry file simply because they are fun and add humor to life. This would include limerick, nonsense verse, and those with clever use of words. The whimsical couplets of Ogden Nash are recorded with musical background. Children especially enjoy his *The Panther* (which ends with "Don't anther") and his *The Octopus*.

A bit of wise-cracking doggerel like this has its place in your file:

MODERN LIGHT

Twinkle, twinkle little star
I know exactly what you are
You're a satellite in the sky
And why my taxes are so high.

Another group of verse in your file would be that which helps the child relate himself to all nature. In the fall, there will be a time when children will sense the rhythm of nature when you read to them Rachel Field's "Something Told The Wild Geese." Once I observed a group of students on a hike who had earlier discovered a deer track on the road and were now listening with true appreciation to "The Tracks" by Elizabeth Coatsworth. The following poem employs delicate and sensitive imagery.

SOFT IS THE HUSH OF FALLING SNOW

I like the springtime of the year
When all the baby things appear;
When little shoots of grass come through
And everything is fresh and new.

But, oh, I like the summer, too.
When clouds are soft and skies are blue
Vacation days are full of fun
I like being lazy in the sun.

But when the fall has once begun
I'm glad that summer then is done
I love the frosty biting air
The harvest yield seen everywhere.

But winter is beyond compare
For though the world seems black and bare
It's rest time for the things that grow
And soft is the hush of falling snow.

—EMILY CAREY ALLEMAN

This one would be appropriate for Arbor Day:

TREES

Trees are the kindest things I know;
They do no harm, they simply grow.
And spread a shade for sleepy cows,
And gather birds among their boughs.
They give us fruit in leaves above
And wood to make our houses of.

And leaves to burn on Halloween;
And in the spring new buds of green.
They are the first when day's begun
To touch the beams of morning sun.
They are the last to hold the light
When evening changes into night.
And when the moon floats in the sky
They hum a drowsy lullaby
Of sleepy children long ago.
Trees are the kindest things I know.
—HARRY BEHN

Poetry has often been the form in which writers have presented an ideal or expressed religious thought. You will want a section of such inspirational material.

A PRAYER FOR LITTLE THINGS

Please God, take care of little things,
The fledglings that have not their wings,
Till they are big enough to fly
And stretch their wings across the sky.

And please take care of little seeds,
So small among the forest weeds,
Till they have grown as tall as trees
With leafy boughs, take care of these.

And please take care of drops of rain
Like beads upon a broken chain,
Till in some river in the sun
The many silver drops are one.

Take care of small new lambs that bleat,
Small foals that totter on their feet,
And all small creatures ever known
Till they are strong to stand alone.

And please take care of children who
Kneel down at night to pray to you
Oh, please keep safe the little prayer
That like the big ones asks Your care.
—ELEANOR FARJEON

Even arithmetic and grammar have been subjects for writers:

COUNTING

Today I'll remember forever and ever
Because I can count to ten.
It isn't an accident any more either,
I've done it over and over again.

I used to leave out five and three
And sometimes eight and four;
And once in a while I'd mix up nine
As seven or two, but not any more.

I count my fingers on one hand first,
And this little pig is one,
And when old thumb goes off to market
That's five, and one of my hands is done.

So when I open my other hand
And start in counting again
From pick up sticks to big fat hen,
Five, six, seven, eight, nine and ten.
—HARRY BEHN

GRAMMAR IN A NUTSHELL

Three little words you often see
Are articles—an, a and the.

A noun is the name of anything
As school, or garden, hoop or swing.

Adjectives tell the kind of noun,
As great, small, pretty, white or brown.

Instead of nouns the pronouns stand—
Her head, his face, your arm, my hand.

Verbs tell of something being done—
To read, count, laugh, sing, jump or run.

How things are done the adverbs tell,
As slowly, quickly, ill or well.

Conjunctions join the word together
As men and women, wind or weather.

The prepositions stand before
A noun, as in or through the door.

The interjections show surprise
As Oh! how pretty! Ah! how wise!

The whole are called the nine parts of speech,
Which reading, writing, speaking, teach.
—UNKNOWN

The effect of reading a poem like "I Wish" by Nancy Byrd Turner or "A Mortifying Mistake" by Maria Pratt after a dull arithmetic period will justify all your efforts to create a poetry file.

A MORTIFYING MISTAKE

I studied my tables over and over, and
    backward and forward, too;
But I couldn't remember six times nine, and
    I didn't know what to do,
Till sister told me to play with my doll, and
    not to bother my head.

"If you call her 'Fifty-four' for a while, you'll
learn it by heart," she said.

So I took my favorite, Mary Ann (though I
thought 'twas a dreadful shame
To give such a perfectly lovely child such a
perfectly horrid name),
And I called her my dear little "Fifty-four"
a hundred times, till I knew
The answer of six times nine as well as the
answer of two times two.

Next day Elizabeth Wigglesworth, who
always acts so proud,
Said "Six times nine is fifty-two," and I
nearly laughed aloud!
But I wished I hadn't when teacher said,
"Now Dorothy, tell if you can."
For I thought of my doll—and sakes alive!—
I answered, "Mary Ann!"

—MARIA PRATT

Sharing poems related to the same
topic will help children see the different
point of view that each of us brings to a
situation.

In these poems each writer is talking
about houses. Do they agree in any way?
Then share with them "Sometimes A Little
House Will Please" by Elizabeth Coats-
worth, "Our House" by Rachel Field, "Our
House" by Dorothy Brown Thompson, and
"Song For A Little House" by Christopher
Morley.

Teachers will find that the building of
such a file increases their own appreciation
of poetic expression. However, what has
been said concerning individual differences of pupils applies to teachers as well.
If you do not truly feel some pleasure and
delight in sharing poetry with children,
possibly it will be well for you to spend
time on those aspects of the curriculum
about which you are enthusiastic. In a few
cases you may learn with the children or
from the children. Start where you are,
even if the only poetry that stirs you in
any way are the words in the "Star Spangled Banner" or "Home on the Range."
That is a beginning.

HOW MAY A VERSE CHOIR ENCOURAGE THE CLASSROOM USE OF POETRY?

The oral reading of poetry has long
been a tradition in the British Isles. The
verse choir in some areas is as highly organized as an orchestra. High and low
voices are balanced to gain special effects
and the number in a choir is limited to
certain voice qualities. A performance by
such a group is as effective as that of a
singing choir. We do not seek the same
standards with verse choirs in the elementary school. Our primary object is to delight those who are taking part rather than
perfecting a performance for the entertainment of others. In accomplishing this the
result will be a satisfying self-expression
that leads to a high degree of appreciation
of the material used.

In achieving this primary objective
there are a number of parallel benefits. The
shy child feels that he is a contributing
member of the group. He is able to participate in a public appearance without any
agonizing emotional pressures. The great-

est benefits are in the area of speech. The
values of precise enunciation and careful
pronunciation are obvious to the most slov-
enly speakers. The slow or fast speaker is
made aware of the effect of such speech
on the listener. Not only is the quality of
voice tone brought to the level of awareness but those whose voices are unpleasant
receive needed attention.

From the beginning the approach
should be one of enjoyment. With any
group start with familiar material so that
there is no problem of memorization. A
favorite with all ages is "Hickory Dickory
Dock." After writing it on the chalkboard
the teacher might point out that the poem
has the rhythm of a clock ticking. Then
add the words, tick-tock three times at the
beginning and end.

Tick-tock, tick-tock, tick-tock
Hickory Dickory Dock
The mouse ran up the clock
The clock struck, One!

San Diego County Schools, Calif.

It was Christmas Eve so the verse choir wore their nightclothes for the program. Waiting for Santa is important when one is in the first grade.

The mouse ran down
Hickory Dickory Dock.
Tick-tock, tick-tock, tick-tock

The teacher might say, "Now watch my arm. I will move it as if it were a clock pendulum or metronome. When I go this way, say *tick,* and this way say *tock.* Let's practice it once to see how much we can sound like a clock." After one round of practice, go ahead: "That was fine! Now we will have one row be a clock and tick all the way through the verse while the rest of us say it. Notice that we must pause after the *dock* to allow time for a *tock* sound. We might say the last *tick-tock* very softly as if the clock were stopping."

Later, a way might be discussed as to how the word *one* might be emphasized. Sometimes emphasis is secured by having only one person say the word, sometimes by clapping hands or ringing a bell, and sometimes simply by having everyone say it louder.

Another verse with a dramatic effect is one with a "wind" idea in it. Have the entire group hum to sound like a wind blowing, then while some continue to hum, the verse is said with the humming quietly fading away at the end. Most children will know "Who Has Seen The Wind?"

Who has seen the wind?
Neither I nor you;
But when the leaves hang trembling
The wind is passing through.

Who has seen the wind?
Neither you nor I;
But when the leaves bow down their heads
The wind is passing by.
—CHRISTINA ROSSETTI

Before saying a verse together it is wise to note the punctuation. If a group pauses at the end of each line an unpleasant sing-song effect destroys the meaning of the poetry. Sometimes this can be avoided by a slight pause after words that should be emphasized, such as *seen* in the first line or *leaves* in the third.

Usually the signal, "Ready, begin" is used for primary children. A hand signal can serve the same purpose. A closed fist opening might be the sign to start.

The simplest type of choral reading is that using a refrain. The teacher usually is the leader and the class gives the refrain.

RED SQUIRREL

Unison:	Flip-flop!
Solo:	Without a stop
(very	A red squirrel runs
rapidly)	To the oak-tree top.
Unison:	Whisk, frisk!
Solo:	He is so shy,
(slowly)	He hides himself in
	The leaves near by.
Unison:	Hip, hop!
Solo:	With acorns brown
(fast)	In his furry cheeks
	He hurries down.
Unison:	Snip, snap!
Solo:	The nuts he cracks
(slowly)	With his long, white teeth
	As sharp as tacks.
Unison:	Pip, pop!
Solo:	He sits quite still
(slow, then	Eating his goodies
very rapidly)	Then runs down the hill.

—GRACE ROWE

THE CHRISTMAS PUDDING

(Read faster and faster with each line.)

Solo:	Into the basin put the plums,
Refrain:	Stirabout, stirabout, stirabout.
Solo:	Next the good white flour comes,
Refrain:	Stirabout, stirabout, stirabout.
Solo:	Sugar and peel and eggs and spice,
Refrain:	Stirabout, stirabout, stirabout.
Solo:	Mix them and fix them and cook them twice,
Refrain:	Stirabout, stirabout, stirabout.

LILLIAN TAYLOR

Another simple form is the two-part arrangement. One-half of the children say one part and the other half the other part. Question-and-answer poetry is often used for the two-part arrangement.

WHISTLE, WHISTLE

Boys:	Whistle, whistle, old wife, And you'll get a hen.

Girls:	I wouldn't whistle if you gave me ten.
Boys:	Whistle, whistle, old wife, And you'll get a flower.
Girls:	I wouldn't whistle if you gave me a bower.
Boys:	Whistle, whistle, old wife, And you'll get a gown.
Girls:	I wouldn't whistle for the best in town.
Boys:	Whistle, whistle, old wife, And you'll get a man.
Girls:	Whhhh! I'll whistle if I can.

A third arrangement is the line-a-child pattern. Each child has a chance to speak one or more lines by himself. In some poems, certain lines can be spoken by individual children and other lines spoken in unison.

THE SONG OF THE POP-CORN

Unison:	Pop-pop-pop!
1st Child:	Says the pop-corn in the pan;
Unison:	Pop-pop-pop!
2nd Child:	You may catch me if you can!
Unison:	Pop-pop-pop!
3rd Child:	Says each kernel hard and yellow;
Unison:	Pop-pop-pop!
4th Child:	I'm a dancing little fellow.
Unison:	Pop-pop-pop!
5th Child:	How I scamper through the heat!
Unison:	Pop-pop-pop!
6th Child:	You will find me good to eat.
Unison:	Pop-pop-pop!
7th Child:	I can whirl and skip and hop.
Unison:	Pop-pop-pop-pop! pop!
	Pop!
	POP!!

—LOUISE ABNEY

The most difficult of all choral reading is that involving the total group. Much practice is required in speaking together and drilling upon articulation, enunciation, inflection and pronunciation, and blending the voices into workable balance while maintaining satisfactory timing. Sometimes it is wise to divide a class into high and low voices. Some of the Bible material, such as Psalm 121 or the Christmas Story of Luke 2 : 1–16, lend themselves to this type of presentation.

BUNDLES

(Good for stressing enunciation)

A bundle is a funny thing
It always sets me wondering;
For whether it is thin or wide,
You never know just what's inside.
Especially on Christmas week,
Temptation is so great to peek;
Now wouldn't it be much more fun
If shoppers carried things undone?

—JOHN FARRAR

LISTEN TO THE WIND

Listen
To the wind
Listen to the wind
Listen to the wind
Wind, wind, wind, wind
He's roaring up the hill
And whirring around the house
He's whistling round the corners
And rattling all the doors
A blustering, boisterous
Monstrous sort of wind
Listen to the wind
Wind, wind, wind, wind
Listen to the wind
To the wind
Sighing.

—MARY M. GREEN

AEROPLANE

1st Group: There's a humming in the sky
There's a shining in the sky.

2nd Group: Silver wings are flashing by
Silver wings are shining by.

All: Aeroplane
Aeroplane
Flying high.

1st Group: Silver wings are shining
As it goes gliding by.

2nd Group: First it zooms
And it booms
Then it buzzes in the sky
Then its song is just a drumming.

All: A soft little humming
Strumming
Strumming.

1st Group: The wings are very little things
The silver shine is gone.

2nd Group: Just a little black speck
Away down the sky.

All: With a soft little humming

And a far away humming
Aeroplane

(softly) Aeroplane
Aeroplane
Good by.

—MARY M. GREEN

THE AMERICAN FLAG

Solo: There's a flag that floats above us,
Wrought in red and white and blue—
A spangled flag of stars and stripes
Protecting me and you.

Unison: Sacrifices helped to make it
As men fought the long months through—

Boys: Nights of marching

Girls: Days of fighting

Unison: For the red and white and blue.

Girls: There is beauty in that emblem

Boys: There is courage in it, too;

Girls: There is loyalty

Boys: There is valor

Unison: In the red and white and blue.

Solo: In that flag which floats unconquered
Over land and sea
There's equality and freedom

Unison: There is true democracy.

Solo: There is glory in that emblem
Wrought in red and white and blue—

Unison: It's the stars and stripes forever
Guarding me and guarding you.

—LOUISE ABNEY

LITTLE ECHO

All: Little Echo is an elf
Who plays at hide and seek.
You never, never find him.
But you can hear him speak:

Low: Hello   *High:* Hello
Low: Hello   *High:* Hello
Low: I'm here   *High:* I'm here
Low: Come near   *High:* Come near
All: I'm here.

—LOS ANGELES CITY SCHOOLS

LOCOMOTIVE

Unison: Mobs of people
Lots of noise,
Rattling baggage.
Porter boys.
Grinding brakes.
Shifting gears.

	Merry laughter,
	Parting tears!
Solo:	All ab-o-o-ard! All ab-o-o-ard!
Dark:	Slowly
	Slowly
	Turning,
	Massive engine moving on.
Medium:	Smoking
	Smoking
	Higher
	Higher
	Smokestacks hurl the smoke anon.
Light:	Fuel
	Fuel
	Fire
	Fire
	Faster
	Faster
	Speed
	Speed!
Unison:	Got to reach my destination.
	Got no time for hesitation.
	Have to please the population.
	I am working for the nation.
	Hurry, hurry to my station.
Medium:	Past the valleys, past the hill-tops.
	Past the river, past the pond.
	Past the farmhouse or the city
	Quickly covering the ground.
High:	I'm racing the sun
	I'm racing the moon
	I'm racing the stars
	I'm faster than time
Low:	The mountains clear away for me.
	They build a bridge across the sea.
	The iron weight above my wheel
Medium:	Trembles even rails of steel
Dark:	Through tunnels, black, a sooty black
	With dusty smoke and grime.
Light:	Faster, faster, night's descending
All:	I must reach my place on time!
	—RODNEY BENNETT

Solo parts should be used to encourage all children rather than to display a few stars. Frequently solo parts should be spoken by small groups of three or four whose voices are similar.

After children are interested in choir work they will accept some special speech exercises such as rolling their heads for relaxation or doing tone exercises, such as saying *ba, be, bi, bo, bu,* toward the front of their mouths. If the teacher starts with these, most children think they are ridiculously funny and no worthy results are achieved.

A verse choir should perform because it motivates both effort and interest but the teacher must avoid the temptation to use material beyond the appreciation level of the children or material unworthy of memorization. At Christmas time little children in their night clothes with candles make an appealing group. A sixth-grade graduation class might prepare a patriotic verse, "I Am an American," from *Book of Americans* by Stephen Vincent Benet. Inviting visitors from another room to hear a choir perform is as motivating as more elaborate presentations.

POETRY COLLECTIONS

Adhead, Gladys, and Anis Duff. *Inheritance of Poetry* (Boston: Houghton, 1948).

Arbuthnot, May Hill. *Time for Poetry* (Chicago: Scott, 1961).

Babbit, Adeline, and Alice Hubbard. *The Golden Flute* (New York: Day, 1937).

De Regniers, Beatrice Schenck. *Something Special* (New York: Harcourt, 1958).

Doane, Pilagie. *A Small Child's Book of Verse* (New York: Oxford, 1948).

McFarland, Wilma. *For a Child* (Philadelphia: Westminster, 1957).

de Angeli, Marguerite. *Book of Nursery and Mother Goose Rhymes* (New York: Doubleday, 1954).

Werner, Jane. *Golden Book of Poetry* (New York: Simon and Schuster, 1947).

Untermeyer, Louis. *Stars to Steer By* (New York: Harcourt, 1941).

Thompson, Blanche J. *Silver Pennies* (New York: Macmillan, 1930).

———. *More Silver Pennies* (New York: Macmillan, 1939).

1. What were some of the poems you memorized in the elementary school? Why did you memorize them?

2. Are the words of any current popular song of poetic quality?

3. Why are so many poems and songs written by men rather than women?

4. What would you do with a poem

brought to school by a child that you considered unworthy of the class?

5. Do you feel that a more analytical approach to poetry should be made in the intermediate grades than suggested in this chapter?

6. What type of tests should be given children with respect to poetry taught?

WHAT VERSE MAY BE USED WITH YOUNG CHILDREN?

The action-verse or finger play is found in all cultures. The Chinese have them, our American Indians have them, and new ones are invented daily. Friedrich Wilhelm August Froebel, the father of the kindergarten, collected many of his time and called them "mothers-play." You may recall the delight you felt as your mother moved your toes and said, "This little piggie went to market, this little piggie stayed home," etc. We suspect that one of the most interesting experiences of childhood is one of self-discovery, and these verses reflect the charm of that experience. The following are among the best known:

PAT-A-CAKE

Pat-a-cake, pat-a-cake, baker's man
Make me a cake as fast as you can.
Roll it, prick it, and mark it with T,
And put it in the oven for Tommy and me.

THUMB MAN

Thumb man says he'll dance,
Thumb man says he'll sing,
Dance and sing my merry little thing,
Thumb man says he'll dance and sing.
(Also *Pointer, Tall man, Ring man, Little man.*)
Where is thumb man? (*hold hands behind back*)
Where is thumb man?
Here I am. (*fist forward with thumb standing*)
Here I am. (*other fist forward, thumb standing*)
How do you do this morning? (*wriggle one thumb in direction of other*)
Very well, I thank you. (*wriggle other thumb*)
Run away, run away. (*hands behind back again*)
(*Can be sung to the tune of "Are You Sleeping?"*)

In using action plays, it is better to use too few than too many. The fun seems to be in repetition of the familiar favorites. The teacher first demonstrates the entire verse, then asks one or two children to come to the front and do it with her. After that, each line is done by the group and repeated until a few have mastered it. Needless to say, parents delight in watching a verse choir use these materials.

After these become old favorites, children will want to make up their own. To do this, start with a movement such as holding up an arm with the fist closed.

"This is an airplane searchlight,"
(*arm held up, wrist bent*)
"It turns to the left," (*open the fist*)
"It turns to the right," (*open the fist*)
"And the airplane came home" (*movement of both hands of airplane landing*)
"On a dark, dark night."

Other movements might be holding the hands together, palms up, with fingers raised as candle on a cake, fingers walking, fists pounding. Soon total body action is needed and eventually one reaches simple pantomime.

When using nursery rhymes, children's names may be substituted for the rhyme characters. Let the children select the person each wants to be, to avoid this being used in a way that might hurt the child. Let children join in on a repeated refrain. This may also be done in a story such as "Little pig, little pig, let me in!" "No, no, no, not by the hair of my chinny-chin-chin." Space permits only a few here. One class found over two hundred known to children in the schools where they were student teachers. *The Rooster Crows* contains many suitable rhymes.

LITTLE JACK HORNER

Little Jack Horner sat in a corner
(*sit straight in chair; left hand held in lap in the pie*)
Eating his Christmas pie.
(*pretend to eat pie with right hand*)
He put in his thumb and pulled out a plum
(*stick thumb of right hand into pie; pull out the plum*)
And said, "What a good boy am I!"
(*hold hands high in air*)

FLAG SALUTE

(This salute to the flag may be used the first semester in school; then gradually introduce our national salute.)

The work of my hands
(*cup both hands in front of you*)
The thoughts of my head
(*both hands on top of head*)
The love of my heart
(*hands folded over chest*)
I give to my flag.
(*extend hands and arms toward flag*)

TWO DICKEY BIRDS

Two little dickey birds sitting on a wall;
(*fists clenched, thumbs erect*)
One named Peter, the other named Paul.
(*nod one thumb, then the other*)
Fly away, Peter; fly away, Paul.
(*one hand, then other moved to behind back*)
Come back, Peter; come back, Paul.
(*one hand, then the other reappears*)

FIVE LITTLE SQUIRRELS

Five little squirrels
Sitting in a tree,
The first one said,
"What do I see?"
The second one said,
"I smell a gun."
The third one said,
"Quick, let's run!"
The fourth one said,
"Let's hide in the shade."
The fifth one said,
"Oh, I'm not afraid."
But—bang! went the gun
Away they did run!

LITTLE TURTLE

There was a little turtle.
(*upper right index finger*)

He lived in a box.
(*place in cupped left hand*)
He swam in a puddle
(*move finger in circle*)
He climbed on the rocks.
(*move up on left fingers*)
He snapped at a mosquito.
(*snap right hand in air*)
He snapped at a flea.
He snapped at a minnow.
He snapped at me.
(*snap toward self*)
He caught the mosquito.
(*close right fist in air*)
He caught the flea.
He caught the minnow.
But he didn't catch me.
(*point toward self, shake head*)

TWO TELEGRAPH POLES

Two tall telegraph poles
(*pointer fingers erect*)
Across them a wire is strung.
(*second fingers outstretched to touch between pointer fingers*)
Two little birds hopped on.
(*thumbs to position against "wire"*)
And swung, and swung, and swung.
(*sway arms back and forth from body*)

CATERPILLAR

Roly-poly caterpillar
Into a corner crept,
Spun around himself a blanket,
Then for a long time slept.
Roly-poly caterpillar
Wakening by and by—
Found himself with beautiful wings,
Changed to a butterfly.

ITSY, BITSY SPIDER

Itsy, bitsy spider went up the water spout.
(*hands make a climbing motion; or thumbs on index fingers of opposite hands, one after the other*)
Down came the rain and washed the spider out.
(*drop hands*)
Out came the sun and dried up all the rain.
(*arms circled overhead*)
Itsy, bitsy spider went up the spout again.
(*make "spider" motion again*)

GRANDMOTHER

Here are grandmother's glasses,

(circle thumb and finger, each hand, over eyes)
Here is grandmother's hat.
(fingertips together on head)
This is the way she folds her hands
And puts them in her lap.

READY FOR BED

This little boy is ready for bed.
(hold up forefinger)
Down on the pillow he lays his head.
(place finger in palm of opposite hand)
Covers himself all up tight,
(fold fingers over forefinger)
Falls fast asleep for the night.
(cock head toward shoulder, close eyes)
Morning comes, he opens his eyes,
(quickly lift head, open eyes)
Throws back the covers with great surprise,
(open palm to uncover forefinger)
Up he jumps and gets all dressed,
(quickly raise forefinger off palm)
To hurry to school to play with the rest.
(move finger off to the side)

FIVE LITTLE SOLDIERS

Five little soldiers standing in a row
Three stood straight and two stood so,
Along came the captain, and what do you think
They all stood up straight just as quick as a wink.

FIVE LITTLE PUMPKINS

Five little pumpkins sitting on a gate.
The first one said, "My it's getting late!"
The second one said, "There are witches in the air."
The third one said, "But we don't care."
The fourth one said, "Let's run, let's run!"
The fifth one said, "Isn't Halloween fun?"
"Woo-oo-oo" went the wind, out went the light.
Those five little pumpkins ran fast out of sight.

Supervisors and principals sometimes use finger play as a means of establishing acceptance on the part of little children. A principal who can teach a new one in the kindergarten will always be welcome. Froebel saw in this common interest a mystic relationship. Perhaps he was right. But it is obvious that these simple verses help children to speak better, notice sounds in words, learn about rhyming endings and gain a social recognition in a way that is pleasant to both the child and the teacher.

Action stories may be developed after the pattern of the old nursery rhyme in which one child says, "I went upstairs," and the other child replies: "Just like me." A leader tells a part of a story and the remainder of the group do the action saying at the same time, "Just like this."

Leader: Goldilocks went for a walk in the forest.
Group: Just like this.
Leader: She stopped to look at a bird.
Group: Just like this.
Leader: The bird said, "Cheer up! Cheer up!"
Group: Just like this, "Cheer up! Cheer up!"

After reading the story *Copy-Kittens* by Helen and Alf Evans, the children may want to act it as it is reread. Other stories of this nature may be "played" as the beginning of creative dramatics.

Suggestions for Projects

1. Review ten books which might be read by children in a single grade to improve their understanding of a foreign land or an ethical value. (A different book for each country or value.)

2. Review ten books which might be read by children in a single grade to improve their historical or geographical concepts of our country.

3. Make a collection of 25 poems that will interest boys in grades 5–6. Indicate in general how such poetry would be introduced and used.

4. Make a collection of ten poems appropriate to the purposes of a verse choir at a grade level.

5. Select three stories or ballads that might be dramatized by children.

6. Make a bibliography of dramatic material to use in the intermediate grades.

7. Indicate the skills needed and how they may be developed with regard to the dramatic presentation of a play.

8. Collect a group of ballads or stories that might be read aloud while a group presented the action in pantomime.

9. Suggest with specific examples ways in which art and literature may be correlated.

10. Plan a summer reading program for children at a specific grade level.

11. Collect and organize program material for use at one of these holidays: Halloween, Thanksgiving, Christmas, Valentine's Day, Arbor Day, Veterans' Day.

12. Prepare material for three flannelboard stories which children might learn to tell.

13. Check a group of books or other reading material used at a specific grade level with respect to readability.

14. Plan a series of lessons with respect to the use of the library for a specific group of children.

15. Make a collection of finger plays to use with young children.

16. Make a bibliography of books to be read aloud to children.

BIBLIOGRAPHY

BOOKS

American Library Association. *Basic Book Collection for Elementary Grades.* Chicago: American Library Association, 1960.

Applegate, Mauree. *Easy in English.* New York: Harper, 1960, chap. 7.

Arbuthnot, May Hill. *Children and Books.* Chicago: Scott, 1957.

Arnstein, Flora J. *Adventures in Poetry.* Palo Alto, Calif.: Stanford U.P., 1951.

Chall, Jeanne S. *Readability.* Columbus: Ohio State. U.P., 1958.

Fenner, Phyllis. *The Proof of the Pudding.* New York: Day, 1957. Chap. SVI.

Hazard, Paul. *Books Children and Men.* Boston: Horn Book, 1960.

Huck, Charlotte, and Doris A. Young. *Children's Literature in the Elementary School.* New York: Holt, 1961.

Smith, Lillian. *The Unreluctant Years.* Chicago: American Library Association, 1953. Chap. 7.

Spache, George. *Good Books for Poor Readers.* Champaign, Ill.: Garrard, 1958.

Turner, Mary C. *Best Books for Children.* New York: Bowker, 1961.

VERSE CHOIR MATERIAL

Abney, Louise. *Choral Speaking Arrangements for the Upper Grades.* Magnolia, Mass.: Expression, 1937.

Barton, Clifford T. *Verse Choir in the Elementary School.* Darien, Conn.: Educational, 1954.

Brown, H. A., and H. J. Heltman. *Let's-Read-Together Poems.* New York: Harper, 1950, pp. 1–6.

———. *Choral Reading for Fun and Relaxation.* Philadelphia: Westminister, 1956.

Pronovost, Wilbert, and Louise Kingman. *The Teaching of Speaking and Listening in the Elementary School.* New York: Longmans, 1959.

Raubicheck, Letitia. *Choral Speaking Is Fun.* New York: Noble, 1955.

Schoefield, Lucille D. *Better Speech and Better Reading.* Magnolia, Mass.: Expression, 1937.

Scott, L. B., and J. J. Thompson. *Speech Ways.* St. Louis: Webster, 1955.

PERIODICALS AND PAMPHLETS

Books for Young Readers. Quarterly. 18288 Prevost Avenue, Detroit 35, Mich.

Horn Book Magazine. 585 Boylston Street, Boston 16, Mass.

Dobler, Lavinia. *Dobler International List of Periodicals for Boys and Girls.* Muriel Fuller, Box 193 Grand Central Station, New York 17, N.Y.

World Book Encyclopedia. "Literature for Children." Chicago: Field, 1954.

Moore, Anne C. "Seven Stories High," reprinted from *Compton's Picture Encyclopedia.* Chicago: Compton, n.d.

CALDECOTT AND NEWBERY MEDAL BOOKS

The Randolph Caldecott Medal, established and endowed by Frederic G. Melcher, is awarded annually by committees of children's librarians of the American Library Association for the most distinguished American picture book for children published during the preceding year. The medal is named in honor of the famous nineteenth-century English artist whose vigorous and delightful picture books have been loved by generations of children.

(Parentheses indicate illustrator, publisher, and date of publication.)

LATHROP, DOROTHY P.
Animals of the Bible (author; Stokes, 1938)

HANFORTH, THOMAS
  Mei Li (author; Doubleday, 1939)
D'AULAIRE, INGRI AND EDGAR P.
  Abraham Lincoln (authors; Doubleday, 1940)
LAWSON, ROBERT
  They Were Strong and Good (author; Viking, 1941)
MC CLOSKEY, ROBERT
  Make Way for Ducklings (author; Viking, 1942)
BURTON, VIRGINIA LEE
  The Little House (author; Houghton, 1943)
THURBER, JAMES
  Many Moons (Louis Slobodkin; Harcourt, 1944)
FIELD, RACHEL
  Prayer for a Child (Elizabeth O. Jones; Macmillan, 1945)
PETERSHAM, MAUD AND MISKA
  The Rooster Crows; A Book of American Rhymes and Jingles (authors; Macmillan, 1946)
MAC DONALD, GOLDEN
  The Little Island (Leonard Weisgard; Doubleday, 1947)
TRESSELT, ALVIN
  White Snow, Bright Snow (Roger Duvoisin; Lothrop, 1948)
HADER, BERTA AND ELMER
  The Big Snow (authors; Macmillan, 1949)
POLITI, LEO
  Song of the Swallows (author; Scribner, 1950)
MILHOUS, KATHERINE
  The Egg Tree (author; Scribner, 1951)
LIPKIND, WILLIAM
  Finders Keepers (Nicolas Mordivinoff; Harcourt, 1952)
WARD, LYND
  The Biggest Bear (author; Houghton, 1953)
BEMELMANS, LUDWIG
  Madeline's Rescue (author; Viking, 1954)
PERRAULT, CHARLES (BROWN, MARCIA)
  Cinderella: or The Little Glass Slipper (author; Scribner, 1955)
RETOLD BY JOHN LANGSTAFF
  Frog Went A'Courtin' (Feodor Rojankovsky; Harcourt, 1956)
SIMONT, MARC
  A Tree is Nice (Marc Simont; Harper, 1957)
MC CLOSKEY, ROBERT
  Time of Wonder (author; Viking, 1958)
CHAUCER, G.
  Chanticleer and the Fox (Barbara Cooney; Crowell, 1959)

ETS, MARIE HALL
  Nine Days to Christmas (author; Viking, 1960)
ROBBINS, RUTH
  Babonshka and the Three Kings (Nicolas Sidjakov; Parnassus, 1961)
HITAPADESA
  Once a Mouse (Marcia Brown; Scribner, 1962)
KEATS, EZRA
  These Snowy Days (author; Viking, 1963)
SENDAK, MAURICE
  Where the Wild Things Are (author; Harper, 1964)

The Newbery Medal is awarded annually for the most distinguished contribution to American literature for children, published during the preceding year. Publisher, date of publication, and grade level are indicated in parentheses. Single asterisk means highly recommended by Children's Catalog; double asterisk, most highly recommended.

VAN LOON, HENDRIK
  *The Story of Mankind (Liveright, 1922, 7–9)
LOFTING, HUGH
  **The Voyages of Dr. Doolittle (Stokes, 1923, 4–7)
HAWES, CHARLES BOARDMAN
  *The Dark Frigate (Little, Brown, 1924, 7–9)
FINGER, CHARLES
  **Tales from Silver Lands (Doubleday, 1925, 5–7)
CHRISMAN, ARTHUR
  *Shen of the Sea (Dutton, 1926, 5–8)
JAMES, WILL
  **Smoky, the Cowhorse (Scribner, 1927, 6–9)
MUKERJI, DHAN GOPAL
  *Gay-Neck: The Story of a Pigeon (Dutton, 1928, 6–9)
KELLY, ERIC P.
  **The Trumpeter of Krakow (Macmillan, 1929, 7–9)
FIELD, RACHEL
  **Hitty: Her First 100 Years (Macmillan, 1930, 5–8)
COATSWORTH, ELIZABETH
  **The Cat Who Went to Heaven (Macmillan, 1931, 4–7)
ARMER, LAURA ADAMS
  *Waterless Mountain (Longmans, 1932, 5–8)
LEWIS, ELIZABETH FOREMAN
  **Young Fu of the Upper Yangtze (Winston, 1933, 7–9)

MEIGS, CORNELIA
Invincible Louisa: The Story of the Author of Little Women (Little, 1934, 7–9)

SHANNON, MONICA
**Dobry* (Viking, 1935, 5–8)

BRINK, CAROL RYRIE
**Caddie Woodlawn* (Macmillan, 1936, 6–8)

SAWYER, RUTH
**Roller Skates* (Viking, 1937, 6–8)

SEREDY, KATE
The White Stag (Viking, 1938, 6–9)

ENRIGHT, ELIZABETH
Thimble Summer (Rinehart, 1939, 5–7)

DAUGHERTY, JAMES
**Daniel Boone* (oversize section) (Viking, 1940, 5–9)

SPERRY, ARMSTRONG
**Call It Courage* (Macmillan, 1941, 5–8)

EDMONDS, WALTER
**The Matchlock Gun* (oversize section) (Dodd, 1942, 4–6)

GRAY, ELIZABETH JANET
**Adam of the Road* (Viking, 1943, 6–9)

FORBES, ESTHER
**Johnny Tremain* (Houghton, 1944, 6–9)

LAWSON, ROBERT
**Rabbit Hill* (Viking, 1945, 3–6)

LENSKI, LOIS
**Strawberry Girl* (Lippincott, 1946, 4–6)

BAILEY, CAROLYN SHERWIN
**Miss Hickory* (Viking, 1947, 4–6)

DU-BOIS, WILLIAM PENE
**The 21 Balloons* (Viking, 1948, 5–9)

HENRY, MARGUERITE
**King of the Wind* (Rand McNally, 1949, 5–8)

DE ANGELI, MARGUERITE
**The Door in the Wall* (Doubleday, 1950, 3–6)

YATES, ELIZABETH
**Amos Fortune, Free Man* (Aladdin, 1951, 6–9)

ESTES, ELEANOR
Ginger Pye (Harcourt, 1952, 4–7)

CLARK, ANN NOLAL
**Secret of the Andes* (Viking, 1953, 4–7)

KRUMGOLD, JOSEPH
**And Now Miguel* (Crowell, 1954, 5–9)

DE LONG, MEINDERT
**The Wheel on the School* (Harper, 1955, 4–7)

LATHAM, JEAN LEE
Carry On, Mr. Bowditch (Houghton, 1956, 6–9)

SORENSEN, VIRGINIA
**Miracles on Maple Hill* (Harcourt, 1957, 5–7)

KEITH, HAROLD
**Rifles for Watie* (Crowell, 1958, 6–9)

SPEARE, ELIZABETH
**Witch of Blackbird Pond* (Houghton, 1959, 6–9)

KRUMGOLD, JOSEPH
Onion John (Crowell, 1960, 6–9)

ODELL, SCOTT
Island of the Blue Dolphins (Houghton, 1961, 6–9)

SPEARE, ELIZABETH
Bronze Bow (Houghton, 1962, 6–9)

'L ENGLE, MADELEINE
A Wrinkle in Time (Farrar, 1963, 6–9)

NEVILLE, EMILY
**It's Like This, Cat* (Harper, 1964, 5–9)

Chapter 8

Written Composition

WHAT IS THE DIFFERENCE BETWEEN PRACTICAL AND CREATIVE WRITING?

Practical writing is done in any situation in which there is need for it. In comparison with creative writing, practical writing is more utilitarian, realistic, or intellectual, and needs the discipline of correct mechanics to be socially acceptable. Correct form seems intrinsically a function of realistic writing because other people are practically concerned. This is the type of writing in which the author works more as a reproducer of known facts, conditions, or ideas presented in his own words. Here the emphasis may be placed upon the mechanics of writing, spelling, penmanship, neatness, punctuation, and similar external items without injury to the child's creative expression.

When a child writes creatively, he expresses one way or another his feelings or his intellectual reactions to an experience —something he has seen, heard, or otherwise come in contact with through his senses. This expression of personal reactions constitutes the quality of originality because no one other than the writer can produce it. It is his own contribution. This type of writing is that of artistic self-expression. It is personal, individual, imaginative, and highly perishable. To keep it alive there must be complete freedom to experiment and complete assurance of a respectful reception of the product regardless of its nature.

Though in a sense the two aspects of writing develop separately and serve different purposes, the child gradually carries over what he has learned of techniques in practical writing and applies it where it suits his purpose in the personal writing. The emphasis is first and last on saying something that is worth saying, and saying it effectively. *A balance between the two types must be maintained, and to give all writing the same treatment is to suppress or inhibit the creative spirit of children.* Lois Lenski stresses the importance of the treatment of creative writing:

It is such a simple thing to help children enter the creative life, to help them to think clearly and to communicate their ideas to others through the spoken or written word. Provide the opportunity—let the child talk and let him write, enjoying both. Share his enthusiasms. All children can and should learn

321

San Diego County Schools, Calif.

This class first dictated a get-well letter to a classmate, then each made his own card and greeting.

the free and easy use of words. Creative expression should never be confused with the teaching of the techniques of writing. These are two distinct procedures.

It should always be remembered that creation is a flowing of ideas. Given a stimulus, ideas come pouring from the mind like water from a fountain. It is all too easy to stop this creative flow. Rules for punctuation, spelling, grammar, and handwriting will stop it. Emphasis on rules is sure to stifle creative thinking.[1]

There are some who would not be as positive with respect to rules as Miss Lenski. Confidence in the craftsmanship of writing and expression also releases cre-

ativity. It is probably true that great writers and artists also have been expert craftsmen. Certainly no great painter has emerged by ignoring the disciplines of his craft. By mastering these disciplines he was able to project his own personal qualities more effectively. Our objective is to use the child's desire to create, to make disciplined craftsmanship acceptable.

1. Do you consider that children can be as creative in such tasks as letter writing as in imaginative writing?
2. To what extent is it true that the skills of language are the skills of conformity?

HOW MAY IMAGINATIVE OR CREATIVE WRITING BE MOTIVATED IN THE PRIMARY GRADES?

The child has two major avenues of expression for his ideas: he can tell them orally or paint a picture. This is where the teacher starts. The child may tell about a

[1] Lois Lenski, "Helping Children to Create," *Childhood Education*, **26** (November 1949), pp. 101–105.

personal experience, tell what he thinks is happening in a picture, tell a story about an object such as a sea shell. Sometimes the experience is completely oral. The teacher makes suggestions with respect to words, important ideas, or the way the story was told. At other times the child makes the picture first then tells what is happening in the picture. This provides a focus for his idea with respect to those that are important and those that are subordinate.

"What would be a good name for Jane's story?" the teacher asks. After several have made suggestions the teacher turns to Jane. "Which one do you like best?" After Jane has decided the teacher writes the name for all to see. With this beginning, children will soon be dictating stories which the teacher writes and the child reads. As the teacher writes she points out where she begins and how each sentence ends. "I'll put the first word here then go to the right. This is the end of the sentence so I will put a period here." A "book" of these stories is placed on the reading table so that chil-dren can read again the stories they have written.

Creative writing can be a class-wide experience, the efforts of a small group, or an individual working alone with the teacher. Such experience usually follows a discussion period where children "think together" and express themselves freely. In the small-group method, the members work faster and the interest factors and feeling of success are high. The teacher is imme-diately able to supply needed words or correct spelling, to stimulate thinking and to build curiosity. In turn, other groups will work with the teacher. Writing experiences which involve the entire class now involve a common topic such as "Thanksgiving." During the discussion period, words that might be used are placed on the chalkboard.

San Diego County Schools, Calif.

Ideas and the freedom to express them have priority over mechanical correctness in this classroom. In time, the child will seek correct form and willingly work to achieve the skills needed, because he wants to write and knows that such discipline is needed to reach his goal.

Specific aspects suitable for writing might be listed such as "My Favorite Thanksgiving," "A Turkey's Ideas About Thanksgiving," "Why I am Thankful." Thus the individual compositions will vary although using a similar vocabulary.

Children learn many things when they write. They become familiar with selecting, eliminating, and arranging words and with "proofreading" or correcting errors. The first efforts usually contain misspelled words, incomplete sentences, meager punctuation and capitalization. The first stories are not corrected, but as the child reads his story to the teacher, his voice indicates beginnings and endings. He then adds, with the teacher's help, his own periods, question marks, and capitals. After children have written many stories and write with ease, the teacher and child correct the first rough draft. The child takes the initiative in finding his errors, or in completing the spelling of a word where only the initial letter is given. The child copies his story and shares it with his classmates. Sometimes the story is placed with others in a bound volume. Children frequently offer stories without a title, probably because a title or name inhibits their ease of writing. The teacher or other children may suggest a title when the child shares his unnamed story with them.

Here is an early effort of an above-average boy in the first grade: [2]

THE DOME BIRD

(as written by Richard, Grade I)

One day dome bird thote two + two was twente. One day men buill schools up. and it was time for dome bird to come to school. One day the teacher put up some arethmatik. then dome bird sat down to rite. The dom bird saw two + two on the board. He put twente on the paper. the teacher saw dome Bird arethmatick so she put an X on the paper so the dome bird saw the X so dom bird Learnd how much two + two was.

THE DUMB BIRD

(as read by Richard)

One day dumb bird thought two plus two was twenty. One day some men built schools and it was time for dumb bird to come to school. One day the teacher put up some arithme-tic. Then dumb bird sat down to write. The dumb bird saw two plus two on the board. He put twenty on the paper. The teacher saw dumb bird's arithmetic, so she put an X on the paper. The dumb bird saw the X, so dumb bird learned how much two plus two was.

As soon as print script has been mastered, the children follow the pattern established by the teacher and write their own story. These will show a great range of interest and expression. But each one is important to the writer.

One will laboriously write "The House" with many smudges and add his name. Another will cover pages as he writes a story like this:

Robert   Jan. 22, 1958

wonts there was a 1 and a half year old girl. her name was tiny because she was so little. One day she saw a dog. she wanted to bathe him because he was so dirty. she asked her mother but she said no get that dirty thing out of here. but tiny brahgt a tub in the yard. then she brahgt some waters and put in it. she bathed him. she got wet and dirty. but the dog was not dirty any more. he went away and he did not come back again because he did not like water.

the end.

The only capital letters Robert knew were those in his name—but that did not

---

[2] South Bay Public Schools, *Our Writing* (San Diego County, Calif., published annually).

stop him. He probably asked for help on "brahgt" and having spelled it wrong once was loyal to his first spelling when the word was repeated. Most revealing of all is a little note in one corner of the page: "I love to make storys."

As children learn to read the pattern of the controlled vocabulary, it is reflected in the material they write. Jon wrote this one:

> Jane and Billy play
> Run Billy
> Billy jumps.

The picture was much more original. Two children were shown with a jumping rope tied to a tree, Billy was jumping while Jane held the rope.

The pattern of teacher made charts soon appears in the writing of children. Peggy produced this story:

> This is Ann and Linda.
> They are looking at the kittens.
> The kittens are in the basket.
> The basket is yellow and red.
> The kittens are cute.

But in the same school another first grade class was writing these stories:

> This is in the Dineohsire's Days. A sea manstre is going to land and eat. a trtaile is under his tail. in those days the were no people.
> —Jeffrey

> This is the sivl war wen the Americans fot the inglish. The Americans wun the wor becas the American's they did not giv up.
> —by Bobby

It is obvious that two different philosophies are at work here. In one there has been an emphasis on form, in the second upon ideas. The natural question to ask is when should these children be expected to spell and write correctly? Teachers who permit the second type of writing say that late in the second grade or sometimes the third grade the children seek correct form. These new standards are the result of wide reading and the gradual mastery of writing mechanics. It is true that unless the prin-

cipal and parents understand the purposes of the teacher there will be criticism. But it should be recognized that children are not going to attempt words like *monster* or *turtle* if they face criticism with respect to spelling and writing.

News reports of the day are popular:

> Donald brought in a
> record for Mrs. Cummins.

> A car hit a teacher's
> parked automobile
> It even hit a house
> It almost poured rain too.
> —by Linda

> Today was a happy
> day. Today Miss Bovee [student teacher]
> came. She will stay until school closes.
> —Belinda

Holidays receive special notice.

> April 7, 1960   Sylvia C.
>
> ### Easter Day
> On Easter Day we had an egg hunt. I found more eggs than my brother. One egg was under the abalone shell. I found an egg in both vases. I had fun on Easter. Most of the eggs were in the living room. But some were in the dining room. The eggs were all different colors. They are very pretty. I helped dye the eggs. I had fun on Easter.

Before this story was written certain words were written on the board as the result of a discussion of words needed. Among these were: dye, Easter, colors. The words *different* and *dining* were corrected before the story was posted. In this class all children wrote on the same topic.

A favorite writing experience at the beginning of second grade is to write, "What I Want to Be" stories. These can be reproduced in a little book for parents' night. If the children will use a ditto pencil or write on ditto masters this also provides an example of the child's writing. These are typical examples:

A JET PILOT

> I want to be a Jet
> pilot. You have to

learn many things
before you can be
a Jet pilot. You must
know how to fly your plane
are you might crash.
If the plane runs
out of gas I will parachute out

             —by BILLY

A FIRE MAN

I want to be a fire man and
put out fires and help
people out of fires.
I want to be a good fire man
I want to slide down the
poles. I want to help
people to be good and not
cause fires

             —by RICKY

A SCHOOL TEACHER

I want to be a school
teacher and teach children
how to spell and do numbers.
I want to teach them how
to tell time and many
other things I want
children who do good work
and not spend their time
talking

             —by DIANE

But second-grade children advance rapidly. By the end of the year some will write this well. The literary pattern now follows that of favorite books.

FLICKA THE FILLY

Dick's father was at the Johnson's farm getting a colt. Dick was going to train it. When his father came home Dick ran to the truck. The colt was beautiful. It was pure white with a black mane and tail and right on its forehead was a gold star. "What will you name her, son?" asked his father.

"I'll call her Flicka," said Dick.

The next day Dick got up early. He ate his breakfast and went to the stable.

"Come on, Flicka," said Dick. "I'm going to train you." Flicka went with Dick to the pasture.

"First you must learn to obey your master," said Dick. Dick walked away and said "Stay."

Flicka did as he said. Flicka obeyed him

with the other tricks, too. And they had lots of fun for the rest of their lives.

             —by JAYNE

After hearing several of the "Just So" stories by Rudyard Kipling, one of the boys wrote this original story:

THE STORY OF THE ELEPHANT THAT HAD NO TRUNK

Once upon a time there lived an elephant. This elephant was very sad because he had no trunk. The way this elephant lost his trunk was.

He was walking along just minding his own business, when out of the blue came a rhinoceros. This rhinoceros was the biggest, fattest, rhinoceros you have ever seen. And the elephant crouched down of fright. The rhinoceros stepped on the trunk and off it came. That's the way the elephant lost his trunk.

             —by DONALD

A teacher may plan a lesson in written composition in a six-step sequence. First, the child is either motivated to write or helped to recognize that he has something to express in writing. Second, the vocabulary needed to express the writer's ideas is made available. Third, forms already taught are recalled, since we want the child to practice correct habits. Fourth, a time is provided for the writing experience. Fifth, the written material is shared. Sixth, improvements are made in the composition appropriate to the writer's purposes.

This six-step procedure cannot always be completed in one language period. A letter might be started in the language class and completed during the spelling or social studies time. A story or poem might be started on one day, completed on a second and revised on a third. The amount of writing will depend on the interest and purpose of those involved. Writing should never become "busy work" or a time-filling activity. A limited amount of writing that has a purpose and is carefully guided to prevent the repetition of error will produce the most satisfying results.

The following classroom procedures have been suggested by teachers for each of these six steps:

1. Motivation

Preprimer Stories—Children are encouraged to make their own preprimers. These may be a compilation of the stories of several students or the work of one. Topics may concern Cowboys, Our Town, My Family, Our Pets, Our School.

Diary or Daily News—At first the children will dictate a report to the teacher on "what we did today." Later they will write their own. This may be a rotating activity. One group may be sharing orally for the day or week, another working on a project, and a third keeping the diary. "Our Friday News" is an excellent way to summarize the work of the week for parents and the principal.

Wishes, Fears, Troubles—Feelings stimulate a great deal of creative thought. Expression of such feelings helps the teacher understand the child as well as helping the child to get problems out in the open. Making pictures, then talking or writing about these topics, illustrate this suggestion.

"If I could have one wish"
"I do not like_____"
"Things that scare me"
"If I could be something else I would be a_____ _____"

Reports—Most adult writing is done to tell what happened, what a person learned, or what a person did. Simple encyclopedias make it possible for children to share interesting information through written reports. Some even call these "term papers" with sources appropriately indicated.

Seasons, Holidays, and Nature—The environment is a natural stimulation for writing. Windy days, storms, rain, are things to tell about. A "Halloween," "Thanksgiving," or "February Hero" book made of a compilation of writing, is a rewarding project. In the second grade and beyond children can print directly on ditto masters so that a book for each child can be assembled.

Titles—All that some children need to start the flow of ideas and the desire to write is a title.

Witches Brew	Vacation Fun
My Pet	My Toys
Adventures of a Penny	Dear Santa
Chimpanaut Tells All	When I was Sick
My Old School	Danger
The Old House	Fire! Fire!

First Lines—Getting started is difficult for many. These first lines reproduced on writing paper will often help a straggler:

1. Dear Santa, Please_____.
2. My name is_____. I live at_____.
3. Once there was a monkey_____.
4. I am_____. I have_____. I can_____.

"If" Stories—suggested plots:

1. If you were a circus pony, what adventures might you have?
2. If you were a lost dog, what might happen to you?
3. If you were a calf that liked to run away, what might happen to you?
4. If you were a dog that saw a turtle in the road, what might happen?
5. If you could go anywhere in the world, where would you go?
6. If you had ten dollars to spend for Christmas, what would you buy?

Tell a story about these facts:

1. I am a crow named Chicago. Tell the story of how I hid some silver and what happened to it.
   Suggested words: thief, chased, claws, dogs, barked, fireman, ladder, afraid, tired
2. I am a fireman named Jim. One day there was a big fire. Tell what happened.
3. I am a monkey named Bimbo. I love to tease my master. Tell how this got me into trouble.
4. I am a baby brother. I got lost one day. Tell what happened to me.

Post Office—Establish a mail box for each child. At any time any child may write a letter to any other child in the class.

The teacher may write a letter as well. Letters may be mailed only at noon and picked up only in the morning before school. To maintain standards it must be understood that no letter will be put in the receiver's box unless it is correctly written. The Postmaster and his staff examine all mail to see if "mailable."

Outer Space Stories—Discuss the following: Today we are going to write a space story. Should we take a trip to Venus or stop at the Moon? Will it be a dream, or an original, or news account in the "Venus Morning News"? Maybe it will be a colony of Pilgrims on the Moon or the diary of one who stayed at home. Perhaps the trip was not planned at all but the result of an accident.

Picture Stimulators are among the best means of motivating a child to write. A picture of a clown cut from a magazine is glued to an idea card. Below it are some stimulating questions: Have you been to the circus? Why is the clown so happy? On the back are words the child might wish to use as he writes a story. Appropriate words might be: clown, circus, tent, laughing, trick, joke, music. These pictures are equally good as stimulators for oral stories prior to writing.

A Writer's Corner in the classroom is a technique used by many teachers to stimulate writing. The corner consists of a table and chairs placed below a bulletin board. Questions, pictures and ideas for word usage can be attractively displayed on the bulletin board for motivation. These are changed frequently. Writing paper, pencils, a dictionary, and needed lists of words are kept on the table. Folders of pictures with words describing the picture are placed on the table. Large sheets of paper with a mimeographed picture in the corner have been successfully used by some teachers to obtain a variety of stories about one picture.

The materials on the writer's table must be introduced to the children so that they know how to use them correctly. The pictures should be used by the class as a regular writing activity before the materials are placed on the writer's table. This does not mean that every new game or picture placed on the writer's table must be introduced to the group first. It does mean that any different type of material that the teacher places on this table should be explained so that the child knows exactly how to use it.

Periodically some recognition should be given to children who are using the writer's desk. Putting up "The Story of the Week," which can be selected by the teacher or the class, or making a booklet of the best stories are two ways that can help stimulate more creative work. Material written may be put in a box which is later read aloud by the teacher. The children guess who is the author in the manner of a television quiz program.

One device for the writer's table is a threefold stand made of cardboard. Each fold is about 9 × 11. The centerfold has a stimulating picture that is slipped behind a sheet of acetate. On the right is a group of words appropriate to the picture also in an acetate envelope. On the left are reminders to the writer. The teacher can change the pictures and vocabulary as she wishes. The reminders might be: "Every story has a title." "All sentences begin with capitals." "All names start with capitals."

The writer's desk can be used by children when they have finished other assigned work. It is desirable to have only one child using the desk at a time. However, if the teacher wishes, children may take certain materials to their desks.

In developing language material for this individual activity, teachers should remember that "above average" or "gifted" children are more likely to use them at first. Since this is so, teachers should plan activities that would be challenging.

2. *Vocabulary Development*

When children write they sometimes wish to use words from their listening

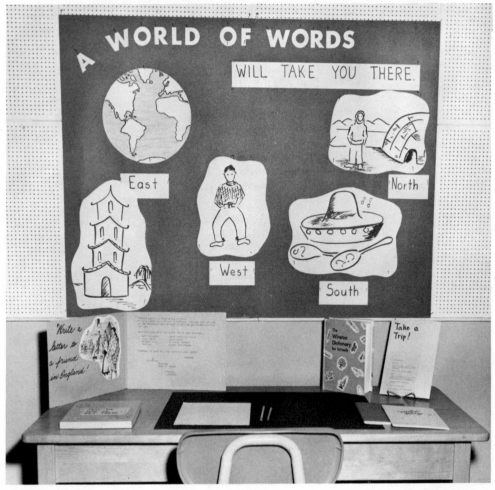

In this writing corner there are: pencil, paper, a simple dictionary, an idea folder of things to write about, a special word list that the class has made—and no one around to bother the author while he works.

vocabulary. One may ask, "What do you call the signs in the newspaper that tell what people have to sell?" He is seeking the word advertisement. The same is true of such words as alfalfa (what do cows eat?) or infinity (space). At such times the teacher provides the word desired.

In other situations the teacher anticipates that the writing and spelling of certain words will be needed and provides convenient references. Interesting words in stories read should be noticed so that they will be available to future authors. Simple picture dictionaries of the names of things may be consulted or created.

Word Cards—Since seasonal words will be needed every year, a packet of cards for Halloween, Thanksgiving, and Christmas can be constructed by older children or the teacher. At the appropriate time these words are spread along the chalkboard to help writers. Pictures on each card, such as a picture of a pumpkin beside the word, will help those still having reading problems.

Word Lists—A folder for each child which contains the words most often used will prevent errors as well as make writing easier for the child. This is a combination of a spelling and reading list.

The Words We Use Most Often

These are the words we use most often.
We use them when we write.
We use them when we read.

We can use this as a dictionary.
We can check the spelling of words here.

Check yourself to see how many you know.
Learn the ones you do not know.
Learn to say them very quickly.

a	Christmas	go	or
about	city	going	other
after	cold	good	our
again	come	great	out
all	comes	had	over
along	coming	happy	people
also	could	hard	place
always	country	has	play
am	days	have	pretty
an	dear	he	put
and	did	heard	ran
another	didn't	help	read
any	do	her	ready
are	dog	here	right
around	don't	may	room
as	door	me	said
asked	down	men	saw
at	each	money	say
away	eat	more	school
back	enough	morning	see
be	ever	most	she
beautiful	every	mother	should
because	father	much	side
bed	few	my	small
been	find	name	snow
before	fire	never	so
best	first	new	some
better	five	next	something
big	for	nice	soon
book	found	night	started
boy	four	no	stay
boys	friend	not	still
brother	from	now	summer
but	fun	of	sure
by	gave	off	take
called	get	old	teacher
came	getting	on	tell
can	girl	once	than
car	girls	one	that
children	give	only	the

their	to	want	while
them	today	wanted	white
then	told	was	who
there	too	water	winter
these	took	way	with
they	town	we	work
thing	tree	week	would
things	two	well	write
think	until	went	year
this	up	were	years
thought	us	what	you
three	use	when	your
through	used	where	
time	very	which	

Other Words That Will Help Us

ask	full	open	stop
ate	funny	pull	ten
black	fall	please	together
brown	far	round	try
blue	fast	red	those
buy	fly	run	thank
both	goes	ride	upon
bring	green	right	under
cut	grow	shall	walk
clean	hold	six	wash
call	hat	show	wish
carry	hurt	sleep	warm
drink	its	seven	why
done	jump	start	yellow
does	myself	sing	yes
draw	own	sit	

A word book or a card file of frequently used words are handy references for words that are used in certain situations.[3] These are usually created by the teacher after discussion with the children. Contents might include some of the following:

Days of Week

Sunday	Thursday
Monday	Friday
Tuesday	Saturday
Wednesday	

Months of the Year

January	March
February	April

Months of the Year

May	September
June	October
July	November
August	December

Sounds that Animals Make

quack	bow wow
mew	oink oink
cluck	whinny
moo	neigh
coo	

Kinds of Weather

foggy	rainy
cloudy	windy
sunny	hot
clear	cold

---

[3] Based upon seminar papers of Catherine Came, Eugene M. Fowler, and Horace McGee, San Diego State College, San Diego, Calif.

Places We Go on Trips

beach	zoo
mountains	harbor
museum	country
desert	farm

Special Words for:

tastes	feelings
color	action
smells	sights

Social Studies Unit Words
Words will vary according to unit.

Training the Five Senses—Play games that emphasize sensory response. Have a child do an act while the others listen. Then tell how it sounded. Such actions as: tap on the desk, tap on the window, drop a book, drum with two pencils, open a window, etc., are appropriate.

Next imagine that you are a bird that could fly anywhere. Tell what you hear and have the class guess where the bird is.

Close your eyes and picture something you saw at home this morning, on the way to school, etc. See if your words will help others see the same thing. The teacher or a student may ask questions until the complete image is visualized.

Match the beginning and ending of sentences such as these:

The door bell	tiptoed softly
The clock	screamed
Mother	hummed
The whistle	clanged
The fire alarm	whimpered
The baby	blew

3. *Standards*

Standards are designed to assist expression of ideas, not interfere with them. Yet we do not value a language anarchy. Security built on a knowledge of proper form will aid any writer.

Reminder Charts—Prior to writing, attention is called to certain skills previously used. These can be reviewed rapidly, then posted as a reminder while writing.

Capital Letters

Names start with capital letters.

Sally, Dick, Paul

Sentences start with capital letters.

See the cat.
Where are you going?

Since all writing involves handwriting skills, the quality practiced is important. Prior to a writing lesson, a five-minute review of handwriting standards with respect to formation of certain letters is valuable. This may involve chalkboard demonstrations by the pupils, an examination of small handwriting reference cards at each student's writing place, or a review of the letter forms usually posted over the blackboard. Second-grade children should know all the letter forms. Primary children should be helped with letters as needed, especially the capital letter forms.

A major use of standards is to direct proofreading of material. Children should not be expected to proofread for all errors. But they should check for certain specifics that have been taught. These would be appropriate:

Did I capitalize the words in my title?
Did I keep a margin?
Did I use my best writing?
Did I put only one line through words I wanted to change? (Prevents erasing or scribbling over a word.)

4. *Laboratory Writing Exercises*

Such activities as the writer's table are individual devices which frees the child from classroom pressures. At other times the guidance of the teacher is desirable as certain skills and understandings are practiced.

Group Composition—This helps to establish security among members of the class, gives the teacher an opportunity to prevent errors in spelling and usage, and builds good human relationships. Some children need this experience before they are able to organize and express themselves independently. Subjects for group composition can develop from a common experience or the social studies. The children contribute ideas which the teacher writes on the chalkboard. Later each child copies the product. Letters to a sick classmate, notes home about a program, or letters to another class are examples of group composition.

Staggered writing assignment—While the writing will frequently be done by the entire class a variation is to have only one group write. This makes it possible for the teacher to give more personal help, evaluate with greater care—since there are fewer papers—and to provide for the individual differences of a group. There is a competitive element in writing as well as reading. Those operating at approximately the same levels profit most by group instruction.

Classroom helpers—At times it will give recognition to a few and help others to appoint one student in each group who may give help with respect to spelling, punctuation, or other problems. Upper-grade children may be given recognition by permitting them to be "human dictionaries" in a lower grade during a writing period.

5. *Sharing the Written Compositions*

Use the sharing time at the beginning of the day to read some of the compositions.

Post compositions on the bulletin board.

Make a booklet such as "Our Halloween Stories."

Some authorities strongly recommend that the teacher or a parent type stories written by children correcting the major errors. This is done so that the self-image is developed and the child can write and has something to say. Lessons concerning errors are taught. There is much testimony that with confidence thus established the children improve with respect to error and expression.

Collect the written efforts in a folder, which is sent home after the parent conference.

Publish in a school newspaper those compositions that have special merit.

Exchange compositions with another class at the same level or a different one (appropriate at the end of a year).

6. *Improving the Composition Skills*

The teacher finds something to praise in each composition. "I like the way you used (a word)". "The ending is good."

But errors are noted as revealing instructional needs of children. The teacher then composes a story that reflects these errors or with the permission of a child uses one of the papers submitted. The problem is presented to the class as "How can we make this interesting paper better?"

The story is written on the board:

Spooky

Spooky was a ghost. He was a friendly ghost. He could be everything. But he could not float. He could not moan. He was a funny ghost. He was a happy ghost too.

After the story is read aloud, the class discusses the sentences and the possibility of joining some of them to make the story sound more interesting and flow more easily.

The class may practice on a written drill of this type:

Name_____

Date_____

Making Our Sentences Sound More Interesting

Make one sentence from these two short sentences:

1. Spooky was a ghost. He was a friendly ghost.

   _____

2. I have a ball. It is a red ball.

   _____

3. John has a pencil. It is green.

   _____

4. Mary is my friend. She is my best friend.

   _____

5. Jane threw the ball. She threw it to me.

   _____

6. This is my wagon. It is big.

   _____

7. I have a doll. She is pretty.

   _____

8. They have the blocks. There are six.

   _____

9. I like your story. It is a good story.

   _____

10. It is on the table. The table is large.

   _____

The children then look over their previous stories and change sentences. Other drills of the following nature may be used:

Name_____

Date_____

Make a sentence by drawing a line from a group of words in List A to a group of words in List B. Be sure they belong together.

	A	B
1.	The dog	me his book.
2.	The little boy	see the game.
3.	John gave	ate some ice cream.
4.	We went to	ran after the cat.
5.	I like	to read.

A	*B*
6. Mary is	you today.
7. The cat	over.
8. I saw	my friend.
9. The chair fell	kick ball.
10. They played	is white.

Name_____

Date_____

Write the words you need to finish each sentence. Choose them from the group of words below.

the red ball	ice cream and cake
We have	splashing down
I wish	three blocks to school
She went	four new dresses

1. I like_____.
2. _____three new girls now.
3. Every day I walk_____.
4. _____I had three dollars.
5. The rain came_____.
6. Mary has_____.
7. _____to the skating party.
8. We are going to have_____.

Paragraph Drills

Name_____

Date_____

Copy these sentences so they tell a story. When you decide which sentence to use first, be sure to indent the sentence. These sentences should make a one-paragraph story.

She ate their porridge and sat in their chairs.
They lived in the woods.
Once there were three bears.
A little girl came to their house.

_____

_____

_____

_____

_____

Name_____

Date_____

Write a paragraph about one of the following things. Then answer the questions below.

A Funny Animal	My Favorite Story
A Rainy Day	My Hobby

_____

_____

_____

_____

Did I write about one thing?	Yes	No
Did I start each sentence with a capital letter?	Yes	No
Did I indent the first word in my paragraph?	Yes	No

1. Why is it better to recognize the situations when a child wants to write than to use a device to motivate him to write? Indicate such a situation.

2. Miss Mauree Applegate broadcasts lessons on creative writing by radio to the rural schools of Wisconsin. Under the circumstances she cannot know each child, yet she inspires excellent writing. Can you explain this success?

3. How do you explain a literal-minded child who seems to have a very limited imagination?

4. Some say that there is a creative element in all writing. For some children writing their name is creative. Do you agree with this? How would you encourage other writing?

5. One of the objectives of the primary grades is to help the child distinguish fact from fantasy. Does creative writing contribute to this?

6. If possible, secure some of your own writing efforts while in grade school and compare it with material being written by children today.

HOW MAY CREATIVE WRITING BE FOSTERED IN THE INTERMEDIATE GRADES?

It takes more than a permissive classroom climate and a teacher interested in children to produce worthy written work in the intermediate classroom. First of all, writing takes time. If a teacher attempts to suggest a topic and have the child write something in a single language period, it means incomplete and hurriedly done papers. Creative writing is a questionable homework assignment. There is a suggestion of coercion in homework that will limit the creative expression of some children. While a child may willingly rework a piece of writing at home, the first draft should be completed under the teacher's supervision. There are a few self-motivated children who like to write, just as others like to study music or play ball. No restrictions should be placed on such children.

A three-day sequence provides adequate time for most writing endeavors. The first period should be used for the stimulation of ideas, discussion of various words and skills needed to develop a topic, and the experimental first drafts of the material. The second period should be a true writing laboratory with each child writing and receiving help as needed. The third day should be used to correct errors, reorganize material, and write the final copy. Some projects will take longer. This means that during the year less written composition may be done, but what is done will have purpose and merit.

The teaching sequence is that of motivation, skill development, refinement, and use. Motivation would involve any experience that started a flow of ideas. The discussion would help the student determine the thought he wishes to develop in his writing. Skill development would involve planned vocabulary materials, reviews of punctuation, writing and spelling skills, and help with organization of ideas.

Refinement would involve making corrections, proofreading and writing to improve content, form, usage, spelling, and handwriting. Use would be the recognition given the final product as it is read to the class, reproduced in a newspaper, placed on a bulletin board, or shared in a way appropriate to the content.

Just as storytelling pictures are used in the primary grades, so they may be used in the intermediate. Those with great human interest, such as the illustrations of Norman Rockwell, are especially good. But pictures expressing beauty, mood, and action are equally motivating. The class discusses two or three before making a choice to use as the basis for a story. The characters are discussed. The children are asked to imagine what is happening now, what happened previously, and what is likely to happen next. Words are selected that describe the action, beauty, or feeling. Possible titles are suggested and first lines written. During a second period the stories are written. Later, children may select pictures from magazines for the writing table or for additional stories.

After the imagination of children has been aroused it sometimes takes only a title to start them thinking of a story. Such titles as these may be put in a box on the writer's table to help some get started:

The Midnight Visitor
The Falling Star
The Hidden Valley
Lost in a Storm
An Animal Friend
A Secret
My Ambition
Flying at Night
Faster than Sound

A Joke on Me
The Dinner Bell
Still Waters

In a similar way, first-sentence starters help a writer get on his way:

"She's gone! Now I am going to find her diary," muttered John to himself as he crept up the stairs noiselessly.

John stood stock still. His legs refused to go. The sweat broke out on his forehead.

Bill walked to the window to let in a little air. As he began to raise it, something outside caught his eye. He stood with his mouth open. There on the lawn below the window was the strangest thing he had ever seen.

At first the noise was very faint and seemed far away. It was an odd noise, one that the boys didn't recognize. As it moved closer they went out to see what it might be.

Mary knew that if her mother found out, she wouldn't be able to sit for days, but she was determined to carry out her plan in spite of this.

The children were playing on the beach when they found the strange footprints in the sand. Their curiosity got the best of them and they decided to follow them along the shore.

"Quick, come here," called Tom, "I want to show you what I've found!" As the others ran to join him, they stopped short, staring in surprise.

When father came home that evening he was whistling happily. The children knew what that meant. He had another of his wonderful surprises.

There was a strange silence about the forest that night. It had an air of waiting for something to happen.

These may be put on cards and placed in an "idea box" to help those who seek ideas.

Some children need only a word to start a series of thoughts that lead to writing:

ghost
fog
gravy
my worst scare
nightmare
rolling waves
little, old lady
a bright idea
late again
mud
some luck
pride
rolling along
long journey
longest day of my life
face like a lion
time to think

The object of writing does not need to be a story. Frequently the purpose is to help children write with vividness and insight. The actual plotting of a story from beginning, characterization, episodes, climax and ending, may be too complex for many in the elementary school. It does not matter if the material be a story, report, autobiography, dramatic play or sketch. It does matter that the child is learning to express ideas in writing effectively.

Painting word pictures will interest students yet not demand the time that story writing involves. Ask the children what pictures the word makes them see. Then have them write a word picture. These are examples:

Variation on old themes will help some get started. What happened to Goldilocks on the next day? What did the three bears do at Christmas? What type of queen was Cinderella? Social studies may motivate historical writing in the form of a news account of such events as Columbus' discovery in the new world or the discovery of gold in California.

A "story formula" will challenge some. A good story has five parts: A beginning, a problem, a high point or climax, a following action or solution, and a satisfactory ending. This chart may be used to check the formula:

A. Does your story have a good beginning? Tell the four "W's": Who, When, Where, and What's the problem?
B. Did you make the reader aware of the problem?
C. Does your story reach a high point or climax?
D. Is there an adequate explanation of how the problem was solved?
E. Do all the parts fit together at the end in a way that satisfies the reader?

Five sentence stories may outline the plot of a story.

A. Mother and I were sitting in the kitchen after dinner one quiet evening.

snow	Snow, soft and cold and white, drifting lazily through the air, rested fluffily upon the boughs of the evergreen trees, and in time covered the earth with quiet beauty.
waves	Waves rolled endlessly toward the shore, crashing thunderously against the gray rocks and sending countless sprays of foam skyward.
airplanes	Airplanes roared down the runways, then effortlessly left the ground and soared majestically into the sky, soon becoming mere specks in the distance.

Objects will start a child's imagination working. One teacher brought in a bag of old shoes—a football shoe, a tennis slipper, a satin pump, etc. With such questions as who wore this shoe? where has it been? why was it thrown away? The class was motivated, and writing of a highly imaginative nature resulted.

B. Suddenly, we heard a scratching noise at the back door.
C. Mother screamed and jumped up on a chair as a gray mouse darted across the floor.
D. I stood there and laughed at the funny sight, while Mother recovered from terror.

E. I imagine the mouse was more frightened than Mother was.

Charts of this nature may be used as guides:

How Stories Begin

1. With conversation to set the stage for action.
2. With the end of the story then going back to the beginning.
3. With the middle of the story then to the actual beginning.
4. A characterization of the chief character or characters.
5. A summary paragraph to tell the point of the story.
6. With description.
7. With the time, place or circumstance.
8. With a question.

Describing Our Characters

1. Simple statement of fact: Bob is lazy.

2. By describing how Bob does things.
3. By telling an episode to prove that Bob is lazy.
4. By telling how little of his work is done.
5. By comparing him with others when lazy.
6. By using synonyms of the word.
7. By reporting what others say.
8. By telling what he is not.
9. By repeating his own characterization of himself.

Self-characterization is easier than describing another. A "Who Am I?" paper that may be read by the teacher while the class identifies the writer may be the beginning of character study.

Strange to say, some of the major interests of children do not lend themselves to creative writing. Baseball and other sports writing apparently calls for greater language power than that possessed by children. The same is true with respect to food. While this is a major interest, children find little inspiration for imaginative writing about the subject.

San Diego County Schools, Calif.

Using new words, imagining an experience, or reliving an event, brings delight to the writer as well as to those with whom the composition is shared.

A major effort in creative writing is directed toward the vocabulary necessary to present the desired thought. As the teacher reads aloud to the children, time is taken to note effective use of language. Sometimes this is done in association with a library book, at other times with examples of children's writing. Approval of vivid ways of saying things sharpens awareness of words and reveals new areas for exploration.

Some children, by virtue of personality, of home, or early school training are alert to the details of the world in which they live; others need help in the development of all five senses. These children must be encouraged to find pleasure in observation and in the discussion of what they see.

It is easy to start an enthusiastic discussion concerning the flavor of certain foods. It's fun, too, to put into words the taste of cod-liver oil, an uncured olive, or a mouthful of the Pacific Ocean. Children soon discover that following one's nose may be an interesting experience leading to the earthy smell of recently turned sod, the tang of the sea, the fragrance of clean linen just off the line, the musty odor of old newspapers stored in the garage.

Vocabulary is increased and power of expression heightened when pupils are helped to see the importance of contrasting words and ideas. They will enjoy trying it, too.

quietness of the forest

> vs. *clang of the city streets*

smooth as the snow-
covered lawn

> vs. *rough and jagged*
> *as the ice on*
> *the pond*

Children are easily helped to understand that whole sentences can be built to reflect contrasting ideas that will best express their own feelings:

The forest was dim. Billy thought of the meadow near his home where a sparkling brook with little minnows rushed down mossy rocks in warm sunshine.

Children enjoy the euphony of a sentence or line in which the same first letter or sound in a group of words is repeated a number of times. Alliteration can become stilted when it is used as a mechanical exercise. With older children it should be encouraged not as a game, but to enhance the meaning of words.

soft slumbering summer
lonely leaf
nodding noon
whispering wind
weird white world

Young children use similes naturally and easily. Although they may not label them as such, older children use metaphors in the same manner. Comparison is a natural method of description for young and old alike. Children enjoy completing these phrases:

as soft as
as loud as
as happy as
as sad as
as stern as
as drowsy as
as bright as
as cold as
as hot as
as muffled as
as slippery as
as long as
as short as
as pointed as

They become conscious of the use of similes in writing about things that "looked like" or were "as gentle as." One class found that the wind today "was as gentle as":

a lamb
my mother's voice
God's voice
a soft, furry cloud
a rose opening
when night falls

Tactile perception can be used to enrich children's writing. Various objects can be passed among the children and their reactions written on the board. One teacher passed a bowl of ice cubes. In seeking to express their reaction, the children sought and found many words to describe what they had touched. Ice is:

> cold
> slippery
> smooth
> hard
> sharp
> shivery

The teacher can use a small figure or figurine, holding it up and asking the class to look at it closely. Then put the figurine behind something. The teacher now asks the class to describe what was seen. The teacher can pretend she has never seen the object, so that she can be very curious about the responses, encouraging accurate, descriptive analysis. After the first attempt, the class tries again, looks at object once more, develops vocabulary to explain, and goes through the entire process. The same thing can be tried with a second object—all responses being verbal. On the third try, using a new object, the class can try writing a description.

After preliminary work on developing "word pictures," the teacher can put three sentences on the board, such as:

> An airplane went up.
> It flew.
> It came down.

The class can be encouraged to develop a more interesting and exciting picture of the situation. Use of action words and descriptive words can be included orally. As a real picture begins to form, children can appreciate the power of such words as "soared," "skimmed," "floated," etc.

As a written work experience, children can take another set of three sentences and see how well they can paint another word picture:

> The wind blew.
> The windows shook.
> The storm came.

Ask the children what pictures the word makes them see. Then let them write a word picture.

RAIN

Rain splashed upon the earth, forming puddles on the ground, pelting against the windows, and dripping endlessly from the eaves of the buildings.

WAVES

Waves rolled shoreward in long unbroken lines, each crest forming for an instant a magic crown of transparent green before toppling over into a churning mass of yellow-white foam.

Children are amused by their first encounter with metaphors. Their practical minds create laugh-provoking pictures when they read such statements as "His eyes dropped," "She turned green with envy," "He put his foot in his mouth," "The doctor was tied up," "Someone spilled the beans." Cartoons can be made to accompany metaphors.

Teach shades of meaning by mounting pictures of increasing size on deepening shades of colored paper. Blow "word bubbles" to get synonyms. Start each row with a word, such as *went, pretty, small,* or *old.* Let children blow their bubbles larger by giving synonyms for each word.

While use of a thesaurus is beyond the ability of most children, it does help to make a "classroom thesaurus" of words to use instead of *said, funny, beautiful,* and other overused words. The study of words separated from the situation where children would use them is an isolated and usually ineffective learning situation. Meaningful exercises of this nature, however, are helpful after the need for adequate vocabulary is felt by a writer.[4]

---

[4] San Diego City Schools, *Oral and Written Language* (1956), with special acknowledgment to Elizabeth Stocker.

To the Pupil:

Life would be pretty dull if we ate the same foods at every meal, or played the same game every day. Life would be equally dull if we said and heard the same words all the time. We need to know enough words so that we don't wear out the same old, tired ones. We can give words a rest by using synonyms. Synonyms are words which have almost the same meaning, like little, small, and tiny.

1. Do you know a word to use in place of "big"? _____

2. Do you know another word which is a synonym for "big"? _____

3. Use your dictionary to help you find three more synonyms for "big."

_____   _____   _____

4. In the exercise below, *circle* the three words that have meanings somewhat alike. Choose the best word to *fill the space* in the sentence. Use your dictionary to help you.

space   distance
expanse   praise   New York is a long_____
place   install   from here.

deposit   plan
crack   split   I will _____ my money in the bank.
break   build   There was a _____ in the plaster.

5. You can find synonyms for these words in the box below. *Write* the correct synonym on the line beside each word. *Check* by using your dictionary.

pair _____   doze _____
jammed _____   funny _____
coast _____   pretty _____
coarse _____   strange _____

nap	lovely	amusing	odd
crowded	shore	couple	rough

To the Pupil:

One day during sharing period Terence told the class this story about his trip to the circus:

"The girl did stunts. Everything she did, the clown tried to do, too. The girl was graceful, but the clown—well, the clown wasn't graceful."

Terence needed a word to tell the opposite meaning of "graceful." He could have used "awkward" or "clumsy," but he just couldn't think of these words. Words which are opposite in meaning to other words are called *antonyms*. To speak and write better we need to know many antonyms.

Circle the word that means the opposite, or almost the opposite, of the first word in each line:

leave	play	sleep	stay
attempt	attach	try	wish
powerful	different	homeless	weak
great	small	large	buff
scarce	plentiful	first	thin
most	least	soft	sweet
expensive	late	next	cheap
damp	clean	strong	dry
good	right	bad	ready
give	grow	take	go

To the Pupil:

Think of the word "apple." Does this word do something to you? Now think of "the juicy, red apple." These added words which tell about the apple make us think about the delicious taste of this fruit. When we describe or tell about something we can make it much more interesting by using words which make our listeners or readers see, hear, touch, taste or smell.

Write a word in the blank in front of each word below which will help to describe that word.

    1. the _____ car (see)
    2. the _____ motor (sound)
    3. the _____ flowers (smell)
    4. the _____ pie (taste)
    5. the _____ satin cloth (touch)

Use these describing words to write in the sentences below:

        howling   rough   sour   pungent   glittering

    1. The _____ floor scratched his feet.
    2. The sky was sprinkled with _____ stars.
    3. Pine needles have a _____ odor.
    4. The _____ dog kept some people awake.
    5. She had a _____ pickle in her lunch box.

To the Pupil:

When we write or speak we paint word pictures in the minds of readers and listeners. These word pictures can be simple black-and-white drawings or they can be wide-screen, 3-D, technicolor, action movies. Compare these two sentences:

1. The fire engine stopped in front of the burning house.
2. Siren screaming and tires screeching, the bright red fire engine braked to a halt in front of the blazing building.

Which sentence painted a better word picture for you? Now see if you can rewrite the following sentences. Make them paint better pictures.

1. John was doing tricks on his bicycle.

_____

_____

2. Susan was playing with her dolls.

_____

_____

3. Bob hit a home run.

_____

_____

4. The girl was wearing a red dress.

_____

_____

5. The horse jumped over the fence.

_____

_____

To the Pupil:

Sometimes we can't think of a good describing word when we need it. One boy discovered a way to help him think of these words. When he thought of a good word, he would write it in a special notebook he kept for this purpose.

See if you can find words to put under the headings below:

Sight	*Sound*	*Taste*
dim	harsh	sweet
bright	rumbling	bitter

_____	_____	_____
_____	_____	_____
_____	_____	_____
_____	_____	_____
_____	_____	_____

Touch	Smell	Color
soft	sweet	rosy
smooth	sharp	dark
_____	_____	_____
_____	_____	_____
_____	_____	_____
_____	_____	_____

You may want to list words under other headings, such as "Action Words" or "Cheerful Words" or "Sad Words." Now you have a good start on a word notebook.

Proofreading and rewriting are aspects of the refinement of ideas. The fact that the first effort to write is a rough draft of ideas or an experiment with ideas needs to be established with children as early as the fourth grade. Because rewriting a long selection can be a burden at this level, the short episode, the humorous incident, the descriptive paragraph or the news item, should be the writing objective.

Standards for proofreading should be established one at a time. These would reflect the language skills being taught at the grade level involved in writing. These items would be appropriate for the fifth grade.

Proofreading My Story

1. Is my paper headed correctly?
2. Did I skip a line after my heading?
3. Did I capitalize the important words in the title?
4. Did I skip a line before I began to write my story?
5. Did I indent for each paragraph?
6. Do I have a margin?
7. Is each word spelled correctly?
8. Is each sentence complete? Did I omit words?
9. Have I a period or question mark after each sentence?
10. Did I include the important points in my story? Did I tell my story in sequence?

A class may be organized so that each writer has an editing partner. This partner then edits the paper. This report is submitted with the original and rewritten paper.

Proofreading

1. Did this person indent?
2. Did this person watch his margin?
3. Have they checked their spelling?
4. Did they use capitals when they were needed?
5. Is this paper neat?
6. Does this person know when to end a sentence and begin a new one?
7. Has this person used too many "ands"?
8. Do you feel this person checked his paper when it was finished?

I checked _____ paper.

My name is _____

Lessons in proofreading should be included in the language period. Exercises of this nature emphasize the skills of proofreading.

Proofread the following story:
Does each sentence start with a capital letter? (There should be twelve sentences.)
Are all the words correctly spelled? (There are five misspelled words.)
Do all the sentences tell about the topic? (There is one that does not belong.)
Are the paragraphs indented?

Once upon a time there lived a boy named Timothy he lived with his mother and father. Once when his father was outside getting water the Indians came along and burned the house.

Only Timothy was alive and then he ran to the mountains and stayed there for five days. Timothy and his famly came from Ohio.

On the fifth day he saw a nest on a rockey cliffth. In the nest he saw a baby eagle. The mother eagle had been shot with an arrow. He took the baby eagle for a pet. Timothy and the eagle grew up in the forrest. They ate together and slept together. They had no famly but they were not alone.

Displays of work "Before Proofreading" and "After Proofreading" will emphasize the improvement possible. A committee of proofreaders can serve the class. Three students are assigned the task of proofreading stories placed in a box at the reading table. When their work is completed the work is placed in a "rewrite" box. Some children who are less imaginative than others are good proofreaders. Of course, the more able students are most helpful at this task. After a visit to a newspaper, the position and role of editor can be dramatized in this way.

Classroom recognition can be given to children's writing in several ways. One school makes a scrapbook of "Our Very Best Writing." When the class feels that something is worthy for this collection the material is added. At the end of the year this is presented to the principal. Scrapbooks made in former years are available on certain occasions.

Children enjoy reading something written by an older brother or sister. Older children are impressed with material they wrote while in a lower grade. Eventually it may be possible for a child to read material written by one of his parents when the parent was in the fifth grade. The teacher must plan so that the best product of each individual is included and that no one is left out. During the year a child might substitute a new selection for one that had been previously selected.

Bulletin boards of children's writing provide recognition and encouragement. Some schools have strict rules about the display of imperfect papers. In light of the objectives of creative writing, it seems that a paper with a few errors checked is still worthy of display. Few children are going to find pleasure in rewriting an entire paper just to have it placed on the bulletin board.

Publication in a school paper or magazine is the ultimate recognition or use for many. Creative writing is not news writing and as such must have a special place in any publication. Many school systems now publish an annual magazine of creative writing. When a selection is considered worthy it is sent to an editing committee. This committee acknowledges the selection with a letter of recognition explaining that the work will be considered, but that not all material submitted will be used. The letter is adequate recognition for many children. If a child's material is selected for the magazine he receives three copies of the publication and another letter. The existence of such a publication influences many teachers to attempt projects involving creative writing who ordinarily would be more secure stressing drill on the mechanics of language.

Perhaps the most important idea that those who work with children in the area of creative or imaginative writing have found to be true is one of the utmost simplicity. You cannot teach children to write creatively—you can only help them express the original ideas within them. Behind the story, poem, or letter—behind the clear, concise sentence or the stumbling search for words—is the child and all that he can become. Creative writing is one more way to understand him.

1. Alvina Burrows reports in the N.E.A. Bulletin No. 18, "Certain procedures have not stood up to the testing of research. Among these are encouraging children to plan stories before they write, checking the mechanics as they write, experimenting with words for the sake of using 'colorful' or 'different' ones, studying vocabulary lists, writing for school newspapers, and requiring self-evalaution of writing." Why do you think some of these have proven unsuccessful?

2. Some years ago it was popular to have "picture study" in the language arts. Small reproductions of great paintings were

made available for each child. Do you think the same idea might work as a stimulation of creative expression?

3. Few children will ever become authors or even reporters. Do you feel, therefore, that a greater effort should be made in the area of practical writing than in creative writing?

HOW MAY THE WRITING OF POETRY BE FOSTERED?

A teacher is an artist at releasing the arts and abilities in others. Truly creative writing cannot be taught; it can only be released and guided. If we see our task as releasing and guiding poetic expression there are certain conditions that must be established. First, there must be a climate in which creative effort is fostered. This can be done by pointing out that certain expressions used by children are imaginative and contain poetic ideas. One day a child mentioned that the sun seemed to be playing peek-a-boo as it hid behind a cloud, then shone again. A comment that this would make a good poem may be enough to get the individual to write. A quiet place to write, away from the group, is another aspect of climate. Then when such expressions emerge the teacher might ask, "Would you like to go to the writing table and write a poem now while the idea is fresh?" A part of the climate in a room is represented by things valued. The fact that the teacher uses a poem as a central theme for a bulletin board, reads poems to the class with personal enjoyment or sends a notice home in verse form makes poetry have significance. Second, the teacher provides stimulations that motivate the writer to get started. Sometimes these dramatize a feeling. One student teacher played a recording of a choir singing "The Battle Hymn of the Republic" then asked, "How would you express your thoughts if asked what the United States means to you?" One verse written under these conditions won a national award. Holidays act as punctuation marks in the humdrum repetition of living. Someone has said that one trouble with life was that it was "so dog-gone daily." When we make some days have special feeling in them it provides all of us with a bit of variety. Halloween,

Thanksgiving, Valentine's Day, Mother's Day and birthdays have emotional associations that stimulate writing.

In addition to a classroom climate that enhances poetry appreciation and personal motivation, the teacher releases creative talents by providing specific writing aids. This includes help with the mechanics of writing and spelling, the development of a vocabulary that expresses the right shade of meaning, and the understanding of poetic form. Before the children write Halloween poetry the class might discuss possible words to use. These would include *ghost, witch, haunting, creeping, scare, afraid*. With older children a rhyming dictionary is a great help. Occasionally after a poem has been enjoyed by the group, take time to look at it as one craftsman admires the work of another. The poem "Trees" can be studied in this way without diminishing its beauty. Notice the rhyme pattern. Then discuss the use of words. Why is "lovely" better than "pretty" in the second line? What image did the writer create by using the words "a nest of robins in her hair" and "lifts her leafy arms to pray"? Ask the group to think of similar images such as "finger chimneys pointing toward the sky" or "little cars pouting in the parking lot."

A combination of words and ideas must be brought together in order to create a poem. No one would deny that some children are more talented with respect to words and ideas than others, but at the same time it seems apparent that all children should be able to achieve this combination to a degree. It would logically follow that the greater the command a child has over words and the more original or varied his ideas, the better would be the quality of the poetry created.

The temptation, then, would be to set up a series of lessons designed to build vocabulary and extend ideas. Before doing so it is well to consider the influence of patterns on creativity. Suppose we set up a series of exercises like this:

1. See the cat
   It wears a _____.
2. I have a bill
   It is from the _____.
3. This boy is tall
   He must be _____.
4. This girl is late
   She must be _____.

It would appear that the child *completed* a rhyme, but did he *create* one? At best he learned a small element of the poet's craft concerning words that rhyme.

Another type of exercise provides an idea in the form of a picture. Usually these are of nursery rhymes. One might be of Jack and Jill, another of Jack Be Nimble or Mistress Mary. Here again the emphasis is not on creativity but on the pleasure of repeating familiar rhyme forms. Still another exercise provides lists of words that rhyme:

day	nice
hay	spice
old	mice
told	ice
ball	sail
tall	mail
wall	pail
all	whale
kitten	tree
mitten	see
bitten	free
written	bee

A suggested verse is given:

> I threw a ball
> High over the wall
> And a boy named Jack
> Threw it right back.

While this is patterned, there is the possibility for a bit of original thinking and the satisfaction of completing a verse. Certainly the rhyme words influenced the idea. Instead of starting with a feeling or something to say, the child was assigned the task of manipulating the words of others. The results have little more emotional appeal than the original list of rhyming words.

Creativity from a child's point of view might be thought of as a personal interpretation of experience. The child might ask "What do certain sounds or sights mean to me? How do I feel when I see or do something? What words can I use that will help others recreate my feelings?"

One group of first-grade children were asked to think of their favorite sounds. The following responses were typical:

> The sound of nice music.
> The sound of the recess bell.

But these were more personal and possibly more creative:

> The sounds my mother makes in the kitchen getting supper ready.
> The sound of the slamming of the car door when my daddy comes home from work.

One of the charming books for and by children is a book of definitions of young children. The title is one of the definitions: *A hole is to dig.*[5] The definition of a principal is an appealing one: "A principal is to pull out splinters."

A third-grade class was fascinated by this book and decided to make some definitions of their own. "A desk is to clean up." "A penny is to lose." They were delighted when the comic strip, "Peanuts," came up with: "Happiness is an A in spelling."

These definitions have the novelty of being functional rather than being descriptive. As a result there is an unexpected quality about them that lends charm to the language. These are probably not poetry, but poetic expression often has this element in it.

From the beginning it would be well to share with children both poetry with and without rhyme patterns. Help them discover the beauty or fun of an idea or word picture in a verse as well as the song

---

[5] Ruth Krause, *A Hole Is to Dig* (New York: Harper, 1952).

of rhyme. "Fog" by Carl Sandburg is a good illustration of poems without rhyme.

I do not want this to sound too complex to a beginning teacher. The caution with regard to patterns and their influence on creativity is only that there are some who would be more harsh in their criticism of this type of procedure. If you can proceed in no other way, then my suggestion is to use the devices you wish. I shall never forget a boy in a rural school I visited as a supervisor who finally completed this verse:

I know a boy whose name is Jack
His horse went away and never came back
So now he rides to school on the bus
And is no better than the rest of us.

I praised his effort and in good school teacher manner asked him to write it over in his best handwriting. The next week I had forgotten, but not Jack. There was the verse ready for me and another verse about "going to town and getting a coat that was brown." This continued throughout the year. Never did Jack produce a poem that is the type teachers send in to be published. But what he did produce made life more interesting and satisfying for him. I suspect that one reason teachers get discouraged about writing poetry in the classroom is that most of the products equal Jack's. As we consider the technique of writing poetry, it might be well to think how some of these suggestions might have helped a boy like Jack.

A type of pattern which is free from emphasis in rhyme would be of this nature:

SPRING MUSIC

Spring is a singing time,
Birds sing in the trees,

. . . .

And I sing too.

THE FEEL OF THINGS

I like the feel of things,
The softness of pussy willows,
The smoothness of velvet,

. . . . .

. . . . .

I like the feel of things.

Children sense the meter of poetry and eventually will want to write with this in mind. The teacher might put a line on the board and have the class count the beats one would hear if each syllable had equal emphasis.

The man in the moon looked down

— —— — —   — —

Then the class experiments with lines like the following and decides which sounds best:

Upon the sleeping little town.
Upon the laughing happy clown.
To see the children gay and brown
To see that snow had fallen over hill and town.

Then they take some words they know and note how these words have similar points of emphasis:

altogether	player
manufacture	remember
tangerine	suggestion
doorkeeper	happiness
pleasant	

This can be changed with the usual markings for accented and unaccented syllables in poetry:

altogether becomes __ __ __′ __
remember becomes __ __′ __

Then note that when some poetry is written some words are as unaccented syllables. If you say the words *ta* for unaccented and *tum* for the accented syllable you can note the meter of a poem.

Then the little Hiawatha (or *tum ta tum ta tum ta tum ta*)
Said unto the old Nakomis
All the hills are edged with valleys

Writing words for songs emphasizes meter. One student teacher interested a group of below average sixth-grade children in writing by using Calypso music. After explaining that the singer made up his song as he went along, the class tried to write "songs." These were the results:

I got a donkey he's a big and fat,
He sits on a pillow and the pillow goes flat.
My donkey, he's a good for nothing beast
Cause he takes all my food for his Sunday feast.

—MAXINE

One class listened to a recorded reading of translations of famous Japanese Haiku. The idea of suggestion, emphasized in the last line and imagery were captured by the Alaskan children who wrote these: [6]

> The boy turned to me
> And he smiled with a cute grin.
> I did the same thing.

> Big Indian Chief
> You are brave but very dumb.
> Let people rule too!

> I hate dogs a lot.
> They bark when someone walks by,
> Especially me.

> I left Alaska, but on the way
> I saw purple mountains
> And turned back.

> A cry is heard. All is still
> A pack of wolves
> Has made its kill. . . . Silence.

> The morning sun
> Chasing night shadows
> Across the awakening world.

The pattern of a Haiku poem consists of three lines, the first having five syllables, the second line seven, and the third line five. Since the syllable in English differs from the Japanese it is not always possible to follow this pattern.

"Cinquains" gain much of the same effect in English. The first line has five words and each succeeding line one less:

> *The white waves bite at*
> *the sandy ocean shore*
> *like a hungry*
> *child eating*
> *cookies.*

or starting with only four words, one gets this result:

> *The empty house stands*
> *among dead grass*
> *lonely and*
> *still.*

Rather than have children start with such a complex task as writing verses about

how they feel or things they saw, some teachers prefer to start with group composition.

A second-grade teacher once asked her children to think of quiet things. As each child made a suggestion she wrote it on the chalkboard. This was the result: [7]

> As quiet as snow falling
> As quiet as buttter melting
> As quiet as a cloud in the sky
> As quiet as a kitten
> As soap bubbles
> A tree growing
> Santa Claus coming
> As quiet as you and I

The children knew that they had created a mood because of the hush in the room. Such experiences can be a step toward individual effort.

A method of group poetry that will give everyone a sense of participation is the word stimulus method. The teacher asks the pupils to get ready for a surprise. First assure the children that this is not a test and that the papers will be ungraded.

"I am going to tell you a word," the teacher continues, "and you are to write the picture that comes to your mind. You may tell what you see, hear, feel or imagine. Just tell me the picture that you see in your imagination. Spell as well as you can, we will get the exact spelling later." Then she gives a word like rain, sunshine, baby, wind, spring, or night.

After the children have finished writing, the papers are collected. Now these individual efforts are assembled into a group poem. This is called a mosaic poem because, like a mosaic painting, it is made from many parts. First the closely related ideas are grouped. One stanza might contain those about gentle rain, another about violent storms, another about the blessings of rain. These are put together with some rearrangement of word order but with no effort to have rhyme. Then the class usually has to add several lines at the bottom that create a conclusion.

The following account by Samuel Gilburt, Principal of The William J. Mor-

[6] Edna B. Garberg, Hunter School, Fairbanks, Alaska.

[7] Based on an experience of Eileen Birch, Campus Laboratory School, San Diego State College, San Diego, Calif.

rison Junior High School, Brooklyn, New York, gives this interesting account of group poetry with older children: [8]

When I use the *cooperative technique* in the classroom, I devote the first lesson to the playing of records. I select songs with strong rhythmic undertones such as *"Surrey With the Fringe on Top"* from *Oklahoma!;* Burl Ives' *"Rock Candy Mountain";* an American folk dance, "Golden Slippers." I encourage the pupils to tap out the rhythm with fingers or to clap. It is rough on the teacher's nervous system sometimes, but I have an aim. It does relax the class. They "let go" inwardly and become much more receptive.

I follow up with Vachel Lindsay's "Congo," Masefield's "Sea Fever," and Kipling's "Boots." These are records supplied by the National Council of Teachers of English with readings superbly done by Norman Corwin. As "Boots" is played, I ask for volunteers to march up and down the aisles in rhythm to the poem. The dullest pupil in the class eventually is aroused to a sensitivity to rhythm and thus grasps the simplest aspect of poetry. Now he is ready to feel and enjoy rhythm, and I suggest he try marching.

I follow up with recordings of Tennyson's "Break, Break, Break," Browning's "Boot and Saddle," and Lanier's "Song of the Chattahoochee."

In ensuing lessons, I read in my best orotund manner: "Casey at the Bat," "The Charge of the Light Brigade," or Poe's "The Bells." "The Barrel-Organ" by Noyes and Psalms XXIV and XLVI are rendreed by the class chorally. Poetry was meant to be read aloud and heard.

We talk about rhythm in nature—the seasons, night and day. The pupils tell me about rhythm in "boogie-woogie" and "be-bop." They bring in their own records and favorite poems. Edgar Guest gets a square deal in my room.

I explain that poetry is far from "sissy stuff." John Masefield was a tough sailor. Joyce Kilmer and Rupert Brook were top-notch soldiers. Sandburg was a truck-driver. We chat about crowbars and steel spikes and we study "Prayers of Steel." I play Corwin's reading of "Fog" and "Lost," and the class reads with him, softly and lingeringly, absorbing the mood and sound pictures.

We play and sing "Trees," "Road to

Mandalay," "Drink to Me Only With Thine Eyes." The class understands by now that songs are poems put to music. We even discuss popular songs and decide whether the lyrics are good or bad. The pupils gradually develop yardsticks of judgment. They select any one poem they enjoyed most for memory purposes.

Throughout, I emphasize the fun, the enjoyment, the movement and the zest of poetry. The feeling for poetry is caught—not taught. The rhythmic exercises, the choral reading, the musical aspects all make for an emotional climate of relaxed interest. These emotional tones, frequently repeated, are associated with poetry and should be retained by the pupil.

By now, the class is eating out of my hand and I come to cooperative writing.

I have had functioning all along in connection with an integrated unit on descriptive writing, a smell committee, a sound committee, a taste committee, etc., who had been compiling actual advertisements from magazines that best reflected these senses in writing. I read Morley's "Smells" or "Swift Things are Beautiful" by Elizabeth Coatsworth and then invite each pupil to write but *one similar line* on the subject of "Noises." In a few minutes I call on the pupils to read their lines. The class either accepts the line as good, or suggests improvements such as a more picturesque word or phrase. As each pupil's line is accepted, the pupil goes up to the board and proudly writes his line.

A volunteer is alerted to write a brief introduction, another to write a concluding stanza while the class is still working on the body of the class poem. The poem that follows was turned out in one forty-five-minute period, with a supervisor observing the lesson. We were caught a little short by the bell, hence the weak ending which was not polished up, marring an otherwise interesting piece of work by a normal eighth-grade class.

NOISES WE LIKE

Most people hate noises,
But a few like them indeed,
Howling, screaming, clicking,
Crying, laughing, walking
These noises some people need.
These be noises one class likes!
The crack of the bat on the first day of spring,
The click of the camera shutter,
The scratch of a pen when writing to a friend,
My dog's bark when he comes to meet me,

[8] S. G. Gilburt, "Cooperative Poetry— A Creative Project," *Language Arts News* (Boston: Allyn, Fall 1957).

The breaking of Rockaway waves at the beach,
The ticking of a clock old and dear,
The beating of drums at a parade,
The tap-tapping of a long wanted typewriter,
The backfiring of a car and the shot of a gun,
The clatter of hoof-beats in the city's streets,
The hoot of a train whistle coming round the
bend,
The crunching of a dollar and the jingling of
a coin,
The light pitter-pat of the rain against the
pane,
The chitter-chatter of people in the street,
The gurgle of a baby in the cradle,
The chirp of the sparrows around a crust of
bread,
The thump of my heart at report card time,
Roller skates whizzing along pavement streets,
The sound of electricity when I comb my
hair,
The crashing and slashing of lightning to
earth,
The hiss of a radiator on a cold winter day,
The crackling of an autumn bonfire,
The moo of cows grazing in the field,
The words of a baby who has just begun to
talk,
The dancing ivory under the fingers of a
"boogie" player.
Hundreds of other noises
Can be acclaimed
But hundreds of others
Cannot possibly be named.

Meanings experienced through poetry call for personal and individual responses. The deep feeling that one person senses in a sentence may be missed by another. We do not seek to have children write a verse in order to please the teacher, to get a good grade, or to participate in a program. Our purpose is to help children discover in poetry some inner satisfaction that is an intimate personal experience. In one fifth-grade room in which a creative climate had been established, a student went to the writer's table and after about fifteen minutes produced the following poem: [9]

A QUESTION TO GOD

When did the first tree start to grow?
When did the first breeze sing so low?
When did the first bird spread his wings?
When was the start of everything?

[9] Reported by Margaret Brydegaard, Fifth Grade Supervisor, Campus Laboratory School, San Diego State College, San Diego, Calif.

When did the first little humming bird hum?
When did the first little creek start to run?
When did the first snow start to fall?
When did the first little cricket call?

When did the first star light the night?
When did the first flower come into sight?
When did the first sunset glow?
When did the first little thing grow?

Oh God, when was the first faintest sound?
When was the beautiful earth made round?
Even though we may never know,
I thank you God, for things made so.
—SUSAN TUCKER

The children in the class recognized that this was a superior poem. Some would have stopped writing because they may have felt unequal to creating material of this quality. Instead of establishing the poem as a standard, the child was praised and honored—much as we praise outstanding musical or athletic talent.

Deserved praise is an important aspect of encouraging children to write. Expect them to present a tremendous range of quality but encourage each child as he creates at his appropriate level.

An equally important aspect is time to write. Providing a quiet time during the course of the week when children may choose to write or read will reward the teacher with worthy contributions. Occasionally this time has to be scheduled, but often it will have to be taken from some other activity. Sometimes the weather is a deciding factor. During a winter snow when the flakes are sinking slowly to earth, or just after a spring rain when every object appears clean-washed, would be excellent occasions for such work. The teacher might say, "Let's have a quiet period now. You may read or write. We will tune in on thirty minutes of silence."

Children like to write poetry in areas that have emotional appeal. Here are some examples:

1. Gripes and Protests

To THE BOY THAT SITS IN FRONT OF ME

You think that you are funny
You think that you're the best

You think that you're a honey
While you're really just a pest.

In arithmetic you're terrible
In reading you're a dunce
And when you talk the teacher must
Remind you more than once!
                    —MERRY LEE TASH, GRADE 5

HOBBIES

They tell me that a hobby
Is to help us make the day
To seem a little shorter
And to pass the time away.

But our teachers seem to think
That we have nothing else to do
But to get one of these hobbies
And then write about it too.

They load us up with homework
And then they go and say,
"Children, you need a hobby
To pass the time away."

"Get yourself a hobby"
That's what the teacher said,
Dear teacher, we need hobbies
Like we need holes in the head.

So when we turn in papers
That don't quite meet perfection—
Don't be angry when we say,
"We are building our collection."
                    MERRY LEE TASH—GRADE 7

POEMS

We're supposed to write a poem for school
But at writing poems I'm a great big fool
Oh! What will I do, Oh Golly Gee
Teacher's going to give me a D.
                    MERRY LEE TASH—AGE 9

2. Personal Experiences

AFTER SCHOOL

I'm staying after school again.
This is an awful mess;
I might as well get down to work
'Til I can leave I guess,
Let's see, arithmetic's all done,
And so is reading work,
(Just think ME staying after school!

I sure feel like a jerk.)
I could improve my writing,
Oh no, I'd just hate that,
If I could just get out of here
I'd gladly eat my hat,
I guess it's just what I deserve
For acting like a fool,
But you won't catch me here again
Staying after school!
                    —SILAS, GRADE 6

COOKIES

Measure
  Sift
    Beat
Cut
  Cook
    Eat.
                    —VERNON, FIRST GRADE (DICTATED)

3. Wonders

GRASS

Green and soft and sweet,
Grass is glistening

Lying on warm grass
I feel relaxed and lazy

With an ant's small size
Grass is probably a kind of jungle.
                    —JANE, AGE 10

4. "If I Were" Poems or Flights of Imagination

If I were a star on the top of the tree,
On Christmas night, here's what I'd see:

Angels and candles, tinsel and balls,
Bright lights and bells and Santa Claus;
Popcorn and long red cranberry strings,
Chains of paper—both red and green.

And if I look closely—I'll take my chances—
I see tiny packages tied to the branches.

Around the tree, all over the floor
Are lots of packages—and there's more—
A train, a bike, a doll, a bat,
A DOG? A puppy—imagine that!!

5. *Special Days*

DEAR MOM

Long years ago, someone decided
That the second Sunday in the month of May,
Should be a day for the women.
Who have taught and guided
Their children. Yes, a Mother's Day!
In return for years of dedication
And love and devotion that has never abated;
One day set apart for the mom's of the nation
To show them that they are appreciated.

The gift we give you is modest indeed,
But with this gift is planted the seed
Of a prayer of hope for this family
To spend the next year in harmony.

For all of us know that there is no other
To take the place of you, our mother.
                    MERRY LEE TASH—GRADE 8

There are others: wishes, surprises, questions, poems "to my doll or dog." But there is one more that should receive special consideration. Sometimes we forget that each child must discover anew the wonders of our world. It is a stimulating experience to watch a group of city boys and girls discovering the beauties of the outdoors in a summer camp. I watched a camp director lead a group that rediscovered the place where the Indians long ago had obtained the clay they used in pottery making. Then as the group rested he asked them to be still and notice what was happening around them. Imaginations were filled with Indians, of course, but these boys and girls looked at the trees, the brook, the clay bank, the birds and squirrels in a new way. Then the leaders asked them how they might share this experience with others. Some sketched the scene, others wrote descriptive letters, but many wrote poems.

The following situation reveals a similar experience of a boy rediscovering the familiar:

HAVE YOU EVER SAT ON THE SHORE OF A HARBOR?

Have you ever sat on the shore of a harbor
And watched the seagulls play?

It's really very interesting
More fun than studying, I'd say.

Have you ever sat on the shore of a harbor
And watched the freighters sway,
Then listened to their whistles
And watched them sail away?
Have you ever sat on the shore of a harbor
And listened to a fog-horn blow,
And wondered where the fog came from
And when and where it will go?

Have you ever watched the sun go down
And have you seen the waves roll in,
Then have you ever wondered,
"When did this all begin?"
                    —BROOKE, GRADE 7

If we accept as our responsibility the releasing of the talents and abilities of the students, there are some teaching practices which should be considered. One does not put a grade on a poem created by a child. Even an evaluative remark such as "Very Good" is not appropriate. It would be much more helpful to the writer to receive guidance and encouragement in other ways. A comment such as "What a novel idea. I never would have thought of that!" or "I can *feel* the snow" indicates the response that a creative talent needs. But young talent will welcome help as well, "instead of *flat* what do you think of the word *level?*" or, "try *inviting* in place of *nice.*"

Praise is powerful if it causes continuous growth. Point out the strength of a creative effort. At first teachers are so pleased to get any completed work that a low level of expectancy can be established by over praise. The expressions "Your first line is especially good," or "The words *lonely lullaby* create a good sound and feeling." Give praise to the points of best quality.

There are two major faults of children's poetry that call for special attention. A child may start with a good idea then come to a dull thump of an ending just to get something that rhymes.

As I looked up at the sky
I saw some planes go flying by
And as I walked home to rest
There came a plane from the west.

After children have achieved some security

in the writing of verse it is well to discuss this problem. Encourage them to write nonrhyming poetry until they have discovered how to use many of the aids available such as rhyming dictionaries and a thesaurus.

The second fault is that of writing parodies on the form of familiar verse. It is fun to write parodies when this is the purpose of writing. The following is questionable as creative poetry. Call it a parody. Then help the child use his idea in a more original form.

> I think that I shall never see
> An airplane tiny as a bee
> A plane that may in summer fly
> Into a piece of apple pie.

Closely related to this is the child who hands in something not his own. Little children sometimes get the idea that the task is to write any poem rather than one of their own creation and some misguided older person helps them and they show up with "Roses are red, violets are blue," etc. When this happens, remember there is no moral issue involved. The child wanted to please. You might say, "That is a cute verse but it has been written before. I think you can write one that no one has ever heard." Or the teacher might suggest,

"Maybe instead of writing a poem you could draw a picture or cartoon of your idea." And the teacher might ask herself if she has made poetry writing a bit too important for the present time if children feel pressured to do this type of thing to gain approbation.

Releasing poetic expression for some who have little inherent talent should not become a challenging burden to the teacher. The object is to release the talent in those so endowed so that all may be enriched by sharing their contributions. Our task is done if we help all to develop this talent to some degree and those gifted in this area to achieve expression in quality that is worthy of them.

1. Assume that you have been selected to judge some children's poetry which is sponsored by a local radio station. What basic criteria would you establish to guide your judgment?

2. Collect five poems which you might use to teach how poems are made to a fifth grade. What would you notice in each poem?

3. One class constructed a mimeographed work book which was the beginning of an anthology made by each student. The collection also served to teach how poetry is written. Some of the material is listed below. Construct similar lessons for your group and report on the results obtained.

Poem	Author or Source	Purpose— To Understand:
Little Snail	Hilda Conkling	Imagery: metaphor and simile
Little Talk	Aileen Fisher	Imagery: empathy
23rd Psalm	Bible	Lyric poetry
Friendly Beasts	Old Coral	Planned repetition
Feather or Fun	John Becker	Cadence
Little Things	James Stephens	Empathy
Swing Song	William Allingham	Rhythm
Near Dusk	Joseph Auslander	Onomatopoeia
Song of the Train	David McCord	Onomatopoeia
Measure Me, Sky	Leonora Speyer	Expression of self
Primer Lesson	Carl Sandburg	Free verse
Spring	William Blake	Lyric rhyme scheme
White Butterflies	Algernon Charles Swinburne	Simile
Cradle Song	Sarajini Naidu	Complex rhyme scheme
High Flight	John G. Magee, Jr.	Imagination
The Wasp	William Sharp	Use of simile and metaphor
Chanson Innocente	e. e. cummings	Experimentation

4. The national poetry day is October 15. Plan a school assembly program for this occasion.

5. A "Junior Author's Tea" sponsored by a school is an annual event in El Cajon, Calif. At such a tea should only the "books" written by those especially talented be displayed? Should awards be made? How would you plan such an event?

HOW ARE CHILDREN TAUGHT TO MAKE REPORTS AND KEEP RECORDS?

Informal reporting of information and observation, and discussion of this information in small or large groups play major roles in the activities of children. Later, these oral expressions may be put into written form. Young children have a need for some written records as they plan together. As the experiences of children grow in complexity, more detailed plans must be made, and children will have further needs for records and reports.

Until such time as children attain sufficient skill in handwriting, the teacher records the information for the group. Later, she transfers this information to charts or booklets. Children may then read the written record when they need to review the steps in specific processes, or simply for the pleasure of reliving the experience.[10]

MAKING BUTTER

We put cream in a jar.
We shook it a long time.
Little yellow lumps of butter
came to the top.

We poured the
buttermilk out and drank it.
We washed the butter and
tasted it. It needed salt.
We added salt. We put it
in a mold.

We ate butter on
crackers. It was delicious!

There are numerous occasions when children are helped to make simple records. They record:

[10] San Bernardino County Schools: *Arts and Skills of Communication for Democracy's Children*, San Bernardino, Calif., 1954, is the source of many examples given here.

The growth of a plant
The date
The daily weather
The daily temperature
The changing appearance of the polliwogs
The days the fish are fed
Monthly height and weight
The number of children present each day

Children enjoy watching the teacher record interesting daily events.

> NEWS
> Today is Monday.
> It is a sunny day.
> We are going on a walk.
> We will look for wild flowers.
> Billy brought a horned toad for us to see.

One group of children carefully recorded the number of days it took for the eggs of the praying mantis to hatch. They recorded:

> Ralph found a green bug.
> It looks like a grasshopper,
>   but it is not a grasshopper.
> It is a praying mantis.

Later, they recorded:

> Our praying mantis laid some eggs.
> It laid them on December 20, 1952.
> Then it died.
> We are counting the days until the eggs hatch.

After listening to a story, seeing a film or filmstrip, taking a trip, or talking with a resource person, children may wish to record information. As they list the information in the order of occurrence, they gain an understanding of sequence.

After they had seen a filmstrip about the truck farmer, one group recorded:

JOBS OF A TRUCK FARMER
The truck farmer plows the soil.
He plants the seeds.
He irrigates the plants.
He sprays the plants.
He harvests the crops.
He sells the produce to a wholesale market.

Children often record individual and group plans for ready reference. The teacher guides the discussion and helps children decide which suggestions will be most helpful. Later, she places these plans on charts for future reference:

How We Clean Up
How We Use Our Tools
How We Go On A Trip
How We Share Together
How We Work Together

Children are helped to organize their thinking by listing questions, recording tentative solutions, testing solutions, and arriving at conclusions. Many of these problems arise in the social studies and related science activities. Problems such as the following may develop after dramatic play:

WE NEED TO FIND OUT
How the gasoline station gets its gasoline
How the groceries get to the store
How people get money from the bank
What do trucks bring to the community

After a group of children had taken a trip to the wholesale bakery, they set up the problem:

What makes bread dough rise?

As children suggested answers to the problem, the teacher recorded their ideas.

JOHN: Because of the warm sun shining on the dough.
SUSAN: Because of the way the baker beats the dough.

SAM: Because of the things that are mixed in the dough.
JEAN: Because of the kind of pan the baker uses for the dough.

This list of suggested answers was held tentative by the group until they could arrive at valid conclusions. The group performed a simple experiment which helped to dismiss the incorrect assumptions and to identify the valid conclusion. They dictated the following story, telling how their final conclusions were reached:

WHAT MAKES BREAD DOUGH RISE?
We wanted to find out what makes bread dough rise.
We took two bowls. We mixed flour and water in one bowl.
We mixed flour, water, and yeast in another bowl.
We took turns beating and stirring the dough in each bowl.
Some of us beat fast and hard. Some of us beat slowly.
We poured the dough from each bowl into two bowls.
The bowls were the same shape and size.
We put the bowls in the sunshine on a table by the window.
Then we went out to recess.
When we came back to the room, we looked at the dough.
We saw that the dough in one bowl was spilling over the edge.
The dough in the other bowl was just as we had left it.
Now we know why bread dough rises. Why? Because there is yeast in the dough!

Girls and boys often wish to record the experiences they have shared or special information they have gained from study trips, special classroom activities, films, filmstrips, or visits of resource people. As children discuss the events which they will include in their story, the teacher guides the group in determining proper sequence, in selecting contributions which best describe the situation, and in choosing words and phrases which are colorful and descriptive.

A group of six-year-olds had carefully watched two caterpillars as each became a chrysalis and later emerged as a "mourning cloak" or purplish-brown butterfly. The teacher put captions near the jar, changing them at appropriate intervals. She recorded the children's observations as they watched this sequence of events. Later, the children discussed all that had taken place from the first day the caterpillars were brought to their room until the beautiful butterflies emerged. The teacher recorded the following story as the group recalled the experience. She helped the children recall the events in sequential order by referring to the changing captions and to the comments the children had made during the past weeks. Later, the group delighted in hearing their story read back to them.

Our Caterpillars

There were two caterpillars eating geraniums when we found them. They were soft and black, and had real pretty spots on them.

We put the caterpillars and some geraniums into a big jar. We gave them fresh leaves to eat.

One day one made a house. He sort of knitted with his head. He shook it up and down, and up and down. Then he went sideways and up and down. We thought he would get dizzy and fall, but he didn't. Pretty soon he had a brownish, grayish colored house without any door and windows.

The other one made a house too, but he made it when we were not looking. Both houses hung down from the geranium.

After a long time, one moth came out. He sat real still and looked at the jar and everything. After recess he was wiggling his wings. The next day he flew in the jar. By the next afternoon the other moth came out.

They were just alike. Maybe they will be a mother and daddy. They visited together. They were pretty black velvet with pretty yellow trimming on the wings. The spots made the trimming maybe. Anyway it's the same color.

We brought them flowers and leaves. They might lay some eggs and then we'd have lots of moths. We are going to keep them a long time to see. They seem to be happy.

The moths didn't live so very long, but we will still keep them.

Shorter stories may be recorded on the chalkboard and later placed on charts.

As children gain in the ability to write down factual experiences, they begin recording their own stories. To the extent that they project their own personalities into their writing, their stories become more than simply stated facts and a recording of information. These stories become creative as they take on the unique character which is distinct to the child who is the writer. As in all other forms of independently written expression, girls and boys are given all the help they need to set down their thoughts with ease.

Jo-Ann wrote:

Our Trip

We went to the trucking terminal today. We saw the big trailers and tractors. I got to see the fifth wheel and the dolly wheels. That's what I wanted to see most of all.

Willis wrote:

The Post Office

The post office is a busy place. There are many workers there. I watched how the mail is sorted and how the letters are canceled.

One man showed us how the mail is put into the boxes. He showed us how the rest of the mail is put into bundles for the mail man.

Taking care of all the mail is a big job.

Nikkie wrote:

Willie's Hamster

Willie brought his little hamster to school. His name is Brownie. His eyes are bright and shiny. When he sleeps, he looks like a little ball of fur. He is brown and white and he wiggles all the time. Willie feeds the hamster two times a day. He feeds it oatmeal and lettuce. The little hamster is asleep now. Shhhh.

The development of reporting and recording clearly, accurately, and interestingly expands as children have many and varied experiences in many and varied activities. Girls and boys are helped to gain in the skills of reporting and recording as they are given opportunity to:

Express themselves orally in many different situations

Dictate and record information which is of real need and value

Set down their own needs and stories independently when they have gained adequate skill and ability in writing.

Children are fascinated with facts. The popularity of information books and children's encyclopedias equals that of story books. This is a report by Debra toward the last months of second grade:

COMETS

Comets are the closest thing to nothing that could be something. Comets are made up of: gas, dust, little molecules of dirt and maybe some sparkes. The closer the comet is to the sun the longer its tail is. The farther away the comet is from the sun the shorter its tail is. Comets tails are formed like this: the comet has a very short tail. Then it get longer, longer, and longer untill it's very long. One Comet comes back every 75 year's. It's called Halley's Comet because he was the man who discovered it. He discovered Comets in 1810 many year's ago.

In the fourth grade, Sammy placed a picture of the Rosetta Stone on the bulletin board next to his report, which started:

For many, many years scholars tried to find out what the old Egyptian hieroglyphics meant. Until 1799 there was absolutely no way of telling what the Egyptians had recorded. In that year the Rosetta Stone was found that contained the same message in three languages. Hieroglyphics were used in one of these. The known languages were used to interpret the meaning of the ancient Egyptian writing.

Reporting is a natural outgrowth of a child's interest in his environment. When the material is pertinent, well-organized, and interestingly presented, the report serves to enrich the on-going experiences of children.

Through this medium children project themselves, their understandings of their world, and their feelings about people, animals, things, or situations. They achieve status with their peers while increasing their own knowledge as well as that of the group.

Maturation and experience are factors which have a cause-and-effect relationship to all communication. Writing a report requires more mature thinking than many of the other written language activities. Because of the difficulties involved, most teachers feel that the written report should not receive much stress until the later elementary years. The background for the organizational thinking required for making written reports, however, is laid during the earlier years in the giving of many oral reports and the occasional writing of group reports.

The writing of a report often serves as a challenge to the exceptional child or to the girl or boy who has some special interest or hobby. Children painstakingly engage in independent research on topics that pique their curiosity. The research and reporting meet individual needs and at the same time add to the fund of knowledge of the entire group.

The following report was made by a sixth-grade boy whose hobby was collecting rocks:

Mr. Fields has over four hundred specimens in his mineral collection. Almost two hundred of these are geodes. What fun and adventure he has making his collection. He said that finding a geode is like receiving a surprise package. You cannot tell from the wrappings what wonderful treasures are inside. When Mr. Fields discovered his first geode, he would have passed it by had a fellow collector not pointed it out to him. It was somewhat round but irregular and no different in color from the rocks and earth around it.

Have you ever seen a geode after it is cut in two? It is filled with six-sided crystals which are called quartz. How these rose and lavendar crystals sparkle! I hope I can find a geode to put in my rock collection.

Facts and imagination can combine to create reports like this:

I WAS THERE WITH LEWIS AND CLARK

I am a flea. I live in Lewis' hat. It all started out in 1803 when Lewis stopped to pet a dog and I jumped on Lewis' leg.

I did not like it there, so I went to higher flesh; that is, his head or hat. Before I knew it, I was boarding a keelboat. From then on I had many adventures. One day we met a grizzly bear. I was going to jump on him, but the men started shooting at him. I then changed my mind. Another time we were going to see the Sioux Indians. Lewis was all dressed up and his boots were shining. All of a sudden the boat hit something and the boat rolled over. I was almost drowned and Lewis was all wet. I never wished I would go to the dogs so badly in my life. But I was saved.

Later on we came to the Mandan Indians. They were much friendlier than the Sioux. More important, we met a French trapper. Lewis found out he could interpret for them, so they took him along. He had an Indian wife name Sacagawea. He was whipping her one night; when I found out, I leaped over to that trapper and bit him so hard I almost set him in orbit. Another time when our boat turned over, Sacagawea saved some very important papers. One time we saw the Rocky Mountains. Then we came to Sacagawea's people who gave us food and ponies. Soon we came to the Pacific Ocean. I was the first American flea to see the Pacific Ocean. Soon we left for home.

Written by Me, the Little Flea.

—DONALD, GRADE 5

Children in the middle grades are "joiners." Organized activity clubs give girls and boys a feeling of belongingness and help them to find their places in the social environment. There are many clubs of this type. Some of the most common are 4-H, Brownies, Cub Scouts, Boy Scouts, Blue Birds, and Campfire Girls. Some clubs are formed around interest and service areas, such as: Science, Reading, Dramatics, Photography, Recreation, and Safety and the Junior Red Cross.

Most of these clubs have secretaries. Although children enjoy being chosen secretary, they have difficulty learning to keep detailed minutes. Girls and boys are generally so interested in the club activities that they feel little need for more than simple records of the happenings.

Mary showed considerable skill as she recorded the following minutes of the sixth-grade Science Club:

The Science Club met in Room 5 Tuesday afternoon at 2:30. Bill called the meeting to order. I read the minutes. Tom showed us the planetarium he made. He helped us find the Big Dipper and Venus. Mary's mother sent cup cakes.

But Mary is not the only one who needs this practice. After the first meeting the entire group should participate in the writing of the minutes under the teacher's leadership. "How do we start a report of a meeting?" the teacher asks. "Yes, we name the club, the place, and the time." After writing these on the board the teacher continues. "Who called the meeting to order? What happened first? And what happened next?" Finally the teacher tells them of the form used by club secretaries. "Respectfully submitted" is not needed at the close of minutes. The secretary's signature is adequate. After they are approved the minutes are an official record."

Simple mimeographed or dittoed newspapers provide an incentive for written reports. Here is a typical page from a monthly paper.[11]

My Letter Brought Results

After I wrote a letter to the Chula Vista Telephone Co., Mrs. O'Neill got my letter and called my teacher about it, then Wednesday, Mrs. Wallace told the class that my letter had brought results and that we would see a film on telephone service and would have a field trip to see the inside of a telephone building. Telephones mean a lot to us, don't you think so too?

—BILLY RINEHART

Mr. Halsema's Girls Won

The girls in Mrs. Wallace's room had a baseball game with Mr. Halsema's girls, Friday, May 2nd. Linda Baker and Carolyn Ferguson were the captains of the two teams. It was a great game. The baseball was flying all over the field. Mr. Halsema's girls won 7 to 6.

—LINDA BAKER

Feeling About Moving to a New School

It is quite interesting, going to different schools, because some schools have more unusual things than others. Some have bigger and better playgrounds for children to play

[11] Selections from the "Emory Epitaph," published by Emory School, South Bay School District, San Diego, Calif.

San Diego County Schools, Calif.

A class paper or magazine may be one sheet reproduced on a mimeograph machine or a section of the class bulletin board. It needs reporters, cartoonists, feature writers, and editors. Before any material is published, the editors require that it be proofread, corrected, and approved.

on. Some have bigger and more colorful rooms and other interesting things. When you first go to a new school, you will probably be afraid, but when you check into school the children will start playing with you, and the second day at school, you will know a lot of kids, and you won't be afraid anymore.

—JUDITH HAWKINS

Book Review

BIG RED, the dog Danny had always wanted is the name of this book. But first, he must teach the Irish Setter the ways of the woods. Together, they roamed the wilderness meeting nature on her own hard terms. When the outlaw bear injures his father, the boy and his dog must hunt him down. How do they do it? Read the book!

—GEORGEANNA MULLIGAN

Play Day

On Friday, April 25, we went on a trip to Imperial Beach School. All the sixth grades in the district met there for Play Day.

We all met in the auditorium where we sang songs of North and South America. Then we went out on the black top for square dancing. The square dances we danced were; Pop Goes the Weasel, Patty Cake Polka, and Parles Vouz. After lunch, we divided up into groups for games, dashes and relays. We came back to school in the afternoon tired but happy. Everyone had a good time.

—BUTCH RURCHES

Our Playground Setup

Our playground setup is the only one of its kind in the South Bay Union School District, and is the best one that Emory has had yet. Each class is assigned certain games to play each week. This saves the time of assigning games each day, and also certain areas won't be overcrowded.

With this new plan, everyone will get a chance to play all the games. By the end of the year, you may learn to like a game you never cared for before. It will save a lot of arguments and confusion.

—SHERRY HUDMAN

WE'D LIKE YOU TO MEET

Mr. Hanavan, our principal likes his job. He taught at Pineville Junior High School in Missouri for eight years. He taught in Imperial Beach sixth grade for two years, and taught one year at Fort Growder.

He has a daughter, Connie, ten years old. She is in the fifth grade. He was born in Pineville, Mo. April 5, 1922.

Mr. Hanavan has been at Emory for two years. His favorite foods are baked ham, mashed potatoes, angel food cake, and chocolate milk.

He served in the army during World War 2 and in the Korean War. He is one of our favorite people.

—LINDA BAKER AND DIANE WILBUR

The teacher should develop, with the class, standards for checking the form and neatness of a written report. This checking method is often called proofreading, editing, or correcting. The standards might be as follows:

Standards for Editing a Report

1. Write the title of the report in the center of the line. Leave a space between the top of the paper and the title. Skip a line after the title.
2. Begin the first word of the title with a capital letter. Capitalize each important word of the title. Do not capitalize *a, an, at, as, the, of, to, in, from, with*, etc., because they are not considered important words.
3. Have good margins at the top, bottom, left, and right.
4. Use clear writing.
5. Use correct spelling and punctuation.
6. Have "sentence-sense." Do not use incomplete, run-on, or choppy sentences.
7. Indent all paragraphs.
8. Sign your name at the bottom of the last page.

The teacher and the class might develop an editing code using those signs familiar to the newspaper office, as well as other signs which might prove helpful. The signs should be charted as follows:

EDITING SIGNS

sp = spelling
c = capital letter
inc = incomplete sentence
෫ = take out
ᔕ = transpose, or turn about
lc = small letter (lower case letter)
Ɔ = join sentences
mb = margins too big
ms = margins too small
// = margins not straight
p = punctuation wrong or omitted
wr = making writing clear
ind = indent paragraph
om = something should be omitted
? = material not clear
= space should be left

One of the most valuable activities in association with a school newspaper is the development of a "style sheet," which summarizes the major rules of punctuation, capitalization, and spelling. The local newspaper will usually give a school a copy of the style sheet which guides their writers.

Longer reports employ two areas of skills which involve gathering information and organizing the material. Textbooks provide adequate guidance with respect to note taking and simple outlining. Neither of these skills should be taught in isolation. It is the report that provides the purpose for taking notes. Planning the report provides the outline. These skills should first be studied in association with oral reports. This permits greater concentrated attention on the problems of gathering and organizing information.

The following standards are suggested with respect to note taking:

1. Read the material through before taking notes.
2. Complete one reference before you read another.
3. Use key words, phrases, or sentences to recall ideas.
4. Record the source of ideas.

With regard to organization, list the big ideas that are to be presented then add the details under each idea. Children find the creation of an outline prior to writing the report very difficult to make but they can outline the report after it has been written. This outlining can be a part of the editing before a report is rewritten. Social Studies materials lend themselves to the study of outlining. Normally this is not a skill to be stressed before junior high school.

This pattern for an outline is an established language procedure:

SIMPLE OUTLINE

Title

I.

   A.

   B.

   C.

II.

   A.

   B.

   C.

Through discussion the children should be made aware of the following:

1. The main topics have Roman numerals. A period is placed after each numeral.
2. The supporting topics (subtopics) are designated by capital letters. A period is placed after each capital letter.
3. The written report contains as many paragraphs as there are main topics.
4. Each subtopic represents at least one sentence within the paragraph.
5. Each main topic and supporting topic begins with a capital letter.
6. There are no periods at the ends of the main topic or supporting topics unless it is a sentence outline.
7. In the simple outline, Roman numerals are kept in a straight column.
8. In the simple outline, capital letters are kept in a straight column.
9. If a topic is two lines long, the second line begins directly under the first word of the topic.

10. All the topics of an outline are written in the same form. That is, they are written *all in the short form* or *all in complete sentences.*

Children should be given many experiences, such as the following:

1. Making a group outline for a report.
2. Making a group outline for a current event.
3. Outlining, as a class, a short article in their readers.
4. Making individual outlines.

Reports are motivated by these activities:

1. Write a riddle about an insect, bird, or animal.
2. Write one paragraph reports on famous people.
3. Write an imaginary news report of an historic event. Or write the news that must have appeared when the historic event took place.
4. Make believe that you are an animal or a famous person. Write a description of yourself.
5. Visit a museum and report on an object observed.
6. Make comparisons of things we have with those in other parts of the world.
7. Write five-sentence reports about a topic in the encyclopedia.
8. A favorite newspaper feature is "Ask Andy." Put a question on the board and let the children write the answers as if they were Andy. Make certain first that adequate reference books are available. Questions like:

    How far is it to the sun?

    What is the brightest star?

    How fast does sound travel?

    What causes a sonic boom?

9. Provide background comments for a current news story. How large is the Congo? How do people make a living there?

10. Make a travel folder for a city, state, park or country.
11. Write an autobiography. Parts might be: My Birthplace, My Parents, My First School, My Pets and Hobbies, My Ambitions. A baby picture on the cover makes these an appealing Parents' Night attraction. Primary children can make a notebook "About My Family and Me."
12. Write a biography. This would involve interviewing a parent, grandparent, or classmate. In addition to place of birth and school experience, items of this nature might be included: Special likes and dislikes, travel, honors, most important event in his life.
13. Make a class record or folder. This is especially appropriate if the sixth grade is the highest grade in a building. Parts might be: History of Our School, Where Our Teachers Were Educated, Our Ambitions, Our Class Will, Twenty Years from Now, Who's Who in the Sixth Grade.
14. The very slow child in the upper grades will find satisfaction in preparing material for young children. Make an alphabet book for the first grade, a farm book for the second, or an animal book for the third grade. These would contain pictures and written explanations. Simple cook books and travel records based upon a road map are within their level of achievement.
15. Surveys of favorite books, opinions about grammar, simplified spelling, or a school problem such as social dancing in the sixth grade, are stimulating and involve a great deal of language learning as the material is gathered, organized and written into a report.

HOW SHOULD LETTER WRITING BE TAUGHT IN THE ELEMENTARY GRADES?

In each classroom beyond those of the first grade there should be a chart or other ready reference illustrating the form of letters appropriate for the grade. Some teachers put a permanent form on the blackboard with crayons. This shows the lines for date, salutation, body of the letter and the closing. Every language textbook provides adequate examples of various letter forms.

In the primary grades the children start by dictating the letter to the teacher who writes on the blackboard. Afterwards, each child copies the completed note to mother or the janitor. As soon as the basic pattern is mastered children are encouraged to write individual messages. These may be to classmates who are ill, to relatives, to the principal, janitor, or to a speaker who visited the class.

The satisfaction of expressing ideas in an accepted social manner seems to be sufficient motivation for most children. But this satisfaction soon ends if the letters are not read and there is no response. Since the post office is usually studied in the second grade, letter writing within the class will interest the children. The letters are carefully written, envelopes prepared, and the letters mailed and delivered as a part of the classroom project. With a little cooperation this can be extended to the second grade in another room or a neighboring school.

As the children advance letter writing is best motivated by real purposes. Pen pals in other states and countries can be located through the *Christian Science Monitor* in Boston, Mass.; the Junior Red Cross in Washington, D.C.; The International Friendship League, 40 Mt. Vernon Street, Boston, Mass.; and the Parker Pen Company in Janesville, Wis. Sources of free and inexpensive materials are listed in "The Wonderful World for Children" by Peter Cardoza, published by Bantam Books. This inexpensive book will be found wherever paperback books are sold. Some of the major corporations such as General Foods, Westinghouse Electric, Union Pacific Railroad, and Goodrich Rubber Company have materials designed for classroom use that will be sent to children who write for them. The highway departments of many state governments will send illustrated highway maps. The National Audubon Society, 1130 Fifth Avenue, New York 28, N. Y., and the National Wild Life Federation, 232 Carrol Street, N. W., Washington 12, D. C., have interesting material for children concerned with conservation.

It should be noted that there are some letters that should not be written. The children's magazines contain many offers to send stamps on approval. Some companies offer free stamps as an incentive. The child who receives such stamps may not understand that he will be expected to pay for them. Another type is the advertisement that offers a bicycle for solving a puzzle. This will involve the child in selling seeds, candy, or other items with a compromise award, such as a box camera.

A second type of letter requiring careful consideration is that written to prominent people. Writing a letter of appreciation to the author of a book is one thing. Writing such a letter to gain information for a book report is another. The author, John Steinbeck, appealed to high school English teachers to stop assigning such letters. He was getting from seventy-five to a hundred on some days. Congressmen have the help and mailing privileges that do not make this a great burden. Few community leaders are in such a comfortable position.

When the need to write a letter has been established, use the lessons in the textbook that deal with the proper form. Some classes make a "Letter Form Handbook." This is a folder that illustrates the blank form of a letter and contains examples of letters which the children have made or brought from home. If the children come from homes where examples of good letters are available, an excellent bulletin board can be made exhibiting these letters. A collection of letters with special offers, which seems to be a modern merchandising practice, might be studied with respect to form and context.

Letters written to express appreciation for a favor or to express interest in a child who is absent, provide opportunities for class discussion of the context of such letters. The teacher might start the discussion with the question, "What are some of the things you would talk about if you could go to the hospital to visit Joe?" "Let me list the ideas on the board."

1. Tell about things that have happened at school.

   The bicycle test.
   The map we finished.
   The new bulletin board.

2. Tell something about ourselves.

   John has a baby brother.
   Mary went to visit Disneyland.
   Jane lost her glasses.

3. Say something about Joe.

   Tell him we miss him.
   Tell him we hope he gets well soon.
   Tell him to have fun at the hospital.

Then discuss the questions: Should all of us write these ideas in the same order? Should all of us write about the bicycle test?

After the letters are written let the children judge the quality of their own letters. None need to be rewritten but some may wish to do so. All should be mailed. Those who wish may read their letters to the group. These ideas might be used in the evaluation:

Does the letter sound like talking?
Would you like to receive the letter yourself?
Does it tell what the reader would want to know?

The pen pal letter to a stranger is an incentive for descriptive writing. The fact that a child in Alaska has never seen the writer, his home, community, or school provides a good reason for writing about the familiar. Unfortunately, doing this as a classroom assignment detracts from the natural rewards of the activity. After the first letter it is wise to permit the activity to continue as a personal choice. Praise those who do continue writing, let them read the letters received to the class, have displays of letters and items received. While intermediate-grade children are interested in foreign lands, the children in non-English speaking countries who wish to write are usually in the upper grades. It thus seems wise to postpone this type of pen pal until the children are in junior high school.

Usually a letter to an adult is much more difficult to write than a letter to another child. This seems especially true of "duty letters." "Thank you" notes or expressions of appreciation require specific patterns of language that apparently seem unnatural to some children. Examples of such letters or notes might be used as the beginning of a discussion.

Which of these letters would you like to receive?

> 1616 Madison
> Albany, N. Y.
> Jan. 6, 1962

Dear Grandmother,

Christmas is so full of surprises. I never expected to have a pair of mittens made by my own grandmother. The colors are just right for my coat. It must have taken you a long time to make them. I'll think of you whenever I wear them.

We gave a Christmas play at school. I was an angel. Daddy says they must have made a mistake to give me a part like that. He is always teasing.

> With love,
>
> Donna

> Newburgh, Ind.
> Jan. 6, 1962

Dear Grandmother,

Thanks for the mittens. I got a sled, a coat, a book, a necktie, a knife, and lots of other things.

I was in a play at school.

> Respectfully yours,
>
> Dan

An incentive for letter writing is provided when a child has his own stationery. This should be lined. Parents might be encouraged to buy such material as birth-day presents for children. The Cub Scouts and Brownies have such stationery for their members. If the teacher gives a gift as a birthday present, it is wise to have a local printer create the type of writing paper the children need.

Tests of this type provide a check of the understanding of letter form.

Correct 10 errors in this business letter form:

> 4854 adams
> chicago illinois
> july 4 1962

Sears Co
1616 Grove St
Denver, Colo.
dear sir,

A chart illustrating the terms used in letter writing should be mimeographed and given to each intermediate child. An example of a friendly letter is shown with these parts identified: heading, salutation, body, complimentary close and signature. A business letter should have these parts identified: inside address, salutation, body, complimentary close and signature.

A challenging task for able students would be to make a list of salutations and complimentary closings. How would one greet the Queen of England, the Archbishop of a church, a Senator, a delegate to the United Nations or a firm of lawyers?

These standards may be placed on a chart and used to evaluate letters.

1. Do I have five parts to my letter?
   A heading
   A greeting
   A message
   A closing
   A name
2. Did I write neatly so that the person who receives my letter can read it easily?
3. Did I indent the first word of each paragraph?
4. Did I leave a straight margin on each part of my letter?
5. Did I tell something interesting?

Worksheets like the following are needed for some children in order to establish understanding:

HEADINGS

NAME_____

A heading tells the place and the date.

1. What is the name of your school?

_____

Did you capitalize each word in the name of your school? Yes _____ No_____

2. What city and state is your school in?

_____

Did you capitalize the city and state? Yes_____ No_____
Did you separate the city and state with a comma? Yes _____ No_____

3. What is the date today?

_____

Did you capitalize the name of the month? Yes _____ No_____
Did you put a comma between the day and the year? Yes_____ No_____

Write in the blanks below the name of your school, the city and state, and the date. Be sure your margin is straight.

_____Name of School
_____City and State
_____Date

GREETING

Begin the first word in the greeting with a capital letter.

Copy over the following greetings correctly.

dear Mary, _____
dear Jane, _____
dear Miss Smith,_____

Use a capital letter at the beginning of such words as Mother, Father, Uncle and Aunt in the greeting.

Copy over the following greetings correctly.

Dear uncle Harry, _____
Dear father, _____
Dear aunt Mary, _____
Dear mother, _____

Put a comma after the greeting.

Copy over the following greetings correctly.

Dear Miss Smith _____
Dear Jane _____
Dear Uncle Harry _____
Dear Mother _____

Name_____

CLOSING AND NAME

Begin the first word in the closing with a capital letter. Copy over the following closings correctly.

your friend, _____

sincerely yours, _____

with love, _____

Write the closing you would use if you wrote a letter to your mother.

_____

Write the closing you would use if you wrote a letter to a friend.

_____

Write the closing you would use if you didn't know the person very well.

_____

Put a comma after the closing. Write the following closings correctly.

Your friend _____

Sincerely yours _____

With love _____

Begin each part of your name with a capital letter. Write the following names correctly.

mary smith _____

jane johns _____

sue jones _____

jack hall _____

1. In addition to reports and letter writing there are other functional language situations when a child needs to write. When would a child need to write a description, an advertisement, a notice, an invitation, a biography, a joke?

2. Do you think writing postal cards should be a part of the letter writing program in school?

3. It is said that women write better letters than men. Is there any factor in our culture that might cause such a difference?

4. Since schools have publications for creative writing, do you feel that outstanding reports, letters, and other such material should receive similar recognition? How might this be done?

Suggestions for Projects

1. Mauree Applegate suggests an I-W-S Formula to start some children in creative writing. This means: Ideas, Words and Stimulators. Use this formula to devise materials that might be used in the classroom.

2. Problems stimulate the able child. Create some folders that present a series of problems and the suggested means whereby the answers may be found to use with such students.

3. Make an anthology of poetry written by children.
4. Evaluate ten films or filmstrips that might be used to stimulate imaginative writing. "The Hunter in the Forest" is suggested in many school courses of study.
5. Evaluate a specific suggestion with respect to creative writing. Such suggestions as these may be used: Have children write the story of a comic-book episode, write a summary of a television show, encourage children to experiment with flannel board characters or puppets as they develop a story or play before writing.
6. Investigate the procedures used with respect to publication of a collection of creative writing. How are the materials selected, who pays for the publication, how is the material distributed?
7. Investigate the way composition is taught in England. The Ministry of Education Pamphlet No. 26, "Language," published by Her Majesty's Stationery Office in London, is an interesting source of such information.
8. Make a study of worthy free materials that may be secured through letters written by children. Use these sources as a guide:

Where to Get Free and Inexpensive Materials, by David L. Byrn, and others. San Francisco, Calif., Fearon Publishers, 1959. (2263 Union St., San Francisco.)

Elementary Teachers Guide to Free Curriculum Materials, by Educators Progress Service. Randolph, Wisconsin. Annual.

Free and Inexpensive Learning Materials. 9th edition. Nashville, Tenn.: Peabody College for Teachers, 1960.

So You Want to Start a Picture File.

Sources of Free and Inexpensive Pictures for the Classroom.

Sources of Free Travel Posters and Geographic Aids.

All the above by Bruce Miller and available from him, c/o Box 369, Riverside, Calif.

Sources of Free and Inexpensive Educational Materials. Chicago: Field Enterprises, 1958. (Merchandise Mart Plaza, Chicago 58, Ill.)

BIBLIOGRAPHY

BOOKS

Applegate, Mauree. *Easy in English.* New York: Harper, 1960.

———. *Helping Children Write.* New York: Harper, 1954.

Arnstein, Flora J. *Adventures into Poetry.* Palo Alto, Calif.: Stanford U.P., 1951.

Bell, Vickars. *On Learning the English Tongue.* London: Faber, 1956.

Board of Education, City of New York. Developing Children's Power of Self-Expression through Writing. Curriculum Bulletin 1952–53 Series No. 2, Brooklyn: New York Public Schools, 1953.

Burrows, Alvina T., June D. Fenebee, Dorothy C. Jackson, and Dorothy O. Saunders. *They All Want to Write.* New York: Prentice, 1952.

Treanor, John H. *English Composition, A Course of Study for Grade 4.* Cambridge, Mass.: Educators Publishing Service, 1960.

———. *Familiar Situations Ideas for Compositions I, II, III.* Boston, Mass.: Educational Advising Center, 1956.

———. *Teaching the Friendly Letter.* Cambridge, Mass.: Educators Publishing Service, 1961.

———. *Workbook for the Friendly Letter.* Cambridge, Mass.: Educators Publishing Service, 1961.

Walter, Nina W. *Let Them Write Poetry.* New York: Holt, 1962.

Wolfe, Don M. *Language Arts and Life Patterns.* New York: The Odyssey, 1961, Chaps. 5–8.

PAMPHLETS AND COURSES OF STUDY

Board of Education Minneapolis, Minn.: "A Guide to the Teaching of Speaking and

Writing," Minneapolis Public Schools, Minneapolis, Minn., 1953.

Board of Education San Diego, Calif.: "Oral and Written Language," San Diego Public Schools, San Diego, Calif., 1956.

Burrows, Alvina Trent: "Teaching Composition," What Research Says to the Teacher Series No. 18, National Education Association, Washington, D. C.

San Barnardino County Schools, San Bernardino, Calif.: "Arts and Skills of Communication for Democracy's Children," 1956.

United Sates Department of Health, Education and Welfare, Office of Education: "How Children Learn to Write," Bulletin No. 2 (1953).

LANGUAGE TEXTBOOKS FOR THE ELEMENTARY GRADES

Dawson, Mildred, Jonnie Mashburn Miller, and Marian Zollinger. *Language for Daily Use.* New York: Harcourt, 1959.

Greene, H. A., and Maude McBroom. *Building Better English.* New York: Harper, 1954.

McKee, Paul, Anne McCowen, and Lucille Harrison. *Language for Meaning Series.* Boston: Houghton, 1959.

Moore, Marion, Ralph G. Nichols, and W.

Cabell Grant. *Listen, Speak and Write.* Chicago: Scott, 1960.

Patton, David H., Georgia Winn, Althea Beery, and Charlotte Wills. *Using Our Language.* Boston: Webster, 1954.

Pollock, Thomas C., and Florence Bowden. *Macmillan English Series.* New York: Macmillan, 1960.

Shane, Harold G., et al. *Good English Series.* River Forest, Ill.: Laidlaw, 1958.

Stauffer, R. G., Alvina Trent Burrows, and Doris Jackson. *American English Series.* New York: Holt, 1960.

Sterling, Edna, Hannah M. Lindahl, and Katherine Koch. *English is Our Language.* Boston: Heath, 1961.

Wolfe, Don, and Lela Hamilton. *Enjoying English Series.* Syracuse, N.Y.: Singer, 1958.

BOOKS FOR PRIMARY TEACHERS

Bailey, Mattilda, Edna M. Horrocks, and Esther Torreson. *Language Learnings Grades 1–2.* New York: American, 1956.

Dawson, Mildred. *Language Teaching in Grades One and Two.* New York: Harcourt, 1949.

Strickland, Ruth G. *English is Our Language, Grades 1 and 2.* Boston: Heath, 1950.

Chapter 9

Grammar, Usage, and Punctuation

WHAT GRAMMAR SHOULD BE TAUGHT IN THE ELEMENTARY SCHOOL?

Since 1935 the National Council of Teachers of English has urged teachers to use the following criteria to determine what is good English:

1. Correct usage must find its authority in the living language of today.
2. It must recognize dialect and geographical variations.
3. It must judge the appropriateness of the expression to the purpose intended.
4. It must recognize social levels of speech.
5. It must take into account the historical development of the language.

Much confusion has resulted in practice from the acceptance of arbitrary standards of English grammar and usage. In the list of basic principles it is apparent that the authoritarian viewpoint of what is correct is not acceptable. Good English, then, is ". . . that form of speech which is appropriate to the purpose of the speaker, true to the language as it is, and comforta-ble to speaker and listener. It is the product of custom, neither cramped by rule nor freed from all restraint; it is never fixed, but changes with the organic life of the language." [1]

One interpretation of this definition for teachers would indicate that in American speech from Maine to California, six levels of language use may be recognized.[2] They are: "(1) the illiterate level, (2) the homely level, (3) the informal standard level, (4) the formal standard level, (5) the literary level, and (6) the technical level." These are not distinct nor mutually

_____

[1] National Council of Teachers of English, *An Experience Curriculum in English* (New York: Appleton, 1935).
[2] Robert C. Pooley, "The Levels of Language," *Educational Method*, 16, March 1937, 290; "What Is Correct English?" *National Education Journal*, December 1960, pp. 12–19. The material from Robert C. Pooley on pp. 371–2 was freely adapted and paraphrased for inclusion in this book.

exclusive. Nor are they entirely arranged in ascending order beyond level (3). The elementary teacher is interested in obtaining more proficiency at the informal standard level and in moving individuals up from the "illiterate" to the "homely" level. The teacher's recognition of the speech level of a child and his parents is necessary if the teaching effort is to be effective.

The most surprising fact about the illiterate level of speech is its widespread uniformity. It is not merely a haphazard series of lapses from standard English, but rather a distinct and national mode of speech, with a fairly regular grammar of its own. It is characterized principally by inversions of the forms of irregular verbs, the confusion of regular and irregular verb tense forms, a bland disregard of number agreement between subject and verb and in pronoun relations, the confusion of adjectives and adverbs, and the employment of certain syntactical combinations like the double negative, the redundant subject, and the widely split infinitive. Some examples of the consistent grammar of illiterate English follow:

1. Inversion of the parts of irregular verbs:
   I *seen, done, come, give*, etc. (past tense)
2. Confusion of regular and irregular verb tense forms: *growed, throwed, swang, clumb*, etc.
3. Reduplicated preterits:
   drownded, attackted, casted
4. Lack of number agreement in subjects and verbs: Four boys *was* arrested.
5. Confusion of number and case in pronouns:
   Us boys went.
6. Confusion of adjectives and adverbs:
   The girl sings *beautiful.*
   I don't feel too *good.*
7. Syntactical combinations:
   That there critter is lame.
   We ain't got *no* bacon.

These are only a few of the typical forms and construction of the illiterate level, but they are practically universal in American speech of this level.

Analogy explains much illiterate us-

age. Since the plural of *hat* is *hats* it is logical to make the plural of *foot, foots*. Since the past tense of *hate* is *hated* it seems to follow that the past of *break* is *breaked*. The fact that such forms as *dived* and *waked* are replacing *dove* and *woke* indicates that the verb forms are changing to correspond to the predominate verb pattern in English.

Many writers on speech levels do not distinguish the homely level from the illiterate level, perhaps with considerable justice. But there seems to be a fairly universal area of speech use lying between the completely vulgar and the informal standard levels. It often has a slightly quaint or old-fashioned cast to it and displays, in many of its specific forms, the survivals of words and idioms once widely used but now dropped from standard speech. Characteristic forms of the homely level are:

It *don't* matter a bit.
I *expect* you're the new teacher.
I *can't hardly* do it.
Now where are we *at?*
Lay down; *set* up to the table.
He *raised* (or *rared*) up and shouted.

To these fairly universal forms must be added the distinct use of regional dialects like: *to home* for *at home,* of New England; the use of *admire* for *like,* of the South; and the use of *pack* in the Western sense of carry or wear (he *packs* a mean gun).

It is exceedingly difficult to draw a sharp line of demarcation between the homely and informal standard levels, on the one hand, and the informal standard and the formal standard on the other. Much of the quibbling over the minutiae of "correct English" among people of some education and culture has its basis in the failure to recognize and allow for differences that exist between the informal standard and the formal standard levels. Worse yet, much of the time spent in English classrooms on "correct usage" is employed in a zealous attempt to replace usages of informal standard English, which are in perfectly good standing, with formal or literary usages, which are indubitably "correct" but frequently out of tune with the spirit of the communication into which they are forcibly injected.

Examples of informal standard English are naturally legion, since this level is the core of the spoken and written English of today. For that reason the examples listed below have been chosen to illustrate the usages that are generally accepted in informal communication, yet excluded from formal standard English.

Examples

He *blamed* the accident *on* me.
Does any one know *if* he *was* there?
I have never seen any one act *like* he does.
Where do you get *those kind* of gloves?
We had just two dollars *between* the four of us.
I *can't help but* go to the store.
Who did you send for?
John is the *quickest* of the two.
It was *good* and *cold* (*nice* and *warm*) in the room.
I *will try and do* it.
They invited John and *myself*.
When did you get *through with* your work?
It *was awfully nice* of you to come.

Formal standard English differs from the informal level principally in a subtle change in the tone and effect of the communication as a whole.

1. More exactness and greater selection in vocabulary, with the definite avoidance of words, constructions, and idioms distinctly associated with informal speech.
2. Greater precision in formal agreement of number, both in subject-verb and pronoun-antecedent relationships, and in case-agreement of pronouns.
3. The avoidance of contractions in speech and writing, and of abbreviations in writing.
4. More precise word order, particularly with respect to the position of modifying words, phrases, and clauses.
5. More varied and complex sentence structure, tending toward periodicity.

In the formal level of English speech will be found the public addresses and formal writing of educated people.

Examples

I *shall* be glad to help you.
Neither of the men *was* injured.
Here are three *whom* we have omitted from the list.
I *had rather* stay at home.
I am rather absurd, *am I not?*
It *behooves* me to complete this work.

The attempt to distinguish a literary level of English use as a form of language recognizably different from the formal standard level is an enterprise fraught with some danger. It requires beyond all doubt a more limited definition of literary English than that usually given in textbooks. It is, therefore, assumed that what is commonly called *correct* English includes the usages of at least three levels: the informal standard, the formal standard, and the literary levels. Correctness within this area rests upon a sensitivity to the appropriateness of the usage, rather than upon an arbitrary right and wrong. The technical level would refer to the type of writing found in most college textbooks and manuals in such areas as science, medicine, or law.

The standard for good English, so far as elementary school is concerned, is the informal standard level. Because many pupils do not use English of this level naturally, the teacher's job is really to help them acquire a new dialect. Their basic dialect has been acquired at an early age, practically entirely by ear. The task of remedial education, or changing these basic patterns, must proceed slowly by listening to and using the higher level of speech. Unless the school program has been effective in altering the level of the student's real or basic speech, little progress has been made, no matter how glibly he may repeat rules of usage.

In some homes the informal standard level would not be accepted as good English. These parents, as well as some who would impose their own definitions of "pure" English, will not agree that the informal standard level should be the goal of the schools.

Others feel that there are actually only two levels: standard English and substandard English, with slang as a kind of no-man's-land in between. The basic point concerning levels of language is that the situation frequently determines what is the correct or best form. Language at a baseball game is quite different from that in a college lecture, yet both are acceptable in their respective milieus. This means that our task or aim is not to have all children speak the "King's English," but to help them express themselves clearly and effec-

meaning of the term is the recognition that much that is done in grammar classes does not help the student speak or write better. Indeed, much of the grammar that is taught applies to Latin and not to English. Among the first to point this out was a Danish teacher of English, Otto Jespersen.[3] As he taught English, Jespersen realized that many "rules" had more exceptions or inconsistencies than applications. He pointed out that English is structurally akin to German, not Latin. While many now agree with Jespersen, there is little agreement as to the best way to inform students about English. Among the most interesting attempts is that presented by Paul Roberts in a book for junior high school students, *Patterns in English*.[4]

Roberts defines the parts of speech in this manner:

"A noun is a word like apple, beauty or desk. That is, it is a word that patterns as apple, beauty or desk. It is a word that occurs in positions like those in which apple, beauty and desk occur such as:

I saw the apple.	I was disappointed in the apple.
I saw the beauty.	I was disappointed in the beauty.
I saw the desk.	I was disappointed in the desk.
I saw the_____.	I was disappointed in the_____.

Her apple is gone.	Apples are plentiful in Washington.
Her beauty is gone.	Beauties are plentiful in Washington.
Her desk is gone.	Desks are plentiful in Washington.
Her_____is gone.	_____are plentiful in Washington.

If we try to fit other words into these patterns, we find some will fit, some will not. *Come, honest,* usually will not and so are not used as nouns."

tively in the classroom and in their daily language situations.

The grammar needed for adequate expression is our next concern. The term *grammar* causes some confusion because it has many meanings. Some think of grammar as the parts of speech, syntax, sentence structure, and paragraph organization. Others prefer to think of grammar as the way our language is used. Some authorities suggest that the term grammar be applied only to the study of language structure, that the matters of correctness be called usage and that matters of form in expression be called conventions.

More important than the present

In the same manner a verb is described as a word that patterns like sing, beautify, or arrive. An adjective is a word that patterns like happy, beautiful, or good.

Soon he arrives at words like *change* that will fit both patterns. In one it is a noun in the other a verb. There are many words of this nature that belong to two "form classes." In order to discover in which class the word is being used the student

---

[3] Otto Jespersen, *Essentials in English Grammar* (New York: Holt, 1933), and *Growth and Structure of the English Language* (New York: Macmillan, 1948).

[4] Paul Roberts, *Patterns in English* (New York: Harcourt, 1956), pp. 19–27.

is directed to note both meaning and pattern.

In the sentence, "Man the pump," the pattern tells us that *man* is a verb and *pump* a noun. But in, "Pump the man," the pattern shows that *pump* is a verb and *man* is a noun. To illustrate that meaning does not tell us the form class, he used nonsense words to show the importance of pattern. "Bool that gloob over there," or "Let's steeker those peanuts." We know from the pattern that *bool* is a verb and is apparently something that can be done to a *gloob*.

It becomes apparent that this is one of the frontiers of the language arts. While few elementary teachers will use such material with children, many will want to examine this material to see if it has any value for them as students of language. It may be that Dr. Roberts has found an approach that is less abstract to young people. Once I worked with a group of fifth-graders and thought they understood the noun. A few days later I asked them for the definitions we had discussed. A Spanish boy waved his hand with enthusiasm so I called on him. "Teacher," said Manuel, "a noun is a person who plays and sings." After recovering, I discovered that my "person, place, or thing" definition meant little more to the others.

Because of experiences similar to this, Robert C. Pooley in his book *Teaching English Grammar* takes a strong stand.[5]

It is my point of view that the foundations of spoken and written English are best laid up to and including the sixth grade without formal instruction in the terminology of grammar—that means learning the parts of speech—or in the practice of identifying and naming the various parts and functions of the sentence. This statement is based upon considerable research and background which will be summarized under the following divisions:

1. The first consideration is the question of time. Time that is used in teaching children the names of parts of speech and the identification and classification of parts of

the sentence is time taken away from the practice of the skills of writing and speaking English.

2. All the evidence of research studies shows that formal grammar has very slight influence on the usage habits of children. Children learn their language by listening to their parents and by the conversation they have with other children in the home and on the playground. By the time a kindergartener reaches school, his patterns of speech are pretty well set up by his experience and have become very largely unconscious. If he has heard excellent English in his home, he speaks excellent English. If he has heard good English with some minor defects, these minor defects will show up in his speech. The child is not responsible in the sense that he is doing anything wrong. He is simply reflecting the background which he brings to school. To change such habits requires more than just knowledge.

3. All the evidence available shows that formal grammar has little or no effect upon the skills of composition in the elementary grades. Many studies have been carried out to determine the relationship between structural grammar and the writing skills of children. As early as 1923 William Asher conducted such an inquiry into the writing abilities of children in the upper elementary grades and derived this conclusion: "We may, therefore, be justified in the conclusion that time spent upon formal grammar in the elementary school is wasted so far as a majority of students are concerned." Other studies working on this same problem have yielded the same conclusions.

4. Various studies which have been conducted over the years indicate that grammatical terminology, when not particularly connected with a skill regularly used by the child, is easily confused and forgotten. To avoid teaching these terms does not mean that the child is unable to learn them. The question is how much effort is required and how valuable is the effort at this point. There is no evidence to show that excellent writing and speaking result, at least through grade six, from teaching the terms of formal grammar. In fact, the reverse seems to be true, that where a great deal of grammar is taught at the expense of practice in writing and speaking, the children make very poor gains in their English expression. It is wasteful of student and teacher time to attempt the mastery

---

[5] Robert C. Pooley, *Teaching English Grammar* (New York: Appleton, 1957), pp. 126–128.

of grammatical terms at least until the beginning of the seventh year.

Despite the truths contained in the above statement, teachers will find in textbooks and courses of study the following sequence of material:

Third Grade	Recognition of nouns
Fourth Grade	Recognition of nouns
	Recognition of verbs
	Recognition of adjectives
	Recognition of adverbs
Fifth Grade	Simple subject
	Compound subject
	Complete subject
	Simple predicate
	Compound predicate
	Complete predicate
	Recognition of nouns
	Common and proper nouns
	Singular and plural nouns
	Possessive nouns
	Nouns in apposition
	Nouns as subjects
	Recognition of verbs
	Agreement with subject
	Principal parts of verbs
Sixth Grade	Correct use of verbs
	Recognition of pronouns
	Singular and plural nouns
	Correct use of pronouns
	Recognition of adjectives

Comparison of adjectives
Correct use of adjectives
Articles
Recognition of adverbs
Comparison of verbs
Correct use of adverbs
Recognition of conjunctions
Correct use of conjunctions
Recognition of prepositions
Correct use of prepositions

Most courses of study outlines for grades seven and eight contain so much grammar that one wonders if the children do any personal writing.

Thus we face a true dilemma. We are required to teach what some authorities feel is of questionable merit. The reaction of teachers has been to place more emphasis on the use of language in the intermediate grades and to seek more meaningful ways to teach the required grammar of the courses of study.

1. Why would you disapprove of a minister or college teacher who used the language of the golf course in the pulpit or classroom?

2. Why do you approve of the school accepting the informal standard level?

3. Which writers of our time would you accept as authorities with respect to use of language?

4. Do you agree with Pooley that the emphasis should be on writing and speaking experience rather than analysis in the elementary school?

HOW IS SENTENCE SENSE TAUGHT IN THE ELEMENTARY SCHOOL?

Throughout the elementary school the emphasis in teaching sentence structure is on how to express ideas and how to assure oneself of being correctly understood. The language conventions that are taught as being correct help to purify a child's language and assure understanding.

As the child uses the language, the experiences build a foundation for the type of analysis that leads to definition. A definition of a sentence such as "a group of words that present a complete thought" is meaningless unless it grows out of experience.

Children are introduced to the punctuation of a sentence long before they are expected to use punctuation themselves. As a teacher writes a dictated group-story on the board, for example, she might point out: "You have given us such a good sentence that I am going to include it in our story. You see, I start the sentence with a capital letter and I put a period at the end. The period tells us to stop before we read the next sentence."

Later a child is helped to gain a sentence sense by the teacher's reading his story with him. It is pointed out that he has told two things about his dog; hence the teacher writes two sentences on the chalkboard. Periods and capitals are added.

Still later, children's sentences may be written on the chalkboard or projected on a screen for examination: Did I tell something? Did I begin with a capital letter? Did I end with the correct punctuation mark?

Number work offers an opportunity for the direct teaching of the question mark. Children learn that a problem has two parts, a telling part and an asking part. When they write their own problems they ask themselves: Did I put a period after the telling part, and a question mark after the asking part?

In order to help children understand sentences, one first-grade teacher held up a picture showing a little girl in a green dress and red shoes, sitting on a chair, looking at a book and eating a big red apple. She seems to be interested and happy.[6]

TEACHER: Would you like to have me tell you a story about this picture?
CLASS: Yes.
TEACHER: Red shoes, a chair, a big red apple, a little girl, a picture book. Does that sound like a good story, boys and girls?
CLASS: (A chorus of No's.)
TEACHER: Did it make sense?
CLASS: No.
TEACHER: Why not?
BOBBY: You just said a lot of words.
TEACHER: Yes, I did. Wasn't that a story?

---

[6] Minneapolis Public Schools, *Communication Curriculum Guide*, 1953.

ANITA: No, you should tell what she is doing.
TEACHER: That's right. I should make a statement that says something. You do it, Anita. What would you say for your story?
ANITA: A girl is reading a book and she is eating an apple.
TEACHER: That is a good statement. You really told us something about the little girl. And what was she doing? Could we say something else?
MARCIA: We could call her Jane and say, "Jane is reading a book."
TEACHER: Yes, that is a good statement.
SAMMY: Jane is wearing a green dress.
DICK: She has red shoes, too.
TEACHER: Good work. Let's *all* make up a story about this picture. I will write it on the board. Each statement will say something about the picture.

The following is the composite story.

Jane is looking at a picture book.
She is eating an apple.
She wears a green dress.
She has pretty red shoes.
Jane is happy.

TEACHER: Here is a picture for each of you. Tomorrow each one may tell a story about his picture.

Sentence recognition is reviewed by a third grade in the following manner.

TEACHER: Today we are going to write a story about our snails. How might we build our story?
CHILDREN: We'll have to have some sentences about our snails.
TEACHER: Do you know what a sentence is?
CHILD: A sentence is a bunch of words.
TEACHER: I'll write a group of words on the board and you decide if it looks like a sentence. (Writes.)
CHILD: No. It doesn't make sense.
TEACHER: Then a sentence is a group of words that tells something.
CHILD: It needs a capital and a period, too.
TEACHER: That's right. That's the way we separate sentences one from the others. As we write our story about our snails,

378 GRAMMAR, USAGE, AND PUNCTUATION

let's check our sentences and ask ourselves: Does it tell something? Does it begin with a capital? Does it end with a stop sign?

The class is introduced to kinds of sentences in grade five.

TEACHER: Your written stories and your reports are improving, but there is still something you can do to make them read more smoothly. You remember that in our spelling lessons the stories we have been reading have longer sentences. We call some of them compound sentences, and some complex sentences. Your ordinary sentences we call simple sentences. Harold, I often hear you using compound sentences. Can you explain what they are?

HAROLD: They're longer.

TEACHER: (*Writing on the chalkboard*) Yes, but they are more than that. Look at these two simple sentences:

Beverly came home last night.
It was getting dark when she arrived.

Who can put them together in one sentence?

JUDY: Beverly came home last night just as it was getting dark.

HAROLD: A compound sentence is two sentences combined.

TEACHER: That's right, only that may also be true of a complex sentence. It all depends on *how* they are put together. Judy's sentence is a complex sentence because she used *just as* to join them, and made the second part of the sentence dependent—as we say—on the first: it merely tells *when* it was she returned; it doesn't add another thought which is just as important as the first. But we won't worry about the difference between complex and compound yet—not until you get used to the idea of combining very short sentences into one longer sentence. Let's try that first. Then we'll look at the various kinds of joining words which make the difference between a complex sentence and a compound sentence.

The terms subject and predicate were introduced by one fifth-grade teacher in this manner:

A pupil was appointed to write on the blackboard what it was he saw the teacher do before the class. He wrote: *She went to the window. She sat on a chair. She picked up a book.*

TEACHER: (*pointing to the statements on the chalkboard*) What are these?

PUPIL 1: Statements.

PUPIL 2: Things the teacher did.

PUPIL 3: They are sentences.

TEACHER: That's right. They are all three, but for our purposes this morning, we'll call them sentences. (*Drawing a vertical line between subject and predicate.*) Notice that each sentence is made up of two parts. What does this much of the sentence (*pointing*) seem to tell you?

PUPIL 1: Who did it.

TEACHER: That's right, and this? (*Pointing.*)

PUPILS: What she did.

TEACHER: Does anyone know the names of each part? (*as pupils hesitate*) if not, I'll tell you. We call the person who does something the *subject;* we refer to what it was the person did, the *predicate.* In these sentences, *I* was the subject. Not all sentences are as simple as this. Let's make them a bit more difficult. This time each of you will be the subject and do something, but instead of just doing it, try to do it in a particular way. How many different ways might I have walked to the window, for example?

PUPIL 1: Slowly.

PUPIL 2: In a hurry.

PUPIL 3: Straight.

TEACHER: Let's do something more exciting than what I did and act it out so that we can see not only what was done but how it was done. As each person acts out his sentence, the rest of us will write down what we see. Later we will compare our sentences and name the parts which we recognize.

The best sentences describing what happened were put on the board and discussed. Adjectives, adverbs, and phrase and clause modifiers appeared in the sentences and were identified and named.

There are many variations of this method: pupils may be asked to include in their dramatizations a gesture or posture that can be referred to by a phrase or clause: *in a haughty manner,* for example, or *as if she were dazed.* To increase interest, groups might compete with each other in acting out and recording complete sentences.

Pictures from magazine covers may be used as the basis for sentence study: What does the picture tell you? *A small boy is pulling a red wagon along the sidewalk. Two girls are jumping rope.* Unless warned, pupils may leave out the verb and say, "A small boy with a red wagon." In such a case, class discussion may center around the incompleteness of the thought, the importance of the verb, or even the various forms, such as *pulling,* which can be made out of a verb.

Children enjoy building sentences. Start with a verb of action such as *break, eat, sew, sing, touch.* Have the children take turns using the word in a statement. When objects are added the sentence can frequently be acted out.

Five basic patterns might be noted with upper-grade children by analyzing some of the material they have written.

1. Subject-verb	*Mary laughed.*	*Mary,* who was watching television, *laughed* frequently.
2. Subject-verb-object	John bought hamburgers.	Having forgotten his lunch John bought the hamburgers with the last money he had.
3. Subject-verb-predicate-nominative	Children are *tax deductions.*	
4. Subject-verb-predicate adjectives	The *teacher is beautiful.*	
5. Expletive-verb (predicate adjective)-subject	There are scholars. It is easy to learn.	

The following activities may be used to teach effective sentence construction:

Some children are challenged by the idea of sentence kits. The idea is based on model car kits which children assemble. Use sentences from the textbooks read in that grade.

Basic sentence:	People	burned	fires
Spare parts:	at the doors some	of caves primitive	to keep animals away

Basic sentence:	houses	were

Spare parts: first   probably   real   houses   lake

Words might be put on cards with flannel backing so that these parts could be used for class demonstrations.

Combining short sentences is excellent practice. Upper grades might take an "Easy to Read" book from the library and summarize the material in longer sentences.

Needs Improvement	*Improved*
We went to the zoo. We saw the monkey. We gave him a banana.	When we went to the zoo we saw a monkey that ate a banana we gave him.

Warn children that *and* can be a sentence spoiler. Use examples of this nature:

We went to see Santa Claus *and* he was at the department store *and* he gave me a book.

A game of "Missing Verb" is liked by children in the intermediate grades.

Purpose:	To give practice in using verbs to complete sentence sense.
Players:	Small group.
Materials:	Two boxes. One box contains a number of cards with incomplete sentences minus the verbs; the other box contains the verb cards.

The man	the tall ladder	climbed

Directions:	The first child draws from the boxes one incomplete sentence card and one verb card. The aim is to fit the verb into the sentence so that it makes good meaning. If the verb does not match the sentence, the sentence is placed face up in the center of the table and other children, in turn, draw a sentence card and a verb card. A player may claim any sentence if his verb completes his sentence or one of the sentences in the center of the table. The child completing the most sentences wins.
Adaptation:	The missing words in the sentences might be adjectives or adverbs.
Caution:	The completed sentences should be checked by the teacher.

1. As you write do the ideas you wish to express dominate your thinking or do you share these with thoughts about sentence structure?

2. Could overemphasis on a sentence pattern result in a monotonous repetition of that pattern in a child's writing?

3. Are some sentences too complex in organization to analyze?

HOW CAN THE PARTS OF SPEECH BE TAUGHT SO THAT THE CHILD WILL SPEAK AND WRITE BETTER?

Let us first look at each part of speech and find ways of teaching the concept. Then we will consider how that knowledge might be used to improve sentences composed by a student.

Rather than waiting until grade four or five to mention nouns, it is sensible to start in the primary grades when children label things. *Doors, windows, desks,* are naming words or nouns. So are *John, Joe* and *Susan.* The same would be true of verbs. Words like *jump, run, play,* are action words or verbs and should be so classified from the first grade on.

With fourth- or fifth-grade children, teachers may start with a picture and have the children list the people they see in the picture, then the places, then the things. In the discussion it is brought out that they *named* these items. There are other things we name, such as ideas like democracy and feelings like happiness. Words that name something are classed as nouns. The same thing can be done by having each child write two sentences about persons, places, things, ideas, and feelings. After the sentences are written the child is asked to underline words that name something. Check by having the children find the nouns in the sentences of a textbook or having them write nouns that they think of when you say "home" or "vacation." Once the idea is taught it should never be permitted to fade from the memories of children. In the spelling list, ask children to use the appropriate words as nouns. In reading ask them to identify nouns. Make a bulletin board on which children add a noun a day.

Most courses of study suggest that singular versus plural forms and possessives be taught in grade five, while compound nouns and concrete versus abstract distinctions are added in grade six. Some teachers feel that this is an arbitrary spread of the concept. Certainly possessives and plural forms will be used by the children long before these grades are reached. One teacher had fifth-grade children keep notebooks titled, "All About Nouns and Verbs." The children brought together all basic information on these two parts of speech during a period of six weeks. Interest did not lag, nor was the material forgotten, since the books were constantly used for reference.

A way to introduce verbs is to put a group of simple sentences on the board and erase the verb. Then discuss what part of the sentence was removed. Develop the idea that these are the words that tell the action.

> Paul *drove* a black car.
> He *went* to see his cousin.
> The cousin *lives* in Yuma.
> He *stopped* in Denver.

Then provide some sentences in which the student adds an action word.

> Mary _____ a new dress.
> My dog _____ the cat.
> Mice _____ cats.
> Mice _____ cheese.
> Cats _____ mice.
> Jack _____ baseball.

Still stressing the action concept, look at sentences in the readers to "spot verbs." Being "verb detectives" has some appeal. A trick to teach children is that if they can put I, you or he, before a word and the two words make a sentence, then the second word is a verb. One can say "I eat," "you draw," "he plays," because the second words are verbs. But you cannot say "I piano," "he birds," or "you newspaper," because the second words are not verbs. This "trick" does assume that the child has a sense of what a sentence is. A variation is to have the children be hunters who put words in noun, verb, and adjective cages.

Very soon the students find sentences that contain only the *to be* verbs. The definition terminology, "verbs of being," rarely makes sense to children. It is best to identify these words as a group. The teacher might say, "There is a group of verbs that are a part of the verb *to be*. I have made a list of them on the board: am, is, are, was, were, have been, shall be, will be. Let us make each one into a sentence."

> I am in the fifth grade.
> He is my teacher.
> We are here.
> I was sad.
> You were happy.

Then discuss the fact that while the words do not show action, they do indicate existing. Students might keep a chart of these nonaction verbs (there are not many) and simply memorize them as one would certain sight words in reading. These verbs are used with action verbs as helpers.

Helping verbs are used to show time:

> Paul is cracking a nut. (*present*)
> Paul will crack a nut. (*future*)
> Paul has been cracking nuts.
> (*past and present*)
> Paul cracked a nut. (*past*)

These words are used as helping verbs:

am	do	might
are	does	must
be	had	shall
been	has	should
can	have	was
could	is	were
did	may	will

In a question the helping verb is frequently separated from the main verb:

> Where *are* you *going*?
> *Did* you *find* it?

No and *not* sometimes separate the verb from its helping verb.

> I *have* not *found* it.

A game called "Employment Agency" provides oral practice in use of helping verbs. It may be played by several children. All except three children are given a verb card such as:

| seem | draw | flown | swim |

The children holding these verb cards are the "Employers." The three other children (the Employees) hold the card with a helping verb such as:

| has | have | had |

Each employer in turn holds his word card in front of the group and says, "Do I need help? Does anyone want a job?" If the word on his card needs a helping word, one of the three helpers who raises his hand may be chosen to stand beside him. The teacher chooses another child to use the word in a sentence.

Exercises like the following stress verb identification:

Replace "tired," often-used verbs with words that are more vivid, such as *trudged* for *walked, consumed* for *ate*, etc.

Cut pictures from magazines that illustrate action verbs and post in a bulletin or use to illustrate a "verb collection."

Combine two words, a noun and a verb, to form a sentence: Boys walk. Turkeys strut. Babies cry. Stars twinkled. Dogs barked.

Keep a record of one morning's activity. Note the use of verbs.

At 9:00 school _____

The teacher _____

I _____

Then the class _____

At recess we _____

After recess I _____

One boy _____

One girl _____

At noon I _____

The term *predicate* is an awkward one. It is used to describe the part of the sentence that tells about the subject. As such it includes more than the verb of most sentences. Yet in writing, the problem is usually the verb alone. It is the verb that fails to agree with the subject in number or the verb is in the wrong tense (time) when related to other sentences in the writing. It is easier for children to understand the verb of the sentence and its operation without including other aspects of the predicate.

The terms *subject* and *object* are much easier to understand. Primary children can locate the subject of a sentence. "What are they talking about?" or "Who is the subject of this sentence?" are natural questions in any reading instruction. Even compound subjects such as, "*John and Joe* bought a dog," are understandable to young children. The one new difficulty added is that of selecting a plural form of the verb. If the oral language patterns are correct this presents little difficulty. When there is difficulty, it is usually restricted to one or two children rather than an entire class. One teacher reported that there were few errors made with this construction until after a lesson had been taught stressing the agreement in number of the verb with the compound subject. In other words, the children were unaware of the problem until it was taught to them. Then it resulted in a concern that produced errors. It might be well to assess the class needs before teaching such a lesson. A simple test having the children supply the correct word will reveal what the teacher needs to know. Use sentences like this: Mary and Jane _____ Girl Scouts. Mother and father _____ there. Where _____ Jane and Jack?

The direct object of the verb is that which receives the action: *John hit Mary*. In this sentence, Mary was *hit* and is therefore the object of the verb. Some children are confused if the teacher says *Mary* is the "object of the sentence." This terminology is too much like, "the meaning or purpose of the sentence." At this point, audio-visual devices help the children see these words as parts of a sentence. The labeling of words in simple sentences will help establish the concepts. Some use the

S-V-O as symbols of the pattern of sentences like this.

The arrow hit the target.
s   v   o

Putting the words on separate pieces of cardboard and reassembling the sentences on the chalk rail or flannelboard helps to dramatize this construction. Pass a different word to each child. One list will be those of nouns, the other of verbs. The teacher asks, "who has a noun that will be the subject of a sentence?" "Who has a verb that will show what the subject did?" Then, "Who has a word that received the action?" Use these nouns: *John, Mary, mother, father, the dog, the cat, the teacher, a bird, an apple, candy.* Use these verbs: *bought, chased, ate, taught, fed, sold.* Objects have a way of getting quite complex, since other parts of speech may have an object, but this type of beginning exercise will help establish the concept.

Children should find adjectives as easy to understand as nouns. Whenever a word describes a noun, as *red* dress, or points out, as *that* grade, it modifies the noun and is an adjective. Adjectives answer the questions: What color? What kind? What size? How many? Which one? After explaining this, have a class think through the following exercise:

Which question does each underlined adjective answer:

The <u>old</u> house was dark.
We sat on <u>three</u> benches.
The <u>back</u> door is open.
I need a <u>wet</u> cloth.
Do you see <u>those</u> girls?

Have an "adjective search" of a page in a reader. See who can find the largest number.

Make lists of adjectives that answer each of the questions that adjectives answer.

Have the children spell only the adjectives in the week's spelling list.

Make a collection of advertisements that use adjectives to make the product attractive.

Put a picture on the bulletin board.

Let each child add one adjective that might be used in telling about the picture.

There is little reason for considering the articles *a, an,* and *the,* as separate parts of speech. Mauree Applegate suggests that they be given some personality by calling them "towing words." This suggestion is appropriate because articles always appear before a noun. The idea also helps children remember that when the word towed starts with a vowel, *a* will not do the towing job —only *an* and *the* want that type of work.[9]

The concept of modification is an important one in understanding the sentence. Ask the children to picture in their minds what they see when they read, "The girl ran down the street." Discuss the various ages each thought the girl and the kind of street that was in their mental pictures. Then ask the children to read this sentence: "The little girl ran down the shady street." Again discuss the mental picture in their minds and note that their ideas are more alike or that the number of meanings have been limited by the use of little and shady. Modification means just that, to limit the meaning. One way of making our meaning more exact is to use modifiers.

Experiment with substitution exercises like the following to see how these words limit the meaning:

The (big) (happy) (dirty) (handsome) boy went to the (haunted) (new) (enchanted) (girl's) house.

As understanding of modification develops, more involved material can be used. It will interest some classes to attempt to construct a sentence that will be so clear that everyone will have exactly the same mental picture:

The dog ran.
The dog ran down the muddy street.
The little yellow dog ran down the muddy street.
The little yellow dog ran down the muddy street barking.
The little yellow dog ran down the muddy street barking at the newspaper boy.

---

[9] Mauree Applegate, *Easy in English* (Harper, 1960).

The traditional diagram form is a good visual aid for adjectives. List a noun on the board and then place a modifier suggested by a child under it. In a series this represents the limiting aspect of modification.

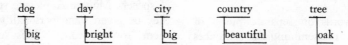

Then point out that in our speech and writing we sometimes use two or more adjective modifications:

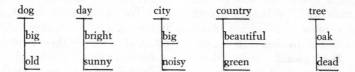

Adverbs have three functions: to modify verbs (run *swiftly*), to modify adjectives (*strangely* silent), or another adverb ("The bell rang unusually long."). Adverbs usually answer the questions *how, when,* or *where*:

How words: slowly, well, neatly, fast.
When words: early, often, once, then.
Where words: inside, up, here, away.

To clarify the use of adverbs, have the children identify *how, when,* and *where* words in sentences like these:

I ran up.
The baby cried loudly.
I ran inside.
I will eat now.
He came early.
He came here.
The cake is light blue.
The boy secretly tasted it.
He very noisily smacked his lips.
The cake was very good.

A few adverbs seem to stand alone because the verb modified is understood rather than spoken: *yes, no, probably, surely, truly, perhaps, indeed, please.*
Some adjectives and adverbs have the same form. The following words can be used either as an adverb or adjective. Chal-

lenge the students to construct two sentences for each word and to label which has the adjective and which the adverb.

best	just
better	late
bright	long
cheap	low
clean	near
close	pretty
deep	quick
direct	right
early	shop
fair	short
far	slow
fast	soft
full	straight
hand	well
high	wide
ill	wrong

Examples would be:

This is the best cake. (Adjective)
Of the three she writes the best.
(Adverb)
He ran fast to catch the plane.
(Adverb)
The jet is a fast plane. (Adjective)

Conjunctions as connectors in such expressions as: "Paul *and* Bill," "We will go to the show *but* you must stay home," cause few identification problems. Neither do exclamations such as: "Oh!" "Ouch!"

"Hello!" Charts can be made of such words and their function illustrated.

Prepositions are more difficult. One child told me that a preposition could be used to describe anything a squirrel could do to a hollow log. A diagram might illustrate such words as *over, under, by, into, in, above, beside, around.* The idea does help define prepositions as directional words. The term is a combination of *pre-*, meaning "in front of" or "before," and *-position,* meaning "place." A preposition is a word that is placed before another word. It is placed before a noun to show relationship between the noun and some other word in the sentence. This relationship can be illustrated in the following expressions:

The hat on the chair.
The dog under the tree.
The cat in the tree.
The boy by the car.
The trailer behind the car.

Make a master list of prepositions:

about	at
above	because of
according	before
across	beyond
after	by
behind	by way of
below	during
beneath	except
beside	for
between	from
in	like
in front of	of
in regard to	on
in spite of	on top of
into	out of
throughout	over
to	through
toward	up
under	up to
until	upon
against	with
along	within
among	without
around	

After the children have looked for preposi-

tions in a story they should note that a preposition always takes an object.

Some prepositions have meanings that need to be clarified. In oral language the following are frequently confused:

Among and *between*

Among applies to *more than two* persons or things:
The baseball equipment was divided *among* all the boys.

Between applies to *only two* persons or things:
Mother placed the flowers *between* the books and the basket.

At and *to*

At means already in place:
The boy is *at* school.

To means going toward a person, place or thing:
The boy is going *to* school.

In and *into*

In means inside or within:
Mary is *in* the pool.

Into means to move from the outside to the inside:
Mary is going to dive *into* the pool.

From and *than*

From is a preposition and shows position in time and space.
Than is a conjunction (a joining word) and not a preposition. It usually joins two parts of a sentence:
I would rather go *than* stay at home.

These sentences are to be read carefully:

This book is different *from* the other books in the room. (correct)
This book is different *than* the other books in the room. (incorrect)

Of and *from*

The prepositions *of* and *from* are never used with the adverb *off* such as:

The men jumped *off* the boat. (correct)

The men jumped *off of* the boat. (incorrect)

The men jumped *off* the log. (correct)

The men jumped *from off* the log. (incorrect)

Posters, charts and bulletin boards, dramatizing these confused meanings (only one group at a time) might be made by intermediate-grade students for a "pure language" week or program.

One part of speech remains to be described—the pronoun. The term means "for a noun." Children can see this when the teacher substitutes pronouns in sentences of this nature: *Mary lost her lamb. Boy Blue went to sleep. The spider sat beside Miss Muffet.* Such sentences become: *She lost her lamb. He went to sleep. It sat beside her.*

When children learn about forming possessives in the third or fourth grade, lessons should be planned on the possessive forms of pronouns. This can be associated with the pronoun definition. "The boy's coat" becomes *his coat,* "the girl's dog" becomes *her dog,* and "the fifth-grade team" becomes *our team.* Contrast the two forms of pronouns:

Pronoun	Possessive Pronoun
I	my
he	his
she	her
we	our
you	your
it	its

The pronoun *it* presents a special difficulty. The possessive of *it* is *its.* There is confusion because of the contraction of *it is* which is *it's.* Since *man* in the plural becomes *men's* by the addition of an apostrophe and an *s,* the logical association is to do the same for *it.* Point out to the children that *its* is like *his.*

The major problem concerning pronouns is the form taken when a pronoun is the object of a verb or preposition. Illustrate the form again with sentences:

Mary hit John.	Mary hit him.
John lost the book.	John lost it.
Mary knew John and Jane.	Mary knew them.
Jane liked Mary.	Jane liked her.
Bring the paper to the teacher.	Bring the paper to her; bring it to her.

Again, contrast the forms in a chart:

Subject Pronouns	Possessive Pronouns	Object Pronouns
I	my	me
he	his	him
she	her	her
we	our	us
you	your (s)	you
they	their (s)	them

But there is a group of words sometimes used as pronouns that are indefinite in that they do not stand for a definite name of something. Among them are *another, anyone, anybody, each, either, everybody, all, everyone, neither, no one, nobody, everything, some one, none, other, somebody, several, both.*

Notice their use in such sentences as these:

Give me another.

Anyone can do this.

Each must give something.

No one is here.

Nobody can do this.

Everything is ready.

One must drive slowly.

Somebody lost it.

Both have finished.

Some like candy.

Some pronouns connect or relate parts of sentences:

	Connecting Pronoun
I have a little dog. He has fleas. I have a little dog who has fleas.	who
I saw the people. Their house burned down. I saw the people whose house burned down.	whose
The dog ran away. He was mine. The dog that ran away was mine.	that

Other pronouns are those used in questions such as, who, what, and which, and the self pronouns which are used for emphasis.

As each part of speech is taught, some useful way to employ that knowledge in speaking and writing needs to be established. At one time a knowledge of the parts of speech was used widely to diagram a sentence. Research has shown that children in the fourth and fifth grades can be taught to diagram, but that this knowledge has little influence on their writing. In the junior high school and beyond, some students profit from their ability to diagram.

As a teacher in the intermediate grades, you will find simple diagrams a help in explaining certain sentences and sentence parts. Do not hesitate to use this visual aid as an aspect of your explanation. But do not expect children to diagram any but simple sentences and a few modification positions.

In the discussion of adjectives and adverbs the relationship of these words was indicated in diagrams. Children find this sentence pattern helpful. At first each major part of the sentence, such as the subject, should be studied separately.

Prepositional phrases are like branches on a tree. A diagram will help the child to identify the related nature of such a group of words.

Here is a simple sentence: *The house burned.*

Here is a simple sentence with a prepositional phrase used as an adjective: *The house by the old mill burned.*

The diagram of the phrase looks like this:

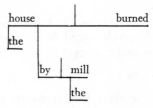

At the beginning the entire phrase could be written on a slanted line under *house* but the form illustrated above is actually easier to write. The concept of the compounds can be illustrated through diagrams.

Here is a simple sentence with a simple subject: *Mary ate an apple.* It would be shown this way:

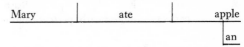

Here is a simple sentence with a compound subject: *Mary and Jack ate the apples.* It would be shown like this:

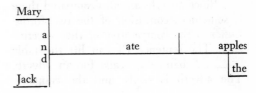

Here is a simple sentence with a compound verb: *The truck rattled and squeaked*. It would be shown like this:

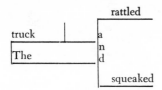

This is a compound sentence made up of two related but independent clauses. With children we would point out that each part is a sentence by itself: The cowboy walked and the lady rode his horse.

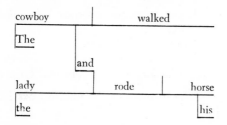

Another use of the knowledge of the parts of speech would be to clarify some common usage errors.

To—too—two

These three homonyms are confused because of sound. The error is a spelling problem. Each has a different meaning and represents a different part of speech. *To* is a preposition, *too* is an adverb, and *two* is an adjective.

> Send the bill to me.
> It is too late.
> I want two dollars. (Note that "twin" also has the *w* in it as a way to remember the meaning and spelling.)

Good—well

> Good is an adjective. This is a *good* cake.
> Well is an adjective only when referring to health: I am *well*. Otherwise it is an adverb: He plays *well*.

Real—really—very

> Real is an adjective meaning genuine. This is *real* gold.
> Really is an adverb meaning actually. Is he *really* (actually) going?
> Very is usually an adverb meaning exceedingly. I am *very* happy.

Both *really* and *very* may be used in the same sentence but the meaning differs.

In the comparison of adjectives typical errors are *most best, beautifulest, more sweeter, more dead*. Children should know the terms used and the standard forms of comparative adjectives.

Positive	Comparative	Superlative
tall	taller	tallest (common form)
beautiful	more beautiful	most beautiful (easier to say with long adjectives)
good	better	best (irregular form)
bad	worse	worst (" ")
little	less	least (" ")
perfect	more nearly perfect	most nearly perfect (for natural superlatives)

The idea that comparison is made between two and superlative among more than two, is easy to illustrate and prevents many errors.

Since adverbs are also compared there is sometimes confusion of the two forms. *Easier* is the comparative of the adjective *easy*. The sentence, "I can lift the table _____ than you," calls for an adverb. The adverb is *easily* and the comparative would be *more easily* rather than *easier*.

There is a group of language errors related to verb tense (time) that concern us as teachers in the language arts.

There are over eight thousand verbs in the English language. Most of these are "regular" verbs—that is, they form the past tense and past participle by adding -*ed* to the present tense:

Present Tense (today)	Past Tense (yesterday)	Past Participle (with I have)
walk	walked	walked
talk	talked	talked
cook	cooked	cooked

But there are enough irregular verbs to cause trouble. Those learning English as a foreign language find this one of the most difficult problems encountered. Fortunately, few children will find all of these a problem. Some are used infrequently while others are so common as to be simple patterns which the child masters in his speech before starting to school. Frequent errors are indicated in parentheses.

Present Tense	Past Tense	Past Participle (with have, has, had)
beat	beat	beaten
begin	began	begun (never used alone)
blow	blew (never *blowed*)	blown
break	broke (not with *have* or *has*)	broken
bring	brought	brought (no word *brang* or *brung*)
burst	burst	burst (no verb *bust, busted or bursted*)
come	came (never with *have* or *has done*)	come
do	did	done (along with *have, has*)
draw	drew (not *drawed*)	drawn
drink	drank	drunk
eat	ate (*et* only in Britain)	eaten
flee	fled	fled
flow	flowed	flowed
fly	flew	flown (nothing to do with *flow*)
go	went (always alone)	gone
grow	grew (not *growed*)	grown
hang	hung	hung
hang	hanged	hanged (used only with reference to executions)
ring	rang (always alone)	rung
swim	swam (always alone)	swum
swing	swung	swung (not *swang*)
write	wrote (always alone)	written
cast	cast	cast (not *casted*)
broadcast	broadcast	broadcast
throw	threw	thrown (not *throwed* or *thrun*)
fall	fell (always alone)	fallen
freeze	froze (always alone)	frozen
run	ran	run
see	saw (always alone)	seen (with *have* or *has*)
sing	sang	sung
speak	spoke	spoken
steal	stole (always alone)	stolen

In English, a verb must agree with its subject in person and number. Thus when the noun or pronoun is changed to show person or number, the verb must also be changed. It will be best to explain this rule with respect to one difficulty at a time. By person we refer to the speaker, those spoken to, and those spoken of.

> I play the piano. (first person speaking)
>
> We sing in school. (first person plural speaking)
>
> You sing well. (second person spoken to)
>
> John plays the piano. (third person spoken of)
>
> These flowers match her dress. (third person spoken of)

By number, we are thinking of the persons or things considered as being one or more than one. These errors will illustrate the problem:

> *The boys was happy.*   for   *The boys were happy.*
> *We was happy.*   for   *We were happy.*

Most indefinite pronouns are singular: *either, neither, each, another, much, one.* All compounds of *one, body* and *thing,* such as *anyone* or *nobody,* are also singular. The pronouns *both, few, many* and *several* are plural. The words *all, any, more, most,* and *such* may be either singular or plural, depending on the noun they represent. When these rules are not understood we find errors like these:

> Each of the boys are to try.
> Neither of the dogs are hungry.
> Nobody who was there are here.

Another problem illustrated above is that the subject and verb are separated. Few would say, "Nobody are here." One help is to suggest enclosing such phrases in parentheses to check the agreement of subject and verb:

> Nobody (who was there) is here.
> A set (of the tools) is very useful.
> One (of the girls) is going home.

Sometimes agreement depends on the idea of the writer. One may write, "Bread and butter are expensive," the writer thinking of two ideas. Compound subjects are usually two ideas but they may be one. The same is true of collective nouns such as *tribe, team, class, club.*

It is difficult for an adult to realize how abstract language becomes when we look at language as a thing apart from the meanings communicated. A teacher needs to place himself in the learner's position in order to understand how complex this can be. Imagine that you are a child again. You have learned to name many of the things you can hear and see. You know the meaning of apple, orange, and banana. In kindergarten or first grade you learned that all of these can be fruit. In time you have learned other generalized meanings for such words as people, animals, games, toys, and house.

At first all these words were learned orally. The sound was the symbol for the thing. Then in reading you learned the printed word which was a symbol for the sound. The printed word is actually a double symbol. It represents both the sound and the meaning. From eight to twelve per cent of the children in school have difficulty understanding this double symbolism and thus are remedial or slow readers. When such a child is asked to use another level of abstraction and classify words as nouns, verbs or other parts of speech, he usually fails. Rather than classification of the sentence parts, these children need opportunities to use the written language with an emphasis upon the ideas expressed. But there are some aspects of sentence structure that can be understood by most of the children in the intermediate grades and which can be applied to improve their written communication.

1. Someone has said we have been teaching language in the same way a coach might teach swimming, by having each person memorize the names of bones and muscles of the body. Is this a fair analogy?

2. The parts of speech were developed by a monk 800 years ago as he analyzed the

Latin of Cicero. Would it be possible to classify our words in other ways?

3. Some writers such as Shakespeare, and in more recent times Sir Winston Churchill, never studied the parts of speech and other grammatical facts. Does it follow that others would write as well as these writers if they had not studied grammar?

4. Check such items as certain irregular verbs and adjectives in a dictionary to see if there is an explanation for their present forms. Is derivation a factor?

HOW MAY CORRECT USAGE HABITS BE ESTABLISHED?

Correct usage is concerned with proper form. The agreement of verb and subject in number and tense, the form of the pronoun in various positions in the sentence, and the word order in sentences are some of the situations that present learning problems of proper form. The child who says "I done my work" is using the wrong verb form. Another who says "Him and me are friends" is using the wrong form of the pronoun. Children use these forms because they hear them at home.

A child cannot learn to *improve* his language unless he first feels free to *use* language. Errors in the use of language, therefore, should be called to his attention only after he feels accepted by the group and sufficiently self-confident so that correction will not silence him. The spirit in which corrections are made is perhaps the most important single factor in the child's language development.

These steps have proven effective in practice:

Listen to the children talk and note the type of errors common to the group and to individuals.

Select the most glaring ones for correction.

Choose a few errors at a time for concentrated effort.

Call attention to the correct use of words as well as to errors in usage.

Correct the child at the time the error is made, but after he has finished what he had to say.

Follow a period of oral expression with a short drill period in which the child hears the correct form repeated several times.

Play games in which the correct form is used over and over again.

Note how Mary is complimented on correct word usage in grade one. The children were saying "I got" repeatedly. Mary said, "I have."

TEACHER: I am so glad to hear Mary say "I have." It sounds pleasing to my ears.

This approval made the others eager to use "I have."

The children correct a common error in grade two:

TEACHER: This morning I heard someone say, "The bird he was building a nest." Let's all think of something you have seen a bird do and see if we can leave out the "he."

CHILD 1: The bird was feeding his babies.

CHILD 2: The bird was hopping on the ground.

TEACHER: This morning I heard someone say, "This here book is mine." It would sound better to say, "This book is mine." Let's all take something out of our desks that belongs to us and tell about it.

CHILD 1: This pencil is mine.

CHILD 2: This chalk is yours.

The children begin to drop "ain't" when assisted to make proper substitutions.

TEACHER: Lately I've been hearing some of you say, "I ain't got a pencil. I ain't going with you." Does anyone know a better way of saying it?

CHILD 1: I haven't a pencil.

CHILD 2: I'm not going with you.

TEACHER: That's better.

The English language is constantly in a period of change. The meaning difference between *shall* and *will* that is still taught in language books has for all realistic purposes disappeared in usage. The use of the pronoun *whom* has reached the stage where those who do use it frequently do so incorrectly and the word is seldom used in conversation.

Some forms, however, do indicate an illiterate and crude level of speech and should be corrected in school, such as the following: yourn, hern, ourn, this here, ain't, a orange, haven't no, he seen, he brung, have wrote, hisself, me and Mary went.

Textbooks, generally speaking, usually provide drill material to teach the correct forms concerning several of the following verbs.

Third Grade

In nearly all series:

> see—saw—seen
> do—did—done
> go—went—gone
> come—came
> are—aren't—ain't
> I have no—I got a
> brung (*eliminated*)

Added in some series:

> run—ran
> was—were
> eat—ate—eaten
> give—gave—given
> wasn't—weren't

Fourth Grade

Retaught in some series:

> see—saw—seen
> do—did—done
> go—went—gone
> come—came
> aren't

Included in some series:

> eat—ate—eaten
> draw—drew
> know—knew
> write—wrote
> can—may
> don't—doesn't
> teach—learn
> wasn't—weren't

Added in some series:

> brought
> took—taken
> let—leave

Fifth Grade

Reteach all items presented in lower grades:

> began—begun
> blow—blew
> break—broke—broken
> fly—flew
> give—gave
> grow—grew—grown
> ring—rang
> say—said
> sing—sang
> set—sit
> speak—spoke
> throw—threw
> take—took

Sixth Grade

Reteach all items taught in lower grades:

> choose
> freeze
> lie—lay
> ought
> ride
> shall—will
> sank—sunk
> dive—dived
> go—goes
> drown—drowned

Sixth Grade

Added in some series:

> drove—driven
> drank—drunk
> began—begun
> tore—torn
> wore—worn
> knew—known

Practice with pronouns varies but the majority of textbooks stress the following items:

Third Grade

Mother and I
those boys rather than them boys
this here corrected

Fourth Grade

himself—themselves
I—me
Avoid *John he went*
Indefinite *they, he* in sentences

Fifth Grade

he—him
she—her
who—which
we—us

Sixth Grade

Pronouns in subject and object positions:

we—us
its—it's

Other usage items included in most textbooks concern the following:

Third Grade

Double negative

Fourth Grade

there—their—they're
a—an
good—well

Fifth Grade

from—off—of

Sixth Grade

to—at
in—into
by—at
misuse of comparatives
than—from

There are very few research studies available on the proper grade placement of usage practice. Those that do exist are usually surveys of city courses of study and textbooks. This means that teacher judg-ment, as much as any other factor, has influenced the grade placement. Textbook writers must consider the practical problem of the total amount of material to be put in a book. As a result the teacher may find an item such as *take-took* listed in an index with three page references. Further examination will reveal that frequently these refer to one sentence in a test of ten items in which the child has to make a choice between two forms. Frequently children guess the correct form in such an exercise even though they misuse the verb in their own speech and writing. *If a child is making an error the teacher must plan more corrective instruction than that found in many textbooks.*

A peculiar problem of usage errors is the fact that a child who has correct speech in the primary grades may start making errors in later grades. Perhaps this is because he hears incorrect usage on television and the playground, or reads it in comic books. Exercises in the textbook may act as a maintenance factor by reinforcing existing correct habits.

One other factor concerning textbook drill material should be noted. The sentence may require the child to select between *was* and *were*. If the problem is only one of selecting between the singular and plural it will not serve the child who says, "you was," or "If I was." The drill or test should concern the error the learner makes.

To correct an error three things are necessary: the error should be identified, oral practice should be stressed until the correct form sounds correct, and written practice should be given to establish the desired habit and to test the learner. Oral exercises provide opportunities in listening to the correct form. The drill is for the listener as well as the speaker. "Game" situations like the following provide such practice.

There Is—There Are—There Was— There Were—Select a pupil to start the game. This pupil asks a question and names another pupil who must answer it. The answer must contain *there is, there are, there was,* or *there were*. If the second pupil does not make a mistake, he calls on another pupil to answer a question, and so on until every pupil has taken part in the game. Players should show, by raising their hands, that they notice an error made by

another. The player who makes a mistake in asking or answering a question loses his turn and has a point counted against him. The pupil with the fewest mistakes wins. This is the way the game goes:

TOM: Bob, how many windows are there in this room?

BOB: There are six windows in this room.

BOB: Fred, how many books are on your desk?

FRED: There is one book on my desk.

FRED: Betty, how many Sundays were there in this month?

BETTY: There were four Sundays in this month.

BETTY: Nellie, how many stars are there in the sky?

NELLIE: There are many stars in the sky.

Thus the game proceeds, each pupil answering and asking questions.

There Aren't—The purpose of this game is to help you to avoid two mistakes that are often made by careless people. These people say, "Are they" when they should say "Are there" and "There ain't" when they ought to say "There aren't."

Arrange the players in two teams, A and B. Put on the blackboard the list of questions given below. The pupils in team A will read the questions, each of which must begin with the words "Are there any." The pupils in team B will answer the questions in turn. Every answer must begin with the words, "No, there aren't any." Thus:

ONE OF THE A's: Are there any lazy boys in our school?

ONE OF THE B's: No, there aren't any lazy boys in our school.

Every mistake counts a point against the side making it. The team with the fewer errors wins. The teacher will act as referee and scorekeeper.

Suggested topics:

1. rabbits in the sea?
2. books on the floor?
3. fairies in the hall?

4. eagles on the roof?
5. lions in this country?
6. jokes in that book?
7. rude boys in our school?
8. fish in trees?
9. cowards in the police force?
10. peanuts in your pocket?
11. careless pupils here?
12. bananas on the desk?
13. whales on a farm?
14. oranges in a meat shop?
15. snakes in the air?
16. pies in a book store?
17. ships on a road?
18. islands in a desert?
19. hockey games in July?
20. flies in winter?

Verb Tense—The teacher will write on the board seven or eight verbs from the following list:

tear, sing, freeze, break, see, do, lay, drink, burst, blow, throw, show, ride, ring, write, catch

The leader will start the game, saying, "I *tore* my coat. I *have torn* it before." The leader then calls on a pupil who stands beside the leader, repeats what he said, and then says, "I *sang* a song, I *have sung* it before." The next person called on repeats what the leader said, what the first pupil said, and then adds, "I *froze* my ears. I *have frozen* them before."

The game continues in this way, each pupil repeating in the proper order what all the others have said, and adding one more, always taking the next word in the list on the board, and using the same forms as were used with the other verbs.

Lie (Lies), Lay, Lain, Lying—A leader is chosen who must leave the room. The pupils in the room watch while the teacher places a small article (pen, book, pencil, ruler) on someone's desk. The leader returns, stands before the class, and has five guesses in trying to locate the article. He asks, "Is the book *lying* on your desk, Susan?" Susan replies, "No, the book isn't *lying* on my desk; you are cold."

If the leader fails to find the article in five guesses, another leader is chosen. If he locates the article, he changes places with the pupil on whose desk it was laid. A pupil whose sentence structure is faulty or who does not use *lying* correctly must drop out of the game.

The children are seated in a circle with the teacher, who holds ten cards, each bearing the picture of a common object. One by one, the cards are displayed quickly to the class. Hands are raised; a child is called on. "What did you see, Tommy?" "I saw an apple." This continues until all cards are used.

Next the teacher holds the cards, two at a time, in random order (Example: orange, first; dog, second) "Which did you see first and which did you see second?" (Hands are raised) "Mary?" "I saw the orange first and then I saw the dog."

"Did and Done" [7]—The teacher, with the children in a circle, asks each one to think of something he or she did the day before with brother or sister or playmate. Example:

TEACHER: What did you do, Jimmy?
JIMMY: I went to the store.
TEACHER: When did you do it?
JIMMY: I did it yesterday.

"Bought and Buyed"—The teacher requests each child, in turn, to think of something he or she bought recently. Example:

TEACHER: What did you buy, Jessie?
JESSIE: I bought some gum.
TEACHER: When did you buy it?
JESSIE: I bought it yesterday.

"My Brother, He . . ."—The teacher asks each child to think of something he or she could tell (that is nice) about a brother, sister, or some member of the class.

---

[7] Adapted from "Creative Language Teaching," by John Maxwell in *Monograph for Elementary Teachers* No. 100 (Evanston, Ill.: Row, Peterson, 1961).

The exercises (as with most oral-aural exercises) should be repeated from time to time, since the problem is deep-rooted and not easily corrected. She asks the class to think through what they are going to say, and to avoid using "he" or "she."

Each child then turns around to his neighbor to the rear and tells his bit of information, with the teacher judiciously correcting each child who uses an incorrect form. The end purpose is to have the correct form used twenty-five to thirty-five times. The problem is deep-seated at this age, and although it will disappear naturally with maturity, the teacher can hasten its disappearance.

"Him and Me," "Her and I"—The teacher gives the class one minute to converse with a neighbor across the aisle to determine what they both like. Each tells the class one of the things he likes.

TEACHER: Donna, what did you and Sam decide?

DONNA: He and I like chocolate ice cream.

TEACHER: Sam, what else do you and Donna like?

SAM: She and I like Zorro.

"Leave and Let"—This problem can be resolved as a game involving the alphabet, knowledge of the noun, use of *leave* and *let*. The class is divided into groups and the game proceeds by rows until one side has finished. When a team errs, the turn goes to the other side. Example:

"He don't" and *"He doesn't"*—One child is sent out of the room while an object (pencil, eraser, eyeglass case, or the like) is given to another child in the room. The first child returns to search for the object. He may look at each person in turn, but must speak to the person behind his "suspect." Example:

"Does he have it?"
"No. He doesn't have it."
"Does she have it?"
"No. She doesn't have it."

Sides may be chosen if desirable and points given for each failure-to-find and a large number of points removed for each finding. The side receiving the smaller number of points wins the game. Use of "he don't" could be a penalty factor.

"Isn't there any" and *"Aren't there any"*—This problem can be made into a fast-moving game. One persons asks, "Aren't there any elephants in the room?" A second person responds as rapidly as possible with "Yes" or "No," depending on the question, and forms a question to be thrown to the next person. If desired, the class may name the objects in alphabetical order: artichokes, billy clubs, copper pennies, dandelions, etc.

Drill material presented on a tape recorder is different enough to appeal to children. The scripts take time to prepare but can be repeated as an individual or group exercise when needed. A class prepared script would provide double instructional opportunities: first as it is prepared by one

Side 1

1. Let me see the apple.
2. I'll leave it in the aisle.
3. Let me see the bun.
4. I'll leave it in the bakery.
5. Leave me see the cauliflower (*error*)

Side 2

Let me see the cherries.
I'll leave them in the box.
Let me see the doughnut.
I'll leave it in the doghouse.
Etc.

Some stress should be placed on the appropriateness of the response (i.e., *where* the item will be left).

group and second as it is used by another. A sixth-grade class prepared the following material:

Script for an Exercise Using "Did" and "Done" Correctly

Good morning. This is station WDSC bringing you another in the series called "Aids to English Usage." Have you ever heard a person say, "I done wrong"? Now, does this sound like a good use of English to you? How about saying it this way? "I have done wrong." The use of *did* and *done* cause a lot of children trouble, so this morning we are going to try and help you use these two words correctly. Listen to the following sentences. Can you explain why we use *done* instead of *did*? Does the word *done* seem to stand alone?

1. I have done the job well.
2. We have done the work quickly.
3. They have done the lesson well.

In these sentences did you notice that *done* has a helper word, *have*? When used, as it was in these sentences, *done* requires a helper word. The word *did* may stand alone. Listen and you will see that *did* stands alone.

1. I did the work for the teacher.
2. We did our homework in the kitchen.
3. Our class did well in arithmetic this week.

Did you notice that the word *did* was able to stand alone? It did not need a helper word. Now, listen to this story and try to fill in the missing word. The speaker will pause when he comes to a place where you could use either *did* or *done*. Write the correct word on your paper. Number your answers from one through five so we may correct them afterwards. Let's begin the story.

John said to Bob, "Look, I (*pause*) my work paper already." Bob laughed and said, "You are slow, John. I have (*pause*) my paper already. Mike has (*pause*) his paper, too." Mike looked up from his desk and smiled. "I (*pause*) mine when the teacher was going over the problem." It looks like all three boys have (*pause*) their lesson well.

Now I shall repeat the story so that you can proofread your answers before we grade the exercise. (*Repeat story.*)

The correct words are: (1) did (2) done (3) done (4) did (5) done. Did you get them all correct? Tune in tomorrow for a special lesson on two more demons, *saw* and *seen*. See you then.

The following games involve simple equipment and may be adapted to various grades:

Build a Sentence (5-6)—This game provides practice in correct usage of irregular verbs. Two teams may play. Irregular verbs written on paper strips about 2 × 10 inches are turned face-down on a table. A player then chooses a strip and must make a sentence containing the word he drew. If he uses it correctly his team scores a point and a player on the other team has a turn. When all the strips are used they may be reshuffled and play may continue. New words may be added as they are studied.

Employment Agency (5-6)—This game provides oral practice in use of auxiliary or helping words. It may be played by several children. All except three children are given a verb card such as:

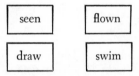

The children holding these verb cards are the "Employers." The three other children, the "Employees," hold the auxiliary word cards such as:

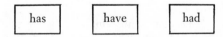

Each "Employer," in turn, holds his word card in front of the group and says, "Do I need help? Does anyone want a job?" If the word on his card needs a helping word one of the three helpers who raises his hand may be chosen by the "Employer" to stand beside him. The teacher or game leader chooses another child from the group to use the words in a sentence. The letters on the cards should be large enough so that words may be clearly seen.

We'll Write It (4-5)—This game provides practice in recognizing contractions in writing. The players are divided into two or more teams. The teacher or leader writes a contraction on the board. A player comes to the board and writes the words from which the contraction is made. If he does so correctly, he scores a point for his team. The leader then writes another contraction and a player on the other team has a turn. Some of the appropriate contractions might be:

let's	can't
I've	I'm
won't	didn't
wouldn't	aren't
doesn't	don't
isn't	it's
there's	we're
haven't	couldn't

Other contractions could be used for advanced pupils. A variation of the game would be to have pupils write the contraction for certain words. The player must also have the words correctly spelled to earn a point for his team. Good writing should be emphasized.

1. One teacher suggests using the parts of a verb as a group might say a football yell. The leader would say the present tense form such as "Ring!" The class then shouts together, "Rang! Rung!" Or the leader points to the present tense and the class gives the yell, "Go! Went! Gone!" Do you think children would learn anything from such an exercise?

2. Another teacher formed an "Ain't Club." Each child had ten milk bottle caps at the beginning of the week. Whenever the child said, "ain't" a cap was forfeited. Those who had bottle caps left on Friday had the last hour free, while the "Ain't Club" met and practiced writing. Do you consider this effective practice?

3. Do you think children should substitute am'nt (am not) for ain't? One great teacher, Dr. Dora Smith, of the University of Minnesota tried to establish this habit.

4. How can correct usage be stressed without having the discourteous habit of correcting each other being established? Should children ever correct adults?

5. In the English language words frequently contain two kinds of symbols. One is the vocabulary symbol or meaning, which can be found in lists such as, table, happy, dolly. The second is the grammatical symbol. In words like walked and babies the -ed and -ies are grammatical signals which indicate time and number. Other grammatical symbols are found in word order and inflection. Some of these are lacking in the written language. Vocal tone, stress, pitch, pauses, repetitions and even facial expression help clarify spoken meanings. Make a list of sentences which may have unclear meanings as written but which

can mean only one thing when spoken. *Example:* He gave her dog biscuits.

6. The best drills to teach English as a foreign-language are known as pattern practice drills. The drills would look something like the following: Suppose the teacher wants to make automatic the use of *there are* and *there is.* The problem, of course, is that the student wants to say, "There is two spoons on the table." We can set up a series of key frames thus:

There's one spoon on the table.
There're two spoons on the table.
There's a spoon on the table.
There're spoons on the table.
There're some spoons on the table.
There're several spoons on the table.

The teacher will say each one of these sentences and then ask the class to repeat each orally. Next she can ask for individual repetition. Then she can extend the exercise by giving a series of cues—words which will substitute in the patterns: toast, dishes, bread, dishes, forks, two vases, several napkins, some food, etc. This can be varied further as follows:

CUE: How many spoons are there on the table?
RESPONSE: There're two spoons on the table.
CUE: Is there a spoon on the table?
RESPONSE: Yes, there's a spoon on the table.
CUE: There's . . .
RESPONSE: There's a spoon on the table. There's a dish on the table.
CUE: There're . . .
RESPONSE: There're forks on the table.

Or take another example: Our problem here is that the student says *them things.* We can set up a series of frames:

I don't like that thing.
I don't like those things.
That book's on the table.
Those books'er on the table.

The students will repeat these and similar frames after the teacher, and then the teacher can proceed thus:

CUE: That man is my friend. (Men.)
RESPONSE: Those men are my friends.
CUE: That thing is on the table. (Things.)
RESPONSE: Those things are on the table.

Later a student may provide cues. What common errors might be attacked in this manner?

HOW SHOULD PUNCTUATION BE TAUGHT?

Have you ever wondered how the punctuation marks came to be? Maybe you have noticed that in pages of Chinese writing there is no punctuation. As recently as 1945 there were no such marks used in the Korean language. However, when they decided to write horizontally rather than vertically the need for such marks was recognized.

meaning, but the sense depends upon the words in such a way, that, if you use the comma, it is too little; if the double point too much. I was thinking to give an example: but, I felt the point had come out plainly enough, in the immediate preceding sentence.

The doubling of the point is next to be considered: the effect of this doubling is, that the mark thus formed takes rank between the

PEANUTS ®   **By Charles M. Schulz**

United Features Syndicate

The ancient Greeks and Romans frequently wrote without separating the words, let alone separating sentences. It was the orators who made the first separations in order to emphasize the thoughts they were expressing. Originally punctuation was built upon a single series of pauses. The comma was for a short or one unit pause, the semicolon for a two unit pause, a colon for a three unit pause and a period for four. The question mark was a sign to raise the voice at the end of the word. The exclamation point was a little dagger similar to that used to fasten important notices to buildings.

One of the first printers, a Venetian named Aldus Manutius, explained the system in this way.[8]

Let us proceed, as it were by steps, from the lowest of the points to the highest.

The least degree of separation is indicated by the comma.

This same mark, if it is used along with a single point, as this is (;) is found in passages in which the words are not opposed in

point used in conjunction with the comma, and the point standing alone.

There remains the single point, with which the sentence is closed and completed. It is not difficult to understand, for one cannot fail to notice with what word a sentence ends, although when it is short and another short one follows, I myself use the double point more freely than the single, as for instance: Make ready a lodging for me: for I shall arrive tomorrow: and so again: I give you no orders concerning my affairs: you yourself will decide what is to be done.

It was this type of punctuation that was used in the King James Edition of the Bible. The Bible was designed for oral reading and was so punctuated. The original Shakespeare folios were punctuated in this manner although the modern editions follow conventional punctuation.

An experiment by E. L. Thorndike illustrates the personal nature of punctuation. Hamlet's soliloquy was punctuated twenty-three different ways by fifty-seven graduate students; the first twenty-four words of The Lord's Prayer were punctuated thirty-two different ways. The study also indicated that after a week the same

---

[8] Quoted in Rudolph Flesch: *How To Make Sense* (New York: Harper, 1954), p. 114–115.

individuals would punctuate these selections differently.[9]

In the primary grades the child first learns about the period. Three uses of the period are taught:

1. At the end of a sentence: *The books are here.*
2. After an abbreviation in titles of persons and things: *Dr. Jones.*
3. After initials in proper names: *H. A. Brown.*

The teacher stresses the period in the first reading the child does and in the first sentence written on the board. "This little dot is called a period," she explains. "It tells us to stop because this is the end of a statement." The other uses are taught as an aspect of spelling.

Two uses of the question mark are taught:

1. At the end of a direct question. "Is this your ball?"
2. After a direct question but within the sentence. "Will you be ready?" the man asked.

The first can be understood and used by beginners in the first grade. The second should not be presented until late in the third grade. This form is less difficult. He asked, "Will you be ready?"

Lord Dunsany once complained that there were so many comma rules that printers could write one of his sentences like this: "Moreover, Jones, who, as, indeed, you, probably, know, is, of course, Welsh, is, perhaps, coming, too, but, unfortunately, alone." In some handbooks one can still find hundreds of rules for the comma. Fortunately for the teacher, eleven seem to be enough to meet the needs of elementary school children.

Four of these eleven rules are those that concern the writing of a letter.

1. To separate the parts of the date and the day of the year: *June 5, 1964.*
2. To set off the name of a city from a state: *Greeley, Colorado.*
3. After a salutation in a letter: *Dear Jim,*

4. After close of a letter: *Your friend,*

Additional comma rules taught in the elementary grades include:

5. To set off short direct quotations: *"We are ready," called the boys.*
6. After clauses of introduction: *"While they were eating, the bell rang."*
7. Between parts of a compound sentence joined by a short conjunction: *"Mr. Smith took Paul, and Jim went in Mrs. Anderson's car."*
8. Before and after appositives: *"The principal, Mr. Nardelli, talked to the parents."*
9. Before and after parenthetical expressions: *"You told your mother, I suppose, about your report card."*
10. Before and after a nonrestrictive clause: *"That boy, who has the dog, is in the fifth grade."*
11. To separate the words in the series: *John, Paul, and Jack are cousins.* (Immediately we run into the problem of the comma before *and*. It seems more exact to use one in that position to prevent a reader from combining Paul and Jack.)

The colon is quite simple to teach, since there are only four ways it is used:

1. After the greeting in a business letter (*Dear Sir:*).
2. Before a long series: (*Mother bought: oranges, lemons, bread, jam and cake.*).
3. To separate the hour from the minutes (2:30 A.M.).
4. To denote examples (A proper name should be capitalized: Mary.).

The apostrophe receives a great deal of attention in spelling. It is used:

1. With the letter *s* to show possession: *Mary's coat, boys' coats.*
2. To show where letters have been omitted: *don't* (do not), *o'er* (over).
3. To show the omission of number from a date: *Class of '64.*
4. To show the plural of figures and letters: *A's, 2's.*

Quotation marks are a special problem for school children. Few adults ever write quotation marks unless they are professional writers. The reader is the best textbook for these marks. After a story has been read, go back and have children take the parts of the story characters. Then while the narrator reads all material not in quotations, the characters read their proper lines. Then examine how the material was punctuated so that each person knew what to read. If the class is engaged in story writing, examples of all the varieties of use should be illustrated on the blackboard as a reference. These are two basic understandings that all children need to learn:

1. The unbroken quotation with the descriptive element preceding the quotation: *He cried, "Get a new man on first base!"*
2. The reverse of the above: *"Get a new man on first!" he cried.*

In order to use a semicolon properly it is necessary to understand conjunctions. Conjunctions may join either words or groups of words. When a conjunction is preceded by a comma (as when joining two clauses) a semicolon may be used instead of the comma and conjunction.

Mary was happy, but Joe was sad, may be written: *Mary was happy; Joe was sad.* Clauses joined by a semicolon must be related and independent, however, the situation must be related in that it affects both Mary and Joe. One may write: *The sea is beautiful at sunset; the water reflects the brilliant glow of the sky.* But not: *The sea is beautiful at sunset; the cry of the seagulls makes me homesick.*

Textbooks contain other rules for the semicolon. It confuses children to present this work as a compromise between a comma and a period.

The hyphen is usually considered an orthographic feature rather than a punctuation mark. It is a growing practice to avoid the hyphen except where a word is divided at the end of a line. Many words formerly hyphenated are now either "solid" (i.e., one word, like *flannelboard*), or two words, like *decision making.* Webster's *Third New*

International is a safe guide to follow in hyphenating. Children in the elementary school are not encouraged to use the dash because they overuse it. Parentheses seldom appear in children's writing.

Interesting exercises in punctuation can be made by taking material from readers and reproducing them without any punctuation. The child is told how many sentences there are. These can be made self-correcting by putting the title of the book and, page number at the bottom of the exercise.

*(Six Sentences, 10 Capital Letters,
5 Commas, 4 Quotation Marks)*

she reached into a big box and pulled out a santa claus suit and held it up it was bright red with real fur trimmings billy could see that there was a cap and a set of whiskers and even boots to go with it
isn't that lovely she said to billy the minute i saw it i thought of you im sure it will fit just perfectly she held it up to him

Since some of the punctuation rules are applied primarily in letters, writing a group letter and then copying it from the board is a good way to introduce the comma rules involved. Practice with letter headings is equally good.

Provide the missing capitals and punctuation:

1.　　　　　　　　　astor hotel
　　　　　　　　　　new york n y
　　　　　　　　　　may 3 1966
　　dear teacher

2.　　　　　　　　　607 adams st
　　　　　　　　　　madison wisc
　　　　　　　　　　june 6 1964
　　dear mother

3.　　　　　　　　　gunnison colo
　　　　　　　　　　dec 5 1960
　　dear santa claus

Charts and bulletin boards which act as constant reminders are valuable in the classroom. The making of these charts should involve the children.

Capitalize These Words

1. The beginning of a sentence.
2. Names of months and holidays.
3. Names of particular streets and schools.
4. First word and important words of a title.
5. Names of people, pets and initials of people.
6. Names of countries, cities, rivers, and mountains.
7. First word in greeting and closing of a letter.
8. References to God.

We saw a show

January, Halloween
Biona Ave., Hamilton School

My Visit to the Farm

Helen, Spot,   A. J. Boyd

Mexico, Mt. Hood, Columbia River

Gentlemen, Yours very truly

Lord, Savior

A Bulletin Board such as this acts as a reminder:

WATCH YOUR COMMAS

713 Olde St.
Austin, Texas
Sept. 19, 1961

Dear Frank,

Your friend,
Bill

One teacher makes punctuation marks come alive through dramatizatioin. A question mark with a face and legs, a comma with a smiling face and wearing a hat, and a chubby little period are placed on a bulletin board, each with a caption telling one thing they do. These characters—Chubby Little Period, Jolly Question Mark, Mr and Mrs. Comma, and Tall Exclamation Point—are introduced via the bulletin board. Each figure with its rule and title is shown. Other rules of punctuation are added as introduced.

This is the way the teacher describes their use:

I have the little people made up into plywood puppets. They are kept on hand in the schoolroom at all times. We use them to point up discussion of punctuation in many ways—in language class, social studies, written work, spelling. For example: in oral reading, we talk about "Chubby Little Period being at the end of a sentence to tell us that we stop here for a short time before going on." "Mr. Comma helps us by telling us this is

the place to pause when we are reading a sentence."

I use this lesson in teaching how to begin and end sentences. In this lesson I also introduce the good English habit. "Use a question mark (Jolly Question Mark) after each sentence that asks a question."

Using the wooden "Chubby Little Period," I say,

Chubby Little Period
Runs and sits,
The end of the sentence
Is always his place.

A sentence is written on the board. Using the puppet, I then demonstrate the period's place.

Jolly Question Mark is introduced in the same way:

Jolly Question Mark says,
"Little Period's place I take—
A *Question* I indicate."

each time a child is called upon and the use of the period and the question mark is dramatized.

The written follow-up work for a time is punctuated with impressive Chubby Little Periods. Other lessons continue with the rules:

"You find me after Mr. and Mrs."
"You find me after the abbreviations of the months and days," etc.

Mr. Comma is then studied. Examples are given to illustrate these uses. "I belong between the number of the day and the year." "Mr. Comma came to help. In an invitation you will find me after 'Dear Mother' and after 'Love.'" "Mr. Comma keeps things apart: "A book, apple, tablet, and pencil were in Mary's desk."

Upper-grade children enjoy a television quiz program in which each punctuation mark appears and is questioned concerning its activities. Or make it a "What's My Line?" format with the punctuation marks appearing as guests. The Master of Ceremonies starts by saying, "Our guest does four things [or ten if it's the comma]. We must name all of them to completely identify him."

Older students enjoy trick sentences like the following:

Bill, when Henry had had *had*, had had *had had*; *had had* had had the teacher's approval. (Omit italics and punctuation when writing this sentence on the chalkboard.)

The fight over the boys came home.

This is the story of walter who has not heard the story through it walter gained lasting fame a beautiful girl and a glorious name he also gained one autumn day on the grassy field in gridiron play the team was losing the clock moved fast any play might be the last of the game injured walter then called his own signal explaining men ill take the blame if we dont score he ran a full ninety yards or more

1. To what extent is punctuation a personal matter?

2. The newspapers frequently carry stories about errors caused by punctuation. At one time a tariff law was passed to admit fruit trees free of duty. A comma between fruit and trees cost the government a great deal of revenue before it was corrected. Do you know of other examples?

3. Why is it possible for two people to punctuate a paper in different ways and both be correct?

4. Do the following three rules cover most, situations?

(*a*) A comma may be used to prevent a possible misreading.

(*b*) A nonessential part of a sentence should be set off with one comma if it comes first or last in the sentence and with two commas if it comes anywhere else.

(*c*) When two or more words or groups of words are similar in form or function they should be separated by commas.

Suggestions for Projects

1. Compare the way five specific correct usage items are presented in different textbooks. These might be: *was-were, do-did-done, went-gone, lie-lay, sit-sat.* Note the amount of drill in the entire book.

2. Illustrate the difference between the inductive and deductive method in teaching correct usage and indicate the one you feel is better. Give reasons for your answer.

3. Make a collection of errors in usage presented to children on the radio, television, comic strips, etc., which will illustrate the cultural competition the schools face in this area.

4. Once correct habits are established with respect to grammar and usage what program of maintenance should the school employ?

5. Compare the way the sentence in each of its forms is introduced in three different language textbooks.

6. How may incorrect forms be used in instructional practices? Cite examples from textbooks.

7. Review the literature on levels of correct usage and indicate how you would explain this to children.

8. Make an annotated catalogue of film strips available for grammar instruction.

Plan a lesson or series of lessons to teach this information:

Man has been speaking for well over 700,000 years. Man has been practicing alphabetic writing only for about 3,450 years. Man has punctuated, in the modern sense, for less than 250 years. He has still not mastered an ideal punctaution. In the system as it stands, the distribution of the marks is as follows:

(*a*) For *linking*, use:

;   semicolon
:   colon
—   linking dash
-   linking hyphen

(*b*) For *separating,* use:

> .   period
> ?   question mark
> !   exclamation point
> ,   separating comma

(*c*) For *enclosing,* use:

> , . . . ,   paired commas
> — . . . —   paired dashes
> (. . .)   paired parentheses
> [. . .]   paired brackets
> " . . ."   paired quotation marks

(*d*) For *indicating omissions,* use:

> '   apostrophe
> .   omission period in abbreviations (or dot)
> —   omission dash
> . . .   triple periods (or dots)
> . . . .   quadruple periods (or dots)

BIBLIOGRAPHY

BOOKS

Applegate, Mauree. *Easy in English.* New York: Harper, 1960, Chap. 11.

Dean, Leonard, and Kenneth G. Wilson. *Essays on Language and Usage.* New York: Oxford U.P., 1959.

Flesch, Rudolph. *How to Make Sense.* New York: Harper, 1954.

Fries, C. C. *American English Grammar.* New York: Appleton, 1940.

Greene, Harry A., and Walter T. Petty. *Developing Language Skills in the Elementary Schools.* Boston: Allyn, 1959, Chap. 14.

Herrick, Virgil, and Leland Jacobs. *Children and the Language Arts,* Englewood Cliffs, N. J.: Prentice-Hall, 1955, Chap. 13.

Jespersen, Otto. *Essentials in English Grammar.* New York: Holt, 1933.

Pooley, Robert C. *Teaching English Grammar.* New York: Appleton, 1957, pp. 1–130.

Roberts, Paul. *Patterns in English.* New York: Harcourt, 1956.

Wolf, Don M. *Language Arts and Life Patterns.* New York: Odyessey, 1961.

PAMPHLETS

Fries, Charles C. "American English Grammar," Monograph No. 10, National Council of Teachers of English. New York: Appleton, 1940.

Marckwardt, Albert H., and Fred G. Walcott. "Facts About Current English Usage," Monograph No. 7, National Council of Teachers of English. New York: Appleton, 1938.

Stageberg, Norman C., and Ruth Goodrich. "Using Grammar to Improve Writing," Educational Service Publications. Cedar Falls, Iowa: Iowa State Teachers College, June 1953.

Treanor, John H.: "Exercises in English Grammar I and II." Cambridge 39, Mass.: Educators Publishing Service, 1958.

TEXTBOOKS CONTAINING HELPFUL IDEAS

Braun, I. H. *Laugh and Learn Grammar.* San Francisco, Calif.: Harr Wagner, 1950.

O'Rourke, L. J. *Self-Aids in English Usage.* Psychological Institute, P. O. Box 118, Lake Alfred, Fla., 1956.

Postman, N. *Discovering Your Language.* New York: Holt, 1963.

Chapter 10

Evaluating and Interpreting the Language Arts Program

HOW ARE STANDARDS ESTABLISHED AND USED IN THE LANGUAGE ARTS?

The term *standard* is used in three different ways in evaluation. One of its meanings is synonymous with *goal.* The children and teacher establish standards one by one that the children use to guide their work. In this sense the standard of achievement is determined by the individual child's stage of development and the personal effort he is able to exert. A second use of standard is as an *average or norm.* A series of tests or experiences establish what most fifth-grade children are doing with respect to a skill, such as the spelling of the word *constitution.* According to the *Iowa Spelling Scale* only ten children out of a hundred in the fifth grade spell this word correctly. Thus a child in the fifth grade who does spell the word is above the standard. The third use of the term is in association with a predetermined level of achievement or expectancy. Teachers or parents decide that we must have higher standards of achievement in the sixth grade. To do this any child who fails to do certain tasks is not promoted to sixth grade. Or a college will decide that only the "upper half" of those graduating from a high school class may seek admission to the institution.

Standards reflect the school's philosophy and purpose. Some countries feel that the schools should act as a filter and eliminate all but the very able. The concept of an educational elite has been a strong influence on all education. Some countries give national examinations at every level and permit only a percentage of those taking it to advance to the next grade, class or form. Other countries feel that education should be made available to all the people at all levels. In order to do this, teachers adjust to the needs of the students rather than being guided by predetermined achievement standards.

Standards also reflect the acceptance or rejection of the teaching of modern psychology. Most teachers accept a concept of individual differences that is based on different levels of intelligence as measured by

405

the IQ cultural experiences of the learner, and the learner's interest. In some countries even an IQ test is rejected. There are parents who have never accepted the concept in the same way that teachers have. While it is recognized that people are different, there is an assumption of lack of effort on the part of either the students or teachers which produces variable results in education.

The area of work also influences the standards. Music teachers must be very tolerant of the untalented who pass through their classrooms. To require a predetermined performance standard would eliminate many pupils from further study, so teachers must accept the fact that music for some students will be an avocation rather than a career. Nearly all teachers have at times determined to improve standards on the playground or in the auditorium. These standards have little relationship to the goals of the children or the aver-

age kind of behavior of children. Within a subject area such as handwriting, we do not expect everyone to write identically, but we do have a minimum standard of legibility.

The elementary teacher has a double task with respect to standards. The young child needs help to understand what the standard means. Then he must be taught to use that standard to guide his work. In the classroom one standard is developed at a time and practice is designed to give some meaning to the standard. During the sharing time the teacher may discuss the problem of being a good listener. After discussing why we listen (to learn, to be courteous) the teacher asks them to think of things a listener should do to help the speaker. The teacher accepts one of the suggestions, such as, "Look at the speaker." "That is a good suggestion, Bill," the teacher remarks. "Let me write that for us so we will remember." Then the

Burbank Public Schools, Calif.

Standards are given meaning, habits of correctness are formed, and the quality of work improves when children are able to assume responsibility for proofreading their work.

teacher writes as the first standard for the group under the title "Good Listeners Do These Things."

At the end of the period after praising those who shared, the teacher asks, "Were we good listeners?" "Why were we good listeners?" The children will thus be reminded of the standards. In time other standards will be added. Some might be: Ask questions at the end. (Do not interrupt.) Laugh *with* the speaker (not *at* him). Sit quietly.

In addition to providing criteria for evaluation, charts of standards remind the student of the factors to consider in preparing an assignment. The following charts developed by teachers and students meet both these needs:

Announcements Can Be Interesting

1. Speak clearly.
2. Speak in a friendly manner.
3. Tell what is going to take place.
4. Tell when and where it will be.
5. Speak briefly.

Ask These Questions About Your Letters

1. Does the letter sound as though you were talking with your friend?
2. Does it tell the things your friend would like to know about?
3. Does it make your friend feel that the letter was especially for him?
4. Does the letter express your opinion about a topic?
5. Is it interesting to read?

Telephone Standards

1. Speak pleasantly, slowly, and distinctly. If people cannot hear you, do not shout. Shouting does not help.
2. Keep your lips an inch or two from the mouthpiece. If you hold the mouthpiece too close, your voice will be muffled or blurred.
3. Hold the receiver lightly against your ear.
4. After the number has been given, keep the receiver at your ear until the person you are calling answers. If you hear a buzzing or clicking sound, it means that the line is busy.

5. Keep the conversation moving and to the point. Do not prolong it.
6. Use correct language.
7. Avoid slang.
8. If the message is for someone who is not at home, write it down.
9. Call someone to the telephone by going to him. Do not yell from one room to the other.

Respecting the Rights of Others When Jokes Are Being Told

1. A good joke never makes fun of another person.
2. A good joke never hurts anyone's feelings.
3. Race, religion, and nationality should never be the subject of a joke.
4. A good joke never makes anyone feel unhappy, uncomfortable, or ashamed.

Language textbooks develop standards that children need to have recalled. Some of the publishers provide bulletin board material which review the standards developed in the lessons. Here are examples of standards developed in a fifth-grade textbook.[1]

When You Write:

1. Make each paragraph in a good report tell something about only one topic. That topic is called the *paragraph* topic.
2. Make each paragraph topic a part of the subject of the report.
3. Make every sentence in a paragraph tell something about one and only one topic, the topic of the paragraph.
4. Put all the sentences that tell about a certain paragraph topic into one paragraph.
5. Use a separate paragraph for each paragraph topic.
6. Place the paragraphs in an order which tells the order in which things happened or are to be done.

---

[1] Paul McKee, *Improving Your Language, Language for Meaning* series (Boston: Houghton, 1951).

*When You Write Business
Letters:*

1. Use the business letter form.
2. Tell everything that the person to whom you are writing must know to do what you want done.
3. Don't waste the time of the person to whom you write. Tell only what he needs to know, and tell it only once.
4. State the purpose of your letter at or near the beginning.

While standards guide children in evaluating the classroom work they are misused if the emphasis is always upon error or failure. The following classroom example indicates how standards might be used to stress positive aspects of work.[2]

Tom struggled to the end of his news report and then finished in a rush with the question, "Does anyone have any criticism?"

The group had been in Miss L.'s room for a week, and to date every report had ended automatically with that same question. Responses, too, were as trite as usual.

"You kept saying *and.*"

"You shouldn't have had your hands in your pockets."

"You didn't look at the class."

"I think it was a very nice report."

"You said, *The submarine officer, he—*"

The stock comments were exhausted and Tom shuffled back to his seat, muttering, "I don't want to make any old reports anyway."

Said Miss L., "I've noticed that all of you ask for criticism. What do you mean by 'criticism,' Tom?"

"Telling what's wrong with the report," was his immediate response.

"Let's see what the dictionary says," suggested Miss L.

"There are two meanings given," said Margaret. "To examine critically and to judge severely."

"Which meaning have you been using most of the time?" asked Miss L.

"The second one," said George, adding,

---

[2] San Diego Public Schools, *Constructive Criticism Bulletin* (San Diego, Calif.: undated).

"I didn't know criticizing might mean finding the good points as well as the bad ones."

"Since you've already mentioned some of the weak places in Tom's report," said Miss L., "let's examine it carefully now to find the strong points."

After a long pause someone offered, "He used the map to show us in what part of the Pacific the submarine was operating."

"And we all want to know about submarines. He chose a good article to tell about," said Henry.

The teacher had already written the first five criticisms on the chalkboard. Now she added these two and paused for the group to read the list.

"Louise found something good about Tom's report the first time. She said it was a very nice report," remarked Marion.

"That's right," mused Miss L. Then, with seeming irrelevance, she questioned, "Why did you ask for criticism, Tom?"

"Everyone does it."

"Why?" queried Miss L., addressing the whole group.

"To help us to do better next time," said Charles.

"Does the statement, 'It was a very nice report,' tell Tom exactly what to do in order to make a better talk?"

The answer was a unanimous "No."

"Louise," said Miss L., "were you really thinking about helping Tom, or were you just saying something that would sound pleasant?"

Louise looked flushed and confused, and Miss L. said kindly, "We all make that mistake, Louise. It's easy to say words without thinking of their meaning, but it's a habit that wastes time and causes a great deal of misunderstanding and confusion. We'll all have to help one another overcome it. Perhaps Tom, too, asked for criticism without really wanting help." Miss L. smiled at Tom and he grinned back sheepishly.

"Now let's get back to these comments," said Miss L., pointing to the chalkboard. "Which seems to you more important: to know how to choose an interesting subject, or to remember not to put an unnecessary word in a sentence?"

"A good topic is far more important," chorused the group.

"And which of these two is more important," continued Miss L., "for the speaker to remember to keep his hands out of his pockets, or to remember to use the map?"

Again there was no doubt in the minds

of the children. Miss L. went on: "Yet these are the very points that the class overlooked completely at first. You see, the audience has an active part in every report. Each of you must be thinking and weighing values while the speaker is talking so that you will be able to choose important points to discuss, and so that you can express your judgment in a way that will be really helpful to the speaker.

"By the way, Tom, there was one thing about your report that puzzled me. Where did they store all of the supplies that you were talking about? Space in a submarine is very limited."

"It's like this," explained Tom, coming to the chalkboard. With quick, sure strokes he illustrated a concise and clear-cut explanation. The class was interested and plied Tom with questions.

When he had finally taken his seat, Miss L. pointed to the first three criticisms on the chalkboard and said, "I didn't notice any of these difficulties when Tom was talking just now."

"He was nervous during his first report," volunteered Marvin: "that's why he looked at the ceiling, kept his hands in his pockets, and kept saying 'and—uh'."

"You didn't seem nervous just now, Tom," said Miss L. "What made the difference?"

"I don't know," said Tom slowly. Then, after considerable thought, "Perhaps it was because I was making a speech the first time and just telling the boys what they wanted to know the second time."

"But that's just the purpose of a speech," said Miss L. "to tell others something that they wish to hear."

As there was no comment, she went on. "Did all of you want to hear Tom's first talk?"

There was division of opinion. However, the consensus was that the subject was interesting, but that Tom didn't tell about it very well.

"A good speech requires teamwork," explained Miss L. "Just now, when you showed your interest by your sitting position, by the expressions on your faces, and by good questions, Tom responded by making an excellent talk. You didn't give him that kind of help the first time he spoke."

At this point the recess bell interrupted the discussion. "Only one news report and no social studies discussion," thought Miss L. Then she relaxed. "We can finish the reports during language time this afternoon and what

we've been doing certainly has social significance."

That afternoon before continuing with the news, the class summarized their morning's discussion as follows:

1. It takes effort on the part of both audience and speaker to produce a good report. If the members of the audience act as though they are interested, the speaker will do his best and will forget to be nervous. The audience must listen carefully, too, in order to criticize wisely.

2. If the speaker really wants help he should ask for it in his own words and not just words he's heard someone else say.

3. The audience should mention what they like about a speech as well as what needs to be improved.

4. The audience should tell the speaker exactly how to improve his talk, not just make general statements that don't mean much.

5. The audience should talk about the most important things first.

The sixth-grade experience just described proved to be the beginning of a campaign to develop habits of thoughtful, kindly criticism. As the occasion demanded in the classroom, on the playground, in the cafeteria, in assemblies, the standards established that first week were referred to and expanded throughout the whole year.

It is difficult to set standards for creative work or assignments in which a student chooses his own subject and form of writing. Such standards almost always must be individual, and must be set up in terms of the kinds of jobs different students are attempting. Considerable reading of good literature, with attention to how effects are achieved, will give some students an idea of what makes a good poem, essay, story, or play. Upper-grade students can also profitably consider standards like these as they write:

1. Did I choose a topic that I knew or could imagine something about?

2. Did I really do what I set out to do—tell how I felt about some experience,

describe something that appealed to me, tell a story in an entertaining way with a rich choice of expressions?

3. Did I end my composition when the job was done, instead of writing just to fill up space?

4. Did I use verbs that will help a reader see what I saw, feel what I experienced?

5. Did I remember that in recreating an experience for other people I could appeal to all five of their senses instead of just the sense of sight?

6. Did I remember that it is often more effective to let a reader draw his own conclusions on the basis of specific things I say rather than to *tell* him how he should feel or how I felt about something? For example, was it necessary for me to say *This was a very thrilling adventure?*

7. Did I use comparisons that were really my own rather than old ones I had heard over and over again?

8. If I used conversation did I use quotation marks, commas, periods and capital letters correctly? Did I indicate change in speakers by paragraphing?

9. Can I give a reason for every mark of punctuation I have used?

10. As I read my paper aloud, do I observe any places in which additional punctuation will help make my meaning clear?

Few teachers would want to use a list of standards as long as the foregoing. They are simply suggestions for the kinds of items a class and teacher might use as basis for the evaluation of certain kinds of imaginative writing.

It will be understood that standards that are set for any kind of writing should be cumulative so that common spelling words, usage, grammar, punctuation, capitalization, mechanics, and form taught in one assignment are reviewed and made part of the expected achievements in the next piece of writing.

1. Are standards established in a textbook as effective as those developed by a class? Why?

2. Are most materials written in a classroom directed toward the teacher as the audience? What other individuals or situations might be used?

3. Some experiments in psychology indicate that people try harder when they know they will be evaluated or a score is being kept. Does this justify grading all classroom assignments?

4. Another term used for standards is expectancies. Are there differences in the meaning of these terms as used in elementary education?

5. What are the advantages and disadvantages in system-wide use of a scale or way of grading papers?

6. Does the following statement contradict what has been said about standards?

> Whether I like the idea or not, there is one hard fact that sticks out whenever I come to consider this business of standards. It is that, in the long run, the standard which I require doesn't matter, because a child will soon be carried beyond my direct influence. What matters is the standard by which the child himself will judge his own words and thoughts, and those of others. . . . He is going to acquire his standards by the light of a growing experience. They will come to him subtly and unseen, and they can't be given to him or forced upon him.*

* Vicars Bell, *On Learning the English Tongue* (London: Faber, 1953), p. 25.

HOW SHOULD COMPOSITION WORK BE EVALUATED?

Certain principles about the correcting and marking of students' work have been recognized by experienced teachers and authorities in the field of English.[3] Some of these are as follows:

1. The teacher who strives only to have students increase their skill is generally wasting her time until she interests them in wanting to write, in having a purpose for writing, and in writing with honesty and responsibility. Until this period is reached, there is little real value in marking papers.

2. In reading any composition, a teacher will want to look first for the answers to the following questions: What prompted the student to write the paper? What limitations did he have? What does the paper really say? What are its strengths and weaknesses?

3. Oral and written criticisms should encourage students and suggest further effort in writing. Any comment made by the teacher, even though it is critical, should indicate respect for what the student has written.

4. A student who truly understands that adherence to the conventions of language is a courtesy to the reader and an aid in conveying the meaning intended by the writer will be more inclined to write correctly than will a student who thinks of spelling, grammar, and so forth as something aside from "thought."

5. If a teacher places undue emphasis on form, he or she is penalizing the bold, original, aggressive thinker whose ideas sometimes get ahead of his command of written language. Teacher and class should have a common understanding of the relative "weight" to be assigned content and form.

6. Marginal symbols are useful in showing a student where his writing is weak.

[3] Denver Public Schools, *Course of Study for the Language Arts, K-12,* (1955), pp. 383–386.

Teachers recognize, however, that certain kinds of weaknesses (particularly in structure of sentences) cannot be easily explained by any symbol but must be discussed orally with the student or elaborated on in a written comment.

7. Teachers in the upper grades need not *make* a correction for a student. Rather they might indicate the point of error or weakness and let the student, with whatever help he needs, work out the correction himself. It is equally important to mark strong points in a student's paper.

8. Teachers will always want to be cautious in suggesting that students "vary sentence patterns," "subordinate" a particular idea, and the like. The relationship of ideas shown in complex sentences by the use of modifying phrases is a highly individual matter. What the writer means to say will determine his sentence structure, as far as subordination is concerned. If the meaning in a given sentence or paragraph is not clear, the student, not the teacher, must decide how sentence structure should be changed to clarify the *student's* ideas. Often this can best be worked out in an individual discussion.

9. The extremely poor speller frequently has some psychological or emotional disturbance. Ignoring his spelling until some diagnostic and corrective work can be done is sometimes the best course of action.

10. Older students should expect to revise and rewrite, or copy, their work. Because revision is important, they must be given time to think about it, time to do it, and help when they need it. However, if a student can correct a minor error or two without completely recopying a paper, he should certainly be allowed to do so.

11. All teachers know that "it is poor teaching to demand what the teacher knows *cannot* be done." Criticism and suggestions for revision, therefore, must be in terms of an individual's capacities.

12. Highly general suggestions for revision are fruitless. To say to a student, "Make

this more interesting (or entertaining, or effective)," will probably result in baffling rather than helping the student.

The busy teacher (a term that describes all teachers) is always seeking ways to make the task of reading and grading papers a little less laborious. The following suggestions have been used with profit.

The more time a teacher spends teaching composition the less time will be spent correcting errors or marking mistakes in students' papers. Teachers know that the purpose of correcting papers is to help students improve their writing, not to catch them in mistakes. If a teacher tries to anticipate the mistakes students might make in a given situation and spends considerable time "preteaching" the items, students' writing will be better and, as a result, the burden of grading is less heavy.

Students should have a chance to do much of their writing in class under the guidance of the teacher. Such classes are true laboratory situations. As students write, a teacher can go from desk to desk offering help where it is needed, assisting students in organizing their ideas, calling their attention to obvious errors, sending them to dictionaries and textbooks for help, and making comments on the strengths and weaknesses of the papers under production. If the teacher discovers a common weakness in the papers, a direct attack on the problem should be made in a class session. Writing done under close supervision is almost "graded" and "corrected" before it is finally submitted.

Students should be held responsible for correction of obvious errors. To insure their meeting this responsibility, a teacher can supervise proofreading sessions before final drafts of papers are written, and again before papers are turned in. A check list of items or criteria will help to guide students' proofreading. For example, one item on every check list would be adherence to whatever manuscript form has been established as standard for a class or school; another would be avoidance of careless omissions or repetitions of words. During part of a proofreading period, students should be told to whisper their words aloud to themselves so that they may hear how it sounds.

Before papers are turned in, have students exchange papers for additional proofreading. The teacher can again circulate in the classroom and act as an arbiter if criticisms are not accepted wholeheartedly or if a difference of opinion cannot be settled by reference to a dictionary or textbook. Occasionally, have the class divide into small groups. Let each student read his paper to this group, ask for suggestions, and make revisions that the group advises. Again the teacher will act as arbiter or final court of appeal in debatable cases.

As a variation of these procedures teachers can occasionally distribute students' papers to the class and have each student write a comment about the paper he reads. The comments are best if they are specifically directed to some major point. For example, if students have written letters to a sick friend, the comment might read: "I would (or would not) like to receive this letter because . . . " The paper and the comment could then be given to the original writer, who would revise his work if necessary.

If a teacher makes a chart of errors that are common to a given set of papers, teaches and reteaches the items in question, and notes with the class the disappearance of these errors in subsequent papers, many students will gradually learn to avoid the mistakes in question.

Students need time in class to consult reference materials, complete certain projects, or read and work with other students. During some periods devoted to these activities, teachers can have individual conferences with certain students, go over written work, point out strengths and weaknesses, and return the paper to the student immediately for revision. Occasionally, it is possible to call together two or three students whose written work shows somewhat comparable characteristics and correct their papers together. No teacher can or should do all the necessary paper work in class, but working directly with students to improve their written work is certainly a valid and useful teaching procedure.

Teachers can save time and decrease the burden of grading papers if they do not try to mark every error on every paper. Gross errors, errors in items specifically pretaught, and in items that have been emphasized repeatedly, should be marked. Other errors can be ignored. What constitutes a "gross error" will be determined by the grade level, the attainment and ability of the class, and the course of study. Conscientious teachers may feel that permitting students to commit errors without correction will be detrimental to the students' work. But common sense suggests that helping students eliminate a few gross errors at a time is a sensible procedure. Able students whose work is superior to that of the average should, of course, be given every chance to improve to the limit of their abilities. Such students can be working on complicated problems of subordination and transition while the bulk of the class is still wrestling with specific forms of verbs.

There is no valid reason for having every student write at exactly the same time. Assigning papers irregularly will help relieve the burden of having a large number of papers that should be marked and returned within a brief period. Although no real saving of time results from this procedure, it relieves the press of work and teachers can find short periods of time more easily than many consecutive hours in which to grade papers.

On most occasions students should decide how long their compositions should be. But if teachers emphasize the virtues of brevity and conciseness, if they help students select subjects that can be easily limited, and if they encourage frequent writing of very short papers instead of less frequent submission of long, involved compositions, the problems of grading seem a bit less formidable. Mature students must at times have a chance to prepare and submit long reports or lengthy themes of one kind or another, but if such long compositions are prepared under fairly close supervision and observation, much of the grading can be done as the job is in progress.

Although it may be understood that the first writing is to be only a rough draft that will be refined through editing or proofreading, some children may resent rewriting the entire paper. Unless there is real motivation for this rewriting, it can appear to be "busy work," especially when only a few major corrections are made by the teacher. Making only a few corrections seems to imply that all of the uncorrected writing or spelling is above criticism and completely acceptable—which, of course, is not necessarily true. Teachers in Grades 3 to 5 should use judgment in requiring material to be rewritten. If the child realizes that rewriting will help him, it should be done. But there is little justification for a complete second draft merely as a matter of policy.

Probably no one system of marking is materially better than another. Most schools find it desirable to establish a reasonably standard procedure so that students (and teachers) can become familiar with the marking procedures used. For young children, evaluative statements by the teacher such as: "This is an improvement," "You are writing more interesting stories," "Your *n*'s still look like *r*'s," "You have written better stories than this one," or "Your spelling is improving" are more informative, and in some cases more remedial, than merely marking the paper "A," "B," "D," or 90, 70, 65, etc.

An occasional faculty or departmental meeting devoted to the subject of grading can be helpful. In such meetings teachers discuss procedures they follow, ask for help on special problems, try to work out a composition scale, examine standardized scales, work as a group in grading a few sample papers, and the like.

Sometimes instead of assigning a grade and marking specific errors, a teacher might simply indicate the number and type of errors, as "10 misspelled words," "3 omissions of necessary capitals," or "1 example of incorrect end punctuation." The students must then take responsibility for finding and correcting mistakes and returning the paper.

Some teachers like to use a three-track system of grading. One grade is assigned for content; the second, for appearance (neatness, handwriting, observance of

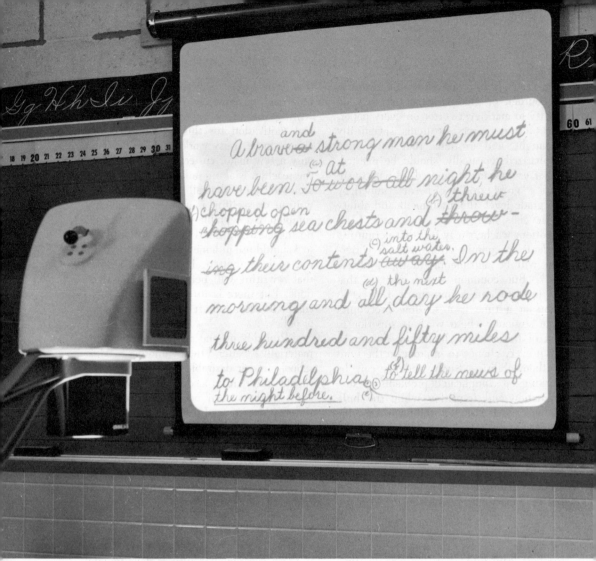

Group evaluation permits the writer to know of possible reader reactions. When properly handled, each class member learns how to improve his own work because of the suggestions given to others.

manuscript form, and the like); the third, for techniques and mechanics (grammar, usage, punctuation). The CAT mark, then covers content, appearance, and techniques. Other teachers like to use two grades, one for general content and one for form. Some teachers believe that a single grade comes closest to expressing the dual importance of "ship and cargo." It is important in any school that teachers agree on some general principle regarding the relative values to be assigned form and content, so that a student's progression from one class to another means no great change in the way in which his progress is evaluated.

Oral and written comments made by a teacher will be in terms of both form and content. Such comments are meant to point the way to improvement, encourage further writing, and help the student understand his grades. Students who have been conditioned to regard the number of "red marks" as the real criteria of strength and weakness in a paper sometimes find it hard to see that a paper which may be mechanically correct is still an inadequate job if the content is weak. A written or oral explanation is due such a student if he is expected to produce better work next time. Challenging unfounded statements, querying the use of foggy words or syntax, pointing up illogical reasoning or praising a discriminating choice of words, keen observation, and use of fresh comparisons—these and many other forms of constructive criticism can be communicated in teacher-written comment.

There are indications that students think that proofreading by the teacher is of greater help than having another child do it or attempting to do this themselves. Instead of "correcting" a paper, it might be well for the teacher to look upon this work as "editing" to assist the writer, similar in kind to the professional copy-editing of manuscripts before publication.

Teachers who type the stories written by the children often observe that a remarkable growth in their expression begins to take place as a result. In typing their stories, the teacher corrects basic errors. This form of editing is especially important if the material is to be used for reading instruction. Improvement takes place largely because the child wants it. First, typing his stories gives him confidence in his ability to write. Then he discovers that the typing makes it easier for him to read his own stories as well as stories written by other children. As the stories are assembled in stapled folders or ring binders, he develops pride of authorship. Eventually, as an "author," he seeks correct spelling, better writing, and more effective expression.

The purpose of all evaluation should be to foster learning. A teacher in England reminds of this when he says: [4]

It is necessary to remind myself now of the basic truth that all education and all learning must partake of the nature of growth. We should all of us repudiate the suggestion that our teaching methods are based upon the injunction, "be like me—now." We should all of us with our hands on our hearts reaffirm that our motto is: "Be like yourself—now and always."

In the teaching of English, it is even more important to act upon this principle than it is in the teaching of any other subject. For we must always regard language as a means whereby the child may honestly, sincerely, and unaffectedly express his own opinions, his own feelings, and—thereby—his own inviolable and unique nature, so far as he has discovered it at a particular moment of time.

I am prepared (and so are hundreds of other teachers who feel as I do) to show, at any time, work written by some of my own nine- and ten-year-olds, which is neat, accurate, correctly spelled, and grammatically well constructed.

And I am equally prepared to show without blush or apology, written work which is untidy, misspelled, badly punctuated, and generally "illiterate."

But in order to satisfy me, there must be one quality apparent in the work of each group. It must be fun to read it. It must have a contact, direct, simple and friendly, between writer and reader.

---

[4] Vicars Bell, *On Learning the English Tongue* (London: Faber, 1953), pp. 20–21.

HOW ARE STANDARDIZED TESTS USED IN THE LANGUAGE ARTS?

Those who make tests seek to establish validity in measurement. The validity of a test means the extent to which it accurately measures what it is designed to test. Some areas of the curriculum allow for such a wide range of personal response, that it is diffcult to find a test which will measure those areas and still be easily scored by a machine or other device. Art appreciation, oil painting, cooking, and enjoyment of poetry are some of the skills or talents for which it is difficult to construct quick-scoring written tests.

There are aspects of the language arts that standardized achievement tests do not measure. Appreciation of literature, creative writing, ability to construct an expressive sentence, oral reading and interpretation, response to poetry, ability to organize a report, ability to organize an interesting talk, and the ability to participate in a conversation or discussion are among those not measured in standardized tests.

Sometimes a principal will report that his school is doing well in language arts. When questioned he will refer to the scores made on an achievement test. It is well for all teachers and parents to know exactly what these tests measure.

The spelling score is often based upon the ability of a child to check the correct spelling from a choice of three or four in items like this:

elefant (4)

An   elefunt (5) is big.

elephant (6)

Check One

(4) (5) (6) (Not given)

Although for many children the ability to detect correct spelling is closely related to the ability to spell, some children can correctly proofread this type of spelling best and yet misspell the word. In the process of standardization, these children are lost in the vast number used to establish the norms.

The language section usually provides a choice between two items such as these:

Denver, Colorado
Denver Colorado

Uncle Jim $\genfrac{}{}{0pt}{}{said,}{said}$ "We can eat here."

I've $\genfrac{}{}{0pt}{}{did}{done}$ my lesson.

Tell Bill and $\genfrac{}{}{0pt}{}{I}{me}$ where it is.

These act as measurements of a child's knowledge of punctuation and correct-usage items. Again it measures an understanding of usage rather than an opportunity to use the knowledge.

One teacher happened to have a set of creative stories to be evaluated at the same time the test was being graded. While many children did not use quotation marks in their stories, approximately half did. There were three who had not put the comma after *said*. Investigation revealed that all of them had checked the correct item in the test.

In situations where teachers are judged by children's responses on standardized tests, it is common practice to have the class work on drill sheets closely related to the usage items tested. If a teacher stresses such work with the upper third of a normal group, they will score so high that the entire class average will be over the expected norm. This result may satisfy some uninformed administrators, but the teacher knows that the test is not a measurement of the children's ability to use language in original speech or writing.

Investigation will reveal that items in many achievement tests are not those taught in the textbooks used by the children tested. Of seventy questions measuring language skills in one test, thirty-seven items were not presented in the fourth-grade language book used in one school, thirty-two were not in the fifth-grade book, and twenty-one not in the sixth-grade book. Twenty-one tested items were not included in the textbooks for the fourth, fifth or sixth grades. The results could mean that a child who had a perfect mastery of all items taught in the books of these grades would still fail in 30 per cent of the items on the test.

If the fifth-grade child answered correctly only the items taught in his textbook, his grade placement on the test would have been below the third grade. To make this point still more vivid, another test which contained items more clearly related to those in the text in use would have measured this knowledge as being in the second month of the eighth grade.

Reading-achievement tests are more apt to measure the skills that have been taught than language tests. Tests of vocabulary and paragraph meaning, together with reading to predict outcomes, understand directions, interpret attitudes, reorganize sentence meaning, note details, use the index, or get information from charts are among the items usually included. In addition to comparative achievement in relationship to established norms, these tests reveal specific strengths and weaknesses that guide the teacher.

But even the best reading tests must be examined critically if they are to be used correctly. Some sections contain only two choices so that there is a strong element of chance present. In some sections, failing to answer one or two questions can make a year's difference with respect to the score. Teachers normally dislike grading standardized tests, but it is only by comparing what they know about a certain child and what he did on each test item that the full value of these teaching instruments is realized.

Interpretation of test results must include a number of factors. In some schools the children in the primary grades frequently test below national reading norms while they are at the norm in grade four and above the national norm in grades five and six. This is due in part to a shorter primary school day than that in other areas and to a different curriculum emphasis during the first two years of school. It is the total growth pattern that needs to be observed. Factors such as part-time school sessions, mobility of population and environmental differences would enter into any interpretation of results.

A positive function that standardized tests serve is that of diagnosis of need. Most manuals for tests indicate action to take if the score in any area is low. It is quite possible that some language skills have not been adequately emphasized as the curriculum has become crowded with science and social studies content.

A grade score of 5.0 on a reading test indicates that the child is reading at the average for beginning fifth grade. If the child's mental age and IQ indicate that he is capable of working at a 6.1 level, this score would be cause for concern because it indicates that his reading achievement is below his ability level. In the same way, the child with a 3.0 ability level who is in the fourth grade and reading at a 3.0 achievement level is working at an expected achievement level.

In the early grades there is a rapid increase in the difficulty of material. Thus a child who is reading at a grade level of 1.5 would find second-grade material difficult, but a child in the sixth grade with a 4.5 reading achievement would have less difficulty because there is not as great an increase in reading complexity at that level.

It seems only fair to inform children concerning the use of a test. Tensions and anxieties concerning promotion or grades can make standardized testing a mental-health hazard. If possible, an individual conference should be held after the test to show where errors were made, to learn the child's explanation of strange interpretations of material, and especially to establish goals in terms of the child's needs. "Here is a section that caused trouble," the teacher will indicate. "Let's see what you need to study." And then teacher and child will determine the next step.

A standardized scale helps a new

418 EVALUATING AND INTERPRETING THE LANGUAGE ARTS PROGRAM

teacher define the expected achievement of a child. To construct a handwriting or composition scale, hundreds of writing samples are judged until a typical one is found for each age or grade level. By careful comparison the teacher can use these selected samples to judge the achievement of her pupils. Composition scales may be based on a single basic quality, as in the samples that follows. The first example is considered good; the second is an example of a child's work that needs greater direction.

A Chart Showing Growth in Ability to Organize Thought [5]

GRADE 2

The Clean-Up Campaign
The children in Hancock School are working to keep Saint Paul a clean city. We started it by cleaning up our school block. We are cleaning up our yards, too.

Clean Up
We are cleaning up this block.
We are trying to have a clean city.
Our school children are taking turns cleaning up our block.

Qualities To Be Noted

1. The title refers accurately to the subject being written about.
2. The first sentence states clearly *what* the composition is about.
3. The order of sentences is good: *from* the general *to* the particular.

Contrasting Points To Be Observed

1. The title is not clear.
2. The first sentence should come second.
3. Sentences one and three overlap.

GRADE 3

A Safe Vacation
We are all going to have a vacation soon. But we must not take a vacation from safety.

_____
[5] Minneapolis Public Schools, *Communication, A Guide to Speaking & Writing*, 1953, pp. 106–107.

Safe things in a home:
  Not to play with matches.
  Not to handle lights if you have water on your hands.

Safety things outdoors:
  Not to play in the streets.
  Not to leaf your toys out after dark.
  Be careful when you are going bearfooted not to walk on glass.
  Be careful not to be hit by a swing.

These are good safety rules. Be careful this summer and make it a good one.

Vacation Safety
Be careful on your bickl on the street. Cross at the corner. Do not go betwy parked cars. Look out where you run so you won't hit people. Cars stop at stop sins so you can cross when the sin ses red. Stay away from moving swings so you won't get hit.

Qualities To Be Noted

1. The opening sentences make a point. The closing sentences clinch it.
2. The illustrations are accurately grouped under the headings.
3. The illustrations aptly support the point made.

Contrasting Points To Be Observed

1. There is no general introductory statement tying the illustrations together.
2. The composition begins and ends abruptly.

3. The fourth sentence is out of place in the sequence.

GRADE 4

A Story About Norway

Norway is a beautiful country. It has big blue mountains, with streams running through them and it is really pretty.

They're greatest sport is skiing. They have the greatest skiers in Norway.

The fiords are so beautiful that thousands of tourists from other countries visit them in summer. They come in ships that sail along the coast inside the skerry guard and make side trips into the fiords.

The Mountains of Norway

It was a beautiful day on the mountains. The little mountain streams were dancing gayly, and looked beautiful in the bright sun. Now if we went down the mountain we might see herds of cattle grazing. But still down farther you would see the winding fiords, they too look beautiful in the sun. When it rains the fiords are often visited by fishermen. Ships are often seen going in and out of the fiords. Someday I hope to go on a ship in and out of the fiords.

Qualities To Be Noted

1. Three points are neatly made, each in a separate paragraph.

Contrasting Points To Be Observed

1. There is a shift in point of view after the fourth sentence and again after the sixth—from *it* to *we* to *you* to *I*.

GRADE 5

What We Believe About Brotherhood

We should not ignore people whose religion is different than ours. They are American people just like we are. Everyone is equal.

Sometimes you will see a group of children playing and having fun. Only it isn't fun for one little girl. She is from a foreign country. She can't talk too well so the children ignore her. It is just like saying, "We can't play with you because you are from a different place than we are."

We should be friends with everyone and not ignore them because they are from a different country or go to a different church, or are of a different race.

Brotherhood

We had some very nice friends in Chicago and we hated to leave them. They were of different nationality and religion, too.

My mother said it would be nice if everybody was of the same religion and nationality. I think so too, but then, like in the olden days, there would be fights, wars and quarrels about the different beliefs. Then the different religions and nations would start all over again. It would be best to stick to the religion and nationality each person believes in. It doesn't make any difference what nationality or race a person is.

Every week should be Brotherhood Week.

Qualities To Be Noted

1. Opening paragraph introduces topic. Closing paragraph clinches point.
2. Second paragraph contains specific illustration. Illustration makes its point.
3. Paragraphing is accurate.
4. Development lives up to the promise of the title.

Contrasting Points To Be Observed

1. Title broad and general. Compare with "What We Believe About Brotherhood."
2. Opening paragraph does not consider the reader, *begins* but does not *introduce*.
3. Relationship between paragraphs 1 and 2 is not clear.
4. Paragraph 2 is jumbled and contradictory.

5. Last sentence not justified by what has gone before.

GRADE 6

The World Is Growing Smaller

Although it still maintains its regular size, the world is growing smaller. This all started when the raft, (which later became the hollowed-out log or makeshift boat), was invented by the caveman. The world got smaller then, because people could go from place to place faster. The world got smaller yet, when beasts were tamed to transport people. As time went on these things were improved on, and finally the airplane and car were invented. All of these helped greatly in shrinking the world. Science is still experimenting, and soon, who knows, if there may be a time when a person can have breakfast in New York, dinner in Paris, supper in London, and be home in time to read the evening paper. The world has grown smaller from the caveman's raft to the jet plane and is continually shrinking from view of yesterday's hardships.

The World Is Growing Smaller

The world is growing smaller because scientists are inventing fast planes and ships that can go around the world in a few days. The world has changed. Its not a large world anymore but a small world. Transportation has changed from slow transportation to fast transportation and transportation is getting faster all the time.

The world is growing smaller and smaller every day. The world is like a midget caught between modern transportation.

Qualities To Be Noted

1. Each succeeding sentence grows out of the preceding; thus the idea of the paragraph grows. It does not, as in composition above, stand still.
2. While the composition might better have divided into two paragraphs—the second one beginning "Science is still experimenting"—the development from sentence to sentence is consistent.

Contrasting Points To Be Noted

1. The thought of this paragraph does not advance. Each succeeding sentence merely repeats what was said before.
2. The final sentence is obscure.

   1. Why are parents apt to accept the results of a standardized test yet reject work samples that indicate immaturity or lack of effort?
   2. What would be gained and what might be lost if all schools used a composition scale to evaluate creative writing?
   3. Why is it important to know the number of students tested to establish a norm in a test? Why is it important to know the locations of the schools used in establishing the norms of a test?
   4. How frequently should standardized tests be used? What is the best time of year to give them?

HOW SHOULD THE LANGUAGE ARTS PROGRAM BE INTERPRETED TO PARENTS?

Since some teachers look upon the nonschool hours in the life of a child as being educationally insignificant, it is well to remind ourselves that the use of language by a child is greater during those hours than during the school day. For this reason and others, it is especially important that parents understand the program in language arts and share in it with their children.

The report card is a report to parents. As such it should communicate information that parents want to know. If they desire a competitive rating that tells them how John performs in relation to others in the class, it must be given to them. If they want to know how John compares with other boys of similar ability, this comparison must be indicated.

On the other hand, there are additional facts that teachers want parents to know about their children and the school program. The schools are a public concern and the teacher's responsibility is not only to the children but also to those who support the schools. When we do a good job of classroom teaching we assume that it will be recognized by the public. But recognition is rather unlikely if the public has no idea of why we use such things as print script, verse choirs, and vast numbers of library books.

To prepare a report on the individual child, the teacher needs a folder of work samples. Children can help by assuming the responsibility for putting samples of writing, creative work, and classroom tests in these folders. In addition to the child's work samples, classroom charts giving information on books read, spelling test scores, and other achievement records should be kept as supporting evidence for evaluation activities.

Teachers are also urged to keep anecdotal records of incidents in the child's school day. This is a burden for a busy teacher, but important because this evidence is needed. Brief notes written in the plan book are a quick means of jotting down short reminders, such as: "John's uncle is in Japan," "Mary seems to resent any mention of her mother," "Billy went out of his way to help the new boy." A crisis in the classroom calls for a more detailed comment. "Mary deliberately spilled paint on Jane's picture. She denied this and accused Jack of the offense. Finally she admitted the offense and agreed that she should not be permitted to paint the rest of this week." Children seldom disclose such events at home, yet they may be part of the material you will wish to share in a parent conference.

The report card, however, is a very limited means of interpreting the school program. Some teachers enclose a bulletin with each report. One calls her's "Kindergarten Confidential." In it are descriptions of expected behavior of this age group as revealed by studies of child growth. School events and policies may be explained. In October parents are informed that the children may come to school in costume for a Halloween celebration. It is also suggested that masks are a safety hazard and should be avoided. At Christmas time an explanation of why gifts are (or are not) exchanged at school is included. A list of songs the children have learned, finger plays to teach at home, and examples of seasonal verse all add to the general attractiveness of the material.

First-grade teachers who want the parents to help children with print script should send home a copy of the alphabet with directions showing how each letter is made. At another time it may be appropriate to explain why the basic reader is not sent home. Simple progress reports contain news the children bring home in their own handwriting. "Everyone in the class now knows twenty-five words." "Everyone in the first grade can write the figures to 10." A parent might be told how to evaluate the early art efforts of a child. Warnings should be given about belittling early efforts or making gratuitous suggestions. Many parents feel that children should be urged to "do better," not realizing that such urging takes all joy out of sharing something with them. Acceptance, recognition, and praise are the rewards sought by a child when he shows his school work. A child should not be constantly reprimanded for his mistakes or errors. Certainly the parents cannot expect him to bring home only perfect papers. Rather than send a paper or two home each day, it is more effective to keep them for a week, then staple together the workbook pages, art, and writing efforts and send them home on Fridays. Beginning teachers should be warned about sending home good work that they wish to use in an exhibit or other purpose. Too many parents will give it due attention and then throw it out with the daily papers.

Upper-grade teachers will find that a school or district-wide pamphlet on "What We Are Doing in Spelling," "When You Buy A Book for Your Child," "Our Reading Program" will meet a common need and be more efficient than a teacher's individual efforts. Many systems now publish parents' handbooks which are distributed at a parent-teacher conference. Those in Denver, Colo., Cincinnati, Ohio, Des Moines, Iowa, Contra Costa County, Calif., and Arlington, Va., are outstanding. The material need not be expensive to be effective. However, some of the mimeographed materials sent from schools leave a poor impression of a group as supposedly well-trained as teachers in language and art. The form is important, but what is said is more important.

An after-school meeting with parents or a demonstration of teaching is an effective way to communicate for some teachers. There are other teachers who do an outstanding job when alone with children but are nervous or ill at ease when adults are present. At all times it is good to remember that modern parents are usually high school or college graduates, are informed about many aspects of education through magazines and study groups, and expect a professional presentation of the school program and the problems being considered. It is not unreasonable for them to expect the teacher to know why she does certain things. Here is a letter that one second-grade teacher sent to parents:

Dear Parents,

Several have asked about the misspelling of children in the written work they bring home. You have probably noticed that the errors are usually phonetic in nature such as *wants* for once or *pepl* for people.

During the primary grades the major task of the children is to learn to read. The phonics taught is to help them sound out words in their books. It is natural then to use this skill when they write a word. Since their oral vocabulary is much larger then their reading vocabulary they write many words that have not been studied in reading.

It helps them think of the ideas that they wish to write if we accept this phonetic spelling. Some would hesitate to write at all if they were to be criticized for not spelling all the words correctly.

We do have a spelling period and some of the words that have been misspelled will be studied. You will find it interesting to keep a collection of the papers your child brings home. There will be a gradual decrease in phonetically misspelled words as he conforms to the conventional forms which he is learning. In the meantime, he is expressing his ideas with ease and confidence. We want him to try to use words like *enormous* and *television* instead of substituting "big" and "T.V." merely because these are easier to spell.

Please read what the child wants to say. Comment about his ideas and share his joys as a creative writer. Do not comment on the spelling of single words.

You might like to visit our spelling class. It is held each day at 2:15.

Respectfully,

Some aspects of the language arts program require the active participation of parents. A child with a speech defect needs to practice at home. Lessons for the parent to use should be created by the school. A child who makes a usage error is reflecting an error heard at home. Send a game home that emphasizes the correct form, and suggest that the family practice it with the child so that the source of the trouble can be corrected. Spelling can be studied at home. A workbook soon becomes tattered and torn after it has been sent home. A better practice is to have the child make a copy of a few words from the list to study at home. This list can be given some importance if he writes it on colored paper or has each word on small individual cards which can be manipulated like flash cards.

Suggestions for enrichment activities might be sent to parents who want to be given a larger role in the formal teaching of their children. These activities might involve the use of encyclopedias, selection and discussion of library books, and application of some of the inexpensive workbook materials available in variety stores. Because children like to read aloud to their parents, some teacher-approved books should be available to read at home. These might be supplementary books, stories taken from discarded material and rebound as little books, or especially prepared story sheets that reinforce the vocabulary of the basic program. Worthwhile books to study with respect to parents are: *Everybody's Business—Our Children* by Mauree Applegate (Harper), *Helping Parents Understand Their Child's School* by Grace Langdon and Irving W. Stout (Prentice-Hall), and *Enjoy Your Children* by Margo Gerke (Abingdon).

It is unfair to beginning teachers, however, to imply by the foregoing that all parents are equally interested in the education of their children. There are certain areas where the parents never visit the school, ignore report cards, do not participate in P.T.A. activities, and in extreme cases, even express disapproval of the entire curriculum. There are, unfortunately, some parents who do not want the responsibility of raising their own children. This rejection often takes peculiar forms. Some parents seem to transfer their own shortcomings and sense of guilt to the schools and teachers. From their point of view it is the fault of the teacher and the school that Joe and Mary are "problem children."

Such criticism of our educational efforts is, of course, most unfair.

In these situations remember that the child is not responsible for his parents. Give him the security, help, and recognition that he may need so desperately. Sometimes teachers must be substitute parents.

1. Should parents be asked to send money to school to buy the "Weekly Reader" for children? To buy library books?

2. Why would it be difficult for some parents to note the difficulties their own child was having as they observed a reading lesson?

3. Modern homework is considered to be an enrichment of the child's experiences rather than a catching-up on competitive assignments. Give examples of this type of homework in a language area.

4. What would be your reply if a parent wanted you to spend an extra half-hour after school working with his child?

5. What would be your reply if a parent wanted to have a birthday party for a child in your classroom at school during school time?

6. How can such days as Christmas, Mother's Day, Father's Day, Education Week, be used to interpret the school program to parents?

WHAT HAS RESEARCH CONTRIBUTED TO THE TEACHING OF THE LANGUAGE ARTS?

Although everyone agrees that the teaching of the language arts is important, the funds available for research have been meager indeed. Most of the research has been financed by individual teachers as they sought to earn advanced college degrees. As a result there are few studies of great magnitude (the Iowa Spelling Scale is a recent exception) or of long duration (the San Diego County Reading Study represents another exception). From 1940 to 1950 research in the language arts remained at a standstill because of the war. At the present time there are a number of studies in process but it will be some years before the work of the classroom teacher will be influenced by it.

Much of the existing research is sub-

ject to valid criticism. Frequently one sees the statement that, according to research, phonics should be taught in kindergarten or that teaching proofreading fails to improve composition. When one reads the studies quoted, one often finds that the "research" was done with a small group of children by a teacher determined to "prove" a theory without realizing that the particular situation is not typical of most classrooms. Much of this research sounds more like testimonials for a patent medicine. Other studies have been subject to so many controls that only a single item of difference may be studied. Teachers usually reject these results as something obtained under unrealistic teaching conditions.

The greatest limitation to most research in child education is that we cannot risk complete failure. In a laboratory many failures are expected before a formula is perfected. As soon as teachers feel that all is not well they either abandon the study or modify procedures. I once asked three teachers to ignore the spelling textbooks and to teach spelling only in association with writing. All expressed fear that the children would not do as well on a standardized test as the nonexperimental classes. It was inevitable that in order to protect their own reputations as teachers they would use word lists and drills that were not related to the writing done by the children.

A related problem is the "Hawthorne" effect. This term is the result of a study of incentive motivation in the Hawthorne plant of the Western Electric Company, located in a Chicago suburb. No matter what was done in the experiment, some improvement was noted. Finally it was decided that the fact that the workers knew an experiment was going on was in itself the motivation, rather than any specific thing done. A change in textbooks often produces the same result in a school program. A year after the change to a new speller it can usually be shown that an improvement has taken place. In a few years the novelty has worn away, the teachers have reduced some of the procedures to routines, and the test results may indicate that spelling achievement is unsatisfactory. A change to any other program, even to the one discarded four years ago, will again produce an apparent improvement.

Hubert C. Armstrong indicates other limitations to educational research: [6]

Research may involve some of the most common interpretations of statistics. We may take average class size, average cost per pupil, average cost per square foot, and yet these averages are no more an indication of what should be than is the average number of colds per child, or the average number of accidents, or the average number of ulcers per elementary school principal.

A conspicuous example of error is the manner in which we interpret test scores. We

measure a group of children of the same age, take the average score and call it a norm. We then refer to the norm as a sort of a standard. We then make two errors in interpretation. The first of these errors is that we interpret a score which is higher or lower than the mean as if it should not be higher or lower. We speak of "retardation" in reading, of being "ahead" in arithmetic. We speak as though the mean were the point that separated the normal from the abnormal. We do not expect all children to be the same height or weight, yet we talk as if we expected all children to be precisely alike in their school work.

The other error we make is in presuming that an average which is based on all sorts of school systems will necessarily give us a desirable standard applicable to any one school, grade, or group including the group on which the test was standardized. We have added elephants and rabbits, and we turn out to have an average what—cow? If we were actuaries and were interested only in prediction, we might use the average as the best measure of what would happen next, provided conditions were not changed. We are not actuaries. It is change, improvement, betterment that we are most concerned with. We are engaged in encouraging a process of growth, in producing greater (or different) learning than the average. We, like the physician, are really interested in an ideal that is entirely different from a central tendency in any sense of that term. The present method of establishing norms of tests is outmoded. Two new types of criteria should take the place of a single "standard."

One of these types is based on criteria from each child himself. We now have available in the field of language—reading, spelling, writing, speech—a means of deriving scores on an *intra*-individual difference basis. Let me illustrate. If a child's hearing vocabulary is known to be 12,000 words and he can read about 6,000, we know that it is only the form of the word, not its meaning, that has to be learned. We might reasonably expect him to learn in visual form as many words as he already knows in auditory form. Similar approaches are possible in other fields.

Another type of criterion may be employed. That criterion will be essentially a means of stating the conditions and circumstances under which any level of achievement was made. We would state what may be expected of children who are healthy, who have had ample opportunities to read books, whose teachers have been well trained,

[6] Hubert C. Armstrong, "The Place of Values in American Education," *Calif. Jour. Elem. Educ.*, February 1955, pp. 141–144.

whose attendance has been regular and at the same school, who have not been subjected to undue emotional stresses or to nervous disorders, and who are within, say, ten points of a stated level of intelligence. We might then have many types of norms based on stated conditions.

We educators have been seduced into this error of misinterpreting measures of central tendency by confusing a major distinction between the physical sciences and the social disciplines. The physical scientist is interested in nature—the nature of nature. He observes and reports and generalizes concerning what nature is like and how it behaves. He never quarrels with the way things are. He is elegantly terse in his reporting. He may write an equation as the shortest way of stating some aspect of nature. He isn't concerned about how nature *ought* to be. He is glad enough to find out about what natural "reality" actually is. The scientist is forever seeking the shortest possible answers to questions as to *how* nature works.

We in education and in other realms of social science began by borrowing methods from the physical sciences. We tried to proceed as the physicist does, that is, to observe, record, relate, generalize, predict, and if possible to control. We, too, observed and took averages. But we were observing not the behavior of matter in the sense that H_2O always means water, or that py equals mk; but we were observing man who is subject to modification.

The educator aims to induce changes in a given direction, to produce results of a given kind, to approach more closely what we want and value. If we ignore change toward values we can easily confuse the way social conditions are with the way we think they ought to be. But we should be clear on these three points. First, it is perfectly legitimate to state in statistical terms the central tendency of data when we are describing that characteristic of a *group*—an existing state of affairs. Second, we cannot necessarily judge an individual deviation from a group average as though that deviation were undesirable. Third, when we are attempting to state standards, ideals, values, or criteria which indicate how we want things to be, we cannot take recourse to a description of things as they are.

Sometimes we attempt to evaluate by comparing the present with the past. We seem to have two contradictory views. One is to glorify the past. We might speak of this as the nostalgic view. When translated in terms

of its root meaning, this may be called the "homesick" view. For those who would like to read a bit of comparative research, I recommend the book, now out of print, but found in many libraries, *Then and Now in Education—1845–1923*, by Otis W. Caldwell and Stuart A. Courtis, describing in abundant detail the first survey in education in this country which was conducted by Horace Mann in Boston in 1845.

Another way of comparing the present with the past is to take the view that progress has been made. This might be dubbed the "look-how-far-we've-come" point of view. There is an implication that change is generally in the direction of the better. This is a tricky method to deal with, for we can easily fall into what Lewis Mumford calls "improved means to unimproved ends," or, in more common parlance "a short cut to a doubtful destination." Either of these methods of comparing the present with the past inevitably leads to the problem of knowing whether any change has been in the right direction; that is, in the direction of what we value.

We sometimes take stock of the present by recourse to a legalistic basis. We often explain or justify present practice by quoting rules, regulations, laws, or even the state or federal constitution. This type of explanation is satisfactory if we have only consistency, or the avoidance of penalties in mind, but it does not indicate to us whether or not a given procedure is a good one, for laws and even constitutions can be changed. We must then ask ourselves if a law or a constitutional provision is good, or if it should be changed.

A related way of judging ourselves and our practices is in terms of habit, custom, and tradition. This is the most pleasant way by far, for there is something about the old, the usual, and the habitual that seems almost as right and true as nature itself. But we are reminded of an instance in which we visited a college professor. She cautioned us about a projecting prong on her desk, pointing out that she had torn her own clothes on it a number of times. It was suggested that perhaps the desk drawer was in backwards. "Oh, no," she said, "it has always been that way ever since it was moved in here several years ago." But on examination we found that changing it end for end was all that was necessary. Apropos of custom, it was Friar Roger Bacon who in the thirteenth century stated four stumbling blocks to truth: (1) the influence of fragile or unworthy authority, (2) custom,

(3) the imperfection of undisciplined senses, (4) and the concealment of ignorance by the ostentation of seeming wisdom.

It is a step forward when educators question so much that has passed as research. The mistakes that have been made will be corrected. Today funds are available in amounts seldom granted in the past, universities and colleges concerned with the training of teachers are providing time and equipment for research, and more school systems are developing research projects.

Action research is used by many schools to improve the curriculum. This research is a cooperative effort of a group of teachers who work together to solve specific problems. Records are carefully kept and the results discovered used to improve practice. Projects may involve such educational problems as these: planning a series of assembly programs to celebrate important holidays, creating drill sheets to use with certain reading textbooks using phonic games, developing a reading record card, or determining a way to teach a child how to transfer from print script to cursive writing.

Action research makes no attempt to proclaim the results of a single study as universal truths. Because it is a shared experience, action research is the basis of theory or opinion on analogous situations, just as conferences among bankers and lawyers help clarify certain aspects of their respective financial and legal activities.

Action research is not as objective, controlled, or well-structured in advance as research of the traditional type. The need for carefully controlled research has not decreased. It is quite possible for action-research projects to lead to problems that must be studied by directed techniques. Action research involves teachers in programs that lead to desired changes, reveals sources of information that might not have been discovered, and satisfies the need to take corrective measures.

1. Under what circumstances may a school research problem risk failure?
2. Make a list of the outstanding authorities in such areas of the language arts as spelling, reading, and handwriting. How would such a list compare in length to a list of authorities in another field that is familiar to you, such as physics?
3. Compare the amount of money available for educational research with that for agriculture, medicine, and business.

HOW IS A BEGINNING TEACHER EVALUATED?

Beginning teachers frequently ask, "What does the person evaluating teaching look for when visiting the class?" Seven basic areas are observed by supervisors.

Area 1: Preparation and Planning

Proper preparation of class material and method of presentation is essential for most effective teaching. Some teachers willingly spend hours planning their day's work, while, it must be admitted, some others prepare little or not at all. Plan books should be kept and checked. Lack of preparation is usually quite obvious to the evaluator in the classroom.

Area 2: Recognition of and Provision for Individual Differences

Recognition of individual differences is almost an instinct of good teachers. Teachers who do not group their pupils according to ability are easily recognized— as are the ones who spare no pains to get to know each of their pupils individually.

Area 3: Motivation

It has been said that two things are essential for pupils' academic success in school: intelligence and motivation, with

motivation being the more important of the two. Some teachers surge far ahead of the others in this area and become sources of inspiration to their pupils. The best motivation results when pupils and teacher have similar purposes.

Area 4: Command of Subject Matter

It is obvious that if teachers are to teach, they must know what they are talking about. The teacher's command of language and ability to put the subject matter across also enter the picture here.

Area 5: Teaching Techniques

These are too numerous to mention, but include such techniques as using a positive rather than negative approach, varying the teaching methods, use of objects and visual aids.

Area 6: Classroom Control

Teachers employ different strategies in controlling behavior in the classroom, some clinging to the despotic approach, others leading their classes with the magic wands of interest, cooperation, fair play, and mutual respect. Unfortunately, a few are never really in control and their school lives become a desperate effort to "hold the line." These indications, of course, can all be perceived and evaluated by a skilled observer.

Area 7: Classroom Atmosphere

Area 7 has to do with the mechanical features of the classroom such as heat and light, neatness, use of bulletin boards, class projects, color combinations, interest centers, displays of children's work and the way the students work.

The skilled supervisor needs only a few minutes in a room to note that the program is proceeding in a well-planned and a purposeful fashion. It takes even less time to notice that this is not happening. Long periods of observation and counseling are required to diagnose the causes of trouble and find a solution. The personality of the teacher, the individual abilities of the children, and the expected results all must be examined in the same way a doctor diagnoses an illness. There are seldom quick solutions or "magic words" that will solve the problems. This type of experience is the process whereby an unsuccessful teacher can improve. It is not especially pleasant to paraphrase Burns: if we could see ourselves as others see us, we probably wouldn't like it.

A beginning teacher's relationship with a supervisor should be based on the premise that the supervisor is genuinely concerned about the children's education. This means that he or she stands ready to give you whatever assistance you require.

It should also be recognized that supervisors are people with human strengths and frailties. Individual differences are as pronounced among adults as they are among children. Some supervisors will appear to be imposing their own methods in seeking to advise you. These methods may not work for you, but at least consider such suggestions with an open mind. Others who are less direct will perhaps outline a philosophical or theoretical approach. Still others may tend to suggest or recommend certain materials. In any case, few supervisors expect every teacher to use a stereotyped formula instead of analyzing each case on its individual merits.

The beginner is always permitted a few mistakes. When you recognize your shortcomings and seek to improve, you will usually be met more than half way. If you cannot see the mistake, or attempt to ignore it, there will be difficult times ahead for you and for your superiors.

As experienced professional people, supervisors can give you considerable assistance in working with the individual child or small group. Their knowledge of materials naturally exceeds that of the new teacher, and they expect to be asked about such matters as third-grade books on Mexico or sources of space pictures. Sometimes new teachers will hesitate to ask these questions for fear that their weaknesses will be criticized. Actually, such questions are evidence of professional concern.

One of the wisest practices a new teacher can follow is to locate an older teacher who is working at the same level. Ask this person if he or she will grant you a few minutes' discussion time after school each day. There is much significant information on the community, school policies, and teaching practices that is not written down which you can gather through this kind of relationship. In turn, share some of the newer materials or techniques that you have picked up in your training. When possible, visit with other new teachers. Nothing brings people together like common difficulties, and your morale will receive a boost when you learn that your troubles are not unique.

The new teacher needs to make special plans for the first weeks of school. Security for both the teacher and the children may be provided during the first day by the familiar. Discuss ways of having the children salute the flag, talk about summer experiences, sing favorite songs, talk about favorite books and show some of the work that was done last year.

Parents and visitors should be told that they will be invited back at another time with an added explanation that during the first few days of school some children are disturbed by too many visitors.

Help the children learn to know each other. Provide games that have to do with learning names. Make a rough map and have children point out where they live. During the first week the children can make a class directory. The children help the teacher decide what should be put into the directory. It may contain facts like these:

Betty Jones　　　Second Grade
4116 Walnut Street
Telephone W 7-1268
I have a dog at home.

Each child during the routine of getting acquainted tells something about himself, his name, where he lives, etc. This information is recorded by the teacher on separate sheets. A child may want to bring a picture of himself and paste on his page. It sustains interest to add to each page the new things children have to tell about themselves. The teacher should have a page too.

It is wise to give little children simple work to take home. Older children should have a specific thing to do at home.

Supplies are sometimes a problem during the first days of a term. A collection of old magazines can be used in many ways. Pictures can be cut out and mounted, words and sounds can be underlined, cartoons might be collected and put on the bulletin board. Among the teacher's resources should be several good books to read aloud. With only one, the teacher always faces the possibility that the children listened to the book last year.

Time spent during the first week establishing social habits and classroom procedures will make both teaching and learning more effective throughout the year.

From the beginning it should be realized that children expect the teacher to be a leader and an arbiter of classroom behavior. Classroom control cannot be divorced from learning. When children are successfully motivated by an important goal, there are few discipline problems.

Emergencies, both major and minor, need to be anticipated. The school will take care of illness, fire drills, and civil defense procedures. The teacher must anticipate such minor catastrophes as spilled ink or paint, broken pencil points, missing lunches or lunch money, emergency phone calls during class sessions, an irate parent's visit, broken projector or torn film, and the many embarrassing moments of childhood that later become anecdotes.

Good discipline is not magic, but merely the application of common sense and past experience. A few simple, direct, and inflexible rules are essential to classroom control. These ten ideas may help you:

1. *Begin right.* Make a good impression. Get the children to feel from the outset that school is going to be a happy place with a friendly but efficient captain at the helm.

2. *Avoid conditions that lead to disorder.* Plan well, have materials ready, be composed, calm, dignified; have variety and surprises in your program; provide enough mental stimulus for even the cleverest children.

3. *Don't let minor incidents go uncorrected.* "Good" children tend to imitate the conduct of "bad" children so that minor incidents become major. Slowness in stopping work, a rough-and-tumble fracas in getting ready for the playground, disobedience in slight matters—such habits may be easily checked at first but soon become established forms of schoolroom behavior. If you allow the children to practice disorder, they will soon become expert at it.

4. *Be tactful.* Tact is a lubricant. It has been called the "art of getting your own ends by the other fellow's means." Children are real persons. Tact is even more effective in dealing with them than with adults.

5. *Be good-natured.* A good-tempered teacher with a sense of humor and a smile can eliminate friction far better than a stern or sarcastic one. Regard all offenses as against the group and not against you personally. Avoid the high-pitched, raspy voice, the authoritative manner, the habitual frown.

6. *Be just.* No quality has a worse effect on children than injustice. They are much keener at reading the minds of adults than adults are at reading the minds of children, and will remember for years the teacher who tore up the paper because the name was written in the wrong place, or who refused to adjudicate a quarrel impartially because of favoritism.

7. *Be persistent.* Peg away at important matters without allowing exceptions until the desired form of conduct is habitual.

8. *Be consistent.* Don't be severe one day and lenient the next. To allow late hours or an outside worry to affect professional conduct is a sign of immaturity, weakness, or lack of poise. Those who show self-control only when they are not under stress are really demonstrating complacency.

9. *Have decision.* "I don't know what I shall do with you if you don't behave yourself" is an oft-heard plaint of distracted mothers. Teachers sometimes feel that way too, but it does no good to let the children know it. *Quiet decision often saves a precarious situation.*

10. *Avoid conflicts.* Do not try to "fight it out" with a child. Tense situations bring hysteria and emotional disturbance. A child simply can't yield when so involved. If a conflict arises between yourself and a child, give him some mental relief. One of the simplest ways to solve a situation is by giving him an either-or choice. Not "you must and shall' but "this must happen or." For example: "Either pick up your clay or I shall ask the class helpers to do it, and you must not have clay again until we so decide." The clay is picked up, all feel that justice has been done, and the emotionally upset child has, instead of a searing experience to recall, a feeling of dissatisfaction at the unreasonableness of his own behavior which will help him to make a better adjustment to the next situation.

Teaching in the elementary school is an art. Techniques and materials can be shared, but the human relationships of the teaching-learning process cannot be learned through words alone. In recent years, printed outline pictures have been designed for "do-it-yourself" painters, using key numbering to indicate which areas are to be painted a certain color. If one follows the directions one can produce a tolerable facsimile of the original painting, but at best it is a mere copy of another's creative expression and planning. Maybe the exercise will teach the rudiments of brush techniques or color combination, as well as the laws of balance and harmony. One's first efforts at original painting will perhaps betray uncertainties of line and form, but the result, however labored, is a creation rather than an imitation. With talent, training, and determination, the amateur painter may in time produce a genuine work of art. In teaching, some start with great talent and seem to know not only how to work with children but also how to use suggestions for the best results. Others start with nothing more than interest and must master the skills supplied by talent. But the rewards are worth the effort. Few professions offer the satisfactions that a teacher knows as children develop the communication skills that will help them face with confidence their responsibilities as adults.

BUILDING WITH CHILDREN A BETTER TOMORROW [7]

The teacher asked of the child,
"What would you have of me?"
And the child replied,
"Because you are you, only you know some
     of the things
I would have of you.
But because I am I,
I do know some of what
I would have of you."

The teacher asked again,
"What would you have of me?"
And the child replied,
"I would have of you what
You are and what you know.
I would have you speaking and silent,
Sure and unsure, seeking for surety,
Vibrant and pensive.
I would have you talking and letting me tell,
Going my way with my wonderings and
     enthusiasms,
And going your way that I may know new
     curiosities,
I would have you leading step by step
Yet letting me step things off in my own
     fashion."
"Teach me," said the child,
"With simplicity and imagination—
Simply that the paraphernalia and the gadgets
Do not get between us;
Imaginatively that I may sense and catch your
     enthusiasm,

_____
[7] Reprinted by permission of the Association for Childhood Education International, 3615 Wisconsin Avenue, N.W., Washington 16, D.C.

And the quickening thrill of never having
     been this way before.
Too, I would have you watching over me,
     yet not too watchful,
Caring for me, yet not too carefully,
Holding me to you, yet not with bindings,
So when the day comes, as it must,
     that we, each, go our separate ways,
I can go free.
Let me take you with me not because
     I must, but because I would have it so.
Let me take you with me because
     you have become, in me,
Not just today—
Tomorrow!"

—LELAND B. JACOBS

From *Childhood Education* (November 1961) 38, No. 3.

Suggestions for Projects

1. Write to the Children's Bureau in the U. S. Office of Education, Health and Welfare in Washington, D. C., for the latest copy of "Research Relating to Children." Report on recent studies in the language arts.
2. Examine a copy of the STEP Essay Test published by Educational Testing Service, Princeton, New Jersey. Use it as a basis for evaluating a set of children's compositions. Report your conclusions.
3. Create a handwriting scale from samples collected in the class you now teach.
4. Survey recent magazine articles with reference to proofreading and editing skills. What suggestions are made to facilitate this practice in elementary classrooms?
5. Examine samples of report cards used in a number of school districts. Note how they differ with respect to reporting achievement in the language arts.
6. Ask teachers for samples of tests they have made and used in the intermediate grades. What similarities and differences exist with respect to emphasis and method?
7. Create a spelling and reading test to be used early in the year to diagnose the needs of children you will teach.
8. Write to the publishers for samples of

testing programs that are keyed to text-books you will use. What would be the strengths and weaknesses of such texts?

9. The Center for Programmed Instruction, 365 West End Avenue, New York, N.Y., publishes information concerning current work relating to teaching machines. Evaluate this material with respect to its use in a language arts class.

BIBLIOGRAPHY

BOOKS

Anderson, Paul S., *et al., Readings in the Language Arts.* New York: Macmillan, 1963.

Burton, W. H. *The Guidance of Learning Activities* 3rd ed. New York: Appleton, 1962, chaps. 20–24.

Remmers, H. H., and N. L. Gage. *Educational Measurement and Evaluation,* New York: Harper, 1955.

PERIODICALS

Early, Margaret J. "What Do They Want To Learn?" *English Journal,* (November 1955), pp. 459–463.

Greene, Harry. "Direct vs. Formal Methods in Elementary English," *Elementary English,* (May 1947), pp. 273–286.

Keene, Katherine. "Students Like Corrections," *English Journal,* (April 1956), pp. 212–215.

Leonard, Roger T. "What Can Be Measured?" *The Reading Teacher,* (March 1962), pp. 326–337.

Shane, Harold G. "Research Helps in Teaching the Language Arts," Association for Supervision and Curriculum Development Report (Washington, D. C.: National Education Association, 1955).

Smith, Dora V. "Evaluating Instruction in English in Elementary Schools of New York," Eighth Research Bulletin of National Conference on Research in Enlgish, 1941.

PAMPHLETS

Grose, Lois M., Dorothy Miller and Erwin R. Steinberg: "Suggestions for Evaluating Junior High School Writing." Champaign, Ill. National Council of Teachers of English, 1961.

National School Public Relations Association: *Conference Time.* Washington, D. C.: National Education Association, 1961.

National School Public Relations Association: *Pebbles.* Washington, D. C.: National Education Association, 1960.

GLOSSARY

absorption unit A unit of reading material which contains words already presented in previous units; materials containing no "new" reading words sometimes called plateau units.

alexia Loss of ability to read; word blindness.

ambidextrous Skilled use of both hands.

analysis Taking apart or breaking down into smaller elements.

antonym A word having the opposite meaning of another word. Example: *good* and *bad* are antonyms.

aphasia Loss or impairment of the power to use or understand speech, caused by brain injury.

articulation Adjustment of the tongue, in relation to the palate, in the production of any speech sound; also, the act of uttering such sounds.

audiometer A device for testing hearing.

auditory discrimination Ability to discriminate between the levels or intensities of sounds, one speech sound from another.

basal-reader approach The development of basic reading abilities and skills by means of special textbooks; the development of initial reading skills and abilities by means of basal readers.

blend The fusion of two (or more) sounds in a word without loss of identity of either sound, as *bl.*

breve A short half circle placed over a vowel to indicate a "short" sound: *cŏt.*

closed syllable A syllable ending with a consonant. Example: *lit.*

compound phonogram A phonic element which does not make a word by itself. Examples: *sl, str, ing, ight, ay,* or *ou.*

configuration Pattern, general form, or shape of a word.

connotation The significance that is suggested or implied in addition to the basic meaning of a word.

consonant trigraph A combination of three successive consonants without vowels in between. Example: *tch* (in *watch*).

deductive Proceeding from general to the specific, as applying a rule in spelling.

dentals Sounds articulated by pressing the tip of the tongue against the teeth. Examples: *d, t, th*.

dextral (or **dextrad**) An innately right-handed individual.

diacritical marks Signs or small characters used to designate a particular sound value of a letter or letters.

digraph Two letters representing one sound, such as *ea* or *ai*. There are consonant and vowel digraphs.

diphthong Two vowel sounds joined in one syllable to form one speech sound, as *oi* and *ow*.

dyslexia The inability to read understandingly, due to a central lesion. (The ability to read may be intact, but there is little or no understanding of what is read.)

euphony Pleasing sound; tendency to greater ease of pronunciation.

extrinsic Outward, external. For example, a gold star for classroom work is an extrinsic reward, whereas the learning acquired is the *intrinsic* reward.

eye-voice span The distance between the point being read (in oral reading) and the point at the right where the eyes are directed. In oral reading the eyes are usually ahead of the voice.

facet Literally, "a little face"; one of a set of small plane surfaces of a polished stone or diamond; by analogy, a sharply defined view or aspect of a subject. Reading, writing, and speaking are facets of the language area.

fixation pause The length of time required for the eyes to fix on a given part of a line in reading.

framing words Isolating a group of words on a printed page by framing with the hands, i.e., placing one hand at each end of the group.

heteronym A word spelled like another, but differing in sound and meaning. Examples: *lead* (a metal and a verb).

homonym A word having the same sound as another but differing in meaning and spelling. Examples: *fair* and *fare*, *bear* and *bare*.

kinesthetic Pertaining to or describing sensations arising from body movements.

labials Sounds articulated mainly by the lips. Examples: *wh, w, f, v, p, b,* and *m*.

legasthenia Inability to make adequate associations with the symbols of a printed page.

linguals Sounds formed with the aid of the tongue. Examples: *l, t, d*.

linguistics Science of language; study of all aspects of speech.

macron Short horizontal mark placed over a vowel to indicate its long sound.

Metronoscope A tachistoscopic device for the controlled time exposure of printed words and phrases for continuous reading (manufactured by the American Optical Company, Southbridge, Mass.).

monosyllabic word A word composed of only one syllable. Example: *bat*.

morpheme A language element (Greek *morphe*, form) that connects images or ideas; a language element showing relationships. Examples: affixes (i.e., prefixes and suffixes), prepositions, conjunctions, accentuation, etc.

myopia A condition of nearsightedness; inability to see clearly without minus lens correction.

nasals Sounds formed by using the tongue and palate to direct the sound into the nose.

onomatopoeic words Words formed by the imitation of natural sounds, such as *buzz*.

open syllable A syllable ending with a vowel. Example: *so*.

Ophthalmograph A device for photographing eye movements during reading (manufactured by American Optical Company, Southbridge, Mass.).

palatals Sounds formed between the tongue and palate. Examples: *k, g, y, q,* and *x*.

palindrome A word, phrase, or sentence that is the same whether read from the left or the right. Examples: *dad; madam*.

philology The study of language; philosophical study of language; linguistic science.

phoneme A group of variants of a speech sound, usually beginning with the same letter but sounded differently because of variations in stress, intonation, and so forth.

phonetic analysis The analysis of a word into its phonetic elements for pronunciation purposes; commonly used as a synonym for *phonics*.

polysyllable A word composed of more than three syllables.

regressive eye-movements Right-to-left return of one or both eyes during reading.

reversal tendency The tendency of immature children, or of children who have practiced immature habits, to reverse or confuse letters and word forms. See *strephosymbolia* below.

root An original word form from which words have been developed by addition of prefixes, suffixes, and inflectional endings.

sight word A word that is memorized or recognized as a whole.

sinistral (or **sinistrad**) An innately left-handed individual.

sonant A voiced sound. Examples: *b, v, w, d*.

stammering Inhibition of speech; involuntary stopping or blocking in speaking.

strabismus Squint, a lack of parallelism of the optical axes; "cross-eyes."

strephosymbolia Literally, "twisted symbols"; a disorder of perception in which objects seem reversed as in a mirror; a special type of reading disability, inconsistent with a child's general intelligence, characterized by confusion between the letters *b* and *d*, *p* and *q*, or the reading of *saw* for *was, left* for *felt.* See *reversal tendency* above.

stuttering Involuntary or spasmodic repetition of a sound or a syllable.

suffix One or more letters or syllables added to the ending of a word to change the meaning. For example: *farm + -ing = farming*.

surd A voiceless sound. Examples: *p, f, wh, t*.

synonym A word that has the same or nearly the same meaning as another word.

synthesis A putting together; combination of modifying elements into inflected words; the opposite of *analysis*.

tachistoscope A device for exposing words, symbols, or other visual stimuli for one-fifth of a second or less.

terminal sound A final sound; frequently referred to as the blend of a vowel with a final consonant as *at* in *cat,* or *ake* in *bake*.

word phonogram A small word, usually learned as a sight word, which serves as a word element in longer words. For example, *at* and *an*.

INDEX

Ability range, 27–35
Accent, use of, 193
Accessories, in dramatics, 65–66, 67–69
Achievement, potential academic of children with various IQ levels, 29
Action research, 426
Activities, block plan for, 36–41
Activities concerning:
  accent, 193
  alphabetization, 189, 195–196
  beginning handwriting, 106–107
  correct spelling, 196
  correct usage, 394–398
  creative writing, primary grades, 327–336
  definitions, 189–192
  diacritical marks, 193
  dictionary skills, 189–198
  guide words, 189
    homonyms, 197
    illustrations, 191
    root words, 192–193
    synonyms, 197
  habits of courtesy and good manners, 72–80
  motivation of reports, 363–364
  phonics, 134–142
  reading:
    first reader, 215–217
    independent, in primary grades, 229–241
    intermediate grades, 272–275
    preprimer, 214–215
    primer, 214–215
    second grade, 241–249
    third grade, 249–256
    word attack skills, 247–249
  sentence sense development, 379–380
  skills in listening, 86–87
  understanding of adjectives, nouns, subjects, verbs and objects, 381–388
  spelling enrichment, 185–186
  spelling in the primary grades, 164
Adjectives, understanding, 378, 383, 384, 388
Adverbs, understanding, 378, 384, 388
"Aeroplane" (poem), Mary M. Green, 313
African influence on English, 15
Aids to children's literature selection, 279–281
Alliteration, use of, 340
Alphabetization, 189, 255

"American Flag, The" (poem), Louise Abney, 313
American Indian influence on English, 15
Anderson, Verna Dieckman, discussion of reading charts, 223–227
Anglo-Saxon influence on English, 11–12
Announcements, standards for, 407
Antonyms, 197–198, 342–343
Applegate, Mauree, 383
Apostrophe, use of, 400
Arabic influence on English, 15
Armstrong, Herbert, 424–426
Art, meaning of, 3
Articles, understanding, 383
Auding, meaning of, 81–82
Auditory-mindedness, 87
Awards, children's book, 280

Barbarisms, 14
Basic reading:
  meaning of, 203
  series, methods of use, 203–204
  textbook series, list of, 277–278
Beginning reading, development of, 212–270
Bequest of Wings, Annis Duff, 289
Bibliography:
  books for bibliotherapy, 282–284
  children's literature, 318–320
  dramatic materials, 71
  handwriting, 126–127
  linguistics (word origins), 186
  listening, 91–92
  phonics, 151
  reading, 277–278
  research and evaluation, 432
  spelling, 198–199
  verse choir material, 318
  written composition, 369–370
Bibliotherapy book list, 282–284
"Big Pig" (poem), 54
Blends, teaching of, 136–138
Block planning in language development, 36–41
Book reports:
  activities for vitalizing, 293–295
  discussion of, 290–295
  intermediate grades, forms for, 294–295
  primary grades, discussion of, 292–293
  primary grades, forms for, 292–293
  purposes of, 291, 293

435